Successful
Writing
at Work

Successful
Writing
at Work

THIRD EDITION

◆

Philip C. Kolin
UNIVERSITY OF SOUTHERN MISSISSIPPI

D. C. HEATH AND COMPANY
LEXINGTON, MASSACHUSETTS • TORONTO

Acquisitions Editor: Paul Smith
Developmental Editor: Holt Johnson
Production Editor: Karen Wise
Designer: Sally Steele
Production Coordinator: Lisa Arcese
Text Permissions Editor: Margaret Roll

Published simultaneously in Canada.

Printed in the United States of America.

International Standard Book Number: 0-669-17796-2

Library of Congress Catalog Card Number: 89-80257

10 9 8 7 6 5 4 3

To
Eric, Kristin, and Janeen
Erica and Pam
Julie and Loretta
and
MARY

Preface

Successful Writing at Work is a comprehensive introductory text designed for use in technical, business, professional, and occupational writing courses. As in the first two editions, the approach in this Third Edition remains practical, emphasizing that communication skills are essential for career advancement and that writing is a vital part of most jobs. The Third Edition even more strongly emphasizes that writing is a problem-solving activity that helps workers meet the needs of their employers, co-workers, customers, and clients. *Successful Writing at Work* presents multiple situations and problems that students as business and technical writers will have to address and asks them to consider the rhetorical options available for solving these problems. As in other editions, the Third Edition gives students detailed guidelines for creating clear, well-organized, and readable writing. It contains a wide range of writing examples drawn from such varied sources as student papers and reports, business correspondence and proposals, and magazine and journal articles.

Consistent with this view of writing in the workplace, the Third Edition places greater emphasis on writing as a process. Students will find clear and concise explanations of the *hows* as well as the *whys* of writing for the world of work. *Successful Writing at Work* helps students develop the crucial skills of brainstorming, researching, drafting, revising, proofreading, and formatting various business and technical documents.

As in prior editions, the Third Edition continues to emphasize audience analysis. Memos, letters, proposals, questionnaires, and reports are considered from the points of view of the intended audience(s); that is, personnel directors, employers, co-workers, customers, and so forth. Students are regarded as professionals seeking advancement at different phases of a business career. For example, students are addressed as job candidates looking for a position in Chapter 7, as employees who must meet the needs of employers and customers with specific problems and requests in Chapter 8, as assistants who have to summarize an article or a report for a superior in Chapter 11, and as business people who must write a persuasive proposal to win a contract in Chapter 15.

The organization of the Third Edition reflects the student's own progress in writing for the world of work. The text moves logically from consideration of basic concepts in writing (audience, tone, message, purpose) to the overall process of writing (brainstorming, drafting, revising) in which these concepts play a vital role. The following chapters on paragraphing, sentence structure, and word choice give students a solid foundation on which to apply their skills of generating ideas, drafting, and revising their work. The text then moves sequentially from shorter assignments (letters and memos) to more complex forms of business writing (instructions, questionnaires, proposals, and reports).

As in the two previous editions, the Third Edition is rich in practical applications useful both to readers who have no on-the-job experience and to those with years of experience. Another continuing strong feature of the Third Edition is the abundance of exercises following each chapter. These exercises give students numerous opportunities to practice a variety of skills from analyzing the strengths and weaknesses of diverse memos, letters, and reports to generating ideas, researching topics, organizing information, drafting, revising, editing, and creating and incorporating visuals.

New Material in the Third Edition

The Third Edition has been improved and expanded to make it a more effective tool for the instructor and a more comprehensive and helpful resource for the student. New examples and exercises have been added throughout to make the discussion of occupational writing more useful and current. Much more information on computers and communication technologies, for example, has been included.

Here is a list of the new items designed to help instructors and students use the Third Edition.

♦ A new Chapter 2 gives an overview of the writing process at work, showing how an employee brainstorms, researches, drafts, and revises an internal proposal.

♦ The process of writing receives increased emphasis throughout; in Chapter 3, for example, students see how a writer generates, drafts, and revises introductory paragraphs for a report on polymers for a general audience.

♦ A new section in Chapter 2 on writing with a computer shows students how using a word processor can help them in the writing process.

♦ Even more examples of unrevised and revised letters and memos illustrate the important techniques of revision.

♦ New examples of and readings on the most recent communication technologies have been added: the feasibility of purchasing a fax machine in Chapter 2, the benefits of desktop publishing in Chapter 11, and the formatting options available from different kinds of software in Chapters 7 and 13.

♦ Additional sections are included on the use of persuasion in occupational writing in Chapter 1, for job letters in Chapter 7, and for proposals in Chapter 15.

♦ Coverage of the AMS letter format in Chapter 6 supplements a sharpened discussion of block and semiblock letter formats.

♦ Expanded coverage of résumé writing in Chapter 7 includes discussion of organizing a résumé by skill area as well as by chronology; two versions of the same individual's résumé help students decide which is best for them.

• The section on computer searches, data bases, and other electronic reference works in Chapter 9 has been greatly expanded.

• Chapter 13 features updated material on computer graphics with additional examples.

• Additional advice and examples are included on avoiding sexist language and on frequently confused words in Chapter 5, adopting the right tone for business correspondence in Chapters 7 and 8, and documenting sources in Chapter 10.

• A more flexible and greatly expanded instructor's guide is available with a new format ($8\frac{1}{2} \times 11$), a classified bibliography of materials on teaching and doing research on occupational writing, additional teaching tips, answers to exercises, transparency masters, and 25 additional models of memos, letters, questionnaires, proposals, and a long report on AIDS and the health care worker. All are suitable for copying and distributing to students for added practice in revising and analyzing their writing.

An Overview of the Chapters

A brief overview of the Third Edition will show how these new materials have been integrated. Section I deals with the overall writing process. Chapter 1, setting the stage for all occupational writing, identifies the basic concepts of audience analysis, purpose, message, style, and tone, and relates these concepts to on-the-job writing.

Chapters 2, 3, 4, and 5 continue this important unit on the basic elements of effective writing. The new Chapter 2 on the writing process at work introduces students to prewriting strategies, drafting, and revising their written work. Chapter 3 explains in detail how to generate effective paragraphs, with special emphasis on the needs of readers in business and industry. Chapter 4, on sentences, gives guidelines on how to create clear and economical sentences, with emphasis on seeing revisions as a key to success. Chapter 5, on words, prepares students to make appropriate choices for their message.

Section II deals with business correspondence. Chapter 6 introduces the nuts and bolts of letter writing and focuses on selecting the appropriate format (including the new section on the AMS letter format), language, and tone. Chapter 7, covering the job search, takes students through the process of preparing a placement file, writing a résumé and organizing it by skill area and/or chronology, writing a letter of application, anticipating interviewers' questions, and accepting or declining a job. For greater teaching flexibility, instructors will find three different letters of application and four résumés from applicants with varying degrees of experience—to help new and veteran job seekers alike. Chapter 8 examines the rhetorical strategies writers must employ to produce a variety of business correspondence—complaint, adjustment, order, sales, and collection letters—with new material on selecting the most effective organizational strategies for good or bad news letters.

Section III provides students with the techniques they need to gather and summarize information. Chapter 9 takes students on a guided tour of the library, shows them how to locate printed and audiovisual materials and how to profit from searching various computer data bases and electronic reference works (a valuable new section of this edition), and provides them with an annotated appendix of useful reference works. Chapter 10 is devoted to several styles of documentation—and particularly to the MLA parenthetical method. A sample student research paper, "Stress and the Computer Programmer," illustrates this method of documentation. In Chapter 11 students will learn how to write clear and concise summaries and abstracts. Chapter 12, on questionnaires, shows how to construct reliable questions, select informants, organize responses, and write a questionnaire survey report. Chapter 13 supplies practical advice on designing visuals, explains how to coordinate visuals with written commentary, discusses and illustrates a variety of visuals students can use in their work, and concludes with a greatly expanded and illustrated section on computer graphics.

In Section IV students are asked to apply the skills they learned in Section III to more complex writing assignments. Chapter 14 covers writing accurate instructions and selecting the most appropriate language and visuals. Chapter 15 focuses on three common types of proposals: an internal proposal for an employer, a sales proposal (solicited and unsolicited) for customers, and a research proposal written for a teacher. Chapter 16 outlines the principles common to all short reports and then discusses specific types, with detailed coverage of test and laboratory reports. Instructors will also find the discussion of unusual occurrence reports especially detailed. Finally, students are cautioned about the legal implications of what they write and are shown how to avoid some legal pitfalls.

To make it more accessible to students, Chapter 17 on long reports has been revised for this edition to emphasize the process of writing such a report. In this chapter students are encouraged to see a long report as the culmination of all their work in the course or on a major project at work. The individual parts of such a report are discussed in detail, with a student-written model report, "The Positive Effects of Robots in American Industry," used as an illustration. Together with the report on "Stress and the Computer Programmer" in Chapter 10, instructors have two complete, fully documented student research papers to use in teaching the long report.

Chapter 18, on the importance of audience analysis in oral communication, offers common-sense advice on handling briefings and on generating, organizing, and delivering formal speeches.

Acknowledgments

I am grateful to the many friends who gave me the benefit of their suggestions as I prepared the Third Edition of *Successful Writing at Work*. At the University of Southern Mississippi, they include Gayle Bracey, LaNelle Daniel, Jeanne Ezell, David Goff, Paul McCarver, Harry McCraw, Linda McDaniel, Mark McElroy, Kathleen Rossman, David Wheeler, and Irmegard Wolfe. I also thank Colby Kullman of the University of Mississippi; David H. Roberts of Samford University; E. D. Lister of California State University at Carson; and Laura Weaver of the University of Evansville.

    I am deeply indebted to the following instructors who offered many valuable suggestions as they reviewed the Third Edition of *Successful Writing at Work:* Albert G. Black, California State University at Long Beach; Eugene R. Cunnar, New Mexico State University; Robert F. Denton, Northern Illinois University; Marlys Hoon, Kirkwood Community College; Terri Johnson, Moraine Park Technical Institute; and John Pennington, Valdosta State College.

    My thanks go to my editors at D. C. Heath for their assistance and friendship—Paul Smith, Karen Wise, Holt Johnson, and Kim Mrazek. I am again indebted to Ann Sykes for her remarkable keyboarding skills.

    Finally, I thank my wife Janeen L. Kolin for once more patiently reading and evaluating every word I wrote and rewrote.

P. C. K.

Contents

Backgrounds

1 Getting Started: Writing and Your Career   3

FOUR KEYS TO EFFECTIVE WRITING   4

Identifying Your Audience / 4   Establishing Your Purpose / 8
Formulating Your Message / 10   Selecting Your Style and Tone / 12

CHARACTERISTICS OF JOB-RELATED WRITING   13

Providing Practical Information / 14   Giving Facts, Not
Impressions / 14   Providing Visuals to Clarify and Condense
Information / 15   Giving Accurate Measurements / 17   Stating
Responsibilities Precisely / 17   Persuading and Offering
Recommendations / 18

HOW THIS BOOK WILL WORK FOR YOU   20

EXERCISES   20

2 The Writing Process at Work   25

WHAT WRITING IS AND ISN'T   25

FOUR ELEMENTS OF THE WRITING PROCESS   26
Researching / 26   Prewriting / 27   Drafting / 29   Revising / 35

COMPUTERS AND THE WRITING PROCESS   35

FOUR BASIC POINTS ON USING A WORD PROCESSOR   40

EXERCISES   40

3 Writing: Paragraphs   43

THE IMPORTANCE OF PARAGRAPHS   43

PARAGRAPHS IN THE WRITING PROCESS   44

FOUR TYPES OF PARAGRAPHS   47

Supporting Paragraphs / 47   Introductory Paragraphs / 49   Transitional
Paragraphs / 49   Concluding Paragraphs / 50

GENERATING TOPIC SENTENCES / 51

THREE CHARACTERISTICS OF AN EFFECTIVE PARAGRAPH / 53
Unity / 53   Coherence / 54   Completeness / 57

THE APPEARANCE OF PARAGRAPHS   59

PATTERNS OF PARAGRAPH ORGANIZATION   61
Examples Pattern / 61   Description Pattern / 62   Time Pattern / 62
Space Pattern / 63   Comparison/Contrast Pattern / 63   Definition
Pattern / 64   Classification Pattern / 64   Cause-to-Effect Pattern / 65
Effect-to-Cause Pattern / 66

THE PARAGRAPH: AN OVERVIEW   66

EXERCISES   66

4   Writing: Sentences   71

CLEAR SENTENCES AND YOUR CAREER   71

WHAT THIS CHAPTER CAN DO FOR YOU   72

CONSTRUCTING AND PUNCTUATING SENTENCES   72
The Difference Between Phrases and Clauses / 72   Sentence Fragments / 73
The Comma Splice / 74   Four Ways to Correct Comma Splices / 75
How *Not* to Correct Commas Splices / 76

USING THE APPROPRIATE VOICE: ACTIVE OR PASSIVE   76
When to Use the Active Voice / 76   When to Use the Passive Voice / 77

USING PARALLELISM   78

WRITING SENTENCES THAT SAY WHAT YOU MEAN   80
Logical Sentences / 80   Sentences Using Contextually Appropriate Words / 81
Sentences with Well-Placed Modifiers / 81   Correct Use of Pronoun
References in Sentences / 82

SEVEN GUIDELINES FOR WRITING READABLE SENTENCES   83

WRITING EFFECTIVE SENTENCES: A BRIEF SUMMARY   87

EXERCISES   87

5   Writing: Words   92

SPELLING WORDS CORRECTLY   92

MATCHING THE RIGHT WORD WITH THE RIGHT MEANING   96

SELECTING PRECISE WORDS   100

CUTTING OUT UNNECESSARY WORDS   102

ELIMINATING SEXIST LANGUAGE   105

AVOIDING JARGON AND SLANG   106
Jargon / 106   Slang / 108

A FINAL NOTE ON USING WORDS EFFECTIVELY   109

EXERCISES   110

Correspondence

6   Letter Writing: Some Basics   117

THE IMPORTANCE OF LETTERS   117

TYPING/PRINTING AND PROOFREADING LETTERS   118

LETTER FORMATS   119

PARTS OF A LETTER   123

Date Line / 123   Inside Address / 125   Salutation / 125   Subject Line / 127   Body of the Letter / 127   Complimentary Close / 128   Signature / 128   Reference Initials / 128   Enclosure(s) Line / 129   Copy or Copies Distributed / 129

ADDRESSING AN ENVELOPE   129

Outside Address / 130   Return Address and Special Instructions / 130

MAKING A GOOD IMPRESSION ON YOUR READER   131

Four Guidelines to Achieving the "You Attitude" / 132

USING THE MOST EFFECTIVE LANGUAGE IN YOUR LETTERS   137

TWENTY QUESTIONS LETTER WRITERS SHOULD ASK THEMSELVES   142

EXERCISES   142

7   How to Get a Job: Résumés, Letters, Applications, Interviews, and Evaluations   147

ANALYZING YOUR STRENGTHS AND RESTRICTING YOUR JOB SEARCH   148

PREPARING A DOSSIER   149

LOOKING IN THE RIGHT PLACES FOR A JOB   153

PREPARING A RÉSUMÉ   154

The Process of Drafting Your Résumé / 155   How Much Should You Include on a Résumé? / 156   What Should You Exclude from a Résumé? / 156   Parts of a Résumé / 156   Organizing Your Résumé by Function or Skill Areas / 165   The Appearance of Your Résumé / 168

WRITING A LETTER OF APPLICATION   171

How the Letter and Résumé Differ / 171   Résumé Facts You Exclude from a Letter of Application / 173   Finding Information About Your Prospective Employer / 173   Drafting the Letter of Application / 174

FILLING OUT A JOB APPLICATION   179

GOING TO AN INTERVIEW   183

Preparing for an Interview / 183   Questions to Expect at an Interview / 183   The Follow-up Letter / 186

ACCEPTING OR DECLINING A JOB   187

EMPLOYMENT EVALUATIONS   187

EXERCISES   190

8 Types of Business Correspondence   196

MEMOS   197

Function of Memos / 197   Memo Format / 197   Strategies for Organizing a Memo / 199

ORDER LETTERS   201

INQUIRY LETTERS   204

SPECIAL REQUEST LETTERS   206

SALES LETTERS   206

Getting the Reader's Attention / 210   Calling Attention to the Product's Appeal / 212   Showing the Customer the Product's Application / 212   Ending with a Specific Request for Action / 214

CUSTOMER RELATIONS LETTERS   214

Planning Your Customer Relations Letters / 215   Being Direct or Indirect / 216

TYPES OF CUSTOMER RELATIONS LETTERS   218

Thank-You Letters / 218   Congratulation Letters / 221   Follow-up Letters / 222   Complaint Letters / 224   Adjustment Letters / 229   Collection Letters / 235

BUSINESS CORRESPONDENCE: SOME CLOSING REMARKS FOR SUCCESS   241

EXERCISES   241

Gathering and Summarizing Information

9 Finding and Using Library Materials   249

THE LIBRARY AND ITS SECTIONS   250

BOOKS   250

The Card Catalog / 250   The Stacks / 255

PERIODICAL HOLDINGS AND INDEXES   257

The *Readers' Guide to Periodical Literature* / 257   Specialized Indexes / 258

USING THE COMPUTER IN YOUR LIBRARY RESEARCH   263

Compact Disks / 264   Online Searches / 264   Suggestions on Using Computerized Searches / 265   Finding a Periodical in Your Library / 266

REFERENCE BOOKS   266

Encyclopedias / 267   Dictionaries / 267   Abstracts / 268
Handbooks, Manuals, and Almanacs / 268

GOVERNMENT DOCUMENTS   268

THE POPULAR PRESS   271

Vertical File Materials / 271   Indexes to Newspapers / 271
NewsBank / 272

AUDIOVISUAL MATERIALS   273

Microfilm / 273   Microfiche / 274

NOTE TAKING   275

How to Prepare Bibliography Cards / 275   How to Prepare Note Cards / 276
To Quote or Not to Quote / 278

APPENDIX: SOME HELPFUL REFERENCE WORKS   280

Indexes / 280   Encyclopedias / 281   Dictionaries / 283
Abstracts / 284

EXERCISES   285

10   Documenting Sources   289

THE WHYS AND HOWS OF DOCUMENTATION   289

Why Is Documentation Important? / 289   What Must Be Documented? / 290

DOCUMENTATION IN THE WRITING PROCESS   290

PARENTHETICAL AND FOOTNOTE DOCUMENTATION   291

PREPARING THE WORKS CITED PAGE   292

How to Alphabetize the Works in Your Reference List / 297

DOCUMENTING WITHIN THE TEXT   298

DOCUMENTATION IN SCIENTIFIC AND TECHNICAL WRITING   302

The Author-Date Method / 303   The Ordered References Method / 303

SAMPLE RESEARCH PAPER USING MLA IN-TEXT DOCUMENTATION   304

EXERCISES   318

11   Summarizing Materials   320

THE IMPORTANCE OF SUMMARIES   320

CONTENTS OF A SUMMARY   322

What to Include in a Summary / 322   What to Omit in a Summary / 322

THE PROCESS OF PREPARING A SUMMARY   323

EVALUATIVE SUMMARIES   334

Evaluating the Content / 334   Evaluating the Style / 335   Minutes / 337
What to Include in Minutes / 340

ABSTRACTS   340

The Differences Between a Summary and an Abstract / 340   Where Abstracts
Are Found / 341

CONCLUSION   342

EXERCISES   342

12   Preparing a Questionnaire and Reporting the Results   349

THE USEFULNESS OF QUESTIONNAIRES   349

Mail Questionnaires Versus Personal Interview Questionnaires / 350
A Questionnaire's Two Audiences / 351

CHOOSING A RESTRICTED TOPIC   352

WRITING THE QUESTIONS   353

Relevant Questions / 353   Two Basic Types of Questions / 355   Reliable
and Valid Questions / 358

WRITING EFFECTIVE INSTRUCTIONS   363

PRESENTING AN ATTRACTIVE QUESTIONNAIRE   365

SELECTING RESPONDENTS   365

Systematic Random Sampling / 367   Stratified Random Sampling / 368
Quota Sampling / 368

DISTRIBUTING A QUESTIONNAIRE   368

TABULATING RESPONSES   371

WRITING EFFECTIVE QUESTIONNAIRE REPORTS   373

Rules for Writing Numbers / 373   Explaining What the Numbers Mean / 378
Using Direct Quotations / 379   Writing a Recommendation / 380

CONCLUSION   386

EXERCISES   386

13   Designing Visuals   391

THE USEFULNESS OF VISUALS   391

CHOOSING EFFECTIVE VISUALS   393

THE GRAPHIC ARTIST'S DESK   394

WRITING ABOUT VISUALS   395

TABLES   397

Preparing a Table / 399   Labeling a Table / 399

FIGURES   400

Graphs / 400   Circle Charts / 404   Bar Charts / 406
Pictograms / 410   Organizational Charts / 411   Flow Charts / 413
Maps / 414   Photographs / 417   Drawings / 419

COMPUTER GRAPHICS   423

Two Ways to Produce Computer Graphics / 424   The Capabilities of
Computer Graphics / 426

GLOSSARY   427

EXERCISES   428

Instructions, Proposals, and Reports

14 Writing Clear Instructions   435

THE IMPORTANCE OF INSTRUCTIONS   435

THE VARIETY OF INSTRUCTIONS: A BRIEF OVERVIEW   436

BEFORE WRITING INSTRUCTIONS   438

SELECTING THE RIGHT WORDS   439

USING VISUALS EFFECTIVELY   440

THE FOUR PARTS OF INSTRUCTIONS   443
The Introduction / 443   List of Equipment and Materials / 446
The Steps in Instructions / 448   The Conclusion / 451

INSTRUCTIONS: SOME FINAL ADVICE   451

EXERCISES   453

15 Proposals   456

WRITING SUCCESSFUL PROPOSALS   456

PROPOSALS ARE PERSUASIVE PLANS   457

TYPES OF PROPOSALS   457
Solicited and Unsolicited Proposals / 458   Internal and External
Proposals / 459

GUIDELINES FOR WRITING A SUCCESSFUL PROPOSAL   459

INTERNAL PROPOSALS   460
Your Audience and Office Politics / 463   The Organization of an Internal
Proposal / 464

SALES PROPOSALS   466
The Audience and Its Needs / 466   Organizing a Sales Proposal / 466

PROPOSALS FOR RESEARCH PAPERS AND REPORTS   474
Writing for Your Teacher / 474   Organization of a Proposal for a Research
Paper / 474

PREPARING PROPOSALS: A FINAL REMINDER   479

EXERCISES   479

16 Short Reports   484

WHY SHORT REPORTS ARE IMPORTANT   484

TYPES OF SHORT REPORTS   484

HOW TO WRITE SHORT REPORTS   485

PERIODIC REPORTS   487

SALES REPORTS   488

PROGRESS REPORTS   493
How to Begin a Progress Report / 498   How to Continue a Progress Report / 498   How to End a Progress Report / 498

TRIP REPORTS   499
Common Types of Trip Reports / 499   How to Gather Information for a Trip Report / 505

TEST REPORTS   505

INCIDENT REPORTS   510
Protecting Yourself Legally / 510   Parts of an Incident Report / 511

MAIN POINTS TO REMEMBER ABOUT SHORT REPORTS   514

EXERCISES   515

17 Long Reports   518
HOW A LONG REPORT DIFFERS FROM A SHORT REPORT   518

THE PROCESS OF WRITING A LONG REPORT   521

PARTS OF A LONG REPORT   522
Front Matter / 522   Text of the Report / 525   Back Matter / 527

THE MODEL LONG REPORT IN THIS CHAPTER   528

EXERCISES   551

18 Oral Reports   552
INFORMAL BRIEFINGS   552

FORMAL SPEECHES   554
Analyzing Your Audience / 554   Speaking for the Occasion / 554   Ways of Presenting a Speech / 555   Preparing the Parts of a Speech / 556   The Speech Outline / 558   Using Visuals / 559   Rehearsing a Speech / 563   Delivering a Speech / 563

SPEECH EVALUATION FORM   565

EXERCISES   567

Index   569

I

Backgrounds

Chapter 1: Getting Started:
Writing and Your Career

◆

Chapter 2: The Writing Process at Work

◆

Chapter 3: Writing: Paragraphs

◆

Chapter 4: Writing: Sentences

◆

Chapter 5: Writing: Words

1

Getting Started:
Writing and Your Career

What skills have you learned in school or on the job this year? Perhaps you have learned techniques of health care in order to become a nurse, respiratory therapist, or dental hygienist. Maybe you have received training in law enforcement to prepare yourself for work with a crime-detection unit or a traffic-control department. Possibly you have studied or worked in industrial technology, agriculture, computer science, hotel and restaurant management, or forestry. Or maybe you have improved skills needed to be an executive secretary, salesperson, office manager, computer programmer, or accountant. Whatever your area of accomplishment, the facts and practical know-how you have acquired are essential for your career.

You need an additional skill, however, to ensure a successful career: you must be able to write clearly about the facts, procedures, and problems of your job. Writing is a part of every job. In fact, your first contact with a potential employer is through your letter of application, which determines a company's first impression of you. And the higher you advance in an organization, the greater the amount of writing you will be doing.

Offices and other workplaces contain numerous reminders of the importance of writing, such as "in" and "out" boxes, file cabinets, typewriters, word processors, printers, and fax machines. Why? Writing keeps business moving. It allows individuals working for a company to communicate with one another and with the customers and clients they must serve if the company is to stay in business. These written communications take the form of memos, letters, summaries, instructions, questionnaires, proposals, and reports. This book will show you, step by step, how to write these and other job-related communications easily and well.

Chapter 1 presents some basic information about writing and offers some questions you can ask yourself to make the writing process easier and more effective. This chapter also describes the basic functions of on-the-job writing.

◆ FOUR KEYS TO EFFECTIVE WRITING

Effective writing on the job is carefully planned, thoroughly researched, and clearly presented. Whether you send a routine memo to a coworker or a special report to the president of the company, your writing will be more effective if you ask yourself four questions.

1. *Who* will read what I write? (Identify your *audience.*)
2. *Why* should they read what I write? (Establish your *purpose.*)
3. *What* do I have to say to them? (Formulate your *message.*)
4. *How* can I best communicate? (Select your *style* and *tone.*)

The questions *who? why? what?* and *how?* do not function independently; they are all related. You write (1) for a specific audience (2) with a clearly defined purpose in mind (3) about a topic your readers need to understand (4) in language appropriate for the occasion. Once you answer the first question, you are off to a good start toward answering the other three. Now let us examine each of the four questions in detail.

Identifying Your Audience

Knowing *who* makes up your audience is one of your most important responsibilities as a writer. In fact, it is important to analyze your audience throughout the composing process. Look for a minute at the American Heart Association posters reproduced in Figures 1.1, 1.2, and 1.3. The main purpose of all three posters is the same: to discourage individuals from smoking. The essential message in each poster—smoking is dangerous to your health—is also the same. But note how the different details—words, photographs, situations—have been selected in order to appeal to three different audiences.

The poster in Figure 1.1 emphasizes smoking problems that are especially troublesome to a teenager: red eyes, bad breath, discolored teeth, and unattractive hair. The smiling teen pictured without a cigarette appears to have avoided these problems. The message at the top of the poster plays on two meanings of the word *heart:* (1) smoking can cause heart disease and (2) smoking can be a deterrent to romance. Teenagers are particularly sensitive to the second meaning.

The poster in Figure 1.2 is aimed at an audience of pregnant women and appropriately shows a woman with a lit cigarette. The words at the top and bottom of the poster appeal to a mother's sense of responsibility as the reason to stop smoking, a reason pregnant women would be especially likely to respond to.

Figure 1.3 is directed toward fathers and appropriately shows a small child seated on his father's lap. The situation depicted appeals to a father's wish for happiness for his child. The words in the poster warn that a father who smokes may die prematurely and make his child's life unhappy.

The copywriters for the American Heart Association have chosen appropriate details—words, pictures, and so on—to convince each audience not to smoke. With their careful choices, they successfully answered the question, "How can we

FIGURE 1.1   No-smoking poster aimed at teenagers.

© Reprinted with permission of the American Heart Association.

best communicate with each audience?" As an indication of their skill, note that details relevant for one audience (teenagers, for example) could not be used as effectively for another audience (fathers).

These three posters illustrate some fundamental points you need to keep in mind when writing for an audience.

- ◆ Members of each audience differ in backgrounds, experiences, needs, opinions.
- ◆ How you picture your audience will determine what you say to them.
- ◆ Viewing something from the audience's perspective will help you to select the most relevant details for that audience.

Some Questions to Ask About Your Audience

You can form a fairly accurate picture of your audience by asking yourself some questions *before* you write. For each audience for whom you write, consider the following questions.

FIGURE 1.2   No-smoking poster directed at pregnant women.

© Reprinted with permission of the American Heart Association.

1. Who is my audience? What is the reader's job title? There's a big difference between writing to a vice-president for industrial relations and writing to a coworker. What specific duties does my audience have to perform? What kind of education, social background, and interests does my audience have?

2. How many people will make up my audience? Is it just one individual (the nurse on the next shift, the desk sergeant) or many (all the users of a product manufactured by my company)? If I write a letter to a customer, will my boss also want to see and approve it? As a general rule, the more diverse your audience is, the less technical your discussion must be.

3. How much does my audience already know about what I am writing about? Are you writing to people who are familiar with all the technical procedures you know? Or are you addressing an employer or customer who, however intelligent, is not an expert in your field and cannot be expected to know technical details and language? Will your reader know as much about a problem or an issue as you do? Most often you will be writing to people who do not know

FIGURE 1.3 No-smoking poster appealing to fathers.

© Reprinted with permission of the American Heart Association.

as much about your job as you do. Such readers need more background information, more definitions of terms, and more explanatory visuals than a technically trained audience would. You may have to provide easy-to-understand comparisons and nontechnical summaries for these readers.

4. What is my audience's reason for reading my work? Is it a part of my readers' routine duties, such as a progress report? Are they looking for answers to special problems? Do they want to find a list of benefits from me that another writer or company cannot offer? Will they want to have complete details or do they prefer a summary of the main points?

5. What is my audience's attitude toward me and my work? Am I writing to readers who are friendly and eager to receive my work—for example, my memo to my boss saying that sales are up? Will my reader be skeptical—for example, a customer whose business I want to attract by selling him or her a new piece of equipment or service? Is my reader antagonistic—for example, a disappointed customer whose request I must refuse? What are the reasons the reader is skeptical or antagonistic? Such readers will want more detailed or more logical explanations than sympathetic readers. It is important to address directly the reasons for their disbelief or complaints.

6. What do I want my audience to do after reading my work? Should they store it for future reference, review it and send it to another office or individual, or act on it at once? Do I want the reader to use my work to purchase something from me or my company, approve my plan for a change within our company, agree with a decision I have made, or gather additional information for me? Have I made clear what I expect next from my reader?

As your answers to these questions will show, you may have to communicate with many different audiences on your job. If you work for a large organization that has numerous departments, you may have to write to such diverse readers as accountants, office managers, personnel directors, engineers, public relations specialists, marketing specialists, computer programmers, and individuals who install, operate, and maintain equipment. In addition, you will need to communicate effectively with customers about your company's products and services. Each group of readers will have different expectations; you need to understand these differences if you want to supply relevant information.

The advertisement in Figure 1.4 concisely illustrates how the writer for a manufacturer of heavy-duty equipment identified the priorities of five different audiences and selected appropriate information to communicate with them. For the owner or principal executive, the writer appropriately stresses financial benefits: the machine is a "money maker" and is compatible with other equipment so additional equipment purchases are unnecessary. A production engineer is more interested in other information. For this reader, the writer emphasizes "state-of-the-art" transmissions, productivity, and upkeep. To appeal to operators, the writer focuses on how easy it is to run the machine—the pressurized cab keeps out environmental problems that interfere with the job. A maintenance worker is concerned about such things as "lube points" and "test ports," not costs or operational comforts. The writer has selected appropriate information about making this worker's job easier and quicker. For the production supervisor, the writer has emphasized the speed and efficiency the machine offers. The lesson of this ad is clear: give each reader the details that he or she needs to accomplish a given job.

In some cases you are not able to identify all the members of your potential audience. Just assume that you have a general audience and keep your message as simple as possible.

Establishing Your Purpose

By knowing *why* you are writing, you will communicate better and find writing itself to be an easier process. The reader's needs and your goal in communicating will help you to formulate your purpose. It will help you to determine exactly what you can and must say. With your purpose clearly identified, you are on the

FIGURE 1.4   An advertisement aimed at the needs of five different audiences.

"The 475C model with TURBO TRANSMISSION is the state of the art in loaders. It's an investment that pays out in productivity. Less upkeep, too."

"I can really do a day's work in this cab. It's insulated, pressurized, and mounted to keep noise, dirt, and vibration out."

"This machine's a money-maker. Its boom size matches our 85-ton trucks, and keeps them hustling."

"I've never seen a machine this size that can move so much material as fast and as easy as this one."

"All the lube points are right here. There's even a test port for the hydraulics. That makes my life easy."

MICHIGAN 475C

CLARK

right track. As you start to write, state for yourself your goal in communicating. Don't worry about the way it sounds. It is more important at this stage to work on ideas.

> I want new employees to know how to log on to the computer.

Think over what you have written. Rewrite your purpose statement until it states precisely why you are writing to your readers and what you want them to do or to know.

> I want to teach new employees the security code for logging on to the company computer.

Since your purpose controls the amount and order of information you include, state it clearly at the beginning of every letter, memo, or report. Such an overview will help the reader to follow and act on your communication.

> This memo is to acquaint new employees with the security measures they must take when logging on to the company computer.

> The following report will give you a detailed account of my progress to date on completing my research study this semester.

In the opening purpose statement below, note how the author clearly informs the reader what the report will and will not cover.

> As you requested at last month's organizational meeting, I have conducted a study of our policies for renting our safe deposit boxes. This report describes, but does not evaluate, our current procedures.

The following preface to a pamphlet on architectural casework details contains a model statement of purpose suited to a particular audience.

> This publication has been prepared by the Architectural Woodwork Institute to provide a source book of conventional details and uniform detail terminology. For this purpose a series of casework detail drawings, . . . representative of the best industry-wide practice, has been prepared and is presented here. By supplying both architect and woodwork manufacturer with a common authoritative reference, this work will enable architects and woodworkers to communicate in a common technical language. . . . It is hoped that besides serving as a basic reference for architects and architectural drafters, it will be an effective training tool for the beginning drafter-architect-in-training. It should also be a valuable aid to the project manager in coordinating the work of many drafters on large projects.[1]

After reading the preface, readers will have a clear sense of why they should use the casebook and what to do with the material they find in it.

Formulating Your Message

Your message is the sum of *what* facts, responses, and recommendations you put into writing. A message includes the *scope* and *details* of your communication. The details are those key points you think readers need to know to perform their

---

[1] Reprinted by permission of Architectural Woodwork Institute.

jobs. Scope refers to how much information you give readers about those key details. Some messages will consist of one or two sentences: "Do not touch; wet paint." "Order #756 was sent this afternoon by Federal Express. It should arrive at your office by March 21." At the other extreme, messages may extend over twenty or thirty pages. Messages may carry good news or bad news. They may deal with routine matters, or they may handle changes in policy, special situations, or problems.

Keep in mind that you will adapt your message to fit your audience. For technical audiences such as engineers or technicians, you may have to supply a complete report with every detail noted or contained in an appendix. For other readers—busy executives, for example—you would be wrong to include such technical details. A short discussion or summary of the financial or managerial significance of these details is what this group of readers would want to have.

Consider the message of the following excerpt from a section of "Tips on Communication" included in a metropolitan telephone book. The message provides factual information about a change in mailing policies, informing the general public about acceptable and unacceptable sizes of first- and third-class mail.

Size Standards for Domestic Mail

Nonstandard Mail

The following material is considered nonstandard mail. First-class mail weighing one ounce or less and single piece third-class mail weighing two ounces or less which

1. exceeds any of the following:
   (a) Height of $6\frac{1}{8}$ inches.
   (b) Length of $11\frac{1}{2}$ inches.
   (c) Thickness of $\frac{1}{4}$ inch.
2. has a height-to-length ratio which does not fall between $1:13$ and $1:25$ inclusive.

A surcharge will be assessed on each piece of nonstandard mail in addition to the applicable postage and fees.

Minimum Sizes

All mail must be at least .007 of an inch thick and mail which is $\frac{1}{4}$ inch or less in thickness must be

1. at least $3\frac{1}{2}$ inches in height and at least 5 inches long.
2. rectangular.

The preceding message is appropriate for a general audience, readers who are given neither less nor more information than is required. However, employees of the U.S. Postal Service or individuals working in the mail rooms of large companies or in mail-order houses need more detailed instructions. Because of their specialized work, these individuals would consult the more technical and elaborate *Postal Service Manual.*

Selecting Your Style and Tone

Style is *how* something is written rather than what is written. Style helps to determine how well you communicate with an audience, how well it understands and receives your message. It involves the choices you make about the construction of your paragraphs, the length and patterns of your sentences, and the choice of your words. (Chapters 3, 4, and 5 discuss each of these elements of style in detail.) For now, keep in mind that you will have to adapt your style to take into account different messages, different purposes, and different audiences. Your words, for example, will certainly vary with your audience. If all your readers are specialists in your field, you may safely use the technical language and symbols of your profession. Your audience will be familiar with such terminology and will expect you to use it. Nonspecialists, however, will be confused and annoyed if you write to them in the same way. The average consumer, for example, will not know what a *potentiometer* is; but by writing "volume control on a radio" you will be using words that the general public can understand.

Tone in writing, like tone of voice, expresses your attitude toward a topic and toward your audience. In general, your tone can range from formal and impersonal (a scientific report) to informal and personal (a letter to a friend or a how-to article for a consumer). Tone, like style, is indicated in part by the words you choose. For example, saying that someone is "interested in details" conveys a more positive tone than saying the individual is a "nit-picker." The word *economical* is more positive than *stingy* or *cheap.* The tone of your writing is especially important in occupational writing, for it reflects the image you project to your readers and thus determines how they will respond to you, your work, and your company. Depending on your tone you can appear sincere and intelligent or angry and uninformed. Of course, in all of your written work, you need to sound professional and knowledgeable about the topic and genuinely interested in your readers' opinions and problems. The wrong tone in a letter or a proposal might cost you a customer.

The following two descriptions of *heparin,* a drug used to prevent blood clots, illustrate two different styles and tones. The first description appears in a reference work for physicians and is written in a highly technical style with an impersonal tone.

HEPARIN SODIUM INJECTION, USP
Description: Heparin Sodium Injection, USP is a sterile solution of heparin sodium derived from porcine intestines, standardized for use as an anticoagulant, in water for injection with sodium chloride, if needed for isotonicity, and may contain 1% benzyl alcohol as a preservative.

Actions: Heparin inhibits reactions which lead to the clotting of blood and the formation of fibrin clots both in vitro and in vivo. Heparin acts at multiple sites in the normal coagulation system. Small amounts of heparin in combination with antithrombin

III (heparin co-factor) can prevent the development of a hypercoagulable state by inactivating activated Factor X, preventing the conversion of prothrombin to thrombin.

Dosage and administration: Heparin sodium is not effective by oral administration and should be given by deep subcutaneous (intrafat, i.e., above iliac crest or into the abdominal fat layer) injection, by intermittent intravenous injection, or intravenous infusion. The intramuscular route of administration should be avoided because of the frequent occurrence of hematoma at the injection site.[2]

The writer has made the appropriate stylistic choices for the audience, the purpose, and the message. Physicians reading the description will understand and need the technical vocabulary the writer uses; these physicians will also require the sophisticated and lengthy explanations in order to prescribe heparin correctly. The author's authoritative, impersonal tone is coldly clinical, which, of course, is also appropriate because the purpose is to convey the accurate, complete scientific facts about this drug, not the writer's or reader's opinions or beliefs. The author sounds both knowledgeable and appropriately objective.

The following description of heparin, on the other hand, is written in a nontechnical style and with an informal, caring tone. This description is similar to those found on information cards given to patients about the drugs they are receiving in a hospital.

Your doctor has prescribed for you a drug called *heparin.* This drug will prevent any new blood clots from forming in your body. Since heparin cannot be absorbed from your stomach or intestines, you will not receive it in a capsule or tablet. Instead, it will be given into a vein or the fatty tissue of your abdomen. After several days, when the danger of clotting is past, your dosage of heparin will be gradually reduced. Then another medication you can take by mouth will be started.

The writer of this description also made the appropriate choices for the purpose and for the readers. Familiar words rather than technical ones are suitable for nonspecialists such as patients. Note also that this audience does not need elaborate descriptions about the origin and composition of the drug. The tone is both personal and straightforward because the purpose is to win the patient's confidence and to explain the essential functions of the drug, a simpler message than the one for physicians.

The trend today in occupational writing is to make letters, reports, and proposals more natural and personal and less impersonal, formal, or stuffy. But adopting a personal tone does not mean that you should address the reader in a chummy or disrespectful way. Quite the contrary, a business letter or report needs to be personal and professional at the same time.

◆ CHARACTERISTICS OF JOB-RELATED WRITING

Job-related writing characteristically serves six basic functions: (1) to provide practical information, (2) to give facts rather than impressions, (3) to provide visuals to clarify and condense information, (4) to give accurate measurements, (5)

---

[2] Copyright © 1979 *Physicians' Desk Reference,* published by Medical Economics Company, Inc., at Oradell, New Jersey 07649.

to state responsibilities precisely, and (6) to persuade and offer recommendations. These six functions tell you what kind of writing you will produce after you successfully answer the *who? why? what?* and *how?* just discussed.

Providing Practical Information

On-the-job writing requires a practical here's-what-you-need-to-do-or-to-know approach. One such practical approach is *action oriented*. In this kind of writing, you instruct the reader to do something—assemble a ceiling fan, test for bacteria, perform an audit, or take an inventory. Another practical approach of job-related writing is to have someone understand something—why a procedure was changed, what caused a problem or solved it, how much progress occurred on a job site, or why a new piece of equipment should be purchased. Examples of such practical writing are a letter sent from a manufacturer to customers to explain a product recall or a memo sent to employees telling them about changes in their group health insurance policy.

The following description of Energy Efficiency Ratio combines both the action-oriented and knowledge-oriented approaches of practical writing.

> Whether you are buying window air-conditioning units or a central air-conditioning system, consider the performance factors and efficiency of the various units on the market. Before you buy, determine the Energy Efficiency Ratio (EER) of the units under consideration. The EER is found by dividing the BTUs (units of heat) that the unit removes from the area to be cooled by the watts (amount of electricity) the unit consumes. The result is usually a number between 5 and 12. The higher the number, the more efficiently the unit will use electricity. You'll note that EER will vary considerably from unit to unit of a given manufacturer, and from brand to brand. As efficiency is increased, you may find the purchase price is higher; however, operating costs will be lower. Remember, a good rule to follow is to choose the equipment with the highest EER. That way you'll get efficient equipment and enjoy operating economy.[3]

Giving Facts, Not Impressions

Occupational writing is concerned largely with those things that can be seen, heard, felt, tasted, or smelled. The writer uses *concrete language* and specific details (discussed on pages 100–02). The emphasis is on facts rather than on the writer's feelings or guesses. The following discussion by a group of scientists about the sources of oil spills and their impact on the environment is an example of writing with objectivity. It describes events and causes without anger or tears. Imagine how much emotion could have been packed into this paragraph by the residents of the coastal states who have watched such spills come ashore.

> The most critical impact results from the escapement of oil into the ecosystem, both crude oil and refined fuel oils, the latter coming from sources such as marine traffic. Major oil spills occur as a result of accidents such as blowout, pipeline breakage, etc.

---

[3] Reprinted by permission of New Orleans Public Service, Inc.

Technological advances coupled with stringent regulations have helped to reduce the chances of such major spills; however, there is a chronic low-level discharge of oil associated with normal drilling and production operations. Waste oils discharged through the river systems and practices associated with tanker transport dump more significant quantities of oils into the ocean, compared to what is introduced by the offshore oil industry. All of this contributes to the chronic low-level discharge of oil into world oceans. The long-range cumulative effect of these discharges is possibly the most significant threat to the ecosystem.[4]

Providing Visuals to Clarify and Condense Information

Visuals are indispensable partners of words in conveying information to your readers. On-the-job writing makes frequent use of visuals such as tables, charts, photographs, diagrams, and drawings to clarify and condense information. Thanks to various computer software packages, visuals can be created easily and inserted into your writing. The use of visuals—including computer visuals—is discussed in detail in Chapter 13. Visuals play an important role in the workplace. As a poster or as an illustration in an employee handbook, Figure 1.5 helpfully reminds readers about correct lifting procedures and thereby prevents injuries.

FIGURE 1.5   Use of a visual to convey information.

© National Safety Council, Chicago.

---

[4] *The Offshore Ecology Investigation*, Galveston: Gulf Universities Research Consortium, 1975: 4.

TABLE 1.1   Commercial TV Stations in Operation, 1965–1987

Year*	Total	VHF	UHF
1965	586	487	99
1966	598	491	107
1967	620	497	123
1968	648	504	144
1969	675	506	169
1970	690	508	182
1971	696	511	185
1972	699	510	189
1973	700	511	189
1974	705	513	192
1975	711	513	198
1976	710	513	197
1977	728	517	211
1978	727	516	211
1979	732	516	216
1980	746	517	229
1981	752	519	233
1982	772	524	248
1983	802	526	276
1984	870	536	334
1985	904	539	365
1986	922	541	381
1987	982	547	435

Source: Reprinted, with permission, from *Broadcasting / Cablecasting Yearbook*.
*The number of stations is as of Jan. 1 of the year noted.

Visuals are extremely useful in making detailed relationships clear to readers. A great deal of information about the growth and diversity of commercial TV stations is condensed into Table 1.1. Consider how many words a writer would need in order to supply the data contained in the table. Note, too, how easily the numbers can be read when they are arranged in columns. It would be far more difficult to decipher them if they were printed like this: Commercial TV stations in operation: 1965, Total 586, VHF 487, UHF 99; 1966, Total 598, VHF 491, UHF 107, and so forth.

In addition to the visuals already mentioned, the following graphic devices (created quickly with the help of a computer) within your letters and reports will make your writing easier to read and follow:

- Headings, such as "Four Keys to Effective Writing" or "Characteristics of Job-Related Writing"
- Subheadings to divide major sections into parts, such as "Providing Practical Information" or "Giving Facts, Not Impressions"
- Numbers within a paragraph, or even a line, such as (1) this, (2) this, and (3) also this
- Different types of s p a c i n g
- CAPITALIZATION
- *Italics* (indicated in typed copy by underscoring)

◆ **Boldface** (darker type for emphasis)
◆ Asterisks * to * separate * items * or to * note key items
◆ Lists with "bullets" (raised dots or other symbols like the diamonds before each entry in this list)

Keep in mind that such visual devices must be used carefully and with moderation. They should never be used just for decoration or to dress up a letter or report. Used properly, they can help you to organize, arrange, and emphasize your material. They make your work easier to read and recall. For example, headings make your outline visible to readers and help them preview your ideas. Use bullets or numbers when you have many related points; by setting your points in a list, you make it easier for readers to follow and compare them.

Giving Accurate Measurements

Much of your work will depend on measurements—acres, bytes, calories, centimeters, degrees, dollars and cents, grams, percentages, pounds, square feet, units. Readers will look carefully at these measurements. Numbers are clear and convincing. An architect depends on specifications to accomplish a job; a nurse must record precise dosages of medications; a sales representative keeps track of the number of customers visited; and an electronics technologist has to monitor antenna patterns and systems. The following discussion of mixing colored cement for a basement floor would be useless to readers if it did not supply accurate quantities.

> The inclusion of permanent color in a basement floor is a good selling point. One way of doing this is by incorporating commercially pure mineral pigments in a topping mixture placed to a 1-inch depth over a normal base slab. The topping mix should range in volume between 1 part portland cement, 1 1/4 parts sand, and 1 1/4 parts gravel or crushed stone and 1 part portland cement, 2 parts sand and 2 parts gravel or crushed stone. Maximum size gravel or crushed stone should be 3/8 inch. Mixing of cement and pigment is done before aggregate and water are added and must be very thorough to secure uniform dispersion and the full color value of the pigment. The proportion varies from 5 to 10 percent of pigment by weight of cement, depending on the shade desired. If carbon black is used as a pigment to obtain grays or black, a proportion of from 1/2 to 1 percent will be adequate. Manufacturers' instructions should be followed closely and care in cleanliness, placing, and finishing must be regarded as essential. Colored topping mixes are available from some suppliers of ready mixed concrete.[5]

Stating Responsibilities Precisely

Job-related writing, since it is directed to a specific audience, must make absolutely clear what it expects of, or can do for, that audience. Misunderstandings waste time and cost money. Directions on order forms, for example, should indicate how and where information is to be listed and how it is to be routed and

---

[5] Reprinted by permission from *Concrete Construction Magazine*, World of Concrete Center, 426 South Westgate, Addison, Illinois 60101.

acted on. The following directions are taken from different job-related communications, showing readers how to perform different tasks.

- Include agency code numbers in the upper-right corner.

- Items 1 through 16 of this form should be completed by the injured employee or by someone acting on his or her behalf, whenever an injury is sustained in the performance of duty. The term *injury* includes occupational disease caused by the employment. The form should be given to the employee's official superior within 48 hours following the injury. The official superior is that individual having responsible supervision over the employee.

- The Journal Tape from each cash register is to be removed on a daily basis. Record the register number and date on the exterior of the Journal Tape as it is removed. Place each day's Journal Tapes, along with the corresponding day's Cashier's Balance Sheets and bank deposit records, in a small bag, i.e., 10 lb. bag. Record the date on the face of this bag, and staple it closed.[6]

Other kinds of job-related writing deal with the writer's responsibilities rather than the reader's. For example, "Tomorrow I will have a meeting with the district sales manager to discuss (1) July's sales, (2) the possibility of expanding our Madison home market, and (3) next fall's production schedule. I will send you a report of our discussion by August 3, 1989." In a letter of application for a job, writers should conclude by asking for an interview and clearly inform a prospective employer when they are available for an interview—e.g., weekday mornings, only on Monday and Tuesday afternoons, or any time after February 15.

Persuading and Offering Recommendations

Much writing in the business world is directed to employers, customers, and clients to persuade them to buy a product or service or to adopt a certain plan of action. In fact, the very first job-related writing you do will likely be a persuasive letter of application to obtain a job interview with a potential employer. Then, once on the job, you may be required to write persuasive sales letters, reports, proposals, brochures, and even advertisements.

Effective persuasive writing involves using all the skills you will learn about audience analysis, tone, organization, research, and the overall process of drafting and revising your work. In much job-related writing you will have to convince readers that you (and your company) can save them time and money, increase efficiency, reduce risks, and improve their image. At the same time you may have to show readers why you are better than your competitors. Writing persuasive letters, proposals, and reports requires that you have a clear sense of your audience's needs, priorities, and preferences. You will have to conduct research, provide logical arguments, and supply concrete examples or appropriate data.

---

[6] Reprinted by permission from *A&P Store Management Manual*, NCR 2125.

FIGURE 1.6   An advertisement using arguments based on cost, time, and convenience to persuade a potential customer to use a service.

GENERAL MEDICAL
WILL STOP THE
UNNECESSARY TRANSPORTING
OF YOUR INMATES.

● We'll bring our X-ray services to your facility,
  7 days a week, 24 hours a day.
    We can reduce your X-ray costs by a
    minimum of 28%.
    X-ray cost includes radiologists's
    interpretation and written report.
    Same day service with immediate results
    telephoned to your facility.
● Save correctional officers' time, thereby saving
  your facility money.
● Avoid chance of prisoner's escape and possible
  danger to the public.
● Avoid long waits in overcrowded hospitals.
● Reduce your insurance liabilities.
● Other Services Available: Ultrasound, Two
  Dimensional Echocardiogram, C.T. Scan, EKG,
  Blood Lab and Holter Monitor.

General Medical Is Your On-Site
Medical Problem Solver

General Medical Services Corp
A subsidiary of

Federal Medical Industries, Inc. O.T.C.
950 S.W. 12th Avenue, 2nd Floor Suite, Pompano, Florida 33069
(305) 942-1111   FL WATS: 1-800-654-8282

Notice how the advertisement in Figure 1.6 offers a persuasively worded list of reasons—based on cost, time, efficiency, and convenience—to convince correctional officials that they should use General Medical's services rather than those of a hospital or clinic.

Much job-centered writing also requires you to be highly persuasive when you make a recommendation to your employer. In many of your memos and reports you will have to evaluate various options and products for your employer. Your reader will expect you to offer clear-cut, logical, convincing reasons for your choice. The reader will want to know why and how you arrived at your recommendation.

Below is the conclusion to one writer's report on why it is better for a company to lease a truck than to purchase one.

After studying the pros and cons of buying or leasing a company truck, I recommend that we lease it for the following reasons.

1. We will not have to expend any of our funds for a down payment.
2. Our monthly payments for leasing the vehicle will be at least $30 less than the payments we would have to make if we purchased the truck.
3. All major and minor maintenance (up to 20,000 miles) is included as part of our monthly leasing payment.
4. Insurance (theft and damage) is also part of our monthly leasing payment.
5. We have the option of trading in our truck every 16 months for a newer model.

Note the persuasive tone and logical presentation of information this writer has used.

◆ HOW THIS BOOK WILL WORK FOR YOU

This book is based on the belief that writing substantially influences your career. Effective writing can help you to obtain a job, to perform your duties more successfully, and to be promoted for your efforts. Guidelines and examples found in this book emphasize the progress you can make in your career by acquiring effective writing skills. Specifically, *Successful Writing at Work* will:

- explain the writing process and show you how planning, drafting, and revising can help you produce a variety of essential job-related communications.
- describe the function and format of these job-related communications.
- teach you how to supply an audience with the information it must have.

The book is organized to coincide with your own progress in writing. After Chapter 2 explores the process of writing, Chapters 3, 4, and 5 present other elements of writing you must master if you are to advance in your profession. From the basics, the book discusses how you should write a business letter (Chapter 6) and a letter of application and résumé for a job (Chapter 7) and then turns to the letters most frequently written on a job (Chapter 8). In your job you will be responsible for gathering, documenting and summarizing information (Chapters 9–12). And most important, you will have to report your findings both in writing (Chapters 13–17) and orally (Chapter 18). In your writing course this term, you can evaluate step by step your progress toward fulfilling professional goals.

Another useful feature of this book is that it frequently represents the view of the audience (prospective employer, customer, supervisor, questionnaire respondent, proposal evaluator) receiving the work you write. Each type of communication is discussed in terms of what readers will be looking for. In Chapter 7, for example, a letter of application and comments appropriate at an interview are discussed in the light of what personnel directors seek when they recruit new employees. In Chapter 8 your readers are customers or agencies from whom you are ordering merchandise or to whom you have supplied merchandise or services. In Chapter 11, which deals with summaries, your reader is a busy executive who does not have the time to read a twenty-page report and will rely on your two-hundred-word summary of it instead. Each of these readers represents a different challenge. The insights you will gain from this book about readers' needs should prove extremely useful. With these insights, you will be able to prepare yourself psychologically for writing assignments in business and industry. You will also learn how to manage your own writing resources to your best advantage.

◆ EXERCISES

1. What is your chosen career field? Make a list of the kinds of writing you think you will encounter or have already encountered in this career.

2. Make a list of the kinds of writing you have done in a history or English class or for a laboratory or shop course.

3. Compare your lists for Exercises 1 and 2. How do the two types of writing differ?

4. Bring to class a set of printed instructions, a memo, a sales letter, or a brochure. Comment on how well the printed material answers the following questions.
   a. Who is the audience?
   b. Why was the material written?
   c. What is the message?
   d. Are the language and ideas appropriate for the audience, the purpose, and the message?

5. Cut out a newspaper ad that contains a drawing or photograph. Bring it to class together with a paragraph (75–100 words) of your own describing how the message of the ad is directed to a particular audience and commenting on why the illustration was selected for that audience.

6. Pick one of the following topics and write two descriptions of it. In the first description use technical vocabulary. In the second use language suitable for the general public.
   a. spark plug
   b. blood pressure cuff
   c. carburetor
   d. scissors
   e. camera
   f. legal contract
   g. electric sander
   h. cement
   i. muscle
   j. protein
   k. compact disc player
   l. word processor
   m. bread
   n. money
   o. fishing reel
   p. soap
   q. calculator
   r. Nintendo game
   s. baby carriage
   t. thermostat
   u. trees
   v. food processor

7. Select one article from a daily newspaper and one article from either a professional journal in your major field or one of the following journals: *Advertising Age, American Journal of Nursing, Business Marketing, Business Week, Computer, Computer Design, Construction Equipment, Criminal Justice Review, Food Service Marketing, Journal of Forestry, Journal of Soil and Water Conservation, National Safety News, Nutrition Action, Office Machines, Park Maintenance, Scientific American, Today's Secretary.* State how the two articles you selected differ in terms of audience, purpose, message, style, and tone.

8. Assume that you work for Appliance Rentals, Inc., a company that rents TVs, microwave ovens, stereo components, etc. Write a persuasive letter to the members of a campus organization or civic club urging them to rent an appropriate appliance or appliances. Include details in your letter that might have special relevance to members of this specific organization.

9. Read the following article and identify its audience (technical or general), purpose, message, style, and tone.

Microwaves

Much of the world around us is in motion. A wave-like motion. Some waves are big like tidal waves and some are small like the almost unseen footprints of a waterspider on a quiet pond. Other waves can't be seen at all, such as an idling truck sending out vibrations our bodies can feel. Among these are electromagnetic waves. They range from very low frequency sound waves to very high frequency X-rays, gamma rays, and even cosmic rays.

Energy behaves differently as its frequency changes. The start of audible sound—somewhere around 20 cycles per second—covers a segment at the low end of the electromagnetic spectrum. Household electricity operates at 60 hertz (cycles per second). At a somewhat higher frequency we have radio, ranging from shortwave and marine beacons, through the familiar AM broadcast band that lies between 500 and 1600 kilohertz, then to citizen's band, FM, television, and up to the higher frequency police and aviation bands.

Even higher up the scale lies visible light with its array of colors best seen when light is scattered by raindrops to create a rainbow.

Lying between radio waves and visible light is the microwave region—from roughly one gigahertz (a billion cycles per second) up to 3000 gigahertz. In this region the electromagnetic energy behaves in special ways.

Microwaves travel in straight lines, so they can be aimed in a given direction. They can be *reflected* by dense objects so that they send back echoes—this is the basis for radar. They can be *absorbed,* with their energy being converted into heat—the principle behind microwave ovens. Or they can pass *through* some substances that are transparent to the energy—this enables food to be cooked on a paper plate in a microwave oven.

Microwaves for Radar

World War II provided the impetus to harness microwave energy as a means of detecting enemy planes. Early radars were mounted on the Cliffs of Dover to bounce their microwave signals off Nazi bombers that threatened England. The word *radar* itself is an acronym for *RA*dio *D*etection *A*nd *R*anging.

Radars grew more sophisticated. Special-purpose systems were developed to detect airplanes, to scan the horizon for enemy ships, to paint finely detailed electronic pictures of harbors to guide ships, and to measure the speeds of targets. These were installed on land and aboard warships. Radar—especially shipboard radar—was surely one of the most significant technological achievements to tip the scales toward an Allied victory in World War II.

Today, few mariners can recall what is was like before radar. It is such an important aid that it was embraced universally as soon as hostilities ended. Now, virtually every commercial vessel in the world has one, and most larger vessels have two radars: one for use on the open sea and one, operating at a higher frequency to "paint" a more finely detailed picture, for use near shore.

Microwaves are also beamed across the skies to fix the positions of aircraft in flight, obviously an essential aid to controlling the movement of aircraft from city to city across the nation. These radars have also been linked to computers to tell air traffic controllers the altitude of planes in the area and to label them on their screens.

A new kind of radar, phased array, is now being used to search the skies thousands of miles out over the Atlantic and Pacific oceans. Although these advanced radars use microwave energy just as ordinary radars do, they do not depend upon a rotating antenna. Instead, a fixed antenna array, comprising thousands of elements like those of a fly's eye, looks everywhere. It has been said that these radars roll their eyes instead of turning their heads.

High-Speed Cooking

During World War II Raytheon had been selected to work with M.I.T. and British scientists to accelerate the production of magnetrons, the electron tubes that generate microwave energy, in order to speed up the production of radars. While testing some new, higher-powered tubes in a laboratory at Raytheon's Waltham, Massachusetts plant, Percy L. Spencer and several of his staff engineers observed an interesting phenomenon. If you placed your hand in a beam of microwave energy, your hand would grow pleasantly warm. It was not like putting your hand in a heated oven that might sear the skin. The warmth was deep-heating and uniform.

Spencer and his engineers sent out for some popcorn and some food, then piped the energy into a metal wastebasket. The microwave oven was born.

From these discoveries, some 35 years ago, a new industry was born. In millions of homes around the world, meals are prepared in minutes using microwave ovens. In many processing industries, microwaves are being used to perform difficult heating or drying jobs. Even printing presses use microwaves to speed the drying of ink on paper.

In hospitals, doctors' offices, and athletic training rooms, that deep heat that Percy Spencer noticed is now used in diathermy equipment to ease the discomfort of muscle aches and pains.

Telephones without Cable

The third characteristic of microwaves—that they pass undistorted through the air—makes them good messengers to carry telephone conversations as well as live television signals—without telephone poles or cables—across town or across the country. The microwave signals are beamed via satellite or by dish reflectors mounted atop buildings and mountaintop towers.

Microwaves take their name from the Greek *mikro* meaning very small. While the waves themselves may be very small, they play an important role in our world today: in defense; in communications; in air, sea, and highway safety; in industrial processing; and in cooking. At Raytheon the applications expand every day.

Raytheon Magazine Winter 1981: 22–23. Reprinted by permission.

10. Explain how the advertisement on the following page illustrates the techniques of occupational writing described in this chapter. Specifically comment on how the ad reveals that the copywriter successfully analyzed the intended audience. Pay attention to advertising copy (words), the photograph (visuals), and the situation depicted. Also explain how the ad illustrates the five characteristics of on-the-job writing.

Courtesy of Trans-Lux Corporation, Norwalk, Conn. Reprinted with permission.

2

The Writing Process at Work

In Chapter 1 you learned about the different functions of writing for the world of work and also explored some basic concepts all writers must master. To be a successful writer, you need to identify your audience's needs, make sure your message meets those needs, and use the most appropriate style and tone for that message. Understanding the importance of audience, message, style, and tone is a major part of being a successful writer. Just as significant to your success is knowing how effective writers actually create their work for their audiences. This chapter will give you some practical information about the strategies and techniques careful writers use when they work. These strategies and techniques are a vital part of what is known as the *writing process.* This process involves such matters as how writers gather information, how they get their ideas down into written form, and how they organize and revise what they have written to make it suitable for their audiences.

◆ WHAT WRITING IS AND ISN'T

As you begin your study of writing for the world of work, it might be helpful to identify some notions about what writing is and what it is not. Writing is not something mysterious done according to a magical formula known only to a few. Even if you have not done much writing before, you can learn how effective writing works. Nor is writing simply a hit-and-miss affair, left up to chance. Successful writing requires hard, thoughtful effort. It is not done well by simply going through an ordered set of steps as if you were painting by number. You cannot sit down for 15 minutes and expect to write the perfect memo, letter, or short report straight through. Writing does not proceed in some predictable way, where introductions are always written first and conclusions last. Also, it is equally misleading to think that once you put something on paper it is there to stay forever and in that exact place in your letter or report.

Writing is a fluid process; it is dynamic, not static. It enables us to discover and evaluate our thoughts. It happens over a period of time and evolves through many changes. It means making a number of judgment calls. In fact, all careful writing involves rewriting and revising. Even experienced writers do not get it right the first time. A rough draft is never a final copy. Writing grows unevenly, sometimes in bits and pieces and sometimes in great spurts. It changes as the writer's thoughts and information change, and as the writer's view of the material changes.

◆ FOUR ELEMENTS OF THE WRITING PROCESS

The writing process involves four elements: (1) researching, (2) prewriting, (3) drafting, and (4) revising. Keep in mind, though, that these elements are not mutually exclusive. Do not expect to complete each of them just once or in that exact order. For example, research goes on throughout the process of preparing your written work, as does revision, since revising means reexamining and improving what you have written. Effective writers add to or delete from their work, coming up with new information or crossing out irrelevant ideas. They also shift paragraphs, sentences, and words around. A careful writer often retraces steps or skips from one section to another to make a piece of work more complete, accurate, and appropriate for an audience.

You will see part of the process one writer engaged in to prepare a piece of on-the-job writing in Figures 2.2 through 2.5. These figures show the successive drafts involved when William Tisch was asked to write a short report for his boss, Melissa Hill. As the office manager for the company, Melissa was concerned about the costs and efficiency in sending information to customers and asked William to investigate some ways of improving communications. His report recommends that the company purchase a fax machine to increase the flow of information to customers.

Researching

Before you start to compose any letter, memo, or report, do some research. Depending on the size of your assignment, your research can be simple or elaborate. Yet whatever the size of the job, researching will help you to obtain the necessary information your audience expects. Take a few minutes to write down what you know about the topic or problem and what you need to know. Don't think you will be wasting or losing time by not starting to write the report or letter immediately. Actually, you will waste more time if you do not find out as much as possible about your topic (and your audience's interest in it).

You might double-check with your employer, client, or teacher to make sure you have the right idea about length (for example, 1 page or 10?), format (memo or letter?), scope (all office practices or just one particular procedure?), and audience (expert or general?) for your work. Find out if your document will be routed to individuals in other departments. Knowing where your letter or report is headed will help you to gather information and say the right things for your audience. If you are working on a group project, confer with teammates to coordinate your activities with theirs. Writing in the world of business is often a collaborative effort in which one writer shows his or her work to coworkers for comments and help. It might also be necessary to interview people outside your company, such as lab researchers or customers. Prepare for such conferences or interviews so that you will ask the right questions of the most appropriate people. In addition, writers in the business world often interact with their readers. Whenever feasible, try to speak to your readers to identify their needs and to target possible problems. You may also need to do library research (such as reading current periodicals), draft a questionnaire, or draw on personal observations and experiences.

Recall that research is not confined just to the start of the writing process; it goes on throughout. As you start to tackle your subject, take a little extra time during this formative period to think about the information you have gathered so you can most effectively adapt it for your audience.

In preparing his report for Melissa Hill, William Tisch realized he had to do some research. In order to make a recommendation, he had to find out something about different kinds of communication technologies. As he read articles in various business journals and magazines, he soon realized that fax machines were receiving a great deal of very favorable attention. As he read more and more about fax machines, he realized they offered some very strong benefits for his company. He visited a few fax dealers in his city and after seeing some demonstrations, became convinced that purchasing a fax was a feasible and economically wise choice. The results of all this research would be reflected in his final report.

Prewriting

At this stage in the writing process your goal is to get something—anything— down on paper. For most writers who are fearful of writer's block, getting started is the hardest part of the job. But you will feel more comfortable and confident once you list your thoughts on paper. It is always easier to clarify and criticize something you can see. Knowing that you have researched your topic should also make getting started less painful because you have something to build on.

Still, getting started is not easy. A number of widely used prewriting strategies, though, can help you to find the right material for your audience and to restrict your message to them. Use any one of the following techniques alone or in combination.

1. Clustering. In the middle of a sheet of paper, write the word or phrase that best describes your topic. Then start writing any words or phrases that come to mind about this topic. As you write, circle each word or phrase and then connect it to the word from which it sprang. Take a look at the clustered grouping in Figure 2.1 to see how one writer used this prewriting strategy to get started on a report encouraging a manager to switch to flex time. (Flex time is a system in which employees may work on a flexible time schedule within certain limits.) The resulting diagram is still an incomplete picture of the final report but it does give the writer a rough sense of some of the major divisions of the topic and where they may belong in the report.

FIGURE 2.1 Clustering on the topic of flex time.

2. Brainstorming. At the top of a sheet of paper describe your topic in a word or phrase and then list any information you found out about that topic—in any order and as quickly as you can. Brainstorming is like thinking aloud except that you are recording your comments on paper. As you brainstorm, don't stop to delete, rearrange, or rewrite anything and don't dwell on any one item. Don't worry about spelling, punctuation, grammar, or whether you are using words and phrases instead of complete sentences. Keep going with the flow of ideas. The result may well be an odd assortment of details, comments, and opinions. After 10 to 15 minutes, stop and take a short break. When you come back to your list, you will want to make some revisions. Some of your points will be irrelevant, so strike them. You may add some ideas, or combine or rearrange others as you start to develop them in more detail. Your list is not final by any means; you have just begun to mine the raw ore.

Figure 2.2 shows William Tisch's initial brainstormed list. After he began to revise it, he realized that some of the items were not relevant for his audience (6, 8, and 13) and that others were pertinent but needed to be adapted for his reader (5). He also recognized that some items were repetitious (1, 2, and 11). As he worked on his list, other relevant points came to mind that were not on his original list—that a fax can transmit and receive messages after 5:00 P.M. when phone rates are lower, that it is small and portable, and that it is compatible with a personal computer.

3. Outlining. A prewriting outline can be brief and very informal—for no one's eyes but yours. You might simply jot down some major points with a few subpoints to identify the major sections and subsections of your paper and to begin to discover relationships between them. Don't worry about a formal outline style with roman or arabic numerals and parallel subdivisions. (Of course, at some later stage, you may have to prepare a formal outline for your employer or coworkers, especially for a longer, more complex project.) Many writers use an outline as a quick way to sketch in their ideas. The outline becomes a handy, convenient form into which writers can plug their ideas. As with a brainstormed list, leave your outline to cool for a while. When you return you can juggle points and add and delete others. Note that William Tisch organized his revised brainstormed list into an outline in Figure 2.3 as a further stage of his prewriting activities.

In addition to these techniques, there are a few others worth trying. You may find that asking and answering a series of questions (who, what, where, how, when, why) about your topic is a good way to get started. Or you might even try some *freewriting* (just plunging into a very early, unplanned draft) helpful. The important point is that there is no one right way to get started. If you are not sure which way works best for you, experiment with a few of these techniques.

Drafting

When you draft, you convert the words and phrases from your outlines, brainstormed lists, or clustered groups into paragraphs. Think of your prewriting jottings as the material out of which the basic building blocks (paragraphs) of your

FIGURE 2.2 William Tisch's initial, unrevised brainstormed list.

Everything I can think of on how a
fax machine could help our business

1. lots of small and big businesses are buying
   fax machines
2. one million of them used in 1988
3. inexpensive models — $1200 to about $1600
   (more with attachments)
4. will scan anything, reproduce signatures,
   blueprints, photographs
5. fast work — 9.6 Kbps
6. used a lot in Japan — M.D.s send prescriptions
   to pharmacies via fax
7. would drastically reduce our cost for overnight
   mail service
8. circuit boards, memory chips — real advance in
   digital technology
9. would give us a record of everything we
   send/receive
10. set up of a fax is quick
11. by 1990, 2.5 million will be installed
12. fax — part of a complete communication system
13. relationship to telex?
14. dual language capability — English/anything
15. no typist needed to transcribe
16. wouldn't interfere with office routines
17. Zap Fax is a good model to choose

drafts will come. During drafting, as elsewhere in the writing process, you will see some overlap as you look back over your lists or outlines to create your rough draft(s).

Keep in mind that drafting is still preliminary to the creation of your final copy. Don't expect to wind up with a polished, complete copy of your paper after

FIGURE 2.3   William Tisch's rough outline made after revising his brainstormed list.

I. Convenience

    A. Transmits over phone lines

    B. Easy to install and operate

    C. All we need is a phone

    D. Small, portable model that fits on a desk

    E. Can send anything--signatures, art, letters, reports

    F. Fits into our work routines

    G. Zap Fax is a good choice

II. Time/Efficiency

    A. Fast speed--400 words in less than a minute

    B. Quick return of documents in less than a day, very good for invoice checking

    C. Quick turnaround of paperwork

    D. Will save time--no need to recopy everything

III. Money

    A. Save on delivery service charges

    B. Can transmit when phone rates are lowest--after 5:00 P.M.

    C. Initial cost of fax cheap

    D. Eliminates (or drastically cuts down on) misunderstood phone orders

working on only one draft. In most cases, you will have to work through many drafts, but each draft should be less rough than the preceding one, moving you ever closer toward your final copy. Figure 2.4 shows only one of the many drafts that William Tisch prepared. Note that he has added an introduction and conclusion that were not included in his outline (Figure 2.3). These are necessary parts

FIGURE 2.4   One of many rough drafts of William Tisch's report.

TO: Melissa Hill, Office Manager

FROM: William Tisch

DATE: November 2, 1988

RE: Improving Communications

As you requested, I have been investigating a variety of ways that we might increase our efficiency and lower the costs of communicating with our customers. The most beneficial and immediate solution I propose is to purchase a fax (facsimile) machine. More and more of our clients have these machines in their offices, factories, and stores, and they are increasingly becoming a part of many companies' communication systems. With a fax machine, we can send our messages almost instantaneously all over the country, and at cheaper rates than we now pay for conventional delivery services. We will realize many advantages.

A fax machine is easy to operate and to set up. All we need is the fax machine and a telephone. Among the number of fax machines I have seen, most are small (about the size of a typewriter) and are portable. They easily fit on a desk. The Zap Fax is a good choice for us. The fax machine sends copies of letters, memos, reports, graphs, blueprints, and artwork over the ordinary phone lines. It is easy to learn to use a fax machine. Using one will not interfere with any existing office routines, and in fact will improve our communications. Many companies in our area sell fax.

Fax machines work efficiently and speedily. They can scan and send a copy of a one-page letter in less than 25 seconds or about 400 words in less than a minute. In even less time they can send a copy of a blueprint or contract. Sending such documents by fax means that we can have a rapid turnaround of paperwork with our clients. In fact, a client can receive a copy of an invoice or an order form and complete it and have it back to us in less than an hour for easy processing on our part here. The fax will also save us secretarial time since we won't have to have someone transcribe a document on either end of a message. The fax prints it exactly. We might therefore cut down on all those embarrassing typos we have seen lately.

The greatest benefit a fax machine has for our company is the amount of money it will save us over time. A small fax machine runs about $800–900, or a little higher with a paper cutter. We spend that amount of money in less than six months on overnight delivery service. So, it should be easy to recoup the initial cost. Moreover, operating a fax machine is also economical. The cost of sending a single letter and piece of artwork over a fax during peak telephone rates (about $.96) is still less than sending it by Nationwide Express or Direct Overnight Service. And we can save even more if we transmit our message after 5:00 when the phone rates are lower. The fax is like an answering machine.

of Tisch's report if he is to accomplish his purpose in writing to his reader. Moreover, Tisch recognized that his draft was still not ready for his boss to see, so he showed it to a coworker for suggestions. Finally, Tisch did not consider his outline as final, so he revised it as necessary at the drafting stage.

The purpose of drafting is to get your main points down in the most logical order for your readers, so at this stage you need to pay careful attention to content and organization. You will make many changes in both areas as you draft your way toward the most satisfactory and satisfying version of your paper. Working on one of his drafts (Figure 2.4), Tisch realized that he had placed one of the most important considerations for his audience (savings) last. In his final version, shown in Figure 2.5, he moved this section to the beginning of his memo because he realized that Melissa Hill would be most interested in costs. As you draft, new and even better ideas will come to you, especially as you continue to research your topic and your audience's needs. You will also discard ideas that you once thought were usable but now appear irrelevant or repetitious.

As you work on your drafts, ask yourself these key questions.

- Is this the best way to start?
- Am I giving my readers too much or too little information?
- Does this point belong where I have it or does it more logically follow or precede something somewhere else?
- Did I forget to tell my readers something they need to know?
- Am I repeating myself?
- Have I contradicted myself?
- Have I ended appropriately for my audience?

Don't forget that effective drafting means making some big decisions about what you say and where you say it. Following are some more suggestions to help your drafting go more smoothly.

- Select a comfortable place to write. Use a pen, typewriter, or word processor—whatever gives you the most satisfying feeling about creating.
- Triple or even quadruple space between lines (if you use a pen or typewriter) to leave enough room to make changes.
- In an early draft, write the easiest part first, regardless of where it may finally end up. Some writers feel more comfortable drafting the body or middle of their work first.
- Then, as you revise in a later draft, write straight through. Do not worry about spelling, punctuation, or the way a sentence sounds. Save these concerns for the revision stages to follow.
- Allow enough time between drafts so that you can evaluate your work with fresh eyes and a clear mind.
- Get frequent "outside" opinions. Show a draft to a fellow student, coworker, or maybe an employer for comment. A new pair of eyes will see things you missed.

FIGURE 2.5   The final copy of William Tisch's report.

TO: Melissa Hill, Office Manager

FROM: William Tisch

DATE: November 2, 1988

RE: Improving Our Communication Cost and Efficiency

As you requested, I investigated some ways to increase efficiency and lower costs of communication with our customers. The most practical solution is to buy a fax (facsimile) machine. A fax scans the image of a document-- including contracts, photographs, blueprints--and transmits a copy over regular telephone lines all over the country or world instantaneously. In the U.S., more than one million companies own a fax. Since many of our clients have a fax, doing business with them should be easier.

The greatest benefit of a fax is the money it will save us. A small fax costs about $800–900, or slightly higher with a paper cutter. We spend that amount in less than six months on overnight delivery services. The cost of sending a letter and artwork over a fax at peak telephone rates (approx. $.96) is far less than sending it by Nationwide Express ($11.25). We can save even more by transmitting messages after 5:00 when phone rates are lower. The fax also takes messages 24 hours a day like an answering machine.

A fax works speedily and efficiently. It can send a one-page letter in less than 25 seconds, or about 400 words a minute. Sending such documents by fax promises a rapid turnaround of paperwork. A client can receive, complete, and return an order or invoice in less than an hour. By reproducing a message exactly, a fax will help to cut down on mistakes with orders taken over the phone. A fax will also give us a written record of our transaction. And by reproducing a message exactly, the fax will save us secretarial time used for transcriptions and help eliminate clerical errors.

A fax system is easy to install. All we need is the fax machine and a telephone. We can choose from among many small models marketed in our area. The Zap Fax, for example, is about the size of a typewriter, can fit on a desk, and is portable. It's easy to learn to use a fax, and it will not interfere with office routines. In fact, a fax can be made compatible with a personal computer to further our communications.

I recommend that we buy a fax immediately. It will improve communicating with our customers.

Revising

Once you are satisfied that your latest draft conveys the appropriate message for your audience, you can start revising. During the drafting stage, you worked hard on getting large units of your work down on paper. At the revision stage, you will be checking everything for accuracy, completeness, easy reading, tone, and voice. Do not be tempted to skip the revision stage just because you have written the required number of words or sections or because you think you have put in too much time already. Revision is an essential stage in the writing process; it requires more than just giving your work a quick glance to check the spelling of a couple of words. When you revise, you *re*see and *re*think your entire document for content, organization, and style. Note the large number of changes William Tisch made between his draft in Figure 2.4 and the final copy of his memo in Figure 2.5.

Because revision is so important, allow enough time to do it carefully. Avoid drafting and revising in one sitting. If possible, wait at least a day before you start to revise. In the meantime, again ask a coworker or friend familiar with the topic to comment on your work.

Plan to read your final draft more than once. Like prewriting or drafting, revision is not done well in one big push. It evolves over a period of time. You will need to examine content for accuracy, completeness, and appropriateness for readers. Is everything proportionate, or have you spent too much (or too little) time and space on one section? Look closely at your organization to see if information is logically divided and easy to follow. At the paragraph level, make sure you have provided clear topic sentences (see Chapter 4) that tell readers what they can expect to find in that paragraph and why. Turning to matters of style, read your sentences out loud to see if they flow logically from each other and to make sure they can be understood on the first reading. Double-check word choices to verify that they establish the right tone and are at the appropriate technical level for your reader. Also, be certain to check spelling and punctuation. A careless mistake here can undermine the hard work you have put in on the bigger units.

After you have made all these checks, you are ready to type or print the final, reader-ready copy. The entire writing process is completed only after you have proofread that copy thoroughly to catch any mistakes at the last minute.

◆ COMPUTERS AND THE WRITING PROCESS

The computer is an essential tool in the workplace. Almost every type of business relies heavily on computers to generate, store, retrieve, and transmit information. Based on computer technology, the automated office today is likely to have word processors, microcomputers, teleconferencing equipment, fax machines, and even voice synthesizers that recognize and translate sounds into writing. Computers increase efficiency, save time, lower costs, and streamline the process of receiving and sending messages.

Knowing how to use a word processor is a requirement for most jobs. Employees either have word processors at their desks or have access to them. Gone are the days when you could do everything in longhand or on a typewriter and then turn over a rough copy to a secretary to edit and produce the finished product. Since you will most likely have access to a word processor, your employer will expect you to create, revise, and print a professional-looking document.

There are a variety of computers on the market, but common to all of them are an illuminated display screen (or monitor), a keyboard, a memory component using a computer chip, and a printer. These parts are known as the *hardware*; the various programs used to give instructions to the computer are known as the *software*. Various software programs will allow you to perform word processing, create graphics, and do accounting ledgers.

The word processor has been misleadingly called a typewriter with a memory. It is more than that; with a typewriter you are stuck with what you type on a given sheet of paper, and if you do not like it you have to start over. With a word processor you can make a large number of changes on a thin, flexible magnetic disk or on the computer's hard disk. The word processor saves what you want to keep while it makes room on the disk for any additions, deletions, or corrections. You are spared the drudgery of retyping a page each time you make a change or a mistake.

With the computer, the appropriate software, and a printer, you can make the following changes any time and anywhere in your document:

- insert or delete words, sentences, paragraphs
- move around lines or entire paragraphs
- search for and replace a word or phrase
- copy part of something in the document or in another document stored in the computer
- design and insert visuals
- use boldface or italic print; change the size of lettering; center headings and put information into columns
- set tabs and margins
- check and verify spelling and punctuation

Since you can watch all these changes on your screen, you will be able to visualize the writing process at work. You are thus able to interact with the text you are creating on the screen. And at any stage in the process you can *scroll* your document—roll the text up or down on the screen—to view different parts of the document.

The word processor assists you in every phase of the writing process by making it easier to complete. When you are prewriting, a word processor can help you to move items in your outline or brainstormed list quickly to organize them into categories. You might even use some of the software packages designed to generate and organize information so you can identify ideas easily. When you draft your document, the word processor can help you get some writing on the monitor screen quickly. In doing this the word processor keeps pace with the speed of your thought process. You will not have to worry about the time-consuming drudgery of having to return a typewriter carriage after every line or of retyping successive drafts. You do not have to stop to check spelling or punc-tuation since you can return to these matters later. And if you run into a snag on any draft, you do not have to stop to fix it and lose momentum. With a single stroke on the keyboard, the word processor will flag items that you want to re-turn to or need more information about. During drafting and revising, some writ-ers in fact move back and forth between a hard copy (the paper copy run off by the printer) and the text on the screen.

When you are revising, the word processor assists you in refining and refo-cusing your thoughts. Using a word processor can actually encourage you to make revisions since they can be accomplished easily and quickly. Again, you will be relieved of the burden of retyping what you want to save each time you make a change or spot an error. Since you can rearrange words, sentences, and para-graphs, or even the appearance of material, you can experiment with a number of versions of your work without having to type each separately. Some software packages even allow you to split your monitor screen into two or four parts (*windows*) to view different versions of a text or several pages of the text simul-taneously. From that perspective you will be able to select the best version of a paper or format for your audience and also to see how a revision on one page might affect another page of your text. Finally, a word processor allows you to print a clean copy at any stage; it is always easier to catch errors on a clean copy than on a marked-up one.

The word processor was created with the needs of the business world in mind. It becomes an invaluable link in any collaborative writing venture; all you have to do is share your disk with a coworker, who can make changes on the disk and then return it to you. And if the boss asks you to change a word or two in the middle of a letter, add a new paragraph, or reverse the order of some paragraphs after seeing your "final" copy, you do not have to do the whole thing over. You can make these changes quickly and have a revised copy ready in no time. Figure 2.6 shows a letter an employee drafted on a word processor and on which her boss made a number of changes in wording, format, and content. Using the appro-priate software, the employee was able to create the revised letter seen in Figure 2.7. If she had mailed the first draft, her reader very likely would not have been impressed with the company's professionalism and would have thought twice about placing an order. The revised final version of the letter is much more effec-tive in its presentation of the material, in its individualized address, and in its for-matting. Good writers benefit from constructive criticism of their drafts and know how to make effective changes during the revision process. In this example the employee benefited from the criticism of her boss. The final copy is the result of the suggested revisions.

Unquestionably, the word processor is a wonderful tool that will help you to increase and improve your writing. But it will not do your writing for you. You may use a software package to help organize your ideas, although you must first do research to discover what ideas are relevant for your audience. The word processor will enable you to produce more writing, but you are the one who must select the right words with appropriate tone and put them into readable sentences and logically organized paragraphs. As we saw, the word processor can greatly assist you in making revisions, but again you must decide what must be

FIGURE 2.6 A draft of a letter prepared on a word processor and edited by an employer.

← ———————————————— November 15, 1989

Terry Tatum
Manager
i Consol**ó**dated Industries
Houston, TX   *add zip code*
    Terry Tatum:
Dear Sir,

Thank you for asking
~~I am taking the opportunity of answering your request~~ for a price list of Servitron   *Consolidated Industries*
products. Servitron has been in business in the Houston area for more than
~~twenty-two~~ years and we offer unparalleled equipment and service to ~~any customer~~.
Utilizing a Servitron will give you both <u>efficiency</u> and <u>economy</u>. *bold face*
22   *can*

Whatever model Servitron you choose carries with it a <u>full one-year warranty</u> on all *boldface*
parts and labor. After the expiration date of your warranty you ~~should~~ purchase our
service contract for $75.00 a year.   *might*

~~Here are the models Servitron offers~~   *—add boldface headings*

Zephyr   81072 $ 459.95
Colt   86085 $ 629.95
Meteor   88096 $ 769.95

Depending on your needs, one of these models should be right for you.

If I might be of further assistance to you, please call on me. I am also enclosing a
brochure giving you more information, including specifications, on these Servitron
products.
                        add phone number

~~Truly,~~ *Sincerely yours,*
                                        reverse
                                        the order
SERVITRON————————*leave 4 spaces*   *of these*
Randy Taylor   *two sentences*
Sales Associate

FIGURE 2.7   The edited, final copy of Figure 2.6.

November 15, 1989

Terry Tatum
Manager
Consolidated Industries
Houston, TX 77005-0096

Dear Terry Tatum:

Thank you for asking for a price list of Servitron products. Servitron has been in business in the Houston area for more than 22 years and we can offer unparalleled equipment and service to Consolidated Industries. Utilizing a Servitron will give you both **efficiency** and **economy**.

Depending on your needs, one of these models should be right for you.

Model Name	Number	Price
Zephyr	81072	$459.95
Colt	86085	$629.95
Meteor	88096	$769.95

Whatever model Servitron you choose carries with it a **full one-year warranty** on all parts and labor. After the expiration date of your warranty you might purchase our service contract for $75.00 a year.

I am also enclosing a brochure giving you more information, including specifications, on these Servitron products. If I might be of further assistance to you, please call me at 580-1689.

Sincerely yours,

SERVITRON

Randy Taylor

Randy Taylor
Sales Associate

revised and how. And never be lulled into thinking that a clean, professionally printed document will hide or make up for incorrect content or poor writing.

◆ FOUR BASIC POINTS ON USING A WORD PROCESSOR

Throughout this book you will find a number of suggestions on how a word processor can help you to write better. But here are four basic points to help you escape some computer users' nightmares.

1. Give yourself adequate time to learn to operate your word processor and any software packages your employer uses. Read the manuals. A few hours of trial and error testing is time well spent.
2. Press the SAVE command every 10–15 minutes or you risk wiping out hours of hard work. Some word processors do so automatically.
3. Make a hard (paper) copy as a backup so that if an electrical storm knocks out the power or you make a keyboard error you will have a written record of your work. Also make a daily backup disk copy of your file.
4. Keep your disks away from magnetized surfaces (e.g., microwave ovens) and heat since these can destroy what you have recorded.

◆ EXERCISES

1. Below is an initial brainstormed list on stress in the workplace.

leads to absenteeism
high costs for compensation for stress-related illnesses
proper nutrition
numerous stress-reduction techniques
good idea to conduct interviews to find out levels, causes, and extent of stress in the workplace
low morale caused by stress
higher insurance claims for employees' physical ailments
myth to see stress leading to greater productivity
various tapes used to teach relaxation
environmental factors—too hot? too cold?
counseling
work overload
setting priorities
wellness campaign
savings per employee add up to $2500 per year
skills to relax
learning to get along with coworkers
need for privacy
interpersonal communication
employee's need for clear policies on transfers, promotion
stress management workshops very successful in California
physical activity to relieve stress
affects management
breathing exercises

Revise this brainstormed list, eliminating any repetition and combining any related items.

2. Prepare a suitable outline from your revised list in Exercise 1 for a report to a decision maker on the problems of stress in the workplace and the necessity of creating a stress management program.

3. From the revised brainstormed list in Exercise 1, write a short memo to a decision maker about the problems and possible solutions related to stress in the workplace.

4. Write a short report (2–3 pages) to the manager of the small company you work for to convince her to establish a system of flex time. Prepare an outline based on the clustered items in Figure 2.1. Add, delete, or rearrange anything in this clustered grouping to complete your outline. Submit your final outline along with your report to your instructor.

5. Compare the draft of William Tisch's report in Figure 2.4 with the final copy of his report in Figure 2.5. What kinds of changes did he make? Were they appropriate and effective for his audience and purpose? Why or why not?

6. Assume you have been asked to write a short report (similar to William Tisch's in Figure 2.5) to a decision maker (the manager of a business you work for or have worked for; the director of your campus union, library, or security force; a city official) about one of the following topics:

   a. computer facilities   f. public transportation
   b. telephone service   g. sporting events/activities
   c. security lighting   h. training programs
   d. food service   i. morale
   e. parking   j. hiring more part-time student
                                        workers

   Do some research and planning about one of these topics and the audience for whom it is intended by writing your answers to the following questions.

   • What is my precise purpose in writing to my audience?
   • What information will my audience expect me to know?
   • What do I know about the topic?
   • Where can I obtain relevant information about my topic to meet my audience's needs?

7. Using one or more of the prewriting strategies discussed in this chapter (clustering, brainstorming, outlining, freewriting), generate a group of items for the topic you chose in Exercise 6. Do your prewriting activities for about 15–20 minutes, or until you have about 10–15 items. At this stage do not worry about how appropriate these items are or even if some of them overlap. Just get some thoughts down on paper.

8. Go through the list you prepared in Exercise 7 and eliminate any items that are inappropriate for your topic or audience or any items that overlap. Try to see how many of them you might expand or rearrange into categories or subcategories. Then create an outline similar to the one in Figure 2.3.

9. Using your outline in Exercise 8, prepare some drafts of your memo report. Submit at least two drafts to your instructor.

10. Revise your drafts as much as necessary to create the final copy of your report.

11. In a few paragraphs, explain to your instructor the changes you made between your early drafts and your revised drafts. Explain why you made them. Concentrate on large changes—adding and moving paragraphs—as well as matters of style, tone, and proofreading.

12. In another memo—addressed to your instructor—explain what major problems you encountered at various phases of working on your report. Also point out what prewriting, drafting, and revising strategies worked especially well for you.

13. Find a piece of writing—a memo, letter, pamphlet, or short report—that you believe was not carefully drafted or revised. In a short memo, point out to your instructor what is wrong with this piece of writing—e.g., not logically organized, inappropriate tone, incomplete or too technical information. Attach a copy of the poor example to your memo.

14. Revise the poor piece of writing you analyzed in Exercise 13. Submit your improved version to your instructor.

3

Writing: Paragraphs

This chapter will show you how to construct, organize, and revise your paragraphs. A paragraph is the basic building block for any piece of writing. If you master the art of writing paragraphs, you should be able to handle any kind of business or technical writing. A *paragraph* is (1) a group of related sentences (2) arranged in a logical order (3) supplying readers with detailed, appropriate information (4) on a single important topic. Each of these points is discussed in detail in this chapter.

◆ THE IMPORTANCE OF PARAGRAPHS

Paragraphs give readers the necessary navigational clues to understand your work. The following three functions of paragraphs are equally important.

1. Paragraphs divide your message into segments. They break complex messages into smaller, more understandable segments for readers. Imagine what a piece of writing would look like without indentations or white spaces to divide it into paragraphs. Without the paragraph breaks, readers would not know where to find key statements and would wonder where one part of a message began and another stopped. Furthermore, an unbroken piece of writing is intimidating to readers; paragraph breaks provide pauses to help refresh your reader.

2. Paragraphs group related details for readers' benefit. Think of a paragraph as an information block. Each block treats only one main idea at a time; that is, it usually contains a general statement and sufficient details to explain that statement. Within each information block you provide readers with only the relevant details they will need to understand that portion of your message. By collecting all related details in one paragraph, you make it easier for readers to understand them in terms of the main idea.

3. Paragraphs link ideas to make your work easier to understand. Paragraphs are not written in isolation. Each paragraph should flow smoothly and logically into the next, linking the different information blocks that make up your message. Transitions (discussed on pages 54–56), especially at the beginning and end of your paragraphs, hook one part of your message to another. In this way, paragraphs show how the different parts of your message are connected and related to each other, how one part "fits" into the next. Paragraphs also help readers to link ideas by saying to them: you have finished one part of the message; now stop to consider what you have read before starting the next section.

◆ PARAGRAPHS IN THE WRITING PROCESS

Paragraphing is a vital activity in the writing process. But writing clear and logical paragraphs is not easy, and it certainly cannot be done in one draft. Our thoughts do not conveniently sort themselves into orderly, ready-made paragraphs. Instead, we have to revise and regroup our ideas, expanding some and subordinating or eliminating others. This process of sorting our thoughts into meaningful chunks of information for readers is what writing paragraphs is all about.

When you are working on your first (or even second) draft, you may not be primarily concerned with paragraph breaks or structure. You want to get your ideas down on paper in order to examine them. But the closer you move toward your final copy the more you must be concerned with the way in which you sort your ideas into paragraphs. Each new paragraph means the writer is treating a new idea, often signaled by a shift in time, place, person, or emphasis. To discover your paragraph breaks you will have to work back and forth between a brainstormed list (or other prewriting plan) and the various drafts of your work. Going through a number of drafts will help you to identify the overall sequence of paragraphs in your report or letter.

Asking (and answering) questions while you are drafting will give you a clearer idea as to what constitutes the paragraphs of your work. Here are some questions to ask yourself about the shape, content, and flow of your paragraphs.

- What function does this paragraph serve that the others do not?
- How does this paragraph relate to what may have gone before or after it?
- Have I signaled to the reader why and how this is a separate paragraph?
- What kinds of information do I need to add for my reader?
- How should I organize this information?
- What do I need to say first in the paragraph?
- How should I end this paragraph?

As you work on various drafts of your paragraphs, expect to make many changes. For example, you might find yourself crowding too much information into one paragraph in an early draft and then splitting that paragraph into two or even three separate ones in a later draft. Or you may do just the reverse and substantially add to a short paragraph in a later draft to answer specific questions a reader may have at this point. You might reverse paragraphs or even combine them. Working on the structure of an individual paragraph, you may move sentences around inside that paragraph or even add a sentence or two from another paragraph. You may also eliminate information from a paragraph because an idea does not belong there.

Below are a few paragraphs from the beginning of a writer's early draft. The writer, an employee at Seacoast Lab, was asked by her supervisor to prepare a short report for the general public on the lab's most recent experiments. These paragraphs represented the writer's first attempt at putting her ideas into paragraphs on the topic for the audience.

> Drag is an important concept in the world of science and technology. It has many implications. Drag occurs when a ship moves through the water and eddies build up. Ships on the high seas have to fight the eddies, which results in drag. In the same way, an airplane has to fight the winds at the various altitudes at which it flies; these winds are very forceful, moving at many knots per hour. All of these forces of nature are around us. Sometimes we can feel them, too. We get tired walking against a strong wind. The eddies around a ship are the same thing. These eddies form various barriers around the ship's hull. They come from a combination of different molecules around the ship's hull and exert quite a force. Both types of molecules pull against the ship. This is where the eddies come in.
>
> Scientists at Seacoast Lab are concerned about drag. Dr. Karen Runnels, who joined Seacoast about three years ago, is the chief investigator. She and her team of highly qualified experts have constructed some fascinating multilevel water tunnels. These tunnels should be useful to ship owners. Drag wastes a ship's fuel.

As she worked on her ideas and thought about the audience's needs, the writer realized that these early paragraphs presented some problems she would have to solve in later drafts. She started asking herself the questions about paragraphs listed on page 44. Answering these questions in turn led her to make a number of major changes.

The writer realized that her first paragraph lacked focus. It was not carefully organized, jumping back and forth between drag on a ship and on an airplane. Consequently, she decided to delete information about planes since Seacoast Lab did not work in this area. In working on the development of this paragraph, she also decided that the information on the effect of drag on a ship was so important it deserved a separate paragraph. So she removed the details on that topic from this long first paragraph and started to develop them separately. In the process, she discovered that her explanation of molecules, eddies, and drag was unclear and would need to be reorganized. While doing some more reading on the topic she came across an interesting analogy that would be appropriate for her audience, so she included it. Working on this explanation, she had to decide how to organize her information. After some deliberation, the topic suggested she follow the pattern, "How does drag work?" So, she developed her paragraph as a cause-effect (drag is the cause and the effect is how it works).

So much for a new second paragraph. But the writer was left with the job of finding an opening for her short report. She wanted to start with something that would both introduce the topic and encourage the audience to continue reading. Buried in the original paragraph was an idea she found worth developing—that we cannot always see the forces of nature but we can feel them. So rather than beginning with a wooden statement about the scientific concept of drag (which she realized over several drafts did not have to be scientifically defined for the audience), she began with a readily understood example about an individual walking against the wind. Through continued drafting and revision she created two useful, carefully organized paragraphs out of one long opening paragraph. And she kept the reader's needs in mind throughout this process.

Working on her original second paragraph, the writer realized that it said very little about the lab's experiments with drag. In fact, what she had initially written might even confuse readers about how and why the tunnels were useful. Once the writer put herself in the reader's place, she asked the question that helped her to develop the paragraph on "What specific things are they doing at Seacoast Lab to reduce drag?" Generating a precise starting sentence from this question made all the difference. Focusing now on the lab's "ways to reduce drag on ships," she found a restricted idea that guided her in choosing specific examples about experiments at Seacoast. Instead of leaving in interesting but unnecessary information (e.g., that Dr. Runnels has been at the lab three years), the writer sought concrete illustrations and appropriately explained their significance to her audience. She also discovered that the last sentence in her original second paragraph did not belong in the new revised paragraph on experiments. The cost of drag was much more appropriately placed in her new opening paragraph.

The final effort of the writer's work is found below. Through drafting and revising, she was able to transform two poorly organized and incomplete paragraphs into the following three carefully separated yet logically connected paragraphs.

> We cannot see or hear many of the forces around us but we can certainly detect their presence. Walking or running into a strong wind, for example, requires a great deal of effort and often quickly leaves us feeling tired. When a ship sails through the water, it also experiences these opposing sources known as <u>drag</u>. Overcoming drag causes a ship to reduce its energy efficiency which leads to higher fuel costs.
>
> It is not easy for a ship to fight drag. As the ship moves through the water, it drags the water molecules around its hull at the same rate the ship is moving. Because of the cohesive force of these molecules, other water molecules immediately outside the ship's path get pulled into its way. All these molecules become tangled rather than simply sliding past each other. The result produces an eddy, or small circling burst of water around the ship's hull, that intensifies the drag. Dr. Charles

Hester, a noted engineer, explains it using an analogy:
"When you put a spoon in honey and pull it out, half the
honey comes out with the spoon. That's what is happening to
ships. The ship is moving and at the same time dragging the
ocean with it."

At Seacoast Lab, scientists are working to find ways to
reduce drag on ships. Dr. Karen Runnels, the principal
investigator, and a team of researchers have constructed
water tunnels to simulate the movement of ships at sea.
The drag a ship encounters is measured from the tiny air
bubbles emitted in the water tunnel. Dr. Runnels's team has
also developed the use of polymers, or long carbon chain
molecules, to reduce drag. These polymers act like a slimy
coating for the ship's hull to help it glide through the
water more easily. When asbestos fibers were added to the
polymer solutions, the investigators measured a 90 percent
reduction in drag. The team has also experimented with an
external pump attached to the hull of the ship, which
pushes the water away from the ship's path.

◆ FOUR TYPES OF PARAGRAPHS

As we have just seen in the Seacoast Lab report, paragraphs are not all alike. Generally speaking, you will use four types of paragraphs: supporting, introductory, transitional, and concluding. Each differs in length, purpose, and position in your work. Each meets your readers' needs in a specific way. The following section describes each type of paragraph, explains how to write it, and provides examples.

Supporting Paragraphs

You will write more supporting paragraphs than any other type. Supporting paragraphs are the workhorses of letters and reports. They carry the information that supports the purpose and message of your writing. They are also called *middle* or *body paragraphs* because they appear between the introduction and conclusion of your work to provide explanations, directions, descriptions, or commentary.

A supporting paragraph expresses one central idea, and its sentences contribute to the overall meaning of that idea. The supporting paragraph does this by giving readers a *topic sentence,* which states the central idea, and *supporting information,* which explains the topic sentence.

The topic sentence is the most important part of the paragraph for readers. It tells readers what your paragraph is about. More specifically, a topic sentence:

- helps you generate sentences that will logically follow in that paragraph.
- summarizes the content of a paragraph.
- forecasts the kinds of information readers can expect to find in the paragraph.
- explains why you included or excluded certain details.

Your topic sentence is a pledge to readers that all the other sentences in the paragraph will support it. You will learn more about writing topic sentences on pages 51–53.

Supporting information includes data to convince readers that what you say about the central idea is accurate and complete. These data can include a range of statistical information—facts about costs, dates, employees, changes in policies—or your interpretation of such facts.

The following is an example of a carefully constructed supporting paragraph. It contains a clear topic sentence (highlighted in color) as well as adequate and relevant supporting details.

> Fat is an important part of everyone's diet. It is nutritionally present in the basic food groups we eat—meat and poultry, dairy products, and oils—to aid growth or development. The fats and fatty acids present in these foods ensure proper metabolism, thus helping to turn what we eat into the energy we need. These same fats and fatty acids also act as carriers for important vitamins like A, D, E, and K. Another important role of fat is that it keeps us from feeling hungry by delaying digestion. Fat also enhances the flavor of the food we eat, making it more enjoyable.

This paragraph contains only one central idea—fat is an important part of everyone's diet. It does not stray from this central topic; every statement refers to the role of fat in the diet. The topic sentence both summarizes and forecasts what readers can expect to learn in the paragraph. The rest of the paragraph uses relevant information (fats are nutritional, ensure proper metabolism, carry vitamins, delay digestion, flavor food) to support the topic sentence.

To picture the structure of a well-made supporting paragraph, visualize a capital T as in Figure 3.1. The topic sentence is like the crossbar (or top) of the capital T; the individual sentences supporting the topic sentence are like the vertical column of the T.

Note how the paragraph about fat in the diet can be visually redesigned to reveal its T-shape.

Fat is an important part of everyone's diet.

provides nutrition

ensures metabolism

carries vitamins

delays hunger

flavors food

The T-shape is just one of many structural shapes paragraphs may take. In other patterns, the topic sentence may come halfway through or at the end of the paragraph or be implied instead of stated. But in business or technical writing, it is customary and desirable to have the topic sentence come first. On pages 51–52 you will learn more about why topic sentences should be placed first.

FIGURE 3.1   A T-shaped paragraph.

```
┌─────────────────────────────────────────────┐
│                                               │
│        TOPIC    SENTENCE                      │
│                                               │
└──────────────────┬──────────────────┬────────┘
                   │  SUPPORTING      │
                   │  SENTENCE        │
                   │                  │
                   │  SUPPORTING      │
                   │  SENTENCE        │
                   │                  │
                   │  SUPPORTING      │
                   │  SENTENCE        │
                   │                  │
                   │  SUPPORTING      │
                   │  SENTENCE        │
                   └──────────────────┘
```

Introductory Paragraphs

Your introductory (or opening) paragraph serves several important functions. It tells your readers what they can expect to find in your letter or report and, like a preview of coming attractions, also sets the tone for your work. Note how the writer's opening paragraph for the Seacoast Lab report (page 46) invites reader interest through a friendly, nontechnical tone.

The introductory paragraph to a memo, a letter, or a short business report is generally brief (one to three sentences) and comes to the point at once. Note how the following introductory paragraph previews what the report will cover. The paragraph also makes a helpful connection for the reader by referring to her previous request.

> Our sales department has compiled the data you recently requested on third-quarter sales. The following brief report provides you with the specific information you need on (1) retail, (2) wholesale, and (3) foreign sales.

A number of introductory paragraphs might be used in a longer report. In the following example, note how the first paragraph establishes the topic and the second describes what readers can expect to learn about that topic.

> The U.S. government is the world's largest buyer of goods and services. One of the major responsibilities of the Small Business Administration (SBA) is to see that small businesses obtain a fair share of this vast government market.
>
> This manual explains how the government buys goods and services, how most businesses sell to the government, and how the SBA helps small business owners sell to federal purchasing agencies and their prime contractors.

Transitional Paragraphs

Transitions move the reader from one idea to another. You can provide transitions through individual words (see pages 54–56) or through sentences at the beginning or end of a paragraph. Another way is to write entire transitional paragraphs to take readers from one section of a letter, memo, or report to another. (They are also called *linking paragraphs* because of this function.) As the following examples show, transitional paragraphs are generally very brief—one or two sentences. Note that transitional words and phrases are italicized.

> *Up to this point* we have considered the engineering advantages of the Rudex system. *Now* we will turn to the financial benefits it offers us.

> The *above process* will so saturate materials with solution that they may be too wet to use properly. *The following instructions* will show you how to dry and recomb the materials.

> The same kind of popularity generated by *the earlier subdivision* can be found at the new construction site. *Below* are some examples.

Concluding Paragraphs

Like introductory paragraphs, concluding ones can be brief—usually only a few sentences. Concluding paragraphs can perform one or all of the following three functions.

1. They can summarize the main points by recapping the key points of your message without giving any new information.

> In summary, the main features of the plan ask the city to reroute traffic on Clinton Avenue, to install a traffic signal on the corner of Adams and Fourth Streets, and to change Concord Place into a one-way thoroughfare.

2. They can draw conclusions by interpreting or emphasizing the significance of the information you have presented.

> In conclusion, then, the soundest investment opportunities for our firm lie in Continental Driftwood securities. They offer the lowest rate of capital, supply the highest interest yield, and have the most stable financial history.

3. They can make recommendations by calling for a specific action.

> After studying the responses of customers to our recent survey, I recommend that we do the following by the last week in May:
>
> + extend our store hours on Friday night from 8:00 P.M. to 9:00 P.M.
> + open on Saturday morning at 8:30 A.M. instead of 9:30 A.M.
> + close at 6:00 P.M. rather than 7:00 P.M. on Monday, Tuesday, Wednesday, and Thursday nights

Remember that you need a concluding paragraph to avoid ending a letter or report abruptly. Concluding paragraphs give readers a sense of completion, of having stopped officially and in a satisfying manner. You can give readers this sense of completion by using such phrases or words as *finally, in conclusion,* or *last of all* in the concluding paragraph.

◆ GENERATING TOPIC SENTENCES

As we saw on pages 47–48, the topic sentence is the most important sentence in your paragraph. Carefully worded and restricted, it helps you to generate and control the kinds of information you need to include in that paragraph. An effective topic sentence also helps your reader to grasp your main idea.

How can you create an effective topic sentence? As with other types of writing, you must work in stages. Usually you will start with brainstorming to collect ideas and facts; then you will draft a topic sentence to explain or summarize these details. You may have to discard some ideas or facts and revise the topic sentence several times. In other words, you will work back and forth, adjusting the content of the paragraph, then the topic sentence, then the content again, and so on. Recall how the writer of the Seacoast Lab report (pages 44–47) generated her topic sentences over various drafts. Again, keep in mind that writing is a process. Your topic sentence, like your paper, evolves from rough early stages that only you see to a completed restricted statement. As you work, pay close attention to the following three guidelines, which will help you produce an effective topic sentence for each paragraph.

1. Make sure you provide a topic sentence. In their rush to supply readers with facts—measurements, working principles, descriptions—some writers forget to include a topic sentence to explain what all the details mean. As it stands, the following paragraph lacks a topic sentence and thus deprives readers of the writer's reason for discussing the mechanics of a wind turbine.

> Sensors found on each machine detect wind speed and direction and other important details such as ice loading and potential metal fatigue. The information is fed into a small computer (microprocessor) in the nacelle (or engine housing). The microprocessor automatically keeps the blades turned into the wind, starts and stops the machine, and changes the pitch of the tips of the blades to increase power under varying wind conditions. Should any part of the wind turbine suffer damage or malfunction, the microprocessor will immediately shut the machine down.

With the addition of a suitable topic sentence, "The MOD-2 wind turbine is designed to be operated completely by computer," readers can more clearly identify the central topic and understand what the details have in common. To make sure you include a topic sentence for every paragraph, ask yourself if the first sentence in the paragraph explains or clarifies everything else in that paragraph. If it does, chances are you have an effective topic sentence.

2. Put your topic sentence first. Place your topic sentence at the beginning—not the middle or end—of your paragraph. Because the beginning sentence occupies an emphatic place, readers are sure to give it their attention. In some business and technical writing, the topic sentence at the beginning of each paragraph is even underscored to help busy readers grasp main points quickly. By seeing that main point up front, readers are not kept in doubt or suspense. Burying the key idea in the middle or near the end of the paragraph makes it harder for readers to act upon your information, as illustrated by the following poorly written paragraph.

In the last two years the cost of insurance on the trucks has increased almost 17 percent. We are now paying $2300 to the Rawlins Agency whereas in March of 1987 we had a bill of $1935. Although it will be impossible to predict the price of gasoline for even one season, let alone a single year, certainly it will go up, too. Also, we have been receiving many orders from customers who live outside a 40-mile radius of Bloomington which makes our policy of providing free delivery even more costly. Whenever one of the delivery trucks is in the shop for repair, we can expect a bill of at least $150, if this year's rates continue. Another major expense is the cost of drivers' overtime. Two of them have logged more than 35 hours of overtime in the last month, amounting to $450.

Eager to assemble all the facts about the firm's delivery trucks, the writer did not consider the reader's need to have the reason for these facts in the first sentence of the paragraph. The writer's main reason for compiling the facts is buried in the fourth sentence of the paragraph—the company's present policy of supplying free delivery to customers is costly and should be changed. If the writer had begun with that fact, the reader would then have been better prepared to follow and interpret the figures about the costs of operating the trucks.

3. Make sure your topic sentence is restricted. If restricted, a topic sentence identifies only one central idea. A broad or unrestricted topic sentence does not zero in on a single idea. Instead, it encourages the writer to stray from one central topic into the territory of numerous other topics. The result is a paragraph that lacks direction and focus. Here are two examples of overly broad topic sentences.

1. Computers have changed the ways we do business.
2. Working conditions are important.

These two sentences, if used as topic sentences, would fail to give readers a clear understanding of the central idea the paragraph will develop. In the first sentence the writer goes astray by using the vague word *ways,* which can apply to almost any computer application in business—producing copy, making graphics, scanning records, storing information. After several drafts, the writer generated a topic sentence that focused on a more precise use of the computer in a particular business context.

The new Aldridge 200 has improved our efficiency in billing customers.

As a topic sentence, sentence 2 above is even more misleading than the first. The phrase "working conditions" suggests many different topics (legal, physical, social, psychological, and environmental conditions) and does not specify for whom or why such conditions are important. An appropriate revision might read as follows:

The increase in rate of overtime pay will boost our employees' morale.

A broad topic sentence leads to a shaky paragraph for two reasons. On the one hand, the paragraph will not contain enough information to support the topic sentence. On the other hand, a broad topic sentence will not be able to summarize or forecast accurately the information available in the paragraph.

It is important to remember that broad topic sentences are part of the process of writing a restricted topic sentence. The first time you write a topic sentence, it is likely to be too broad. The next step is to revise, rework, and rephrase the sentence until it is restricted. A broad topic sentence is one starting point for a restricted topic sentence.

◆ THREE CHARACTERISTICS OF AN EFFECTIVE PARAGRAPH

Effective paragraphs have **unity, coherence,** and **completeness.** In the following pages, each of these characteristics is described, together with techniques you can follow to achieve these characteristics in your paragraphs.

Unity

A unified paragraph sticks to one topic without wandering from it. Every sentence and every detail in the paragraph supports, explains, or proves the central idea stated in the topic sentence. A unified paragraph includes only relevant information and excludes unnecessary or irrelevant comments. However, a unified paragraph offers readers more than just pertinent details. It assures them that the appropriate information they need is included in that paragraph and not lodged elsewhere. For example, in a progress report a paragraph on the work you have already completed should not include details about work you hope to accomplish during the next report period. These are two separate topics and hence deserve separate paragraphs.

Let's say you are writing a report for an insurance company about the increasing popularity of recreational vehicles (RVs). You might include sections (and paragraphs) about the variety of RVs, their costs, the training and licensing of dealers, and the amount of taxes RV owners pay. You might want to include a section on the convenience and advantages of RVs to show why they are popular. In fact, one of your supporting paragraphs in such a section might have the following topic sentence: RVs offer owners the comforts of a home on wheels. Which of the following points from a writer's brainstormed list would support that central idea?

1. RVs can come equipped with showers.
2. Ad valorem taxes on RVs have increased 13 percent in the last three years.
3. Some RVs come equipped with microwave ovens.
4. RVs get fairly decent mileage on the highway—around 16 miles per gallon.
5. Dealers can customize any van to suit an owner's taste.
6. The number of RV dealerships in the state has doubled over the last six years.
7. RVs often have large swivel chairs—captain's chairs—comparable to recliners.
8. Financing is an important part of the dealer's job.
9. RVs carry their own air-conditioning units equipped with thermostat control for steady-state cooling.
10. Some RVs offer built-in desks.

11. RVs come in many forms—vans, motor homes, trailers, slide-in pickup trucks.

12. RVs can be small and compact (sometimes even crowded) or large and spacious.

Only points 1, 3, 7, 9, and 10 would be relevant for a paragraph whose central idea was on the comforts of home that RVs offered buyers.

The other points in the list would destroy the unity of that paragraph because they are not directly related to the topic sentence. Point 2 raises a comparison between homes and RVs—they both require the owner to pay taxes—but information on a tax increase would hardly support the idea of home comfort in an RV. Point 4 expresses an advantage of owning an RV but not a relevant one. A house does not travel by gasoline. Points 5, 6, and 8 would belong in a paragraph on RV dealers. Point 5 appears to be relevant, but note that the emphasis in it is on the dealer's ability, not the RV's comparison with a home. Point 11 belongs in a separate paragraph because it does not support the topic. And as it is currently worded, point 12 contradicts the idea expressed in the topic sentence. The writer needs to stress the comforts an RV offers; saying that some RVs are crowded does not support that idea.

Coherence

A paragraph is coherent when all its sentences flow smoothly and logically to and from each other. Sentences in a paragraph need to serve as the links of a chain. By showing the connections, you will help readers understand the precise relationship a sentence has with the one preceding it. By making clear the relationships that exist between sentences, you help to make clear the relationship that exists between your ideas.

Four Ways to Achieve Coherence

You can clarify relationships between your sentences (and paragraphs) by using transitional words and phrases, by repeating key words and ideas, by using pronouns and demonstrative adjectives, and by using parallel grammatical structures.

1. Use transitional words and phrases. One of the easiest ways to achieve coherence in a paragraph is to use traditional words and short phrases like those included in Table 3.1. Note how these words are arranged according to the types of relationships they signal to readers. For example, when readers see words like *also, furthermore, in addition,* the message the writer conveys is, "Go ahead; you are on the right track." Words used to contrast ideas—*however, on the other hand, in contrast*—prepare readers for this message: "Go in the opposite direction from the one you have been following." And transitional words and phrases signaling that your work is coming to an end—*finally, in short, to summarize*—tell readers "Prepare to stop; here comes a wrap-up." Be careful how you use these transitional devices. They should be logical and natural.

TABLE 3.1   Transitional Words and Phrases

Addition	also and besides furthermore	first, second, third in addition many moreover	next too
Cause/Effect	and so accordingly as a result because of	consequently due to hence if	on account of since therefore thus
Comparison/ Contrast	but conversely equally however	in contrast in the same way likewise on the contrary	on the other hand similarly still yet
Condition	although even though granted that if	of course provided that to be sure unless	
Conclusion	at last finally in conclusion	in short in summary to conclude	
Emphasis	above all after all again as a matter of fact	indeed in fact of course obviously	to repeat unquestionably
Illustration	for example for instance in effect in other words	in particular specifically that is to illustrate	
Place	alongside of at this point behind below	here in front of next to there	where wherever
Time	afterwards at the same time at times beforehand currently during	earlier later meanwhile next now once	presently soon then until when while

A paragraph without such transitional words and phrases lacks coherence as the following example demonstrates.

Advertising a product on the radio has some advantages over using television. Radio rates are much cheaper. A one-time 60-second spot on television can cost $750. Advertisers can purchase nine 30-second spots on the radio. The production costs are low on radio. Advertisers can pay extra for models and voice-overs. Radio offers advertisers immediate scheduling. Ads appear the same week a contract is signed. Television stations are booked up months in advance. Radio gives advertisers a greater opportunity to reach potential buyers. Radio follows listeners everywhere—in their homes, at work, and in their cars. Television is popular. Television cannot do that.

Readers will find this paragraph hard to follow because the writer did not point out relationships (especially contrasts) between advertising on radio as opposed to advertising on television. To remedy the problem, effective transitional words and phrases must be added. Note how smoothly and logically the revised version reads, thanks to such transitions (in italics):

> Advertising a product on the radio has many advantages over using television. *For one thing,* radio rates are much cheaper. *For example,* a one-time 60-second spot on local T.V. can cost $750. *For that money,* advertisers can purchase nine 30-second spots on radio. *Equally attractive* are the low production costs for radio advertising. *In contrast,* television advertising often includes extra costs for models and voice-overs. *Another* advantage radio offers advertisers is immediate scheduling. *Often* the ad appears during the same week a contract is signed. *On the other hand,* television stations are *frequently* booked up months in advance, so it may be a long time *before* an ad appears. *Furthermore,* radio gives advertisers a greater opportunity to reach their potential buyers. *After all,* radio follows listeners everywhere—in their homes, at work, and in their cars. *Although* it is very popular, television cannot do that.

2. Repeat key words or ideas. Restating key words or ideas in a paragraph provides continuity for readers by keeping important ideas constantly before them. Key words link different parts of the paragraph for readers and show how the paragraph is put together. The following paragraph effectively repeats the key words *fringe benefits* or *benefits* for readers.

> *Fringe benefits* are an important part of recruiting and retaining qualified employees. In a highly competitive job market, such *benefits* rather than salary may determine if a talented professional accepts or declines a job. Traditionally, *fringe benefits* were limited to basic hospital and surgical insurance and to pension plans. But today they extend to dental and optical riders on company insurance policies. Other more lucrative *fringe benefits* include the financial rewards companies offer loyal employees—profit-sharing options to buy stock at reduced rates and generous bonuses for diligent sales activities.

Notice how the writer's lively use of transitional words (*but, also, for example*) prevents the four references to *fringe benefits* from becoming dull or redundant. The reader is made aware of the controlling sense of fringe benefits in the paragraph without being overwhelmed by the repetition of the phrase.

3. Use pronouns and demonstrative adjectives. The use of personal pronouns (*he, she, him, her, they,* and so on) also contributes to the coherence of a paragraph. When readers connect the pronoun with its antecedent (the noun to which it refers), they tie sentences and ideas together. Demonstrative adjectives (*this, that, these, those*) also help readers to link related pieces of information. As their name implies, these adjectives emphasize and distinguish specific objects or features for readers. In the paragraph that follows, the connections that pronouns and demonstrative adjectives make between sentences are graphically emphasized through boxes and lines.

any contemplated move.

4. Use parallel grammatical structures. Writers can provide a great deal of coherence by using parallel grammatical structures. When readers see how ideas are related grammatically, they can more easily see how they are related logically. (See pages 78–80 for a discussion of parallel grammatical structures.) Note the use of parallelism in the following paragraph.

> Orientation sessions accomplish four useful goals for trainees. First, they introduce trainees to key personnel in accounting, data processing, maintenance, and security. Second, they give trainees experience logging into the data base system, selecting an appropriate menu, editing core documents, and getting off the system. Third, they explain to trainees the company policies affecting the way supplies are ordered, used, and stored. Fourth, they help trainees understand their responsibilities in such sensitive areas as computer security and use.

In this paragraph parallelism is at work on a number of levels. The four sentences about the four goals start in the same way grammatically ("... they introduce/give/explain/help trainees ... ") to help readers categorize the information. Within individual sentences, the repetition of *present participles* (logg*ing*, select-*ing*, edit*ing*, gett*ing*) and of *past participles* (order*ed*, us*ed*, stor*ed*) helps the writer to summarize information and to see the related nature of the activities being explained. Note that the transitional words *first, second, third, fourth* convey a sense of parallelism as well as of sequence.

Completeness

Completeness means that your paragraph provides a well-developed and satisfying information block for your reader. In a complete paragraph you provide readers with a restricted topic sentence and sufficient information to clarify, analyze, support, defend, or prove the central idea expressed in your topic sentence.

A complete, carefully developed paragraph is an information block—containing the following types of supporting information for readers:

- names of specific individuals
- dates
- examples of a term, plan, situation

* measurements—size, shape, designs, temperatures, etc.
* costs and other figures
* descriptions
* statistical details

You gather these facts from your research and through your prewriting strategies, such as brainstorming and outlining (see pages 27–29).

Individually, these facts might not mean much to readers. But when linked in your paragraph, they provide the support readers need. Readers need these specific supporting details to understand a concept, perform a task, or evaluate a plan you are proposing. Without such supporting details, your paragraph will be underdeveloped, undernourished, incomplete.

One sure sign of an incomplete paragraph is that it leaves readers with questions, not answers. "Have I missed something?" "Is that the whole story?" "How did the writer arrive at that conclusion?" "Why is X better than Y?" For instance, the following skimpy paragraph is incomplete because it lacks the specific details necessary to explain and prove the assertion made in the topic sentence.

> Farmers can turn their crops and farm wastes into useful, cost-effective fuels. Much grown on the farm can be converted to energy. This energy can have many uses and save farmers a lot of money in operating expenses.

The writer did not consider the readers' needs. Farmers would expect to find examples of energy-rich fuels and specific farm uses of these fuels. Instead the farmer is left with the following questions: "What specific materials lend themselves to energy use?" "How can crops and farm wastes be turned into energy?" "What are some specific uses of this new energy?"

In the revised version that follows, the writer answers these questions through specific examples and explanations.

> Farm crops and wastes can be turned into fuels to save farmers money on their operating costs. Alcohol can be distilled from grain, sugar beets, potatoes—even from blighted crops. Converted to gasohol (90 percent gasoline, 10 percent alcohol), this alcohol can be used to run such farm equipment as irrigation pumps, feed grinders, and tractors. Similarly, through a biomass digestion system, farmers can produce methane from animal or crop wastes. This methane can be an important source of the natural gas used for heating and cooking. Finally, cellulose pellets, derived from plant materials, are an important solid fuel that can save farmers money in heating barns.

How will you know if your paragraph is complete? Chances are that a series of skimpy shoestring paragraphs lack necessary supporting data. But measuring length alone is not the only way to determine if a paragraph is developed sufficiently. Even a paragraph of four or five sentences can be incomplete if it contains a series of generalities and does not provide factual details. A paragraph is complete when it leaves no confusion in the reader's mind about what you intended, about how the reader is supposed to respond, and about why such a response is both necessary and appropriate.

◆ THE APPEARANCE OF PARAGRAPHS

Readers appreciate well-designed paragraphs and will respond more favorably to you and your message if you construct them carefully. The appearance of your paragraphs is especially important in the business world, where an excessively long paragraph is as unappreciated as a skimpy one. Your paragraphs should look professional and inviting. With the help of a word processor you can quickly change the size and shape of your paragraphs. But more than format changes are required to write appropriately constructed paragraphs. The following guidelines on the appearance of your paragraphs and the writing skills involved will help you to write readable and complete paragraphs.

1. Avoid excessively long paragraphs. Long paragraphs, especially long opening paragraphs, turn readers off. A full-page paragraph jammed with information is not user friendly and will cause readers to conclude that your work is too technical and that it will require a lot of hard work to get through. Long paragraphs tend to repeat the same idea (though in slightly different words) or to include information that belongs in another paragraph. Another cause of excessively long paragraphs may be overly broad topic sentences. By narrowing your topic sentence, you will shorten the paragraph.

Perhaps an excessively long paragraph signals that you have two or even three other paragraphs packed into one oversize block, as the writer for Seacoast Lab discovered (pages 44–47). When you suspect this, mark off parts of the long paragraph into smaller sized sections and see if each of these can be developed.

Keep in mind that a paragraph is the right length and size when it contains only the details readers need to understand the main point of the paragraph. Anything that does not directly support the topic sentence would make the paragraph too long.

2. Avoid stringing together a series of short paragraphs. An entire letter or report made up of one- and two-line paragraphs does not make the reader's job easier. On the contrary, making each sentence or two into a new paragraph may frustrate your reader. Such "shoestring" paragraphs suggest that your subject is trivial or that you could not find enough information about it. If your paragraphs are too short because of lack of supporting details, include additional relevant facts for readers (see the earlier section on paragraph completeness, pages 57–58). A string of short paragraphs may also tell you that you have chopped a complete paragraph into unnecessary smaller ones. Try to find a topic sentence in your short paragraphs to see whether they might be combined into one paragraph under that central idea.

3. Use visual clues to show emphasis and organization. Headings make organization visible and prepare readers for the information found in a group of related paragraphs. Headings also emphasize the major ideas of a memo or report. Within paragraphs, use italics, boldface type, bullets, and numbering to emphasize points as well as to break them down into smaller, easier-to-understand units. Figure 3.2 gives examples of these visual clues.

FIGURE 3.2   Use of visual clues to show emphasis and organization.

Audio Interference and Remedies

INTERFERENCE TO AUDIO DE-VICES (TELEPHONE, STEREOS, AM/FM RADIOS)

Telephones, electronic organs, stereo/hi-fi equipment, or AM/FM radios can be susceptible to interference. The source of interference will determine the effect on your audio device. For instance, if the equipment is picking up a nearby radio transmitter, you may hear the voice of the operator. When electrical interference is present, you may hear a sizzling or popping sound.

If you are receiving interference from a nearby radio transmitter, you should contact the operator and provide the Radio Operator Guidelines section of this handbook.

1. Generally, internal modification of your equipment must be made to eliminate the interference.
2. For **safety** reasons, it is recommended that any modification be made by a qualified service representative. The service representative should make the modifications in the home while the interference is occurring, in order to locate the point at which the interfering signal is entering the equipment.

Telephone Interference

Transmissions from a nearby radio transmitter can be picked up by your telephone system. The interference could enter the system at the following points:

1. drop wire leading to the house
2. telephone wiring inside the house
3. in the telephone instrument itself

Customer Owned Telephones

If you own your telephone and interference is occurring, the dealer or manufacturer should be contacted to assist you with modifications that will eliminate the interference.

Note: All telephone equipment must meet FCC registration standards and any internal filtering or modifications must be made by the manufacturer of the equipment or by other companies authorized by the FCC to do so.

Some states permit a telephone company to charge customers for service visits when they determine that the equipment is customer-owned.

Federal Communications Commission, *How to Identify and Resolve TV Interference Problems.* 2nd ed. Washington, D.C.: U.S. Government Printing Office, 1982.

4. Make your paragraphs visually attractive. Readability is enhanced when you use relatively neat segments of prose with plenty of white space surrounding them. Paragraphs of 6 to 8 lines, with 40 to 60 spaces per line, are easiest to read. White space on the page makes readers feel comfortable and shows that you have not crowded ideas together. Thanks to word processors, you may be able to experiment with the most pleasing format for your readers. More specific guidelines on spacing will be found in Chapter 6 (pages 119–129).

If possible, you might also try varying the length of your paragraphs to create a pleasant visual effect. As mentioned earlier, a series of long paragraphs is hard for readers to digest, while a string of short, skimpy paragraphs is annoying and jarring. When you combine long and short paragraphs you stand a better chance of holding the reader's interest. Generally, your first and last paragraphs will be shorter than your supporting paragraphs.

◆ PATTERNS OF PARAGRAPH ORGANIZATION

As you have seen, information in a paragraph should be unified, coherent, and complete. That information must also be presented in a logical and orderly sequence. Without organization each paragraph would be simply a list of unrelated ideas, which would not explain how the ideas are related. To explain the relationship of the ideas within a paragraph, you will have to choose an appropriate pattern of organization. The ones you select will depend on three things about the writing assignment: (1) the nature of your message, (2) the purpose of your work, and (3) the needs of your audience. In a short letter or memo, you may be able to develop your ideas using only one or two patterns for all the paragraphs. However, in a longer report you may use many patterns, and you may also combine patterns.

In the following pages, examine how paragraphs can be organized by means of these commonly used patterns: examples, description, time, space, comparison and contrast, definition, classification, and cause and effect.

Examples Pattern

To use the examples pattern, begin your paragraph with your restricted topic sentence and then offer examples proving or explaining that statement. (You may find it easier to generate your topic sentence *after* you think of a list of examples.) In the following paragraph, the author wants to prove that owning and operating an automobile is an escalating expense. To do that, the author found examples of the costs a driver will encounter over the life of the car.

> The cost of owning and operating a motor vehicle is of major significance as Americans experience increasing demands on their incomes. It costs more than $14,300 to purchase a car. If the car is driven 120,000 miles over a period of 12 years, the total cost to the owner will be $35,853 as the following expenses show. During the 12 years it will cost about $8,604 (excluding taxes) for some 7,059 gallons of gasoline. To maintain and repair the car, the owner can expect to pay another $6,232. Insurance will run about $3,991. Expenses for parking and tolls will be about $939. And, finally, the driver can expect to pay $1,787 in taxes.[1]

---

[1] U.S. Department of Transportation, *Cost of Owning and Operating Automobiles and Vans.*

Description Pattern

Use the description pattern to explain what something—a tool, a site, any object—looks like. Start your paragraph with a topic sentence that identifies what you will describe. Then provide a part-by-part practical description giving readers precise details about size, shape, color, function, or other relevant information. Your description may also emphasize any special features. The following paragraph describes the appearance and function of a golf ball.

> A golf ball has three interrelated parts that make it function effectively—the center, the threads, and the cover. The center of the golf ball, a liquid of clay, glycerine, and water, gives the ball its bounce. This small but compact center is like a ball within a ball. Wound around the center of the golf ball are hundreds of tiny rubber threads. When the ball is hit by a golf club these threads at first contract and then expand to give the ball its velocity. The cover, two hemispherical shells made of thermoplastic, contains indentations, or dimples, that affect the way the ball spins in flight. Without them, the ball would not travel as far or as fast.

Time Pattern

A paragraph organized by a temporal pattern discusses events in the order in which they occurred. This pattern is very versatile. You might use a chronological sequence to summarize events for a progress report or to analyze how a certain problem developed. For instance, you might use this pattern to outline the steps in a physical process such as continental drift or radiation. Or you might employ the temporal pattern to give instructions on how to do something. Note how the following paragraph arranges information about women's participation in the U.S. labor force chronologically.

> Over the last 40 years, the number of women in the U.S. labor force has steadily increased. In fact, since the end of World War II, women have accounted for about 60 percent of the net growth of the American labor force. According to the Bureau of Labor Statistics, in 1950 slightly less than 34 percent of all American women were employed outside the home. By 1960 that number was 38 percent. In 1970 the percentage of women in the labor market had increased to 43.4 percent. And by 1980 one woman out of two, or 51.6 percent, was a member of the U.S. labor force. It is estimated that by the year 2000 as many as 80 percent of all American women will be in the U.S. labor force.

A chronological pattern is also essential when readers have to follow instructions in a strict order. To point out that sequence, label each step.

> To clean a storage tank, follow these steps exactly. First, ventilate the tank to release noxious fumes. Second, wash out the tank with water to dispel flammable vapors and to further reduce the chances of an explosion. Third, remove any sludge or deposits with Anixyl 345 or Metathine 45XT. Finally, allow the tank to air for at least 36 hours.

Space Pattern

A paragraph with a spatial pattern of development arranges information according to a particular view of an object or its location. Consider the many perspectives or views possible—from top to bottom, from bottom to top, from inside to outside, from outside to inside, from front to back, from back to front, from left to right, or from right to left. Choose a view that is most appropriate for your topic and your reader. In the paragraph below, the writer arranges the types of protective clothing worn by industrial workers from helmets to shoes, or from top to bottom. This head-to-toe order helps readers follow the information in a familiar sequence; the writer does not jump from goggles to overalls to helmets.

> Protective clothing is available for every part of the industrial worker's body. Hard hats protect the worker's head from the impact of falling objects when the individual is handling stock. Caps and hair nets keep the worker's hair from catching in machinery. Face shields, safety goggles, glasses, and similar kinds of clothing guard the worker's eyes from splashing chemicals or flying debris. Protective vests, jackets, aprons, and overalls shield the worker's body from cuts or bruises from heavy or rough-edged stock. The worker's hands are protected from the same kinds of injuries with special gloves. Finally, safety shoes and boots shield the worker's feet from being injured by falling stock.[2]

Comparison/Contrast Pattern

This pattern for organizing the ideas can show readers the similarities (comparisons) and the differences (contrasts) between objects, plans, locations, or the like. In a single paragraph you show either similarities or differences or both. You can also use this pattern to explain an unfamiliar concept or object by comparing it to one known to readers. When you use this pattern, always identify in the topic sentence the points or objects you are comparing or contrasting. The following paragraph both compares and contrasts two types of home mortgages.

> Before making a loan application, prospective home buyers need to know the two most popular types of mortgage: the conventional mortgage and the adjustable-rate mortgage (ARM). The conventional mortgage gives buyers a fixed rate of interest over the life of the loan, for example, 11 1/2 percent for 30 years. The ARM, however, has interest rates that vary as the rate of interest paid on Treasury Bills varies. For example, an ARM may begin at 9 percent but in a year or two either escalate or decrease by 2 percent or more. With a conventional loan, monthly mortgage payments are fixed. With an ARM, on the other hand, they can change each year, depending on the financial market. A conventional loan may be more expensive for home buyers to obtain than would be an ARM. Lending institutions generally demand higher discount points (costs to rent the money) for fixed-rate mortgages than for ARMs. Therefore, home buyers will have to decide between the stable but initially higher rate of a conventional mortgage and the fluctuating, initially lower rate of an ARM.

---

[2] U.S. Department of Labor, *Concepts and Techniques of Machine Safeguarding* (1980): 10.

Or you can use a separate paragraph for each subject of the comparison and contrast.

> The traditional office exists in a one-to-one environment: each manager has a secretary. Each secretary has nonspecialized functions—typing, filing, copying, scheduling, answering telephones, and doing correspondence with an electric typewriter and a copier, resulting in much retyping and duplication of effort. The manager waits for the secretary, and the secretary waits for the manager. The situation always generates more paperwork. The traditional solution is to hire more people, use more overtime, or miss more deadlines.
>
> The automated office, however, is no longer a one-to-one arrangement. One secretary supports several managers and oversees several people, each with a different specific function. Managers use automation (telephone, dictation equipment) to create or implement ideas. The secretary, using automated equipment such as word processors or transcription equipment, distributes information largely through electronic means (terminals). In this modern office, the skills of existing personnel, particularly those performing secretarial functions, are used most effectively.[3]

Definition Pattern

When you use the definition pattern, you organize your paragraph around what a term or concept means. Definition is especially useful in on-the-job writing because of the many technical words you may have to explain to customers or to professionals outside your field. Some of the elements that may appear in a definition paragraph, depending on the situation, include: (a) what the term means; (b) where and when the term originated; (c) what its applications or characteristics are; and (d) what examples or illustrations of the term will help readers to understand it. Note how the following paragraph on flex time uses many of these techniques.

> Flex time refers to a policy of replacing the traditional fixed work hours with a more flexible schedule set by employees within certain prescribed limits. These limits typically include a *core time* and *flexible time.* During core time, such as 9:30 A.M. to 3:00 P.M., all employees are required to be at work. Flexible time is a period before or after core time when employees can exercise their option to start or leave work. Flexible time is usually between 7:00 A.M. and 9:30 A.M., and 3:00 P.M. and 6:00 P.M..[4]

Classification Pattern

To classify is to sort *related* objects (types of wrenches or types of microcomputers) into mutually exclusive groups according to a consistent principle. In libraries, the Dewey decimal system classifies all books into one of ten large branches of knowledge. The same objects can usually be classified according to

---

[3] *USAF Medical Service Digest* Nov.–Dec. 1982: 15–16.
[4] *Supervisory Management* Feb. 1984: 38.

several different principles as long as the classification is done systematically and logically. For example, items on a shopping list can be arranged in one of several ways; in one classification, you may list items according to how essential they are to you: essential—items that are needed immediately (milk, bread), less essential—items needed at some time in the future (more soap, more dog food), and luxuries—items you can live without (snack foods, extra cookies). Or using a different classification, you may list items on your shopping list according to how many calories they contain: high calorie (chocolates), medium calorie (bread, milk), and low calorie (lettuce). Or yet another shopper may classify items according to their location in the supermarket in order to avoid retracing steps.

For on-the-job writing, the classification pattern is especially helpful when you have to identify or evaluate different products, sites, or plans for an employer. The following paragraph classifies for a store manager different types of burglar alarms.

> An appropriate burglar alarm system can help protect the merchant. Basically the merchant can choose from two types of alarms. The central alarm alerts a security or police agency but does not warn the burglar. The local alarm, usually a siren or bell, goes off at the site of the break-in. Whether the alarm is central or local, the merchant has a wide choice of alarm-sensing devices. Among them are radar motion detectors, invisible photo beams, detectors that work on ultrasonic sound, and vibration detectors. Also, there is supplemental equipment such as an automatic phone dialer. This device phones the police and the store owner to give them verbal warning when an alarm is breached.[5]

Cause-to-Effect Pattern

In a cause-to-effect pattern, the paragraph starts with why something occurred (the cause) and then tells readers what resulted (the effect). This pattern is useful as the structure for a letter of complaint, an investigative report, or a proposal. In writing a proposal you try to convince readers that if your plan (the cause) is adopted, certain good things will follow (the effects). With this pattern you can describe any problem or decision, and then trace its effects. In the following paragraph the writer begins with the causes of the employees' problems (the improperly positioned video display terminals, or VDTs) and then lists some of the effects of that action (glare, backache, decreased productivity).

> When new VDTs were put in a month ago, they were installed incorrectly. They were placed too low, at the wrong angle, and in the wrong lighting conditions. As a result, our employees have experienced a number of problems. They have complained of an annoying glare from the reflection of room lighting on the screen. In addition to experiencing eyestrain, employees have had low backaches because they have to slump in their chairs to focus on the screens, which were not tilted up and not placed high enough on the desks. Consequently, our employees' efficiency dropped 15–20 percent during the last month.

---

[5] Small Business Administration, "Preventing Burglary and Robbery Loss" 1965.

Effect-to-Cause Pattern

To use an effect-to-cause pattern, begin the paragraph with the effect—the result or outcome of something—and then identify its causes. This pattern is especially useful when substantiating why something happened. Make sure that you document the relationship between effects and their causes with specific, relevant information. In the following paragraph, the writer links increased tourism (the effect) to its multiple causes.

> Over the last eighteen months tourism has continued to increase in Hillview. A major reason for this increase is the opening of the Rocky Mountain Theme Park. Attendance at this park has grown each year since its opening in 1988. The completion of the Dodge County Metro Center in March of last year also contributed to increased tourism. Residents from nearby states frequently attend rock concerts at the center and often spend an extra day or two in Hillview to shop or to sightsee. Three new hotels have also increased tourism. In the past year five conventions were held in Hillview, two more than last year.

◆ THE PARAGRAPH: AN OVERVIEW

Paragraphs are essential to the success of your written work. Effective paragraphs result from the process of sorting your thoughts into meaningful groups for your audience. Paragraphs can introduce, support, provide transitions between, and conclude your ideas. A key part of your paragraph is the topic sentence, which should be suitably restricted and placed first in the paragraph to help readers grasp your central idea quickly. One simple model to follow is the T-shape, particularly useful for supporting paragraphs.

In their final form, your paragraphs should be coherent, complete, unified, and the appropriate length for your message. Depending on that message, you may organize your paragraphs according to any of the patterns explained on pages 61–66. A long piece of writing will contain paragraphs following many or all of these patterns. Once you can construct a paragraph as a unified information block, you will have mastered one of the basics in the process of writing.

◆ EXERCISES

1. The following sentences would be poor choices for topic sentences because they are too broad. They do not help a reader focus on a single, unified topic. Revise these sentences to make them suitable topic sentences by restricting the topic. The first one has been done for you.
   a. Highway safety saves lives. (Traffic engineers have found that artificial lighting can reduce night accidents.)
   b. Cable stations offer many benefits to subscribers throughout America.
   c. Our company would be interested if conditions were right.
   d. The Social Security System is under attack.
   e. Accounting (or welding, or any field) is an exciting profession.

f. A job applicant's qualifications mean a lot.

g. Banks play a significant role in the economy.

h. Medical science can perform wonders.

i. Knowledge of chemistry will help all students.

j. This is a big year for our school.

k. Vacations can be taken anywhere and at any time.

2. Write a complete, unified, and coherent paragraph on one of the topic sentences you revised for Exercise 1. Submit at least two drafts with your final copy.

3. The topic sentence is buried in each of the following paragraphs. Find it and rewrite it if necessary and then put it first in the paragraph. If necessary, revise the other sentences in the paragraph to account for the change.

   a. For a noise barrier to work, it must be high and long enough to block the view of a road. Noise barriers do very little good for homes on a hillside overlooking a road or for buildings that rise above the barrier. Noise barriers can have functional limitations. Openings in the noise barrier for driveway connections or intersecting streets destroy its effectiveness, too. In some areas, homes are scattered too far apart to permit noise barriers to be built at a reasonable cost.

   b. Sometimes shoplifters have special hooks or belts on the insides of their coats; or they wear tricky aprons and undergarments, which are designed to hold innumerable articles. Some sleight-of-hand thieves slip merchandise into packages or into boxes that have a hinged top, bottom, or end. Salesclerks should know how to spot devices used by shoplifters. Employees should also be suspicious of and watch shoppers who carry bulky packages, knitting bags, shopping bags, and umbrellas. These are handy receptacles for items that a shoplifter purposely knocks off counters.

4. The following paragraphs lack unity. Rewrite them to eliminate unnecessary or irrelevant information.

   a. The Hanks Company has decided to construct its new lighting store in Burton Hills to attract more customers. This location will serve a busy market of 200,000 customers from Pasco, Downers Grove, and Middletown. Customers in these areas will no longer have to make an hour-long drive to Omaha for special lighting. The new lighting center offers them 23,000 sq. ft. of display space and gives the Hanks Company one of the largest stores in the region. This new location will also attract customers from the Portersville community, who must frequently drive to Omaha. The financing of the lighting center will be done by Perry and Associates of Fort Worth.

   b. A person does not need extensive training to operate the new microcomputer effectively. In many ways, it is no more difficult to operate than a typewriter. Our employees did object, however, to giving up their typewriters; some of these machines have been in the company for 10 years. The microcomputer uses a very simple language called BASIC. This language was developed about 25 years ago and has worked well in other offices like ours. Written in English, BASIC can be taught to our operators in less than a day. Storage capacity and speed will make the microcomputer a valuable addition in the office for our operators.

5. The following paragraphs lack coherence. Rewrite them using the four techniques discussed in this chapter: transitional words and phrases, repetition of key words, the use of personal pronouns and demonstrative adjectives, and grammatical parallelism.

   a. High-altitude photography has many uses. Land forms are measured and mapped.

Accuracy is important for the measurement of water and other resources. Foresters find out the volume of trees, and foresters will be interested in knowing whether the trees are infested. Wildlife can be measured. Future highways and pipelines are always sketched out on the drawing board. Aerial photography helps city planners and geologists. Applications include shoreline changes. Geologists can measure the damage caused by floods. Changes in the landscape come from storms and hurricanes. Aerial photography records important data.

b. Our company prefers the Lodex word processors. The other models are expensive. About $300 separates the price of a Lodex from the prices charged by other vendors. The service contract provides us with good terms. Repairs are made free of charge for the first 90 days. A discount on parts is available at 30 percent. Flexible software will help our efficiency. Other vendors have limited means. Lodex provides 12 hours of free instruction for our staff.

6. Below is the first draft of a paragraph on foot care. Assume that you have been asked to write a short pamphlet on this topic for a local public health agency. Using the process and techniques of paragraphing discussed in this chapter, work on this draft until you have developed two complete, unified, and coherent paragraphs from this early draft. Delete or add any details as necessary.

Feet need breathing room. Common foot problems include corns and calluses, athlete's foot, bunions, ingrown toenails, and chronic blistering. Over a lifetime the feet hold up a weight that more than equals several million pounds. We all feel tired at the end of the day at the office or plant. A nurse or a police officer must stand on their feet for at least an 8–12 hour shift. Diseases can be detected from examining the feet. Podiatrists (foot doctors) are called to hospitals to trim the toenails of diabetic patients. Diabetes makes people extra sensitive to foot infections. Standing, stretching, walking, and strenuous exercise are good for the feet. Shoes need to be selected carefully. Skin irritations easily result. Sitting with legs crossed or wearing tight clothing affects the feet. Gym tights can hurt the feet. Wading through cold water or having pressure on the feet from poor-fitting shoes causes poor circulation. Over-the-counter medicines are often advertised as cures for some problems. Foot problems tend to get worse the older we get. But shoes made of leather and low-heeled shoes can help skin and circulation problems. Hot baths work to speed flow to the feet. Improved care helps circulation.

7. For each of the following topic sentences, explain which pattern(s) of paragraph organization would be most appropriate and why.

a. Computer time-sharing offers the small business many financial advantages over buying its own hardware.

b. Vandalism is behavior that defaces or destroys property.

c. Over the last seven years video games have become more sophisticated.

d. Enzymes in our mouth help us to digest the food we eat.

e. The living room was redecorated from floor to ceiling.

f. Computer graphics offers a business many advantages over traditional, manual graphics.

g. Ergonomics is the applied science of designing equipment to meet the needs of workers.

h. After inspecting the property on November 30, I found that the major deterioration had begun in the basement and spread upstairs.

i. For many workers coffee is a necessary evil.

j. A door lock has a number of important, interconnected parts.

k. For all practical purposes, ours is a paperless office.

l. A large oak tree looks like a multicolored umbrella.

m. The U.S. Postal Service instituted the nine-digit zip code to speed the delivery of mail.

n. Over-the-counter drugs are packaged to protect consumers from poisoning.

o. Music videos are mini-musicals.

p. If not used properly, pesticides are poisonous to people and pets.

q. Because the park was not carefully kept up, patron use dropped 18 percent in the last six months.

r. Based on their prices, houses in our town fall into one of four categories.

s. A roof includes more than just shingles.

8. From the topic sentences in Exercise 7, select three which follow different patterns of organization and write an appropriate paragraph for each of these.

9. Analyze the paragraphs included in the following article, "Emergency Preparedness via Cable TV." Classify them according to the four types and according to pattern(s) of organization. Discuss the use of transitional words or phrases used to link paragraphs.

Emergency Preparedness via Cable TV
By William Rushton

(1) In any kind of emergency, most Americans turn first to their television sets. Because 98 percent of U.S. homes have TV sets, television is the most immediate and available communications resource we have. Proper understanding of emerging communications technologies and some advance planning on the local level would enable us to enhance significantly the usefulness of this resource for emergency purposes.

(2) Chief among these new technologies is cable television, which currently is capable of bringing 50 or more channels by wire into homes. In the past these American households could at best receive only a dozen or so channels "over the air." Cable is the highway of the new telecommunications environment. It distributes programs from broadcast stations, satellites, microwave feeds, and local nonbroadcast origination studios ("access centers"). These cable services offer a wide variety of traditional kinds of entertainment and a new world of nonentertainment services. By the end of this decade, virtually all American households will have access to cable services.

(3) Cable's multiplicity of channels gives rise to "narrowcasting," or the targeting of a small segment of an audience and programming its specific needs. Access channels, particularly government access channels, can be used for programs that discuss very narrow and specific issues, with phone-in discussion by the target audience involved. Cable's initial role, therefore, might be in planning for energy emergency preparedness. Phone-in cable shows, for example, offer a mechanism by which the government can *interact* with its citizens.

(4) Another major advantage in using cable in emergency situations is its local-ism. In most states, cable utilities are franchised by local municipalities, offer-ing access channels (similar to a local community TV "station") to communities that might not have a local broadcast station. During the blizzard of 1978, for example, the town of Danbury, Connecticut (which had no broadcast television station) effectively used its cable system as a 24-hour emergency information center.

(5) Many cable systems have specific emergency facilities built in, such as an emergency command station or a direct feed from such a facility. Moreover, the centralized nature of cable distribution (from a processing center called a "head end") allows a cable operator to run an electronic message (or "crawl") along the bottom of the screen on all channels simultaneously, announcing an emergency and calling public attention to a specific channel for relevant emergency details. In the case of a derailed tank car of hazardous chemicals, for example, or a zone downwind from a nuclear power plant accident, it might be easier to reach the affected area by phone calls or electronic messages directly to a cable system or two than to try to reach all the broadcast stations, running the risk of panic in nonaffected areas. Instructions to one zone might be vastly different from instruc-tions to another. Moreover, new devices are on the market now that would allow your cable to signal you even if the television set is off, a service no other broad-cast outlet can offer.

(6) Another advantage of cable TV is that in the event of a severe long-term emergency—such as disruptions of imported oil supplies, with resulting restric-tions on private auto use—cable television offers what may be our only long-term solution for certain public information-dissemination and service-delivery tasks. "Teleconferences," "telecourses," and "telemedicine" (preventive medical care and social work activities) can be offered over cable without making the viewer travel. Not all information or social service activities can be conveyed on cable, of course, but enough of them can be so that any medium-to-long-range energy cri-sis could be made more manageable. In the long term, cable might be our only alternative to curtailing or eliminating such services altogether in an emergency.

(7) In conclusion, cable television can provide many emergency services for the public good. The technology is here, and its applications are proven and helpful.

U.S. Department of Energy, *The Energy Consumer* Dec. 1980–Jan. 1981: 24.

Writing: Sentences

A successful paragraph depends on successful sentences. And as is the case with constructing a successful paragraph, writing effective sentences takes time and work. In all likelihood you will not find yourself writing logical, polished sentences in your first or even second draft. Recall from Chapters 2 and 3 how many times William Tisch and the writer for Seacoast Lab revised their sentences to make their work clear and easy to read for their audience. By developing your skills in drafting and revising sentences, you will make valuable progress toward writing successfully on the job.

◆ CLEAR SENTENCES AND YOUR CAREER

The way in which you construct and revise your sentences can determine whether you succeed or fail in the world of work. Your sentences reveal a lot about you. They tell readers how well or how poorly you can convey a message and how much you value your reader's time and energy. If your sentences are clear, concise, and varied, readers will find your message easier to understand and to act on. They will thank you for not having to reread your work in order to understand your message. If you write readable sentences, you predispose your reader to respond positively to you and your message. Clear writers earn high marks from both employers and customers and are in great demand in the workforce.

On the other hand, if your sentences are unclear, immature, or crowded with excessive baggage, readers will dread receiving memos and letters from you. Such sentences will make your reader's job hard and unpleasant. Because of poor sentences, readers may also question your powers of reasoning and action. Employers certainly do not look favorably on writers who embarrass them or cost the company time and money because of unclear or misleading sentences.

◆ WHAT THIS CHAPTER CAN DO FOR YOU

The goal of Chapter 4 is to help you write clear and readable sentences. It starts out with some basics in sentence structure and punctuation and then turns to ways of helping you revise your sentences until they become clear and lean. By studying this chapter carefully, you will learn to:

- ◆ construct and punctuate sentences correctly.
- ◆ use the appropriate voice (active or passive).
- ◆ use parallel constructions.
- ◆ write sentences that say what you mean.
- ◆ write sentences that are economical and easy to read.

◆ CONSTRUCTING AND PUNCTUATING SENTENCES

A *sentence* is a complete thought, expressed by a subject and a verb, that can make sense standing alone. The first step toward success in writing sentences is learning to recognize the difference between phrases and clauses.

The Difference Between Phrases and Clauses

A *phrase* is a group of words that does not contain a subject and a verb; phrases cannot make sense standing alone. Phrases cannot be sentences.

in the park	**No subject:** Who is in the park?
	No verb: What was done in the park?
for every patient in intensive care	**No subject:** Who did something for every patient?
	No verb: What was done for the patients?

A *clause* does contain a subject and a verb, but *not every clause is a sentence.* Only *independent* (or *main*) *clauses* can stand alone as sentences. Here is an example of an independent clause that is a complete sentence.

       subject   verb   object

The president closed the college.

A *dependent* (or *subordinate*) *clause* also contains a subject and a verb, but does not make complete sense and cannot stand alone. Why? A dependent clause contains a subordinating conjunction—*after, although, as, because, before, even though, if, since, unless, when, where, whereas, while*—at the beginning of the clause. Such conjunctions subordinate the clause in which they appear and make the clause dependent for meaning and completion on an independent clause.

After ⎫
Before ⎪
Because ⎬   the president closed the college
Even though ⎪
Unless ⎭

"After the president closed the college" is not a complete thought. This dependent clause leaves us in suspense. It needs to be completed with an independent clause telling us what happened "after."

dependent clause	independent clause		
	subject	verb	phrase
After the president closed the college,	we	played	in the snow.

Sentence Fragments

Complete sentences do not leave the reader hanging in midair, wondering who did something, how it was done, or under what conditions it was done. An incomplete sentence is called a *fragment.* Fragments may be phrases or dependent clauses. They either lack a verb or a subject or have broken away from an independent (main) clause. A fragment is isolated; it needs an overhaul to supply missing parts to turn it into an independent clause or to glue it back to the independent clause from which it became separated.

You can avoid writing sentence fragments by following a few rules. In the next few pages, incorrect examples are preceded by a minus sign; corrected versions, by a plus sign.

1. Every sentence must have a subject telling the reader who does the action.

− Being extra careful not to spill the water. (Who?)
+ The aide was extra careful not to spill the water.

2. Every sentence must have a complete verb. Watch especially for verbs ending in *-ing.* They need another verb (some form of *to be* or *have*) to make them complete.

− The woman in the blue uniform. (What did she do?)
+ The woman in the blue uniform directed traffic.
− The machine running in the computer department. (Did what?)

You can change the last fragment into a sentence by supplying the correct form of the verb.

+ The machine *is* running in the computer department.
+ The machine *runs* in the computer department.

Or you can revise the entire sentence, adding a new thought.

+ The machine running in the computer department handles all new accounts.

3. Do not detach prepositional phrases (beginning with *at, by, for, from, in, to, with,* and so forth) **from independent clauses.** Such phrases are not complete thoughts and cannot stand alone. Correct the error by leaving the phrases attached to the sentence to which they belong.

- − By three o'clock the next day. (What was to happen?)
- + The supervisor wanted our reports by three o'clock the next day.

- − For every patient in intensive care. (What was done?)
- + Nurses kept hourly reports for every patient in intensive care.

4. Do not use a subordinate clause as a sentence. Even though it contains a subject and a verb, a subordinate clause standing alone is still a fragment. To avoid this kind of sentence fragment, simply join the two clauses (the independent clause and the dependent clause containing a subordinating conjunction) with a comma—*not* a period or semicolon.

- − Unless we agreed to the plan. (What would happen?)
- − Unless we agreed to the plan; the project manager would discontinue the operation. (A semicolon cannot set off the subordinate clause.)
- + Unless we agreed to the plan, the project manager would discontinue the operation.

- − Because safety precautions were taken. (What happened?)
- + Because safety precautions were taken, ten construction workers escaped injury.

Sometimes subordinate clauses appear at the end of a sentence. They may be introduced by a subordinate conjunction, an adverb, or a relative pronoun (*that, which, who*). Do not separate these clauses from the preceding independent clause with a period, thus turning them into fragments.

- − Some of the new employees selected the high-risk option in their policy. While others did not.
- + Some of the new employees selected the high-risk option in their policy, while others did not. (The *while* subordinates the clause, and therefore that clause cannot stand alone.)

- − An all-volunteer fire department posed some problems. Especially for residents in the southern part of town.
- + An all-volunteer fire department posed some problems, especially for residents in the southern part of town. (The word *especially* qualifies *problems,* referred to in the independent clause.)

The Comma Splice

Fragments occur when you use only bits and pieces of complete sentences. Another common error that some writers commit involves just the reverse kind of action. They weakly and wrongly join two complete sentences (independent clauses) with a comma as if those two sentences were really only one sentence. This error is called a *comma splice.* Here is an example.

- − Gasoline prices have risen by 10 percent in the last month, we will drive the car less often.

Two independent clauses (complete sentences) exist:

> Gasoline prices have risen by 10 percent in the last month.
> We will drive the car less often.

A comma alone lacks the power to separate independent clauses. As the preceding example shows, many pronouns—*I, he, she, it, we, they*—are used as the subjects of independent clauses. A comma splice will result if you place a comma instead of a semicolon between two independent clauses where the second clause opens with a pronoun.

> − Rosa approved the plan, she liked its cost-effective approach.
> + Rosa approved the plan; she liked its cost-effective approach.

However, relative pronouns (*who, whom, which, that*) are preceded by a comma, not a period or semicolon, when they introduce subordinate clauses.

> − She approved the plan. Which had the cost-effective approach.
> + She approved the plan, which had the cost-effective approach.

Four Ways to Correct Comma Splices

1. Remove the comma separating two independent clauses and replace it with a period. Then capitalize the first letter of the first word of the newly reinstated sentence.

> + Gasoline prices have risen by 10 percent in the last month. We will drive the car less often.

2. Delete the comma and insert a semicolon.

> + Gasoline prices have risen by 10 percent in the last month; we will drive the car less often.

The semicolon is an effective and forceful punctuation mark when the two independent clauses are closely related, that is, when they announce contrasting or parallel views, as the two following examples reveal.

> + The union favored the new legislation; the company opposed it. (contrasting views)
> + Night classes help the college and the community; more students can take more credit hours. (parallel views)

3. Insert a coordinating conjunction (*and, but, or, nor, for, yet*) **after the comma.** Together, the conjunction and the comma properly separate the two independent clauses.

> + Gasoline prices have risen by 10 percent in the last month, and we will drive the car less often.

4. Rewrite the sentence (if it makes sense to do so). Turn the first independent clause into a dependent clause by adding a subordinate conjunction; insert a comma and add the second independent clause.

+ <u>Because</u> gasoline prices have risen by 10 percent in the last month, we will drive the car less often.

(Of the four ways to correct the comma splice, the last example is the most suitable for the sample sentence, because the price of gasoline affects how much a car is driven.)

How *Not* to Correct Comma Splices

Some writers mistakenly try to correct comma splices by inserting a conjunctive adverb (*also, consequently, furthermore, however, moreover, nevertheless, then, therefore*) after the comma.

− Gasoline prices have risen by 10 percent in the last month, consequently we will drive the car less often.

Because the conjunctive adverb (*consequently*) is not as powerful as the coordinating conjunction (*and, but, for*), the error is not eliminated. If you use a conjunctive adverb—*consequently, however, nevertheless*—you still must insert a semicolon or a period before it, as the following examples show.

+ Gasoline prices have risen by 10 percent in the last month; consequently, we will drive the car less often.
+ Gasoline prices have risen by 10 percent in the last month. Consequently, we will drive the car less often.

◆ USING THE APPROPRIATE VOICE: ACTIVE OR PASSIVE

"Voice" refers to whether the subject of a sentence performs the action or receives it. In the active voice a subject performs the action and so appears in the first (and subject) part of the sentence. In the passive voice the subject becomes the recipient of the action and no longer occupies the first part of the sentence, but now appears in the last part or is even omitted.

Active voice **1.** The recruiting staff made three visits.
Passive voice **2.** Three visits were made by the recruiting staff.
Passive voice **3.** Three visits were made.

In sentence 1 the writer stresses the actions of the staff. In sentence 2 and especially in 3 the writer is more interested in the number of visits than in who made them.

When to Use the Active Voice

The active voice is usually more forceful and direct than is the passive voice. It generally requires fewer words than the passive voice. Sentence 2 contains two more words than are in sentence 1: *were* and *by*. These extra words show how passives are formed. Verbs in the passive voice are constructed with some form of the verb *to be* followed by a *past participle* (here, *made*); often a prepositional phrase with *by* indicates the presence of a passive verb: *by the recruiting staff.* You can often change the passive into the active voice by making what is included in the *by* phrase the subject of the sentence: *The recruiting staff made three visits.*

Since both the active and the passive voices have advantages, use both in your work. The active voice, however, offers writers these benefits:

1. The active voice gives instructions authority and clarity.

Active   Remove the hex nut.
Passive   The hex nut should be removed.

Active   Wear protective eyeglasses.
Passive   Protective eyeglasses should be worn.

2. The active voice can eliminate awkwardness.

Active   I completed two years of technical training.
Passive   Two years of technical training were completed by me.

Active   Ms. Rodgers spoke about the new design.
Passive   The new design was spoken about by Ms. Rodgers.

3. The active voice lets readers know that another person, not a machine, is writing to them in letters and reports.

Active   The tour director arranged the plans for your travel.
Passive   Plans have been arranged for your travel.

Active   I can make an appointment for you.
Passive   An appointment can be made for you.

You will find that using sentences in the active voice will make your letters and reports easier to read and to follow. The active voice shows exactly who is in charge and who has accomplished certain tasks. For this reason, be careful that you do not overuse the passive voice as you revise your work.

When to Use the Passive Voice

Scientists often use the passive voice in order to emphasize the experiment or the procedure rather than the individual performing it. They believe that references to "I" detract from the objectivity of the work. Many scientists would prefer the second of the following two sentences:

Active   The biologist performed the experiment three times in forty-eight hours.
Passive   The experiment was performed three times in forty-eight hours.

Clearly, some contexts call for the "I" and the active voice in reporting scientific data. But the passive voice does have its advantages when you are writing about a process—changing hydrogen and oxygen into water, for example—when the emphasis is not on the human actor, but on the changes brought about through scientific law.

The passive voice also serves the following useful functions.

1. The passive voice can be used when the actor is unknown.

The car was stolen at noon. (The thief's identity is not known.)

The practice was started in 1955. (Who started it is not known.)

Monthly house payments are scaled down during the first five years of the mortgage. (By whom?)

2. The passive voice can be used when the object is more important for the reader than is the actor.

The injection of insulin was given at 6:30 A.M.

Pieces of the bullet were found in the dining room wall.

The generator was periodically inspected.

3. The passive voice can be used as a business strategy when anonymity is necessary or when emphasis on the subject has unfavorable ethical implications. Compare these two sentences.

Mr. Corcoran fired the mechanic.

The mechanic was fired.

The first sentence emphasizes the fact that it was Mr. Corcoran who dismissed the mechanic; the second sentence does not even mention Mr. Corcoran. Sometimes for legal reasons a person's identity must be kept secret.

The juvenile was arraigned in court.

The suspect's identity was not revealed by the police.

The pilot's license was suspended by the Board.

◆ USING PARALLELISM

Parallelism expresses the similarity of ideas by placing them in the same grammatical form. Parallel forms may use the same part of speech or the same type of phrase or clause. Using parallel grammatical units for parallel ideas enables you to group related points, to clarify relationships, and to emphasize your message for readers. Readers seeing repeated grammatical forms will find it easier to read your work and to understand the comparisons you are making. To use parallelism effectively, make sure that the grammatical forms are the same and that the ideas actually are equal and related. The following examples show parallelism in grammatical forms:

Present participle	listening	reading	writing	speaking
Infinitive	to listen	to read	to write	to speak
Noun	listener	reader	writer	speaker
Lack of parallelism	to listen	reading	writing	to speak

Note how parallelism is violated in the following example in which each duty of a proposal writer is expressed in a different grammatical form.

The specific duties of a proposal writer involve

• defining the problem for readers.
• the need to describe the solution.
• establishment of a schedule.
• is responsible for budget plans.
• has assigned personnel.
• writes progress reports.

Suitably revised, the writer's duties in the following list are parallel because they have equal importance and because they are expressed with the same grammatical form (all start with present participles).

The specific duties of a proposal writer involve

• defining the problem for readers.
• describing the solution.
• establishing a schedule.
• planning a budget.
• assigning personnel.
• writing progress reports.

Note how the writer of the following sentence calls attention to the report's characteristics through the series of adjectives.

The report was clear, concise, and informative.

Compare the following faulty sentences (in which words are not parallel) with the corrected versions.

− The student was enthusiastic, cooperative, and she knew the material very well. (After two parallel adjectives, the writer introduces an independent clause and thus destroys the parallelism.)

+ The student was enthusiastic, cooperative, and knowledgeable. (all adjectives)

When you list a group of parallel words in a series, be sure that you are consistent in using *the, a, in,* or *that* with them. Use the article, preposition, or pronoun either before each element or before only the first element.

− We have stores in Cleveland, Detroit, Kokomo, and in Chicago.

+ We have stores in Cleveland, in Detroit, in Kokomo, and in Chicago.
+ We have stores in Cleveland, Detroit, Kokomo, and Chicago.

Parallelism is used with prepositional phrases to group related information.

− The new lights were installed within the hallways, on the roof, and they were included in the parking lot, too.

+ The new lights were installed within the hallways, on the roof, and in the parking lot.

Parallelism of clauses works well as long as you warn readers by beginning each clause in exactly the same way.

− Hiring qualified employees is a matter of screening applicants carefully, interviewing them diplomatically, and then to run a reference check. (two present participles followed by an infinitive)

+ Hiring qualified employees is a matter of screening applicants carefully, interviewing them diplomatically, and running a reference check.

Establishing proper parallelism can be especially tricky in sentences that use the following *correlative conjunctions: either/or, neither/nor,* and *both/and.* Keep in mind that the information on either side of these correlatives has to be grammatically identical. Study the following faulty examples and their revisions.

− He told the operator to either repair the equipment or to replace it. (*Either* is *in the middle of* one infinitive and its counterpart *or* is *in front of* the other infinitive.)
+ He told the operator either to repair the equipment or to replace it. (Both *either* and *or* have the same position: before the infinitive.)

− All employees are entitled to both fifteen vacation days and to eight holidays. (This is confusing; do the employees receive two fifteen-day vacation periods?)
+ All employees are entitled both to fifteen vacation days and to eight holidays.

◆ WRITING SENTENCES THAT SAY WHAT YOU MEAN

Your sentences should say exactly what you mean, without double talk, misplaced humor, or nonsense. Sentences are composed of words and word groups that influence each other. Like molecules, they bump and rub into each other, exerting a strong reciprocal influence.

It's easy to overlook the kinds of errors discussed below when you first write a sentence or even after you have finished a draft of a letter or memo. But you can eliminate these errors by reminding yourself, as you are revising your work, to read your sentences to see how one group of words fits into and relates to another. If you are composing on a word processor, don't be lazy. Scroll the text of your letter or report up and down to see how one sentence connects to another.

Logical Sentences

Sentences should not contradict themselves or make outlandish claims. The following examples contain such errors; note how easily the suggested revisions handle the problem.

Illogical The manager's order established a new precedent for our time. (A precedent is something that has already been established; hence it cannot be new.)

Revision The manager's order established a precedent.

Illogical Steel roll-away shutters make it possible for the sun to be shaded in the summer and to have it shine in the winter. (The sun is far too large to shade; the writer meant that a room or a house, much smaller than the sun, could be shaded with the shutters.)

Revision Steel roll-away shutters make it possible for owners to shade their living rooms in the summer and to admit sunshine during the winter.

Sentences Using Contextually Appropriate Words

Sentences should use the combination of words most appropriate for the subject matter you are writing about. Here are some illustrations of sentences containing inappropriate words, together with suggested revisions.

Inappropriate The building materials need to be explained in small, concrete steps. (The writer was thinking of "concrete" in terms of teaching; the context, though, encourages the reader to picture cement stairs.)

Revision The building materials need to be explained separately and carefully.

Inappropriate The members of the Nuclear Regulatory Commission saw fear radiated on the faces of the residents. (The word "radiated" is obviously ill-advised; use a neutral term.)

Revision The members of the Nuclear Regulatory Commission saw fear reflected on the faces of the residents.

Inappropriate The game warden is shooting for an increase in the number of nonresident licenses this year.

Revision The game warden hopes to increase the number of nonresident licenses this year.

Sentences with Well-Placed Modifiers

A *modifier* is a word, phrase, or clause that describes, limits, or qualifies the meaning of another word or word group. A modifier can consist of one word (a *green* car), a prepositional phrase (the man *in the telephone booth*), a relative clause (the woman *who won the marathon*), or an *-ing* or *-ed* phrase (*walking three miles a day,* the student was in good shape; *seated in the first row,* we saw everything on stage). You will learn more about modifiers and readability on page 86.

A *dangling modifier* is one that cannot logically modify any word in the sentence.

   − When answering the question, his notebook fell off the table.

One way to correct the error is to insert the right subject after the *-ing* phrase.

   + When answering the question, he knocked his notebook off the table.

You can also turn the phrase into a subordinate clause.

   + When he answered the question, his notebook fell off the table.
   + His notebook fell off the table as he answered the question.

A *misplaced modifier* illogically modifies the wrong word or words in the sentence. The result is often comical.

   − Hiding in the corner, growling and snarling, our guide spotted the frightened cub. (Is our guide growling and snarling in the corner?)
   − All travel requests must be submitted by employees in green ink. (Are the employees covered in green ink?)

The problem with both of the examples above is word order. The modifiers are misplaced because they are attached to the wrong words in the sentence. Correct the error by moving the modifier where it belongs.

+ Hiding in the corner, growling and snarling, the frightened cub was spotted by our guide.
+ All travel requests by employees must be submitted in green ink.

Misplaced modifiers may also be corrected by recasting the sentence.

+ While the frightened cub was hiding in the corner, growling and snarling, our guide spotted it.
+ Our guide spotted the growling and snarling, frightened cub, which was hiding in the corner.

Note that each "correct" version has a slightly different emphasis; the choice depends on the aspect of the situation you wish to stress.

Misplacing a relative clause (introduced by such relative pronouns as *who, whom, that, which*) can also lead to problems with modification.

− Our firm decided not to move to the office in Salem that needs remodeling. (It is the office, not the town, that needs remodeling.)
+ Our firm decided not to move to the office that needs remodeling in Salem.

− The salesperson recorded the merchandise for the customer that the store had discounted. (The merchandise was discounted, not the customer.)
+ The salesperson recorded the merchandise that the store had discounted for the customer.

To avoid problem sentences like those above, always place the relative clause immediately after the word it modifies.

Correct Use of Pronoun References in Sentences

Sentences will be vague if they contain a faulty use of pronouns. When you use a pronoun whose *antecedent* (the person, place, or object the pronoun refers to) is unclear, you risk confusing your reader. At the revision stage, double-check pronouns to make sure they clearly refer to the correct antecedent. Here are some examples of unclear pronoun references, with revisions following.

Unclear After the plants are clean, we separate the stems from the roots and place them in the sun to dry. (Is it the stems or the roots that lie in the sun?)

Revision After the plants are clean, we separate the stems from the roots and place the stems in the sun to dry.

Unclear The park ranger was pleased to see the workers planting new trees and installing new benches. This will attract more tourists. (The trees or the benches?)

Revision The park ranger was pleased to see the workers planting new trees and installing new benches, for the new trees will attract more tourists.

Unclear When Bill talked with his boss, he became angry. (Who became angry, Bill or his boss?)

Revision When he talked with his boss, Bill became angry.

You can correct faulty pronoun references by replacing the unclear pronoun with the noun it stands for as in the last example where the vague *he* in the independent clause is replaced by the clear and specific *Bill.* The reader will then know exactly which word is the subject or object of the sentence. Another way to correct misleading pronouns is to rewrite the sentence.

◆ SEVEN GUIDELINES FOR WRITING READABLE SENTENCES

Use of correct grammar and punctuation alone cannot guarantee that your sentences will be easy to read and understand. Wordy, unclear sentences in the passive voice will only frustrate your reader. No one wants to waste time rereading an unclear sentence. Furthermore, your reader will suspect that you cut corners in the writing process. Perhaps you skipped the revising or proofreading stage. Maybe you did not put your work aside for a while so you could come back to it with "fresh eyes" or have someone else look it over. Remember that writing readable sentences takes time, especially at the beginning of the revision process.

This section will give you seven specific guidelines to follow during revision to help you write easy-to-read—lean and clean—sentences. As you study these guidelines, keep in mind that readability depends on:

- the length of your sentences.
- the order in which you list information in your sentences.
- the way in which you signal the relationship among your sentences.

1. Write sentences that tell who does what to whom or what. The clearest sentence pattern in English is the subject-verb-object (*s-v-o*) pattern.

> s   v   o
> Sue mowed the grass.

> s   v   o
> Today's newspaper contains a special supplement on our school.

This pattern tells who does what to whom. Readers find this pattern easiest to read and understand because it provides direct and specific information about the action. Hard-to-read sentences obscure or scramble information about the subject, the verb, or the object. Poor writers, for example, bury the subject in prepositional phrases in the middle or the end of the sentence, smother the verb in phrases, or allow an object to act like a subject.

Not all clear sentences, however, follow the subject-verb-object pattern. You might use a subordinate clause in addition to the subject, verb, and object in the independent clause. Regardless of your sentence pattern, make sure that your sentences give readers clear information about who performs what action to whom.

To write sentences that tell readers clearly what's going on, follow these steps. First, identify the subject: the person, place, or concept that controls the main action. (Avoid using vague words such as *factors, conditions, processes,* or *elements* for subjects; these words will lead to ambiguity.) Next, select an action-packed verb that shows what the subject does. Then specify the object that is acted upon by the real subject through the verb.

In the following unclear sentences, subjects are hidden in the middle of their sentences. Revised, these sentences clearly tell what has happened.

Unclear The preparation of the patient for surgery was done correctly by the nurse. (Who did what to whom?)
Revision The nurse correctly prepared the patient for surgery.

Unclear An assessment of the market helped our company design its new food blender. (The main action is designing. Who did it?)
Revision Our company designed its new food blender by assessing the market.

Unclear The fact that delivery schedules were changed hurt our business. (Who is the subject—*the fact that? delivery schedules?* What actually hurt business?)
Revision Changes in delivery schedules hurt our business.

Unclear The control of the ceiling limits of glycidyl ethers on the part of the employers for the optimum safety of workers in the workplace is necessary. (Who is responsible for taking action? What action did they take? For whom was that action taken?)
Revision For the safety of workers, employers must control the ceiling limits of glycidyl ethers.

Start your sentence with its real subject. Don't delay the subject by putting unimportant or unnecessary words ahead of it. You give readers a false and slow start by beginning with a dummy subject such as *there is/there are, it appears that, it seems that.* These impersonal constructions push the real subject back and make it harder to read the sentence. The result is a wordy and less emphatic sentence, as the following examples show.

Dummy subject There is only one option that is feasible.
Real subject Only one option is feasible.

Dummy subject There were many times during the trial when the defense attorney asked for a recess.
Real subject The defense attorney asked for a recess many times during the trial.

Dummy subject It is essential to realize that each quarter the manager needs accurate figures to prepare the budget.
Real subject The manager needs accurate figures each quarter to prepare the budget.

2. Arrange information logically within your sentences. The order in which you list information within a sentence can help or hinder a reader in understanding your message. You cannot list details in just any order. Draft different versions of your sentences to make sure readers receive information in the most logical, helpful way. The pattern you use will, of course, depend on your topic. The content of the sentence will help you to choose the more logical pattern: chronological, cause to effect, action to reaction, and the like.

Poor They shut off the computer once they finish with their program.
More logical Once they finish their program, they shut off the computer. (Since finishing the program precedes shutting the computer off, give readers the information in this order.)

Poor My strengths are in neurological and geriatric nursing to give you some background about my work experiences.

More logical To give you some background about my work experiences, my strengths are in neurological and geriatric nursing. (Tell readers why you are giving them the details first, so that they know what the details mean.)

3. Avoid needlessly complex or lengthy sentences. How long should your sentence be? The answers to this question vary, depending on the educational level of your audience and the subject you are writing about. You can be guided by one safe rule, however: write so that it is easy for your reader to understand you. Generally, the longer the sentence, the more difficult it is to understand; therefore, do not pile one clause on another. Instead, break one overly long sentence into two or even three more manageable ones.

Most readers have very little trouble with sentences ranging from 8 to 15 words. On the other hand, readers find sentences over 20 to 23 words much more difficult. As a general rule, keep your sentences under 18 words in order to reach most readers. The first sentence below is too long for readers to understand, even the second time through. The revision is much easier to read.

Too long The planning committee decided that the awards banquet should be held on May 15 at 6:30, since the other two dates (May 7 and May 22) suggested by the hospitality committee conflict with local sports events, even though one of those events could be changed to fit our needs.

Easier to read The planning committee has decided to hold the awards banquet on May 15 at 6:30. The other dates suggested by the hospitality committee—May 7 and May 22—conflict with two local sports events. Although the date of one of those sports events could be changed, the planning committee still believes that May 15 is our best choice.

4. Combine a series of short, choppy sentences. Avoiding long, complex sentences only to write short, simplistic ones will not make your reader's job easier. In fact, a memo, letter, or report written exclusively in short, staccato sentences sounds immature and makes for boring reading. To avoid this error, vary your sentences both in length and structure. The most effective on-the-job writing blends short sentences with longer ones to achieve variety and to reflect different logical relationships. For example, a sentence containing a subordinate clause followed by an independent clause may signal a cause-to-effect relationship to readers. A sentence with a series of parallel independent clauses points to the equality of the ideas spelled out in these clauses. A short sentence at the end of a paragraph can emphatically summarize a main idea. Don't be afraid to trim your sentences as you revise or to split one long sentence into two shorter ones. But when you find yourself writing a series of short, choppy sentences, such as in the following example, combine them where possible and use connective words similar to those italicized in the revision.

Choppy Secretaries have many responsibilities. Their responsibilities are important. They must answer telephones. They must take dictation. Sometimes the speaker talks very fast. Then the secretary must be quick to transcribe

what is heard. Words could be missed. Secretaries must also prepare letters. This will take a great deal of time and concentration. These letters
are copied and stored properly for reference.

Smoother Secretaries have many important responsibilities. *These* include answering
the telephones and taking dictation. *When* a speaker talks rapidly, the secretary will have to transcribe quickly *so* that no words are omitted.
Among the most demanding of their duties are preparing letters accurately *and then* making copies of them and storing those copies properly
for future reference.

**5. Use active verbs rather than verb phrases with verbs disguised as
nouns.** In trying to sound important, many writers avoid using simple, graphic
verbs (see page 102). Instead, these bureaucratic writers add a suffix (*-ation,
-ance, -ment, -ence*) to a direct verb (*determine*) to make a noun (*determination*) and then couple the new noun with *make, provide,* or *work* to produce a
weak verb phrase (for example, *make a determination of, provide maintenance
of, work in cooperation with*). Such a verb phrase imprisons the active verb inside a noun. The following sentences with weak verb phrases are rewritten to
make them more readable and emphatic.

Weak The officer made an assessment of the damages the storm had caused.
Strong The officer assessed the damage the storm had caused.

Weak The investigators made an entrance into the wilderness site at dusk.
Strong The investigators entered the wilderness site at dusk.

Weak The city provided the employment of two work crews to assist the strengthening of the dam.
Strong The city employed two work crews to strengthen the dam.

6. Avoid piling up modifiers in front of a noun. It's hard for readers to
grasp your message when you string a series of modifiers in front of a noun.
Modifiers are subordinate units that should clarify and qualify the noun to which
they refer. When you put too many of them in the reader's path to the noun, you
confuse the reader who does not know how one modifier relates to another
modifier or to the noun. To avoid this problem, rephrase the sentence by placing
some of the modifiers in prepositional phrases after or before the nouns they
modify.

Crowded The ordinance contract number vehicle identification plate had to be
checked against inventory numbers.
Spaced The ordinance contract number on the vehicle identification plate had to
be checked against the inventory numbers.

Crowded The vibration noise control heat pump condenser quieter can make your
customer happier.
Spaced The quieter on the condenser for the heat pump will make your customer
happier by controlling noise and vibrations.

7. Avoid unnecessary *that/which* clauses. Wordiness can be the writer's
greatest weakness and reader's most common complaint. (Chapter 5 will help
you find the words and phrases you need for a more concise, direct style.) *That/
which* clauses using some form of the verb *to be* (*is, are, were, was*) are infamous

for adding words but not meaning. They are popular with bureaucratic writers, who like to draw out an idea beyond the number of words needed. The information contained in *that/which* clauses can often be adequately represented by an adjective, as the following wordy sentences and their revisions show.

Wordy The pain medication that was prescribed by the doctor was very helpful to her father.

Concise The pain medication prescribed by the doctor helped her father. (Note how the revision reduces "was helpful to" to "helped" to further save words and time.)

Wordy I think the news magazine, which appears bi-monthly, will be one which keeps employees up to date on current events at Balko Industries.

Concise I think the bi-monthly magazine will keep employees informed about current events at Balko Industries.

Wordy The organizational plan that was approved last week contains a number of points which are considered to be especially important for new employees.

Concise The organizational plan approved last week contains important points for new employees.

◆ WRITING EFFECTIVE SENTENCES: A BRIEF SUMMARY

To write clear, readable sentences, remember the reader's needs. A reader wants to be able to get through a sentence and understand its message on the first attempt. To help readers do this, make sure that you follow the strategies in this chapter for revising your sentences for correctness, clarity, and conciseness. Specifically, make sure that you punctuate sentences correctly, select verbs in the appropriate (usually active) voice, identify all pronoun references accurately, and follow the seven guidelines found on pages 83–87.

◆ EXERCISES

1. Punctuate the following sentences correctly.
   a. Cooking can kill many bacteria in food, it cannot kill them all.
   b. Bass fishing attracts many tourists to the lake. Not just during the summer but also during the fall.
   c. No new accounts will be opened today, therefore the credit office is closed.
   d. The charges for our service are reasonable, they come to barely $35.
   e. Ms. Jones-Fairley likes our contract, she will sign it and mail it tomorrow.
   f. The Land Rover is popular with sports enthusiasts partly because it is economical. And partly because it is so rugged.
   g. The patient received an injection for pain, however, he said that it did not help.
   h. Because real estate values soared; many buyers were unable to own their own homes. Which angered them.

    i. The college is offering five sections of Business English this term, many of them are in the late afternoon and night.

    j. The sales manager had to prepare her report by that afternoon. Because the buyer wanted to review it before the conference tomorrow.

    k. Buses leave for Dayton punctually. On the hour and on the half.

2. The following sentences contain an awkward use of the passive voice. Rewrite them using the active voice to make them less awkward and easier to read.

    a. Little attention has been paid by your office to our request for additional information.

    b. The enclosed forms should be completed by you no later than August 15.

    c. The dinner was planned by her staff to celebrate her thirtieth birthday.

    d. A comet was seen by those citizens who stayed up late last evening.

    e. Discretion should be exercised by employees when answering complaint letters.

    f. Faster ways of notifying customers have been found by one of our employees.

    g. Appropriate uniforms are to be worn by all police officers attending the ceremony.

    h. The blocking of the canal had been planned by the Corps of Engineers for two years.

    i. It was determined by management not to approve a new employees' health center.

3. The following sentences contain errors in parallelism. Correct these sentences to make the grammatical units in them parallel.

    a. Willard likes swimming, hiking, and to fish.

    b. Silver is used in aerial photography, microfilming, for medical and industrial x-rays, and printers use it, too, to make photographic plates.

    c. Please return overshipments promptly and also I want you to reimburse any amounts paid over charges.

    d. You either must repair the circuit or it has to be replaced.

    e. Use a visual to emphasize key points, as a way of arousing interest, and when you want to summarize a lot of statistical data.

    f. The agency did not know who was responsible, where the individual lived, or the time the individual would return.

    g. In the saddle stitch method, printed material is bound using metal staples or cloth stitches are inserted.

    h. Once a conference is on our schedule, the personnel director is responsible for sending out announcements, the seating arrangements, what type of menu to serve, and also has to provide information on housing.

    i. We received questions from customers on how long it takes to complete the process, the cost required for additional safety features used in the process, and whether marketing advantages associated with the process were present.

    j. The shipment neither was on time nor could it have been accurate.

    k. The local television station either had to change its programming or it would be in trouble with the FCC.

4. The following sentences are contradictory or contain words that are inappropriate for the context. Rewrite these sentences to correct the errors.
    a. In metric terms, our new olympic swimming pool is twenty-five feet long.
    b. His report discusses the differences in jogging between the United States and Great Britain.
    c. The operator fed the load onto the truck using a hydraulic fork.
    d. Sampling all of the residents of Cherry Hill, we found that 25 percent wanted the zoning laws to remain the same, 40 percent wanted them modified to include multiple family housing, and the other 45 percent wanted changes in housing and transportation.
    e. The watch commander was happy to report that convictions exceeded arrests.
    f. The local committee threw its spirited support behind the opposition to the new liquor laws.
    g. The nonsoluble retaining wall will let in only a small amount of water.
    h. New drilling techniques make it possible to create oil faster.
    i. The applicant did not plan ahead and was, therefore, ready for the interviewer's questions.
    j. Health food stores take a great interest in nuts.

5. Rewrite the following sentences to correct dangling and misplaced modifiers.
    a. When preparing school papers, your dictionary will be a great aid.
    b. Using the Heimlich maneuver, a piece of food will be forced out of a person's airway.
    c. We purchased a new model from the salesclerk with adjustable arms.
    d. Topped with a tasty hollandaise sauce, the waiter brought us a delicious salad.
    e. Allowing for a 3 percent margin for error, the specifications arrived on the builder's desk this morning.
    f. Before turning the patient, intravenous solutions are given.
    g. The bank almost closed before we got there.
    h. Fastened securely, the officer left the compound.
    i. The teacher gave the test to the new student that covered the first third of the textbook.
    j. The plumber repaired the sink in our office that was stopped up since last week.
    k. The show dog ran away from the trainer with a leash around his neck.
    l. All travel requests must be submitted by employees in triplicate.
    m. The meal is prepared by the chef delicately seasoned with oregano.
    n. Almost maintenance-free, the housekeeper liked the new electric broom.
    o. Before placing the specimen under the microscope, proper care has to be taken.
    p. About the size of a quarter, most Americans did not like the Susan B. Anthony dollar.

q. My neighbor went to see the dentist with a huge cavity.

r. Turning the machine counterclockwise, the springs were loosened.

s. The tax collector sent a bill to every property owner in Madison County that was due by April 1.

6. Rewrite the following sentences to correct faulty pronoun references.

   a. The head nurse ordered the aide and the technician to help the patient in Room 334. She came at once.

   b. The boss sent four different memos to the maintenance department about the problems with refuse on the weekends. They really made an impact on the department.

   c. When Barbara saw Mary, she shouted with joy.

   d. The filter was placed over the vent, but it was too small.

   e. The machine had to be primed and oiled regularly, which ensured a quick start.

   f. An all-purpose battery would be better in this car than an expensive one.

   g. The white mice were placed in the new cages, and they were to be cleaned daily.

   h. Mr. Martin told Mr. Rodriguez that he had found his glasses.

   i. A check-up is important for good health. That is something you want to have.

   j. Fourteen recruits joined the force in the months of July, August, and September. They will not be forgotten.

7. Rewrite the following sentences to make them easier to read. They contain one or more of the errors discussed on pages 83–87 of this chapter.

   a. There are a number of businesses that have succumbed to failure recently due to the fact of their being mismanaged.

   b. The work activities classification internal quarterly notification report is due at the end of this week.

   c. Long open conveyor belts, which are used for the transportation of coal particles, can be considered to be a significant source of pollution.

   d. It is, therefore, expensive to secure the importation of food from abroad because so much of it is shipped by costly carriers.

   e. It seems apparent that there are a number of inconsistencies between the reports from Baxterville and New Platz.

   f. The continuation of the fluoridation of the city water supply is advocated strenuously by the residents of West Allentown.

   g. Evasive action roadblock techniques diminish the promotion of terrorist activities.

   h. Flowing from hot to cold substances, heat is a form of energy.

   i. The power is supplied by a six-cylinder, in-line, liquid-cooled, standard-regulation, gasoline-powered engine located in the front of the truck.

   j. To rotate the auger at a slower speed with more power, place the transmission in first gear.

   k. Relative to emissions from the iron and steel processes, inspection techniques have certain fundamental characteristics regarding costs which are the same for every technique so used.

l. The recent purchase of a Multi-Writer can lead to the improvement of routine office data-processing functions, which will save the company many hours of time and dollars in costs, provided that effective training programs accompany the acquisition of the Multi-Writer and that it does not become dated and that it is compatible with our existing data-processing equipment, which resulted in a large expenditure for the firm last year.

m. If it has the appearance of being spoiled or gives an emission of an odor, the destruction of the food shipment is imperative.

n. There are a number of precautions that it is believed by the Department of Public Safety must be put into effect within the next year.

Writing: Words

The decisions writers make about word choice are usually secondary to the larger concerns of overall organization, development, and arrangement of ideas into coherent paragraphs. But then, having also established the scope, technical level, and audience for their piece, writers can better understand the specific context in which their words will be read. Writers may make several passes through their work as they revise to see if their words are accurate and appropriate for the reader. In the process, they will add, delete, and substitute words as they check spelling, usage, clarity, and conciseness.

Remember, however, that the writing process does not refer to a series of steps that must follow in sequence. Writers can—and usually do—leap back and forth from one element of the process to another. Thus the ideal word or phrase may occur to the writer at any point from first draft to final copy. Chapter 5 discusses some of the most common problems writers face in selecting their words and offers practical suggestions on how and why to make these choices. Specifically, after reading this chapter and applying its principles to your writing, you will learn to:

- check the spelling of words carefully.
- match the right word with the right meaning.
- select precise words.
- cut unnecessary words.
- eliminate sexist language.
- avoid jargon and slang.

◆ SPELLING WORDS CORRECTLY

Your written work will be judged in part on how well you spell. A misspelled word may seem like a small matter, but on an employment application, incident report, or letter, it stands out to your discredit. Readers will inevitably wonder about other skills if your spelling is incorrect.

Your professional work places a double duty on you as a speller. You must learn to spell correctly the technical terms of your field as well as the common words of the English language. The following suggestions can help to improve your spelling.

1. Keep a college-level dictionary at your desk (not on a shelf where you have to reach for it) and use it. Better yet, buy a small pocket dictionary and carry it with you.
2. Also keep on your desk a specialized dictionary or manual that lists the technical vocabulary you use on your job.
3. Make a list of the words you have most trouble spelling as well as any new and difficult words you encounter. Write them down in a small spiral notebook for easy reference.
4. Double-check your spelling before submitting your work.

If you prepare your work on a word processor, you may have the option of using a spell-checking program. Spell checkers are very handy for flagging potential problem words. But beware! Spell checkers only recognize words that have been listed in them. A proper name or infrequently used word may be flagged as an error even though the word is spelled correctly. You should compile a list of technical words you use regularly and words that you find particularly difficult and add them to the spell-check program. Even then the spell checker cannot tell you if a word is the right one for the context. For example, it will not differentiate between *too* and *two* or *there* and *their.* In short, do not rely exclusively on spell checkers. It is your responsibility to make sure your words are spelled correctly. You must be the final judge.

The following suggestions can help you become a better speller. The chances are that many of the words that cause you difficulty are the same ones that give others trouble. Attention to these danger areas will pay dividends.

1. **Silent letters.**

a*c*quaint	fas*c*inate	lei*s*ure
ai*s*le	for*e*arm	man*e*uver
as*c*end	gau*g*e	min*i*ature
*c*holesterol	hemor*rh*age	mor*t*gage
cod*ei*ne	hyg*ie*ne	n*e*utral
colum*n*	*k*napsack	vacu*u*m
diaphra*g*m	li*k*ely	We*d*nesday

2. **Use of *ei* and *ie*. In general, *i* before *e*, except after *c*.**

ie	*ei*	*exceptions*
believe	ceiling	ancient
cashier	weight	conscience
chief	deceive	deficient
experience	perceive	financier
yield	receive	society

3. **Double consonants.** Many words double a consonant when a verb

changes from present to past tense (*prefer* / *preferred*) or when the root form changes from verb to noun (*occur* / *occurrence*).

admit / admitted / admittance
commit / committed / *but* commitment
omit / omitted
plan / planning
repel / repelling / repellent
write / written / *but* writing
profit / *but* profited

4. **Prefixes and suffixes.** When adding a prefix (*il-*, *mis-*, *un-*), do not change the spelling of the word to which it is attached.

*il*logical
*mis*spell
*un*necessary

Watch out for the following suffixes.

-able	-iable	-ible
acceptable	appreciable	audible
dependable	justifiable	combustible
noticeable	negotiable	edible
profitable	reliable	eligible
serviceable	variable	visible

5. **Plurals.**

- When a word ends in *y*, drop the *y* and add *-ies* if the *y* follows a consonant: *apology* / *apologies; army* / *armies; history* / *histories; library* / *libraries; party* / *parties.* If the word ends in *y* and the *y* follows a vowel, just add *s*: *bay* / *bays; toy* / *toys; turkey* / *turkeys.*

- Words that end in *f* or *fe* usually change these letters to *v* before adding *-es*: *calf* / *calves; half* / *halves; knife* / *knives; life* / *lives; leaf* / *leaves; self* / *selves; shelf* / *shelves; wife* / *wives.*

- Nouns ending in *o* after a vowel form their plurals by adding *s*: *patio* / *patios; stereo* / *stereos; studio* / *studios; zoo* / *zoos.* When the *o* follows a consonant, add *-es* to form the plural: *echo* / *echoes; hero* / *heroes; potato* / *potatoes; tomato* / *tomatoes.* Exception: *lasso* / *lassos; piano* / *pianos; tobacco* / *tobaccos.*

- Some nouns do not form their plural by adding *-s* or *-es.* Instead, they use an older kind of plural (*ox* / *oxen; child* / *children*), or they indicate a change in number in the middle of a word rather than at the end (*foot* / *feet; man* / *men*), or they use a foreign plural (*criterion* / *criteria; curriculum* / *curricula; phenomenon* / *phenomena; syllabus* / *syllabi*). Some nouns for animals are the same for both singular and plural: *fish, deer, sheep, snipe.* Finally, some words are "false" plurals; they end in *s*, leading you to think that they are plural. These nouns, however, are always singular in meaning and are never spelled without the final *s*: *economics, measles, pediatrics, scissors.*

6. Apostrophes.

- To form a contraction, the apostrophe takes the place of the missing letter or letters: *I've = I have; doesn't = does not; he's = he is; it's = it is. Its* is a possessive pronoun (the dog and its bone), not a contraction. There is no such form as *its'.*
- To form a possessive, follow these rules.

  (a) If a singular or plural noun does not end in an **-s**, add **'s** to show possession.

Mary's locker	the woman's jacket
the truck's battery	the women's jackets
San Francisco's streets	anybody's time
children's books	the company's policy

  (b) If a plural noun ends in **-s**, add just the **'** to indicate possession.

employees' benefits	computers' speed
lawyers' fees	police officers' training
horses' auction	the boss's schedule (singular noun)

  (c) If a proper name ends in **-s**, use **'s** to form the possessive.

Jones's account	Keats's poetry
the Williams's house	James's word

  (d) If it is a compound noun, add an **'** or an **'s** to the end of the word.

brother-in-law's business	Ms. Allison Jones-Wyatt's order

  (e) If you wish to indicate shared possession, add just **'s** to the last name.

Warner and Kline's Computer Shop	Sue and Anne's major

  If you want to indicate separate possession, add an **'s** to each name.

John's and Mary's transcripts	Shakespeare's and Byron's poetry

- To form the plural of numbers and capital letters used as nouns, including abbreviations without periods, just add **s**.

during the 1980s	all perfect 10s
his SATs	several local YMCAs

For abbreviations with periods, however, and for lower-case letters used as nouns, form the plural by adding **'s**.

p's and *q*'s	Ph.D.'s

◆ MATCHING THE RIGHT WORD WITH THE RIGHT MEANING

The English language contains many common words that are frequently mistaken for each other because they are pronounced alike but spelled differently. These words are called homonyms. *Meat* (food) and *meet* (to greet) are examples. When a dispatcher orders employees to keep overtime to a "bear minimum," no reference to a grizzly is intended; rather, *bear* has been confused with *bare*. Similarly, the mechanic who writes on a work order to "idol" down a car has confused *idol* (religious image) with *idle* (a verb meaning to slow down). Remember, your word processor's spell checker can never tell you if you have confused *bear* for *bare* or *idol* for *idle*.

The words in the following list frequently are mistaken for one another. Some are true homonyms; others are just similar in spelling, pronunciation, or usage. By studying the correct spelling, part of speech, and meaning of each, you will save yourself time and embarrassment.

accept (v) to receive, to acknowledge: *We accept your proposal.*
except (prep) excluding, but: *Everyone attended the meeting except David.*

access (n) the right to use: *We don't have access to all of their files.*
excess (adj) superfluous: *Please remove all excess materials from this file.*

adapt (v) to adjust to: *We will have to adapt to the new phone system.*
adept (adv) skillful: *Cheryl is very adept at word processing.*
adopt (v) to follow by choice: *Let's adopt a new technique.*

advice (n) a recommendation: *I should have taken Leroy's advice.*
advise (v) to counsel: *Our lawyers advised us not to sign the contract.*

affect (v) to change, to influence: *Has the detour on Route 22 affected your travel plans?*
effect (n) a result: *What was the effect of the new procedure?*
effect (v) to bring about: *We will try to effect a change in company policy.*

attain (v) to achieve, to reach: *My sister soon attained the position of partner at the law firm.*
obtain (v) to get, to receive: *You must obtain an accident report form from the personnel office.*

beside (prep) next to: *I keep a dictionary beside my word processor.*
besides (prep) in addition to: *Besides Juan and Suzanne, who will attend the seminar?*

brake (v) to stop: *I always wear my seat belt in case I need to brake suddenly.*
brake (n) a mechanism to stop a vehicle: *She hit the brakes just in time.*
break (v) to split, to crack: *He always breaks pencils when he's angry.*

break (n) a split, a separation: *Let's take a short break before Hal's presentation.*

capital (adj) major, chief: *I think that is a capital idea.*
capital (adj) upper-case: *Always begin names of cities and states with a capital letter.*
capital (n) wealth in money or property: *We can't start a new business without some capital.*
capital (n) the governing city of a state or country: *Concord is the capital of New Hampshire.*
capitol (n) the building where a state legislature meets: *My cousin is a secretary at the capitol.* (Note: *Capitol* is always capitalized when it refers to the Capitol building in Washington, D.C.)

cent (n) one penny: *My old car isn't worth a cent.*
scent (n) smell: *I detected the scent of ammonia coming from the supply room.*
sent (v) transmitted (past tense of *send*): *I sent the blueprints by overnight express.*

cite (v) to document: *Please cite several examples to support your claim.*
site (n) place, location: *They want to build a parking lot on the site of the old theatre.*
sight (n) vision: *I will never forget the sight of our general manager changing her flat tire on the highway.*

coarse (adj) rough: *This paper is too coarse to use for our new brochure.*
course (n) class: *She should take a course in computer programming.*
course (n) plan of action: *We must decide immediately what course to take.* (Also, *of course,* meaning certainly: *Of course, I'll take you to the airport.*)

complement (v) to add to, to fill out: *His graphs and charts complemented my proposal.*
compliment (v) to praise: *The customer complimented us on our courteous staff.*

continually (adv) frequently and regularly: *This answering machine continually disconnects the caller in the middle of the message.*
continuously (adv) constantly: *The air conditioning is on continuously during the summer.*

discreet (adj) showing respect, being tactful: *The manager was discreet in answering the complaint letter.*
discrete (adj) separate, distinct: *Put those figures into discrete categories for processing.*

dual (adj) double: *A clock-radio serves a dual purpose.*
duel (n) a fight, a battle: *The argument almost turned into a real duel.*

eminent (adj) prominent, highly esteemed: *Dr. Rollins is the most eminent pediatrician in our community.*

imminent (adj) about to happen: *A hostile takeover of that company is imminent.*

fair (adj) just, legal: *It would be fair to give our employees extra sick leave benefits.*
fare (n) price of travel: *We should try to make early reservations so we can get a discount fare.*

hear (v) to listen: *The members in the back of the auditorium couldn't hear the speaker.*
here (adv) in this place: *Let's post the bulletin here so everyone can see it.*

imply (v) to suggest: *Mr. Chin implied that I had taken too long for my lunch break.*
infer (v) to draw a conclusion: *We can infer from these sales figures that the new advertising campaign is working.*

it's (noun + verb) contraction of *it* and *is*: *Do you think it's too early to tell?*
its (adj) possessive form of *it: That old typewriter is on its last legs.*

lay/laid/laid (v) to put down: *Lay aside that project for now. He laid aside the project. He had already laid aside the project twice before.*
lie/lay/lain (v) to recline: *I think I'll lie down for a while. He lay there for only ten minutes before the firefighter rescued him. She has lain out in the sun too often.*

lose (v) to misplace, to fail to win: *Be careful not to lose my calculator. I hope I don't lose my seat on the planning board.*
loose (adj) not tight: *The printer ribbon was too loose.*

maybe (adv) perhaps: *Maybe we can sell them our top-of-the-line model.*
may be (v) two-word verbal phrase, *may + be: I may be home late tonight if the meeting runs over.*

pair (n) two, a couple: *We could use a pair of new copy machines.*
pare (v) to cut down: *Try to pare down that list so it will fit on one page.*
pear (n) a fruit: *Chris has a pear for dessert every day.*

passed (v) went by (past tense of *pass*): *He passed me in the hall without recognizing me.*
past (n) time gone by: *We've never used their services in the past.*

peace (n) calm: *There was peace in the office while the phones were dead.*
piece (n) a portion: *They just ordered a new piece of equipment to make the job go more smoothly.*

personal (adj) private: *She closes her door only if she's making a personal phone call.*
personnel (n) staff of employees: *All personnel must take part in tomorrow's fire drill.*

perspective (n) view: *From the customer's perspective, we are a fair and courteous company.*

prospective (adj) expected, likely to happen or become: *Send the new brochure to all prospective customers.*

plain (adj) simple: *The plain truth is that they just don't want to spend the money on repairs.*

plains (n) a flat, open area of land: *Miguel grew up on the plains of Texas.*

plane (n) short for *airplane*: *He took an early plane to Phoenix.*

plane (n) a device used to make a surface smooth and level: *I'll borrow their plane so we can finish sanding this door.*

precede (v) to go before: *A slide show will precede the open discussion.*

proceed (v) to carry on, to go ahead: *Proceed as if we had never received that letter.*

principal (adj) main, chief: *Sales of washers and dryers constitute their principal source of revenue.*

principal (n) the head of a school: *She was a high school principal before she entered the business world.*

principle (n) a policy, a belief: *Salesclerks should operate on the principle that the customer is always right.*

respectfully (adv) with esteem: *One should always treat managers respectfully.*

respectively (adv) in the order mentioned: *Paragraphs and sentences are discussed in Chapters 3 and 4, respectively.*

right (adj) correct: *You're on the right track.*

right (adj) the opposite of left: *His right hand started to ache from so much writing.*

rite (n) a ceremony or ritual: *The rite of marriage is a sacred one.*

write (v) to form letters: *Tony had to write up a report summarizing his findings.*

stationary (adj) not moving: *Kim rides a stationary bicycle for an hour every morning.*

stationery (n) writing supplies, such as paper and envelopes: *Please stop off at the stationery store and buy some more address labels.*

than (conj) as opposed to (used in comparisons): *He is a faster typist than his predecessor.*

then (adv) at that time: *First she called the client, then she summarized their conversation in a letter.*

their (adj) possessive form of *they*: *All of the lab technicians took their vacations during January.*

there (adv) in that place: *Please put the file cabinet in there.*

they're (noun + verb) contraction of *they* and *are*: *They're our two best customer service representatives.*

two (n) a number: *I sent her two copies of the proposal.*
to (prep) toward: *Akiko was already on her way to the bank when we discovered the error.*
too (adv) also: *You can come along too.*

wear (v) to dress: *All employees must wear the same uniform.*
where (adv) at what place: *Where did I leave my coffee cup?*

weather (n) climate: *The fall weather is beautiful in Boston.*
whether (conj) if: *I don't know whether she plans to attend.*

weak (adj) not strong: *My opening argument was too weak.*
week (n) seven days: *Marco was out sick all week.*

who's (noun + verb) contraction of *who* and *is*: *Who's up next for a promotion?*
whose (adj) possessive form of *who*: *Whose idea was that in the first place?*

you're (noun + verb) contraction of *you* and *are*: *You're going to like their decision.*
your (adj) possessive form of *you*: *They agree with your ideas.*

◆ SELECTING PRECISE WORDS

Clear writing can save an employer time and money, and it can save you the frustration of additional explanations over the phone or in rewriting your work. Precise writing gets the job done right the first time. You can be precise, though, only if your words are. After all, your words take the place of the references they describe. Your words should answer the questions readers ask themselves as they read.

- ◆ How big?
- ◆ How expensive?
- ◆ How much?
- ◆ What color?
- ◆ How many?
- ◆ Who?
- ◆ Where?
- ◆ When?

To write precisely, use concrete, specific words rather than vague, general ones. Choose words that appeal to the reader's five senses—words that help a reader to see, hear, smell, taste, and touch. For example, "piece of office equipment" is vague. "An IBM microcomputer with a 14-inch green phosphor screen" is precise.

Words such as *aspect, condition, creature, factor, nice, thing,* and *ways* raise more questions than they answer. Is a "nice" house made of brick or covered with aluminum siding? Does it have gas or electric heat? Will you find it in the city, suburbs, or the country? Here is another example of the advantage of using exact words:

General With adequate storage fish keeps for some time.
Specific If refrigerated at 32°F (0°C) and covered with crushed ice, fresh fish may be stored up to three days.

Unlike the first sentence, the second sentence provides helpful, practical information.

There is a wide range between "general" and "specific." In Table 5.1 note that the general terms in the far left column gradually become more precise as you proceed to the right.

How can you be sure that your words are precise, that they are specific and not vague? Follow these three simple procedures as you revise your work for the reader.

1. Circle all your nouns. Do they point to a specific person, place, or object? Could your reader separate that person, place, or object from all others like it? If so, you have a specific word. If readers or listeners cannot quickly identify an object, person, or place from your description, you have used a general word.

2. Underline all your adjectives. Do they tell readers the exact color, size, texture, quantity, or quality you want to convey? Adjectives like *bad, fantastic, nice, good, great, interesting, numerous, serious,* or *small* will not help your audience see vividly or measure accurately. Next, see if you need every adjective you have underlined. A noun or verb may render some adjectives unnecessary; the adjective or adverb may be repeating what the noun or verb has already said—for example, "shout loudly" (shouts are always loud), "a big Saint Bernard" (such dogs are always big), "a small 3″ × 5″ card" (is there a large 3″ × 5″ card?).

3. Star all your verbs. Do they show lively movement or have they fallen limp on the page? Check your verbs for their activity level; they should be full of

TABLE 5.1   The Range Between General and Specific Terms.

General←			→Specific
vehicle	truck	pickup	Dodge wide cab
medication	injection	barbiturate	Seconal 100 mg.
food	protein	poultry	Chicken Kiev
residence	house	cottage	Tudor cottage
official	federal agent	USDA inspector	Mary Whitton
reasonable	inexpensive	bargain	20 percent off $500 sale price
circumstance	disaster	storm	Hurricane Frederic

information for readers about how and why something happened. Give readers something specific and concrete to watch. Vague verbs such as *appear, concern, consider, evidence, exist, relate, seem,* or any of the forms of *to be* (*is, are, was were*) lack information about specific action. These verbs are especially sluggish when combined with "there are" and "it is" constructions such as the following: "It appears that there are some troubles with the company truck." This sentence would move any employer to scream "What happened?" Note the increased action level in the revised sentence: "The company truck ran over a roofing nail, which punctured the right front tire." Choose graphic verbs such as *accelerate, complete, carry out, direct, duplicate, increase, force, juggle, mount, program, push, scatter, squeeze, support, streamline, test.* If your starred verbs vibrate with action, you help readers to grasp your meaning precisely. You will also make reading your work easier and more lively.

◆ CUTTING OUT UNNECESSARY WORDS

Too many people in business and industry think the more words, the better. Nothing could be more self-defeating. Your readers are busy; unnecessary words slow them down. Make every word go to work; when a word takes up space and gives no meaning, cut it. Cut out any words you can from your sentences; if the sentence still makes sense and reads correctly, you have eliminated wordiness.

The phrases on the left should be replaced with the precise words on the right.

Wordy	Concise
at a slow rate	slowly
at an early date	early
at the point where	where
at this point in time	now
be in agreement with	agree
bring to a conclusion	conclude, end
bring together	combine, join
by means of	with
come to terms with	agree, accept
due to the fact that	because
express an opinion that	believe
feel quite certain about	believe
for the length of time that	while
for the period of	for
for the purpose of	to
in an effort to	to
in such a manner that	so
in the area / case / field of	in
in the event that	if
in the neighborhood of	approximately
look something like	resemble
serve the function of	function as
show a tendency to	tend

take into consideration	consider
take under advisement	consider
take place in such a manner	occur
with reference to	regarding, about
with the result that	so

The following tips will help you eliminate other kinds of wordiness just as easily.

1. Replace a wordy phrase or clause with a one- or two-word synonym.

Wordy   The college has parking zones for different areas for people living on campus as well as for those who do not live on campus and who commute to school.

Revision   The college has different parking zones for resident and commuter students. (Twenty words of the original sentence—everything after "areas for"—have been reduced to four words: "resident and commuter students.")

Wordy   Many banks use a system of tubes to move small items by means of air pressure from one place to another.

Revision   Many banks use pneumatic tubes to send small items from one place to another. (Using the phrase "pneumatic tubes" will save many words and identify the system more precisely—provided, of course, that your reader knows what pneumatic tubes are.)

2. Combine sentences beginning with the same subject or ending with an object that becomes the subject of the next sentence.

Wordy   I asked the inspector if she were going to visit the plant this afternoon. I also asked her if she would come alone.

Revision   I asked the inspector if she were going to visit the plant alone this afternoon.

Wordy   Homeowners want to buy low-maintenance plants. These low-maintenance plants include the ever-popular holly and boxwood varieties. These plants are also inexpensive.

Revision   Homeowners want to buy such low-maintenance and inexpensive plants as holly and boxwood. (This revision combines three sentences into one, condenses twenty-four words into fourteen, and joins three related thoughts.)

Another kind of wordiness comes from using redundant expressions. Being redundant means that you say the same thing a second time, in different words. "Fellow colleague," "component parts," and "corrosive acid" are phrases that contain this kind of double speech; a fellow *is* a colleague, a component *is* a part, and acid *is* corrosive. Redundant expressions are uneconomical and are often clichés. The suggested revisions on the right are preferable to the redundant phrases on the left.

Redundant	Concise
absolutely essential	essential
advance reservations	reservations
basic necessities	necessities, needs
cease and desist	stop

Redundant	Concise
close proximity	proximity, nearness
each and every	each, every, all
end result	result
eradicate completely	eradicate
exposed opening	opening
fair and just	fair
final conclusions / final outcome	conclusions / outcome
first and foremost	first
full and complete	full, complete
grand total	total
null and void	void
passing fad	fad
personal opinion	opinion
prerecorded	recorded
over and done with	over
tried and true	tried, proven
unexpected surprise	surprise

Watch for repetitious words, phrases, or clauses within a sentence. Sometimes one sentence or one part of a sentence needlessly duplicates another.

> **Redundant** The post office hires part-time help, especially around the holidays, to handle the large amounts of mail at Christmas time.
>
> **Revised** The post office often hires part-time help to handle the large amounts of mail at Christmas time. ("Especially around the holidays" means the same thing as "at Christmas time.")

> **Redundant** The fermenting activity of yeast is due to an enzyme called zymase. This enzyme produces chemical changes in yeast.
>
> **Revised** The fermenting activity of yeast is due to an enzyme called zymase. (The second sentence says vaguely what the first sentence says precisely; delete it.)

> **Redundant** To provide more room for employees' cars, the security department is studying ways to expand the employees' parking lot.
>
> **Revised** The security department is studying ways to expand the employees' parking lot. (Since the first phrase says nothing that the reader does not know from the independent clause, cut it.)

Adding a prepositional phrase can sometimes contribute to redundancy. The italicized words below are redundant because of the unnecessary qualification they impose on the adverb or adjective. Delete the italicized phrases.

audible *to the ear*	hard *to the touch*
bitter *in taste*	honest *in character*
fly *through the air*	light *in weight*
orange *in color*	soft *in texture*
rectangular *in shape*	tall *in height*
second *in sequence*	twenty *in number*
short *in duration*	visible *to the eye*

Certain combinations of verbs and adverbs are also redundant. Again, the italicized words should be deleted.

advance *forward*

burn *up*

cancel *out*

circle *around*

close *off*

commute *back and forth*

combine *together*

continue *on*

drop *down*

funnel *through*

join *together*

lift *up*

merge *together*

open *up*

plan *ahead*

probed *into*

prove *conclusively*

refer *back*

repeat *again*

reply *back*

revert *back*

write *down*

◆ ELIMINATING SEXIST LANGUAGE

Sexist language unfairly assigns responsibilities, jobs, or titles to individuals on the basis of sex. Such language discriminates in favor of one sex at the expense of the other, usually women. Sexist language is often based on sexist stereotypes that show men as superior to women. For example, calling politicians "city fathers" or "favorite sons" follows the stereotypical picture of politicians as male; such phrases discriminate against women who do or could hold public office. Sexist phrases assume engineers, physicians, or pilots are male (*he, his, him*) and social workers, nurses, and secretaries are female (*she, her*) although members of both sexes belong to these professions. Sexist language offers a distorted view of our society and deprives women of their equal rights. Sexist phrases include *gal Friday, little woman, lady of the house, the best man for the job, the weaker sex, working wives,* and *young man on the way up.* Using such sexist terms, you will not only offend but exclude many members of the audience you want to reach.

One way to eliminate sexist language from your writing is to replace sexist words with neutral ones. Neutral words do not refer to a specific sex; they are genderless. Note how the sexist words on the left can be replaced by neutral, nonsexist ones on the right.

Sexist	**Neutral**
authoress	writer, author
businessman	business executive, manager, business-person
chairman	chair, chairperson
craftsman	skilled worker
fireman	firefighter
foreman	supervisor
janitress	cleaning person
landlord, landlady	owner
mailman / postman	mail carrier
mankind	humanity
manmade	synthetic, artificial
manpower	strength, effort, power
men	human beings, people
policeman	police officer
salesman	salesperson, clerk
stewardess	flight attendant

Using the masculine pronouns (*he, his, him*) when referring to a group that includes both men and women is also sexist.

Every worker must submit his travel expenses by Monday.

Workers may include women as well as men, and to assume all workers are men is misleading and unfair to women. You can avoid such sexist language by doing one of the following.

1. Make the subject of your sentence plural and thus neutral.

   Workers must submit their travel expenses by Monday.

2. Use *his or her* instead of *his*.

   Every worker must submit his or her travel expenses by Monday.

3. Reword the sentences using the passive voice.

   All travel expenses must be submitted by Monday.

Moreover, in some contexts exclusive use of the masculine pronoun might invite a lawsuit. For example, you would be violating federal employment laws prohibiting discrimination on the basis of sex if you wrote the following in a help-wanted advertisement for your company.

Each applicant must submit his transcript with his application. He must also have 3 letters of recommendation sent to our office from individuals familiar with his work.

From the language of this ad, one would assume that only men could be applicants for the position.

There are other sexist uses of language you need to avoid. Eliminate such sexist salutations as Dear Sir or Dear Gentlemen from your letters (see pages 125–127). Do not single out a woman's physical appearance (a tall blonde), marital status (a divorcee), or age (middle-aged mother). It is unjust and insulting to introduce sexist distinctions.

◆ AVOIDING JARGON AND SLANG

Jargon

Jargon is shop talk, the specialized vocabulary of a particular occupation. Jargon includes, for example, an *IPPB* (Intermittent Positive Pressure Breathing) *machine* in respiratory therapy, *hard water* (water containing more than 85.5 parts per million of calcium carbonate) in geology, or *pixel* (minimum amount of light on a VDT screen) in computer science. Such technical terms are necessary, but should be used only when the following three conditions are met.

1. The audience understands jargon and expects the writer to use it.
2. A technical term or phrase conveys a precise idea that could not be adequately described with a common word or phrase—for instance, flange pan instead of cake pan.

3. The kind of form or report you are completing requires jargon—for example, a patient's hospital record, a specification sheet, or a legal description.

The word *jargon* has another meaning besides the legitimate technical language of a profession. More often, it refers to phony, inflated, and uselessly complex language. Jargon is a label attached to pompous words (pseudoscientific jawbreakers) some writers use instead of the much more simple, natural, and direct vocabulary their readers better understand and value. Jargon is language that puts on airs; it reeks of the stuffiness found in some business letters (see page 139). People who favor jargon dislike pleasantly clear and direct verbs. For the unassuming verb *get,* they substitute *procure;* for *simplify* or *ease,* they choose (or *elect,* in jargon) *facilitate;* rather than *join* or *connect,* they prefer to *interface.* They also use trendy, bureaucratic nouns instead of much more clear and direct ones—*parameters,* for *limits* or *scope; viability* for *possibility* or *likelihood; domicile* for *residence; ambiance* for *atmosphere;* and *input* for *advice, suggestion,* or *contribution.*

Here are three characteristics of jargon, together with suggestions for doing away with it.

1. Pompous words. Use short, serviceable words instead of pompous expressions (*verbiage* in jargon). Your readers will appreciate your clarity and your honesty. Cut a three-word smoke screen (*scholastic achievement profile*) to one word (*transcript*). *Aquatic support system* could be written *life jacket.*

Note how the original, clear first sentences of Herman Melville's *Moby-Dick* lose their clarity and directness in the jargon translation that follows.

The Original:

Call me Ishmael. Some years ago—never mind how long precisely—having little or no money in my purse and nothing in particular to interest me on shore, I thought I would sail about a little and see the watery part of the world.

The Translation:

You may identify me by the nomenclature of Ishmael. At a point in time several years previous to the current temporal zone—the precise number of which is extraneous information—devoid of sufficient monetary resources and lacking physical and/or psychical stimuli within the confines of my sphere of activity on land, I initiated several thought processes and concluded that I would commandeer a vessel of navigation with which to explore the aquatic component of this planet.[1]

2. Use of -ize and -ation words. Avoid words such as *finalize* (for conclude); *hypothesize, energize, personalize, conceptualize* (for think); *optimize* (for improve); *prioritize* (for rank); *visualize* (for see); *utilize* (for use); *verbalization* (for statement); *conflagration* (for fire); *democratization* (for democracy); *socialization* (for acceptance); *precipitation* (for rain, sleet, or snow); *illumination* (for light); *institutionalization* (for company policy).

3. Excessive or unclear abbreviations. Do not use abbreviations that,

---

[1] The example originally appeared in the *Brown Alumni Monthly;* by the permission of Debra Shore.

while they may be understood by professionals in your field, will confuse readers unfamiliar with such shorthand. For example, if a nurse told patients that they would have to be NPO (initials indicating that patients are to have nothing by mouth) for a GB vis. (X-ray of the gallbladder), the patients would certainly be baffled and perhaps terrified. The writer of the following letter to Ann Landers sums up the situation well.

Dear Ann Landers: The growing tendency to call everything by initials is extremely irritating. I've discussed this with others and find that I am not alone.

It wasn't so bad when there were just a few, such as the CIO, the AFL and the CIA. Now we have the IRS, the ERA, the IUD, the NAACP, HEW, MIT, ORT and DNA.

Where I work, quarterly meetings are mandatory. We must sit and listen for an hour and a half to talk like this: "The IAM met with the TQA and discussed the YTD. We must now check back with the IRA and do something about the LTC." I become thoroughly confused trying to sort out the meaning of the initials.

What's more, I feel like a fool because I don't know what's going on. Will you please tell those double-dome intellectuals to call things by their names and not assume that because THEY know what all the initials mean, everybody else does?—Abbreviated into Oblivion in Kalamazoo

Dear Kal.: IOU warm thanks for writing such an OK letter. I am printing it PDQ.[2]

For those readers who might be unfamiliar with an abbreviation, the writer should give the full name once, followed by the abbreviation in parentheses: political action committee (PAC). From that point on, the writer can use the abbreviation.

Before you use technical terms or inflated words that you think will sound important, consider your reader. That reader will appreciate your choosing words that are easy to understand and that express your ideas clearly and quickly. As you revise your work, make a special effort to keep your words simple, direct, and familiar.

Slang

All of us use slang when we talk to our friends. It is a sign that we are comfortable with the people we know best. Slang, however, is out of place in professional communication, written or oral. Slang is playful, irreverent, and sometimes vulgar—qualities not appreciated in business communication. You need not be a stuffed shirt, but don't be too casual, either. Here are examples of slang terms to avoid in your professional writing; a more formal equivalent is given in parentheses.

---

[2] Reprinted by permission of Ann Landers and Field Newspaper Syndicate.

airhead (absent-minded or stupid person)
bad (good)
bag (avoid confronting, skip)
baloney, bull (nonsense, exaggeration)
blow off (ignore)
chill [out] (relax)
cool, neat (interesting, exciting)
cop out (take the easy way out, let down)
dump on (unload one's problems on)
geek, nerd (socially inept person)
get on someone's case (check up on someone)
goof off (slack off, be lazy)
peel out (drive off recklessly)
rip off (steal)
spaced out, spacy (absent-minded)
stressed out, uptight (tense, nervous)
ticked off (angered)

The following poem laments, with numerous examples, the invasion of slang into our language.

Remember when hippie meant big in the hips,
And a trip involved travel in cars, planes, and ships?
When pot was a vessel for cooking things in,
And hooked was what grandmother's rugs may have been
When fix was a verb that meant mend or repair,
And be-in meant merely existing somewhere?
When neat meant well-organized, tidy, and clean,
And grass was a ground cover, normally green?
When groovy meant furrowed with channels and hollows,
And birds were winged creatures, like robins and swallows
When fuzz was a substance, really fluffy, like lint,
And bread came from bakeries and not from the mint?
When roll meant a bun, and rock was a stone,
And hang-up was something you did with the phone?
It's groovy, man, groovy, but English it's not.
Methinks that our language is going to pot.

                                        Anonymous

◆ A FINAL NOTE ON USING WORDS EFFECTIVELY

Words are the essential building blocks of any piece of writing. This chapter has given you some practical advice on how to become an effective wordsmith as you compose and revise your work. If you choose words skillfully to say exactly what you want, your writing will be more effective. Choose words that are lean and clean, precise and concise. Precise words provide readers with the information they need to grasp your message; concise words avoid wordiness that wastes a reader's time. Spell words correctly and be careful not to confuse one word with another. Finally, eliminate any sexist or discriminatory language from your work as well as unnecessary jargon or slang. By following these guidelines, you will write more readable and professional correspondence, instructions, proposals, and reports—the subjects of later chapters.

◆ EXERCISES

1. The following sentences contain misspelled words. Find these words and correct them.
   a. The superviser did not find our performance acceptible on the new equiptment.
   b. Unusual occurance reports help safety commitees make thier decesions.
   c. If the carburator is not adjusted proparly, the timing will be alwrong.
   d. Students must recieve twenty-five hours of instruction to become familar with trafic control problems.
   e. Only the patience family is admited to the intensive care unit.
   f. To describe the suspect's physical apparance, aquaint your self with the correct descripters.
   g. Eat high nutriant foods containing protiens, carbohidrates, and sufficeint ruffage.
   h. Unflammable liquids could be dangerus.
   i. Some freindly newly weds occupyed the bridel suit.
   j. These archetectural designs are unexpensive.
   k. According to City Ordnance 67, combustables cannot be storred on open shelfs.
   l. I will have a zerox copy of the order preparred for you.
   m. We have printed new calandars with pictures of wild turkies and deers on them.
   n. Gasaline prices will reach a cieling before autum.

2. The following sentences contain mistakes in using apostrophes. Find and correct these mistakes.
   a. We tried to survey everybodies opinion but couldnt include all the members who work the night shift. Well try tomorrow to find them.
   b. The mens locker room was painted last March, wasnt it?
   c. Freud and Einstein's theories changed the way we'ved looked at the world.
   d. The Smiths new house is much larger than the Sanders.
   e. He's report had too many words and contained too many Is.
   f. When the mayors conference was held in Detroit last year, the keynote speakers notes embarrassingly fell to the floor.
   g. Marion and Beatrice's daughters both attended the accelerated math student's seminar in Kalamazoo, which wasnt too far away.
   h. The bolt came off it's shaft during the first cycle. It's too bad we didnt double-check the system.
   i. Because the print was so light, all the x's looked like y's on everyones's copy. The vendors repair crew wasnt able to fix the word processor today.
   j. Adkins's and Kaplan's new restaurant on Broadway Street is a big success.

k. Margaret Bridges'-Bowers new office is on the second floor. It's walls still need to be painted.

3. Select the appropriate word in the following sentences and briefly explain your choice.
   a. My new listings book is larger (then / than) last year's.
   b. All new (personnel / personal) reported to pick up (there / their) identification cards.
   c. Regardless of (it's / its) price, buy the property so the firm does not (lose / loose) it. We must (attain / obtain) it.
   d. She kept her (stationary / stationery) on the desk (beside / besides) her printer where she could easily reach it.
   e. The fabric was (course / coarse) and cheap, and the buyer refused to (choose / chose) it.
   f. Please (except / accept) this (complementary / complimentary) offer with our best wishes.
   g. The (principle / principal) reason given was that our test scores were (to / too) low and the superintendent was afraid none of us would (pass / past) the test.
   h. Corn grows well on the flat (plains / planes) of Illinois.
   i. Smoking (affects / effects) blood pressure.
   j. Our squad had to (sight / cite) every violation so that it could be reported in the district commander's log.
   k. Unusually hot days in March often cause a lot of bad (weather / whether).
   l. (Its / It's) possible to find a (peace / piece) of metal in the shop.
   m. The applicant (who's / whose) credentials were so suitable for our position took another job working for a (pare / pair) of attorneys.
   n. She was very (adept / adapt) at (adapting / adopting) the new guidelines to suit our agency.
   o. The customer made the (rite / right) choice in selecting our firm; we have the (capitol / capital) to develop the project correctly.
   p. The new floor manager was on her feet (continually / continuously) during the month of August to assist customers.

4. The following sentences contain vague and abstract words. Replace them with concrete ones. The first sentence has been done for you.
   a. The individual saw the occurrence. (The police officer from the second district saw the young boy steal Ms. Saliba's purse.)
   b. Three factors disturbed the crew when it had to deliberate.
   c. The case she outlined sounded interesting. *She outlined an interesting case.*
   d. Circumstances indicated that we follow another course of action in handling this matter.
   e. The nature of the area is such that alternative measures must be sought.
   f. It happened this week.
   g. The materials were incomplete; we found defects, too. *We found defects in the incomplete materials.*
   h. The causes of the action seemed to be good.
   i. The phenomenon she discussed happened occasionally in our area.
   j. The individual sought an immediate solution to the problem.

5. The following sentences contain limp, sluggish verbs. Rewrite these sentences replacing vague verbs with active, precise ones. The first one has been done for you.
   a. Tourists are on the beach each August. (Tourists crowd the beach each August).
   b. The writer seemed concerned. *was filled with*
   c. All the points in the proposal relate to our expansion plans. *strongly support*
   d. There exist three possible solutions that appear attractive.
   e. Obtaining appraisals is important.
   f. There are many problems that appear to be significant.
   g. Computers are tools that exist in each business office. *revolve around*
   h. It is apparent that the new equipment has its purpose.
   i. A computer timesharing program will get work accomplished.
   j. The new law is harmful to our district. *detrimental*

6. The following sentences contain wordy expressions. Rewrite them to cut these expressions out.
   a. Due to the fact that the bus was late, we did not get home until after midnight. *We didn't get home until midnight due to a late bus.*
   b. In an effort to correct some health violations, we fixed the refrigerator in such a way that it would not cause us any more trouble. *to comply to health regula*
   c. You will have to connect together the terminals with the assistance of a Phillips screwdriver.
   d. In terms of our ability to meet the demands of those individuals living in the Thames district, all that we can articulate adequately at this date on the calendar is that every effort will be made to find appropriate work crews to find, gather, and remove the refuse left by the storm.
   e. Our manager is very supportive of our efforts to expand our line of coats, hats, shirts, pants, blouses, dresses, and socks for young children between the ages of two weeks and one year.
   f. For the length of time that the powder is left around the edges of the room, you might want to check the walls and doors.
   g. The patient's arm was soaked in warm water with the result that she felt much better and in such a way that the doctor discharged her.
   h. I am in agreement with the terms in your letter of July 25 and I feel quite certain the manager will respond favorably in an effort to secure the contract.

7. The following sentences contain redundancies. Rewrite these sentences to remove unnecessary repetition.
   a. It was a foreign import.
   b. The owner's car was light azure blue in color and a convertible model.
   c. The president told them to terminate the plan and end it.
   d. A student delivered an oral talk to fellow classmates.
   e. The crew was traveling and in transit; therefore, it could not be reached.
   f. The troops advanced forward even when they were confronted face-to-face with hazardous dangers staring them in the eyes.

g. The chemistry major had to reread the chapter on bonding again.

h. The chief canceled our leaves when the major requested additional, further officers.

i. The clamp was connected together with the hose.

j. After explaining the new policy, the office manager centered her discussion around the ways of implementing and carrying out that policy in our routine, daily activities.

k. When the technician walked into the room, the patient was really bleeding profusely.

l. She came to her final conclusion after referring back to the occurrence report.

m. Although the diamond was oval in shape, it still would satisfy the buyer.

n. First and foremost, the guests received a complimentary bottle of wine, which did not cost them a cent.

o. He received personalized and individual care.

p. A knife, tent, and food supplies are basic necessities on an outdoor camping trip in the woods.

q. The report will specifically and exclusively deal with urban problems affecting the city.

r. The local, neighborhood commission gave sufficient and adequate reasons for letting the carpenter work independently and use her own resources.

s. They have legal recourse as promised by the law.

8. The following sentences contain sexist language. Rewrite them to eliminate all sexist words and phrases.

a. The Constitution of the United States promises each man freedom of speech.

b. The city will hire more firemen and policemen at the beginning of the fiscal year.

c. In the last five years, our company has been a leader in developing manmade fibers.

d. Taylor Community College enrolled more than 2000 coeds last term.

e. Our office advertised for a couple of girls to work part-time as receptionists in a 20-man department.

f. Each pilot is required to have his physical examination this month.

g. All attorneys and their wives are invited to attend the reception.

h. Job applicants should always spell the employer's name correctly or he may not respond favorably to their letter.

i. On the medical-surgical floors, every nurse is required to rotate her work shift.

j. Every shopper should realize the value of her coupons.

k. The businessman's lunch offers a variety of specials.

l. The new financial program is designed to help the common man.

m. The foreman believes that a woman's work is never done.

n. A new copywriter must learn to take criticism like a man.

9. The following paragraphs are wordy and full of jargon. Rewrite these paragraphs to make them more readable and concise by replacing the jargon with clear and appropriate words.

a. It has been verified conclusively by this writer that our institution must of necessity install more bicycle holding racks for the convenience of students, faculty, and staff. These parking modules should be fastened securely to walls outside strategic locations on the campus. They could be positioned there by work crews or even by the security forces who vigilantly patrol the campus grounds. There are many students in particular who would value the installation of these racks. Their bicycles could be stationed there by them, and they would know that safety measures have been taken to ensure that none of their bicycles would be apprehended or confiscated illegally. Besides the precaution factor, these racks would afford users maximized convenience in utilizing their means of transportation when they have academic business to conduct, whether at the learning resource center or in the instructional facilities.

b. On the basis of preliminary investigations, it would seem reasonable to hypothesize that among the situational factors predisposing the Smith family toward showing pronounced psychological identification with the San Francisco Giants is the fact that the Smiths make their domicile in the San Francisco area. In the absence of contrariwise considerations, the Smiths's attitudinal preferences would in this respect interface with earlier behavioral studies. These studies, within acceptable parameters, correlate the fan's domicile with athletic allegiance. Yet it would be counterproductive to establish domicility as the sole determining factor for the Smiths's preference. Certain sociometric studies of the Smiths disclose a factor of atypicality which enters into an analysis of their determinations. One of these factors is that a younger Smith sibling is a participant in the athletic organization in question.

Correspondence

Chapter 6: Letter Writing: Some Basics

◆

Chapter 7: How to Get a Job:
Résumés, Letters, Applications,
Interviews, and Evaluations

◆

Chapter 8: Types of
Business Correspondence

6

Letter Writing: Some Basics

Letters are probably the kind of writing you will do most frequently on your job. Because letters are so important, Chapters 6, 7, and 8 are devoted exclusively to ways of writing letters effectively. This chapter introduces the entire process and provides some guidelines, definitions, and strategies common to all letter writing.

◆ THE IMPORTANCE OF LETTERS

A letter can be defined as a formal or informal written message that is carefully prepared and addressed to a specific audience and that has a clearly announced function. Letters are more formal than the memos that are written to people who work in your office. They are both a personal and professional means of communication. Effective letters clearly announce their purpose and are written in complete sentences in a style that (1) follows an appropriate format, (2) courteously addresses the reader, and (3) selects the most precise language.

Companies annually spend millions of dollars writing letters. In terms of materials and time, the average business letter now costs between eight and twelve dollars to compose, dictate, type, proofread, mail, store, and retrieve. Not surprisingly, many companies own fax machines that allow them to send a letter across the country in a few minutes. But even with such machines, businesses need people to write and proofread the letters. Numerous companies offer their employees seminars on how to write clear and appropriate letters. The skill of good letter writing can be learned and can lead you to advancement and rewards.

Why are letters so important to the employer and the employee? Letters represent the public image of the company and the professional competence of the writer. They can influence people favorably or unfavorably. Basically, letters serve the following five functions.

1. Letters provide information. They can give instructions and can inform readers about a new policy, a change in time for deliveries, an alteration in procedures, a new product, or a service.

2. Letters prompt action. They can help the writer collect money from overdue accounts, alter a city ordinance, speed the shipment of new parts, initiate a policy, call a meeting, or waive a requirement.

3. Letters establish goodwill. They can thank someone, convey congratulations, respond to a complaint, settle an account satisfactorily, or provide a recommendation.

4. Letters sell. They can sell a product, a service, or the writer's own skills.

5. Letters follow up on telephone calls and other types of conversation. They can also provide documentation and clarification of oral agreements.

Letters accomplish all these goals by following certain conventions (rules or customary practices). These conventions are the ways in which businesses and their readers expect letters to look and to be written. This chapter will show you how to use these conventions and will also provide numerous examples for you to study.

◆ TYPING/PRINTING AND PROOFREADING LETTERS

The first thing a reader notices about a letter is how the words and paragraphs are arranged on the page. Your audience is influenced by the way your letter looks even before they read its contents. A neat, clean, and professional looking letter tells the reader that the work, service, or skill the writer promises to deliver will be done in the same way. Strikeovers (crossing out one letter by typing another letter on top of it), messy erasures that leave the paper bare in one spot, blotches of liquid corrector smeared across the page, and handwritten changes inserted to correct errors all look unprofessional and distract the reader from understanding your message quickly and accurately.

The way in which a letter is typed or printed on the page significantly affects the visual impression it makes. If using a typewriter, you can avoid crowded or lopsided letters if you take a few minutes to estimate the length of the message before you type it. You do not want to start a brief letter at the top of the page and leave three-fourths of the page blank. Plan to start near the center of the page. Also avoid cramming a long letter onto one page; sometimes you will have to use a second sheet. A letter that is squeezed onto one page will deprive the reader of necessary and pleasant white space.

Specific typing instructions are included later in the chapter. Here are a few general hints. Leave generous margins of approximately $1\frac{1}{2}$ inches all around your letter. Have more white space at the top than at the bottom, and watch right-hand margins in particular, since it is easy to exceed their limits. Shorter letters may require wider margins than longer letters, but don't exceed a margin of $1\frac{1}{2}$ inches on the right-hand side.

Be especially careful about the typewriter or printer you use. Make sure that all the keys work and that none of them produces a broken or half letter. Clean your keys and buy a new ribbon so that your typed letter will not be fuzzy or messy. If you are using word processing equipment to prepare your letter, use a letter-quality printer. Letters run off on a dot matrix printer generally do not look as crisp, fresh, or professional. Choose a space density that will be pleasant and inviting to the eye. Crowding too many letters on a line will not inspire your reader's confidence. Your letter will look like it's hard to read.

Proofread everything that has your name on it, even if you did not type it. You cannot blame a typist for spelling mistakes or other errors. As the writer, you are responsible for the final product. When a letter goes out with your signature, you are telling the reader that you are accountable for everything in it. Typographical errors can be costly and embarrassing. If you want to tell a steady customer that "the order will be hard to fill" and you type instead that "the order will be hard to bill," confusion will result. Poor typing and proofreading can also lead to omitted letters (the "ill arrived" for "the bill arrived"), transpositions ("hte" for "the," "nad" for "and," "sti" for "its"), or omitted words ("the market value of the was high").

Proofreading is reading in slow motion. Here are eight ways to proofread effectively. You may want to combine all of them to ensure accuracy.

1. Read the letter word for word from the bottom to the top.
2. Read the letter from start to finish aloud. Pronounce each word carefully to make yourself more aware of typographical errors or omitted words. Look at every letter of every word. Don't skim.
3. Place your finger under each word as you read the letter silently.
4. Double-check the spelling of all names and the accuracy of dates, costs, addresses, and other factual details. Errors here are sure to cause problems. Watch for inconsistencies (e.g., Phillip in one place; Philip in another).
5. Have a friend read the letter. Four eyes are better than two.
6. Have your friend read the original copy of the letter aloud while you follow the typed copy.
7. If you have the time, proofread the letter the following day.
8. Never proofread when you are tired, and avoid reading large amounts of material in one sitting.

◆ LETTER FORMATS

Letter format refers to the way in which you type a letter—where you indent and where you place certain kinds of information. A number of letter formats exist. Two of the most often used in the business world are the full block format (Figure 6.1) and the semiblock format (Figure 6.2). Gaining popularity is a third format known as the Administrative Management Society (AMS) simplified style, illustrated in Figure 6.3. Before you choose a letter format, find out if your employer has a preference.

The full block style is the easiest to use because all information in the letter is typed flush against the left-hand margin. You will not have to worry about indenting paragraphs or aligning dates with signatures. Figure 6.1 shows a full block let-

FIGURE 6.1   Full block letter format.

RICHARD E. FELTS   CAMERON E. WILLIAMS, CPCU   RICHARD L. PHILLIPS, CPCU
Chairman Emeritus   Chairman   First Vice Chairman

Ohio Insurance Institute / 620 EAST BROAD STREET, P.O. BOX 632, COLUMBUS, OHIO 43216 / PHONE (614) 228-1593

JOHN C. WINCHELL, CPCU   NOREEN R. WILLS   ALAN V. RINARD, CPCU   CAROLINE KASLER
President   Vice President,   Vice President,   Assistant Vice President,
    Public Information   Research & Education   Education & Research

April 3, 1985

Ms. Molly Georgopolous, C.P.A.
Business Manager
Diversified Industries
3400 South Madison
Akron, OH 44324-6652

Dear Ms. Georgopolous:

All typing/
printing
lined up
against
left-hand
margin

As I promised in our telephone conversation this afternoon, I am enclosing a study of the Ohio financial responsibility law. I hope that it will help you prepare your report.

I wish to emphasize again that probably 95 percent of all individuals who are involved in an accident do obtain reimbursement for hospital and doctor bills and for damages to their automobiles. If individuals have insurance, they can receive reimbursement from their own carrier. If they do not have insurance and the other driver is uninsured and judged to be at fault, the State Bureau of Motor Vehicles will revoke that party's driver's license and license plates until all costs for injuries and damages are paid.

Please call upon me again if I may be of help to you.

Sincerely yours,

John C. Winchell

John C. Winchell, President

JCW/pck

Encl.

Letterhead reproduced by permission.

ter typed on letterhead stationery (specially printed stationery giving a company's name, address, telephone number, and sometimes the names of its chief executives or the company logo). The use of letterhead stationery eliminates the need to type a writer's address. On plain stationery, the writer's address is typed flush with the left-hand margin, directly above the date.

FIGURE 6.2   Semiblock letter format.

```
                          Writer's address ⎤  7239 East Daphne Parkway
                          and date are     ⎬  Mobile, AL 36608-1012
                          indented.        ⎦  January 31, 1989



Mr. Travis Boykin, Manager
Scandia Gifts
703 Hardy Street
Hattiesburg, MS 39401-4633

Dear Mr. Boykin:

I would appreciate knowing if you currently stock the Crescent
pattern of model 5678 and how much you charge per model
number. I would also like to know if you have special prices
per box order.

The name of your store is listed in the Annual Catalog as the
closest distributor of Copenhagen products in my area. Would
you please give me directions to your shop from Mobile and the
hours you are open.

I look forward to hearing from you.

                                      Sincerely yours,

              Complimentary      ⎤
              close and writer's ⎬  Arthur T. McCormack
              name are indented. ⎦
                                    Arthur T. McCormack
```

In contrast, the semiblock style (Figure 6.2) has the writer's address (if it is not imprinted on a letterhead), date, complimentary close, and the signature at the right-hand side of the letter. The typist must make a number of adjustments to align the date with the complimentary close and must remember to go back to the left side to note any enclosures with the letter. Paragraphs within a letter in the semiblock style can be flush against the left-hand margin or indented.

FIGURE 6.3   AMS simplified letter format.

OFFICE PROPERTY MANAGEMENT ASSOCIATES
2400 SOUTH LINCOLN HIGHWAY
LIVINGSTON, NJ 07040–9990

April 17, 1989

Mr. W. T. Albritton
Albritton and Sharp Accounting Services
Suite 400
Suburban Office Complex
Livingston, NJ 07038-2389

IMPROVED SERVICES AT SUBURBAN OFFICE COMPLEX

At our April meeting, Office Property Management Associates discussed a number of requests you and other tenants made at the Suburban Office Complex. I am happy to inform you that the following improvements in services will go into effect at the Suburban Office Complex within 45 days.

1. Effective June 5, you will have an on-site manager, Judy Fiorelli, who will be happy to answer any questions you may have about the Complex and will help you solve any problems.
2. The parking lot on the southwest side will be resurfaced during the week of June 12–18. During this time, we ask that you and your staff please park your vehicles in the north or the east lots.
3. A new outdoor security lighting system will be installed by June 16. Work on this system should not inconvenience you.

I welcome your comments on these changes or suggestions for additional ones. Please feel free to call or write me.

Gladys T. Mullins-Osborne

GLADYS T. MULLINS-OSBORNE, VICE PRESIDENT

tc

The AMS style follows the block format in which every line begins at the left-hand margin, including any numbered items such as those in Figure 6.3. But unlike the block format, the AMS style omits the salutation and complimentary close. In place of the salutation it includes a subject line (without using the word *subject*), typed or printed in all capital letters, three spaces down from the inside address. Three spaces after the subject line comes the first paragraph of the letter. The writer's name and title are typed in capital letters on the same line four lines after the last paragraph of the letter. The typist's initials appear two lines beneath the writer's name. Because the AMS style saves the typist time (and thus the company money), many offices now use it.

If your letter runs to a second page, use a sheet of plain white bond paper rather than company letterhead. About nine lines, or $1\frac{1}{2}$ inches from the top of the page, type the reader's name on the left-hand side, a simple arabic 2 in the center, and the date of the letter on the right-hand side.

```
Patricia Riordan-Sanchez        2        April 30, 1990
```

Alternatively, put "Page 2" and the date directly under the recipient's name on the left-hand side. However, never number the first page of a letter, even if your letter is just one page long.

◆ PARTS OF A LETTER

A letter must contain many parts to communicate its message. These parts and their placement in your letter form the basic conventions of effective letter writing. Your reader will be in the habit of looking for certain information in certain places in your letter. It is your responsibility as a letter writer to meet your reader's expectations. By doing so you will create a good impression.

In the following discussion, those parts of a letter marked with an asterisk are found in every letter you will write. Figure 6.4 contains a sample letter displaying all the parts discussed below. Note where each part is placed in the letter.

*Date Line

Where you place the month, day, and year depends on the format you are using. If you are using the full block style or the AMS simplified style, the date line is flush with the left-hand margin. If you are using the semiblock style, the date can be placed at the center point, centered under a company letterhead, or flush with the right-hand margin.

FIGURE 6.4   A sample letter, full block format, with all parts labeled.

Letterhead	**MADISON AND MOORE, INC.** Professional Architects 7900 South Manheim Road Crystal Springs, NE 71003-0092
Date line	December 11, 1990
Inside address	Ms. Paula Jordan Systems Consultant Broadacres Development Corp. 12 East River Street Detroit, MI 48001-0422
Salutation	Dear Ms. Jordan:
Subject line	SUBJECT: Request for alternate duplex plans, No. 32134
Body of letter	Thank you for your letter of December 3, 1990. I have discussed your request with the officials in our Planning Department and have learned that the forms we used are no longer available. In searching through my files, however, I have come across the enclosed catalog from a Nevada firm that might be helpful to you. This firm, Nevada Designers, offers plans very similar to the ones you are interested in, as you can tell from the design I checked on page 23 of their catalog. I hope this will help your project and I wish you success in your venture.
Complimentary close	Sincerely yours,
Company name	MADISON AND MOORE, INC.
Signature	*William Newhouse*
Writer's name and title	William Newhouse Office Manager
Typist's identification	WN/kpl
Enclosure	Encl. Catalog
Copy to	cc: Planning Department

Spell out the name of the month in full; type "September" and "March" rather than abbreviating to "Sept." or "Mar." Most frequently the date line is typed this way: November 14, 1989. Yet many international firms prefer to date correspondence with the day followed by month and year (14 November 1989), with no commas separating the day, month, and year.

*Inside Address

The inside address, which is the same address that goes on the envelope, is always placed against the left-hand margin. It contains the name, title (if any), company, street address, city, state, and zip code of the person or company to which you are writing. If possible, try to write to a specific individual in a company instead of using "Sales Manager" or "President." Check correspondence, telephone directories, or annual reports. Call the company if you have to. You will get off to a bad start if you do not spell that person's name right; don't put Anderson for Andersen, Kean for Keen, or MacDermott for McDermott.

Single-space the inside address, but do not use any punctuation at the end of the lines. The name of the individual, together with a courtesy title such as Mr., Ms., Dr., Professor, goes on the first line. When writing to a woman, use Ms. unless she expressly asks to be called Mrs. or Miss. A woman's marital status is not an issue. The initials M.D., Ph.D., or D.P.H. should not be added after you use Dr. Use either Janice Howell, M.D. or Dr. Janice Howell, *not* Dr. Janice Howell, M.D. Any military titles (Captain, Corporal), academic ranks (Professor, Assistant Professor), or religious designations (Reverend, Father, Sister) should be written out in full and the first letter capitalized.

If the individual to whom you are writing holds an office or has a title within the company, put a comma after the person's name, followed by the title: Ms. Kathy Buel, President. Use the courtesy title Ms. and capitalize the "P" in President. If the title contains more than one word, put the title on the next line: Mr. Henry Gerald/Director of Computer Services. If you do not know the individual's name or if you are writing to an entire corporation or section of a company, put the department or company name on one line and the street address on the next line: Public Relations Department/The Doulet Brace Company/1343 Jackson Street/Chicago, IL 60624–1205.

The last line of the inside address contains the city, state, and zip code. Table 6.1 lists the official U.S. Postal Service abbreviations—two capital letters without periods—for the states and territories of the United States. Acceptable abbreviations for the provinces of Canada are listed below the table. Pay special attention to those abbreviations beginning with the same letter. For example, mail going to Jackson, Mississippi (MS), could go astray if a letter without a zip code used the same abbreviation for Michigan (MI). Also note the difference between AR (Arkansas) and AK (Alaska). If you are writing to someone in a foreign country, type the name of that country in capital letters alone on the last line of the inside address.

Salutation

The greeting part of your letter, or the salutation, is typed flush against the left-hand margin in both the full block and semiblock formats and is omitted in the AMS simplified format. Begin with *Dear,* a convention showing respect for your reader, and then follow with a courtesy title, the reader's last name, and a colon (Dear Mr. Brown:). A comma is used only for an informal letter. The salutation is

TABLE 6.1   U.S. Postal Service Abbreviations

U.S. state / territory	Abbreviation	U.S. state / territory	Abbreviation
Alabama	AL	Montana	MT
Alaska	AK	Nebraska	NE
Arizona	AZ	Nevada	NV
Arkansas	AR	New Hampshire	NH
American Samoa	AS	New Jersey	NJ
California	CA	New Mexico	NM
Colorado	CO	New York	NY
Connecticut	CT	North Carolina	NC
Delaware	DE	North Dakota	ND
District of Columbia	DC	Ohio	OH
Florida	FL	Oklahoma	OK
Georgia	GA	Oregon	OR
Guam	GU	Pennsylvania	PA
Hawaii	HI	Puerto Rico	PR
Idaho	ID	Rhode Island	RI
Illinois	IL	South Carolina	SC
Indiana	IN	South Dakota	SD
Iowa	IA	Tennessee	TN
Kansas	KS	Trust Territories	TT
Kentucky	KY	Texas	TX
Louisiana	LA	Utah	UT
Maine	ME	Vermont	VT
Maryland	MD	Virginia	VA
Massachusetts	MA	Virgin Islands	VI
Michigan	MI	Washington	WA
Minnesota	MN	West Virginia	WV
Mississippi	MS	Wisconsin	WI
Missouri	MO	Wyoming	WY

Canadian province	Abbreviation	Canadian province	Abbreviation
Alberta	AB	Nova Scotia	NS
British Columbia	BC	Ontario	ON
Labrador	LB	Prince Edward Island	PE
Manitoba	MB	Quebec	PQ
New Brunswick	NB	Saskatchewan	SK
Newfoundland	NF	Yukon Territory	YT
Northwest Territories	NT		

determined by the first line of the inside address and must be consistent with it. If you are not sure of the sex of the reader, use the reader's full name: "Dear Terry Banks."

If you are writing to a large group of readers, use an individual's relevant designation: Dear Pilot, Dear Homeowners. When writing to a company, use the company name—Dear Macy's, Dear Saperstein Textiles—not the sexist "Dear

Gentlemen." Similarly, if you are writing to a group that includes both men and women, use Dear Ladies and Gentlemen, but not the sexist "Dear Sirs." (For a discussion of sexist language and how to avoid it, review pages 105–06).

And finally, if you are on a first-name basis with your reader and using his or her last name would be awkward, simply write "Dear Bill" or "Dear Sue."

Subject Line

The subject line can provide a concise summary of the letter (something like a title) or it can list account numbers, order notations, or referral numbers so that the reader can at once check the files and see what the status of your account or policy is. Your most recent letter can then be placed accurately in your file. In both the full block and semiblock formats, the subject line, preceded by the word SUBJECT in capital letters, is placed two spaces below the salutation, flush with the left-hand margin:

```
Dear Ms. Hogan:

SUBJECT: Repair of model 7342
```

Or it can be moved to the right-hand side of the letter, on the same line with the salutation:

```
Dear Ms. Hogan:                    SUBJECT: Repair of model 7342
```

Review page 123 and Figure 6.3 for style and placement of the subject line in an AMS simplified style letter.

*Body of the Letter

The body of a letter contains the message. In the full block format, paragraphs are never indented; in the semiblock and AMS simplified formats, paragraphs may or may not be indented five spaces. Whichever style you choose, single-space within the paragraph, but double-space between paragraphs.

While some of your letters will be only a few lines long, many of them will extend to three or more paragraphs. Always begin your letter with your purpose. Tell readers in the first paragraph why you are writing to them and why your letter is important to them. In a second (or subsequent) paragraph, develop your message with factual support. But don't bury important points within the middle or end of your paragraph. Follow the techniques of paragraph writing discussed in Chapter 3. In your last paragraph, bring readers to a true sense of conclusion. Tell them what you have done for them, what they should do for you, what will happen next, when they will hear from you again, or any combination of these messages. Don't leave readers hanging.

Consider the appearance of your paragraphs, too. Review pages 59–61.

Complimentary Close

Except in an AMS simplified style letter (where the complimentary close is omitted), the complimentary close always appears two spaces below the body of the letter, flush with the left-hand margin in the full block format and at the center point, aligned with the date, for the semiblock format. As the term suggests, the complimentary close ends the letter politely. For most business correspondence, the standard close is *Sincerely yours, Sincerely, Yours sincerely, Best wishes,* or *Respectfully.* Avoid flowery closes such as *Faithfully yours* or *Forever yours.* Capitalize only the first letter of the complimentary close, and follow the entire close with a comma.

*Signature

The typed name appears four spaces below the complimentary close (or, in an AMS simplified style letter, below the last line of the body), either on the left side (full block or AMS simplified format) or at the center point (semiblock format). You need four spaces so that your name, when you write it out, will not look squeezed in. Always sign your name in ink, just as it is typed. Your name not only indicates who you are, but also verifies that the contents of your letter have your approval. An unsigned letter indicates carelessness or, worse, indifference.

Some firms like to have the company name as well as the employee's name in the signature section. If so, type the company name in capital letters two spaces below the complimentary close, and then sign your name. Add your title underneath your typed name. Here is an example:

```
Sincerely yours,

THE FINELLI COMPANY
```

Robert Stavropoulos

```
Robert Stavropoulos
Cover Coordinator
```

Reference Initials

When a letter is typed for you, the typist's initials are placed two spaces below your typed signature. The typist's initials are typed in lower-case letters and follow your initials, which are typed in capital letters. The notation WBT/vgh or WBT:vgh, for example, means that Winnie B. Thompson's letter was typed by Victor G. Higgins. The company thus has a record in its files of who dictated the letter and who typed it. Do not list any initials if you typed your own letter.

Enclosure(s) Line

The enclosure line is typed two spaces beneath the reference initials (or your typed signature if you typed your own letter). This line informs the reader that additional materials (brochures, diagrams, forms, job descriptions, a proposal) accompany your letter. You can type the word "Enclosure" in full or abbreviate it to "Encl." Most writers indicate briefly what is being enclosed (Encl. Incident report; Encl. Résumé) or at least give the number of enclosures (Encl. 3). Sometimes the title of an enclosure is given, for example, Encl. "The 1989 Sales Report to the Management of Powers Industries."

Copy or Copies Distributed

The initials "cc" or "xc" (typed in lower-case letters with no space between them) indicate that a letter has been duplicated and sent to other people or departments. Type these initials, followed by a colon and the appropriate names, two spaces below the enclosure line.

```
cc: John Bandy
    Service Dept.
```

Letters are copied and sent to a third party for a variety of reasons. You may be required to send copies of all your correspondence to your boss. Additionally, you may send copies of certain letters to a specific individual who needs to be kept apprised of an ongoing situation, or another department in your firm may be interested in your letter. When you are sending a copy of your letter to more than one individual, list these individuals in alphabetical order or by corporate rank.

```
cc: Janice Algood          xc: Plant Superintendent Swarr
    Peter Lemon                Comptroller Algood
    Robbie Swarr               Shift 1 Supervisor Lemon
```

Often letters are copied for other readers without the knowledge of the person to whom the letter is addressed. Such copies are called "blind copies." But professional courtesy dictates that you tell the reader that a copy of your letter is being sent to someone else.

◆ ADDRESSING AN ENVELOPE

When addressing an envelope, use a standard $9\frac{1}{2}'' \times 4\frac{1}{8}''$ white envelope or, as most firms do when they mail statements, an envelope measuring $6\frac{1}{2}'' \times 3\frac{5}{8}''$ with a window (a transparent cellophane opening) showing the customer's address. Because most mail is sorted by optical scanning machines, the United States Postal Service has established regulations concerning envelope size. In particular, avoid odd-shaped envelopes and small, invitation-sized ones. Review the regulations listed on page 11 for proper envelope sizes.

Outside Address

An envelope has two parts: the outside address and the return address, as shown in Figure 6.5. The outside address, the same as the reader's inside address on your letter, should be typed single-spaced and centered on the envelope. Although the Postal Service recommends using all capitals and no punctuation on the envelope, most companies still prefer to use standard capitalization and punctuation on both the inside and outside addresses. Leave at least one-half inch of white space between the last line of the address and the bottom of the envelope. Never exceed five lines for an address, and make sure that all lines of the address are lined up flush left. If an individual's address contains both a street address and an apartment, room, or suite number, put all this information on the same line: 809 Troup Street, Apt. 7B. If an individual does not live at an address permanently, you will have to send the letter in care of (c/o) the permanent resident.

> Ms. Mary Jane Truax
> c/o Ms. Faye Jelinick
> 33 West 91st Street
> New York, NY 10072-3678

Always use a zip code, even if a letter is going to someone in your city, because a letter with a zip code will arrive at its destination sooner.

All mail delivery areas in the United States now have a nine-digit zip code. The first five digits direct mail to a particular geographic location (a neighborhood or area in New York City or San Francisco) while the last four digits provide a further geographic breakdown (a unit within a company, a floor of a large office building, a college post office box).

Return Address and Special Instructions

The return address is your address. It should appear at the upper left-hand side of the envelope (not on the back flap), single spaced, and without any courtesy title.

FIGURE 6.5   A properly addressed envelope.

```
Thomas Addington
45 Simmons Road, Apt. 2B  } Return address
Medvale, VT 05402-1521



                          Ms. Patricia Barnes
                          Office Manager
      Outside address  {  Courtesy Motors
                          1700 Lakewood Street
                          Boston, MA 02127-3160
```

FIGURE 6.6   An envelope with an attention line.

```
Kathy Kooperman
769 East 45th Street
Baltimore, MD 21224-6025




                    The Placement Office
                    Attention: Ms. Faye Gladstone
                    East Central Community College
                    Baltimore, MD 21228-0710
```

Sometimes special mailing directions are also required. In such cases, one of the following designations is added to the envelope.

- **Hold for Arrival.** Individuals may be away on business or on vacation, and you want the letter to reach them on their return. Perhaps, too, you are writing to someone who will arrive at a hotel or firm after your letter does. The notation "Hold for Arrival" ensures that your letter is not returned or thrown away.
- **Personal** or **Confidential.** This designation indicates that only the individual to whom you are writing should open and read your letter.
- **Attention.** This word on the envelope is followed by the name of the individual to whom you are writing. The attention line is particularly helpful when you have been dealing regularly with one section, department, or individual in a large company—credit officer, parts warehouse, or statistics office. An attention line also helps a company sort and route its mail faster.
- **Please Forward.** This designation asks that your letter be sent on to a new address after an individual has moved.

All such special instructions, except the attention line, are placed at the top left, two spaces below the return address. The attention line is typed on the second line of the reader's address, as shown in Figure 6.6.

◆ MAKING A GOOD IMPRESSION ON YOUR READER

You have just learned about the mechanical requirements your letter must fulfill. Now we will discuss the content of your letter—what you say and how you say it. Writing letters means communicating to influence your readers, not to alienate or antagonize them. Keep in mind that writers of effective letters are like successful diplomats in that they represent both their company and themselves. The image you want readers to have of you and your company is projected through your letter. You want readers to see you as courteous, credible, and professional.

To write an effective letter like that, first put yourself in the reader's position. What kinds of letters do you like to receive? You would at once rule out letters that are vague, impersonal, sarcastic, pushy, or condescending. You want letters addressed to you to be polite, businesslike, and considerate of your needs and requests. If you have questions, you want them answered honestly, courteously, and fully. You do not want someone to waste your time with a long, puffy letter when a few well-chosen sentences would have done the job much better.

What do you as a writer have to do to send such effective letters? Adopt the "you attitude"; in other words, signal to readers that they and their needs are of utmost importance. Incorporating this "you attitude" means that you should be able to answer "Yes" to these two questions: (1) Will my readers receive a positive image of me? (2) Have I chosen words that convey both my respect for the readers and my concern for their questions and comments? The first question deals with your overall view of readers. Do your letters paint them as clever or stupid, practical managers or spendthrifts? The second question deals with specific language and tone conveying your view of the reader. Words can burn or soothe. Choose them carefully.

Figures 6.7 and 6.8 contain two versions of the same letter. Which one would you rather receive? Why?

Four Guidelines to Achieving the "You Attitude"

The following four guidelines will help you make a good impression on your reader. Keep them in mind as you draft and revise your letters.

1. Never forget that your reader is a real person. Avoid writing cold, impersonal letters that sound as if they were form letters or tape-recorded messages on a telephone. Let the readers know that you are writing to them as individuals. Neglecting this rule, a large clinic once sent its customers this statement: "Your bill is overdue. If you pay it by the 15th of this month, no one except the computer will know that it was late." Similarly, the letter below violates every rule of personal and personable communications.

> It has come to our attention that policy number 342q765r has been delinquent in payment and is in arrears for the sum of $302.35. To keep the policy in force for the duration of its life, a minimum payment of $50.00 must reach this office by the last day of the month. Failure to submit payment will result in the cancellation of the aforementioned policy.

This example displays no sense of one individual writing to another, of a customer with a name, personal history, or specific needs. The letter uses cold and stilted language ("delinquent in payment," "in arrears for," "aforementioned policy"). Revised, this letter contains the necessary personal (and human) touch.

> We have not yet received your payment for your insurance policy (#342q765r). By sending us your check for $50.00 within the next three weeks, you will keep your policy in force and can continue to enjoy the financial benefits and emotional security it offers you.

FIGURE 6.7   A letter lacking the "you attitude."

BROWN COUNTY
Office of the Tax Assessor
County Building, Room 200
Ventura, Missouri 56780-0102

March 4, 1989

Mr. Ted B. Ladner
451 West Hawthorne Lane
Morris, MO 64507-3005

Dear Mr. Ladner:

You have made a mistake by writing to the wrong office here at the County Building. There is no way we would even attempt to verify the kinds of picky details you are demanding from Brown County.

Simply put, by carefully examining the 1988 tax bill you said you received, you should have realized that it is the Tax Collector's Office, not the Tax Assessor's, that will have to handle the problem you claim exists.

In short, call or write the Tax Collector of Brown County, not us.

Thank you!

Tracey Kowalski

Tracey Kowalski

The benefits to the particular reader are stressed, and the reader is addressed directly as a valued customer.

Don't be afraid of using "you" in your letters. Readers will feel more friendly toward you and your message. (Of course, no amount of "you's" will help if they appear in a condescending context such as the letter in Figure 6.7.) In fact, you might even use the reader's name or the name of his or her company within your letter to create goodwill and to show your interest.

FIGURE 6.8   A you-centered revision of Figure 6.7.

BROWN COUNTY
Office of the Tax Assessor
County Building, Room 200
Ventura, Missouri 56780-0102

March 4, 1989

Mr. Ted B. Ladner
451 West Hawthorne Lane
Morris, MO 64507-3005

Dear Mr. Ladner:

Thank you for writing about the difficulties you encountered with your 1988 tax bill. I wish I could help you, but it is the Tax Collector's Office that issues your annual property tax bill. Our office does not prepare individual homeowners' bills.

If you will kindly direct your questions to Paulette Sutton at the Brown County Tax Collector's Office, Room 100, County Building, Ventura, Missouri 56780-0100, I am sure that she will be able to assist you. Should you wish to call her, the number is 458-3455.

Respectfully,

Tracey Kowalski

Tracey Kowalski

2. Keep the reader in the forefront of your letter. Make sure that the reader's needs control the letter. This is the essence of the "you attitude." No one likes people who talk about themselves all the time. What is true about conversation is equally true of letters. Stress the "you," not the "I" or the "we." Again, try to find out about your readers. Here is a paragraph from a letter that forgets about the reader.

I think that our rug shampooer is the best on the market. Our firm has invested a lot of time and money to ensure that it is the most economical and efficient shampooer available today. We have found that our customers are very satisfied with the results of our machine. We have sold thousands of these shampooers, and we are proud of our accomplishment. We hope that we can sell you one of our fantastic machines.

The example above talks the reader into boredom by spending all its time on the machine, the company, and the sales success. Readers are interested in how *they* can benefit from the machine, not in how much profit the company makes from selling it. To win the readers' confidence, the writer needs to show how they will find the product useful, economical, and worthwhile at home or at work. Here is a reader-centered alternative.

Our rug shampooer would make cleaning your Happy Rest Motel rooms easier for you. It is equipped with a heavy–duty motor that will handle your 200 rooms with ease. Moreover, that motor will give frequently used areas, such as the lobby or hallways, a fresh and clean look you can be proud of.

3. Be courteous and tactful. However serious the problem or the degree of your anger at the time, refrain from turning your letter into a punch through the mail. Capture the reader's goodwill, and the rewards will be greater for you. The following words can create a bad taste in the reader's mouth.

it's defective	unprofessional (job, attitude, etc.)
I demand	your failure
I insist	you contend
we reject	you allege
that's no excuse for	you should have known
totally unacceptable	your outlandish claim

Use words that emphasize the "you attitude," and avoid offensive language. Compare the discourteous sentences on the left with the courteous alternatives on the right.

Discourteous	Courteous
We must discontinue your service unless payment is received by the date shown.	Please send us your payment by November 4 so that your service will not be interrupted.
You completely misunderstood my letter.	I am sorry that my letter did not explain that more clearly.
Your claim that our product was defective on delivery is outlandish.	We are sorry to learn that you were dissatisfied with the condition of our product when it reached you.
The rotten coil you installed caused all my trouble.	The trouble may be caused by a malfunctioning coil.
You are sorely mistaken about the warranty.	We are sorry to learn about the difficulty you experienced over the service terms in our warranty.

Discourteous

The new printer you sold me is third-rate and you charged first-rate prices.

Obviously your company is wrong. I wonder if all the people at Acme are as inept as you.

Needless to say, you have misread your warranty agreement.

It goes without saying that your suggestion is not worth considering.

Courteous

Since the printer is still under warranty, I hope that you can make the repairs easily and quickly.

I would appreciate receiving a more detailed explanation from your home office about this matter.

Clause 17 in your warranty agreement does not cover the problem you have called to our attention.

It was thoughtful of you to send me your suggestion but unfortunately we cannot implement it right now.

The last two examples above begin with phrases that frequently set readers on edge. It's best to avoid using *needless to say* or *it goes without saying* since they can quickly set up a barrier between a reader and writer.

4. Be neither boastful nor meek. These two strategies—one based on pride and the other on humility—often lead inexperienced letter writers into trouble. On the one hand, they believe that a forceful statement will make a good impression on the reader. Or perhaps they think that a cautious and humble approach will be the least offensive way to earn the reader's respect. Both paths are wrong.

Aggressive letters, filled with boasts, rarely appeal to readers. Letters should radiate confidence without sounding as if the writer had written a letter of self-recommendation. Letters should let the facts speak directly and pleasantly for themselves. The sentences on the left boast; those on the right capture confidence with grace.

Boastful

You will find me the most diplomatic employee you ever hired.

The Sun and Sea unqualifyingly promises the nicest rooms on the Coast.

I have performed that procedure so many times I can do it in my sleep.

The Check-Pack offers you incomparable customer convenience.

Graceful

Much of my previous work has been in answering and adjusting customer complaints.

Each room at the Sun and Sea has its own private bath and bar refrigerator.

I have performed all kinds of IV therapy as part of standard procedure.

The Check-Pack gives you a free safe-deposit box.

At the other extreme, some writers stress only their own inadequacy. Their attitude as projected in their letters is "I am the most unworthy person who ever lived, and I would be eternally grateful if you even let my letter sit on your desk, let alone open it." Readers will dismiss such writers as pitiful, unqualified weaklings. Note how the meek sentences on the left are rewritten more positively on the right.

Meek	Positive
I know that you have a busy schedule and do not always have time to respond, but I would be appreciative if you could send me your brochure on how to apply Brakelite.	Please send me your brochure on how to apply Brakelite.
I know the season is almost over, but could you possibly let me know something about rates for the rest of the summer.	I am interested in renting a cabin in late August (24–30) and would like to know about your rates for that week.
I will be grateful for whatever employment opportunities you could kindly give me.	I will welcome the opportunity to discuss my qualifications with you.

◆ USING THE MOST EFFECTIVE LANGUAGE IN YOUR LETTERS

For many people, the hardest part of writing letters is putting their ideas into the right language. An effective letter may require several drafts and revisions. Even a short letter (1–2 paragraphs) needs to be revised until it sends the exact message conveyed in the right tone to your reader. Three simple suggestions can help. Your letters should be (1) clear, (2) concise, and (3) contemporary. Regard these principles of letter writing as the three C's.

1. Be clear. Clarity obviously is the most important quality of a business letter. If your message cannot be understood easily, you have wasted your time. Confusion costs time and money. Plan what you are going to say—what your objective is—by taking a few minutes to jot down some questions you want answered or some answers to questions asked of you. Doing this will actually save you time. Review pages 26–27 in Chapter 2.

Choose precise details appropriate for your audience. In choosing exact words, answer the reader's five fundamental questions—who? what? why? where? and how? Supply concrete words, facts, details, numbers. On the left are some examples of vague sentences that will puzzle a reader because necessary details are missing. These sentences have been revised on the right, with exact words replacing unclear ones.

Vague	Clear
Please send me some copies of your recent brochure I can use at work.	Please send me 4 copies of your brochure on the new salt substitute to share with my fellow dietitians.
You can expect an appraisal in the next few weeks.	You will receive an estimate on the installation of a new 50,000 BTU air-conditioning unit no later than July 12.
One of our New York stores carries that product.	Our store at 856 East Fifth Avenue sells the entire line of Texworld gloves.

Vague	Clear
I would like some information about your scheduling policies to Rio de Janeiro.	Please let me know if Worldwide Air has a weekday morning flight to Rio de Janeiro and how far in advance reservations would have to be made for that flight.
The fee for that service is nominal.	The fee for caulking the five windows on the first floor will be $45.

2. Be concise. "Get to the point" is one of the most frequent commands in the business world. A concise letter does not ramble; instead, it is easy to read and to act on. As you draft and then revise your letter, ask yourself these two questions: (1) What is the main message I want to tell my reader? (2) Does every sentence and paragraph stick to the main point? The secret to efficient correspondence is to get to the main point at once, as in the following examples.

Your order will be delivered by July 26, as you requested.

I am happy to confirm the figures we discussed in our telephone conversation last Wednesday.

I request an extension of two weeks in paying my note.

Please accept our apologies for the damaged Movak shipped to you last week.

Here is the report you asked our accountant to prepare. It does contain the new figures on the Manchester store you wanted.

Many letter writers get off to a deadly slow start by repeating, often word for word, the contents of the letter to which they are responding.

First Draft
I have your letter of March 23 before me in which you ask if our office knows of any all—electric duplexes for rent less than five years old and that would be appropriate for senior citizens. You also ask if these duplexes are close to shopping and medical facilities.

Revised
Thank you for your letter of March 23. Our office does rent all—electric duplexes suitable for senior citizens. We have two units, each renting for $375 a month, that are four blocks from the Mendez Clinic and two blocks from the Edgewater Mall.

Another way to write a concise letter is to include only material that is absolutely relevant. In a letter complaining about inadequate or faulty telephone service, mentioning color preferences for extension telephones would be inappropriate. In a request for information on transferring credits from one college to another, do not ask about intramural sports.

Finally, make sure that your letter is not wordy (review the pertinent sections of Chapters 4 and 5, pages 83–87, 102–05). By taking a few minutes to revise your letters before they are typed, you can write shorter, more useful letters.

3. Be contemporary. Being contemporary does not mean you should use slang expressions ("I had a tire ripped off"; "That rejection was a bummer") or informal language that is inappropriate ("Doing business with Bindex is a hassle"). Nor should you go to the other extreme and become too stiff and formal. Sound friendly and natural. Write to your reader as if you were carrying on a professional conversation with him or her. Business letters today are upbeat, simple, and direct. A business letter is readable and believable; it should not be old-fashioned and flowery.

Often individuals are afraid to write naturally because they fear that they will not sound important. They resort to using phrases that remind them (and the reader) of "legalese"—language that smells of contracts, deeds, and starched collars. The following list of words and phrases on the left contains musty expressions that have crept into letters for years; the list on the right contains modern equivalents.

Musty Expression	Modern Equivalent
aforementioned	previously mentioned
ascertain	find out
at this present writing	now
I am in receipt of	I have
attached herewith	enclosed
at your earliest possible date	soon
I beg to differ	I disagree
we beg to advise	we believe, think
I am cognizant of	I know
contents duly noted	we realize
forthwith	at once
hereafter, heretofore, hereby	(drop these three "h's" entirely)
we humbly request	we ask
immediate future	soon
in lieu of	instead of
kindly advise	let us know
pursuant	concerning
please be advised that	I am happy (or sorry) to tell you that
please find enclosed	I'm enclosing
pending your reply	until I hear from you
per our conversation	when we spoke
prior to	before
we regret to inform you that	we are sorry that
remittance	payment
remuneration	cost, salary, pay
rest assured that	you can be sure that
your letter arrived and I have same	I have your letter
thanking you in advance	thank you
the undersigned / the writer	I
under separate cover	I'm also sending you
the wherewithal	the way
yours of recent date	your recent letter
your communication	your phone call, your memo, your order

FIGURE 6.9   A letter using stilted, old-fashioned language.

```
    23 Babson Court
    Chicago, IL 60648-1489
    May 1, 1990

    Professor Bernard Jackson
    Department of English
    Harrison College
    Chicago, IL 60649-1672

    Dear Professor Jackson:

    Please accept my humblest apologies for being absent on the
    24th when the examination you were giving was in progress. Per
    your request at the commencement of the term, I am cognizant
    of my responsibility to advise you about the cause of my
    absence. Herewith is an explanation to that effect.

    I am sorry to inform you that my automobile was impaired due
    to the fact that one of the tires was punctured when I was en
    route to your classroom. Please be advised that I took every
    precaution to avoid this puncture but the burden of travel
    made such attention on my part ineffective. Lest you doubt my
    excuse, I herewith enclose a copy of my indebtedness to a
    local repair shop for road service. My situation was such that
    I was forced to accompany the mechanic to the repair facility.
    Accordingly, I thereby failed to attend your class.

    The aforementioned disruption in my schedule will not occur
    again this term. But I beg permission to take the examination
    in question at your earliest possible convenience. Pending
    your reply, this writer will diligently prepare for said
    examination.

    At this present point in time, I wish to express my sincerest
    gratitude to you and eagerly anticipate our future meeting.

    Your dedicated student,

    Roger Hayes
    Roger Hayes

    Encl.
```

Figure 6.9 contains a flowery letter from Roger Hayes to his English teacher. Note how many old-fashioned, pompous expressions he uses. Figure 6.10 contains a modern translation of the same letter.

FIGURE 6.10   A clear and concise revision of Figure 6.9.

```
23 Babson Court
Chicago, IL 60648-1489
May 1, 1990

Professor Bernard Jackson
Department of English
Harrison College
Chicago, IL 60649-1672

Dear Professor Jackson:

I am sorry that I missed the examination you gave on Moby-Dick
last Tuesday (April 24), but I do have a valid excuse. On my
way to class, I had a flat tire, and I had to go with the
mechanic when he repaired it. A copy of the bill is enclosed.

I would appreciate your allowing me to take a make-up
examination. I will come to your office during your office
hour on Monday to discuss this possibility with you.

Sincerely yours,

Roger Hayes

Roger Hayes

Encl.
```

If you can be clear, concise, and contemporary, your letters will be well writ-ten and well received. These three C's will establish your reputation as a com-petent writer whose letters are easy to understand and easy to answer courte-ously and promptly.

◆ TWENTY QUESTIONS LETTER WRITERS SHOULD ASK THEMSELVES

Here is a checklist of twenty questions you need to ask yourself before you send your letter out. If you answer "No" to any one of these questions, you need to do some more rewriting, remembering all elements of the writing process. These questions deal with the format, style, and content of your letter. If you can answer each one satisfactorily, you will be off to a good start at communicating effectively with your reader.

1. Does my letter look neat and professional?
2. Have I followed one letter format (full block, semiblock, or AMS simplified) consistently?
3. Are my margins wide enough—at least $1\frac{1}{2}$ inches all the way around?
4. Did I spell every word, including the reader's name, correctly?
5. Have I corrected every typographical error?
6. Did I tell the reader exactly why I am writing?
7. Does my letter adopt the "you attitude"?
8. Are my words clear and precise?
9. Is my letter free from flowery and stuffy language?
10. Do I get my message across politely and sincerely?
11. Have I answered the reader's questions without including irrelevant material?
12. Have I eliminated unnecessary repetition?
13. Are all my facts—costs, policy numbers, model types, dates, addresses—correct?
14. Have I included all necessary information—dates, quantities, locations, names, costs, references to previous orders or letters?
15. Does my last paragraph sum up my letter appropriately?
16. Have I chosen an appropriate complimentary close (for the full block or semiblock format)?
17. Did I sign the letter in ink?
18. Have I indicated an enclosure line if I am sending something with the letter?
19. Is my return address on the upper left front of the envelope?
20. Does the reader's name and address on the envelope match the inside address?

◆ EXERCISES

1. What kinds of letters do you receive addressed to you at home? At your work? Write a paragraph about one of these kinds of letters, indicating why it was sent to you and what it wanted you to do.

2. Find two business letters and bring them to class. Be prepared to identify the various parts of a letter discussed in this chapter.

3. Bring to class letters following the full block format, the semiblock format, and the AMS style. How do they differ in format?

4. Find a form letter that is addressed to "Dear Customer," "Postal Patron," or "Dear Resident" and rewrite it to make it more personal.

5. Correct the following inside addresses.

   a. Dr. Ann Clarke, M.D.
   1730 East Jefferson
   Jackson, MI. 46759

   b. To: Tommy Jones
   Secretary to Mrs. Franks
   Donlevey labs
   Cleveland, O. 45362

   c. Debbie Hinkle
   432 Parkway
   N. Y. C. 10054

   d. Mr. Charles Howe, Acme Pro.
   P.O. Box 675
   1234 S. e. Boulevard
   Gainesville, Flor. 32601

   e. Alex Goings, man.
   Pittfield Industries
   Longview, TEXAS 76450

   f. ATTENTION: G. Yancy
   Police Academy
   1329 Tucker
   N. O., La. 3410–70122

   g. David and Mahenny
   Lawyers
   Dobbs Build.
   L.A. 94756

   h. CONFIDENTIAL
   Jordon Foods, INC.
   Miller Str.
   Lincoln, Neb. 2103

6. Write appropriate inside addresses and salutations to (a) a woman who has not specified her marital status; (b) an officer in the armed forces; (c) a professor at your school; (d) an assistant manager at your local bank; (e) a member of the clergy; (f) your congressperson.

7. Which of the following complimentary closes is suitable for a business letter to someone you have never written to before and do not know?

Yours,	Cordially,	Very truly yours,
Gratefully yours,	Blissfully,	Happily yours,
Sincerely,	Thankfully yours,	Patiently yours,
Faithfully,	Yours truly,	Truly,

8. Find and correct the typographical errors in the following letter.

Dear MR. Jones;

I am very much enterested in finding a copy of your most recent brochure on nutrition. I am najoring in in foodscience at Westgatte Community Colledge and would appreciate obtainning some infornation about your polcies and procedurs in the disrtibution of hot lucnchs in teh elemantery grades. Your extenaive operatiom in this area has been priased for its thoroghness nad flexibilty.

If you have any copies of this borchure, or other instructons I mihgt see, I would like to use them in my class repotrs. With yoor permision, I would like to shafe these materials with my homeeconomics calss.

Sincerly yours,

J. P. Allen

J. P. Allen

9. Rewrite the following sentences to make them more personal.
   a. It becomes incumbent upon this office to cancel order #2394.
   b. Management has suggested the curtailment of parking privileges.
   c. ALL USERS OF HYDROPLEX: Desist from ordering replacement valves during the period of Dec. 19–29.
   d. The request for a new catalog has been honored; it will be shipped to same address soon.
   e. Perseverance and attention to detail have made this writer important to company in-house work.
   f. The Director of Nurses hereby notifies staff that a general meeting will be held Monday afternoon at 3:00 P.M. sharp. Attendance is mandatory.
   g. Reports will be filed by appropriate personnel no later than the scheduled plans allow.

10. The following sentences are discourteous, boastful, excessively humble, vague, or do not reflect the "you attitude." Rewrite them to correct these mistakes.
    a. Something is obviously wrong in your head office. They have once more sent me the wrong model number. Can they ever get things straight?
    b. My instructor wants me to do a term paper on safety regulations at a small factory. Since you are the manager of a small factory, send me all the information I need at once. My grade depends heavily on all this.
    c. It is apparent that you are in business to rip off the public.
    d. I was wondering if you could possibly see your way into sending me the local chapter president's name and address, if you have the time, that is.
    e. I have waited for my confirmation for two weeks now. Do you expect me to wait forever or can I get some action?
    f. Although I have never attempted to catalog books before, and really do not know my way around the library, I would very much like to be considered at some later date convenient to you for a part-time afternoon position.
    g. It goes without saying that we cannot honor your request.
    h. May I take just a moment of your valuable time to point out that our hours for the next three weeks will change and we trust and pray that no one in your agency will be terribly inconvenienced by this.
    i. Your application has been received and will be kept on file for six months. If we are interested in you, we will notify you. If you do not hear from us, please do not write us again. The soaring costs of correspondence and the large number of applicants make the burden of answering pointless letters extremely heavy.

j. My past performance as a medical technologist has left nothing to be desired.

k. Credit means a lot to some people. But obviously you do not care about yours. If you did, you would have sent us the $49.95 you rightfully owe us three months ago. What's wrong with you?

11. The following letter, wordy and awkward, is filled with musty expressions. It buries key ideas and does not consider the reader's needs. Rewrite this letter to make it shorter, clearer, and more reader-centered.

Dear Ms. Granedi:

This is in response to your firm's letter of recent date inquiring about the types of additional services that may be available to business customers of the First National Bank of Bentonville. The question of a possible time frame for the implementation of said services was also raised in the aforementioned letter. Pursuant to these queries, the following answers, this office trusts, will prove helpful.

Please be advised that the Board of Directors at First National Bank has a continuing reputation for servicing the needs of the Bentonville community, especially the business community. For the last fifty years—half of a century—First National Bank has provided the funds necessary for the growth, success, and expansion of many local firms, yours included. This financial support has bestowed many opportunities on a multitude of business owners, residents of Bentonville, and even residents of surrounding local communities.

The Board is at this present writing currently deliberating, with its characteristic caution, over a variety of options suggested to us by our patrons, including your firm. These options, if the Board decides to act upon them, would enhance the business opportunities for financial transactions at First National Bank. Among the two options receiving attention by the Board at this point in time are the creation of a branch office in the rapidly growing north side of Bentonville. This area has many customers who rely on the services of First National Bank. The Board may also place a business loan department in the new branch.

If this office of the First National Bank of Bentonville might be of further helpful assistance, please advise. Remember banking with First National Bank is a community privilege.

Soundly yours,

M. T. Watkins

M. T. Watkins
Public Relations Director

12. Write a business letter to one of the following individuals and submit an appropriate envelope with your letter.
   a. your mayor, asking for an appointment and explaining why you need one
   b. your college president, stressing the need for more parking spaces or computer terminals in a library
   c. the local water department, asking for information about fluoride supplements
   d. an editor of a weekly magazine, asking permission to reprint an article in a school newspaper
   e. the author of an article you have read recently, telling why you like or dislike the views presented
   f. a disc jockey at a local radio station, asking for more songs by a certain group
   g. a computer dealer, asking about software packages and explaining your company's special needs

How to Get a Job:
Résumés, Letters, Applications,
Interviews, and Evaluations

Obtaining a job today involves a lot of hard work. Before your name is added to the payroll, you will have to do more than simply walk into a personnel office and fill out an application form. Furthermore, finding the *right* job takes time. And finding the right person to fill that job also takes time for the employer. From the employer's viewpoint, the stages in the search for a valuable employee include the following:

1. deciding on what duties and responsibilities go with the job and determining the qualifications the future employee should possess
2. advertising the job
3. reading and evaluating résumés and letters of application
4. having candidates complete application forms
5. requesting further proof of the candidates' skills—letters of recommendation, transcripts
6. interviewing selected candidates
7. offering the job to the best-qualified individual

Sometimes these steps are interchangeable, especially steps 4 and 5, but generally speaking, employers go through a long and detailed process to select employees. Step 3, for example, is among the most important for employers (and the most crucial for job candidates). At this stage employers often classify job seekers into one of three groups: those they definitely want to interview; those they may want to interview; and those they have no interest in.

As a job seeker you will have to know how and when to give the employer all the kinds of information the seven steps require. You will also have to follow a certain schedule in your search for a job. The following eight procedures will be required of you:

1. analyzing your strengths and restricting your job search
2. preparing a dossier (placement file)
3. looking in the right places for a job
4. constructing a résumé
5. writing a letter of application
6. filling out a job application
7. going to an interview
8. accepting or declining a job

Your timetable should match that of your prospective employer.

Chapter 7 shows you how to begin your job search and how to prepare appropriate letters that are a part of the job-search process. You will need to write a letter of application, letters requesting others to write recommendations for you, letters thanking employers for interviews, and letters accepting or declining a position. In addition to discussing each of these kinds of letters, this chapter shows you how to assemble the supporting data—dossiers, résumés—that employers request. You will also find some practical advice on how to handle yourself at an interview. The chapter concludes with the kinds of evaluations—of yourself and of others—that you can expect to write once you have worked on your job.

The eight steps of your job search are arranged in this chapter in the order in which you are most likely to proceed when you start looking for a job. By reading about these stages in sequence, you will have the benefit of going through a dry run of the employment process itself.

◆ ANALYZING YOUR STRENGTHS AND RESTRICTING YOUR JOB SEARCH

Individuals who advise students about how to get a job have isolated two "fatal assumptions" that many job seekers hold. If you assume the following two points, chances are that you will *not* be very successful in your job search.[1]

1. I should remain loose (vague) about what I want so I'm free to respond to any opportunity.
2. The employer has the upper hand in the whole process.

The first "fatal assumption" will disqualify you for any position for which your major has prepared you. Your first responsibility is to identify your professional qualifications. Employers want to hire individuals with highly developed technical skills and training. Your education and experience should help you to identify and emphasize your marketable skills. Make an inventory of your accomplishments in your major or job and then decide which specialty within your chosen career appeals to you most. If you are enrolled in a criminal justice program, do you want a position as a corrections officer, a security official, or a member of the local police force? If you are in a nursing program, do you want to work in a large

---

[1] Lewis E. Patterson and Ernest M. Schuttenberg, *College Board Review* (Fall 1979): 15.

hospital, a nursing home, or a state health agency; what kinds of patients do you want to care for—geriatric, pediatric, psychiatric? If your major is food science, do you want to be a caterer or a restaurant owner, or would you rather work for an industrial or hospitality employer? If you already hold a position and want to advance yourself professionally, ask yourself where you would like to relocate and what type of additional responsibilities you want to assume. In short, ask yourself: Where do I want to work and why?

Avoid applying for positions for which you are either overqualified or under-qualified. If a position requires ten years of on-the-job experience and you are just starting out, you will only waste the employer's time, and your own, by applying. On the other hand, if you have two or three years of experience in the food industry, for example, you would not apply for a position that calls for someone who has no training.

The second "fatal assumption"—assuming that the employer controls the entire job-search process—is equally misleading. To a large extent, you can determine whether you are a serious contender for a job by the letters and résumés you write and the self-image you present. Even in today's highly competitive job market, you can secure a suitable job if you keep in mind that the basic purpose of all job correspondence is to sell yourself. Letters and résumés are sales tools to earn you an interview and eventually the job. Be confident and convincing. Employers almost always have a shortage of good, qualified employees.

◆ PREPARING A DOSSIER

The job placement office or career center at your school will assist you by providing counseling; notifying you of available, relevant jobs; and arranging on-campus interviews. The job placement office may also help you establish your dossier, sometimes referred to as your placement file.

The *dossier,* a French word for a bundle of documents, is your own personal file that is stored at the placement office. This file contains information about you that substantiates and supplements the facts you will list in your résumé and letter of application. Your dossier should contain your letters of recommendation; copies of these letters are made and sent out to prospective employers, thus relieving those who have recommended you of writing an original letter each time you apply for a job. You may also want to include unsolicited letters—those awarding you a scholarship, praising you as the employee of the month, or honoring you for some community service. Be very selective about these kinds of letters; you do not want to crowd your dossier with less important items that will compete for attention with your academic recommendations. The dossier also contains biographical information, a listing of your job experiences, and your academic transcript(s). You may ask that your dossier be sent to an employer; or employers may request it themselves if you have listed the placement office address on your résumé.

The most important part of your dossier is the letter-of-recommendation section. Whom should you ask to recommend you? Your present or previous employer (even for a summer job) is a logical choice, but be cautious here. If your current employer knows that your education is preparing you for another profession, or if you are working at a part-time job while you are in school, you should obtain a letter of recommendation to be included in your dossier. If you are happily and successfully employed and are looking for a new position only for professional advancement or a better salary, you may not want your present employer to know that you are searching for a new job. You have the right to request a prospective employer to respect your confidence (for instance, not to call you at work) until you become a leading candidate. At that point you may be happy to have your current employer consulted for a reference. On the other hand, if you are on bad terms with your current employer and want very much to find a new, more suitable position, you need to inform the prospective employer as honestly and professionally as you can with the least damage to yourself. No sure solution exists.

Be sure to ask two or three of your professors to be references. Choose teachers who know and like your work, have graded your papers, and have supervised you in fieldwork or laboratory activities. Superiors who knew your work in the military are also likely candidates. Recommendations from these individuals will be regarded as more objective than a letter from a member of the clergy or from a neighbor. Of course, if you are asked specifically for a character reference, by all means ask a member of the clergy.

Make sure that you ask permission of these individuals before you list them as references. This is a courtesy, and it will also give them time to write an appropriate letter for you. Imagine how damaging it would be for you if a prospective employer called one of your teachers whom you had not yet asked to serve as a reference. What if the teacher responded that he or she did not even know you were looking for a job or, worse yet, said you had not had the courtesy to ask to use his or her name as a reference? When you ask for permission in a letter or in person, stress how much a strong letter of support means to you and find out if the individual is willing to write such a letter. It is important to emphasize that you need a strong letter of recommendation; a general or weak one will hurt your chances in your job search. As a help to your references, tell them what kind of jobs you are applying for and keep them up to date about your educational and occupational achievements. Figure 7.1 shows a sample letter requesting an individual to serve as a reference.

You have a legal right to determine whether you want to see your letters or not. If you have read your recommendations, that fact is noted on the dossier. Some employers feel that if the candidates see what is written about them, the writers of the letters of recommendation will be less frank and even unwilling to volunteer critical information. If you waive your right to see the letters written about you, you must sign an appropriate form, a copy of which is then given to the individual recommending you. Keep in mind, too, that some individuals may refuse to write a letter that they know you will see; they may prefer absolute confidentiality. Figure 7.2 shows a confidential evaluation form. Before you make any decision about seeing your letters, get the advice of your instructors and your placement counselor.

FIGURE 7.1   Request for a letter of recommendation.

```
5432 South Kenneth Avenue
Chicago, IL 60651
March 30, 1990


Mr. Sonny Butler, Manager
A&P Supermarket
4000 West 79th Street
Chicago, IL 60652-4300

Dear Mr. Butler:

As you may recall, I was employed at your store from September
1988 through August 1989. During the school year, I worked
part-time as a stock clerk and relief cashier, while in the summer
months I was a full-time employee in the produce department,
helping to fill in while Bill Dirksen and Vivian Rogers were away
on their vacations.

I enjoyed my work at A&P, and I learned a great deal about
ordering stock, arranging merchandise, and assisting customers.

This May I expect to receive my A.A. degree from Moraine Valley
Community College in retail merchandising. I have already begun
preparing for my job search for a position in retail sales. Would
you be kind enough to write a letter of recommendation for me in
which you mention what you regard as my greatest strengths as one
of your employees? If you agree, I will send you a letter of
recommendation form from the Placement Office at Moraine Valley.
Your letter will then become a part of my permanent placement
file.

I look forward to hearing from you. I thought you might like to
see the enclosed résumé, which shows what I have been doing since
I left A&P.

Sincerely yours,

Robert B. Jackson
Robert B. Jackson

Encl. Résumé
```

Do not wait until you begin applying for jobs to establish your dossier. Most placement offices recommend that candidates set up their dossiers at least three to six months before they begin looking for jobs. You will thus ensure that your letters of recommendation are on file and that you have benefited from the placement office's services. In counseling you, the placement office will ask that you

FIGURE 7.2   A confidential evaluation form.

Return this form to:

**OFFICE OF CAREER DEVELOPMENT & PLACEMENT
VALDOSTA STATE COLLEGE
Valdosta, Georgia 31601**

CONFIDENTIAL EVALUATION

TO THE CANDIDATE: (type in)

Candidate's
Full Name _____   Name of
              first   middle   last   Reference _____

Courses under this instructor (title, quarter, year) or Period of employment _____

_____

Today's date _____ Your (anticipated) date of graduation _____ Degree program _____

TO THE TEACHER OR EMPLOYER:

Please note that this is a confidential evaluation. The candidate has waived his or her right of access to this evaluation. We shall appreciate both a rating and a statement regarding the candidate's suitability for employment. Your evaluation will become a permanent part of his or her placement record which is made available to employers and graduate schools. *Do not show it to the candidate.* Also, *please type* this form if possible. Blue ink does not duplicate clearly. Once this form is on file you may refer future requests concerning this candidate to the Career Development & Placement Office for a reply.

Indicate degree of acquaintance with candidate:

Length of acquaintance: _____

☐ Know personally

☐ Know as a student

☐ Know only as a member of a large class

☐ Know as an employee

	Unable to Observe	Excellent	Above Average	Average	Below Average	Poor
Appearance						
Academic Performance (within subject (s) under your supervision)						
Promptness in assignments; regularity of attendance						
Ability to communicate: Orally						
In Writing						
Initiative						
Leadership						
Social qualities (congeniality, interest in others)						
Promise in _____ (specify field)						
Suitability for graduate school						

STATEMENT: (Please elaborate on the above and comment on any other appropriate points. This statement is considered an <u>important</u> part of the total evaluation.)

Signature _____

Title & Dept. _____

Institution or Organization _____

Date: _____   Address _____

Reprinted by permission of Office of Career Development and Placement, Valdosta State College.

complete a confidential questionnaire about your geographic preferences, salary expectations, and the types of positions for which you are qualified. With this information on hand, the placement office will be better prepared to advise you and to notify you of appropriate openings.

Some placement offices will charge a small fee for their services, while others provide their services free of charge.

◆ LOOKING IN THE RIGHT PLACES FOR A JOB

One way to search for a job is simply to send out a batch of letters to companies you want to work for. But how do you know what jobs, if any, these companies have available, what qualifications they are looking for, and what application procedures and deadlines they want you to follow? You can avoid these uncertainties by knowing where to look for a job and knowing what a specific job requires. Such information will make your search easier and, in all likelihood, more successful. Here are a number of sources to consult.

1. Do not overlook the obvious: the newspaper. Look at local newspapers as well as papers with a wide circulation: the *New York Times,* the *Chicago Tribune,* the *Los Angeles Times,* the *New Orleans Times-Picayune,* the *Cleveland Plain Dealer.* The Sunday editions usually advertise positions available all over the country. The *National Business Employment Weekly,* published by the *Wall Street Journal,* lists jobs in many different areas, including technical and managerial. The ads you find may list the name, address, and phone number of the company seeking employees or may be "blind," that is, listing only a post office box to conceal the employer's identity.

2. Investigate openings listed in professional journals in your major. The *American Journal of Nursing,* for example, carries notices of openings arranged by geographic location in each of its monthly issues; and *Food Technology* prints in each issue a section called "Professional Placement," which lists jobs from all over the country.

3. Visit your college's placement office. Counselors keep an up-to-date file of available positions and can also tell you when a firm's recruiter will be on campus to conduct interviews. They can also help you locate summer and part-time work, both on and off campus.

When you visit the placement office, also examine a current issue of the *College Placement Annual,* a useful catalog that lists the addresses of more than one thousand employers in business, industry, and government. The *CPA* also gives information on the kinds of requirements job candidates are expected to have for these positions.

4. Check with your state and local employment offices. They also have a current file of positions and offer some counseling (free of charge). Some educational television stations even broadcast information (qualifications, salary) about positions on file at a state employment office. If you are interested in working for the U.S. government, visit a Civil Service Commission Office, a Federal Job Information Center, or any government agency. Get the addresses from the white pages of your phone book.

5. Visit the personnel department of a company or agency to see if there are any current openings or if any vacancies are anticipated. Often you will be given an application to fill out even if there is not a current opening, or your name will be placed on a list. But do not call employers asking about openings. A visit shows a more serious interest. Also, they are more likely to re-member you if a job does develop. New openings often arise unexpectedly in business and industry.

6. Let your relatives, friends, neighbors, and professors know that you are looking for a job. They may hear of something and can notify you. Bet-ter yet, they may recommend you for the position—with a phone call, a trip to the personnel department (if they work for the company), or a letter. A respected employee can open the door for you. John D. Erdlen and Donald H. Sweet, ex-perts on the job search, cite the following as a primary rule of job hunting: "Don't do anything yourself you can get someone with influence to do for you."

7. Write to your local Chamber of Commerce. Though not a placement center, the Chamber of Commerce can give you the names and addresses of em-ployers likely to hire individuals with your qualifications, as well as information about these companies to use in a letter of application or at an interview.

8. Register with a professional employment agency. Some agencies list two kinds of jobs—those that are found for the applicant free of charge (be-cause the employer pays the fee) and those for which the applicant pays a fee. Sometimes that fee can be stiff—for example, a percentage of your first year's salary. Employment agencies often find out about jobs through channels already available to you. Before turning your search over to a professional employment agency, however, make sure that you have exhausted all the previously men-tioned services and be sure to ask who pays the fee for the service.

◆ PREPARING A RÉSUMÉ

The résumé, sometimes called a data sheet or curriculum vitae, is a factual and concise summary of your qualifications for the job. It is not your life's history or an emotional autobiography, nor is it a transcript of your college work. The résumé is a one-page (no more than two-page) outline accompanying your letter of application for a job. Résumés are never sent alone. You may, however, bring one with you to an interview. The main function of the résumé is to present in-formation about your education, experience, and other achievements accurately and quickly so that a busy personnel manager or department head will want to in-terview you. The résumé should make a good first impression.

The Process of Drafting Your Résumé

As with other types of writing, preparing your résumé requires that you work through a process. You cannot produce a polished résumé in an hour. But having a clear idea about the type of job you want and your qualifications for it should get you off to a good start.

Begin with the prewriting strategies discussed in Chapter 2 (pages 27–29) to identify your strengths and achievements. Write down everything you think is a skill or achievement—from jobs (full- or part-time, summer), school (course-work, workshops, labs, extracurricular activities, sports) the military, or community work. Do not overlook skills you have in operating equipment (particularly computers). Circle or underline any awards or honors as well as responsibilities you have had. Don't be worried if you produce a rather lengthy list of seemingly unrelated activities. From this brainstormed list (or clustered grouping) you will have a working inventory of accomplishments from which you can begin to restrict and organize material for the final copy of your résumé.

The next step is to be highly critical of your working inventory. Cross off any repetitions, eliminate unimportant or irrelevant items, try to sort items into related categories, and add whatever information you think is valuable.

As you criticize and supplement your list, examine your accomplishments the way a prospective employer might. The chief question an employer will ask about you (and all other applicants) is: "What can this person do for our company?" Employers are results-oriented; they read résumés looking for clear proof of your marketable skills. You have to convince your reader (or group of readers, since résumés often circulate among a hiring committee) that you have succeeded in the past and will do so in the future. Pay special attention to your four or five most significant, job-worthy strengths and work especially hard on them. While not everything you have done might relate directly to a particular job, indicate how your own achievements might be relevant to the employer's specific needs. For example, responsibility in handling money or supervising others in a grocery store establishes your ability to do the same things in another business context.

Keep in mind that all employers are looking for employees who are intelligent, cooperative, and responsible. Employers want to hire people who can communicate well, organize effectively, learn material quickly, and be team players. Your résumé (like your letter of application) needs to demonstrate that you have done these things in a previous job, in school, or in another organization. Again, by revising your résumé with the employer's needs in mind, you can be appropriately selective and persuasive.

When you have what seems like a final draft, show your résumé to two or three people whose opinion you value, individuals who may have what is called "business sense." Ask a teacher, placement counselor, or someone who has worked in the profession for a number of years to criticize your résumé the way a prospective employer would. You might also ask someone you know who is already employed by the company you are interested in to read your résumé and point out things you need to add, delete, emphasize, or rearrange.

How Much Should You Include on a Résumé?

How much should you include on your résumé? Both experienced candidates and recent graduates with limited experience ask this question. The dangers involve including too much or putting in too little. If you have years of experience and have recently returned to school, you may risk flooding your prospective employer with too many details. You cannot possibly include every detail of your job(s) for the last ten or twenty years. Therefore, you must be selective and emphasize only those skills and positions most likely to earn you the job. Figure 7.3 shows a résumé from Anna Cassetti, an individual who had years of job experience before she returned to school.

Many job candidates who have spent most of their lives in school are faced with the other extreme: not having much job experience to put down. The worst thing to do is to write "None" for experience. Any part-time or summer job, as well as volunteer work done at school for a library or science laboratory, shows a prospective employer you are responsible and knowledgeable about the obligations of being an employee. Figure 7.4 shows a résumé from Anthony Jones, a student with very little job experience; Figure 7.5 shows one from Maria Lopez, a student with a few years of experience.

What Should You Exclude from a Résumé?

Knowing what to exclude from a résumé is as important as what to include. Here are some details to exclude from your résumé:

- salary demands or expectations
- preferences for work schedules, days off, or overtime
- comments about fringe benefits
- travel restrictions
- your photograph (unless you are applying for a modeling or acting job)
- comments about your family, spouse, or children
- height, weight, hair or eye color

Save any questions or preferences you have for the interview. The résumé should be written appropriately to get you that interview.

Parts of a Résumé

Name, Address, Phone

Center this information at the top of the résumé under the word RÉSUMÉ. (Capitalize the word RÉSUMÉ and be sure to add the two accent marks by hand if your typewriter or printer cannot.) Capitalize all the letters of your name to make it stand out, but do not capitalize every letter of your address. Include a zip code and telephone number with a proper area code so a prospective employer can

FIGURE 7.3 Résumé from an individual with ten years' job experience.

RÉSUMÉ
Anna C. Cassetti
6457 South Blackstone Avenue
Fort Worth, Texas 76321-6733
(817) 234-5657 (Home)
(817) 432-7211 (Office)

Career Objective Full-time sales position with large real estate office in the Phoenix or Tucson area with specific opportunities in real estate appraisal and tax counseling.

Experience

1988–present *MacMurray Real Estate, Haltom City, Texas*
Real estate agent. Worked in small office (two salespersons plus broker) with limited listings; sold individually $850,000 in residential property; appraised both residential and commercial listings.

1982–1987 *Dallman Federal Savings and Loan, Inc., Fort Worth, Texas*
Chief Teller. Responsible for supervising, training, and coordinating activities of six full-time and two part-time tellers. Promoted to Chief Teller, March 1985.

1982 (Jan.–May) *H&R Block, Westover Hills, Texas*
Tax consultant.

1979–1981 *Cruckshank's Hardware Store, Fort Worth, Texas*
Salesperson.

1975–1979 *U.S. Navy*
Honorably discharged with rank of Petty Officer, Third Class. Served as stores manager.

Education

1981–1987 *Texas Christian University, Fort Worth, Texas*
Awarded B.S. degree in Real Estate Management. Completed thirty-three hours in business and real estate courses with a concentration in real estate finance, appraising, and property management. Also completed nine hours in computer science and data processing. Wrote reports on appraisal procedures as part of supervised training program in my last term.

call you for an interview. If you have two addresses (home and school) it is wise to list them both. It is also perfectly acceptable to list two phone numbers if one of them is where you receive messages during the day and the other in the evening.

FIGURE 7.3   (Continued)

Cassetti 2

1980 (Sept.–Dec.)	*H&R Block, Westover Hills, Texas* Earned diploma in Basic Income Tax Preparation after completing intensive ten-week course.
1976–1977	*U.S. Naval Base, San Diego, California* Attended U.S. Navy's Supply Management School. Applied principles of stores management at Newport Naval Base.
Personal	Texas Realtor's License: 756a2737
Hobbies and Interests	Chair, Financial Committee, Grace Presbyterian Church, Fort Worth. Have also worked with Junior Achievement advising teenagers in business management. Enjoy golfing and hiking.
References	My complete dossier is available from the Placement Office, Texas Christian University College, Fort Worth, Texas 76119-6811.

Career Objective Statement

One of the first things a prospective employer reads is your career objective statement. Such a statement involves self-evaluation and will influence everything else you list. To write an effective one, ask yourself four basic questions: (1) What kind of job do I want? (2) What kind of job am I qualified for? (3) What kinds of

FIGURE 7.4   Résumé from a student with little job experience.

RÉSUMÉ

ANTHONY H. JONES
73 Allenwood Boulevard
Santa Rosa, California 95401-1074
(707) 464-6390

CAREER OBJECTIVE:
Full-time position as a layout artist with a commercial publishing house.

EDUCATION:
1988–1990
Will receive A.S. degree in June from Santa Rosa Junior College, majoring in industrial graphics illustration with a specialty in layout design. Completed more than forty hours of classwork in design principles, layout and lettering, graphic communications, and photography. Am very familiar with both layout techniques and electromechanical illustration. Major projects included assisting layout editors at McAdam Publishers during an apprenticeship program completed in May 1990 and writing a detailed report on the kinds of designs, photographs, and artwork used in two local magazines--Living in Sonoma County and Real Estate in Sonoma County. Made Dean's List in 1989 with a GPA of 3.4.

1984–1988
Attended Santa Rosa High School. Took electives in drawing, photography, and industrial arts. Provided major artwork for student magazine, Thunder.

EXPERIENCE:
1988–1990
Worked part-time as salesperson at Buchman's Department Store while attending Santa Rosa Junior College full-time. Duties included assisting customers in sporting goods and appliance departments. Also assisted sport shop manager with displaying merchandise.

PERSONAL:
Volunteer work for Santa Rosa Humane Society-- designed posters for 1989 fund drive.

REFERENCES:

Mr. Albert Kim
Art Department
Santa Rosa Junior
  College
Santa Rosa, CA
  95401-1099
(707) 464-6300
	Ms. Margaret Feinstein
	Layout Editor
	McAdam Publishers
	Santa Rosa, CA 95401-1079
	(707) 453-8699

Dr. Gloria Cernek-Willis
Art Department
Santa Rosa Junior College
Santa Rosa, CA 95401-1099
(707) 464-6300

FIGURE 7.5   Résumé from a student with some job experience.

RÉSUMÉ

Maria H. Lopez
1725 Brooke Street
Miami, Florida 32701-2121
(305) 372-3429

Career Objective	Full-time position assisting dentist in providing dental health care and counseling and performing preventive dental treatments; especially interested in learning more about pedodontics.
Education August 1987– May 1989	**Miami-Dade Community College, Miami, Florida** Will receive A.S. degree in dental hygiene in May. Have completed nine courses in oral pathology, dental materials and specialties, periodontics, and community dental health. Currently enrolled in clinical dental hygiene program. Am familiar with procedures and instruments used with oral prophylaxis techniques. Subject of major project was proper nutrition for preschoolers. Minor area of interest is psychology (twelve hours completed). Received excellent evaluations in business writing course. GPA is 3.2. Plan to take American Dental Assistants Examination on June 2.
1980–1984	**Miami North High School, Miami, Florida** Took electives in electronics and secretarial science.
Experience April 1985– July 1987	**St. Francis Hospital, Miami Beach, Florida** Full-time unit clerk on the pediatric floor. Duties included ordering supplies, maintaining records, transcribing orders, and greeting and assisting visitors.
June 1984– April 1985	**Murphy Construction Company, Miami, Florida** Secretary-receptionist. Did light typing, filing, and mailing in small office (four employees).
Summers 1982–1983	**City of Hialeah, Florida** Water meter reader.
Personal	Health: Excellent; Bilingual: Spanish/English.

skills do I possess? (4) What kinds of skills do I want to learn? Do not apply for a position that requires experience you lack or demands skills you do not possess. On the other hand, do not give the impression that you will take anything.

Define your job goal precisely so that prospective employers can measure your experience and education against their needs. You may even want to tailor your career objective statement to correspond more closely to the description of

FIGURE 7.5   (Continued)

Lopez 2

Hobbies and   Swimming, reading (especially applied psychology), and
Interests   tennis. Have done volunteer work for church day-care
                         center.

References   The following individuals have written letters of
                         recommendation for my placement file, available from the
                         Placement Center, Miami-Dade Community College, Medical
                         Center Campus, Miami, FL 33127-2225.

Sister Mary James   Professor Mitchell Pellborne
Head Nurse, Pediatric Unit   Department of Dental Hygiene
St. Francis Hospital   Miami-Dade Community College
10003 Collins Avenue   Medical Center Campus
Miami Beach, FL 33141-4041   Miami, FL 33127-2223
(305) 432-5113   (305) 421-3872

Mildred Pecos, D.D.S.   Mr. Jack Murphy
9800 Exchange Avenue   Owner, Murphy Construction
Miami, FL 33167-6028   1203 Francis Street
(305) 421-1039   Miami, FL 33157-6819
                             (305) 421-6767

---

each specific job you are applying for. Rather than simply saying "sales work" or "law enforcement," concentrate on specific immediate and long-range goals within your chosen career, for example: "Full-time position with urban police force, eventually allowing me to gain experience in correctional counseling"; "Management trainee in personnel department, providing opportunity for professional growth and advancement in insurance counseling"; "Full-time position as staff nurse on medical-surgical unit with opportunity for primary care nursing." Demonstrate to your prospective employer your current level of competence and through a career objective statement, show your willingness to advance in the organization.

The order of the next two categories—education and experience—can vary. If experience is your best selling point, list it before education, as Anna Cassetti did in Figure 7.3. List education first if you are short on job experience, as Anthony Jones did in Figure 7.4.

Education

In listing your educational experiences, begin with your most recent education, and list everything significant since high school. Indicate when you received your latest degree, diploma, or certificate or when you expect to receive it. You need not list every school if you have transferred frequently. Do indicate your major and minor in college work and emphasize written and oral communications courses you have completed. Employers are impressed by students who can write and speak well. But remember, a résumé is not a transcript. Do not simply list a series of courses. Your goal is to convince your prospective employer that you have special abilities. Simply listing standard courses will not set you apart from hundreds of other applicants taking similar courses across the country. Moreover, an employer may not know exactly what might be covered in your college's advanced accounting course. Mention the number of credit hours you have completed and then indicate by subject area the courses in your major most relevant for the position for which you are applying.

Try to avoid vague titles such as Science 103 or Nursing IV. Instead, concentrate on the kinds of skills you learned. For example, "30 hours in planning and development courses specializing in transportation, land use, and community facilities and 12 hours in field methods of gathering, interpreting, and writing a description of survey data were required." Or state that "24 hours in my major included courses in business marketing, management, and materials in addition to 12 hours in computer science." Any computer skills you have are especially important to employers because of the increased use of computers in all areas of business and industry. Also note any laboratory work, fieldwork, internship, or cooperative educational work. It is important to an employer looking for someone with previous practical experience. List your GPA (grade point average) only if it is 3.0 or above and your rank in class only if you are in the top 35 percent. Otherwise, indicate your GPA in just your major or during your last term, if it is above 3.0.

Also list any academic honors you have won (dean's list, department awards, school honors, scholarships, grants, or honorable mentions). Indicate membership in any honor societies in your major because such participation will show that you are professionally active. You also should mention military schools, training programs (E.M.T., secretarial), institutes or special workshops, company-sponsored seminars you have attended, or any apprenticeships you have completed. If you have attended many of these learning programs, do not list your high school. Applicants with limited educational experience may include their high school, the date of graduation, and, if helpful, any special training related to their current work (shops, labs, trips) and any honors. As a rule, though, high school activities should be deemphasized.

Experience

This is the most important category for many employers. It shows them that you have held jobs before and that you are responsible. Beginning with your most recent position, include both full- and part-time work, and list the dates, company name, titles you held, and major responsibilities. Do not mention why you left a job. Give the most attention to your latest, most relevant position. If it happens to be your second most recent position, keep the correct order, but spend more time on it. Discuss jobs that you held eight or nine years ago only if your experiences then are relevant to the position you are looking for now. If these jobs were not relevant, just list the places of employment or do not mention them at all.

In describing your position, emphasize any responsibility you had that involved handling money, other employees, customer accounts, services, programs, or writing letters and reports. Prospective employers are interested in your leadership abilities, financial shrewdness, tact in dealing with the public, and communication skills. They are also favorably impressed by promotions you may have earned. Use strong, action verbs to pinpoint your duties and achievements. Here is a list of some attention-getting verbs:

administered	conducted	improved	oversaw
arranged	coordinated	increased	performed
assembled	developed	initiated	prepared
built	directed	instituted	researched
calculated	established	maintained	served
collected	handled	managed	supervised
completed	implemented	operated	wrote

Note that résumés are generally written in short sentences that omit the subject "I." See how this is done in Figures 7.3 and 7.4.

Don't just say you "worked for a newspaper"—your prospective employer won't know if you wrote editorials, sold advertising space, or delivered papers. Perhaps you were an assistant to the ads editor and were responsible for arranging and verifying copy. Say so. That is impressive and informative. Rather than saying that you were a secretary, indicate that you wrote business letters, organized files, prepared schedules for part-time help in an office of twenty-five people, or assisted the manager in preparing accounts. Of course, do not inflate your role to the point of calling a receptionist a "communications consultant" or a waiter a "food service manager." In describing your responsibilities, try to indicate how your work improved sales, service, or otherwise enhanced your former employer's business; for example, "Increased sales volume" or "Improved machine efficiency."

If you have held many jobs, which ones should you list, and which ones should you omit? As a general rule, indicate whatever positions are most relevant for the job you are seeking. Your summer job as a lifeguard who knew life-saving techniques may help you in getting a position as a respiratory therapist. Waiting on tables is good experience for candidates who want to obtain a position with a hospitality chain or a food-service organization. Do not forget jobs you may have had at school—stacking books in the library, typing for a teacher, cleaning buildings, tutoring. Employers are not impressed by baby-sitting or lawn-mowing jobs, however, unless you can relate those duties to the position you are seeking.

If you have had several jobs in the last ten or twenty years, list only those in which your responsibilities were significant and relevant to your present search for a job. Avoid stringing out five or six temporary jobs (each under three months). Combine all of them into one brief statement or omit them. Remember, space is at a premium on your résumé. If you have been a full-time mother of three for ten years before returning to school or the job market, list this information and note why you are reentering the business world. Indicate the management skills you developed in running a household.

Personal (Optional)

Federal employment laws prohibit discrimination on the basis of sex, race, national origin, religion, or marital status. But if you think that any of this personal information might help land you the job, then you are free to include it. For example, if you are applying for a sales position requiring extensive travel, mentioning that you are single would inform the employer that you do not have family obligations to restrict you. Moreover, if you are applying for a position in a child day-care center or one as a teacher's aide, the fact that you have children may be important to your employer. Other pertinent personal details include any foreign languages you speak or any special licenses and certificates you hold. For example, if you are bilingual in Spanish, Vietnamese, or French and are applying for a position in customer relations work in a bank or hospital, list that fact. It will be a drawing card with your employer. If you have already passed nursing state boards or earned a pilot's license, state that by indicating your appropriate license numbers. Ultimately, common sense dictates that you reveal only personal information that is required or that underscores your qualifications for the job.

Hobbies or Interests (Optional)

This category is of least value to a prospective employer, *if there is no connection between it and the rest of your résumé.* Of course, if a pastime, sport, or hobby has a direct bearing on the kind of job you are applying for or the kinds of subjects you studied in school, then by all means list and briefly describe it. For example, the following activities may be appropriate for careers listed after them: weight lifting for construction work; photography for advertising; volunteer work for nursing or social work; gardening for a horticultural position; civic work for law enforcement. Include extracurricular activities or community service especially if you held some office (treasurer of the local Lions Club, manager of a college basketball team). Exclude such obvious interests as reading, meeting new people, or traveling.

References

You can inform readers of your résumé that you will provide references on request or that they can obtain a copy of your dossier from your placement center; or you can list the names, titles, addresses, and telephone numbers of three or four individuals directly on your résumé. Prospective employers can then write to you, ask for your dossier, or directly write or call the individuals whose names have been given. Listing the names of your references is useful only when they are well known in a community or belong to the same profession in which you are seeking employment. In these cases you profit from the magic a recognizable name or title gives you.

Organizing Your Résumé by Function or Skill Areas

The résumés in Figures 7.3–7.5 are organized chronologically. Information about the job applicants is listed year by year under two main categories—Education and Experience. This is the traditional way to organize a résumé. It is straightforward, easy to read, and employers find it acceptable. The chronological sequence works especially well when you can show a clear continuity toward progress in your career through your job(s) and in schoolwork or when you want to apply for a similar job with another company. A chronological résumé is appropriate for students with limited experience who want to emphasize recent educational achievements.

But there are other ways to organize a résumé. Depending on your experiences and accomplishments, you might organize your résumé according to *function* or *skill areas*. According to this plan, you would *not* list your information chronologically within categories labeled "Experience" and "Education." Instead, you would sort your achievements and abilities—whether from coursework, jobs, extracurricular activities, or technical skills—into two to four key skill areas. Some of these areas might be labeled "Sales," "Public Relations," "Training," "Management," "Research," "Technical Capabilities," "Counseling," "Group Leadership," "Communications," "Working with People," and so forth. The important feature of a functional résumé is that you try to discover and emphasize those major strengths or skills that you believe a prospective employer is most interested in. In order to draft a functional résumé successfully, you must first have a clear idea about the type of job you are seeking.

Figure 7.6 shows what Anna Cassetti's chronological résumé (Figure 7.3) might look like if she had organized it according to function. Note how the three functional areas she selected ("Sales/Financial Management," "Public Relations," and "Business Communication") effectively allowed her to capitalize on her diverse experiences.

When you prepare a functional or skills résumé, start with your name, address, telephone number, and career objective, just as in a chronological résumé. To find the two to three functional areas, use the prewriting strategies (especially clustering and brainstorming) discussed in Chapter 2. Think of your skills areas as the common denominators that cross job and educational boundaries—the common threads that link and highlight your diverse experiences. After you discover

FIGURE 7.6   Résumé organized by function, or skill areas.

RÉSUMÉ
ANNA C. CASSETTI
6457 South Blackstone Ave.
Fort Worth, TX 76321-6733
(817) 234-5657 (Home)
(817) 432-7211 (Office)

CAREER OBJECTIVE	Full-time sales position with large real estate office in the Phoenix or Tucson area with specific opportunities in real estate appraisals and tax consulting
SALES/ FINANCIAL MANAGEMENT SKILLS	• Licensed (Texas) real estate appraiser with extensive knowledge of real estate codes, appraisal procedures, and market conditions • Achieved notable success in selling residential property in Fort Worth • Served as a tax consultant with special interest and competence in real estate sales • Performed general banking procedures as chief teller • Responsible for maintaining, purchasing, and ordering supplies for ship's stores in U.S. Navy
PUBLIC RELATIONS SKILLS	• Have developed positive, professional image in helping clients select appropriate property for their needs and income • Counseled commercial and individual clients in tax matters • Supervised, trained, and coordinated the activities of eight bank tellers • Established rapport in assisting customers with their banking needs • Chaired a financial committee at Grace Presbyterian Church, Fort Worth, Texas
BUSINESS COMMUNICATION SKILLS	• Prepared standard real estate appraisals • Wrote in-depth business reports on appraisal procedures, property management problems, and banking policies affecting real estate transactions

---

and suitably revise the information to be included in these categories, only briefly list your educational and work experiences, as Anna Cassetti does in Figure 7.6, without repeating details found earlier in the résumé.

A functional résumé has a number of advantages for some job seekers. Since it does not tie a job candidate to a strict chronological account, a functional

FIGURE 7.6   (Continued)

Cassetti 2

- Organized and maintained files using Corpsheet and other spreadsheet programs
- Addressed small groups successfully and frequently in both training and sales sessions

EDUCATION

B.S. in real estate management, 1987
Texas Christian University, Fort Worth.
Advanced course work taken in business, finance, and real estate; completed a minor in data processing

Diploma, Basic Income Tax Preparation, 1980
H&R Block, Westover Hills, Texas

EMPLOYMENT HISTORY

MacMurray Real Estate, Inc., Haltom City, Texas:
1988–present; one of two agents

Dallman Federal Savings and Loan, Inc., Fort Worth, Texas:
1982–1987; promoted to Chief Teller in 1985

H&R Block, Westover Hills, Texas:
Sept.–Dec. 1980; consultant, tax preparer

Cruckshank's Hardware Store, Fort Worth, Texas:
1979–1981; salesperson

U.S. Navy, San Diego, California (last duty station):
1975–1979; stores manager; honorably discharged with rank of Petty Officer, Third Class

HOBBIES AND INTERESTS

Golfing; hiking; have worked with Junior Achievement advising teenagers about business management

REFERENCES

Complete dossier is available from the Placement Office, Texas Christian University, Fort Worth, Texas 76119-6811.

résumé can offer a useful way to fill in gaps in education or employment. If you were laid off, left school for a year, or moved around, you do not have to worry about the gaps in time. A functional résumé also clearly emphasizes general skills acquired over a long period of time, so individuals with widely differing job experience may find it preferable to a chronological résumé. Finally, unlike a chronological résumé, a functional résumé does not force the job seeker to emphasize his or her most recent experience or educational achievements at the expense of an earlier accomplishment.

You might want to prepare two different versions of your résumé—a chronological as well as a functional one—to see which sells your talents best. Again, get the advice of your instructor or placement counselor about which one works best for you.

The Appearance of Your Résumé

The appearance of your résumé is as important as its content. It should be inviting and pleasing to the eye. Employers may receive as many as 200 résumés for one position and spend as little as 60 to 90 seconds on each. Preparing a résumé involves skills highly valued on the job—neatness, the ability to organize and summarize, and most important, a sense of proportion. If your résumé is professional looking, employers will predict that the work you do for them will be done the same way. A résumé can make that good first impression for you; a poorly prepared one assures that you will not get a second chance.

Given the short time employers spend scanning each résumé, you cannot expect them to hunt and peck for information about you. Help potential employers spot your achievements by making your résumé easy to read with wide margins, dark type, and clearly divided sections with headings. Employers will also be looking for accuracy (a spelling mistake can be fatal) and consistency.

There are a variety of ways you can prepare your résumé. You can take it to a printer, who for a relatively modest fee will phototypeset your résumé, giving it a highly professional look. This is what Anna Cassetti did (Figures 7.3 and 7.6). You will reap many advantages this way—your résumé will look neat, professional, crisp—but you will have to buy at least 25 to 50 copies of the same one. There is no way to tailor your résumé if the need arises; you cannot add, delete, or emphasize information as your job search progresses.

Another option is to have your résumé done on a word processor, as Maria Lopez did (Figure 7.5). You can take advantage of different sizes of type and use boldface or italics to separate and highlight information. Be careful, though, that you do not overuse these visual effects. You can also justify your margins (that is, make the right side of your résumé line up just as the left-hand side does). Perhaps the greatest advantage of putting your résumé on a disk is that you can easily add or delete information without having to type the entire résumé over again. Some software programs can even make your word-processed résumé look like it was typeset by a printer.

Still another option is to hire a professional typist to do your résumé. Be sure to explain in detail how you want it to look.

Whatever method you choose, keep in mind these important rules. Avoid the twin dangers of crowding information all over the page or of leaving huge, highly conspicuous chunks of white space at the bottom and sides. A crowded résumé suggests that you cannot summarize, whereas too much blank space points to a lack of achievements. You should, of course, leave white space between categories to emphasize certain points and to make reading your résumé easier. Study Figures 7.3–7.6 again. Type or print a number of rough drafts to experiment with spacing.

FIGURE 7.7 A poor résumé.

RÉSUMÉ

JAMES L. McPHERSON
33 North Platte Road *Poor alignment*
Noland, New Mexico *No zip code*
No telephone number

Spelling
PERSONNEL:

Spelling
Age: 22yrs. 6 mos. Wieght: 156 lbs
Not needed Marital Status: Engaged Height: 5'10" *Abbreviation*
Religion: Presbyterian Health: O.K. *Slang*

CAREER OBJECTIVE: I like to work outdoors and want
Poor typing to get any suitable job *Too broad*
in the forrestry industry.

EDUCATION: *Spelling*
1985–1989 Attended Noland Junior College,
Noland, N.M. 84546. I took courses
in English, Outdoor Recreation,
Listing courses at random Forrest Surveying, Forrest *Spelling*
says nothing about specific Management, Forest Economics,
skills Park Administration, Human
Spelling Rolations, Recreation
Margin Maintenance, Communications
and Mathematics, and Science. I
Why did better my secondyear *Typing*
mention? than my first. In my English and
Communications courses I wrote
Spelling papers and delivered sppeeches
about the forrest. Also, I went on
two or three lengthy field trips /
in the north. *Margin*
What skills did he learn?
Wrong 1885 I attended Noland Junior College
century part-time. *Why a separate entry?*

1984 I graduated from Noland High *Hyphen*
School, where I played basket*missing*
ball my third year and fourth year.
I also was the team co-captain.
Vague phrase Helped out with The Torch.
What is it?

FIGURE 7.7 (Continued)

Underscore EXPERIENCE: Worked for Walgreen's. Address:
             1984—1985 *Doing what?* 754 South Loma Blvd. Also I joined
           Abbreviation the N. Mexico National Guard. We
                            were sent to Ft. Carson for our
                            basic training.*Why mention Ft. Carson?*
                            What does he do in the Guard?

Capitalize <u>Hobbies:</u>   I like swimming, jogging, and water
                            polo.   *So what?*

           <u>REFERENCES:</u>

          Mr. Henry R. Pepeer   Dr. John Lyons   Alice McPherson
No   P.O. Box 768   Noland Junior College 33 N. Platte
telephone   Noland, N.M.   Noland, N.M.   Noland, N.M.
numbers   *Who is he?*   *What department?*   *Relative is not an*
or zip   *impartial reference*
codes

Print or type your résumé on good quality $8\frac{1}{2}'' \times 11''$ white or off-white bond paper (at least 20 lb. stock). In fact, recruiters in one study preferred white to colored paper.[2] Never use flimsy computer paper with perforated strips. If you use a word processor, avoid running your résumé off on a dot matrix printer. Use a letter-quality (or laser) printer.

Unlike your letter of application, you will not have to retype your résumé for each job you seek. Your prospective employer will not expect an original copy, but will expect a professional-looking copy. Never send a carbon, mimeographed, or thermofaxed copy of your résumé. And avoid rushing to the nearest photocopy machine in the library or student union to make a copy. It may come out with black dots or streaks on it. Try to locate the best-working photocopier you can.

Proofread your résumé to make sure that it is letter perfect. Ask two or three people to check it for you, too. Because you will be supplying many prospective employers with a copy of your résumé, a single error in it would appear each time you sent it out. Check and double-check the spelling of any words or names about which you may be unsure. Avoid strikeovers, crossed-out letters, or crookedly printed lines. Figure 7.7 contains a poorly prepared résumé and the reasons why it is bad. Figure 7.8 shows an evaluation form used by six experts from business, industry, and education who judged student résumés prepared for a workshop at the University of Colorado, Boulder. After you complete a final draft of your résumé, evaluate it according to the ten criteria on the form. Then revise until it satisfies these criteria and is ready for final typing or printing.

◆ WRITING A LETTER OF APPLICATION

Along with your résumé, you must send your prospective employer a letter of application, one of the most important pieces of correspondence you may ever write. Its goal is to get you an interview and ultimately the job. Letters you write in applying for jobs should be personable, professional, and persuasive—the three P's. Knowing how the letter of application and résumé work together and how they differ can give you a better idea of how to begin your letter.

How the Letter and Résumé Differ

The résumé is a compilation of facts—a record of dates, your important achievements, names, places, addresses, and jobs. You will have your résumé duplicated, and you will send a copy to each prospective employer. Your letter of application, however, is much more personal. You must write a new, original letter to each prospective employer. Photocopied letters of application say that you did not care enough, that you did not want to spend the time and energy to answer

---

[2]John Penrose, "A Discrepancy Analysis of the Job-Getting Process and a Study of Résumé Techniques," *Journal of Business Communication* 21 (Summer 1984): 3–15.

FIGURE 7.8   A résumé evaluation form.

1. Clarity of job objective	not on résumé ☐	very unclear	extremely clear
		1 2 3 4 5	
2. Essence of educational information	not on résumé ☐	too much or too little information	extremely concise and informative
		1 2 3 4 5	
3. Description of job experience with skills emphasis	not on résumé ☐	poor description of skills	excellent description of skills
		1 2 3 4 5	
4. Additional positive information that supports job objective	not on résumé ☐	irrelevant additional information	very supportive additional information
		1 2 3 4 5	
5. Correctness of typing, spelling, and grammar		poorly written and typed	well written and typed
		1 2 3 4 5	
6. Organization		poorly organized	extremely well organized
		1 2 3 4 5	
7. Ease of reading (layout)		very difficult to read	very easy to read
		1 2 3 4 5	
8. Quality of reproduction (paper, print)		poor quality	excellent quality
		1 2 3 4 5	
9. Attractiveness		not attractive	very attractive
		1 2 3 4 5	
10. Overall rating		poor résumé	excellent résumé
		1 2 3 4 5	

Journal of Employment Counseling 16 (September 1979):156. Copyright 1979 American Personnel and Guidance Association. Reprinted with permission.

the employer's ad personally. Each letter of application should be tailored to a specific job. It should respond precisely to the kinds of qualifications the employer seeks. The letter of application is a sales letter emphasizing and applying the most relevant details (of education, experience, and talents) on your résumé. In short, the résumé contains the raw material that the letter of application transforms into a finished and highly marketable product—you!

Résumé Facts You Exclude from a Letter of Application

The letter of application should not simply repeat the details listed in your résumé. In fact, the following details belong only on your résumé and should not be restated in the letter: (1) personal data including license or certificate numbers, (2) the specific names of courses in your major, (3) your hobbies, and (4) the names and addresses of your references. Duplicating these details in your letter gives no new information to help persuade prospective employers that you are the individual they are seeking.

Finding Information About Your Prospective Employer

One of the best ways to sell yourself to future employers is to demonstrate that you have some knowledge of their company. A number of years ago, a college was looking for an instructor and was pleased with one candidate who referred to the college's specific courses by their numbers in her letter of application. This individual went to the profitable trouble of reading the college's catalog before applying. Do a little similar homework; investigate the job and the company. Consult such reference works as *Industry Surveys, Directory of Corporation Affiliations,* or *Standard and Poor's Corporation Records* for information on company activities. Figure 7.9 reprints part of a page from *Standard and Poor's Corporation Records,* which supplies useful details on the history, financial status, location of plants, subsidiaries, products, and officers of a company. You can also find information about prospective employers in the *Thomas Register of American Manufacturers, Forbes* magazine (especially the "Annual Directory" issue published in May), and the issue of *Fortune* magazine listing the "Fortune 500" companies. The *Business Periodicals Index* (see pages 260–63) is also a helpful guide to stories written about different companies in various business publications (e.g., the *Wall Street Journal* or *Money* magazine). You can also obtain information from the company itself by writing for brochures, descriptions, and annual reports a number of months before you actually apply. Check with the Chamber of Commerce. Ask people who work in the company.

Except in response to a blind ad, write directly to the individual responsible for hiring—the personnel officer, the supervisor, the director of nurses, the district manager. You can call the company and ask the switchboard operator to give you the name of this individual. Ask for the correct spelling of the name, too, so there is no mistake when you write to this individual.

FIGURE 7.9   A company description from *Standard and Poor's Corporation Records.*

Silicon Graphics, Inc.

CAPITALIZATION (June 30 '88)
LONG TERM DEBT- $35,201,000 (incl. $120,000 curr.), including $35,000,000 5¾% Conv. Subord. Debs., due 2012.

STOCK-	Auth. Shs.	Outstg. Shs.
Preferred	2,000,000	None
Common $0.001 par.	*25,000,000	15,622,000

*Incl. 3,968,830 optioned to employees, with 3,218,670 for future grants; and 1,153,213 for conversion of Debs.

LINE OF CREDIT provides up to $11,000,000 with int. at the bank's reference rate, the interbank offered rate plus .75%-1.25%, or the banker's acceptance bid rate plus 0.40%-0.85%- none taken down at June 30, 1988.

CORPORATE BACKGROUND
Company designs, makes, sells and services a family of computer systems called superworkstations which are used by engineers, scientists, and creative professionals for conceptual design, analysis, and simulation of 3D objects. Applications for Co.'s systems include conceptual design and engineering analysis of aircraft and automobiles, molecular modeling, computational fluid dynamics, flight simulation, factory floor simulation, military systems simulation, consumer product package design, and special graphics effects for movies and television advertising. Products are sold and serviced in the U.S., Can., Western Europe and the Far East.
Hardware products include the IRIS 3000 and 3100 series superworkstations and the 40 series Superworkstation; and software include AT&T's UNIX System V operating system and the IRIS Graphics Library.

SUBSIDIARIES- Numerous subsidiaries with the name Silicon Graphics in their titles.
PROPERTY- Research and development and manufacturing facilities are leased in Mountain View, Calif.
EMPLOYEES- June 30, 1988, 1,055.
INCORPORATED in Cal. in Nov., 1981.
OFFICERS-
J.H. Clark, Chrm
E.R. McCracken, Pres & Chief Exec Officer
M.W. Perry, Exec V-P
K.L. Coleman, Sr V-P
Ralph Mele, Sr V-P
D.P. McBride, V-P & Contr
R.L.S. McKeithen, V-P, Gen Counsel & Secy
-V-Ps-

Forest Baskett	E.W. Nelson
T.A. Jermoluk	T.J. Oswald
Jennifer A. Konecny	Michael Ramsay
G.L. Lauer	H.J. Smith

DIRECTORS- J.H. Clark, C.R. Kramlich, E.R. McCracken, J.A. McDivitt, G.M. Mueller, Gil Williams.
OFFICE- 2011 N. Shoreline Blvd., Mountain View CA 94039-7311 (Tel.: 415-960-1980). ANNUAL MEETING- In Nov.

BOND DESCRIPTIONS
5¾% CONV. SUBORD. (S.F.) DEBS.: Due Apr. 1, 2012
Auth. & outstg.. $35,000,000
INDENTURE DATED Apr. 1, 1987. INTEREST PAYABLE Apr. & Oct. 1, to holders registered the preceding Mar. & Spet. 15, respectively. PRINCIPAL PAYABLE at the Trustee's office in Boston or at its office or agency in NYC. INTEREST GRACE PERIOD- 30 days.
TRUSTEE- First National Bank of Boston.
DENOMINATIONS- Fully registered, $1,000 and multiples thereof.
SINK... ...res retirement on 30 days' ...e Debs. each Apr. 1

Reprinted from Standard & Poor's "Corporation Records," vol. 50, No. 5, by permission.

Drafting the Letter of Application

The letter of application should follow the standard conventions discussed in Chapter 6. It should be typed neatly on a plain white sheet of good bond paper, $8\frac{1}{2}'' \times 11''$. Make sure that your typewriter or printer works perfectly and that the type does not appear faded. Proofread meticulously; a spelling error here will harm your chances. Avoid abbreviations ("thru" for "through," "nite" for "night"), slang expressions, or unnecessary jargon. Don't forget the "you attitude." Employers are not impressed by boastful proclamations ("I am the most efficient and effective safety engineer," "I am a natural-born nurse"). On the other hand, trying to appeal to an employer's sympathies will not work either. One student wrote that he needed the job to pay tuition and a car loan. The employer was not impressed. Another applicant spent so much time on advantages to her that she forgot the employer entirely: "I have worked with this kind of equipment before, and this experience will give me the edge in running it. Moreover, I can adjust more quickly to my working environment."

The best letters of application are to the point and are readable. Your letter will be seen as an example of your writing skills. Keep in mind that employers will receive many letters and that yours will have to compete for their time. You want your letter to be placed in the "definitely interview" category discussed on page 147. A letter of application should not exceed one page; it is to your advantage to make it shorter. On the other hand, you should not write a telegraphic message of only two or three sentences. Strive for brevity and clarity. Emphasize your qualifications with specific evidence; don't let them get lost in a sea of words. A three-paragraph letter will be sufficient for most candidates. Figure 7.10 contains a model letter—Maria Lopez's application for a job. Compare her letter with her résumé (Figure 7.5). Then compare her letter with the letter in Figure 7.11, written by Anthony Jones, who has little relevant job experience; see his résumé, Figure 7.4. He must rely mainly on his educational training.

Above everything else, remind yourself to take advantage of the techniques involved in the process of writing. In your eagerness to get your letter of application in the mail, don't be tempted to send a prospective employer your first draft. A first or even second draft can rarely sell your abilities as well as a third, fourth, or even fifth one can. Write and rewrite your application letter until you are convinced it presents you in the best light possible.

The discussion that follows will give you some suggestions on how to do just that.

The First Paragraph

The first paragraph of your application letter is your introduction. It should answer three questions: (1) why you are writing (by mentioning the specific position you are applying for), (2) where or how you learned of the job, and (3) what your most important qualification is for the job. Begin your letter by stating directly that you are writing to apply for a job. Don't say that you "want to apply for the job," for such an opening raises the question "Why don't you then?" And avoid starting off in an unconventional or boastful way: "Are you looking for a dynamic, young, and talented photographer?" Do not begin with a question; be more positive and professional. If you learned of the job through a newspaper or journal, make sure that you underscore its title.

> I am applying for the food-service manager position you
> advertised in the May 10 edition of the Los Angeles Times.

Do not waste the employer's time and your space on the page by repeating verbatim the words of the advertisement. If you learned of the job from a professor, friend, or employee at the firm, state that fact also. Next, indicate your chief qualification—you will soon graduate with an A.A. in food service, you have worked in the large restaurant of a major hotel chain, or you have ten years' experience managing a cafeteria. Select one fact that justifies your suitability for the job.

FIGURE 7.10   Letter of application from a student with some job experience.

1725 Brooke Street
Miami, FL 32701-2121
May 14, 1990

Dr. Marvin Hendrady
Suite 34
Medical/Dental Plaza
839 Causeway Drive
Miami, FL 32706-2468

Dear Dr. Hendrady:

Mr. Mitchell Pellborne, my clinical instructor at Miami-Dade Community College, informs me that you are looking for a dental hygienist to work in your northside office. I am writing to apply for that position. This month, I will graduate with an A.S. degree in the dental hygienist program at Miami-Dade Community College, and I will take the American Dental Assistants Examination in early June.

I have successfully completed all course work and clinical programs in oral hygiene, anatomy, and prophylaxis techniques. During my clinical training, I received intensive practical instruction from a number of local dentists, including Dr. Mildred Pecos. Since your northside office specializes in pedodental care, you might find the subject of my major project--proper nutrition for preschoolers--especially relevant. I have also had some related job experience in working with children in a health care setting. For a year and a half, I was employed as a ward clerk on the pediatric unit at St. Francis Hospital, and my experience in greeting patients, filling out forms, and assisting the nursing staff would be valuable to you in running your office. You will find more detailed information about me and my experience in the enclosed résumé.

I would welcome the opportunity to talk with you about the position and my interest in pedodontics. I am available for an interview any time after 2:30 until June 13. After that date, I could come to your office any time at your convenience.

Sincerely yours,

Maria H. Lopez

Maria H. Lopez

Encl. Résumé

The Second Paragraph

To show why and how you are qualified for the job, the second paragraph of your application letter emphasizes your education and work background. Recent graduates with little work experience will, of course, spend more time on their education, but even if you have much experience, don't forget your education. Stress

FIGURE 7.11   Letter of application from a student with little job experience.

73 Allenwood Boulevard
Santa Rosa, CA 95401-1074
May 25, 1990

Ms. Jocelyn Nogasaki
Personnel Manager
Megalith Publishing Company
1001 Heathcliff Row
San Francisco, CA 94123-7707

Dear Ms. Nogasaki:

I am applying for the layout editor position advertised on
May 25 in the San Francisco Chronicle. Early next month, I
will receive an A.S. degree in industrial graphics
illustration from Santa Rosa Junior College.

With a special interest in the publishing industry, I have
successfully completed more than forty credit hours in
courses directly related to layout design, where I acquired
skills in drafting, reproduction processes, and production
techniques. You might like to know that many of the design
patterns of Megalith publications were used as models in my
graphic communications and photographic technology classes.
My studies have also led to practical experience at McAdam
Publishers, as part of my Santa Rosa apprenticeship program.
Working at McAdam's, I was responsible for assisting the
design department in photo research and in the preparation of
mockups. Other related experience I have had includes artwork
and proofreading for the student magazine, Thunder. As you
will note on the enclosed résumé, I have also had experience
in displaying merchandise at Buchman's Department Store.

I would appreciate the opportunity to discuss with you my
qualifications in industrial graphics. After June 12 I will
be available for an interview at any time that is convenient
for you.

Sincerely yours,

Anthony H. Jones

Anthony H. Jones
Encl. Résumé

your most important educational accomplishments. Employers want to know
what skills and expertise your education has given you and how those skills apply
to their particular job. Simply saying that you will graduate with a degree in criminal justice does not explain how you, unlike all the other graduates of a criminal
justice program, are best qualified for the job. Indicate that in thirty-six hours of

course work you have specialized in industrial security and that you have twelve hours in business and communications. That says something specific. Rather than boasting that you are qualified, give the facts to prove it. If your GPA is relatively high or if you have won an award, mention that. Do not worry about repeating important information in both your letter and résumé.

After you discuss your educational qualifications, turn to your job experience. The best letters show how the two are related. Employers like to see continuity between a candidate's school and job experience. Provide that link by showing how the jobs you have held have something in common with your major—in terms of responsibility, research, customer relations, community service. Say that your course work in data processing helped you to be a better programmer for your previous employer, that your summer jobs for the local park district reinforced your studies in human services. However, do not dwell on being a nurse's aide three years ago when you have nearly completed a degree program to be an R.N. Busing tables in a restaurant is good experience, but do not let that job overshadow your current work as a management trainee for a large hotel chain.

Above all, the second paragraph of your application letter must relate your education and experience directly to the employer's job. Tell exactly how your school work and job experience qualify you to function and advance in the job advertised. Here, your homework on what the company is like should pay off. Note in Figure 7.10 how Maria Lopez uses her knowledge of Dr. Hendrady's specialty to her advantage; in Figure 7.11 Anthony Jones profitably emphasizes how he gained his knowledge of and respect for Megalith publications.

Your second paragraph may run to six or seven sentences. You might want to spend three sentences on your educational qualifications and three on your job experience; or perhaps your work experiences are so rich that you will spend four sentences on them. At any rate, do not neglect education for experience or vice versa. Refer to your résumé, and do not forget to say that you are including it with your letter.

The Third Paragraph

The third paragraph has three functions: (1) to emphasize once again your major qualification, (2) to ask for an interview, and (3) to indicate when you are available for that interview. Paragraph three is short—about two or three sentences. End gracefully and professionally. Don't leave the reader with just one weak sentence: "I would like to have an interview at your convenience." Such a sentence does nothing to sell you. Say that you would appreciate talking with the employer further to discuss your qualifications. Then mention your chief talent. Indicate your interest in the job and give the times you are available for an interview. If you are going to a professional meeting where the employer might be present, or if you are visiting the employer's city, say so. Following are some poor ways to close the letter and reasons to avoid them.

> Pushy: I would like to set up an interview with you. Please phone me to arrange a convenient time. (That's the employer's prerogative, not yours.)

Too Informal: I do not live too far from your office. Let's meet for coffee sometime next week. (Say that since you live nearby, you will be available for an interview.)

Too Humble: I know that you are busy, but I would really like to have an interview. (Say you would like to discuss your qualifications further.)

Introduces I would like to discuss other qualifications you have in mind for
New Subject: the job. (How do you know what the interviewer might have in mind?)

Note how the professional closing paragraphs in Figures 7.10 and 7.11 avoid these errors.

◆ FILLING OUT A JOB APPLICATION

At some point in your job search, you will be asked to complete a prospective employer's application form. A recruiter may hand you a job application form at a campus interview, or you may be mailed a form in response to your letter of application. Most often, though, you will be given an application to complete when you are at the employer's office. The job application form, your letter of application, and your résumé are the three key written documents employers use to screen applicants.

Application forms can vary tremendously. But they all ask you to give information about your education, any military service, present and previous employment, references, general state of health, and reasons for wanting to work for the company or agency. Since these topics overlap those on your résumé, bring the résumé with you to the employer's office to make sure you don't omit something important. Some forms even require you to attach your résumé. But *under no circumstances* should you attach a résumé to a blank form instead of filling the form out. Employers want their own forms completed by job seekers.

The following general guidelines can help you to complete an application form.

1. Read the instructions before you begin. Then quickly scan all the questions so you won't supply information in one spot only to find that it's asked for specifically later in the questionnaire.
2. Answer all the questions. Some forms instruct you to put N/A (not applicable) rather than leave a space blank.
3. Print neatly, using a black or blue ball-point pen. Do not use a felt-tip pen or a pencil.
4. Double-check numbers—Social Security, driver's license, area and zip codes, registration numbers, union certificates.
5. Do not write in spaces marked "For Office Use Only."
6. Check spelling and punctuation.
7. Be as neat as you can. Do not write over the lines or in the margins or insert asterisks indicating further clarification. If you need more room to answer a

question, attach a separate sheet of paper. Make sure that your name and the specific question number appear on the attached sheet.

8. Be truthful. Don't say you can type seventy words a minute when you have trouble with thirty.

9. Be as precise as possible. For "previous experience," do not just say "construction worker"; indicate "building inspector," "mason," "carpenter."

10. When asked about salary expectations, avoid extremes. If you have done your homework, you will have a sense of the established range. Do not put "minimum wage"; an employer has to give you that anyway.

11. Many applications ask you to comment on your training and education, giving you one or two inches of space for your answer. Fill the blank space with facts, not padding. Giving just one or two small details will not sell your talents and will only point to your lack of self-expression and confidence. Many employers, including the federal government, rank prospective employees on the basis of their answers to such a question. So, as a rule of thumb, provide as much relevant information as space allows, and make sure that you are positive, not negative, about your previous position and employer.

12. Sign the application, verifying that what you have written is true and complete. Your signature is essential if you must have a security clearance or if the company has to release any of the information you have provided or obtain your permission to find out more about you.

Individuals desiring to work for one of the many branches of the United States government complete a "Personal Qualifications Statement." That form contains many of the kinds of questions you can expect future employers to ask you. The government, like so many employers, expects job candidates to have done their homework. The first question asks the applicant to identify the desired job by title and number—information readily available from a civil service or governmental agency. Since the federal government is the largest employer in the nation, many users of this book will complete this form. You can obtain a copy of the form from a Federal Job Information Center.

Figure 7.12 contains an application form similar to ones used by private companies. This form asks applicants to give reasons for leaving previous jobs and also requires them to write a "personal essay" stating why the company should hire them. Both of these questions will require tact and thought. If you were fired from a past job, it is not to your advantage to simply state that fact. Indicate further relevant information, such as that the industry suffered a recession. More frequently, though, your reasons for leaving a job will be financial, educational, or geographic. You may have received a better offer, decided to return to school, or planned to move to another town.

Writing the personal essay will require that you convince the employer of your sincerity and qualifications. In doing so, do not dwell on what the company can do for you. Concentrate on how your previous experience and education will help your employer; emphasize, too, your willingness to learn new techniques and skills on the job. Do not be afraid to cite specific accomplishments; your success will depend on it.

FIGURE 7.12   Sample job application form.

APPLICATION FOR EMPLOYMENT

Date _____

PERSONAL INFORMATION

SS# _____

Name _____
      Last   First   Middle

Present address _____

Phone no _____

Height _____ Weight _____

If related to anyone in our company,
state name, relationship, and position _____

EMPLOYMENT DESIRED

Position applying for _____ or _____

Health Status   Good _____ Fair _____ Poor _____

EDUCATIONAL BACKGROUND

Name and location of school	Years attended	Date graduated	Subjects studied
High school			
College			

Other

_____

Military service _____ Duties _____

_____

Dates _____

In case of emergency, notify:

Name _____

Address _____

Phone number _____

FIGURE 7.12   (Continued)

EMPLOYMENT RECORD

Former employer	Address	Salary & position	Reason for leaving	Dates employed

REFERENCES

Give the names of three persons not related to you whom you have known for at least one year:

Name	Address	Business	Years acquainted

Why did you leave your last job? Explain your answer in detail.

_____

_____

_____

PERSONAL ESSAY

Please state why you feel we should hire you for the position desired, including any qualifications not mentioned above. Attach another sheet if necessary.

_____

_____

_____

_____

_____

_____

DO NOT WRITE BELOW THIS LINE—FOR OFFICE USE ONLY

Date interviewed _____ By _____

General appearance _____

Attitude _____

Date hired (if any) _____

Salary _____

Position _____

◆ GOING TO AN INTERVIEW

An interview can be challenging, threatening, friendly, or chatty; sometimes it is all of these. By the time you arrive at the interview stage, you are far along in your job search. Basically, there are two kinds of interviews. One is a *screening interview,* to which numerous applicants have been invited so that a company can narrow down the candidates. Campus interviews are an example of screening interviews. The other kind of interview is known as a *line interview;* the employer invites only a few select applicants to the company's office for a tour and detailed conversation.

Preparing for an Interview

An interview gives the employer a chance to see how you look, act, and react. Once in a while interviewers intentionally create stressful situations for you, such as inviting you to smoke and not providing an ashtray. But most employers do not want to trick you. They want to see how well you can talk about yourself and your work; they also want to see how well you listen and respond to their answers. At some interviews job candidates are shown a film about the company and are then given a quiz about that film. Interviewers expect applicants to be nervous, but you can free yourself of some anxiety if you know what to expect.

Interviews can last half an hour or extend to two or three days. Most often, though, an interview will last about one hour. It has been estimated that the applicant will do about 80 to 90 percent of the talking. Since you will be asked to speak at length, make the following preparations before your interview.

1. Do your homework about the employer—history, types of products or services provided, location of main and branch offices, contributions to industry or the community.
2. Review the technical skills most relevant for the job. You might want to reread sections of a textbook, study some recent journal articles, or talk to a professor or an employee you know from the company.
3. Prepare a brief (one- or two-minute) review of your qualifications to deliver orally should you be asked about yourself.
4. Bring your résumé with you. Your interviewer will have a copy on the desk, so you can be sure that its contents will be the subject of many questions. Be able to elaborate on and supplement what is on your résumé. Any extra details or information that bring your résumé up to date ("I received my degree last week"; "I'll get the results of my state board examinations in one week") will be appreciated.

Questions to Expect at an Interview

You can expect questions about your education, job experience, and ambitions. An interviewer will ask you questions about courses, schools, technical skills, and job goals. Through these questions an interviewer attempts to discover your good points as well as your bad ones. A common interviewer strategy is to postpone questions about your bad points until near the end of the interview. Once a relaxed atmosphere has been established, the interviewer thinks that you may be less reluctant to talk about your weaknesses. The following fifteen questions are typical of those you can expect from interviewers.

1. Tell us something about yourself. (Here's where your prepared one-minute oral presentation of yourself comes in handy.)
2. Why do you want to work for us? (Recall any job goals you have and apply them specifically to the job under discussion.)
3. What qualifications do you have for the job? (Mention educational achievements in addition to any relevant work experience.)
4. What could you possibly offer us that other candidates do not have? (Say "enthusiasm," being a team player, and problem-solving abilities in addition to educational achievements.)
5. Why did you attend this school? (Be honest—location, costs, programs.)
6. Why did you major in "X"? (Do not simply say financial benefits; concentrate on both practical and professional benefits. Be able to state career objectives.)
7. Why did you get a grade of "C" in a course? (Do not hurt your chances of being hired by saying you could have done better if you tried; that response shows a lack of motivation most employers find unacceptable. Explain what the trouble was and mention that you corrected it in a course in which you made a B or an A.)
8. What extracurricular activities did you participate in while in high school or college? (Indicate any duties or responsibilities you had—handling money, writing memos, coordinating events; if you were not able to participate in such activities, tell the interviewer that a part-time job, community or church activities, or commuting a long way to school each day prevented your participating. Such answers sound better than saying that you did not like sports or fraternities or clubs in school.)
9. Did you learn as much as you wanted from your course work? (This is a loaded question. Indicate that you learned a great deal but now look forward to the opportunity to gain more practical skill, to put into practice the principles you have learned; say that you will never be through learning about your major.)
10. Why was your summer job important? (Highlight skills you learned, people you helped, employers you pleased.)
11. What is your greatest strength? (Being a team player, cooperation, willingness to learn, ability to grasp difficult concepts easily, managing time or money, taking criticism easily, and profiting from criticism are all appropriate answers.)
12. What is your greatest shortcoming? (Be honest here and mention it, but then turn to ways in which you are improving. You obviously don't want to say something deadly like, "I can never seem to finish what I start" or "I hate being criticized." You should neither dwell on your weaknesses nor keep silent

about them. Saying "None" to this kind of question is as inadvisable as rattling off a list of wrongdoings.)

13. How much did you earn at your last job and what salary would you expect from us? (Some job counselors wrongly advise interviewees to lie about their past salaries in order to get a larger one from the future employer. But if the prospective employer checks your last salary and finds that you have lied, you lose. It is better to round off your last salary to the nearest thousand. As far as present salary is concerned, if you did your homework, you should have a sense of the salary range.)

14. Why did you leave your last job? (Usually you will have educational reasons: "I returned to school full-time" or geographical reasons: "I moved from Jackson to Springfield." *Never attack your previous employer.* This only makes you look bad.)

15. Is there anything else you want to discuss? (Here is your opportunity to end the interview with more information about yourself. You might take time to reiterate your strengths, to correct an earlier answer, or to indicate your desire to work for the company.)

Of course, you will have a chance throughout the interview to ask questions, too. Do not forget important points about the job: responsibilities, opportunities for further training, security, and chances for promotion. You will also want to ask about salary (but do not dwell on it), fringe benefits, schedules, vacations, and bonuses. If you spend time on these subjects, especially during the first part of the interview, you tell the interviewer that you are more interested in the rewards of the job than in the duties and challenges it offers. Do not go to the interview with dollar signs flashing in your eyes.

Some questions an interviewer may not legally ask you. Questions about your age, marital status, ethnic background, race, or any physical handicaps violate equal opportunity employment laws. Even so, some employers may disguise their interest in these subjects by asking you indirect questions about them. A question such as "Will your husband care if you have to work overtime?" or "How many children do you have?" could probe into your personal life. Confronted with such questions, it is best to answer them positively ("My home life will not interfere with my job," "My family understands that overtime may be required") rather than bristling defensively, "It's none of your business if I have a husband."

Keep in mind some other interview "dos" and "don'ts." *Be on time.* If you are unavoidably delayed, telephone to apologize and set up another interview. Go to the interview alone. Dress appropriately for the occasion. Speak slowly and distinctly; do not nervously hurry to finish your sentences, and never interrupt or finish an interviewer's sentences. Do not smoke, even if the interviewer offers you a cigarette. Also refrain from chewing gum, fidgeting, or tapping your foot against the floor or a chair. Maintain eye contact with the interviewer; do not sheepishly stare at the floor or the desk. Body language is equally important. For instance, don't fold your arms—that's a signal indicating you are closed to the interviewer's suggestions and comments. And one last point: When the interview is over, thank the interviewer for considering you for the job.

The Follow-up Letter

Within a week after the interview, it is good strategy to send a follow-up letter thanking the interviewer for his or her time and interest in you. The letter will keep your name fresh in the interviewer's mind. Do not forget that this individual

FIGURE 7.13   A follow-up letter.

```
        2739 East Street
        Latrobe, PA 17042-0312
        September 10, 1990



        Mr. Jack Wong
        Personnel Manager
        Transatlantic Steel Company
        1334 Ridge Road N.E.
        Pittsburgh, PA 17122-3107

        Dear Mr. Wong:

        I enjoyed talking with you last Wednesday and learning more about the
        security officer position available at Transatlantic Steel. It was
        especially helpful to take a tour of the plant's north gate section to see
        the types of challenges it presents for the security officer stationed
        there.

        As you noted at my interview, my training in surveillance electronics has
        prepared me to operate the sophisticated equipment Transatlantic has
        installed at the north gate. I was happy that Ms. Turner took time to show
        me this equipment.

        I am looking forward to receiving the brochure about Transatlantic's
        employees' services. Would it also be possible for you to include a copy of
        the newsletter introducing the new security equipment to the employees?

        Thank you for considering me for the position and for the hospitality you
        showed me. I look forward to hearing from you. After my visit last week, I
        know that Transatlantic Steel would be an excellent place to work.

        Sincerely yours,

        Marcia Le Borde

        Marcia Le Borde
```

interviewed other candidates, too—some of them probably on the same day as you. In your follow-up letter, you can reemphasize your qualifications for the job by showing how they apply to conditions described by the interviewer; you might also ask for some further information to show your interest in the job and the employer. You could even refer to a detail, such as a tour or film that was part of the interview. A sample follow-up letter appears in Figure 7.13.

◆ ACCEPTING OR DECLINING A JOB

Even if you have verbally agreed to take a job, you still have to respond formally in writing. Your letter will make your acceptance official and will probably be included in your permanent personnel file. Accepting a job is easy. Make this communication with your new employer a model of clarity and diplomacy. Respond to the offer as soon as possible (certainly within two weeks). Often a time limit is specified. A sample acceptance letter appears in Figure 7.14. In the first sentence tell the employer that you are accepting the job, and refer to the date of the letter offering you the position. Indicate when you can begin the job. Then mention any pleasant associations from your interview or any specific challenges you are anticipating. That should take no more than a paragraph. Do not douse your letter with praise for the employer or the job.

In a second paragraph express your plans to fulfill any further requirements for the job—going to the personnel office, taking a physical examination, having a copy of a certificate or license forwarded, sending a final transcript of your college work. A final one-sentence paragraph might state that you are looking forward to starting your new job.

Refusing a job requires tact. You are obligated to inform an employer why you are not taking the job. Since the employer has spent time interviewing you, respond with courtesy and candor. For an example of a refusal letter, see Figure 7.15.

Do not bluntly begin with the refusal. Instead, prepare the reader for bad news by starting with a complimentary remark about the job, the interview, or the company. Then move to your refusal and supply an honest but not elaborate explanation of why you are not taking the job. Many students cite educational opportunities, work schedules, geographic preference, health reasons, or better, more relevant professional opportunities. End on a friendly note, because you may be interested in working for the company in the future and do not want to cause any bad feelings.

◆ EMPLOYMENT EVALUATIONS

Even after you have been hired and have been working at your job for a while, you may be expected to write convincingly about your qualifications for that job. In the past, employee evaluations for promotions and salary increases were handled by supervisors and administrative personnel. Today, many companies annually ask employees to grade themselves in addition to having supervisors do an

FIGURE 7.14   Letter accepting a job.

73 Park Street
Evansville, WI 53536-1016
June 29, 1990

Ms. Melinda A. Haas, Manager
Weise's Department Store
Janesville Mall
Janesville, WI 53545-1014

Dear Ms. Haas:

I am pleased to accept the position of assistant controller that you offered
me in your letter of June 22. Starting on July 16 will be no problem for me.
I look forward to helping Ms. Meyers in the business office. In the next few
months I know that I will learn a great deal about Weise's.

As you requested, I will make an appointment for early next week with the
Personnel Department to discuss travel policies, salary payment schedules,
and insurance coverage.

I am eager to start working for Weise's.

Cordially,

Kevin Dubinski

Kevin Dubinski

assessment. The two evaluations are then compared, and employees are given the
opportunity to see and respond to what their supervisors have written about
them. Employees may also be asked to evaluate their supervisors. Thus employees
must know how to evaluate themselves and others effectively. For this reason
it is a good idea to keep a record of your achievements and commendations on
the job.

FIGURE 7.15   Letter refusing a job.

```
345 Melba Lane
Bellingham, WA 98225-4912
March 8, 1990



Ms. Gail Buckholtz
Assistant Editor
The Everett News
Everett, WA 98421-1016

Dear Ms. Buckholtz:

I enjoyed meeting you and the staff photographers at my recent
interview for the photography position at the News. Your plans
for the special weekend supplements are exciting, and I know
that I would have enjoyed my assignments greatly. But because
I have decided to continue my education part-time at Western
Washington University in Bellingham, I have accepted a
position with the Bellingham American. Not having to commute
to Everett every day will give me more time for my studies and
also for my free-lance work.

Thank you for your generous offer and for the time you and the
staff spent explaining your plans to me. I wish you much
success with the supplements.

Sincerely yours,

George Alexander
George Alexander
```

What kinds of questions can you expect your employer to ask? Here are a few of the most common.

1. What are your current duties?
2. How well do you perform them?
3. What improvements can you make?

4. What would you like to accomplish in the next year?
5. Where would you rank yourself in comparison with others in your department?
6. What special contributions have you made to the company (or agency) in the last year?
7. Why do you deserve a raise or a promotion?

Before you answer such questions, keep in mind that your readers know you are automatically prejudiced in your behalf; objectivity, therefore, will be deemed a virtue. Rather than only saying that you are invaluable or that you are a hard worker, tell your employer why you hold this view of your work. Give relevant facts—cite how many customers you visited and sold products to, mention any exceptional services you performed for clients, or any ways you saved the company money or improved communication. Indicate how your work benefited the company and your fellow employees. Did you make any suggestions that improved services or schedules? If your supervisor praised your work, cite his or her comments and give dates.

Keep your assessment short and to the point. Also make sure that your comments about your accomplishments directly pertain to your assigned duties. At the other extreme, do not sell yourself short by saying that you did what was expected of you or that you accomplished what you were told. Tell your reader how you performed routine tasks with skill and to the benefit of the company. A credible answer to question 3 would indicate that you have made a mistake, but would also indicate what you have done to correct it and to ensure that it will not occur again.

When asked to evaluate your supervisor, be objective. Avoid cheap shots or any attempts to get even for grievances. Questions of leadership, honesty, respect, and clarity in explaining job goals are usually found on evaluations of one's supervisors. Respond according to these criteria with facts and with honesty.

Your employer may supply you with a form (or checklist) for your evaluation of yourself, your supervisor, or for both. Or you may be instructed to write a formal letter of assessment. In either case, proofread what you write carefully for spelling and punctuation. You should also make a copy for your own records.

◆ EXERCISES

1. Make a brainstormed list of your marketable job skills. To do this, first concentrate on the specialized kinds of skills you learned in your major or on your job (for example, giving injections, fingerprinting, preparing specialized menus, keeping a ledger book, operating a· computer, learning a computer language). List as many of these skills as you can think of; then organize them into three or four separate categories that reflect your major abilities.

2. Using at least three different sources, compile a list of 10 employers for whom you would like to work. Get their names, addresses, phone numbers,

and the names of the managers or personnel officers. Then select one company and write a profile about it—location, services, kinds of products or services offered, number of employees working for it, clients served, types of schedules used.

3. Tell your college placement office when you will begin your job search. The office will almost certainly give you some forms to complete. Bring these forms to class and discuss the kinds of questions they contain and the most effective ways to answer them.

4. Obtain some personal evaluation forms from your placement office. Write a sample letter to a former or current teacher and employer, asking for a recommendation. Tell these individuals what kinds of jobs you will be looking for and politely mention how a strong letter would help you in your job search. Make sure that you bring them up to date about your educational progress and any employment you have had since you worked for them.

5. Request an application form for employment from a local store, hospital, government agency, or company. Bring the form to class and be prepared to discuss the best ways of completing it.

6. Which of the following would belong on your résumé? Which ones would not belong? Why?

    a. student I.D. number
    b. Social Security number
    c. the zip codes of your references' addresses
    d. a list of all your English courses in college
    e. section numbers of the courses in your major
    f. statement that you are recently divorced
    g. subscriptions to journals in your field
    h. the titles of any stories or poems you published in a high school literary magazine or newspaper
    i. your GPA
    j. foreign languages you studied
    k. years you attended college
    l. the date you were discharged from the service
    m. names of the neighbors you are using as references
    n. your religion
    o. job titles you held
    p. your summer job washing dishes
    q. your telephone number
    r. the reason you changed schools
    s. your current status with the National Guard
    t. the name of your favorite professor in college
    u. your work for the Red Cross
    v. hours a week you spend reading science fiction
    w. the title of your last term paper in your major
    x. the name of the agency or business where you worked last

7. Indicate what is wrong with the following career objective statements and rewrite them to make them more precise and professional.
   a. Job in a dentist's office.
   b. Position with a safety emphasis.
   c. Desire growth position in a large department store.
   d. Am looking for entry position in health sciences with an emphasis on caring for older people.
   e. Position in sales with fast promotion rate.
   f. Want a job working with semiconductor circuits.
   g. I would like a position in fashion, especially one working with modern fashion.
   h. Desire a good-paying job, hours: 8–4:30, with double pay for overtime. Would like to stay in the Omaha area.
   i. Insurance work.
   j. Computer operator in large office.
   k. Personal secretary.
   l. Job with preschoolers.
   m. Full-time position with hospitality chain.
   n. I want a career in nursing.
   o. Police work, particularly in suburb of large city.
   p. A job that lets me be me.
   q. Desire fun job selling cosmetics.
   r. Any position for a qualified dietitian.
   s. Although I have not made up my mind about which area of forestry I shall go into, I am looking for a job that offers me training and rewards based upon my potential.

8. Rewrite the following bad résumé to make it more precise and persuasive. Include additional details where necessary and exclude any details that you think would hurt the job seeker's chances. Also correct any inconsistencies.

RÉSUMÉ OF

Powell T. Harrison
8604 So. Kirkpatick St.
Ardville, Ohio
345 37 8760
614 234 4587

PERSONAL   Confidential

CAREER   Seeks good paying position with progressive Sunbelt
OBJECTIVE   company.

EDUCATION
1987–1990   Will receive degree from Central Tech.
                Institute in Arch. St. Earned high average
                last semester. Took necessary courses for

```
                    major; interested in systems, plans, and
                    design development.

1983-1987           Attended Ardville High School, Ardville, OH;
                    took all courses required. Served on several student
                    committees.

EXPERIENCE          None, except for numerous part-time jobs and student
                    apprenticeship in the Ardville area. As part of
                    student app. worked with local firm for two months.

HOBBIES             Watching MTV, playing Nintendo video games. Member
                    of Junior Achievement.

REFERENCES          Please write for names and addresses.
```

---

9. Determine what is wrong with the following sentences in a letter of application. Rewrite them to eliminate any mistakes, to focus on the "you attitude," or to make them more precise.
   a. Even though I have very little actual job experience, I can make up for it in enthusiasm.
   b. My qualifications will prove that I am the best person for your job.
   c. I would enjoy working with your other employees.
   d. This letter is my application for any job you now have open or expect to fill in the near future.
   e. Next month, my family and I will be moving to Detroit, and I must get a job in the area. Will you have anything open?
   f. If you are interested in me, then I hope that we make some type of arrangements to interview each other soon.
   g. I have not included a résumé since all pertinent information about me is in this letter.
   h. My GPA is only 2.5, but I did make two B's in my last term.
   i. I hope to take state boards soon.
   j. Your company, or so I have heard through the grapevine, has excellent fringe benefits. That is what I care about most, so I am applying for any position which you may advertise.
   k. I am writing to ask you to kindly consider whether I would be a qualified person for the position you announced in the newspaper.
   l. I have made plans to further my education.
   m. My résumé speaks for itself.
   n. I could not possibly accept a position which required weekend work, and night work is out, too.
   o. In my own estimation, I am a go-getter—an eager beaver, so to speak.
   p. My last employer was dead wrong when he let me go. I think he regrets it now.
   q. When you want to arrange an interview time, give me a call. I am home every afternoon after four.

10. Why is the following letter of application ineffective? Rewrite it to make it more precise and appropriate.

Apartment 32
Jeggler Drive
Talcott, Arizona

Monday

Grandt Corporation
Production Supervisor
Capital City, Arizona

Dear Sir:

I am writing to ask you if your company will consider me for the position you announced in the newspaper yesterday. I believe that with my education (I have an associate degree) and experience (I have worked four years as a freight supervisor), I could fill your job.

My school work was done at two junior colleges, and I took more than enough courses in business management and modern packaging. In fact, here is a list of some of my courses: Supervision, Materials Management, Work Experience in Management, Business Machines, Loading and Landing Tactics, Introduction to Packaging, Art Design, Modern Business Principles, and Small Business Management. In addition, I have worked as a loading dock supervisor for the last two years, and before that I worked in the military in the Quartermaster Corps.

Please let me know if you are interested in me. I would like to have an interview with you at the earliest possible date, since there are some other firms also interested in me, too.

Eagerly yours,

George D. Milhous

George D. Milhous

---

11. From the Sunday edition of your local newspaper, clip ads for two or three jobs you are qualified to fill and then write a letter of application for one of them.

12. Write a chronologically organized résumé to go along with the letter you wrote for Exercise 11 above.

13. Write a functional résumé to accompany your application letter in Exercise 11.

14. Write an appropriate job application letter to accompany Anna Cassetti's résumé in Figure 7.3.

15. Write a letter to a local business inquiring about summer employment. Indicate that you can work only for one summer and that you will be going back to school by September 1.

16. Rewrite this follow-up letter to make it more professional.

Dear Mr. Gage:

It was good talking to you yesterday. The job is even more attractive than I thought. I had no idea that the salary was in the $21,000 to $22,000 range. That is excellent money for someone starting out.

I am sorry that I did not know the answers to your questions on the use of the new laser printers. After checking with my instructor, Dr. Patricia Holmes, I can give you a full and complete answer now. If you would like me to put it in writing, please let me know, and I shall be happy to oblige you. I do not want you to think that I am not properly trained.

I am really excited about working for your company. And I am staying glued to the phone in the hopes that you will give me that call that will start me on a great career.

Absolutely yours,

C. K. Randolph

C. K. Randolph

Types of
Business
Correspondence

Receiving and answering business correspondence—memos and letters—are vital to the success of a company and its employees. The way you prepare your correspondence will reflect on your professional abilities and your company's reputation. When memos and letters are written clearly, effectively, and promptly, you and your employer profit. When they are done poorly, everyone suffers. For this reason, being an effective writer of memos and letters is a necessary and prized skill. In fact, the higher up the corporate ladder you climb, the more you will be expected to write—and write well.

Chapter 8 discusses six of the most common types of business correspondence that you will be expected to write on the job:

1. memos
2. order letters
3. inquiry letters
4. special request letters
5. sales letters
6. customer relations letters

These six kinds of correspondence will introduce you to a variety of formats and a number of writing strategies and techniques. Generally speaking, memos, the least formal type of correspondence, convey brief notes or instructions; order, inquiry, and special request letters give and request information in differing contexts; sales letters require a description of your product or service and a convincing argument for your reader; and customer relations letters are vital to company image and customer satisfaction.

◆ MEMOS

Memorandum, from which the noun "memo" comes, is a Latin word signifying that something is to be remembered. The Latin meaning points to the memo's chief function: to record information of immediate importance and interest in the busy world of work. Memos are in-house correspondence sent up and down the corporate ladder—from managers to employees and from employees to managers. They are also sent to and from co-workers. Memos allow a business or agency to communicate with itself in its day-to-day operations.

Function of Memos

Memos have a variety of functions. They are written to ask or to respond to questions affecting daily work. They notify employees about the date of a meeting or the main points raised at that meeting. They inform readers about appointments, policies, or new procedures. They alert the staff to a forthcoming order and any special problems in handling it. Or they can provide figures necessary to honor a customer's request, confirm what has been decided in a telephone conversation, or offer suggestions or recommendations. Memos are also used for short reports; see Chapter 16 for examples of field, trip, or progress reports in memo format. Many internal proposals (pages 460–65) are written as memos, too.

Memo Format

Memos can vary in format. Some companies use standard, printed forms (Figure 8.1) while others have their names (letterhead) printed on their memos as in Figure 8.2. Memos can be written on $8\frac{1}{2}'' \times 11''$ sheets of paper or on half sheets.

FIGURE 8.1   Standard memo form without any letterhead.

```
TO:        All RN's

FROM:      Margaret Wojak, Director of Nurses   M.W.

DATE:      August 14, 1990

SUBJECT:   RN identity patches


Effective September 1, 1990, all RN's will have the choice of wearing their caps
or an identity patch. Patches should be sewn on the upper right arm of lab coats
or uniforms so that staff and patients can easily identify you as an RN. Those
RN's wishing to wear identity patches may obtain them for one dollar apiece at the
Health Uniforms Shop directly across from the hospital on Ames Street. Please call
me at Extension 732 if you have any questions.
```

FIGURE 8.2   Memo on letterhead stationery.

BILL'S CATERING SERVICE
56 North Jones
Canton, Ohio 45307-0299

TO: Marge Adcox   DATE: November 23, 1990

FROM: Roger Blackmore *RB.*   SUBJECT: Review of Management
                                                   Training Seminar

As you requested, I attended the Management Training Seminar (November 19–20).
Here is a review of the major points made by the director, Jack Lowery.

1. The individual conducting the training sessions should always talk in a loud voice
   so that the trainees can hear him or her.

2. The main purpose of the training session should always be announced so that the
   trainees can focus on a specific set of topics.

3. Instructors should allow at least a ten-minute break for each two-hour session. A
   brief break will help to increase the trainees' attention span and allow for better
   learning.

4. The easiest tasks should be assigned first; more complicated ones should follow.

5. The instructor should provide feedback to the trainees at the end of each major
   section.

I will be happy to meet with you to discuss these points in detail. These training
techniques could be used in our orientation program. Let me know when it would be
convenient for you to discuss these points.

The smaller size paper is useful for shorter communications and encourages the
writer to be concise. You can make your own memos by including the necessary
parts discussed below.

As you can see from looking at Figures 8.1 through 8.4, memos look different
from letters. They are more streamlined and less formal. Because they are sent to
individuals within your company, memos do not need the formalities necessary in

business letters. Memos, therefore, do not contain an inside address, salutation, complimentary close, or signature line.

Basically, the memo consists of two parts: the identifying information at the top and the message following this information. The identifying information includes these easily recognized parts: the *To, From, Date,* and *Subject* lines.

```
TO:   Aileen Kelly              DATE:  January 31, 1990
      Data Processing Manager

FROM: Stacy Kaufman  S.K.       SUBJECT: Progress report on
      Operator, Level II                 preparing fall
                                          schedule
```

On the *To* line write the name and job title of the individual(s) who will receive your memo or a copy of it. If you are on a first name basis with the reader, just use his or her first name. Otherwise, include the reader's first and last names. In some companies memos are sent to everyone whose name is on a distribution list. If your name is on the list for receiving information on a given project or from one or more departments, you will get every memo from these sources. Your name may appear on a number of lists. Don't send copies of your memos to individuals who don't need them. You will only increase the paper inflation in an office.

On the *From* line write your name (first name only if your reader refers to you by it) and your job title (unless it is unnecessary for your reader). Some writers put their handwritten initials after their typed name to verify that the message comes from them.

On the *Subject* line write the title and the purpose of your memo. Be precise so that readers can file your memo correctly. Vague subject lines such as "New Policy," "Operating Difficulties," or "Shared Computer Time" do not identify your message accurately and may suggest that your message is not carefully restricted or developed. "Shared Computer Time," for example, does not tell readers if your memo will discuss new equipment, corporate arrangements, or vendors; offer additional or fewer hours; or warn employees about abusing the system.

On the *Date* line do not simply list the day of the week. Give the calendar date and year—June 5, 1990.

Just because a memo is an in-house communication, do not think that the quality of your writing is unimportant. Your employer and co-workers deserve the same clear and concise writing and attention to the "you attitude" that your customers do. In fact, your job may depend upon preparing correct, persuasive, and readable memos. Keep in mind that memos require the same care and follow the same rules of effective writing as letters do.

Strategies for Organizing a Memo

Your memos need to be drafted and organized so that readers can find information quickly and act on it promptly. For longer, more complex communications, such as the memos in Figures 8.2–8.4, the message of your memo might be divided into three parts: (1) introduction, (2) discussion, (3) conclusion.

FIGURE 8.3   A memo that uses headings.

RAMCO INDUSTRIES
"Where Technology Shapes Tomorrow"

TO: Harrison Mohler   SUBJECT: Ways to Increase
        Vice-President, Corp. Affairs   Ramco's Community
                                               Involvement

FROM: Trudy Snowden   *TS.*   DATE: March 3, 1989
        Public Relations Chief

At our planning session in early February, our division managers stressed the
need to generate favorable publicity for our new Ramco plant in Mayfield.
Such publicity would help to highlight Ramco's anticipated community
involvement. You asked me to investigate ways in which Ramco's visibility in
the Mayfield community might be enhanced. This memo suggests three
plans we might pursue.

Create a Scholarship Fund
Ramco would receive favorable publicity by creating a scholarship at
Mayfield Junior College for any student interested in a career in industrial
technology. A tuition scholarship for one year at Mayfield Junior College
would cost Ramco $2800. The scholarship could be awarded by a committee
composed of Ramco's executives and administrators at Mayfield Junior
College. Such a scholarship would emphasize Ramco's support for industrial
education and our interest in a local college.

Offer Factory Tours
Short guided tours of the Mayfield factory would introduce the Mayfield
community to Ramco's products and innovative technology. The tours might
be organized for community and civic groups—the members of the YMCA
and YWCA, senior citizens' clubs, schools. On these tours, individuals would
see the care we take in our production, our equipment, and the speed with
which we ship our products. Of special interest to visitors would be Ramco's
use of industrial robots. These tours must be scheduled well in advance so
they do not conflict with our production schedules. A question-and-answer
period could follow each tour.

Provide Guest Speakers
A number of our employees would be excellent guest speakers at social and
educational meetings in Mayfield. Possible topics would include the
technological advances Ramco has made in manufacturing and engineering
and how these advances help consumers. It would be relatively easy to
compile a list of interested speakers from our engineering, safety, and
transportation departments.

Please give me your comments on these suggestions as soon as possible. If we
are going to put one or more of them into practice before the plant opens,
we'll need to take action by the end of this month.

In the introductory section of your memo, tell readers clearly about the problem, procedure, question, or policy that prompted your writing to them. Link the first sentence of your memo to the subject line. Explain briefly any background information the reader needs to know. Be specific about what you are going to accomplish in your memo. Note, for example, how the writer in Figure 8.2 tells the reader why he is providing a list of items or why recommendations are included in the memo in Figure 8.3. Do not be afraid to come right out and say "This memo explains new parking procedures" or "This memo summarizes the action taken at the industrial site near Evansville to reduce air pollution."

In the discussion section, explain with relevant detail the procedures, policies, or problems you are calling to the readers' attention. Tell them why a problem or procedure is important, who will be affected by it and why, what caused it, why changes are necessary, and what those changes are. Give precise dates, times, and locations. For example, note how carefully the writer of the memo in Figure 8.4 explains the problem and procedure in cleaning the brake machine.

Provide a conclusion that states specifically how you want the reader to respond to your memo. To get readers to act appropriately, you can do one or more of the following in your conclusion.

1. Ask the readers to call you if they have any questions.
2. Request a reply—in writing, over the telephone, or in person—by a specific date.
3. Provide a list of recommendations that the readers are to accept, revise, or reject.

Throughout your memo use organizational markers (see pages 16–17) to make information easy for readers to follow. When you have a large number of related points, as the writer of the memo in Figure 8.2 does, number them so that the reader can comprehend them more easily. Lists in a memo point out comparisons and contrasts easily. Underlining or using boldface type for key sentences will also help readers by emphasizing important points. But do not abuse this technique by underlining or boldfacing too much. Only underline or boldface points that contain summaries or draw conclusions. Memo reports, such as in Figure 8.3, use headings to separate information for readers so that they can find it more quickly. Headings (often discovered from brainstorming) will also help you organize information as you write.

◆ ORDER LETTERS

Order letters are straightforward notices informing a seller that you want to purchase a product or service. To make sure that you receive exactly what you want, your letter must be clear, precise, and accurate. Double-check the seller's brochure, catalog, or agency manual before you write your order letter.

Order letters address the following five points.

1. Description of the product or service. Specify the name, model or stock number, quantity, color, weight, height, width, size, or any special features

FIGURE 8.4   Memo with a clear introduction, discussion, and conclusion.

MEMORANDUM

Dearborne Equipment Company
204 South Mill St.
South Orange, NJ 02341-3420

TO: Machine Shop Employees   DATE: September 26, 1989

FROM: Janet Hempstead   SUBJECT: Importance of
Shop Supervisor   Keeping
Brake Machines Clean

During the past two weeks I have received a number of reports
that the brake machines are not being cleaned properly after
each use. Through this memo I want to emphasize and explain
the importance of keeping these machines clean for the safety
of all employees.

When the brake machines are used, the cutter chops off small
particles of metal from the brake drums. These particles
settle on the machines and create a potentially hazardous
situation for anyone working on or near the machines. If the
machines are not cleaned before being used again, these metal
particles could fly into an individual's face when the brake
drum is spinning.

To prevent accidents like this from happening, please make
sure you vacuum the brake machines after each use. You will
find two vacuum cleaners for this purpose in the shop--one of
them is located in work area 1-A and the other, a reserve
model, is in the storage area. Vacuuming brake machines is
quick and easy; it should take no more than a few seconds. I
am sure you will agree that this is a small amount of time to
make the shop safer for all of us.

I appreciate your cooperation in this matter. If you have any
questions, please call me at Extension 123 or come by my
office.

that separate one model from another (e.g., chrome as opposed to copper handles). Make your letter easy to read by itemizing when you order more than one product. Listing the products or materials in tabular form will set them apart and allow the seller an opportunity to check off each item as it is being prepared for shipment.

FIGURE 8.5   An order letter.

DAVIS CONSTRUCTION COMPANY
1200 South Devon
Millersville, Pennsylvania 17321

April 2, 1990

E. F. Johnson and Associates
820 Frontage Road
P.O. Box 1007
St. Louis, MO 64211-1007

PLACING AN ORDER

Please send us by first-class mail the following materials as listed in your 1990 catalog entitled *Personnel Forms for Monitoring Selection, Administration, and Evaluation*:

Catalog Number	Title	Number of Copies	Total Cost
P-4	Personnel Interviewer's Survey	25	$10.00
P-5	Health Information Questionnaire	100	24.00
EA-4	Personnel Application Forms	25	12.00
ATS-6	Health History	1	1.50
			$47.50

When you mail these forms, send them to the Personnel Department in care of my attention. Please send these forms within the next ten days and telephone me collect if there will be any delay.

A check for one half the amount ($23.75) is enclosed and the balance will be paid upon receipt of the materials.

Roberta Youngblood

ROBERTA YOUNGBLOOD, PERSONNEL OFFICER

Encl.: Check 3467 for $23.75

---

2. Price of the product or service. Indicate precisely the price per unit, per carload, per carton, and then multiply that price by the number you are ordering. For example, ask for "twelve units @ $5 a unit." Do not put down the cost of one item ($5) for the dozen you are requesting. You will receive only one.

3. Shipping instructions. Do you want the product sent by first-class or fourth-class mail, Federal Express, by priority mail? Specify any special handling instructions—Do not fold; Use hand stamp; Refrigerate or Pack in Dry Ice; Ship to the Production Department.

4. Date needed. Is there a rush date?

5. Method of payment. Businesses with good credit standing are sent a bill. Individuals, however, may be required to pay beforehand. If so, are you enclosing a check or money order? Is the product to arrive COD (cash on delivery)? If you use a charge card, specify which card, and include your account number. Will you be paying in installments? State how much you are including and when and how the balance is to be paid.

Orders can be considered external or internal. An external order is sent to an individual or company you do not work for or with. You will refer to the five points just discussed and use a letter or sometimes a form provided by the company from which you are ordering the product. Figure 8.5 shows a sample order letter written in the AMS format for letters discussed on page 123.

An internal order, often called a *requisition,* asks one individual or department or section of your company to supply another with necessary materials, equipment, service, or publications. A letter is not necessary for an internal order; instead, use a memo or a specially provided form.

◆ INQUIRY LETTERS

An inquiry letter asks for information about a product, service, publication, or procedure. Businesses frequently exchange such letters. As a customer, you too have occasion to ask for catalogs, names of stores in your town selling a special line of products, and the price, size, and color of a particular object. Businesses are eager to receive such inquiries and will answer them swiftly because they promise a future sale.

Figure 8.6 illustrates a letter of inquiry. Addressed to a real estate office managing a large number of apartment complexes, Michael Ortega's letter follows the three basic rules for an effective inquiry letter. It:

1. states exactly what information the writer wants.
2. indicates clearly why the writer must have this information.
3. specifies when the writer must have the information.

Whenever you request information, be sure to supply appropriate stock and model numbers, pertinent page numbers, or exact descriptions. You might even clip and mail the advertisement describing the product you want. Vague or general letters delay a response to you. Had Michael Ortega written the following letter to Acme, he would not have helped his family move: "Please send me some information on housing in Roanoke. My family and I plan to move there soon." Such a letter does not indicate whether he wants to rent or buy, whether he is interested in a large or small apartment, furnished or unfurnished, where he

FIGURE 8.6   A letter of inquiry.

403 South Main Street
Kingsport, TN 37721-0217
March 2, 1990

Mr. Fred Stonehill
Property Manager
Acme Property Corporation
Main and Broadway
Roanoke, VA 24015-1100

Dear Mr. Stonehill:

Please let me know if you will have any two-bedroom furnished
apartments available for rent during the months of June, July,
and August. I am willing to pay up to $425 a month plus
utilities. My wife, one-year-old son, and I will be moving to
Roanoke for the summer so that I can take classes at Virginia
Western Community College. If possible, we would like to have
an apartment that is within two or three miles of the college.
We do not have any pets.

I would appreciate hearing from you within the next two weeks.
My phone number is (606) 273-8957. The best time to reach me
is between 6:00 p.m. and 9:00 p.m.

If you have any suitable vacancies, we would be happy to drive
to Roanoke to look at them and give you a deposit to hold an
apartment for us.

Sincerely yours,

Michael Ortega

Michael Ortega

would like it to be located, or the rent he is willing to pay. Similarly, a letter asking a firm to "Send me all the information you have on microwave ovens" might bring back a detailed service manual when the writer wanted only prices of the top-selling models.

◆ SPECIAL REQUEST LETTERS

Special request letters make a special demand, not a routine inquiry. Among other things, these letters can ask a company for information that you as a student will use in a paper, an individual for a copy of an article or a speech, or an agency for facts that your company needs to prepare a proposal or sell a product. The person or company being asked for help stands to gain no financial reward for supplying this information; the only reward is the goodwill such a response creates.

Make your request clear and easy to answer. Supply readers with addressed, postage-paid envelopes and a telephone number for any questions.

Saying "please" and "thank you" will help you get the information you want. Also, do not expect your reader to write the paper or proposal for you. Asking for information is quite different from asking readers to organize and write it for you. Follow these seven points when asking for information in a special request letter.

1. State who you are and why you are writing.
2. Indicate clearly your reason for requesting the information.
3. Give the reader precisely and succinctly the questions you want answered. List, number, and separate the questions.
4. Specify exactly when you need the information. Allow sufficient time—at least three weeks.
5. Offer to forward a copy of your report, paper, or survey in gratitude for the help you were given.
6. If you want to reprint or publish the materials you ask for, indicate that you will secure whatever permissions are necessary. State that you will keep the information confidential if that is appropriate.
7. Thank the reader for helping.

Figure 8.7 gives an example of a letter that follows these guidelines.

◆ SALES LETTERS

A sales letter is written to persuade the reader to buy a product, try a service, support some cause, or participate in some activity. A sales letter can also serve as a method of introducing yourself to potential customers. You have undoubtedly received numerous sales letters from military recruiters, local merchants, charitable organizations, and campus groups. Sales letters face a lot of competition that you will have to overcome.

To write an effective sales letter, you have to do three things.

1. Identify and limit your audience.
2. Find out exactly what the needs of this group are.
3. Determine precisely what you want your readers to do after reading your sales letter.

These three points require that you do adequate homework about both your audience and the product or service you are selling.

FIGURE 8.7   A special request letter.

234 Springdale Street
Rochester, NY 14618-0422
February 7, 1990

Ms. Victoria Stanton
Research Director
Creative Marketing Association
198 Madison Avenue
New York, NY 10016-0092

Dear Ms. Stanton:

I am a second-year student at Monroe College in Rochester and
I am preparing a term paper on the topic "Current Marketing
Practices." As part of my research for this paper, I am
writing an overview of marketing practices for the past
twenty-five years. Two of your publications would be of great
help to me. Would you please send me the following two
pamphlets:

1. A History of Marketing in the United States (CMA 15)
2. Creative Marketing Comes of Age (CMA 27)

I would appreciate receiving these materials by February 28
and will be pleased to send you a copy of my paper in late
May. Creative Marketing Association will, of course, be fully
cited in my bibliography.

Thank you for your assistance. I look forward to hearing from
you.

Sincerely yours,

Julie Kawatsu

Julie Kawatsu

FIGURE 8.8   A sales letter sent to a selected group of readers.

MOSBY
TIMES MIRROR

THE C. V. MOSBY COMPANY · 11830 WESTLINE INDUSTRIAL DRIVE, ST. LOUIS, MISSOURI 63141
314-872-8370 · CABLE ADDRESS "MOSBYCO"

Dear Doctor:

After you look it up, do you really know which drug is best for YOUR patient . . . and WHY?

It all depends on where you look. If you consult standard "cookbook" guides to current drug therapy, you'll have only the personal opinions of one or two physicians on which drug they prefer to treat a specific disease.

However, if you consult the new DRUGS OF CHOICE, you'll have an authoritative, critical, unbiased appraisal of all drugs in current use, written specifically to support and verify your selection of the optimum drug for a specific patient in a particular clinical situation.

DRUGS OF CHOICE is the only drug therapy book that recognizes that you alone can fit drug and patient together, and thus gives you all the facts necessary to assist you in that "fitting." Dr. Modell and his 45 eminent contributors discuss all drugs available for a particular condition, based on their specialized knowledge and experience, substantiated by selected references. You will note updating in every chapter, particularly those on diuretics and drugs for cardiac arrhythmias.

You'll find a more complete description of the new DRUGS OF CHOICE on the specially prepared brochure enclosed, including table of contents, distinguished contributors, and 54 timesaving tables. Take a moment now to examine it; then examine the book itself for 30 days at our expense. Just complete the examination certificate and return it to us in the postage-paid envelope provided.

Each time you sign a prescription, you, and you alone, endorse the safety and quality of the drug prescribed. If you're going to look it up, you want the whole story. And only one book offers you that . . . DRUGS OF CHOICE. Can you afford to be without it?

Sincerely,

William J. DeRoze

William J. DeRoze
for The C. V. Mosby Company

WJD:ne

Letter adapted courtesy of the C. V. Mosby Company.

In deciding whom you want to reach, you will also be investigating the needs of your audience. Do you want to write a letter to all the nurses in your state district nurses' association or only the pediatric nurses at a particular hospital? Are you writing to all homeowners who purchased aluminum siding from your company in the last three years or just in the last three months? Sometimes a sales letter will be duplicated and sent to hundreds of readers, as in Figure 8.8; sometimes you may write to only one reader, as in Figure 8.9. Some helpful considerations in

FIGURE 8.9 A sales letter addressed to an individual.

Faithful Answering Service
4300 South Wabash
Lincoln, Oregon 97407-6028

September 27, 1990

Ms. Katherine Eubanks
Eubanks Pest Control
18 West Gannon Drive
Lincoln, OR 97411-4219

Dear Ms. Eubanks:

How much business do you lose when your telephone rings and you are not there to answer it? A prospective client or steady customer might call one of the other 22 exterminators listed in the Lincoln Yellow Pages.

You will never miss a call if you use the Faithful Answering Service. Our courteous and experienced operators are on duty twenty-four hours a day, every day of the year. They are prompt, too. Your telephone will be answered before the caller hears the third ring.

You tell us when we are needed by simply calling and giving us your identifying code number. We will then be ready to take your messages or to transfer calls to any number you give us. When you are out of the office, a quick call to us can save you extra trips, time, and gas. Your customers will also be happier, knowing that you can be reached whenever they need you to solve their pest problems.

All this convenience and peace of mind can be yours, Ms. Eubanks, for less than 90 cents a day. And if you act by October 4, you can have your Faithful service installed free of charge and save the $25 installation fee. We promise to have your phone connected within three days after we hear from you.

I urge you to call us at 657-3434 by October 4. You can call us at any time, day or night. Don't forget, we are here twenty-four hours a day.

Sincerely yours,

Samuel Heywood

Samuel Heywood, Owner

audience analysis are occupation, age, consumer needs or habits, geographic location, and memberships. Your employer may have a mailing list that you should consult. Once you have selected those who should receive your letter, you have made a great deal of headway in knowing what you will say to that audience.

The "you attitude" is crucial. A sales letter is not written to provide elaborate explanations about a product. That kind of information comes after the sale. Nor is a sales letter written to proclaim the merits of your company. Here is a safe rule to follow: Don't boast or be a bore. The sales letter is written to persuade readers to buy, support, or join. Everything in the letter should be directed toward that goal. Appeal to readers' emotions, pocketbooks, or self-images. Entertain, amuse, coax, inform, or flatter the reader. The central question is: What are we trying to do for you, our customer? Ask yourself that question before you begin writing and you will be using effective reader psychology.

Sales letters follow a time-honored and workable plan; that is, each sales letter follows what can be called the "four A's":

1. gets the reader's *attention*
2. highlights the product's *appeal*
3. shows the customer the product's *application*
4. ends with a specific request for *action*

These four parts may be handled in less than four paragraphs. Holding a sales letter down to one page or less will keep the reader's attention. Television commercials and ads in magazines provide useful models of this fourfold approach to the customer. The next time you see one of these ads, try to identify the "four A's."

Getting the Reader's Attention

Your opening sentence is crucial. If you lose readers here, you will have lost them forever. A typical television commercial has thirty to sixty seconds to sell viewers; your first sentence has about two to five seconds to catch the readers' attention and prompt them to read on. That first sentence is bait on a hook. It must show readers how their problems could be solved, their profits increased, or their pleasures enriched. The reader's attitude will be "What's in this for me?"

Avoid an opening that is flat, vague, or lengthy. Beginning with a statement such as "I have great news for you" tells the readers nothing. They are more likely to toss your letter away if it does not contain something personally relevant in the first sentence. Tell them what the news is by selecting something that will appeal to their wallets, their emotions, or their chances to look better in the eyes of others. A letter for a pesticide that begins "The cockroach could become the next endangered species if a California manufacturer has its way" offers some interesting, specific news. Keep your opening short, one or two sentences at most.

The following five techniques are a few of the many ways to begin a sales letter. Each technique requires you to adapt it to your product or service.

1. Asking a question. Mention something that readers are vitally concerned about that is also relevant to your product or service. Look, for example, at the opening question in Figure 8.8. Avoid such general questions as "Are you happy?" or "Would you like to make money?" Use more specific questions. For example, an ad for a home-study training course in crime investigation and identification asked readers "Are you promotable? Are you ready to step into a bigger job?" And an ad for Air Force Reserve Nursing asked nurses "Are you looking for something 30,000 feet out of the ordinary?" These are precise questions relevant to the offers they introduce. Similarly, a sales letter beginning with "Could you use $100?" zeroes in on one particular desire of the reader. Since your main goal is to persuade readers to continue reading your letter, choose a question that they will want to see answered.

2. Employing a "how to" statement. This is one of the most frequently used openers in a sales letter. The reason for its success is simple—the letter promises to tell readers something practical and profitable. Here are some effective "how to" statements: "We can show you how to increase all your plant growth up to 91%." "Here is how to save $75 on your next vacation." "This is how to provide nourishing lunches for less than eighty cents a person." These "how to" statements attract the readers' attention by introducing a subject that promises rewards and then shows how to gain those rewards.

3. Using flattery. Appeal to the reader's ego. But remember that readers are not naive; they will be suspicious of false praise. Select some compliment that affects the reader professionally or that praises the reader for some specific actions. An effective sales letter for a school supply shop was sent to every new member of a campus sorority announcing, "You've made the right choice in joining Delta Zeta. Now, let us make the right choice in helping you select your supplies this term."

4. Offering a free gift. Everyone likes to receive something for nothing or to boast about a bargain. Often you can lure readers further into your letter by telling them that there is a sale going on and that they can save a lot of money or that they can get the second product free or at half price if they purchase the first one at full price. One book club promises prospective customers, "We'll give you three books for $1 and a free tote bag to put them in with membership." An automobile dealer promises $50 to every customer who test drives a new car. A local realtor tempts customers to see lots for sale with, "Enclosed is a coupon worth $25 in gas for seeing Deer Run Trails Estates."

5. Using a comparison. Compare your product or service with conventional or standard products or procedures. For instance, a jacket firm told police officers that if they purchased a particular jacket from them, they were really getting three in one, since their product had a lining for winter and a covering used for greater visibility at night.

Calling Attention to the Product's Appeal

Once you have aroused the reader's attention, introduce the product or service. Make it so attractive, so necessary, and so profitable that the reader will want to buy or use the product or service. Don't lose the momentum you have gained with your introduction by boring the reader with petty details, flat descriptions, elaborate inventories, or trivial boasts. Appeal to the reader's intellect, emotions, or both, while introducing the product. In Figure 8.8 Mosby Company's mass-mailing letter appeals to the physician's professional requirements for an up-to-date book. Here is an emotional appeal by the Gulf Stream Fruit Company.

> Can you, when you bite into an orange, tell where it was grown? If it tastes better than any you have ever eaten . . . full of rich, golden flavor, brimming with juice, sparkling with sunshine . . . then you know it was grown here in our famous Indian River Valley where we have handpicked it, at the very peak of its flavor, just for your order.[1]

From a leading question, the sales letter moves to a vivid description of the product, name of the supplier, and the customer's ability to recognize how special both the product and he or she is to the Gulf Stream Fruit Company. Using another kind of appeal, the manufacturers of Tree Saw show how their product can decrease customers' fears and increase their safety.

> The greatest invention since the ladder, and a lot safer. With the Tree Saw, you can cut branches thirty feet above the ground. No need to call in a tree surgeon. And you don't have to risk your life on a shaky ladder. Just toss the beanbag weight of the flexible Tree Saw over a branch. Pull on each end of the control rope to make a clean cut. Spring pruning is quick and safe with this perfect tool.[2]

Showing the Customer the Product's Application

The third part of your sales letter lets the readers know how and why the product is worthwhile for them. Here is the place where you give evidence of the value of what you are selling. You have to be careful, though, that you do not overwhelm readers with facts, statistics, detailed mechanical descriptions, or elaborate arguments. The emphasis is still on the use of the product and not on the company that manufactures or sells it. The shift from your company to your prospective customer is essential to any sale. The sales letter in Figure 8.8 emphasizes the importance of the physician's role in the prescribing drugs: "You alone can fit drug and patient together." The Fisher-Price Toys sales message on the following page is addressed to parents who are worried about children damaging a phonograph. Note how the details about the phonograph are all related to that reader-centered issue.

---

[1] "Gifts from Gulf Stream," Oct. 1980, Gulf Stream Fruit Company, Ft. Lauderdale, Florida. Reprinted by permission.
[2] Reprinted courtesy Green Mountain Products, Inc., Norwalk, Conn.

Fisher-Price knows that children begin to appreciate music at a very early age. Usually, a little before they fully appreciate how to handle delicate things like tone arms and fragile records. That's why we designed our new phonograph with lots of features other record players don't offer. To assure that this phonograph can take the toughest treatment young music lovers can hand out and keep playing in fine tune year after year:

1. There's a real, replaceable diamond needle that lasts five times longer than a sapphire needle.
2. The needle cartridge actually retracts when the tone arm is forced down, to prevent deep scratches.
3. The tone arm is solidly constructed so it can be pulled and tugged and still work smoothly.
4. The detachable case cover is specially designed to gently guide the tone arm back in place even if the cover is slammed shut.
5. The phonograph's 4″ speaker provides a nice clear sound. And there are just two simple controls for volume and record speed (33 and 45 rpm) plus a built-in storage space for the electrical cord.

So you can see, the Fisher-Price Phonograph is not a toy. It's a really dependable piece of audio equipment that's made especially for children. So you, and they, can relax and enjoy its wonderful sound for years to come. And that should be music to your ears.

Reprinted courtesy Waring & LaRosa, Inc., and Fisher-Price Toys, Inc.

What evidence should you use to convince the reader? Concentrate on descriptions of the product or service that emphasize convenience, usefulness, and economy. Any special features or changes in the product or service that make it more attractive for the customer should be mentioned. For example, an ad for a greenhouse manufacturer stressed that in addition to using its structure just for a place to grow plants, customers would also find it a "perfect sun room enclosure for year-round 'outdoor' activities, gardening or leisure health spa."

Testimonials—endorsements from previous customers as well as from specialists—may also convince readers to respond favorably to your letter. Rather than saying that hundreds of customers are satisfied with your product, get two or three of those happy customers to allow you to quote them in your letter. A large nursing home published residents' compliments about the food and care to show that it was a good place to live. A private boarding school printed a brief biography (with now and then pictures) of a successful graduate to prove that the school inspires students to leadership. A roach powder firm tells customers that its product is used at the White House. You might also cite awards, honors, accreditations, or citations that your product or service has won.

Worth mentioning also are warranties, guarantees, services, or special considerations that will make the customer's life easier or happier. One store advises readers: "As usual, there is no charge for local deliveries when purchases are over $100." Tell the reader that labor and parts are good for a year, two years, or however long they last. Emphasize that you will refund the price if the customer is not completely satisfied. Tell customers that they do not have to wait for parts or that you will loan them a replacement if they do.

You may be obligated to mention costs in your letter. Postpone discussion of them until the reader has been shown how appealing and valuable the product is. Of course, if price is a key selling point, mention it early in the letter. Readers will react more favorably to costs after they have seen the reasons why the product or service is useful. Do not bluntly state the cost. Relate prices, charges, or fees to the benefits provided by the services or products to which they apply. Customers then see how much they are getting for their money. An electric blanket ad tells customers that it costs only four cents a night to be warm and comfortable. That sounds more inviting than just listing the cost of the blanket as $40. A dealer who installs steel shutters does not tell readers the exact price of the product, but does indicate that they will save money by buying it: "Virtually maintenance free, your Reel Shutters also offer substantial savings in energy costs by reducing your loss through radiation by as much as 65% . . . and that lowers your utility bills by 35%." Relate costs to the reader's profit or convenience.

Ending with a Specific Request for Action

This last section of your letter is vital. If the reader ignores your request for action, your letter has been written in vain. Tell readers exactly what you want them to do and make it easy and pleasurable to do it. Do you want them to fill out a postcard ordering your product, send for a brochure, come into your store, take a test drive, participate in a meeting? Tell them if they have to sign an order blank or merely initial it. Is there an enclosed stamped envelope for their convenience? Is there a deadline for taking advantage of a sale price or bonus? "Come to our store tomorrow between 10 A.M. and 10 P.M. to get your free lounge chair with the purchase of any bedroom suite." As with price, link the benefits the customers will receive to their responses. "Respond and be rewarded" is the basic message of the last section of your letter. Note that in Figure 8.8 the call to action is made in the next-to-last paragraph, but is followed by a brief reminder of the significance of the action. Figure 8.9 shows a call-to-action statement in the last paragraph. The letter urges the reader to act immediately in order to take advantage of the free installation.

◆ CUSTOMER RELATIONS LETTERS

Much business correspondence deals explicitly with establishing and maintaining friendly working relations. Such correspondence, known as customer relations letters, sends readers good news or bad news. Good news tells customers that you have the product or service they want at a reasonable price, that you agree with them about a problem they brought to your attention and that you are solving it exactly the way they want, that you are approving their loan, or that you are grateful to them for their business. Thank you letters, congratulations letters, or adjustment letters saying "Yes" are examples of good news messages.

Bad news messages inform readers that you are not approving their loan, that you do not like the work or equipment they have sold you, that you do not have the equipment or service they want or you cannot provide it at the price they want to pay, that you cannot refund their purchase price or perform a service again as they requested, that you are raising their rent or not renewing their lease, or that you want them to pay what they owe you now. Bad news messages can come to readers through complaint letters, adjustment letters that say "No," or collection letters.

Regardless of the type of news—good or bad—you have to convey to readers, you need to be a diplomatic and persuasive writer. Customer relations letters show how you and your company regard the people with whom you do business. These letters should reveal your sensitivity to their needs. After all, you want to keep them as customers and you never know when you may work with them again. Writing effective customer relations letters requires skill in human relations and reader psychology. The first lesson to learn is that you cannot look at your letter only from your (the writer's) perspective. You have to see the letter from the reader's perspective and anticipate the reader's needs and reactions. Ask yourself how you would feel if you received the same letter. What would be your view of the writer and the writer's company?

As you read this section, keep in mind the two basic principles captured in the words "the customers always write":

1. Customers will write about how they would like to be or have been treated—to thank, to complain, to request an explanation.
2. Customers have certain rights that you must respect in your correspondence with them. They deserve a prompt and courteous reply, whether they are correct or not. If you refuse their request, they deserve to know why; if they owe you money, you should give them an opportunity to explain and a chance, up to a point, to set up a payment schedule.

Planning Your Customer Relations Letters

Whether you are sending good news or bad, you have to determine what to say and how to say it. As with your other written work, do some preliminary planning. Outline for a few minutes to find your ideas. Your outline does not have to be formal or even neatly written—a few scribbles sometimes will be enough to get you started. By outlining, you will save (not lose) time, for you can identify your main points, exclude unnecessary or unimportant ones, and avoid the risk of forgetting something essential. Fortified by your outline, you will feel more confident as you draft your letter. In the process of drafting and revising that letter, consider whether your reader will bristle at or accept the words you use. Your choice of words will determine the success or failure of your letter. You might want to review the appropriate discussions on tone (pages 12–13) and the "you attitude" (pages 132–37).

Being Direct or Indirect

Your message, tone, and knowledge of your reader are essential ingredients in a successful customer relations letter. But success involves something more than knowing how to use the right words to get across your main ideas. It is also cru-

FIGURE 8.10　An ineffective bad news letter.

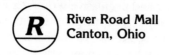

River Road Mall
Canton, Ohio

December 1, 1990

Mr. Daniel Sobol
Flowers by Dan
Lower Level
River Road Mall

Dear Mr. Sobol:

This is to inform you of a rent increase. Starting next month your new rent will be $850.00, resulting in a 15 percent increase.

Please make sure your January rent check includes this increase.

Sincerely yours,

A. J. Griffin

A. J. Griffin
Manager

cial to know where and how to start, and especially, where to present your main point. Not every customer relations letter starts by giving the reader the writer's main point, judgment, conclusion, or reaction. Where you place your main idea is determined by the type of letter you are writing. Good news messages require one tactic; bad news another.

FIGURE 8.11   A diplomatic bad news letter.

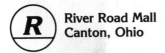

River Road Mall
Canton, Ohio

December 1, 1990

Mr. Daniel Sobol
Flowers by Dan
Lower Level
River Road Mall

Dear Mr. Sobol:

In the past two years we have been delighted to have the name of Flowers by Dan on our mall directory. It's been a pleasure to have you as a tenant and we look forward to serving you in the future.

Over the last two years we have seen a dramatic increase here at River Road Mall in the costs of maintenance, pest control, utilities, insurance premiums, and taxes. Last year we tried to absorb these increases and so did not have to raise your rent. Unfortunately, we find that we cannot do it again for 1991 and so regretfully we must raise your rent by 15%, to $850 a month.

We do not like to raise rents, and we know that you do not like it either. But we also know that you do not want us to compromise on the quality of service that you and your customers have come to expect from River Road Mall.

Please let us know how we can assist you in the future. We wish you a very successful and profitable 1991.

Cordially,

A. J. Griffin

A. J. Griffin
Manager

If you are writing a good news letter, use the direct approach. Start your letter with the welcome, pleasant news that the reader wants to hear. Don't postpone this opportunity to put your reader in the right frame of mind. Then provide any relevant supporting details, explanations, or commentary. Being direct is advantageous when you have good news to convey.

But if you have bad news to report, do not open your letter with it. Be indirect. Prepare your reader for the bad news. Do everything you can to keep the tension level down. If you throw the bad news at your reader right away, you run the risk of jeopardizing the goodwill you want to create and sustain. Again, put yourself in the reader's place. Consider how you would react to a letter that began "We regret to inform you that . . . ," "Your order cannot be filled," or "Your application for a loan has been denied." Having been denied, disappointed, or even offended in a first sentence or paragraph, the reader is not likely to give you his or her attentive cooperation thereafter.

Notice how A. J. Griffin's bad news letter in Figure 8.10 curtly starts off with the bad news of a rent increase. Receiving such a letter, the owner of Flowers by Dan could certainly not be blamed for looking for a new place of business. Or if he did pay the increase, Griffin's letter would hardly ensure that Mr. Sobol would remain a happy tenant at River Road. Griffin was too direct when he should have been diplomatically indirect. He did not consider his reader's reaction; all he was concerned about was delivering his message.

Compare the revised version of Griffin's letter in Figure 8.11 with his curt message in Figure 8.10. In the revised version, Griffin begins tactfully with a few pleasant, positive words designed to put his reader in a good frame of mind about the management of River Road Mall. Then Griffin gives some background information the owner of Flowers by Dan can relate to. A businessperson himself, Mr. Sobol doubtless has experienced some recent increases in his own costs. Griffin makes one more attempt to encourage Sobol to recall his good feelings about the Mall—last year they did not raise rents—before introducing the bad news of a rent increase. And even after giving the bad news Griffin softens the blow by saying that the Mall knows it is bad news. Griffin's tactic here is to defuse some of the anger that Sobol will inevitably feel. Griffin then ends on a positive, upbeat note: a prosperous future for Flowers by Dan.

◆ TYPES OF CUSTOMER RELATIONS LETTERS

Thank-You Letters

A thank-you letter tells how much a person's acts or words have meant to you. In the business world thank-you letters show that the writer is a responsible individual who values human relations. Even if you have already expressed your gratitude in person or over the telephone, a letter further emphasizes your thoughtfulness and courtesy.

Obviously, you will not write a thank-you letter for every kindness shown you or your firm. Reserve a letter for the special occasions when an individual or company does something extra—something that did not have to be done or that was especially helpful. Thank-you letters also figure significantly in a job search. The individuals who write your letters of recommendation, as well as the prospective employers who interview you, deserve thank-you letters. Figure 8.12 contains a thank-you letter to Mr. Butler, to whom Robert Jackson wrote (in Figure 7.1) for a reference. Also review the letter in Figure 7.13 to a prospective employer after the candidate has been interviewed.

Thank-you letters are easy to write. Your main concerns are being specific about what you liked and explaining why you are grateful. Begin with a simple, direct statement of gratitude identifying what has pleased you. Indicate how and when this service was provided. Mention the names of individuals responsible for the work and why their work was so helpful. Also indicate why this service deserves special thanks—that is, how the action helped you or your company.

FIGURE 8.12   A thank-you letter.

```
    5432 South Kenneth Avenue
    Chicago, IL 60651-0396
    April 30, 1990


    Mr. Sonny Butler, Manager
    A&P Supermarket
    4000 West 79th Street
    Chicago, IL 60652-4300


    Dear Mr. Butler:

    Thank you very much for writing a letter of recommendation to
    be included in my dossier at the Placement Office at Moraine
    Valley Community College. I appreciate your taking the time to
    do this, and I am especially grateful for the many kind things
    you said you had included in your letter. Your high praise of
    my work for A&P will certainly help me in finding a job in
    retail sales.

    Once again, thank you for your recommendation. I will let you
    know how my job search goes.

    Sincerely yours,

    Robert B. Jackson

    Robert B. Jackson
```

The letter in Figure 8.13 illustrates an apt thank-you letter. A local merchant thanks a glass company for the exceptional service she received. When the Dole Glass Company has any need of hardware parts, it will certainly be favorably disposed to order from Granger Hardware because of Ms. Stovall-Granger's kind and welcome thank-you letter.

FIGURE 8.13   A thank-you letter.

Serving Fair View Since 1945

Granger Hardware Store
20 N.E. Hasse Road
Fair View, NJ 02386-0691

February 27, 1990

Mr. Randolph Della Sinta, Manager
Dole Glass Company
Managers Highway
Kensington, NJ 02384-8205

Dear Mr. Della Sinta:

I am grateful to the Dole Glass Company for giving me outstanding service last Sunday night, February 25. My store's front plate-glass window (21 feet by 12 feet) was smashed by flying debris. Your crew, Paula Romero and Tim Tulley, were at my store thirty minutes after I phoned them late Sunday night. They quickly cleared away the glass and measured my window. Realizing that the plates they had on their truck would not fit my window, they drove all the way back to your Devonshire warehouse to locate a suitable piece. They could have waited until the next day to do this, but they returned and installed the new glass window in record time.

Their service was exceptional. It allowed me to open my store on Monday morning for business as usual. If your crew had not worked so quickly and made that extra trip, I would have been forced to board up my store and close on Monday to have the repairs made.

I have the highest opinion of Dole Glass and your two employees who came to my store two days ago.

Cordially,

Barbara Stovall-Granger

Barbara Stovall-Granger
Owner

Congratulation Letters

When you put your praise into a letter, you show considerable thoughtfulness. You could call the individual on the telephone or speak to him or her in person to extend your congratulations. But a letter shows that you have made an extra effort. This personal touch also says far more than a greeting card with a pre-printed message.

The occasions for such letters are many. In the business world you might congratulate someone for being promoted, opening a new business or expanding an existing one, or being honored for an accomplishment (for example, having the highest sales record of the month or year). When you honor someone for a distinction, you also honor his or her company. In your own community you create goodwill by congratulating someone for being elected to public office, serving on a civic committee, or receiving an award. In addition to complimenting people for professional or civic achievements, you may congratulate them for engagements, marriages, births, graduations, and anniversaries.

Congratulatory letters must arrive at the right time. Write as soon after the accomplishment as you can. Good news travels fast; acknowledging the individual's honor quickly shows that you are keeping track of events and are eager to express your congratulations. A late letter will say that you did not have the time to write, that the news was not very important to you, or that you belatedly joined everyone else in sending your good wishes.

Keep your letters short and sincere. But a one-sentence letter—"Congratulations on your promotion"—is inappropriate. A letter this short looks as if you sent it not because you were sincerely interested in the individual, but because you felt obligated to write something.

You need not write four or five long paragraphs. A long congratulatory letter with flowery language and backslapping smacks of insincerity. Excessive praise is doubtful praise.

A sincere yet brief letter of congratulation praises one or two significant points of the individual's accomplishment. The following two paragraphs provide a suitable congratulatory letter.

Dear Ms. Bozanich:

Congratulations on being promoted to branch manager of the Powersville store. Your work in the field for the Jordan Company will profit you and us in your new position.

I wish you great success as branch manager. Please call me if I can help you in any way.

Sincerely,

Casey Meyer

Casey Meyer

This next congratulatory letter selects a few details, including the place where the writer learned of the reader's achievement, to show the writer's sincere interest.

Dear Mr. Goshin:

Congratulations on your new title of Certified Insurance Counselor just announced in the <u>Midtown Financial Record</u>. It certainly is an honor to be among only two thousand agents in the country who can sign C.I.C. after their name.

You have my best wishes for continuing success in your insurance business.

Sincerely yours,

Jennifer Rodriguez

Jennifer Rodriguez

One last point about congratulatory letters: Do not use them to sell a product or service. By calling attention to your company's services, you reveal your congratulations are only a gimmick, not a sincere expression of goodwill.

Follow-up Letters

A follow-up letter is sent by a company after a sale to thank the customer for buying a product or using a service and to encourage the customer to buy more products and use more services in the future. A follow-up letter is, therefore, a combination thank-you note and sales letter. The letter in Figure 8.14 is sent to customers soon after they have purchased an appliance and offers them the option of a continued maintenance policy. The letter in Figure 8.15 shows how an income tax preparation service attempts to obtain repeat business. Both of these letters follow helpful guidelines.

1. They begin with a brief and sincere expression of gratitude for having served the customer.
2. They discuss the benefits (advantages) already known to the customer. Then, they transfer the company's dedication to the customer from the product or service already sold to a new or continuing sales area.
3. They end with a specific request for future business.

Occasionally a follow-up letter is sent to a good customer who, for some reason, has stopped doing business with the company. Perhaps the customer has closed an account of long standing, no longer comes to the store, discontinues a subscription, or fails to send in an order for a product or service. Such a follow-up

FIGURE 8.14   A follow-up letter to sell a maintenance agreement.

 Dynamic Appliance Company
100 Walden Parkway
Denver, Colorado 80203-4296
(303) 588-9681

February 9, 1989

Mr. John H. Abbott
3715 Mayview Drive
Cottage Grove, MN 53261-1852

Dear Mr. Abbott:

We are delighted that you have purchased a Dynamic appliance. To help ensure your satisfaction, this appliance is backed by a Dynamic warranty. At the same time, we realize that you bought the appliance to serve you not just for the period covered by the warranty but for many years to come. That's why the purchase of a Dynamic Maintenance Agreement at this time is one of the wisest investments you can make.

A Dynamic Maintenance Agreement provides savings benefits many cost-conscious customers want and look for today. It helps extend the life of the appliance through an annual, on-request maintenance checkup. And if you need service, **it provides for as many service calls as necessary for repairs due to normal use—at no extra charge to you.**

All this coverage is now available to you at a special introductory price of $40 a year. This price takes into consideration the warranty coverage you have remaining. Act now, by filling out and returning the enclosed form.

Sincerely

Carole Morrow

Carole Marrow
Sales Representative
Extension 285

Encl.

letter should try to find out why the customer has stopped doing business and to persuade that customer to resume business dealings. Study the letter in Figure 8.16, in which Jim Margolis first politely inquires whether Mr. Janeck has experienced a problem and then urges him to come back to the store.

FIGURE 8.15   A follow-up letter to encourage repeat business.

TAYLOR TAX SERVICE
HIGHWAY 10 NORTH
JENNINGS, TX 78326

December 1, 1985

Ms. Laurie Pavlovich
345 Jefferson St.
Jennings, TX 78326

Dear Ms. Pavlovich:

Thank you for using our services in February of this year. We were pleased to help you prepare your 1984 federal and state income tax returns. Our goal is to save you every tax dollar to which you are entitled. If you ever have any questions about your return, we are open all year long to help you.

We are looking forward to serving you again next year. The new federal tax laws, which go into effect January 1, will change the kind of deductions you can declare. These changes might appreciably increase the size of your refund. Our consultants have studied these new laws and are ready to explain them to you and apply them to your return.

Another important tax matter influencing your 1985 returns will be any losses you may have suffered because of the hailstorms and tornadoes that hit our area three months ago. Our consultants are specially trained to assist you in filing proper damage claims with your federal and state returns.

To make using our services even easier next year, we have started an appointment policy for your convenience. Please call us at **884-3457** or **885-7853** as soon as you have received all your forms in order to set up an appointment. We are waiting to serve you any day of the week from 9:00 A.M. to 9:00 P.M.

Sincerely yours,

TAYLOR TAX SERVICE

J. P. Sanchez

J. P. Sanchez
Manager

Complaint Letters

Each of us at some time has been frustrated by a defective product, inadequate service, or incorrect billing. Usually our first response is to write a letter dripping with juicy insults. But a hate letter rarely gets results and can in fact hurt the

FIGURE 8.16 A follow-up letter to maintain customer goodwill.

BROADWAY CLEANERS
Broadway at Davis Drive
Baltimore, Maryland 21228-6210
422-1962

April 3, 1990

Mr. Edward Janeck
34 Brompton Lane
Apartment 143
Baltimore, MD 21227-0102

Dear Mr. Janeck:

Thank you for allowing us to take care of your cleaning needs for more than
three years now. It has been our pleasure to see you in the store each week
and to clean your shirts, slacks, and coats to your satisfaction. Since you
have not come in during the last month, we are concerned that we may have in
some way disappointed you. We hope not, because you are a valuable customer
whose goodwill we do not want to lose.

If there is something wrong, please tell us about it. We welcome any
suggestions on how we can serve you better. Our goal is to have a spotless
reputation in the eyes of our customers.

The next time you need some garments cleaned, won't you please bring them to
us, along with the enclosed coupon worth $10 on your next cleaning bill. We
look forward to seeing you again--soon.

Sincerely yours,

Jim Margolis

Jim Margolis, Manager

Encl.

---

writer and create an unfavorable image of the company being represented. A
complaint letter is a delicate one to write.

A complaint letter is written for more reasons than just blowing off steam.
You want some specific action taken. By adopting the right tone, you increase
your chances of getting what you want. Do not call the reader names, hurl insults,

or refuse to do business with the company again. Register your complaint courteously and tolerantly. Companies want to be fair to you in order to keep you as a satisfied customer and correct defective products so that other customers will not be inconvenienced. The "you attitude" is especially important here to maintain the reader's goodwill.

An effective complaint letter can be written by an individual consumer or by a company. Figure 8.17 shows Michael Trigg's complaint about a defective fishing reel; Figure 8.18 expresses a restaurant's dissatisfaction with an industrial dishwasher. Present your case logically, and provide enough detail to obtain a speedy settlement. To accomplish this objective, follow these five steps.

1. Begin with a detailed description of the product or service. Give the appropriate model numbers, size(s), quantity, color. Indicate when and where (specific address) you purchased it, and also how much warranty time remains. Indicate if you are returning the product to the company and how you are sending it—U.S. mail, UPS, or the like. If you are complaining about a service, give the name of the company, the date of the service, the personnel providing it, and their exact duties.

2. State exactly what is wrong with the product or service. Precise information will enable the reader to understand and act on your complaint. How many times did the machine work before it stopped, what parts were malfunctioning, what parts of a job were not done or were done poorly, and when did all this happen? Stating that "the brake shoes were defective" tells very little about how long they were on your car, how effectively they may have been installed, or what condition they were in when they ceased functioning safely. Reach some conclusion, even if you qualify your remarks with words like "apparently," "possibly," or "seemingly" when you describe the difficulty.

3. Briefly describe the inconvenience you have experienced. In this section of the complaint letter, show that your problems were directly caused by the defective product or service. To build your case, give precise details about the time and money you lost. Don't just say you had "numerous difficulties." If you purchased a calculator and it broke down during a mathematics examination, say so (but do not blame the calculator company if you failed the course). Did you have to pay a mechanic to fix your car when it was stalled on the road, did you have to take time away from your other chores to clean up a mess made by a leaky new washing machine, did you have to buy a new telephone answering machine?

4. Indicate precisely what you want done. Do not simply write that you "want something done," that "adequate measures must be taken," or that "the situation should be corrected." State that you want your purchase price refunded, your model repaired or replaced, or a completely new repair crew provided. Maybe you want only an apology from the company for some discourteous treatment. If you are asking for damages, state your request in dollars and cents, and include a copy of any bills resulting from the problem. Perhaps you had to rent a car, were forced to pay a janitorial service to clean up, or had to rent equipment at a higher rate because the company did not make its deliveries as promised.

FIGURE 8.17 A complaint letter from a consumer.

17 Westwood
Magnolia, MA 02171
September 15, 1990

Mr. Ralph Montoya, Manager
Customer Relations Department
Smith Sports Equipment Company
P.O. Box 287
Tulsa, OK 74109-1014

Dear Mr. Montoya:

On August 31, 1990, I purchased a Smith reel, model 191, at
the Uni-Mart Store on Marsh Avenue in Magnolia. The reel sold
for $24.95 plus tax. Since the reel is not working effec-
tively, I am returning it to you under separate cover by
first-class mail.

I had made no more than five casts with the reel when it
began to malfunction. The button that releases the spool and
allows the line to cast will not spring back into position
after casting. In addition, the gears make a grinding noise
when I try to retrieve the line. Because of these problems, I
was unable to continue my participation in the Gloucester
Fishing Tournament.

I am requesting that a new reel be sent to me free of charge
in place of the defective one I returned. I would also like
to know what was wrong with this defective reel.

I would appreciate your handling my claim within the next two
weeks, if at all possible.

Sincerely yours,

Michael Trigg

Michael Trigg

5. Ask for prompt handling of your claim. Ask that an answer be provided to any question you may have (such as finding out where calls came from
that you were billed for but did not make). And ask that your claim be handled as
quickly as possible. You might even specify a reasonable time by which you want
to hear from the writer or need the problem fixed.

FIGURE 8.18 A complaint letter from a business.

The Loft
Cameron and Dale
Sunnyside, California 91793-4116

213-316-7500

June 18, 1990

Priscilla Dubrow
Customer Relations Department
Superflex Products
San Diego, CA 93141-0808

Dear Ms. Dubrow:

On September 15, 1989, we purchased a Superflex industrial dishwasher, model 3203876, at the Hillcrest Store at 3400 Broadway Drive in Sunnyside, for $2,000. In the last three weeks, our restaurant has had repeated problems with this machine. Three more months of warranty remain on this dishwasher.

The machine does not complete a full cycle; it stops before the final rinsing and thus leaves the dishes still dirty. It appears that the cycle regulators are not working properly because they refuse to shift into the next necessary gear. Attempts to repair the machine by the Hillcrest crew on June 3, 12, and 16 have been unsuccessful.

Our restaurant has been greatly inconvenienced. The kitchen team has been forced to sort, clean, and sanitize utensils, dishes, pans, and pots by hand. Moreover, our expenses for proper detergents have increased.

We want your main office to send another repair crew at once to fix this machine. If your crew is unable to do this, we want a discount worth the amount of warranty life on this model to be applied to the purchase of a new Superflex dishwasher. This amount would come to $400, or 20 percent of the original purchase price.

So that our business is not further disrupted, we would appreciate your resolving this problem within the next week.

Sincerely yours,

Emily Rashon

Emily Rashon
Manager

Adjustment Letters

Adjustment letters tell customers dissatisfied with a product or service how their claim will be settled. Adjustment letters should reconcile the differences that exist between a customer and a firm and restore the customer's confidence in that firm.

Rather than ignoring or quarreling with complaint letters, most companies view answering them as good for business. Many large firms maintain separate claims and adjustment departments just to respond to disappointed customers. By writing to complain about a product or service, the customer alerts your company to a problem that can be remedied to avoid similar complaints in the future. Customers who have taken the time to put complaints in writing obviously want and deserve a reply. If you do not answer the customer's letter politely, you may lose a lot of business—not just the customer's business, but also that of his or her friends, family, and associates, who will all have been told about your discourtesy.

An effective adjustment letter requires diplomacy; be prompt, courteous, and decisive. Do not brush the complaint aside in hopes that it will be forgotten. Investigate the complaint quickly and determine its validity by checking previous correspondence, warranty statements, guarantees, and your firm's policies on merchandise and service. In some cases you may even have to send returned damaged merchandise to your firm's laboratory to determine who is at fault.

A noncommittal letter signals to the customer that you have failed to investigate the claim or are stalling for time. Do not resort to vague statements like the following.

- We will do what we can to solve your problems as soon as possible.
- A company policy prohibits our returning your purchase price in full.
- Your request, while legitimate, will take time to process.
- We will act on your request with your best interest in mind.
- While we cannot now determine the extent of an adjustment, we will be back in touch with you.

Customers want to be told that they are right; or if they cannot get what they request, they will demand to know why, in the most explicit terms. At the other extreme, do not overdo an apology by agreeing that the company is "completely at fault," that "such shoddy merchandise is inexcusable," or that "it was a careless mistake on our part." An expression of regret need not jeopardize all future business dealings. If you make your company look too bad, you risk losing the customer permanently. When you comply with a request, a begrudging tone will destroy the goodwill created by your refund or replacement.

Adjustment Letters That Tell the Customer "Yes"

If investigation reveals the customer's claim to be valid, you must write a letter saying "Yes, you are right; we will give you what you asked for." Such a letter is easy to write if you remember a few useful suggestions. As with a good news message, start with the favorable news the customer wants to hear and that will put him or her in a positive frame of mind to read the rest of your letter. Also, make the customers realize that you sincerely agree with them—not to feel as if you are reluctantly granting their request. The two examples of adjustment letters saying "Yes" show you how to write this kind of correspondence. The first example, Figure 8.19, says "Yes" to Michael Trigg's letter in Figure 8.17. You might

FIGURE 8.19   An adjustment letter saying "Yes."

Smith Sports Equipment
P.O. Box 287
Tulsa, Oklahoma 74109-1014
(918) 881-0164

September 21, 1990

Mr. Michael Trigg
17 Westwood
Magnolia, MA 02171

Dear Mr. Trigg:

Thank you for alerting us in your letter of September 15 to the problems you had with one of our model 191 spincast reels. I am sorry for the inconvenience the reel has caused you. A new Smith reel is on its way to you.

We have examined your reel and found the problem. It seems that a retaining pin on the button spring was improperly installed by one of our new soldering machines on the assembly line. We have thoroughly inspected, repaired, and cleaned this soldering machine to eliminate the problem. Our company has been making quality reels since 1935. We hope that your new Smith reel brings you years of pleasure and many good catches, especially next year at the Gloucester Fishing Tournament.

We appreciate your business and look forward to serving you again.

Respectfully,

SMITH SPORTS EQUIPMENT

Ralph Montoya

Ralph Montoya, Manager
Customer Relations Department

want to reréad the Trigg complaint letter to see what problems Ralph Montoya faced when he had to write to Mr. Trigg. The second example of an adjustment letter that says "Yes" is in Figure 8.20. It responds to a customer who has complained about an incorrect billing. The following four steps will help you write a "Yes" adjustment letter.

FIGURE 8.20 An adjustment letter saying "Yes."

Brunelli Motors
_____
Route 3A   Giddings, Kansas 62034-8100   (913) 241-1521

October 6, 1989

Ms. Kathryn Brumfield
34 East Main
Giddings, KS 62034-1123

Dear Ms. Brumfield:

We appreciate your notifying us, in your letter of September 30, about the problem you have experienced regarding warranty coverage on your new Phantom Hawk GT. The bills sent to you were incorrect, and I have already canceled them. Please accept my apologies. You should not have been charged for a new shroud or for repairs to the damaged fan and hose, since all these parts, and labor on them, are covered by warranty.

The problem was the result of an error in the way charges were listed. Our firm has just begun using a new system of billing to give customers better service, and the mechanic apparently punched the wrong code number on your account. I have instructed our mechanics to double-check their code numbers before submitting them to the Billing Department. We hope that this policy will help us to serve you and our other customers more efficiently.

We value you as a customer of Brunelli Motors. When you are ready for another Phantom, I hope that you will once again visit our dealership

Sincerely yours,

a. y. O'Donnel

A. Y. O'Donnel
Service Manager

1. Admit immediately that the customer's complaint is justified and apologize. Briefly state that you are sorry and thank the customer for writing to inform you.

2. State precisely what you are going to do to correct the problem. Are you going to cancel a bill, return a damaged camera in good working order, repaint a room, enclose a free pass, provide a complimentary dinner, or give the customer credit toward another purchase? Do not postpone the good news the customer wants to hear. The rest of your letter will be much more appreciated and convincing. In Figure 8.19 Michael Trigg is told that he will receive a new reel; in Figure 8.20 Kathryn Brumfield is informed that she will not be charged for parts or service.

3. Tell customers exactly what happened. They deserve an explanation for the inconvenience they suffered. Note how the explanations in Figures 8.19 and 8.20 give only the essential details; they do not bother the reader with side issues or petty remarks about who was to blame. Don't threaten to fire one of your employees because of a customer's problem. Assure customers that the mishap is not typical of your company's operations. While your comments should not shift the blame, they should center on the unusual reason or circumstance for the difficulty. Avoid promising, however, that the problem will never recur. Such an admission is not only unnecessary but may also be beyond your control.

4. End on a friendly, and positive, note. Do not remind customers of the trouble they have gone through. Leave them with a good feeling about your company. Say that you are looking forward to seeing them again, that you will gladly work with them on any future orders, or that you can always be reached for questions.

Adjustment Letters That Tell the Customer "No"

Writing to tell customers "No" is obviously more difficult than agreeing with them. You are faced with the sensitive task of conveying bad news, while at the same time convincing the reader that your position is fair, logical, and consistent. Do not accuse or argue. Avoid remarks such as the following that blame, scold, or remind customers of a wrongdoing and hence may cost you their business.

- You obviously did not read the instruction manual.
- Our records show that you purchased the set after the policy went into effect.
- The company policy plainly states that such refunds are unallowable.
- You were negligent in running the machine.
- You claim that our word processor was poorly constructed.
- Your error, not our merchandise, is to blame.
- You must be mistaken about the merchandise.
- As any intelligent person could tell, the switch had to be "off."
- Your complaint is unjustified.

The following five suggestions will help you say "No" diplomatically. Practical applications of these suggestions can be found in Figures 8.21 and 8.22. Contrast the rejection of Michael Trigg's complaint in Figure 8.21 with the favorable response to it in Figure 8.19.

FIGURE 8.21   An adjustment letter saying "No."

Smith Sports Equipment
P.O. Box 287
Tulsa, Oklahoma 74109-1014
(918) 881-0164

September 21, 1990

Mr. Michael Trigg
17 Westwood
Magnolia, MA 02171

Dear Mr. Trigg:

Thank you for writing to us on September 15 about the trouble you experienced with our model 191 spincast reel. We were sorry to hear about the difficulties you had with the release button and gears.

We have examined your reel and have found the trouble. It seems that a retaining pin on the button spring was pushed into the side of the reel casing, thereby making the gears inoperable. The retaining pin is a vital yet delicate part of your reel. In order to function properly, it has to be pushed gently. Since the pin was not used in this way, we are not able to refund your purchase price.

We will be pleased, however, to repair your reel for $6.98 and return it to you for hours of fishing pleasure. Please let us know your decision.

I look forward to hearing from you.

Respectfully,

SMITH SPORTS EQUIPMENT

Ralph Montoya

Ralph Montoya, Manager
Customer Relations Department

FIGURE 8.22   An adjustment letter saying "No."

HEALTH AIR, INC.
4300 Marshall Drive
Salt Lake City, Utah 84113-1521
(801) 877-6028

August 20, 1990

Ms. Denise Southby, Director
Bradley General Hospital
Bradley, IL 60610-4615

Dear Ms. Southby:

Thank you for your letter of August 10 explaining the problems you have encountered with our Puritan Bennett MAII ventilator. We were sorry to learn that you could not get the high-volume PAO_2 alarm circuit to work.

Our ventilator is a high-volume, low-frequency machine that is capable of delivering up to 40 ml of water pressure. The ventilator runs with a center of gravity attachment that is on the right side of the diode. The trouble you are having with the high oxygen alarm system is due to an overload on your piped-in oxygen. Our laboratory inspection of the ventilator you returned indicates that the high-pressure system had blown a vital adaptor in the machine. Our company cannot be responsible for any type of overload caused by an oxygen system of which we are unaware. We cannot, therefore, send you a replacement ventilator free of charge. Your ventilator is being returned to you.

We would, however, be very glad to send you another model of the adaptor, which would be more compatible with your system, as soon as we receive your order. The price of the adaptor is $600, and our factory representative will be happy to install it for you at no charge. Please let me know your decision.

We welcome the opportunity to assist you in providing quality health care at Bradley General.

Sincerely yours,

R. P. Gilford

R. P. Gilford
Customer Service Department

1. Thank customers for writing. Make a friendly start by putting them in a good frame of mind. The letter writers in Figure 8.21 and 8.22 say that they are thankful that the customers brought the matter to their attention. As with other bad news letters, never begin with a refusal. You need time to calm and convince customers. Telling them "No" ("We regret to inform you") in the first sentence or two will negatively color their reactions to the rest of the letter. Also, never begin letters with "I was surprised to learn that you found our product defective (*or* our service inefficient)" or "We cannot understand how such a problem occurred. We have been in business for years, and nothing like this has ever happened." Such openings put customers on the defensive. Use the indirect approach discussed on pages 216–18.

2. State the problem so that customers realize that you understand their complaint. You thereby prove that you are not trying to misrepresent what they have told you.

3. Explain what happened with the product or service before you give customers a decision. Provide a factual explanation to show customers that they are being treated fairly. Convince them of the logic and consistency of your point of view. Rather than focusing on the customer's mishandling of merchandise or failure to observe details of a service contract, state the proper ways of handling a piece of equipment or the terms outlined in an agreement. Instead of writing "By reading the instructions on the side of the paint can, you would have avoided the streaking condition that you claim resulted," tell the customer that "Hi-Gloss Paint requires two applications, four hours apart, for a clear and smooth finish." In this way you remind customers of the right way of applying the paint without pointing an accusing finger at them. Note how the explanations in Figures 8.21 and 8.22 emphasize the right way of using the product.

4. Give your decision without hedging. Do not say that perhaps some type of restitution could be made later or that further proof would have been helpful. Indecision will infuriate customers who believe that they have already presented a sound, convincing case. Never apologize for your decision. Avoid using the words *reject, claim,* or *grant. Reject* is too harsh and impersonal. *Claim* implies your distrust of the customer's complaint and suggests that questionable differences of opinion remain. *Grant* signals that you have it in your power to respond favorably but decline to do so; a grant is the kind of favor a ruler might give a subject. Instead, use words that reconcile.

5. Leave the door open for better and continued business. Whenever possible, help customers solve their problem by offering to send them a new product or part, and quote the full sales price. Note how the second-to-last paragraphs of the letters in Figures 8.21 and 8.22 do this diplomatically.

Collection Letters

Collection letters are, unfortunately, a part of every business's concern. They require the same tact and fairness as do complaint and adjustment letters. While the majority of your customers will pay their bills promptly, some will not pay on time, and a few others may not pay until they are threatened with legal action or harassment from a collection agency.

Each nonpayment case should be evaluated separately. A nasty collection letter sent after only one month's nonpayment to an otherwise good customer can damage your relationship and send that customer elsewhere. On the other hand, three overly cordial, easygoing letters sent over three or four months to a customer who is a poor credit risk may encourage that individual to postpone payment, perhaps indefinitely.

Many businesses send four letters to customers before turning matters over to an attorney or a collection agency. Letters to poor credit risks are sent at shorter intervals than letters to good credit risks. Each letter in the series employs a different technique, ranging from giving compliments and offering flexible credit terms to issuing demands for immediate payment or threats of legal consequences. One small hospital uses four collection letters (illustrated in Figures 8.23 through 8.26) to encourage ex-patients to pay their bills.

The letter in Figure 8.23 typifies the function of a first collection letter. It is a friendly reminder that an account is due. The tone of the letter is cordial and sincere—now is not the time to say "Pay up or else!" A first collection letter should stress how valuable the customer is, as does the first paragraph in Figure 8.23. Note also that the first paragraph underscores how pleased the hospital is to have provided the care the patient needed. The last sentence of that paragraph unobtrusively introduces the word "finances" in the context of service. The second paragraph, after allowing for possible questions concerning the bill, makes a request for payment. Inducements to make that payment are offered: (1) a flexible payment schedule and (2) an escape from the inconvenience (or embarrassment) of receiving past-due notices. The bottom of the letter conveniently lists payment-schedule options available to the patient.

If after a month to six weeks, a customer still does not make a payment, send a second letter, such as the one illustrated in Figure 8.24. This letter begins with a gentle reminder that the balance due has not yet been paid. The second paragraph politely inquires if something is wrong, thus acknowledging that not all nonpayments stem from willful neglect. While this second collection letter understands that there might be some "difficulty," it firmly reminds the patient to pay if there is no financial trouble. The last sentence makes another strong appeal to the patient's community obligation. Note that unlike the first letter, no payment schedule appears at the bottom of the letter, thus giving the reader a chance to explain any delay.

When still more time elapses and no payment is made, creditors send a third letter, an example of which appears in Figure 8.25. The creditor's tone and tactics have changed. From the cooperative tone of "What's wrong; can we help?" in the second collection letter, the third letter switches to the much more direct "We have waited a long time. Pay, or at least begin to pay, your bill now." The third collection letter, which must be more forceful than the second, announces that serious consequences will result if the creditor does not receive a payment from the customer. The vague threat, "further action," wisely does not commit the hospital to take legal action or to speak to a collection agency, its last resort. The

FIGURE 8.23   A first collection letter.

➕ **Baldwin County Hospital**   P.O. Box 222   Notown, MA 02138-1098   (617) 281-3000

May 15, 1990

Mr. Howard Peterson
318 Brook Avenue #8A
Notown, MA 02146-1074

Re: Inpatient Services
Date of Hospitalization: April 1–5, 1990
Balance Due: $3725.48

Dear Mr. Peterson:

We are grateful that we were able to serve your health needs during your recent stay at the Baldwin County Hospital. It is our continuing goal to provide the best possible hospital care for residents of Baldwin County and its vicinity. You will readily understand that to do so we must keep our finances up to date.

Our records show that the above balance remains due on your account. Unless you have a question concerning the figure, we would appreciate receiving your prompt payment. If you are unable to pay the full amount at this time, we will be happy to set up a schedule of partial payments. Just fill in the appropriate blanks below, and return this letter to me. That will enable us to avoid billing you on a "Past Due" basis. Thank you for your cooperation.

Sincerely,

Morris T. Jukes

Morris T. Jukes
Accounts Receivable Department

(   ) I will pay $_____ (   ) weekly; (   ) monthly, on my account.

(   ) Enclosed is a check for full payment in the amount of $_____ .

_____
Signature

---

third letter should still give the delinquent customer a way out, and so this one contains some useful, face-saving options listed at the bottom of the letter.

If after receiving these three letters, a customer still does not respond, the creditor sends a fourth letter containing a specific threat that will be carried out.

FIGURE 8.24   A second collection letter.

 Baldwin County Hospital   P.O. Box 222   Notown, MA 02138-1098   (617) 281-3000

June 19, 1990

Mr. Howard Peterson
318 Brook Avenue #8A
Notown, MA 02146-1074

Re: Inpatient Services
Date of Hospitalization: April 1–5, 1990
Balance Due: $3725.48

Dear Mr. Peterson:

Since we have not received a reply to our letter of May 15, we want to remind you of the balance that remains on your account.

If there is some difficulty, drop by and see us today; we will do our best to help. Otherwise, we would appreciate receiving your payment in full by return mail.

Our ability to provide health services to others depends to a great extent upon your cooperation. Please do not let us down.

Sincerely,

Morris T. Jukes

Morris T. Jukes
Accounts Receivable Department

Note, though, how the letter in Figure 8.26 does not begin with that bad news. Instead, it reminds the patient of all the efforts the hospital has expended to collect its bills. The letter clearly points out that the time for concessions is over. Then it announces what consequences will result if the patient still does not pay. The letter gives proper legal notification that the patient has ten days to respond.

FIGURE 8.25   A third collection letter.

**Baldwin
County
Hospital**   P.O. Box 222   Notown, MA 02138-1098   (617) 281-3000

July 24, 1990

Mr. Howard Peterson
318 Brook Avenue #8A
Notown, MA 02146-1074

Re: Inpatient Services
Date of Hospitalization: April 1–5, 1990
Balance Due: $3725.48

Dear Mr. Peterson:

We regret that we have received no response from you to our letters of May 15 and
June 19 concerning your outstanding balance.

Because so much time has elapsed, we must now require full payment (or your signed
agreement to make regular installment payments) within the next ten days.

If we have not heard from you by August 23, it will become necessary for us to take
further action.

Sincerely,

Morris T. Jukes

Morris T. Jukes
Accounts Receivable Department

(   ) I will pay $_____ (   ) weekly; (   ) monthly, on my account.

(   ) Enclosed is a check for full payment in the amount of $_____.

_____
Signature

The fourth collection letter attempts to frighten the customer into payment and
does not have to seek or give any explanations. If the hospital, or any company,
fails to carry its threat to turn delinquent accounts over to a collection agency or
attorney, however, it will quickly get a reputation for having all bark but no
bite—a reputation that would make it difficult to collect its debts in the future.

FIGURE 8.26   A fourth and final collection letter.

**Baldwin
County
Hospital**   P.O. Box 222   Notown, MA 02138-1098   (617) 281-3000

August 27, 1990

Mr. Howard Peterson
318 Brook Avenue #8A
Notown, MA 02146-1074

Re: Inpatient Services
Date of Hospitalization: April 1–5, 1990
Balance Due: $3725.48

Dear Mr. Peterson:

During the past few months we have written to you several times concerning your
outstanding balance.

As you may recall, we offered to arrange for installment payments or to help you in
any way that we could. Since you have not responded, we must demand your payment
in full at this time.

If we do not hear from you within ten days, we will have no alternative but to turn
your account over to our collection agency.

Sincerely,

Morris T. Jukes

Morris T. Jukes
Accounts Receivable Department

◆ BUSINESS CORRESPONDENCE: SOME CLOSING REMARKS FOR SUCCESS

This chapter has shown you how to prepare some of the most common types of business correspondence. Regardless of the kind of letter or memo you have to write, you will increase your chances for success if you adhere to the following four guidelines.

1. Plan what you are going to say. Take a few minutes to plan your message before you draft it. Think before you write. If you are responding to a letter or memo, have a copy of it before you so you don't forget to include information the reader needs.

2. Organize your information in the most effective way for the reader. Letters and memos should follow reader-effective strategies. Always begin your correspondence by explaining why you are writing; don't make readers wade through several paragraphs to find out. When you have good news to report, tell them right away; when you have bad news to convey, be diplomatically indirect.

3. Emphasize the "you attitude" with every reader—employer, customer, or co-worker. Make the reader feel that you are interested in him or her. A personable, courteous approach will increase your chances of getting the reader to do what you suggest.

4. Be timely and accurate. Answer all correspondence promptly. A late letter might jeopardize a sale, irritate a customer or an employer, or reflect poorly on your own performance on the job. Remember to give readers reasonable time to receive and answer your correspondence.

◆ EXERCISES

1. Write a memo to your employer saying that you will be out of town two days next week and three the following week for one of the following reasons: (a) to inspect some land your firm is thinking of buying, (b) to investigate some claims, (c) to look at some new office space for a branch your firm is thinking of opening in a city five hundred miles away, (d) to attend a conference sponsored by a professional society, or (e) to pay calls on customers. In your memo, be very specific about dates, places, times, and reasons.

2. Send a memo to your public relations department informing it that you are completing a degree or work for a certificate, and indicate how the information could be useful for its publicity campaign.

3. Write a memo to the payroll department notifying it that there is a mistake in your last paycheck. Explain exactly what the error is and give precise figures.

4. You are a manager of a local art museum. Write a memo to the Chamber of Commerce in which you put the following information into proper memo format.

Old hours: Mon.–Fri. 9–5; closed Sat. except during July and August when you are open 9–12

New hours: Mon.–Th. 8:30–4:30; Fri.–Sat. 9–9

Old rates: Adults $1.50; senior citizens $1.00; children under 12 free

New rates: Adults $2.50; senior citizens $1.00; children under 12 free but must be accompanied by an adult

Added features: Paintings by Thora Horne, local artist; sculpture from West Indies in display area all summer; guided tours available with a party of six or more; lounge areas will offer patrons sandwiches and soft drinks during May, June, July, and August

5. Select some change (in policy, schedule, or personnel assignment) you encountered in a job you held in the last two or three years and write an appropriate memo describing that change. Assume you are your former employer explaining the change to employees.

6. Write a letter in which you order merchandise from a company. Specify the quantity, size, stock number, cost, and also include delivery instructions, the date by which you must receive the merchandise, and the way in which you will pay for it.

7. Write a letter of inquiry to a utility company, a safety or health care agency, or a company in your town, asking for a brochure describing its services to the community. Be specific about your reasons for requesting this information.

8. In which course(s) are you or will you be writing a paper or report? Write to an agency or company that could supply you with helpful information for the paper and request its aid. Indicate why you are writing, indicating precisely what information you need, why you need it, and offer to share your paper or report with the company.

9. Examine an ad in a magazine or a TV commercial and then write a one-page assessment in which you identify the four parts of a sales message.

10. Choose one of the following and write a sales letter addressed to an appropriate audience on why they should:
   a. major in the same subject you did.
   b. live in your neighborhood.
   c. be happy taking a vacation where you did last year.
   d. dine at a particular restaurant.
   e. shop at a store you have worked for or will work for.
   f. have their cars repaired at a specific garage.
   g. give their real estate business to a particular agency.

11. Find at least two sales letters you or your family have received and evaluate

them according to how well they follow the four parts of a sales letter discussed in this chapter. Attach these sales letters to your evaluation.

12. Write a sales letter about the effectiveness of sales letters to an individual who has told you that almost everyone throws them away as soon as he or she gets them.

13. Rewrite the following sales letter to make it more effective. Add any details you think are relevant.

Dear Pizza Lovers:

Allow me to introduce myself. My name is Rudy Moore and I am the new manager of Tasty Pizza Parlor in town. The Parlor is located at the intersection of North Miller Parkway and 95th Street. We are open from 10 a.m. to 11 p.m., except on the weekends, when we are open later.

I think you will be as happy as I am to learn that Tasty's will now offer free delivery. As a result, you can get your Tasty Pizza hot when you want it.

Please see your weekly newspapers for our ad. We also are offering customers a coupon. It is a real deal for you.

I know you will enjoy Tasty's and I hope to see you. I am always interested in hearing from you about our service and our fine product. We want to take your order soon. Please come in.

14. Write a thank-you letter in response to one of the following:
    a. a gift you have received from a coworker
    b. a letter of recommendation someone wrote for you
    c. some business that was directed to you or your employer
    d. a dinner or other social occasion to which you were invited by a customer or your employer or agency

15. Write a congratulation letter to someone for one of the following:
    a. being promoted
    b. winning an award at school
    c. being named salesperson of the month
    d. completing a special course or degree
    e. being elected to public office
    f. concluding a business deal (selling a product, renegotiating a contract)
    g. opening a new store or branch
    h. joining your firm or agency

16. Send a follow-up letter to one of the following individuals:
    a. a customer who informs you that he will no longer do business with your firm because your prices are too high
    b. a family of four who stayed at your motel for two weeks last summer
    c. a church group that used your catering services last month

    d. a customer who exchanged a dress or coat for the purchase price

    e. a customer who bought a new car from you one year ago

    f. a company that bought a year's supply of pens from you nine months ago

17. Write a bad news letter to an appropriate reader about one of the following:

    a. Your company has to discontinue Saturday deliveries because of rising labor and fuel costs.

    b. You are the manager of an insurance company writing to tell one of your customers that because of reckless driving, his or her rates are going to increase.

    c. You have to refuse to send a bonus gift to a customer because that customer sent in an order after the expiration date for providing that bonus gift.

    d. You have to refuse a young couple a mortgage.

    e. You have to notify residents of a community that a bus route is being discontinued.

    f. You represent the water department and have to tell residents of a community that they cannot water their lawns for the next month because of a serious water shortage problem in your town.

    g. You cannot send customers a catalog—which your company used to send free of charge—unless they first send $5 for the cost of that catalog.

    h. You cannot repair a particular piece of equipment because the customer still owes your company for three previous service visits.

18. Write a good news letter about the opposite of one of the situations listed in Exercise 17 above.

19. Write a complaint letter about one of the following:

    a. an error in your utility or telephone bill

    b. discourteous service you received on an airplane or bus

    c. a frozen food product of poor quality

    d. a shipment tha arrives late and damaged

    e. an insurance payment to you that is fifty dollars less than it should be

    f. a public television station's policy of not showing a particular series

    g. junk mail that you are receiving

20. Write the complaint letter to which the adjustment letter in Figure 8.20 responds.

21. Write the complaint letter to which the adjustment letter in Figure 8.21 responds.

22. Rewrite the following complaint letter to make it more precise and less emotional.

Dear Sir:

We recently purchased a machine from your Albany store and paid a great deal of money for it. This machine, supposedly the best model in your line, has caused us nothing but trouble each time we used it. Really, can't you do any better with your technology?

We expect you to stand by your products. The warranties you give with them should make you accountable for shoddy workmanship. Let us know at once what you intend to do about our problem. If you cannot or are unwilling to correct the situation, we will take our business elsewhere, and then you will be sorry.

Sincerely yours,

23. Write an adjustment letter saying "Yes" to the manager of The Loft whose letter is in Figure 8.18.

24. Write an adjustment letter saying "No" to the customer who received the "Yes" adjustment letter in Figure 8.20.

25. Rewrite the following ineffective adjustment letter saying "Yes."

Dear Mr. Smith:

We are extremely sorry to learn that you found the suit you purchased from us unsatisfactory. The problem obviously stems from the fact that you selected it from the rack marked "Factory Seconds." In all honesty, we have had a lot of problems because of this rack. I guess we should know better than to try to feature inferior merchandise along with the name–brand clothing that we sell. But we originally thought that our customers would accept poorer quality merchandise if it saved them some money. That was our mistake.

Please accept our apologies. If you will bring your "Factory Second" suit to us, we will see what we can do about honoring your request.

Sincerely yours,

26. Rewrite the following ineffective adjustment letter saying "No."

Dear Customer:

Our company is unwilling to give you a new toaster or to refund your purchase price. After examining the toaster you sent to us, we found that the fault was not ours, as you insist, but yours.

Let me explain. The motor in our toaster is made to take a lot of punishment. But being dropped on the floor or poked inside with a knife, as you probably did, exceeds all decent treatment. You must be careful if you expect your appliances to last. Your negligence in this case is so bad that the toaster could not be repaired.

In the future, consider using your appliances according to the
guidelines set down in warranty books. That's why they are
written.

Since you are now in the market for a new toaster, let me suggest
that you purchase our new heavy-duty model, number 67342, called
the Counter-Whiz. I am taking the liberty of sending you some
information about this model. I do hope you at least go to see one
at your local appliance center.

Sincerely,

27. Assume that you work in a student services department at a local college and
that you have been asked to write collection letters to those graduates who
are not paying off their student loans on time. Write a series of four collection letters to be sent at appropriate times. The first letter is sent after the
student misses only one payment, the second letter after two nonpayments,
the third letter after three nonpayments, and the fourth letter after four nonpayments.

28. Rewrite the following collection letter twice, the first time making it appropriate for a first notice and the second time making it suitable for a second
notice.

Dear Customer:

You may recall that you owe us the slight sum of $64.56 for the
plumbing work we did for you in January. To you such bills may
appear trivial, but in order to stay in business we have to
collect from everyone, from the little guy like you to the big
companies we help.

Do not be a problem for us. Pay what you owe. If you do not send us
a check for the above amount in the next few days, we will somehow
get the money out of you. Whether you pay the easy way by sending
us a check now or whether we put a hard-nosed collection agency on
your case is entirely up to you.

Sincerely yours,

Gathering and Summarizing Information

Chapter 9: Finding
and Using Library Materials

◆

Chapter 10: Documenting Sources

◆

Chapter 11: Summarizing Material

◆

Chapter 12: Preparing a
Questionnaire and Reporting the Results

◆

Chapter 13: Designing Visuals

9

Finding and Using Library Materials

A personnel director asked an applicant during a job interview to name the titles of two or three major journals in the applicant's field. When the applicant could not come up with any titles, chances for employment at the company became slim. The question was typical, fair, and relevant. The interviewer knew that an applicant's success in the job depends on the quality of information supplied to the employer. Employers expect carefully researched answers; they will not be satisfied with guesses.

Research, or the careful investigation of material found in books, magazines, pamphlets, films, and other sources (including resource people), is a vital part of every occupation. Companies expect their employees to be able to research a problem, find information, and prepare bibliographies for any number of reasons, such as writing proposals and long reports. You might conduct research by telephoning someone in the next department for information or by thumbing through a company catalog. Or you might engage in research by studying reference works in a library or by preparing statistical or analytical surveys. You must be informed about the latest developments in your field, and you must be able to communicate your findings accurately and concisely. Doing research is a practical skill like swimming, running, or typing. Once learned, it is easy to perform. Knowing how to do research in your field offers lifelong benefits.

The information in Chapter 9 can save you from suffering the embarrassment experienced by the job applicant described above. Specifically, Chapter 9 discusses major reference works—where to find them and how to use them. The appendix to this chapter (pages 280–85) contains information about specific reference works (indexes, encyclopedias, dictionaries, and abstracts) that will be extremely valuable to you in your research.

◆ THE LIBRARY AND ITS SECTIONS

You may think of your library as a single building, but that building is divided into many sections. When you walk into a library, probably the first section you see is the circulation desk—in many ways, the business center of the library. You go to the circulation desk to borrow or return books, to pick up materials you may have ordered from another library, or to find out if a book has been checked out. From the circulation desk you can move to any one of the following parts of the library to use materials. (The page numbers after each area refer to the page numbers of this chapter where you will find a description of the particular unit and the materials in it.)

- the card catalog (pages 250–55)
- the stacks (pages 255–57)
- periodical holdings and indexes (pages 257–66)
- reference books (pages 266–68)
- government documents (pages 268–71)
- the popular press (pages 271–73)
- audiovisual materials (pages 273–75)

◆ BOOKS

The Card Catalog

The card catalog, your guide to the library, will be located in a prominent place, usually near the entrance. Traditionally housed in cabinets with numerous drawers, the card catalog contains three-by-five-inch index cards for each book, filmstrip, tape recording, or microfilm your library owns. The card catalog does not contain information about articles in magazines or journals. For information on the contents of individual magazines or journals, you will have to consult your library's periodical holdings list and the periodical indexes discussed later in this chapter.

At some firms and libraries, the cabinets of the card catalog have been replaced by a computer terminal. The computer links the user to the online catalog, or database, containing information about the books and other materials in the library. With access to this database, the user can find information about titles, authors, subject areas, and location of materials as well as learn whether a book has been checked out, is placed on reserve, or is available to be checked out. Computerized card catalogs will be used increasingly in the future.

How Material in the Card Catalog Is Alphabetized

You can use three methods to find a book in the card catalog. You can look for it under the author's name, under the title, or under the subject it discusses. Some libraries may have separate cabinets for each of these three designations (author, title, subject), while at other libraries, especially small ones, all three designations are included in one cabinet. Information in all three categories is listed alphabetically, either letter by letter or word by word. These two ways of alphabetizing entries can make a big difference, as the following examples show.

Letter by letter		Word by word	
fire	fire escape	fire	fire wall
firearm	firefly	fire drill	firearm
fire drill	firetrap	fire escape	firefly
	fire wall		firetrap

The letter-by-letter method is based on the sequence of individual letters regardless of whether an entry contains one word or two. Hence, *firearm* comes before *fire drill*. Under the word-by-word method, each entry is alphabetized according to the letters in the first word, whether that entry is made up of one word or two. *Fire wall* comes ahead of *firearm* and *firefly* because the word *fire* is a part of both of these words and alphabetically precedes them. Find out which method your library uses so you can look up entries more quickly and more accurately. The following alphabetical rules apply to both methods and will help you search for an entry in the card catalog.

1. An author's last name beginning with *Mc* is listed as if the *Mc* were spelled *Mac*; so *McDonald* will be listed in the card catalog as if it were *MacDonald*. Hyphenated last names are found at the end of the alphabetical letter beginning the first of two hyphenated names. A book by Alan Jones-Davies, for example, would be listed at the end of the J's, not under the D's.

2. Disregard definite and indefinite articles—*the, a,* or *an*—at the beginning of a title. A book with the title *A New Fashion Guide* will be found in the N's.

3. Abbreviations, acronyms (NATO, VISTA, and other words formed from the first letters of several words), and numbers can be alphabetized in one of two ways. They can be alphabetized as if they were spelled out in full, so a book entitled *Mr. and Mrs. Average American* would be found in the title section of the card catalog under *Mister* and *22 Ways to Better Health* would be listed under *Twenty-Two*. A book written by IBM would be listed under *International Business Machines*. And a study put out by the ANA would be found in the author section under *American Nurses Association*. But some libraries file acronyms alphabetically at the beginning of the letter (*NASA, NATO, native*).

Author Card

One way to find a book is to locate the author card in a card catalog. Spell the author's name correctly and record first names or initials accurately. If you know only the last name, and if it is a common one, your search may take a great deal of extra time. An *author card* for a book by Martin Meyerson can be seen in Figure 9.1. To find Meyerson's book, you would look under the M's until you come to Meyerson and then find Martin. The author card(s) tells you what titles by that author are in your library. Each card will tell you where to find the book, when it was written, who published it, and where. Figure 9.1 is coded to show you what each number, abbreviation, and symbol means.

FIGURE 9.1   An author card in the card catalog.

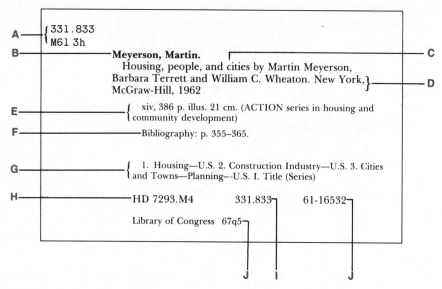

A   The *call number* locates the book in the library. In this case the library has filed the book according to the Dewey decimal system.

B   The *author's name* is always listed with the last name (surname) first. Sometimes a card also gives the author's date of birth and, if the author is deceased, the date of death. If a book has more than one author or editor, only the author whose name appears first in the book is listed in the upper-left-hand corner of the card.

C   The *title* of the book.

D   The names of any *coauthors or coeditors and pertinent publication information*—city, publisher, and date of publication.

E   A *physical description of the book*—number of pages from the preface (usually numbered in lower-case roman numerals) through the index, whether the book is illustrated (illus.) and the height (in centimeters) of the book. Also noted is whether the book is part of a special series or is issued under a special imprint (or publishing arrangement).

F   This book contains a *bibliography* on pages 355 to 365.

G   List of the *other headings in the subject catalog under which the book is listed.*

H   The *Library of Congress designation* for this book would be in the A position if the library followed the Library of Congress system of classification rather than the Dewey decimal one. "Library of Congress" means that a copy of the book is in the national library.

I   The *Dewey decimal number.*

J   *Identification numbers used by librarians.* You need not be concerned with this designation.

Title Card

Figure 9.2 shows a *title card.* It is identical to an author card except that the title of the book is listed twice—once as a heading on top of the card and again as part of the entry itself. It is easy to find this card when you know the first word of the title. Keep in mind that the articles *a, an,* or *the* at the beginning of the title are

FIGURE 9.2   A title card in the card catalog.

```
331.833
M613h                    Housing, people and cities.

         Meyerson, Martin.
              Housing, people, and cities by Martin Meyerson,
         Barbara Terrett and William C. Wheaton. New York,
         McGraw-Hill, 1962.

              xiv, 386 p. illus. 21 cm. (ACTION series in housing and
         community development)

              Bibliography: p. 355–365.
              1. Housing—U.S. 2. Construction Industry—U.S. 3. Cities
         and Towns—Planning—U.S. I. Title (Series)

         HD 7293.M4        331.833        61-16532

         Library of Congress   67q5
```

omitted in alphabetizing. With the Meyerson book you do not have an article for the first word of the title; just search for the book under the H's in the title section of the card catalog.

Subject Card

Figure 9.3 shows the *subject card* for the Meyerson book. Again, the subject card is identical to the author card except that a subject heading—marked with distinctive red or black ink—is located at the top of the card. Many times students start with the subject section of the card catalog since they do not have titles or authors in mind early in their search. The subject catalog also lists reference

FIGURE 9.3   A subject card in the card catalog.

```
331.833
M613h       CONSTRUCTION INDUSTRY–UNITED STATES

         Meyerson, Martin.
              Housing, people, and cities by Martin Meyerson,
         Barbara Terrett and William C. Wheaton. New York,
         McGraw-Hill, 1962.

              xiv, 386 p. illus. 21 cm. (ACTION series in housing and
         community development

              Bibliography: p. 355–365.


              1. Housing—U.S. 2. Construction Industry—U.S. 3. Cities
         and Towns—Planning—U.S. I. Title (Series)

         HD 7293.M4        331.833        61-16532

         Library of Congress   67q5
```

works (abstracts, bibliographies, dictionaries, handbooks, and indexes) that will guide you to specific titles.

The subject section divides a topic into subheadings or groups and alerts readers to other, related topics. Looking under the subject section for "construction," you would first find a cross-reference, or "see also," card, illustrated in Figure 9.4. This card alerts you to other subject categories (references) you should check for information in addition to the cards gathered under the "construction" heading. Next, you would find the following breakdown of the topic with appropriate books listed for each:

* construction dictionary
* construction equipment
* construction handbook
* construction, housing
* construction industry

Stopping at the last subheading, "construction industry," you could find even more subclassifications:

* accounting
* automation
* contracts
* costs
* data processing
* law and legislation
* management
* personnel
* subcontracting
* United States

Meyerson's book would be found under this last subheading, "United States."

FIGURE 9.4 A "see also" card in the card catalog.

```
                    see also

                    CONSTRUCTION—UNITED STATES
                    BUILDING
                    ENGINEERING
```

Subject cards break down topics into subcategories and list appropriate titles under each subcategory or refer readers to other parts of the subject catalog. They also list on the entry card beneath the title of the book other relevant topics to consult directly. Examine the Meyerson card in Figure 9.3. Following the bibliographic information, the card lists three other subject areas that will help readers find additional information: (1) housing, (2) construction, and (3) cities and towns.

The Stacks

The majority of space in a library is taken up by the rows of bookshelves, called stacks. Your library may have open or closed stacks. If the stacks are open, you are free to walk along the rows to find the books you need. If they are closed, a member of the library staff will find a book for you after you present a call slip identifying—by author, title, and number—the book you want.

Call Numbers

Regardless of which system your library uses, you will have to know the call number of the book you want. Call numbers or letters are found in the upper left-hand side of the card in the catalog. Your library may use either the Library of Congress (abbreviated LC) or the Dewey decimal system. Table 9.1 shows a section of the LC system and some of the divisions in the Dewey decimal system. The LC system divides all areas of knowledge into twenty-one categories that are differentiated by capital letters of the alphabet. Subdivisions are labeled with a combination of letters and numbers. As its name implies, the Dewey decimal system divides knowledge into ten large categories indicated by numerical groups ranging from 000 to the 900s. Each large division is divided into groups of ten subdivisions. The first number in a Dewey classification indicates the large category of knowledge in which a book is found, and the second and third numbers specify exact areas of that large group.

Meyerson's book, *Housing, People, and Cities,* is classified in the LC system by the letters HD. The letter H indicates that the book falls into the large category marked "Social Sciences," and D signifies that the book belongs in the subcategory "Economics," as opposed to "Statistics" (HA) or "Sociology" (HM–HX). The Dewey number for Meyerson's book is 331.833—that is, it falls into the 300s, "Social Sciences"; the 30s of the 300s is the subdivision "Economics."

Shelves

Once you know the call number, you should check where the book is shelved if your library has open stacks. Your library may post maps that show the location of books by their call numbers. When you know the approximate location of a book, go to that section of the library and look at the markers posted at the end of each row of stacks. Then walk down the appropriate row to find your book.

TABLE 9.1   A Sample of Headings from Call-Number Sections

Library of Congress		Dewey Decimal	
Q	Science	500	Pure sciences
Q	Science (General)	510	Mathematics
QA	Mathematics	520	Astronomy and allied sciences
QB	Astronomy	530	Physics
QC	Physics	540	Chemistry and allied sciences
QD	Chemistry	550	Sciences of earth and other worlds
QE	Geology	560	Paleontology
QH	Natural History	570	Life sciences
QK	Botany	580	Botanical sciences
QL	Zoology	590	Zoological sciences
QM	Human anatomy	600	Technology (Applied sciences)
QP	Physiology	610	Medical sciences
QR	Microbiology	620	Engineering and allied operations
		630	Agriculture
R	Medicine	640	Domestic arts and sciences
R	Medicine (General)	650	Managerial services
RB	Pathology	660	Chemical and related technologies
RK	Dentistry	670	Manufactures
RT	Nursing	680	Miscellaneous manufacturing
		690	Buildings
S	Agriculture		
S	Agriculture (General)		
SB	Plant culture		
SD	Forestry		
SF	Animal culture		

Library of Congress, Subject Cataloging Division, *LC Classification Outline,* 3rd ed. (Washington, D.C.: U.S. Government Printing Office, 1975); Melvil Dewey, *Decimal Classification and Relative Index: The Second Summary* (New York, 1971), 450.

FIGURE 9.5   Spine of a book with call number.

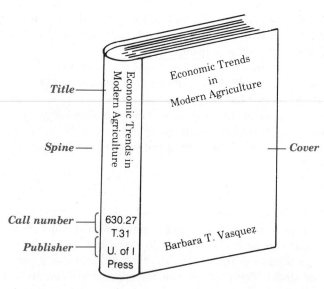

Most books will have their call numbers on the spine, or the place where the book is bound, as illustrated in Figure 9.5. Some especially thin books have their call numbers on the outside front cover.

If the book you are looking for is not on the shelf, go to the circulation desk to see if it has been checked out. If so, you can ask the librarian to hold it for you when it comes back. Perhaps the book can be used only in the library (then it is said to be "on reserve"), in which case you will have to sign it out from the circulation desk. If the librarian discovers that the book has not been checked out or is not on reserve, it may be misshelved. Check with the library in the next few days to see if it has been found.

◆ PERIODICAL HOLDINGS AND INDEXES

Your research will not be confined exclusively to books. Some of it will lead you to the wealth of information contained in periodicals. A *periodical* is a magazine or journal that is published at established, frequent intervals—weekly, bimonthly (once every two months), quarterly. The word *magazine* refers to periodicals— *Gentleman's Quarterly, Redbook,* or *Time*—that appeal to a diverse audience and that treat popular themes. The word *journal* characterizes technical or scholarly periodicals, such as the *American Journal of Nursing* or the *American Waterworks Journal,* whose audiences read them for professional or scientific information in special fields.

Periodicals have certain advantages over books when it comes to research. Because they take less time to produce than books, periodicals can give you more recent information on a topic. Further, periodicals are not as restricted as books. A book usually discusses one subject from one point of view, but a periodical can contain ten different articles, each covering a separate topic and each offering a different perspective. This is not to imply that you should ignore books and focus solely on magazines or journals. Use both, but be aware of the differences.

To find appropriate articles in magazines and journals, you need to use indexes. An *index* is a listing by subject, and sometimes also by author, of articles that have appeared within a specified period of time. An index tells you what articles have appeared on your subject, where they were published, who wrote them, and whether they contain any special information, such as bibliographies, illustrations, diagrams and maps, or portraits. You would be lost without indexes. You could never successfully thumb through all the periodicals in the library to determine which ones contain an article you could use. Furthermore, your library might not subscribe to all the journals and magazines that contain articles related to your subject. The indexes let you know what is available beyond your own library's holdings.

The *Readers' Guide to Periodical Literature*

One of the most basic indexes is the *Readers' Guide to Periodical Literature,* which has been listing information on periodicals since 1900. The *Readers' Guide* indexes information from more than 200 periodicals, mostly popular magazines and a few scientific journals. The *Guide*'s main purpose is to list periodicals of interest to the general, not technical, reader. Therefore, you will find articles from *Good Housekeeping, Parents' Magazine,* and *Reader's Digest* indexed, but not articles from *Hospitals, Journal of Petroleum Technology,* or *Professional Safety.* For journal articles, you will have to consult the more specialized indexes discussed later in this chapter.

The *Readers' Guide* is published every month. Every three months the *Guide* combines issues to form a cumulative index for that period. Every year these three-month indexes are collected and bound into one large yearly index that can weigh as much as a large dictionary.

The *Readers' Guide* allows you to search for an article by topic, subtopic, author's name, and, whenever appropriate, title. At the beginning of every issue you will find two important keys. One key tells you which periodicals were surveyed for that particular issue of the *Readers' Guide.* Along with this information is a list of abbreviations that will be used for those periodicals throughout the issue. For example, *Saturday Review* will be listed as *Sat R* and *Working Woman* will be found as *Work Wom.* The other key lists abbreviations for months, bibliographic facts, and titles. Refer to both these keys as you "decode" the entries in an issue.

Figure 9.6 contains an excerpt from the *Readers' Guide* for May 1988. This excerpt, which indexes articles on the eye, will show you how the *Readers' Guide* is organized and how abbreviations are used. Like the subject designations in the card catalog, the *Readers' Guide* refers users to other, related topics in the issue. In this excerpt, the reader is told to "see also" entries under "cornea," "vision," and other headings. The articles on the eye covered by this issue are then divided into appropriate categories—care and hygiene, diseases and defects, and so forth.

In addition to listing articles under the subjects they discuss, the *Readers' Guide* indexes articles according to author. Some authors also have articles written about them. In this case the *Readers' Guide* first lists the works by the author and immediately following those articles lists works about the author. Look at Figure 9.7. The excerpt from Bill Cosby's book (a work *by* him) comes first, followed by five articles *about* him and an interview. Note that portraits and/or photographs ("pors") accompany each article about him.

Specialized Indexes

While the *Readers' Guide* is a good source to consult, remember that the *Guide* is limited to "periodicals of general interest published in the United States." Your research may require you to read professional journals in your field—journals that the *Readers' Guide* does not index. To find information published in professional journals, you will need to consult a specialized index. These indexes are guides to the literature in particular subject areas—business, farming, food service, nursing, public safety, respiratory therapy, and many others. Some indexes (print versions as opposed to online versions discussed below) cover sixty or more years of work (*Applied Science & Technology Index* or *Index Medicus*); other indexes were established within the past five to ten years (*Criminal Justice*

FIGURE 9.6   An excerpt from the *Readers' Guide*.

EXTRATERRESTRIAL LIFE *See* Life on other planets
EXTRATERRESTRIAL MATERIAL *See* Matter, Interstellar
EXTRATERRESTRIAL SIGHTINGS *See* UFOs
EXTRAVEHICULAR ACTIVITY *See* Space flight—Extravehicular activity
EYE
 See also
 Cornea
 Retina
 Rods and cones
 Vision
 Visual Purple
          Amphibia
Multipotent precursors can give rise to all major cell types of the frog retina. R. Wetts and S. E. Fraser. bibl f il *Science* 239:1142–5 Mr 4 '88
          Animals
 See also
 Vision—Animals
          Care and hygiene
Eye openers. il *Glamour* 86:200–3 F '88
          Crustaceans
Taking a crab's-eye view of the world [work of Dan-Erik Nilson] D. D. Edwards. il *Science News* 133:167 Mr 12 '88
          Diseases and defects
 See also
 Cataracts (Eye defect)
 Glaucoma
 Retinitis pigmentosa
 Xerophthalmia
A gift of sight for newborns [cryotherapy to prevent retinopathy of prematurity] J. Carey. il *U.S. News & World Report* 104–59 Ap 11 '88
Longevity has created a new villain—a mysterious eye disease [age-related macular degeneration] il *Aging* no357:31–2 '88
Viewing with alarm. J. H. Tanne. il *New York* 21:54+ F 8 '88
          Psychological aspects
She's got the blinding blues [central serous chorioretinopathy; research by Gary S. Gelber and Howard Schatz] D. Pine. il *Health (New York, N.Y.)* 20:20 Ja '88
          Movements
In the blink of an eye [blink rate relates to mental processes; research by John A. Stern] S. Chollar. il *Psychology Today* 22:8+ Mr. '88
          Protection
Laser advances spur Pentagon efforts to protect flight crewmembers' eyes. B. D. Nordwall. il *Aviation Week & Space Technology* 128:73+ F 22 '88
          Surgery
 See also
 Cataracts (Eye defect)—Surgery
 Cornea—Surgery
EYE DONORS
A child's gift, a mother's message [K. Coolican] B. Lindeman. il *50 Plus* 28:4–5 F '88

Periodical Index or *Environmental Index*). You will find a list of some important specialized indexes in the appendix of this chapter. But perhaps the two most important specialized indexes are the *Applied Science & Technology Index* and the *Business Periodicals Index.*

FIGURE 9.7 Entries from the *Readers' Guide* for articles by and about one person.

```
COSBY, BILL, 1937-
   Lead us not into McDonald's [excerpt from Time flies] il
     The Saturday Evening Post 260:58–9 Ja/F '88
                          about
   Bill Cosby calls for a closer look at violence after New York
     rape case. il por Jet 73:52 F 29 '88
   The Cosbys give $1.3 million to four black universities. il
     pors Jet 73:24 Ja 11 '88
   Morehouse inaugurates new president; Cosby boosts black
     colleges. il pors Jet 73:12–13 Mr 14 '88
   Talking with Cos [interview] M. Collins. il por Ladies' Home
     Journal 105:113+ Ja '88
   Three great love stories. I. Norment. il pors Ebony 43:150+
     F '88
   Who's making the big bucks? A. D. Frank. il Reader's Digest
     132:118–22 Ja '88
```

Readers' Guide to Periodical Literature, Vol. 88 No. 5, May 1988, p. 179. Copyright © May 1988 by the H. W. Wilson Company. Material reproduced by permission of the publisher.

Applied Science & Technology Index

If you need to locate information about a technical subject, you would be wise to start with the *Applied Science & Technology Index.* The *Index* is a guide to more than 300 specialized journals in a wide range of scientific and technical fields. The prefatory note to each issue of the *Index* reminds readers of this breadth of coverage.

> Subject fields indexed include aeronautics and space science, atmospheric sciences, chemistry, computer technology and applications, construction industry, energy resources and research, engineering, fire and fire prevention, food and food industry, geology, machinery, mathematics, metallurgy, mineralogy, oceanography, petroleum and gas, physics, plastics, textile industry and fabrics, transportation and other industrial and mechanical arts.

Like the *Readers' Guide,* the *Index* is organized alphabetically by subject. Many of these subjects are subdivided to assist users further. Take a look at Figure 9.8, which reprints a section of the *Index,* to see how useful these subclassifications can be. Information published about helicopters is categorized according to blades, design, engineering use, fuselage, manufacture, and so forth. The subclassifications in the *Applied Science & Technology Index* might give you an idea for a research paper and then assist you in gathering relevant and thorough information on that topic.

Business Periodicals Index

Published since 1958, the *Business Periodicals Index* is invaluable when you are researching a topic in or about business and industry. The *Business Periodicals Index* surveys more than 300 business publications published in English. Subjects that are indexed include accounting, advertising, communications, computer technology and applications, finance, industrial relations, management, occupa-

FIGURE 9.8   An excerpt from *Applied Science & Technology Index*.

Heavy oil *See* Petroleum — Heavy oil
Heavy water *See* Water — Heavy water
Helical springs *See* Springs (Mechanism)
Helices *See* Spirals
Helicopter pilots
                   Training
   Bristow buys five Robinson R22 IFT trainers. *Air Prog*
     50.25 Mr '88
Helicopters
   Helicopter manufacturers foresee small but steady sales
     gains. B.A. Smith. il diags *Aviat Week Space Technol*
     128:18–19 F 15 '88
   New financing program offered for R22 helicopters. il *Air*
     Prog 50:30 My '88
                  Blades
   Tiltrotor tries its composite blades [XV-15] il *Mach Des*
     60:16 Ja 21 '88
                  Design
   Helicopter manufacturers divided on development of new
     aircraft. B. A. Smith. il *Aviat Week Space Technol* 128:58–9
     F 29 '88
   McDonnell Douglas develops preproduction Notar
     helicopter. B. A. Smith. il *Aviat Week Space Technol* 128:24
     Ja 25 '88
   McDonnell Douglas steps up work on proposed MDX
     helicopter program. *Aviat Week Space Technol* 128:58 F
     29 '88
              Engineering use
   Can concrete fly? K. Basham and J. Groom. il *Conor Constr*
     33:299+ Mr '88
                 Fuselage
   Prototype helicopter tests innovative composites. il *Mach Des*
     60:10+ Mr 24 '88
               Manufacture
   Commercial helicopter firms foresee steady recovery from
     7-year slump. il *Aviat Week Space Technol* 128:218–19+
     Mr 14 '88
   Material handling system improves worker safety [Sikorsky
     Aircraft] il *Ind Eng* 20:62–3 Mr '88
   Vacuum-type lifter improves safety [Sikorsky Aircraft] il
     Mater Handl Eng 43:89 Ap '88
              Military use
   See Military helicopters
              Police use
   Commercial helicopter firms foresee steady recovery from
     7-year slump. il *Aviat Week Space Technol* 128:218–19+
     Mr 14 '88
                Rotors
   See Helicopters — Blades
             Specifications
   1988 helicopters [with specification charts] il *Bus Commer*
     Aviat 62:103–15 Ap '88
   International rotary wing aircraft [tables] *Aviat Week Space*
     Technol 128:137–9 Mr 14 '88
   U.S. rotary wing aircraft [tables] *Aviat Week Space Technol*
     128:135–6 Mr 14 '88
Helicopters, Pilotless *See* Airplanes, Pilotless
Helicopters in medical service
   Commercial helicopter firms foresee steady recovery from
     7-year slump. il *Aviat Week Space Technol* 128:218–19+
     Mr 14 '88
Heliotropism *See* Plants, Effect of light on
Helium
   Dielectric constants for hydrogen, helium, and one-electron
     ions. S. A. Studniarz and J. P. Crawford. bibl diag *J Phys*
     Chem 92:1429–31 Mr 24 '88
   Effects of helium addition to an argon glow discharge
     plasma on emmission lines of sputtered particles. K.
     Wagatsuma and K. Hirokawa. bibl *Anal Chem* 60:702–5
     Ap 1 '88

FIGURE 9.9   An excerpt from the *Business Periodicals Index.*

Word processing equipment
> *See also*
> Dictating machines
> Typewriters, Automatic
> Word stations (Office automation)

Document reader eases law firm's work load [Oppenheimer Wolff Foster Shepard & Donnelly] il *Office* 97:78 + Je '83

New word processors to get token-passing local network [Harris Corporation's new 9000 series] il *Data Commun* 12:163–4 + Jl '83

Paper processors speed work of automated office systems [Institute of Nuclear Power Operations] il *Office* 97:102–3 Je '83

Turning typewriters into input stations with OCR [Wharton Econometric Forecasting Associates] G. J. Marquez. *Office* 97:68 + Je '83

Add-ons
> *See* Word processing equipment—Plug compatible equipment

Plug compatible equipment
ACS moves in on Wang peripherals [Applied Computer Sciences Inc.] J. Levine. *Venture* 5:94 S '83

Prices
IBM cuts tags up to 30% on Displaywriter. I. Sager. *Electron News* 29:26 + Je 13 '83

Printers
> *See* Printers (Data processing systems)

Programs
Climbing to the top of the charts [top 10 in business software] A. Solomon. *Inc* 5:141 + S '83

Does your printer work with Wordstar? C. Stevenson. *Byte* 8:411–12 + S '83

IBM cuts tags up to 30% on Displaywriter. I. Sager. *Electron News* 29:26 + Je 13 '83

Innovative office automation training [program for word processing operators] *Train Dev J* 37:10 S '83

Word processing: it's never been easier [tables] D. R. Roman. il *Comput Decis* 15:152–4 + Je '83

Selection
Word-processing systems: the matter of selection [Arrow Electronics] *Office* 97:110 Je '83

Word processing equipment industry
> *See also*
> Compucorp
> Data General Corp.
> Harris Corp.
> Lanier Business Products, Inc.
> NBI Inc.
> NCR Corp.
> Wang Laboratories Inc.

Acquisitions and mergers
Harris to buy Lanier for $415M in stock. L. Antelman. *Electron News* 29:1 + Jl 25 '83

Office automation's new marriage [proposed Harris-Lanier merger] M. Price. *Ind Week* 218:20–1 Ag 8 '83

Competition
ACS moves in on Wang peripherals [Applied Computer Sciences Inc.] J. Levine. *Venture* 5:94 S '83

Exhibitions
Syntopican bounces back with a record turnout [San Francisco] J. B. Dykeman. *Mod Off Proced* 28:34 Ag '83

Marketing
Product switch saves company [Systel Computers Inc.] A. Heller. *Venture* 5:17 + S '83

tional health and safety, office automation, personnel, real estate, telecommunications, and transportation. Like the *Applied Science & Technology Index,* the *Business Periodicals Index* is organized alphabetically by subject and offers many useful subheadings. Note how the excerpt from the *Business Periodicals Index* contained in Figure 9.9 arranges and classifies information about word processors and how it helps users to find information about companies and individuals.

◆ USING THE COMPUTER IN YOUR LIBRARY RESEARCH

A computer can make your library research easier, more accurate, and far more comprehensive. Computers are essential guides to the ever-expanding number of publications available today. More than 40,000 books are published in America each year, and the number of articles and reports in technical journals published in just one month alone is staggering. Thanks to computer technology it is possible to search through this mountain of information and locate the materials you need on your topic. As we have already seen, many libraries have switched to a computerized card catalog to help patrons find out a variety of things about a given book. Furthermore, many businesses regularly conduct computer searches to find the most current information on a topic before preparing a proposal or a report.

A computerized search offers many advantages. It is a fast alternative to a manual search through an index or abstract, since you can go through 5–10 years of an index in just a few minutes. A computer search can also help you locate items that you may otherwise miss and can give you access to materials your library does not have.

Conducting a computer search usually begins by consulting a trained librarian who will either perform the search for you or assist you in doing your own search. Basically, the procedure is simple. Information found in various indexes and abstracts is stored in online databases. (A database is an electronic index service that contains a file of information from which the computer then retrieves the key citations you need.) Several hundred databases exist. In fact, almost every professional discipline has its own database—criminal justice (*Criminal Justice Periodical Index*), nursing (*Nursing and Allied Health*), chemistry (*Chemistry Abstracts*), business (*Business Periodicals Index; Trade and Industry Index;* etc.), psychology (*Psychological Abstracts*), engineering (*Compendex*), and so forth. In order to search an appropriate database you must first narrow your topic and then give the librarian a key word or phrase (as well as some alternates) that summarizes your topic. For example, to find out specific information about such broad topics as child abuse, artificial intelligence, or laser printers, you would need to restrict your focus more. Also, you may want to put chronological limits on your search, say to articles published after 1985. Or perhaps you are interested in finding films, reports, or conference proceedings as well as articles. The librarian will then enter this key phrase or word, along with any restrictions you have indicated, into the computer to search the database(s) for materials about your topic. Having completed its search, the computer will list on the display screen the number of entries (articles, books, reports, etc.) that are filed under this key word or phrase. With another command, the computer will then print out a list of bibliographic citations, thus saving you the trouble of having to write them out by hand.

Now we will take a look at the two ways you can search databases using a computer. One of these uses a compact disk and the other employs an online search.

Compact Disks

This type of computerized reference work is known as a CD-ROM ("compact disk, read-only memory"), meaning that information about the periodicals, encyclopedias, books, and other reference works is stored on a self-contained disk. The 12-inch laser-driven disk is about the size of a 45 rpm record and is played on a video disk player. It is a closed system; that is, you are restricted to information placed on the disk. In many instances, this information is updated each month or two and a new disk is then made available for library patrons.

One of the most frequently used compact disk retrieval systems is InfoTrac, available from the Information Access Company. This electronic periodical index far surpasses any printed index in coverage. A single 12-inch InfoTrac disk, for example, stores bibliographical information about more than 500,000 articles published in over 1,000 periodicals in business, technology, psychology, and education. Like printed indexes, InfoTrac is organized into subject categories with subheadings in each main subject category. InfoTrac begins coverage with articles published in 1980 and supplies two disks to cover the 10-year period from 1980–1990. Updated disks are sent to libraries each month. To use InfoTrac you may not need the help of a librarian, but you still must enter a key phrase or word into the computer for it to search the database file and to identify all the appropriate citations to the articles listed on the compact disk. It does this in less than a minute. With another simple command, InfoTrac prints a list of complete bibliographic citations of these articles.

Online Searches

Online searches are available at many libraries. An online search works like this. A library subscribes to a particular computerized information retrieval service that has numerous databases stored in its host, mainframe computer. Via its computer terminal your library is able to dial into these databases. There are more than 3000 different databases, and while no one retrieval service offers access to all of them, these services do supply their customers with vast amounts of information. Many of the databases correspond to printed indexes (e.g., *Business Periodicals Index*), while others are available only through online searches—that is, there is no print equivalent for them. An online search can offer you bibliographic information (a list of articles and other references for a preliminary working bibliography), copies of abstracts of articles included in certain databases, and, in some cases, even copies of the publications themselves.

Online searching differs from compact disks by giving you access to more current material, since information can be continuously fed into the mainframe computer. Furthermore, an online search will give you more search options (ways of pulling information out of a database) than you would have using a disk. Finally, some online searches offer more specialized (and technical) databases than disks do. Keep in mind, though, that many online search services are now making their databases available on disks as well.

Below are four online searches that you might be likely to use; note that there is some overlap among these different services.

1. DIALOG gives you access to more than 300 bibliographic databases (with more than 120 million entries) in a wide range of fields: agriculture and food sciences (*AGRICOLA*), chemistry (*Chemical Industry Notes)*, medicine *(MEDLINE*), oceanography (*Oceanic Abstracts*), business (ABI/INFORM), and social sciences (SOCIAL SCISEARCH). Using DIALOG you can quickly (within a microsecond) search five or six years' worth of *Financial Times, Business Week, Fortune, Forbes,* or *Chemicalweek,* and many other publicatons for information relating directly to your topic. DIALOG also gives users access to information from federal agencies (e.g., *IRS Taxinfo*), professional societies, commercial organizations, and a variety of products and services (especially through the *Electronic Yellow Pages*).

2. WILSONLINE offers subscribers computerized access to the bibliographic information contained in many of the indexes published by the H. W. Wilson Company. Some of these indexes are *Applied Science & Technology Index, Book Review Digest, General Science Index, Readers' Guide to Periodical Literature, Index to Legal Periodicals,* and the *Social Science Index.* WILSONLINE, like most databases, is not cumulative—it does not go back forty or fifty years. Coverage on WILSONLINE varies and will probably change continuously as more information (and years) are added to the individual databases.

3. Bibliographic Retrieval Service (BRS) provides patrons with access to more than 135 different databases from government agencies, professional organizations, and publishers. Among the databases available through BRS are *AIDS Articles, Books in Print, Computer & Mathematics Search, Family Resources, Magazine Index, MEDLINE, National Technical Information Service, RIVE (Resources in Vocational Education), Sports Database,* and *Robotics Information Database.*

4. Dow Jones News/Retrieval supplies access to articles and other information found in the *Wall Street Journal* and *Barron's.*

Suggestions on Using Computerized Searches

Here is some practical advice on running a computer literature search.

1. Prepare for your search. Do not just walk into the library and tell the librarian you are interested in taxes, credit cards, drug enforcement, or another large topic. Rather than asking for all the information on acid rain, first decide on what restricted area of acid rain you need to research in detail—its effect on crops, its prevention, its danger to the ozone layer, its political effects on neighboring countries, etc.

2. Conduct a preliminary manual search first to find out approximately how much is written on the topic. Thus you will have some idea whether you will be asking for 10 entries or 100.

3. Be prepared to work with the librarian to refine your search even further. Often the librarian can use two or three different key phrases or words, or a combination or modification of them.

4. Realize that there are limits to the periods of time that databases scan. In some cases, databases will not cover more than the last few years.

5. Understand that libraries often will charge for a computer search. Patrons are usually charged per citation retrieval and per minute for each minute spent connected (via telephone lines) to the database. It is not uncommon to spend $30–$40 for a search on DIALOG, for example.

6. Recognize that your library may have limited access to databases in your field.

Finding a Periodical in Your Library

Once you find an article in an index or through a computer search, your next job is to locate and read it. Libraries list their periodical holdings in different ways. Some libraries list them in a separate catalog; others maintain a holdings list in the form of a computer printout. The holdings list will tell you to which journals and magazines your library subscribes and how far back the subscription goes. If the journal you are looking for is not on your library's periodical holdings list, you will have to go to another library or seek assistance through interlibrary loan.

If the library has the periodical you are looking for, it may be in a number of places, depending on the date of the issue. Recent periodicals are often housed in a periodicals reading room. Older back issues may be bound with other issues for that year and gathered together in a hard, permanent cover and shelved like a book. Many libraries shelve bound periodicals according to subject matter or alphabetically by title in an area of the library separate from the stacks. Another method of storing back issues is to put them on microfilm or microfiche, which stores information concisely and economically. (Microfilm and microfiche are discussed on pages 273–75.)

◆ REFERENCE BOOKS

The works discussed in this section are kept in the reference room in the library. Reference books usually may not be checked out of the library. More detailed information on specific reference works is given in the appendix to this chapter.

Encyclopedias

The work *encyclopedia* comes from a Greek phrase meaning "general education." Some encyclopedias provide information on an incredibly broad range of subjects. These comprehensive encyclopedias take years to produce and are written by a staff of experts from every major field of knowledge. The information in an encyclopedia is arranged alphabetically, with some subjects receiving as much as twenty pages of coverage. A general encyclopedia can get you started in your research by explaining some key terms, offering a quick summary, and supplying you with a list of further readings. Another advantage of encyclopedias is the colorful and varied illustrations they offer. Three useful general encyclopedias are *Collier's Encyclopedia, Encyclopedia Americana,* and *Encyclopaedia Britannica.*

Do not attempt to do all your research using only encyclopedias, however. They have their limitations. For one thing, the information in them is designed for the general reader, not the specialist. For another reason, general encyclopedias, however good, do not contain the most current information on a subject, especially on technical matters. For that kind of up-to-date material, you must consult periodicals and specialized reference books. Finally, relying on encyclopedias alone reveals your lack of ability to find and use more specialized and restricted sources.

Dictionaries

Dictionaries are perhaps the most important reference tool, since they help you to understand the information gathered from the other works (books, periodicals, pamphlets) that make up the bulk of your research. In addition to giving the meaning of words, dictionaries indicate spelling, pronunciation, etymology (word history), and usage. Generally speaking, dictionaries fall into two categories: general English-language dictionaries and more specialized dictionaries used by a specific profession.

English-language dictionaries are either unabridged or abridged. An unabridged dictionary is a large, comprehensive guide to all the words of the language. The following unabridged dictionaries are excellent references: *Funk & Wagnalls New Standard Dictionary of the English Language,* the *Oxford English Dictionary,* the *Random House Dictionary of the English Language* (2d ed.), and *Webster's Third New International Dictionary of the English Language.* The *Oxford English Dictionary* is a historical dictionary; that is, it lists the dates when a word was first used and how it was used and supplies illustrative quotations.

Abridged dictionaries are much smaller. They can range from a pocket dictionary to a large compilation with photographs and other illustrations. The following abridged dictionaries are useful: the *American Heritage Dictionary,* the *Random House College Dictionary, Webster's New Collegiate Dictionary,* and *Webster's New World Dictionary.*

You will frequently use dictionaries, such as those described in the appendix, that contain the specialized vocabulary of your profession. These specialized, or field, dictionaries not only define the words used in the literature of a profession but also help to characterize that profession's scope and importance.

Abstracts

An *abstract* is a short summary. In addition to listing the author's name, title, and publication data, an abstract will give a brief (usually a few sentences) summary of the content and scope of the book, article, or pamphlet. By condensing this information, an abstract can save users hours of time by letting them know if the work is relevant to their topic.

Use abstracts with caution, however, for they are not a substitute for the article or book they summarize. A few sentences highlighting the content of a book or article obviously omit much. When in doubt about what is omitted, read the original work to uncover the details, the rationale, and the dimensions of the whole problem. Never quote from an abstract; always cite material from the original work.

Not every field has an abstracting service, nor is every article or book always abstracted. The titles of abstracts found in the appendix to this chapter will give you a clear idea of the range of fields that do offer this valuable service.

Handbooks, Manuals, and Almanacs

Handbooks, manuals, and almanacs supply you with definitions of terms in your field, statistical facts, explanations of procedures, and authoritative reviews of the kinds of practical and professional problems and solutions you will encounter on the job. In the card catalog these works will be marked *Ref.* or *R.*, indicating that they are shelved in the reference section of your library.

When you look for the reference books in your field, make sure that you use the most up-to-date ones. Also, consult more than one manual or handbook in your field. Compare their discussions of the same topic; different approaches or emphases will help you to research a given procedure more accurately.

◆ GOVERNMENT DOCUMENTS

The U.S. government, through its diverse agencies and departments, engages vigorously in conducting research and in publishing its findings. This published material, collectively referred to as *government documents,* can be in the form of journal articles, pamphlets, research reports, transcripts of government hearings, speeches, or books. These materials have immense practical value for the research you do in your field. Government reports, for example, will discuss care of the aged, flood insurance, farming techniques, fire precautions, housing costs, outdoor recreation, and urban development.

Three indexes to government documents are especially helpful in guiding you through this vast store of information.

1. The *Monthly Catalog of U.S. Government Publications.* Published since 1895 by the GPO (Government Printing Office), this index lists government documents published during that month. The catalog is arranged by agen-

FIGURE 9.10 Sample entry with explanation of codes from the *Monthly Catalog* of U.S. Government Publications.

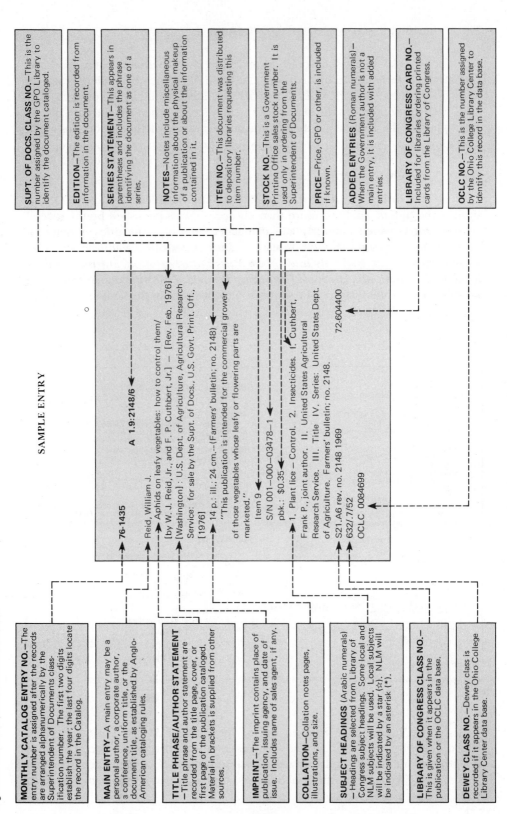

SAMPLE ENTRY

SUPT. OF DOCS. CLASS NO.—This is the number assigned by the GPO Library to identify the document cataloged.

EDITION—The edition is recorded from information in the document.

SERIES STATEMENT—This appears in parentheses and includes the phrase identifying the document as one of a series.

NOTES—Notes include miscellaneous information about the physical makeup of a publication or about the information contained in it.

ITEM NO.—This document was distributed to depository libraries requesting this item number.

STOCK NO.—This is a Government Printing Office sales stock number. It is used only in ordering from the Superintendent of Documents.

PRICE—Price, GPO or other, is included if known.

ADDED ENTRIES (Roman numerals)—When the Government author is not a main entry, it is included with added entries.

LIBRARY OF CONGRESS CARD NO.—Included for libraries ordering printed cards from the Library of Congress.

OCLC NO.—This is the number assigned by the Ohio College Library Center to identify this record in the data base.

MONTHLY CATALOG ENTRY NO.—The entry number is assigned after the records are arranged alphanumerically by the Superintendent of Documents classification number. The first two digits establish the year; the last four digits locate the record in the Catalog.

MAIN ENTRY—A main entry may be a personal author, a corporate author, a conference, uniform title, or the document title, as established by Anglo-American cataloging rules.

TITLE PHRASE/AUTHOR STATEMENT—Title phrase and author statement are recorded from the title page, cover, or first page of the publication cataloged. Material in brackets is supplied from other sources.

IMPRINT—The imprint contains place of publication, issuing agency, and date of issue. Includes name of sales agent, if any.

COLLATION—Collation notes pages, illustrations, and size.

SUBJECT HEADINGS (Arabic numerals)—Headings are selected from Library of Congress subject headings. Some local and NLM subjects will be used. Local subjects will be indicated by a star (☆). NLM will be indicated by an asterisk (*).

LIBRARY OF CONGRESS CLASS NO.—This is given when it appears in the publication or the OCLC data base.

DEWEY CLASS NO.—Dewey class is recorded if it appears in the Ohio College Library Center data base.

76-1435

A 1.9:2148/6

Reid, William J.
    Aphids on leafy vegetables: how to control them/
[by W. J. Reid, Jr., and F. P. Cuthbert, Jr.] – [Rev. Feb. 1976]
[Washington] : U.S. Dept. of Agriculture, Agricultural Research
Service: for sale by the Supt. of Docs., U.S. Govt. Print. Off.,
[1976]
    14 p.: ill., 24 cm.–(Farmers' bulletin; no. 2148)
    "This publication is intended for the commercial grower
of those vegetables whose leafy or flowering parts are
marketed."
    Item 9
    S/N 001–000–03478–1
    pbk.: $0.35
    1. Plant lice – Control. 2. Insecticides. I. Cuthbert,
Frank P., joint author. II. United States Agricultural
Research Service. III. Title IV. Series: United States Dept.
of Agriculture. Farmers' bulletin; no. 2148.
S21.A6 rev. no. 2148 1969   72-604400
632/.7/52
OCLC 0084699

cies that publish or sponsor works (for example, the departments of Agriculture, Commerce, Interior, State, and so forth). At the back of each issue there is also an index to subjects, authors, titles, key words in titles, reports, and contract numbers. Each entry provides the author's or agency's name, the title, the date, a brief description of the contents of the document (including whether it contains a bibliography, maps, or index), when and where the research was conducted, who sponsored it (including a contract number), the price, and how to order a copy. Figure 9.10 shows you how to interpret a sample entry.

   2. The *Index to Government Periodicals*. Published since 1970, this subject and author guide to more than 200 periodicals published by the federal government is issued quarterly and cumulated annually. The titles of some of these periodicals suggest their research value: *American Rehabilitation, Fire Management Notes, Highway and Urban Mass Transportation, Marine Fisheries Review, Occupational Outlook Quarterly, Pesticides Monitoring Journal,* and *Tree Planters' Notes.* Figure 9.11 shows some entries from this index.

FIGURE 9.11   Some entries from *Index to Government Periodicals*.

GRAHAM, Thomas K.
   How do you fit? il Approach 32 7 13 My **87-013**
GRAHAM, Vickie M.
   Getting S. A. savvy. il Airman 31 6 17-22 Je **87-009**
   Mountain medics. il Airman 31 3 36-39 Mr **87-009**
   Testing our high-tech future—now! il Airman 31 1 29-33 Ja **87-009**
GRAIN
   Look ahead byproducts and markets. Farmline 8 4 5 Ap **87-253**
   Measuring government's role in agriculture around the world. Doug Martinez, il, ref, tab Farmline 8 5 3-5+ My **87-253**
      Byproducts
   Despite obstacles, potential exists for sorghum sales. For Agric 25 5 9-11 My **87-052**
   Feed grains project a success in Middle East. For Agric 25 5 2 My **87-052**
      Consumption
   Biggest potential grain markets are middle-income countries. Mervin Yetley and Suzanne Marks, il, ch For Agric 25 4 1£ Ap **87-052**
   Rising incomes encourage coarse grain use in developing world. Gary Vocke, For Agric 25 4 20 Ap **87-052**
      Diseases
   Preserving the stuff of life. Stephen Berberich, ch Agric Res 35 4 6-9 Ap **87-004**
      Drying
   Plans afoot to expand grain storage capacity. For Agric 25 4 22 Ap **87-052**
      Exports
   Export growth markets for U.S. grain

GRAMM-RUDMAN-HOLLINGS Act See
   Balanced Budget and Emergency Deficit Reduction Act
GRANADE, H. Ray
   Gambierdiscus toxicus from the Caribbean: a source of toxins involved in ciguatera. Joseph P. McMillan and others, ref, tab Marine Fish Rev 48 4 48-52 **86-065**
GRAND Duchy of Luxembourg See
   Luxembourg
GRANITE
   Radon vs. lung cancer: new study weighs the risks. Richard E. Toohey, il, gr Logos 5 1 7-11 Spr **87-340**
GRANT, Cheryl E.
   Hickman catheter clots: a common occurrence despite daily heparin flushing. Anita Johnson Anderson and others, ref, tab Cancer Treat Rep 71 6 651-653 Je **87-176**
GRANT, Don
   Great Lakes forest fire compact. Don Grant and Art Sutton, mp Fire Man Notes 48 1 21 **87-184**
GRANT, Ulysses S.
   Dismantling the myth. Harry J. Maihafer, il, por Mil Rev 67 6 58-62 Je **87-283**
GRANTS See
   Federal aid
   Foundations
   Scholarships and fellowships
GRANU...urogenital tumor cells.
   ...or J Nat

Index to Government Periodicals (April–June 1987): 153. © Infodata International. Chicago, 1987.

   3. The *Index to Publications of the United States Congress*. Published monthly since 1970 by the Congressional Information Service (CIS), this reference work indexes and abstracts House and Senate documents, reports, hearings, investigations, and other publications. It is a particularly valuable guide to legislative investigations and decisions.

States and counties also engage in research and publish their findings. The Library of Congress publishes the *Monthly Checklist of State Publications,* which lists, according to the individual states, such materials as pamphlets, statistical studies, yearbooks, and histories. At the county level, practical advice and publications are available on a wide range of topics in agriculture, education, food science, housing, and water resources.

◆ THE POPULAR PRESS

The "popular press" includes reading material written in nontechnical language for the general public. Pamphlets, brochures, consumer manuals, and newspapers constitute the popular press. This section will show you where to find them indexed and how to obtain copies of specific articles.

Vertical File Materials

Every library receives, as part of its collection of "popular press," materials that are best classified as temporary, or "ephemeral," documents. These materials— pamphlets, catalogs, promotional materials, posters, charts, and maps—are stored in the library's *vertical files*, often one or a series of file cabinets. Although these materials may not be listed in the card catalog, the titles (and sources) may suggest the kinds of topics they cover: "A Guide to the New Jelico Drill" (from a manufacturer), "High Blood Pressure" (from the American Heart Association), "Highway Safety" (from a state highway department), "So You Want to Be a Geologist" (from a professional society), "A Map of the Olympic Sites" (from an Olympic committee). In addition, you will find clippings from newspapers and magazines on topics that the librarian believes are of interest to patrons.

You may also want to consult the *Vertical File Index* (1936–), which lists these pamphlets, posters, maps, charts, brochures, and so forth under subject headings, along with a title index. Another especially helpful feature of the *Vertical File Index* is that it lists the addresses of the companies and associations from whom you may obtain a copy of the publication, sometimes free of charge.

Indexes to Newspapers

In many ways newspapers provide a valuable source of information relevant to the research you do in school or on the job. Newspapers provide information about community projects, financial changes, or recreational facilities that might be useful. Newspapers can also help you to locate new markets or sites or expand those your company or agency already has.

A thorough guide to the newspapers published in the United States and Canada is the *Gale Directory of Publications,* formerly known as the *Ayer Directory of Periodicals.* This work, issued annually, lists the date a paper began publication; its current address, rates, and circulation; and its religious or political preference. The directory also includes a capsule history of the community served by the paper. Unfortunately, it will not refer you to specific stories. For that information you need to consult an index. The best one is the *New York Times Index,* which indexes by subject and author stories that have appeared in its paper since 1851. This index also summarizes stories and reprints the photographs, maps, and other illustrations that accompanied some of the stories. Still another advantage this comprehensive index offers is that you can find the date of an event in it and then use that date to see how a local newspaper covered the story. Many libraries have the back issues of the *New York Times* on microfilm.

In addition to the *New York Times Index,* you should also look at the indexes to the stories published in four newspapers representing four main areas of the country: the East Coast (*Washington Post*), the Midwest (*Chicago Tribune*), the South (*New Orleans Times-Picayune*), and the West Coast (*Los Angeles Times*). You might also consult the very valuable *Wall Street Journal* and *Christian Science Monitor* which publish their own indexes.

Almost every newspaper is indexed. Often you can find the index to your local newspaper in that section of a newspaper office called the "morgue," where all the back issues of a paper are stored. To use the index, all you need is the date of the story you are interested in. Newspapers gladly allow readers access to back issues, often help by conducting computerized searches of topics, and may even photocopy a story for you.

NewsBank

Begun in 1982, NewsBank is an extremely useful newspaper reference service that offers both a collection of newspaper stories and indexes to the topics in them. NewsBank supplies the full text of selected articles and reviews found in newspapers from over 450 cities across the United States. It reprints stories on microfiche (transparent four-by-six-inch cards on which the pages of the newspaper are greatly reduced; see page 274). While you will not find stories from the readily available *New York Times, Wall Street Journal,* or *Christian Science Monitor* in NewsBank, you will be able to locate articles that have appeared in major newspapers in cities such as Atlanta, Cincinnati, Houston, Kansas City, Las Vegas, Oakland (CA), Providence (RI), and many others. The articles that NewsBank selects for inclusion deal with a wide range of topics including business and economic development, consumer affairs, employment, the environment, films and television, health, housing and land development, the performing arts, social relations, and transportation. NewsBank makes stories from across the country easy to obtain and to read and allows the researcher to see how a story may be reported differently from one section of the country to another.

The *NewsBank Index,* which is issued monthly, offers a multilevel index system to allow researchers to scan the material for different aspects of a subject. The *Index* is organized by subject headings and by geographic regions. But it is important to keep in mind that the particular citations from NewsBank in the *Index* refer to the NewsBank microfiche card numbers and not to the page numbers or sections from the original newspapers from which they are taken. Since News-

Bank makes materials from these 450 newspapers easily available to library users, it may not be too long before documenting by NewsBank microfiche numbers is widely accepted. In addition to the *Index,* NewsBank's *Reviews in the Arts* and *Names in the News* (both for individuals and groups) are essential guides to the collection.

◆ AUDIOVISUAL MATERIALS

Audiovisual materials include records, cassettes, tape recordings, photographs, films, and microforms. These materials are shelved in a separate part of the library that contains the proper equipment to use them conveniently and properly. Audiovisual titles are listed in the card catalog and perhaps also in a separate audiovisual catalog. One particular type of audiovisual material, microforms, deserves special attention.

The name *microforms* refers to a number of research tools—microfilm, microfiche, microcards—that all make use of microphotography. Each of these library tools presents a great deal of information reduced from its original size and stored compactly on film or tape. The microform process saves the library space, increases the durability of the documents, and offers libraries a wider range of titles for far less money. Microforms are used frequently in business and industry as well. Hospitals can store patients' records much more economically and banks can put canceled checks on microforms for safe storage and easy reference.

Microfilm

A microfilm is a strip of black-and-white film on which reduced images are found. Microfilm is stored on reels, cartridges, or cassettes, as shown in Figure 9.12. These reduced images are microscopic pictures of the pages of books, articles, newspapers, court proceedings, and so forth. The size of these pages has been reduced by microphotography to a fraction of their original size. Believe it or not,

FIGURE 9.12   Examples of microfilm stored on (a) reels, (b) cartridges, and (c) cassettes.

(a)   (b)   (c) "a 1,245-page Bible can be reproduced on a one-inch square piece of microfilm. If the Library of Congress chose, it could store its 270 miles of books and other reference material in six standard filing cabinets"[1]. A library could save 95 percent of its space if it converted all its holdings to microfilm.

The advantages microfilm offers are many. Without it, no library could possibly save all the back issues of a local newspaper, let alone a large, nationally famous paper such as the *New York Times*. Moreover, newspapers tear, yellow, and crumble after being used by readers for a few weeks. Using microfilm, a library can store a newspaper's daily issues from an entire month on one reel. A special machine called a *microfilm reader* enlarges the images for reading. Your library has at least one or two of these machines and possibly more. Your librarian will be pleased to show you how to operate one.

Microfiche

Microfiche (pronounced "micro feesh") is a close cousin to microfilm. The microfiche process, as described in our discussion of NewsBank, reduces the pages of books, articles, or any other printed materials and puts them on film. Each fiche (or film card) may hold as many as 90 to 100 pages. Superfiche, an even more

FIGURE 9.13 A sample microfiche.

E. Stevens Rice, *Fiche and Reel* (Ann Arbor, MI.: Xerox, n.d.): 13. Used by permission.

---

[1] *Nation's Business* (Mar. 1971): 20.

compact method of reproduction, can put 300 to 400 pages on a single four-by-six-inch card. A common reduction rate is 24:1. Figure 9.13 shows a sample microfiche. More than fifty-five pages of a periodical are placed on this single card. As with microfilm, you need a special machine to see the material condensed onto microfiche. Using a microfiche reader, you slide the four-by-six-inch card onto a tray, push the tray underneath a magnifying lens, and see the material projected and enlarged on a lighted screen. To find the page you want, you simply slide the tray up or down or from right to left.

A *microcard* is identical to a microfiche except that the film is printed on an opaque, not transparent, card.

◆ NOTE TAKING

Once you have consulted the appropriate sources, you need some systematic way to record relevant information from them in preparing your paper or report. Before you can begin drafting your work, you must be able to organize and classify data from your research efficiently. (Even after you start to draft your report, you will probably need to continue your research and take additional notes.)

Note taking is the crucial link between finding sources and writing a report. Never trust your memory to keep all your research facts straight. Taking notes is time well spent. Do not be too quick in getting it done or too eager to begin writing your paper. Careless note taking may cause you to forget page numbers, publishers, dates, or even titles; you might need this information at 2:00 A.M. when the library is closed and your paper is due at 8:00 A.M.. Not copying accurately from a source could lead you to omit key words in a quotation or even worse, misrepresent or contradict what the author has said. Carelessness could result in crediting one author with another's work.

Basically, you will be preparing two kinds of notes. One type, on the sources you read, will become your working bibliography. The other type will be reserved for the specific information you take from these sources in the form of direct quotations, paraphrases, or summaries.

How to Prepare Bibliography Cards

Look at the sample card shown in Figure 9.14. To record accurate and meaningful information, follow these practical guidelines.

1. Use only three-by-five-inch index cards. Do not be tempted to use slips of paper or looseleaf notebook paper; cards are less likely to get lost, and they will help you to organize, alphabetize, and label material.
2. Write on only one side of the card. It is easier to copy and check information when you list it all on one side.
3. Use a ballpoint pen to write your notes. Felt-tip pens or pencils may smudge. Write legibly; print if necessary.
4. Put only one title (article or book or film) on each card. These cards will later have to be arranged in alphabetical order for your Works Cited page

FIGURE 9.14   Card containing bibliographic information on a source.

(see pages 292–98); if you place two titles on one card, you could end up retyping your entire Works Cited page (to put these "missing" entries in), or you could run the risk of omitting one of the titles.

5. Include full bibliographic information for each source. For books, list author, title, chapter titles, edition, date, city of publication, publisher, and page numbers; for articles, supply author, title, journal, volume number, date, and page numbers.

6. Decode and spell out any periodical index or journal abbreviations. Record periodical entries with their full and accurate bibliographic information. (See Chapter 10 on documentation.) The abbreviated entries in indexes such as the *Readers' Guide* or the *Applied Science & Technology Index* are not in acceptable format for parenthetical documentation or Works Cited page entries in your paper or report.

7. Write down the call numbers of the book or periodical in the upper left-hand corner of the card so you will know where to find the source again if you need it. If you are using more than one library, also indicate at which library you found the source.

How to Prepare Note Cards

While your bibliography cards will give you important facts about authors, titles, and publication data, your note cards will give you the specific information from these sources that you need to write your paper. Your note cards will contain direct quotations from, or paraphrases of, your sources. Quotations and paraphrases

FIGURE 9.15   Note card containing a direct quotation.

> Jenkes 46   DISCOVERY OF VITAMINS
>
> "The discovery, isolation, and synthesis of vitamins was one of the great scientific and public health achievements of the 20th century. They [nutritionists] made it scientifically possible to eliminate the nutritional deficiency diseases that had plagued human beings for centuries. This was an immediate and complete victory, unlike the incessant and on-going war against malaria, diabetes, cancer, and heart disease."

are discussed on pages 278–80. Here are some guidelines to follow when preparing note cards like those shown in Figures 9.15 and 9.16.

1. Use four-by-six-inch cards to keep them separate from the three-by-five bibliography cards.
2. Write on only one side of the card. It will be easier for you to arrange the cards in the order you may need them for your paper.
3. Don't include notes from two different sources on one card.
4. Copy names, facts, dates, statistics accurately from the source. Be sure, too, that you record the author's words correctly; you may want to quote these words verbatim in your paper. Always compare what you have written with the original.
5. Make sure that you distinguish quotations from your own paraphrase by placing quotation marks around any words you record directly from a source.
6. Write a code word or phrase in the upper-right-hand corner of the card to identify the topic treated by the source or the information written on the card from that source. Using code words such as "characteristics," "function of," "history of," or "location of" on your cards will help you to organize when you write your paper. Figure 9.15 shows how one writer used these code words.
7. You might indicate on the card why the material is significant to your argument or where you might include such information in your report or paper. In Figure 9.16 the writer has identified a possible use for the Dampier paraphrase.
8. Write a short title of the book or journal article in the upper-left-hand corner or include the author's last name so that the note card is coded to your bibliography card.

FIGURE 9.16   Note card containing a paraphrase.

To Quote or Not to Quote

Before recording information from sources, ask yourself these three questions: (1) How much should I take down? (2) How often should I copy the author's words verbatim to use direct quotations? (3) When should I paraphrase or summarize? A safe rule to follow is: Do not be a human photocopying machine. If you write down too many of the author's own words, you will simply be transferring the author's words from the book or article to your paper. That will show that you have read the work but have not evaluated its findings. Do not use direct quotations simply as a filler.

Direct quotations should be used sparingly and saved for when they count most. When an author has summarized a great deal of significant information concisely into a few well-chosen sentences, you may want to quote this summary verbatim. Or if a writer has clarified a difficult concept exceedingly well, you may want to include this clarification exactly as it is listed. And certainly the author's chief statement or thesis may deserve to be quoted directly. Figure 9.15 contains such an important statement. Just be careful that you do not quote verbatim all of the evidence leading to that conclusion. The conclusion may be pointedly expressed in two or three sentences; the evidence could cover many pages. If you are worried about exactly how much to quote verbatim, keep in mind that no more than 10 to 15 percent of your paper should be made up of direct quotations. Remember that when you quote someone directly, you are telling your readers that these words are the most important part of the author's work as far as you are concerned. Be a selective filter, not a large funnel.

There will be times when a sentence or passage is particularly useful, but you may not want to quote it in its entirety. You may want to delete some words that are not really necessary for your purpose. These omissions are indicated by using ellipsis dots (three spaced dots within the sentence to indicate where the words are omitted). Here are some examples.

> Full Quotation: "Diet and nutrition, which have been studied by researchers, significantly affect oral health."
>
> Quotation with Ellipsis: "Diet and nutrition . . . significantly affect oral health."

When the omission occurs at the end of the sentence, you must include the end-of-sentence punctuation after the ellipsis. In the following example, note how the shortened sentence ends with four spaced dots: a period and the three dots for the ellipsis.

> Full Quotation: "Decisions on how to operate the company should be based on the most accurate and relevant information available from both within the company and from the specific community that establishment serves."
>
> Quotation with Ellipsis: "Decisions on how to operate the company should be based on the most accurate and relevant information available. . . ."

At times you may have to insert your own information within a quotation. This addition, known as an *interpolation,* is made by enclosing your clarifying identification or remark within brackets inside the quotation; for example, "It [the new transportation network] has been thoroughly tested and approved." In other words, anything within brackets is not part of the original quotation.

Most of your note taking will be devoted to paraphrasing rather than writing down direct quotations. A paraphrase is a restatement in your own words of the author's ideas. Even though you are using your own words to translate or restate, you still must document the paraphrase because you are using the author's facts and interpretations. You do not use quotation marks, though. When you include a paraphrase in your paper, you should be careful to do four things.

1. Be faithful to the author's meaning. Do not alter facts or introduce new ideas.
2. Follow the order in which the author presents the information.
3. Include in your paraphrase only what is relevant for your paper. Delete any details not essential for your work.
4. Use paraphrases in your report selectively. You do not want your work to be merely a restatement of someone else's.

Figure 9.16 shows a note card containing a paraphrase of the following quotation.

> While the effects of acid rain are felt first in lakes, which act as natural collection points, some scientists fear there may be extensive damage to forests as well. In the process described by one researcher as "premature senescence," trees exposed to acid sprays lose their leaves, wilt and finally die. New trees may not grow to replace them. Deprived of natural cover, wildlife may flee or die. The extent of the damage to forest lands is extremely difficult to determine, but scientists find the trend worrisome. In Sweden, for example, one estimate calculates that the yield in forest products decreased by about one percent each year during the 1970s.[2]

---

[2] Bill Dampier, "Now Even the Rain Is Dangerous," *International Wildlife* 10 (Mar.–Apr. 1980): 18–19.

Paraphrased material can be introduced in your paper with an appropriate identifying phrase, such as "According to Dampier's study," "To paraphrase Dampier," or "As Dampier observes."

 ## APPENDIX: SOME HELPFUL REFERENCE WORKS

After the title of each of the following reference works is a brief annotation indicating, sometimes with a direct quotation taken from the particular work, its audience, organization, and coverage. The dates in parentheses after indexes and abstracts refer to the year in which they began publication.

Indexes

Bibliographic Index: A Cumulative Bibliography of Bibliographies (1937). Issued three times a year, this index lists bibliographies on people, technical and popular subjects, and organizations that have appeared in journal or magazine articles, books, or separately.

Biological and Agricultural Index (1945). This index is published monthly with quarterly and yearly cumulative issues. Formerly called *Agricultural Index,* this work indexes about 200 periodicals in such fields as agricultural economics, animal husbandry, ecology, food science, forestry, horticulture, marine biology, nutrition, soil science, and veterinary medicine.

Criminal Justice Periodical Index (1975). Published yearly, this index contains both an author and subject list. It is a guide to articles in more than 100 journals in the fields of law enforcement, corrections, paralegal work, security, and traffic enforcement.

Cumulative Index to Nursing & Allied Health Literature (1955). Published bimonthly, this index surveys over 250 journals and magazines in the nursing and allied health fields. Nurses, respiratory and physical therapists, social workers, radiological and medical technicians will find this index a convenient guide to literature in their fields.

Education Index (1929). This index is published every month except July and August. It lists periodicals that deal with all aspects of education from driver training to adult and continuing education.

Environmental Index (1971). Published annually, this index "offers *keyword direct access* to more than 55,000 citations appearing in 2,000 of the world's most significant environmental publications. The index compiles and cross-references environmental material from major scientific, technical, professional, trade, and general periodicals, government documents, proceedings, research reports, newspapers, books and speeches."

Hospital Literature Index (1945). Published quarterly, this "is a subject-author index of literature about the administration, planning, financing of medical care facilities and about administrative aspects of medical, paramedical, and prepayment fields." While it does not survey nursing literature, it does cover administrative and educational issues in allied health fields.

Index to Legal Periodicals (1926). This index is published monthly, except September, and contains a subject and author index to more than 350 law journals published worldwide. "Case notes or discussions of recent cases are listed by the name of the case discussed at the end of the subheading 'Cases.'" It also includes a book review index.

Index Medicus (1879). Published monthly by the National Library of Medicine in Washington, D.C., this index surveys more than 2,500 journals published worldwide in medicine and ancillary fields (for example, medical technology, medical records, respiratory therapy, etc.). It contains subject and author sections and translates titles of articles not written in English.

Index of Supermarket Articles (1935). Published by the Supermarket Institute in Chicago, this index surveys articles on supermarkets and food suppliers published in such journals as *Chain Store Age, Grocery Editions, Progressive Grocer, Supermarket Merchandising,* and *Supermarket Manager.*

Social Sciences Index and *Humanities Index* (1907). Known as the *International Index* from 1907 to 1965 and the *Social Sciences and Humanities Index* from 1965 to 1974, these two works now list articles in many of the social sciences (for example, sociology, political science) and the humanities.

Encyclopedias

The Arnold Encyclopedia of Real Estate, edited by Alvin Arnold and Jack Kusnet. Boston: Warren, Gorham & Lamont, 1978. A topical "Entry Finder" at the back "classifies selected entries into twelve major subjects"; contains annual yearbook updates.

Encyclopedia of Animal Care, edited by Geoffrey P. West. 15th ed. London: A. & C. Black, 1985. This work gives information on "the diseases, breeding, and health of domesticated animals and is intended for farmers, public health officials and breeders who do not need a veterinary reference work or who need more detail than a popular magazine provides."

Encyclopedia of Architectural Technology, edited by Pedro Guedes. New York: McGraw-Hill, 1979. "Architect, art historian, and engineer" as well as the "concerned" layperson should profit from this book. It is divided into six sections: stylistic periods; building forms and building types; structures; structural, mechanical and environmental systems; building materials; and tools, techniques, and fixings. The encyclopedia offers 800 illustrations.

Encyclopedia of Careers and Vocational Guidance. 6th. ed. Chicago: J. G. Ferguson, 1984. 3 vols. Provides useful overviews of the kinds of requirements and responsibilities necessary for numerous technical and managerial positions.

Encyclopedia of Computer Science and Engineering, edited by Anthony Ralston. 2d ed. New York: Van Nostrand Reinhold, 1983. This work has a helpful list of titles on related subjects at the beginning of each section. It also has appendixes on abbreviations, acronyms, mathematical notations, numerical tables, and key high-level languages.

Encyclopedia of Food Technology and Food Service Series. Westport, Connecticut: Avi Publishing. Vol. 1 *The Encyclopedia of Food Engineering,* edited by C. W. Hall, A. W. Farrall, and A. L. Rippen, 1971. Vol. 2 *The Encyclopedia of Food Technology,* edited by Arnold H. Johnson and Martin S. Peterson, 1974. Vol. 3 *The Encyclopedia of Food Science,* edited by Arnold H. Johnson and Martin S. Peterson, 1978.

Encyclopedia of Marine Resources, edited by Frank E. Firth. New York: Van Nostrand Reinhold, 1979. Information on the "most significant aspects of the ocean's resources" will be of interest to biologists, food technologists, fishery management specialists, and others.

Encyclopedia of Materials Handling, edited by Douglas Woodley. New York: Pergamon, 1964. 2 vols. It contains valuable chapters on machines (conveyors, elevators, cranes, hoists, trucks, etc.), unitization, and loading and transportation.

Encyclopedia of Practical Photography, edited by Eastman Kodak Company. Garden City, NY: Amphoto, 1979. 14 vols. In this work the "emphasis . . . is on practical advice and instruction in using light, film, and chemicals to get the most of your equipment. Here you will find the how-to information necessary for actual production of photographic images."

Encyclopedia of Textiles, edited by the editors of *American Fabrics Magazine.* 3d ed. Englewood Cliffs, New Jersey: Prentice-Hall, 1980. This is a "reference guide for every person concerned with the producing and marketing of fibers and fabrics, and for the professions of designing and advertising which service the textile industry." A lavishly illustrated work, this encyclopedia contains information on the history, production, and manufacturing of natural and synthetic fibers, colors and dyes, and textile printing.

Encyclopedia of Urban Planning, edited by Arnold Whittick. New York: McGraw-Hill, 1974. Reprint. Huntington, NY: R. E. Krieger, 1980. A preface describes and defines urban planning. Numerous pictures, maps, and drawings and a bibliography at the end of each section are included in this encyclopedia, which provides information on international projects, urban renewal, legislation, and other topics.

Food & Nutrition Encyclopedia, edited by A. H. Ensminger et al. Clovis, CA: Pegus Press, 1983. 2 vols; 1600 illustrations. The goal of this work is "to produce the most complete and in-depth foods and nutrition source ever." Containing over 2,800 entries, it "covers all aspects of food-nutrition-health with adequate historical and interpretive context. Each article includes all relevant aspects of the topic."

Goodheart-Wilcox Automotive Encyclopedia, edited by William K. Toboldt, Larry Johnson, and Steven W. Olive. South Holland, Illinois: Goodheart-Wilcox, 1989. Detailed guide to auto repair and maintenance.

McGraw-Hill Encyclopedia of Energy, edited by Daniel N. Lapedes. New York: McGraw-Hill, 1981. This encyclopedia is divided into two sections: "Energy Perspectives" and "Energy Technology." The encyclopedia "with its more than 300 articles written by specialists is designed to aid the student, librarian, scientist, engineer, teacher, and lay reader with any information on any aspect of energy from the economic and political to the environmental and technological."

McGraw-Hill Encyclopedia of Environmental Science, edited by Daniel N. Lapedes. New York: McGraw-Hill, 1974. This work contains 300 alphabetically arranged articles, most of which include a bibliography. There is also an analytical index.

McGraw-Hill Encyclopedia of Food, Agriculture & Nutrition, edited by Daniel N. Lapedes. New York: McGraw-Hill, 1977. Following five feature articles are 400 alphabetically arranged articles on subjects dealing with "the cultivation, harvesting, and processing of food crops; food manufacturing; and health and nutrition—from the economic and political to the technological."

McGraw-Hill Encyclopedia of Science and Technology, edited by Sybil P. Parker. 6th ed. New York: McGraw-Hill, 1987. 20 vols. Extremely wide-ranging, this is the most comprehensive encyclopedia you can consult for scientific and technological subjects.

The New Encyclopedia of Furniture, edited by Joseph Aronson. New York: Crown, 1967. This work contains numerous drawings and designs of period pieces. A bibliography and a glossary of designers is found at the end of the work.

The New York Botanical Garden Illustrated Encyclopedia of Horticulture, edited by Thomas H. Everett. New York: Garland Publishing, 1982. 14 vols. This work provides a "comprehensive description and evaluation of horticulture as it is known and practiced in the United States and Canada by amateurs and by professionals, including those responsible for botanical gardens, public parks, and industrial landscapes."

Dictionaries

Dictionary of Architecture and Construction, edited by Cyril M. Harris. New York: McGraw-Hill, 1975. This dictionary provides definitions of terms "encountered in the everyday practice of architecture and construction and in their associated fields." It emphasizes terms from the building trades and includes information on "building products and materials, and related terms dealing with their design, appearance, performance, installation, and testing"; it also covers construction equipment.

Dictionary of Computers, Data Processing, and Telecommunications, edited by Jerry M. Rosenberg. 2d ed. New York: Wiley, 1987. Offering more than 10,000 entries, "this work contains terms that relate directly or indirectly to usage of hardware and software, including the broad categories of computers, data processing, distributed data processing, home computers, information transmission, microprocessors, minicomputers, personal computers, programming languages, telecommunications, and word processing."

Dictionary of Nutrition and Food Technology, edited by Arnold E. Bender. 5th ed. Boston: Butterworths, 1982. This dictionary is for students in agriculture, commerce, food science, dietetics, home economics, sociology, and medicine. "The purpose of this dictionary is to assist the specialist from one field to understand the technical terms used by the variety of specialists in the food fields."

Dictionary of Practical Law, edited by Charles F. Hemphill, Jr. and Phyllis D. Hemphill. Englewood Cliffs, New Jersey: Prentice-Hall, 1979. "This dictionary was prepared for the needs of law students, paralegal courses, legal secretaries, and students in the administration of justice, corrections, and rehabilitation. It was also written for the needs of working police officers, and for those who simply want a definition of legal terms in everyday language."

Fairchild's Dictionary of Textiles, edited by Isabel B. Wingate. 5th ed. New York: Fairchild, 1979. It includes "terms, often of several words used or once used in the textile industry, to identify the thousands of fiber-based products employed for either the consumer or industrial purposes, along with the fibers and production processes and major equipment." It is useful to "people in all branches of industry: manufacturing, sales, producers, designers."

Stedman's Medical Dictionary. 24th ed. Baltimore, Maryland: Williams and Wilkins, 1982. Illustrated. This is a highly technical work that contains terms from all medical specialties. Heavily illustrated, it provides information on pronunciations, etymologies, spellings, and word groups.

McGraw-Hill Dictionary of Scientific and Technical Terms, edited by Sybil P. Parker. 3d ed. New York: McGraw-Hill, 1984. It includes terms used by professionals in agriculture, ecology, data processing, food engineering, graphic arts, medicine, microbiology, navigation, oceanography, petrology, and veterinary medicine; it supplies "also known as" terms and emphasizes definitions rather than pronunciation.

Mosby's Medical & Nursing Dictionary, edited by Walter P. Glanze. St. Louis: C. V. Mosby Company, 1986. According to the preface, this is "a reference book of consummate usefulness to nurses and other health professionals." Contains full-sentence definitions, includes information about etymology and pronunciation, and provides extensive cross-references and illustrations.

Modern Dictionary of Electronics, edited by Rudolf F. Graf. 6th ed. Indianapolis: Howard W. Sams, 1984. This work supplies detailed definitions of words, concepts, and abbreviations used by many professionals in electronics and electrical engineering.

Office Automation: A Glossary and Guide, edited by Nancy MacLellan Edwards. White Plains, New York: Van Nostrand Reinhold, 1983. Intended for office service managers, operations managers, purchasing agents, or "anyone who is not a professional in any of the technical areas, but who must understand their applications, their abbreviations, their symbols, and their jargon when undertaking needs analyses, evaluating equipment, talking with vendors, implementing systems, and training personnel."

Prentice-Hall Dictionary of Business, Finance, and Law, edited by Michael Downey Rice. Englewood Cliffs, New Jersey: Prentice-Hall, 1983. Intended "for business people who deal with the law, and for lawyers who deal with business," this work is also useful for students of business and law, engineering, economics, and public administration.

Private Secretary's Encyclopedic Dictionary, edited by the Prentice-Hall Editorial Staff; revised by Mary A. DeVries. 3d ed. Englewood Cliffs, New Jersey: Prentice-Hall, 1984. This work contains information on all aspects of secretarial practice, covering everything from "color coding" to "records management" to word processing.

Abstracts

Abstracts for Social Workers (1965). Published quarterly by the National Association of Social Workers, this abstract contains a subject and author index. Topics are divided into six categories, of which "Fields of Service" is the largest.

Abstracts on Criminology and Penology (formerly *Excerpts Criminologica*) (1961). This is "an international abstracting service covering the etiology of crime and juvenile delinquency, and control and treatment of offenders, criminal procedure, and the administration of justice."

Air Pollution Abstracts (1970–1976). Compiled by the Air Pollution Technical Information Center of the Environmental Protection Agency, this work contains a subject and author index and surveys periodicals, books, hearings, investigations, and other legislative actions.

Applied Ecology Abstracts (1974). Compiled monthly by Information Retrieval Limited, this abstract reviews 5,000 journals for appropriate articles. Subject categories include terrestrial and aquatic resources, control, agrochemicals, grasslands, wetlands, and pollution and pollutants.

Biological Abstracts (1926). This work surveys more than 5,000 journals in every biological field; it also lists new books.

Communication Abstracts (1977). Issued four times a year, this work provides a "comprehensive source of information about communication-related publications worldwide," including articles, reports, and books. Subject categories include advertising, broadcasting, communication theory and practice, journalism, public relations, and radio and television (for example, audiences, effects, programming). It excludes "general film-related topics."

Computer & Control Abstracts (1966). Issued monthly, this work "forms the world's major, English-language abstracting service covering the fields of computer and control engineering." It includes more than 40,000 items per year and contains subject, author, and subsidiary indexes.

Criminal Justice Abstracts (1968). Issued quarterly by the National Council on Crime and Delinquency, this volume contains an author and subject index.

Employment Relations Abstracts (1958). Published monthly, this abstract covers a wide variety of work-based issues in management, labor and union relations, etc.

Metals Abstracts (1968). Previously known as *Metallurgical Abstracts* (1934–1967), this abstract covers more than 1,000 journals.

Nursing Research. Beginning with the 1960 volume, each issue of this journal has carried "Abstracts of Reports of Studies in Nursing"; the Spring, 1959 issue contained "Abstracts of Studies in Public Health Nursing, 1924–1957."

Oceanic Abstracts (1964). This work surveys information on oceans (pollution, food source, oil exploration, geology) found in periodicals, books, and reports from government and private agencies. It was known as *Oceanic Journal* (1964–1967) and *Oceanic Citation Journal* (1968–1971).

Psychological Abstracts (1927). This abstract appears in two bound volumes a year and offers "nonevaluative summaries of the world's literature in psychology and related disciplines"; it includes a subject and author index. Some of the topics are nervous disorders, motor performance, sex differences, and sleep disorders.

Safety Sciences Abstracts Journal (1974). Issued quarterly, this journal abstracts articles on industrial safety, environmental conditions affecting the work site and workers, transportation, and occupational risks.

Sociological Abstracts (1952). Issued five times a year, this work divides sociological literature into 31 categories (for example, poverty, violence, women's studies). Issues are bound every three months; it contains a subject and author index.

Solar Energy Update (1978). Published monthly by the Technical Information Center of the Department of Energy (Oak Ridge, Tennessee), these abstracts cover current scientific and technical reports, journal articles, conference papers and proceedings, books, patents, theses, and monographs.

◆ EXERCISES

1. Find out if your library gives patrons a map or description of its holdings. If it does, bring a copy of the map or description to class. If the library does not offer such a map or description, draw one of your own indicating the location of the circulation desk, the card catalog, the reference room, the stacks, the periodicals room or section, vertical files, government documents, and audiovisuals.

2. Find any book in the library and write a brief description of the steps you took to locate that book—from your search in the card catalog to your actually checking the book out of the library. Refer to your map you used in Exercise 1.

3. Using the materials discussed in this chapter, locate the following works in your major. If your library does not have them, select titles that are most closely related to your major and explain how they would be useful to you. Prepare a separate bibliography card for each title.
   a. an index to periodicals
   b. titles of three important journals
   c. an abstract of an article appearing in one of these journals
   d. a term in a specialized dictionary
   e. a description or illustration in a specialized encyclopedia
   f. a film or tape recording
   g. two government documents
   h. a story in the *New York Times* or one of the newspapers covered by NewsBank which, in the last year, discussed a topic of interest to students in your major

4. In the subject section of the card catalog find a topic that is subdivided in the way books on construction are listed in Figure 9.3. After you do this, divide these subdivisions even further until you have a restricted topic for a research report. Bring your topic to class.

5. Using the subject, author, and title catalogs, find four or five books on the topic you selected for Exercise 4. Write a bibliography card for each book.

6. Prepare a list (providing full bibliographic information) of 15 articles for the restricted topic you selected for Exercise 4. At least five of these articles should come from periodicals not listed in the *Readers' Guide.*

7. Write a short memo (2–3 paragraphs) to your instructor describing the types of computer searches your library offers and how such a search would assist you in researching the topic you selected in Exercise 4.

8. Choose a term that is frequently used in your profession—a technical, scientific, or occupational word or phrase. Then look up its meaning in a (a) specialized dictionary or encyclopedia and (b) general dictionary or encyclopedia. You might also check the *Oxford English Dictionary.* Write a brief report (one or two paragraphs) on how these definitions are alike and how they differ—that is, what's left out in the general dictionary and why?

9. Using appropriate reference works discussed in this chapter, answer any five of the following questions. After your answer, list the specific works you used. Supply complete bibliographic information. For books, indicate author or editor, title, edition, place of publication and publisher, date, and volume and page number. For journals and magazines, include volume and page number; for newspapers, precise date and page number.
   a. Who invented the digital computer?
   b. What is biomass?
   c. How many calories are there in an orange?
   d. List three interviews that Henry Kissinger granted between 1968 and 1975.

   e. Whom did *TIME* magazine select as "Man of the Year" for 1988?
   f. What is the boiling point of coal tar?
   g. What was the headline in the *New York Times* the day you were born?
   h. List three publications issued by the U.S. Department of the Interior from 1985 to the present on outdoor recreation.
   i. What was the population of Spokane, Washington, in 1970?
   j. List three articles published between 1985 and 1988 on the advantages of teleconferencing.
   k. Who discovered the neutrino?
   l. What is the first recorded (printed) use of the word *ozone?*
   m. List three articles giving job applicants information on the effective use of body language during an interview.
   n. Who wrote *The Advance of American Nursing* in 1978?
   o. Give the title, date, and page number and author (if listed) of a story in your local newspaper that focused on child abuse.
   p. When was Sandra Day O'Connor appointed to the Supreme Court? Give the exact date.
   q. List the titles of three articles on the abuse of credit cards that have appeared in professional journals within the past two or three years.
   r. What is a high key photograph?.
   s. Name five plants that have the word *fly* as part of their common name.

10. Write a paraphrase of two of the following paragraphs.
   a. Deep-fat frying is a mainstay of any successful fast-food operation and is one of the most commonly used procedures for the preparation and production of foods in the world. During the deep-frying process, oxidation and hydrolysis take place in the shortening and eventually change its functional, sensory, and nutritional quality. Current fat tests available to food operation managers for determining when used shortening should be discarded typically require identification of a change in some physical attribute of the shortening, such as color, smoke, foam development, etc. However, by the time these changes become evident, a considerable amount of degradation has usually already taken place.[3]
   b. Ponds excavated in areas of flat terrain usually require prepared spillways. If surface runoff must enter an excavated pond through a channel or ditch, rather than through a broad shallow drainageway, the overfall from the ditch bottom to the bottom of the pond can create a serious erosion problem unless the ditch is protected. Scouring can take place in the side slope of the pond and for a considerable distance upstream in the ditch. The resulting sediment tends to reduce the depth and capacity of the pond. Protect by placing one or more lengths of rigid pipe in the ditch and extend them over the side slope of the excavation. The extended portion of the pipe or pipes may be either cantilevered or supported with timbers. The diameter of the pipe or pipes depends on the peak rate of runoff that can be expected from a 10-year frequency storm. If you need more than one pipe inlet, the combined capacity should equal or exceed the estimated peak rate of runoff.[4]

---

[3] Vincent J. Graziano, "Portable Instrument Rapidly Measures Quality of Frying Fat in Food Service Operations," *Food Technology* 33 (Sept. 1979): 50. Copyright © by Institute of Food Technologists. Reprinted by permission.
[4] U.S. Department of Agriculture, Soil Conservation Service. *Ponds for Water Supply and Recreation* (Washington, D.C.: U.S. Department of Agriculture Handbook No. 387, 1971) 48.

c. Police administrators have long recognized the value of computers for records management, crime analysis, manpower deployment, and other vital areas. The ability to manage information over short and long terms is directly proportional to the success of an individual or an agency. Until recently, however, computers have not been financially feasible for most police agencies. The National Crime Information Center (NCIC), established by the FBI in 1967, provided the only computerized resource for many departments. Other police agencies were able to use their state government's computer, but they were required to share it with other agencies. Consequently, only a few programs for law enforcement could be developed.[5]

[5] Lee McGhee and Glenn Whiteacre, "Microcomputers for Law Enforcement," *FBI Law Enforcement Bulletin* (Mar. 1983): 24.

10

Documenting Sources

Documentation is at the heart of all the research you will do at school or on the job. To document means to furnish readers with information about the materials (books, articles, pamphlets, films, interviews, questionnaires) you have used for the factual support of your statements.

This chapter will give you practical and precise directions on what to document and how to do it efficiently and consistently. Of the various systems (or formats) of documentation, perhaps footnoting is the one most familiar to you. In this chapter you will learn about other methods of documenting your sources. The major emphasis, however, will be on the *parenthetical documentation* system advocated by the Modern Language Association. You will find a sample research paper using parenthetical documentation at the end of this chapter.

◆ THE WHYS AND HOWS OF DOCUMENTATION

Before looking at the specific techniques you need to use when you document, it's necessary to understand why documentation is so important and the major role it plays in your writing strategies.

Why Is Documentation Important?

Documentation is important for at least three reasons.

1. Documentation informs your readers that you have done your homework. It proves that you have consulted experts on the subject and have relied on the most current and authoritative sources to build your case.
2. Documentation gives proper credit to these sources. Citing works by name is not a simple act of courtesy; it is an ethical requirement and, because so much of this material is protected by copyright, a point of law. By documenting your sources, you will avoid being accused of *plagiarism*—that is, steal-

ing someone else's ideas and listing them as your own. If you are found guilty of plagiarism, you could be expelled from school or fired from your job.

3. Documentation informs readers about a specific book or article you used. They may want to read it themselves for additional information or to verify the facts you have listed from that source.

What Must Be Documented?

This question often puzzles writers. If you document the following materials, you will be sure to avoid plagiarism and to assist the reader of your research paper or report.

- any direct quotations, even if it is a single phrase or key word. Quotations from the Bible, from Shakespeare, or any literary text should be identified according to the specific work (*Exodus, Merchant of Venice*) and the place in that work (for example, act 3, scene 4, line 23, listed as 3.4.23).
- any paraphrase or summary of another individual's written work
- any opinions—expressed verbally or in writing—that are not your own
- any statistical data that you have not compiled yourself
- any visuals that you have not constructed yourself—photographs, tables, charts
- any software programs that you did not develop yourself

Of course, do not document obvious facts, such as normal body temperature, well-known dates (the first moon landing in 1969; Ronald Reagan was the fortieth president of the U.S.), formulas (H_2O; the quadratic formula), or proverbs from folklore ("The hand is quicker than the eye").

◆ DOCUMENTATION IN THE WRITING PROCESS

Documentation is a vital activity in the process of writing a research paper or report. Documentation begins as you start researching your topic and continues on during the course of organizing, drafting, and even editing your work. You need to keep a careful record of the sources you use and the exact material you take from them. By listing this information on note and bibliography cards (see pages 275–80), you are able to create such a record. Then as you begin organizing and drafting your paper, selecting appropriate details and ideas from your sources, you transfer information from your note and bibliography cards to the text of your paper. Throughout various drafts you need to be sure you document precisely what you are using and then add every source you refer to in the text of your paper on the Works Cited page (discussed below). During revision (and editing) be careful to check and double-check the accuracy of your documentation. This means making sure page numbers, dates, and quotations are correct and that bibliographic information mentioned in the text of your paper matches that on your Works Cited page(s).

◆ PARENTHETICAL AND FOOTNOTE DOCUMENTATION

Numerous formats exist for documenting sources. Two of these formats are *parenthetical documentation* and *footnote documentation.* The following section will introduce you to parenthetical documentation by contrasting it with the footnote method.

A widely used system of parenthetical documentation is found in the *MLA Handbook for Writers of Research Papers,* Third Edition, edited by Joseph Gibaldi and Walter S. Achtert (New York: Modern Language Association, 1988). Although used primarily by individuals in the humanities, the MLA system is in many ways very similar to the methods of documenting sources in the sciences, technological fields, and business. For that reason this method will be emphasized in this chapter. The MLA system does not recommend footnotes or endnotes to document sources, nor does it contain a bibliography of works the writer may have consulted but has not cited directly in the paper.

Instead, the MLA method uses parenthetical, or in-text, documentation. According to this method, the writer tells readers directly in the text of the paper, at the moment the acknowledgment is necessary, what reference is being cited—by including the author's last name in parentheses together with the appropriate page number(s) from which the information is borrowed. Seeing the citation "(Morgan 205)," for example, the reader knows that the writer has borrowed information from a work by Morgan, specifically from page 205 of that work. Such sources (authors' names with page numbers) refer to an alphabetical list of works that the writer has cited in the text of the paper. This list—called "Works Cited" or "References Cited"—is placed at the end of the paper.

As you may recall from other writing courses, when you document using footnotes or endnotes, you insert a slightly raised numeral immediately after the information you wish to document, like this: [1]. In many books, the source of the information is provided in a footnote at the bottom (or "foot") of the page, preceded by the same raised numeral [1]. In other books and in most papers and reports, all of the sources are listed together on an endnotes page at the end of the entire paper. The order in which the endnotes are listed must correspond exactly to the order in which the information is cited within the paper. When readers see a [7], for instance, they expect to find information about the particular source for that information at [7] on the endnotes page. Footnotes and endnotes provide the same details: author's name, title of the work, and date and place of publication.

Figure 10.1 shows a paragraph that uses endnote documentation and a section of the endnotes page containing information about the sources. Figure 10.2, on the other hand, shows how the same paragraph is prepared using parenthetical documentation and reprints the relevant section of the Works Cited page.

FIGURE 10.1   A paragraph using endnotes to document sources.

Technical writing has expanded rapidly since World War II. The newest market seeking technical writers is data processing. In fact, it is "one of the fastest growing fields for technical writers."[1] Technical writers are especially in demand to prepare the documentation necessary for computer software systems manufactured by many different companies.[2] In preparing this documentation, the technical writer often has to explain complex information to audiences totally unfamiliar with computers. This obstacle is increasingly difficult to overcome because of the growing complexity of computers. To solve this problem, "the technical writer must function like a computer specialist while thinking like a layperson."[3]

Endnotes

[1] Julie Teunissen, "Opportunities for Technical Writers," Computer Outlook 10 (1985): 98.

[2] George Tullos, "Technical Writers and the Needs of the Computer Industry," Journal of Computer Operations 17 (1985): 13.

[3] Mary Bronstein, The New Generation of Technical Writers San Francisco: Harbor House, 1982) 45.

To provide accurate parenthetical documentation for your readers, you must first prepare a careful Works Cited page and then include the documentation in the right form and place in your text. Preparing the Works Cited page and documenting within the text of a paper are discussed in the next two sections.

◆ PREPARING THE WORKS CITED PAGE

Before you can document your sources parenthetically you must first establish what those sources are. Even though the list of references cited comes at the end of your paper, it is important that you prepare this list before you start to document. By preparing the list first you will know what sources you must cite and what page numbers you must list. You will also avoid accidentally omitting a source.

When you prepare your list of references, you must include the information in the following order.

FIGURE 10.2   The same paragraph using parenthetical documentation of sources.

> Technical writing has expanded rapidly since World War II. The newest market seeking technical writers is data processing. In fact, it is "one of the fastest growing fields for technical writers" (Teunissen 98). Technical writers are especially in demand to prepare the documentation necessary for computer software systems manufactured by many different companies (Tullos 13). In preparing this documentation, the technical writer often has to explain complex information to audiences totally unfamiliar with computers. This obstacle is increasingly difficult to overcome because of the growing complexity of computers. To solve this problem, "the technical writer must function like a computer specialist while thinking like a layperson" (Bronstein 45).

> Works Cited
>
> Bronstein, Mary. The New Generation of Technical Writers. San Francisco: Harbor House, 1982.
>
> Teunissen, Julie. "Opportunities for Technical Writers." Computer Outlook 10 (1985): 98-99.
>
> Tullos, George. "Technical Writers and the Needs of the Computer Industry." Journal of Computer Operations 17 (1985): 13.

Books
author(s)
editor(s)
title (underscored)
edition (if second or subsequent)
place of publication
publisher's name
date of publication

Articles
author(s)
title of article (put in quotation marks)
name of journal (underscored)
volume number (in arabic numerals)
date of publication
page number(s)

The examples below show you how to list different types of books and articles.

• Book by one author

Enockson, Paul G. A Guide for Selecting Computers and Software for Small Businesses. Reston, VA: Reston Books, 1983.

Note that no page numbers are listed in this citation because the appropriate page numbers to Enockson's book would be included parenthetically in the paper.

◆ *Two or more books by the same author*

Flesch, Rudolf. <u>Art of Readable Writing</u>. New York: Harper, 1974.

———. <u>Say What You Mean</u>. New York: Harper, 1972.

When you cite two or more works by the same author, do not repeat the author's name in the second or subsequent reference. Type three hyphens in place of the name and then a period. (List the works in alphabetical order.)

◆ *Book by two or three authors*

Muggins, Carolyn, and Keith Applebauer. <u>The Art of Interviewing</u>.

　　　Chicago: General Books, 1990.

Both authors' names are listed in the order they appear on the title page; do not worry about alphabetical order. But make sure that the first author's name is listed in reverse order.

◆ *Book by more than three authors*

Andreoli, Kathryn G., et al. <u>Comprehensive Cardiac Care: A Text</u>

　　　<u>for Nurses, Physicians, and Other Health Care Practition-</u>

　　　<u>ers</u>. St. Louis: Mosby, 1978.

When there are more than three authors, list only the first author's name in reverse order and add "et al." ("and others") after the comma following the first author's name. Note that when a book has a subtitle, you must include it. Separate the title and subtitle by a colon as in the above example.

◆ *Corporate author*

National Institute for the Foodservices Industry. <u>Applied</u>

　　　<u>Foodservice Sanitation</u>. Lexington, MA: Heath, 1978.

A corporate author refers to an organization, society, association, institution, or government agency that publishes a work under its own name, for example, the Federal Aviation Administration. In the example above, the institute (often cited as NIFI) wrote the book. Notice how the state is given after the city to tell readers that the book was published in Lexington, Massachusetts, as opposed to Lexington, Kentucky, or Lexington, Virginia. The name of the state is not used after well-known cities such as Boston, Chicago, or San Francisco. For this reason the writer using the Enockson book—see the example under *Book by one author*—cites the state, Virginia.

◆ *An edited collection of essays*

Tyson–Jones, Sandra, ed. <u>The Ten Best Ways to Invest in Stocks</u>

　　　<u>and Bonds</u>. New York: Merrimack, 1990.

The abbreviation "ed." for *editor* follows the editor's name listed in reverse order.

♦ *An essay included within a collection*

Holcomb, Barry T. "Municipal Bonds: A Good Investment

Opportunity." The Ten Best Ways to Invest in Stocks and

Bonds. Ed. Sandra Tyson—Jones. New York: Merrimack, 1990.

321–29.

The name of the author of the article in this collection comes first—in reverse order—then the title of the article in quotation marks. Next comes the title of the collection underscored. The editor's name is listed after the title, with "Ed." before her name to indicate that she is the editor. Do not list the editor's name in reverse order.

♦ *An article in a professional journal*

van Holland, Phyllis. "Why Banks Fail." Bank Administration 59

(1988): 36–38.

Note how a reference to a journal article differs from one citing a book. The title of the article is in quotation marks, not underscored; no place of publication is listed. The volume number immediately follows the title of the journal with no intervening punctuation. And the page number(s) on which the article is found follow the colon placed after the publication information within parentheses.

♦ *A signed magazine article*

Marcial, Gene G. "Bulls Who Snort at IBM Bears." Business Week 2

July 1984: 78.

Unlike the more scholarly journal articles, popular and frequently issued magazines (such as *Business Week, TIME, U.S. News & World Report*) are listed by date and not volume number. Note again, the page number(s) following the date; no "p." or "pp." should be used with them.

♦ *An unsigned magazine article*

"When Dream Homes Turn into Nightmares." U.S. News & World Report

11 Dec. 1978: 43.

Many magazine articles do not carry an author's name (or by-line) because they are written by one of the staff members of the magazine. If this is the case, begin with the title of the article. Unsigned works are always listed according to the first word of their title (excluding *a, an,* or *the*).

An article in a newspaper

Wittington, Delores. "The Dollar Buys More Vacation Overseas

This Year." <u>Springfield Herald</u> 30 Mar. 1988, late ed.,

sec. A: 10.

Give the title of the newspaper as it appears at the top of the first page of the newspaper, including the name of the city if it is part of that title. List the article by day, month, and year, not according to the cumbersome volume and issue numbers. Identify section, page, and edition information for readers. In the example above, readers know that the story appeared in the late edition on page 10 in section A. Sometimes the story you cite will not require these details. The example below cites an article found on page 2 of a paper that issues only one edition per day.

Bulkeley, William M. "Data General Corporation Is Ready to

Introduce Portable Computers with 25–Line Display." <u>Wall</u>

<u>Street Journal</u> 4 Sept. 1984: 2.

An article in an encyclopedia

Truxal, John. "Telemetering." <u>McGraw–Hill Encyclopedia of</u>

<u>Science and Technology</u>. 6th ed. 1987.

Because it is a multivolume, alphabetical work, only the particular edition and year of an encyclopedia has to be listed on the Works Cited page. If you cite the name of the author of an article in an encyclopedia, begin your reference with his or her last name. Some encyclopedia articles are not signed.

A pamphlet

Boone, Roberta T. <u>Ghetto Children and Their Diets</u>. Washington,

DC: U.S. Children's Bureau, 1968.

Document a pamphlet the same way you would a book.

A film

<u>Understanding Asthma</u>. Sound filmstrip. Philadelphia: Health

Care Media, 1988. 37 min.

Underscore the title of a film and include the distributor and order number. If you indicate the length of the film, include this information last.

Radio or television program

<u>60 Minutes</u>. CBS News. 16 Oct. 1988.

"The Dilemma." <u>Rich Man, Poor Man</u>. PBS. WTQA, Lincoln. 21 Apr.

1987.

Underscore the title of a program but put an individual episode in a series within quotation marks, as in the title from *Rich Man, Poor Man* above. (In your Works Cited page, *60 Minutes* would be listed under "S" for "Sixty.")

◆ *Computer program*

> Smith, Judith. A Learner's Guide to Computer Graphics. Com-
>
> puter software. Tulsa: General Computers, Inc., 1989.

◆ *Cartoon or advertisement*

> Lees, Charlotta. Cartoon. Miami Magazine. Feb. 1989: 36.
>
> American Resort Council. "Leisure Life Pays Off." Adver-
>
> tisement. Vacation Life Aug. 1990: 71.

◆ *A published interview*

> Zeluto, Thomas. "Interview with Former Budget Director."
>
> Findlay Magazine Oct. 1988: 2–4.

Begin with the name of the individual being interviewed. Then indicate the title of the interview.

◆ *An unpublished interview*

> Jensen, Barbara. Professor of Physics, Berry College. Telephone
>
> interview. 15 May 1990.

Begin with the name of the individual—in reverse order—and then indicate how and when the interview was conducted.

◆ *A questionnaire*

> Questionnaire for Secretaries. Distributed between 6–10 Nov.
>
> 1989. Seager Construction Company.

How to Alphabetize the Works in Your Reference List

Your list of references must be in alphabetical order to enable readers to find them quickly. Here are some guidelines to follow when you alphabetize your list.

1. Make sure that each author's name is in correct alphabetical sequence with the author's (or the first of multiple authors') names in reverse order. Thus, you would have Jones, Sally T., not Sally T. Jones.

2. Hyphenated last names should be alphabetized according to the first of the hyphenated names.

   Grundy, Alex H.
   Mendez-Greene, A. Y.
   Mundt, Jill

3. List corporate authors as you would names of individuals, but do not invert the corporate name.

Marine Fisheries Association
Nally, Mark
National Bureau of Standards
Nuttal, Marion

4. List names beginning with the same letters according to the number of letters in each name—the shorter names precede the longer ones.

Lund, Michael
Lundford, Sarah
Lundforth, Jeffrey

5. Disregard the article (*a, an, the*) when you list an unsigned article or a film.

The Cable Television Guidebook (an unsigned pamphlet, listed under C on the Works Cited page)
The Godfather, Part II (film, listed under G)
"An Improved Means of Detecting Computer Crime" (unsigned article, listed under I)

◆ DOCUMENTING WITHIN THE TEXT

The Works Cited list does not, of course, tell readers what you actually borrowed from your sources or where that information is located within a source. To give readers that information you must include documentation within the text of your paper or report. As you write your rough draft(s), make sure that you insert the author's name and appropriate page number(s) for each one of the sources that you use. Be sure also that the information you include parenthetically within the text—names, page numbers, short titles—precisely matches the information you supplied under Works Cited at the end of your paper or report. Double-check the spelling of names, page numbers, and publication data against the titles on your Works Cited page. Remember, if you fail to document within your text, you are guilty of plagiarism; and if your documentation is incorrect or incomplete, readers will have trouble finding the source and may doubt the reliability of your work.

Parenthetical, or in-text, documentation is relatively simple. Keep your documentation brief and to the point so you do not interrupt the reader's train of thought. In most cases, all you will need to include is the author's last name and appropriate page number(s) in parentheses, usually at the end of the sentence. For unsigned articles or radio and television programs, you would use a shortened title in place of an author's name. Note in the following example that no mark of punctuation appears before the parentheses and that a period follows them. Also, no "page" or "p." or comma comes between the author's name and the page number within the parentheses.

About 5 percent of the world's population has diabetes mellitus,
and 25 percent of the world's population acts as carriers of the
disease (Walton 56).

Seeing this parenthetical documentation, the reader will expect to find the title
and publication information about Walton's study correctly listed after Walton's
name on your Works Cited page.

Walton, J. H. Common Diseases of the World. New York: Medical
    Books, 1988.

The number after Walton's name in the parenthetical documentation refers to the
page number where the information you cite can be found.

You may refer to the same work more than once in your paper or report. For
second or subsequent references you will use the same method of documentation. As in the Walton example above, you will place Walton's name and the appropriate page number—even if it is the same as in the previous reference(s)—
within parentheses following the borrowed information. Of course, if you include
Walton's name within the sentence, there is no need to repeat it in the parentheses; all you need do is give the page number. The exact placement of the author's
name within the sentence will be discussed later.

If you are using a work that has two authors, list both their last names parenthetically.

Tourism has increased by 21 percent this last quarter, thanks to
individuals passing through our state on their way to the World's
Fair (Muscovi and Klein 2–3).

If one of the works you use has three or more authors, list just the first author's
last name in parentheses followed by et al. or "and others" and the page num-
ber(s).

An understanding of ergonomics has revolutionized the design of
office furniture (Brodsky et al. 345–47).

If the work you are borrowing from has a corporate author, use a shortened version of the name within the parentheses as in the following example where
"Commission" replaces "Commission on Wage and Price Control":

Salaries for local electricians were at or above the national
average (Commission 145).

In all of the preceding examples, the names of the authors have appeared in
parentheses. However, you may cite the author's name within your text. If so,
there is no need to repeat it parenthetically. Include only the appropriate page
number(s) within parentheses. The following examples show three different, acceptable ways of citing an author's name in the text and indicate how writers can
document page references.

Clausen sees the renovation of downtown areas as one of the most
challenging issues facing city governments today (29).

As Clausen notes, the renovation of downtown areas is one of the most challenging issues facing city governments today (29).

The renovation of downtown areas, according to Clausen, is one of the most challenging issues facing city governments today (29).

Similarly, if you list the title of a reference or anonymous work within the text of your paper, you need not repeat it for your parenthetical documentation.

According to the Encyclopaedia Britannica, Cecil B. De Mille's King of Kings was seen by nearly 800,000,000 individuals (3: 458).

The first number in parentheses refers to the volume number of the *Encyclopaedia Britannica;* the second points to the page number of that volume. In this case, the writer wisely gives both volume and page numbers to indicate that the information is listed under deMille and not the title of the film.

If you are citing information from two or more works by the same author, you will have to inform readers clearly from which work a particular fact or opinion comes. Let's say that you used information from the following works.

Howe, Grace. The Management of an Office. New York: Business
    Publications, 1989.

———. "Systems Control for Small Businesses." The Modern Office
    15 (1988): 67–81.

You have a number of ways to tell readers from which specific work by Grace Howe you are borrowing material.

1. Cite the author's name, short title, and page number parenthetically.

Communication stations are important in an office to provide a maximum flow of information (Howe, Management 132).

Note that a comma follows the author's name when you also cite a title within parentheses.

2. Mention the author's name in your sentence and a short title and page number within parentheses.

Howe thinks communication stations in an office are important to provide a maximum flow of information (Management 132).

3. Give the author's name and a shortened title in the text with only the page number included parenthetically.

According to Howe's article "Systems Control," productivity increases by at least 20 percent after each training session involving data processing techniques (71).

Occasionally you will have to cite two sources at the same time to document a point. Include the names of the authors of both sources just as if you were listing them individually but separate each source with a semicolon.

The use of salt domes to store radioactive wastes has come under severe attack (Jelinek 56–67; McPherson and Wong 23–29).

Be careful, though, that you do not overload readers by including a long string of references in your parenthetical documentation as the following example does.

Wind energy has been successfully used in both rural and urban settings (Bailey 34; Henderson 9; Kreuse 78; Mankowitz 98–99; Olsen 456–58; Vincenti 23; Walker and Smith 43).

Rather than interrupting the reader and crowding references together, consider revising your sentence to make the subject more precise and the references more restricted.

Wind energy has long benefited the farm community (Kreuse 78; Walker and Smith 43). But recent experiments in New York City have shown the effectiveness of this form of energy for apartment dwellers, too (Bailey 34; Henderson 9). Similar experiments in San Francisco also show how wind power helps urban residents (Mankowitz 98–99; Olsen 456–58; Vincenti 23).

If you include a quotation, place the parenthetical documentation at the end of the sentence containing the quotation.

Pilmer has observed that coffee "is only mildly addictive in the sense that withdrawal will not harm you or produce violent symptoms" (16).

Note that the period follows the parentheses, not the quotation marks. Even if the quotation is short and appears in the middle of the sentence, place the documentation at the end of the sentence.

Alvin Toffler uses the phrase "third wave" to characterize the new scientific and computer revolution (34).

If the material you quote runs to more than four typed lines, set the quotation apart from the text by indenting it ten spaces and by eliminating the quotation marks. Double-space the quotation. Place the parenthetical documentation after the quotation as in the following example.

L. J. Ronsivalli offers this interesting analogy of how radiation can penetrate solid objects:

One might wonder how an x-ray, a gamma ray or a cosmic ray can penetrate something as solid as a brick or a piece of wood. We can't see that within the atomic structures of the brick and the wood are spaces for the radiation to enter. If we look at a cloud, we can see its shape, but because distance has made them too small, we

can't see the droplets of moisture of which the cloud is

made. Much too small for the eyes to see, even with the

help of a microscope, the atomic structure of solid

materials is made of very small particles with a lot of

space between them. In fact, solids are <u>mostly</u> empty

spaces. (20–21)

If you omit anything from a quotation, follow the rules governing ellipses on pages 278–79.

If you take a quotation from any place but the original source (if, for example, the quotation you want to use is included in the book you are citing but originally came from another book or article), you should document that fact by including "qtd. in" in your parenthetical documentation.

The monthly business meeting serves a number of valuable
functions. In fact, perhaps the most important one is that
"chain-of-command meetings provide the opportunity to pass
information up as well as down the administrative ladder" (qtd.
in Munroe 87).

This documentation lets readers know that you found the quotation in Munroe, not in the original work from which these words come.

◆ DOCUMENTATION IN SCIENTIFIC AND TECHNICAL WRITING

Numerous other formats exist for documenting sources. Many professions publish their own style sheet or book to provide such instruction (for example, the *Publication Manual of the American Psychological Association,* the *Council of Biology Editors' Style Manual,* the American Institute of Physics's *Style Manual for Guidance in the Preparation of Papers*) or recommend that writers follow the format used in a specific technical or scholarly journal. Every professional group, however, would advise writers *against* using the formats and abbreviations found in periodical indexes such as the *Readers' Guide* or the *Applied Science & Technology Index.* The way information is listed in these sources is not offered as a model in documentation. Before you write a paper or report, ask your instructor or employer about the format they prefer.

Many professions use the author-date method of documentation or the ordered references method. Like the MLA style just discussed, both methods rely on parenthetical documentation; that is, rather than using footnotes or endnotes with raised arabic numerals, the particular information about the source is placed directly in the text within parentheses. A brief overview of these two methods will show you how this is done.

The Author-Date Method

With this method the writer does not use notes or note numbers at all. Instead, information about a reference or quotation is placed in the text of the paper or report.

> The theory that new housing becomes increasingly expensive as buyers move farther north has been recently advanced (Jones, 1988, p. 13).

The reader sees that Jones advanced this theory on page 13 of a work written in 1988. If Jones's name were mentioned in the text, "Jones advances the theory that new housing . . . ," only "(1988, p. 13)" would be listed. To find Jones's work, readers turn to an alphabetical list of references at the end of the paper, report, or article where, under *Jones,* they find a bibliographic entry for the work. As in the MLA system, only works actually cited in a paper are listed in the reference list. If two works by Jones were cited, the references for both of them are given. If they were done in the same year, they are differentiated in the text *and* in the list of references by a lower-case letter *a* and *b.* For example:

> Housing is increasingly more expensive on the north side than on the south (Jones, 1988a, p. 22).

> A recent study has established a demographic pattern for small cities in the Midwest (Jones, 1988b, p. 73).

In the accompanying list of references, the two works by Jones might be listed as follows:

> Jones, T. 1988a. The cost of housing on Lincoln's northside. Urban Studies, 72: 10–24.

> Jones, T. 1988b. Demographic density in three Midwestern small cities. Columbia: University of Missouri Press.

According to this method of documentation, only the first word of the title (even if it is *a, an,* or *the*) and proper nouns are capitalized in the reference list. Titles are neither underscored nor put into quotation marks. The volume number of a journal is often underscored or italicized and followed by a colon to distinguish it from the page numbers that are listed immediately thereafter.

The Ordered References Method

Like the author-date method, the ordered references method uses parenthetical documentation, but relies on numbers rather than authors' names to identify a source. The references in a paper are numbered in the order in which they appear. For example,

```
Three new products help reduce bacterial infection in restaurant
kitchens (7:47).
```

The "7" indicates that this is the seventh source found in the reference list; "47" refers to the page number of that source. Sources, therefore, are not listed in alphabetical order, as they are in the author-date method. Each time a source is mentioned, the same number is used. If your first cited source is listed again near the middle or end of your paper, or if it is cited three times in a row, it is still listed parenthetically as (1:   ). The page numbers after the colon may or may not change.

◆ SAMPLE RESEARCH PAPER USING MLA IN-TEXT DOCUMENTATION

Study the following sample research paper on stress and computer programmers to see how the student author has successfully used the MLA documentation. Compare the references mentioned in the text with the Works Cited page to see how the writer has handled documentation appropriately. The sample long report on pages 305–17 also uses the MLA system of parenthetical documentation.

1 inch

Janet Hempstead

Type double-space throughout

Professor Smith

Business Writing 112

December 7, 1988

Stress and the Computer Programmer   ←*1 inch*→

←*1 inch*→Since computers were born in the middle of the 1940s, they have gradually become a part of everyone's life. Once computers were used "primarily to construct and control our nation's missiles and spaceships" (Fisher, Origins 6). But now they have made their way into corporations, classrooms, and homes. It is a rare business that does not own at least one microcomputer.

The computer's enormous capacity for processing information offers us more control over our lives, greater freedom of choice, and the opportunity for richer interactions with one another and the world around us (Fisher, "Freedom" 11). But computers could not perform the numerous tasks they do without human management. Without being programmed to do a specific job, the computer would be worthless. In the world of business and industry, the importance of such programming functions makes the computer programmer essential. According to the Bureau of Labor Statistics, there were more than 266,000 jobs for computer programmers in the 1980s, and the opportunities for future positions are excellent (179).

The computer programmer's job, however, is neither easy nor calm. It is misleading to view the programmer as a cold, robot-like creature who acts more like a machine than a human being. The programmer is often wrongly seen as an individual unthreatened by emotions or untouched by the conflicts and demands that affect other workers. On the contrary, programmers are under considerable stress on their highly technical jobs. This paper will study the problems of job-related stress that affect computer programmers by discussing (1) the symptoms that can result from stress involved in programming a computer, (2) the causes of that stress, (3) the effects of that stress for programmers and their employers, and (4) the specific techniques programmers can use to reduce or control stress on the job.

Symptoms of Stress Related to Computer Programming

Stress is any disturbance or reaction that alters the body's normal functions. Katherine Lodjac, a noted researcher on stress management, has said that "Everyone needs some stress to function, but the major question is how we handle that stress" (qtd. in Holden 182). Some people are naturally stress prone; others are not. Recent research has shown that individuals' reactions to potentially stressful situations vary greatly, depending on their personalities (Rice 84-85). What is true for the general population is equally true for programmers. Those workers who bury themselves in

3

programs, instructions, and codes will be more likely
to exhibit the symptoms of stress than those who do
not. Programmers who allow separate time for work and
relaxation will be less prone to experience stress than
their colleagues who do not. Yet regardless of how it
is handled, stress is an inescapable part of every
computer programmer's life.

Because of their particular work, programmers are
especially susceptible to symptoms linked to stress.
They have to spend long hours at their terminals, often
straining their eyes to focus images on a moving VDT
screen. This eye movement can trigger tension around
the eyes, headaches, blurred vision, nausea, and
fatigue, many of the symptoms identified in a study by
Wong and Johnson (108-10). Programmers often complain
of severe lower backaches from having to sit for hours
in poorly designed chairs and having to slouch into
uncomfortable positions to read VDT screens clearly.
Perhaps in the future ergonomically designed office
furniture will relieve some of this stress for the
programmer (Overton 89-90).

If the programmer does not identify and treat
stress-related symptoms, even more serious ones may
develop. Many symptoms of prolonged or severe stress
include spastic colitis, gastritis, migraine headaches,
urinary problems, and rashes (Danner and Dworkin 66).
For the programmer under constant stress, the risk of

4

hypertension, or high blood pressure, is especially great (Danner and Dworkin 68). If the programmer has a family history of blood pressure problems, of course the danger is greater. But even if the computer programmer does not have such a history, a few years immersed in the pressures of the job may cause a dangerously elevated blood pressure (Wong and Johnson 109). Besides these physical problems, the programmer under prolonged stress can develop emotional problems that adversely affect job performance, lifestyle, and family life (Rice 81).

Causes of Stress on Computer Programmers

    Computer programmers are under almost constant stress. As we have seen, part of that stress may come from the kinds of hardware programmers use. But the full cause of the programmer's stress goes far beyond hardware. Stress is built into the programmer's very occupation. According to a recent computer science graduate from Northeast Community College, now a computer programmer at Denver Industries, "The stress starts from the day you accept the position" (Ricks, interview).

    Companies have high expectations for their programmers. They demand perfect work and may not always allow the programmer sufficient time to debug a

5

program. The importance a company assigns to
programming is, of course, justified. A company depends
on the programmer to develop and test programs and to
prepare instruction sheets for computer operators. The
following job description for a computer programmer
issued by the Bureau of Labor Statistics points to the
stress-producing responsibilities placed on the
individual choosing programming as a career.

> In hiring programmers, employers look for
> people who can think logically and are
> capable of exacting analytical work. The
> ability to work with abstract concepts and to
> do technical analysis is especially important
> for systems programmers because they work
> with the software that controls the
> computer's operation. The job calls for
> patience, persistence, and the ability to
> work with extreme accuracy even under
> pressure. Ingenuity and imagination are
> particularly important when programmers must
> find new ways to solve a problem. (179)

One of the most significant causes of stress for
programmers is working under a deadline to produce a
highly technical document, often on very short notice.
The programmer knows that a delay can seriously affect
his or her work--creating a terrifying backlog--or the
work of another individual or department in the

6

company. As Bob Turnbull, the chief programmer at Data Processing Corporation, aptly observed, "I once was given an hour to write a program for an important set of instructions when I could have used at least three hours to get the job finished" (Turnbull, interview).

The way in which programmers work with others can also elevate their stress level. In some companies, programmers work in groups or teams for large, highly technical projects. This working arrangement may be easy and pleasant for the programmer who enjoys interacting with others, thus lessening an individual programmer's tension and stress. But not every programmer prefers to work as part of a team. As Lee A. Norris pointed out, the team approach may be more frustrating for the programmer than the deadline (32). Disagreements and potential delays may result from such team interaction. And when two or more programmers disagree, because of either egos or errors, they may not be able to meet deadlines, and so their stress levels may increase. "The Group Stress Syndrome is ... a frequent and disturbing occurrence at many large plants" (Norris 33).

Effects of Stress for Programmers and Their Employers

Stress on the job can have many serious side effects for both programmer and employer. On-the-job

7

stress can force employees to adopt potentially
unhealthy ways of handling stress. In a survey
published in Industrial Psychology Review, the most
frequently reported harmful methods for coping with
stress were overeating, overdrinking, smoking, drug
use, and "perpetual anger to thwart what the individual
perceives as a growing number of personal attacks"
(Danner 73). These unhealthy reactions can seriously
hurt programmers and their work.

When stress attacks the programmer, the employer
also suffers. A weakened or rushed programmer is more
likely to make mistakes. Brown and Rosenbaum argue that
repeated exposure to highly stressful situations--like
programming--can temporarily lower an individual's IQ
(112). This may be the reason why more mistakes are
made by employees under stress. Even a slight error by
a programmer can cost the company time and money: "Last
year a single programming error resulted in our having
to redo the payroll for the first week of March--a
six-hour job" (Ricks, interview). If only 1 percent of
the more than 266,000 computer programmers--2,660--made
one error each week, companies could stand to lose
millions of dollars each year.

Illnesses caused by stress can also significantly
increase absenteeism. The physical ravages of stress--
ulcers, fatigue, hypertension--are responsible for many
lost workdays. An employee suffering from stress-
induced illness may lose as many as ten to thirty

8

working days each year ("High Costs of Stress" 29).
This lost time spells trouble for the employer worried
about decreased productivity. When the programmer is
ill, work in a number of departments may fall behind or
an additional burden is placed on other employees.

How the Computer Programmer Can Control Stress

Stress has been correctly called a disease (Danner
73; Rice 78; Wong and Johnson 106). As we have seen, it
is a disease to which programmers may be particularly
vulnerable. In order to control this disease
successfully, programmers must acknowledge that their
symptoms are stress-related and then take steps to
control these symptoms. To do this, programmers must be
prepared to make changes in their work habits and in
their attitudes toward work.

On the job, the programmer should in Fisher's
words be aware of "working for long periods of time
without a single restful break" ("Freedom" 12). A few
rest periods throughout the day will help to relieve
the programmer's tension and reduce the level of
stress. These rest periods do not have to be long or
costly for the company. Some might be taken right where
the programmer works--"minute vacations," as Ricks
calls them (Interview). Relaxation or breathing
exercises, such as those advocated by Jablonski (8-10),
take only a few minutes and can quickly refresh and

9

relax the programmer. A brief change of scenery--a short walk to the water cooler or around a desk--will relieve eyestrain. "Escape from the computer or the desk even for a few seconds heightens the worker's spirits" (Jablonski 9).

Vigorous physical activity in the middle of the day can reduce stress, which, without release, can build up to monstrous proportions by the end of the day. During lunch breaks many executives are beginning to jog, play a quick game of handball or do calisthenics. Some companies like Southwest Industries have built gyms on their plant site to help employees work off stress before and after work ("Killer Stress"). Programmers need to exercise often to reduce their stress levels.

Many companies now also have stress-reduction programs or psychological counseling services for employees (Rice 84). If these sessions are available, the programmer should take advantage of them. These services benefit both the employee and the company by defusing the worker's tension and thereby increasing productivity. As Fisher points out in his influential study The Origins and Development of the Computer in the Modern World, "Sophisticated hardware can solve many of our technological problems but the ultimate success of this hardware depends upon the mental health of human beings who use it" (169).

The programmer also needs to have a healthy attitude about work. Perhaps one of the greatest causes of stress in the lives of technical workers is "their desire for perfection" (Danner and Dworkin 65). Some programmers believe that they will be regarded as failures if they write just one bad program. This "Win-or-Lose-Everything Syndrome," as Danner calls it (75), can be devastating. Programmers should not judge their future careers on the outcome of a single program. If a program fails, the programmer should adopt an optimistic attitude that the next one will be better (Norris 34).

Conclusion

Because of their highly technical and demanding positions, computer programmers are frequent victims of stress. The symptoms of stress may be eyestrain, fatigue, backaches, ulcers, or even more serious, hypertension. Stress may be caused by computer hardware, by unrealistic expectations of employers, and by the programmers' own desire for job perfection. The effects of stress in the workplace are serious for programmers and employers. Confronted with stress, the programmer may develop unhealthy coping mechanisms. Moreover, stress-related diseases can lead to employee absenteeism, costing an employer time and money. While programmers cannot eliminate stress from their lives,

11

they can alleviate it by taking "minute vacations"
(Ricks, interview) devoted to relaxation and exercise
techniques. Perhaps, though, the most effective
antidote for the problems of stress on the job is for
programmers to put a healthy distance between their job
and their home life.

                                                                12
                              Works Cited

Brown, Bernard, and Lilian Rosenbaum. "How Stress
     Lowers IQ Scores." Science Digest Oct. 1983:
     112-14.
Bureau of Labor Statistics. "Computer Programmers."
     Occupational Outlook Handbook. 1984-85 ed.
Danner, G. T. "Wrong Ways of Coping with Stress: A
     Survey." Industrial Psychology Review 32 (1988):
     73-89.
Danner, G. T., and Martin Dworkin. "A Correlation of
     Physical Diseases with Stress Factors." Journal of
     Health and Society 11 (1987): 63-70.
Fisher, Harold. "Computers and Personal Freedom."
     Computer World 31 Jan. 1988: 11-12.
---. The Origins and Development of the Computer in the
     Modern World. San Francisco: Data-Master, 1987.
"The High Costs of Stress." U.S. News & World Report 10
     May 1983: 29.
Holden, W.A. "When Stress Can Hurt Your Health."
     McCalls Apr. 1981: 182-84.
Jablonski, Margaret. "Exercise Your Stress Away."
     Healthy Executive May 1988: 8-10.
"Killer Stress: How Business Deals with It." Inside
     Business Today. CBS. WBCK, Middletown, TX. 5 Nov.
     1988.
Norris, Lee A. "Together or Apart?: Group Dynamics and
     Deficiencies in the Computer Center." Computer
     Science 7 (1986): 31-35.

13

Overton, James P., Jr. "Ergonomics, Office Design, and
    Stress." Today's Office Feb. 1983: 89-92, 101-2.

Rice, Berkeley. "Can Companies Kill?" Psychology Today
    June 1981: 78-85.

Ricks, Larrisa. Personal interview. 2 Nov. 1988.

Turnbull, Bob. Personal interview. 8 Nov. 1988.

Wong, Carl, and Janis Johnson. "Stress and Health in
    Silicon Valley." Industrial Management 14 (1987):
    106-11.

◆ EXERCISES

1. Ask a professor in your major what he or she regards as the most widely respected periodical in your field. Find a copy of this periodical and explain with examples its method of documentation. How does it differ from the MLA method?

2. Put the following pieces of bibliographic information in proper form according to the MLA method of documentation for Works Cited.

   a. New York, Hawthorn Publishing Company, John Anderson, 1988, pages 95–97, second edition, *A New Way to Process Film.*

   b. *American Journal of Nursing,* Karen E. Forbes and Shirlee A. Stokes, July 1984, pages 884–88, "Saving the Diabetic Foot." vol. 84.

   c. *The FCC Procedures and Manual Book,* the Federal Communication Commission, the Government Printing Office, price $8.50, available after June 1976, page 32, Washington, D.C.

   d. *Southern Living,* Steve Bender, page 72, "Native Magnolias," June 1988.

   e. an interview with your local police chief that took place in the college auditorium after he delivered a talk on crime prevention on Wednesday, January 10, 1990.

   f. today's editorial in your local newspaper.

   g. Pyramid Films, Inc., *Pulse of Life,* 1986, Santa Monica, California, order number 342br.

   h. *Essays on Food Sanitation,* John Smith (editor), Framingham, Massachusetts, 3rd edition, pages 345–356, Mary Grossart (author), Albion Publishing Company, "Selection of Effective Chemical Agents," 1988.

   i. *TIME,* "Nature Aids the Alaska Cleanup," page 84, May 8, 1989.

   j. January to February of 1989, pages 43–53, "Smoke Detectors and Alarms," Bertschinger, Susan, *Fire Journal.*

3. Put the bibliographic references you listed in MLA format in Exercise 2 into the format that one of the periodicals in your major uses.

4. Convert the bibliographic information given for one article in the periodical you chose for Exercise 1 to the MLA parenthetical style.

5. The following passage contains mistakes in the MLA method of documentation. Find these mistakes and explain how they might be corrected.

> More and more companies are allowing employees to
> "telecommute" (see Smith; Dawson; Brown; Gura and Keith; and
> Allen). One expert defines telecommuting as "home-based work"
> (13). Having terminals in their homes "allows employees to work
> at a variety of jobs" ("New Employment Opportunities"). It has
> been estimated that currently 700,000 employees work out of their
> homes (Pennington, p. 56). That number is sure to increase as
> computer-based businesses multiply in the 1990s (Brown). In one
> of her recent articles on telecommuting, Holcomb found that "in

the last year alone 43 companies in the metropolitan Phoenix area made this option available to their employees" (167).

Employees who telecommute cite a variety of benefits for such an arrangement (see in particular articles by Gura, Smith, and Kaplan). One employee of a mail order company whose opinion was quoted observed that "I can save about 15—17 hours a week in driving time" (from Allen). Working at home allows the telecommuting employee to work at his or her optimum times ("The Day Does Not Have to Start at 9:00 A.M."). Also, in articles by Kaplan and Keith the benefits of not having to leave home are emphasized: "A telecommuting parent does not have to worry about child care" (39). Telecommuting may "be here to stay" (quoted in a number of different sources).

6. Submit your preliminary list of references for a research paper or long report to your instructor.

11

Summarizing Material

A summary is a brief restatement of the main points in a book, report, article, meeting, or convention. A summary saves readers hours of time, because they do not have to study the original or attend a conference. A summary can reduce a report or article by 85 to 95 percent (or even more) or capture the essential points of a three-day convention in a one-page memo. Moreover, a summary can tell readers if they should even be concerned about the original; it may be irrelevant for their purposes. Finally, since only the most important points of a work are included in a summary, readers will know they are given the crucial information they need.

◆ THE IMPORTANCE OF SUMMARIES

Summaries can be found all around you. Television and radio stations regularly air two-minute news broadcasts—sometimes called "newsbreaks"—to summarize in a few sentences the major stories covered in more detail on the evening news. Popular news magazines such as *TIME, Newsweek,* or *U.S. News & World Report* have a large readership because of their ability to condense seven days of news into short, readable articles highlighting key personalities, events, and issues.

Newspapers also employ summaries for their readers' convenience. Daily newspapers such as the *Wall Street Journal* or weekly papers such as *Barron's: A Business and Financial Weekly* or the *National Law Journal* print on the first page brief summaries of news stories that are discussed in detail later in the paper. Some newspapers simply print a column entitled "News Summary" on the first or second page of an issue to condense major news stories. *Facts on File*'s *News Digest* comprehensively summarizes world news every week. Figure 11.1 illustrates a summary that appeared in *Facts on File* about copyright status for computer-colored films. Note how a few paragraphs capture and emphasize the most significant data that may have taken weeks and numerous reports or stories to record. The *Readers' Digest,* one of the most widely read publications in Amer-

FIGURE 11.1   A summary of the copyright status of colorized films.

> **Copyrights Approved for "Colorization."**
> Computer-colored films would be granted copyright status if those tinted versions revealed a certain degree of human creativity and were produced by existing computer-coloring technology, the U.S. Copyright Office of the Library of Congress ruled June 19.
>   The ruling came after months of debate surrounding the "colorization" process, a debate that had reached all the way to the U.S. Senate.
>   The copyright office ruled that computer-colored versions of black-and-white films were entitled to copyright protection as "derivative works." Such protection gave a studio the right, generally for 75 years, to distribute a colored version of a movie through broadcast and cable-TV outlets and to sell videotape copies. The studio could also collect damages from companies that copied the colored films.
>   Films would not be eligible for copyright protection if the tinting "consists of the addition of only a relatively few number of colors to an existing black-and-white motion picture."

ica, is devoted largely to condensing articles, stories, and even books while still preserving the essential message, flavor, and wording of the original.

On the job, writing summaries is a regular and important responsibility. Each profession has its own special needs for summaries. Chapter 16 discusses a variety of reports—progress, sales, periodic, trip, test, and incident—whose effectiveness depends on a faithful summary of events. You may be asked to summarize a business trip lasting one week into one or two pages for your company or agency. A busy manager may ask you to read and condense a ninety-page report so that she will have a knowledgeable overview of its contents. To cite another example of using summaries on the job, acute-care nurses must write a one- or two-page discharge summary for patients who are being referred to another agency (home health, nursing home, rehabilitation center). These nurses must read the patient's record carefully and summarize what has happened to the patient since admission to the hospital. They must note any surgeries, treatments, diagnoses, and prognoses and indicate necessary follow-up treatments (medication, office visits, outpatient care, x-rays).

◆ CONTENTS OF A SUMMARY

The chief problem in writing a summary is deciding what to include and what to omit. As we have just seen, a summary, after all, is a much abbreviated version of the original; it is a streamlined review of *only* the most significant points. You will not help your readers save time by simply rephrasing large sections of the original and calling the new version a summary. That will only supply readers with another report, not a summary. You need to make your summary lean and useful by briefly telling readers about the main points: the purpose, scope, conclusions, and recommendations. A summary should concisely answer the readers' two most important questions: (1) What findings does the report or meeting offer? and (2) How do these findings apply to my business, research, or job?

How long should a summary be? While it is hard to set down precise limits about length, effective summaries are generally 5 to 15 percent of the length of the original. The complexity of the material being summarized and your audience's exact needs can help you to determine an appropriate length. To help you know what is most important for your summary, the following suggestions will guide you on what to include and what to omit.

What to Include in a Summary

1. Purpose. A summary should indicate why the article or report was written or why a convention or meeting was held. (Often a report is written or a meeting is called to solve a problem or to explore new areas of interest.) Your summary should give the reader a brief introduction (even one sentence will do) indicating the main purpose of the report or conference.

2. Essential specifics. Include only the names, costs, codes, places, or dates essential to understanding the original. To summarize a public law, for example, you need to include the law number, the date it was signed into law, and the name(s) of litigants.

3. Conclusions or results. Emphasize what was the final vote, the result of the tests, the proposed solution to the problem.

4. Recommendations or implications. Readers will be concerned especially with important recommendations—what they are, when they can be carried out, why they are necessary.

What to Omit in a Summary

1. Opinion. Avoid injecting opinions—your own, the author's, or a speaker's. You distract readers from grasping main points by saying that the report was too long or that it missed the main point, or that a salesperson from Detroit monopolized the meetings, or that the author in a digression took the Land Commission to task for failing to act properly. A later section of this chapter (pages 334–41) will deal with evaluative summaries.

2. New data. Stick to the original article, report, book, or meeting. Avoid introducing comparisons with other works or conferences, because readers will expect a digest of only the material being summarized.

3. Irrelevant specifics. Do not include any biographical details about the author of an article. Although many journals contain a section entitled "notes on contributors," this information plays no role in the reader's understanding of your summary.

4. Examples. Examples, illustrations, explanations, and descriptions are unnecessary in a summary. Readers must know outcomes, results, and recommendations, not the specific details leading up to those results.

5. Background. Material in introductions to articles, reports, and conferences can often be excluded from a summary. These "lead-ins" prepare the reader for a discussion of the subject by presenting background information, anecdotes, and details that will be of little interest to readers who want a summary to give them the big picture.

6. Reference data. Exclude information found in footnotes, bibliographies, appendixes, tables, or graphs. All such information supports rather than expresses conclusions and recommendations.

7. Jargon. Technical definitions or jargon in the original may confuse rather than clarify the essential information the general reader is seeking.

◆ THE PROCESS OF PREPARING A SUMMARY

To write an effective summary, you need to proceed through a series of steps. Basically, you will have to read the material very carefully, making sure that you understand it thoroughly. Then you will have to identify the major points and exclude everything else. Finally, you will have to put the essence of the material into your own words. This process demands an organized plan. Follow these steps in preparing your summary.

1. Read the material once in its entirety to get an overall impression of what it is about. Become familiar with large issues, such as the purpose and organization of the work, and the audience for whom it was written. Look at visual cues—headings, subheadings, words in italics or boldface type, notes in the margin—that will later help you to classify main ideas and summarize the work. Also see if the author has included any mini-summaries within the article or report or if there is a concluding summary after an article or a chapter of a book.

2. Reread the material. Read it a second time or more often if necessary. To locate all and only the main points, underline them in the work; or, if the work is a book or an article in a journal that belongs to the library, take notes on a separate sheet of paper. (You may find it easier to photocopy articles so that you can underline.) To spot the main points, pay attention to the key transitional words (see page 55 in Chapter 3). Such words often fall into the following categories.

- *Words that enumerate:* first, second, third, initially, subsequently, finally, next, another
- *Words that express causation:* accordingly, as a result, because, consequently, therefore, thus
- *Words that express contrasts and comparisons:* although, by the same token, despite, different from, furthermore, however, in contrast, in comparison, in addition, less than, likewise, more than, more readily, not only . . . but also, on the other hand, the same is true for, similar, unlike
- *Words that signal essentials:* basically, best, central, crucial, foremost, fundamental, indispensable, in general, important, leading, major, obviously, principal, significant

Also pay special attention to the first and last sentences of each paragraph. Often the first sentence of a paragraph contains the topic sentence, and the last sentence summarizes the paragraph or provides some type of transition to the next paragraph.

You also have to be alert for words signaling information you do *not* want to include in your summary, such as the following.

- *Words announcing opinion or inconclusive findings:* from my personal experience, I feel, I admit, in my opinion, might possibly show, perhaps, personally, may sometimes result in, has little idea about, questionable, presumably, subject to change, open to interpretation
- *Words pointing out examples or explanations:* as noted in, as shown by, circumstances include, explained by, for example, for instance, illustrated by, in terms of, learned through, represented by, such as, specifically in, stated in

3. Collect your underlined material or notes and organize the information into a rough-draft summary. At this stage do not be concerned about how your sentences read. Use the language of the original, together with any necessary connective words or phrases of your own. You will more than likely have more material here than will appear in the final version. Do not worry; you are engaged in a process of selection and elimination. Your purpose at this stage is to extract the principal ideas from the examples, explanations, and opinions surrounding them.

4. Read through your rough draft and delete whatever information you can. See how many of your underlined points can be condensed, combined, or eliminated. You may find that you have repeated a point. Check your draft against the original for accuracy and importance. Make sure that you are faithful to the original by preserving its emphases and sequence.

5. Now put the edited version into your own words. Again, make sure that your reworded summary has eliminated nonessential words. Connect your sentences with conjunctive adverbs (*also, although, because, consequently, however, nevertheless, since*) to show relationships between ideas in the original.

Compare this final version of your summary with the original material to double-check your facts.

6. Do not include remarks that repeatedly call attention to the fact that you are writing a summary. You may want to indicate initially you are providing a summary, but avoid such remarks as: "The author of this article states that water pollution is a major problem in Baytown"; "On page 13 of the article three examples, not discussed here, are found."

7. Identify the source you have just summarized. Do this by including pertinent bibliographic information in the title of your summary or in a footnote or endnote. Doing this gives proper credit to the original source and informs your readers where they can find the complete text if they want more details.

Figure 11.2, a 1,500-word article entitled "Counting on the Census," appeared in the *Journal of American Insurance* and hence would be of primary interest to individuals in the insurance field. Assume that you are asked to write a summary of this article for your boss, a busy insurance executive. By following the steps outlined previously, you would first read the article carefully two or three times and then underscore the most important points, signaled by key words. Note what has been underscored in the article. Also study the comments in the margins; these explain why certain information is to be included or excluded from the summary.

FIGURE 11.2   The original article with important points underscored for use in a summary.

Counting on the Census

Delete introductory material, here used to provide a background

> Probably no other people but Americans have such as obsession with constantly counting and cataloguing themselves. With help from computers, we've now got more information about ourselves than ever before: an awe-inspiring amount of information, highly sophisticated and often very specific in nature
>
> With so much data-mania around, it's no wonder that the most well-known survey, that just-completed once-a-decade population count conducted by the Census Bureau, is generating more interest than ever. Aside from the controversies—questions about its accuracy and debate over the problem of illegal aliens— Americans are paying attention to the 1980 Census because not only will it confirm our own notions of what we as a nation have become,

Delete details of lesser importance

Important conclusion

> but also because there's a lot of cold hard cash riding on the results.

Include significant point

> This massive survey will document, on both a large and local scale, the far-reaching social changes of the 1970s. It will chronicle

Delete explanations and examples

what has happened to each of us over the past ten years: if, like other Americans, we've moved often, and ever south and westward; if we've had smaller families, and bought larger homes. The population count will lend a certain sense of continuity or historical perspective to these changes measuring them against nearly 200 years of American demographic history. The

Important finding

fact that the twentieth census will find a majority of one- and two-person households (they numbered nearly half in 1970 and have been on the rise ever since) is all the more remarkable in light of the 1790 count, in which half of all those fledgling American households consisted of six or more people, and only a tenth had one or two persons living alone.

Delete explanation and following quotation

Results from the head count will add depth and specificity to what we already know, filling in the outlines of our broadbrush figures. "Surveys may tell you what's happened," says Roger Herriot of the Census Bureau, "the census tells you to whom and where."

Include important information

The final tally will reveal both small group and small area data—important, useful information that is available nowhere else. A house-

Delete statistics

wife's decision to return to work is significant as part of a national trend (since 1978, half of all American women age 16 and older—42 million of them—were in the labor force); yet it's even

Significant conclusion

more meaningful when also placed in the context of how many other women of the same age, living in the same state, town, or even neighborhood, are also working.

Key words signaling important application

On the more pragmatic side, the census appeals to our more avid interests, as we are urged to stand up and be counted to get our fair share—of political representation, and fed-eral money. The constitutionally mandated

Delete facts indicating former use

count is no longer just a means of changing the boundaries of congressional districts to reflect population shifts; since 1970, it also has been

Include financial use

used to determine where and how more than $50 billion in public welfare and federal rev-enue-sharing money will be spent. Of special interest to insurers are federal programs on vo-

Combine types of programs

cational rehabilitation, highway safety, law en-forcement assistance, energy research and de-velopment, and alcohol and drug abuse, which are among the more than 100 programs using census statistics to guide the allocation of funds to states and local communities. Funding

Delete examples

for the Cooperative Extension Service, for example, hinges upon a state's rural and farm population; while spending for the Headstart program relies on the number of children of poverty-level families in a particular community.

Key words "also much" introducing important idea

There is also much that the insurance industry, the property/casualty side of the business included, can cull from the reams of data generated by the census. The count will be industry's first opportunity for a look at the demographic trends of the next decade, trends which will play a major role in shaping business in the years just ahead. This glimpse into the future will allow insurers, known for their sophisticated application of data, to evaluate—and anticipate—these changes on a local level, where business is actually conducted.

Include reason why census is so important to insurers

Include relevant change affecting insurers; delete statistics

One change in store for this country is that, in the 1980s, the elderly as a group will be getting larger. Between 1950 and 1978, that part of our population age 65 and older doubled in size, and it is expected to increase even further in the coming years. This means a growing need for more resources to meet the financial and medical requirements of the elderly—two areas where the insurance industry will play a vital role.

Include these "two areas" significantly highlighted by key words "vital role"

Another important point, but delete the statistics

Also getting its first few gray hairs will be the "baby boom" generation, whose members now fall into the 25 to 34 age group. The fastest-growing segment of the population, its ranks swelled by 35 percent between 1970 and 1978, according to census figures. Members of this group, who have dominated the social changes of the past 20 years, will again set the pace in the next decade. They'll enter their prime years in terms of earning and buying power, pumping up demand for both durable goods and housing, as well as property insurance to cover their investments.

Emphasize insurance needs

Include main point here

Indeed, property/casualty insurers will be able to glean some valuable information from the questions asked on this year's census. Although only two relate directly to property insurance (one asks homeowners the annual premium for fire and hazard insurance on their property; another inquires whether the regular monthly mortgage payment includes these payments or not), more than half of all the questions are concerned with housing. Some are general, requesting information on owning or

"Although" points to subordinate idea; delete it and examples

Include major observation

Delete examples of types of questions

renting, the number of rooms in living quarters, and the type of building; while others are quite specific, asking how you heat your home, which fuel you use for cooking, house and water heating, and how much you pay each month for electricity, water, gas, oil or coal (interestingly, census tests have shown that people tend to overestimate their utility costs).

Restatement of main point

Delete explanation

Compiling housing data has been a census assignment since 1850, yet the emphasis placed on the topic on this year's questionnaire is unprecedented. This is due, in part, to the growing number of requests the Census Bureau has received about housing in general, and shelter costs in particular, according to Census housing expert Bill Downs, who says that federal agencies, as well as state and local governments, are among the big users of this type of information.

Delete example

A 1976 bureau survey found, for example, that the average owner of a mortgaged home was paying 18 percent of his/her annual income in that year for the mortgage, real estate taxes, property insurance, utilities, fuel, and trash collection. How much that figure will change in 1980, in light of soaring fuel costs, and other factors such as the 45 percent jump in the average price of a new, one-family home,

Include main point relevant to insurance agents/executives

Of less significance, but still include

should be of wide interest to property insurers, among others.

Also of interest but of somewhat more limited use, will be both the number and size of America's homes. Analysts predict that the 1980 count will find that the number of housing units in this country has increased 20 percent since the last census was taken in 1970: twice the rate of the population growth. Along with an increase in the number of households (at a rate three times as fast as that of the rise in population between the years 1970 and 1978 alone), these figures reflect a continuing decline in the average size of households.

Delete statistics

Include main points

Delete statistics following this point

At the same time people are choosing to live with fewer other people, they are also living in larger houses. Between 1970 and 1976, the number of five-room housing units (homes, mobile homes and trailers, apartments, and condominiums) rose from 16.9 to 19.2 million; while homes with seven or more rooms grew in number from 11.9 to 15.9 million.

Unless a change is imminent, this trend,

| | | 1970 | 1980 | % Change |

Delete opinion and qualification

which reflects to a degree the self-indulgent and free-spending lifestyle cultivated by many during the 1970s, has dire implications for our energy needs in the future. Fewer people in bigger living areas means energy inefficiency, wasting the energy and resources needed to construct and heat these homes—a loss that increased conservation can only partly remedy.

Parallel point
Key phrase for audience

Include essential point

Delete statistics

Key word indicating another conclusion

Delete clarifying statistics

Key word emphasizing results

Key reference to audience's use of information

Equally ominous in view of the energy crunch, and of interest to automobile insurers, is the fact that the 1980 census should show no let-up in America's dependence on the car as a means of transportation. In 1975, of the 73 million households in the U.S., nearly 63 million had at least one automobile, according to census bureau figures. Further, owning a home seems to go hand in hand with owning a car: nearly all homeowners have at least one car, while renters are considerably less likely to purchase a vehicle. Moreover, the number of two-car households more than doubled between 1960 and 1975, and is expected to have jumped even higher in the years since.

The final report, however, may shed light on one transportation alternative. Questions on the number of one-ton trucks and vans, and on whether people who use cars, trucks, or vans to get to work ride with other people (and if so, how many) will give transportation planners as well as auto insurers some insight into the extent of car and van pooling. This information is the first step in learning how to encourage more people to try this energy-efficient way for commuting.

Not an essential point

Brief restatement of article thesis

Of course, insurance companies use many sources of information other than the once-a-decade census to keep themselves abreast of important demographic changes. Yet insurers, like many other businesses, still count on the census and the more than 300,000 pages of resulting statistics to tell them where we've been and where we as a nation are going.

Delete information in tables; used only for support

	1970	1980	% Change
Population of the U.S.	207,976,452	222,000,000 (est.)	9%
No. of Housing Units in the U.S.	69,000,000	86,000,000 (est.)	23%
No. of Households in the U.S.	64,000,000	79,000,000 (est.)	26%

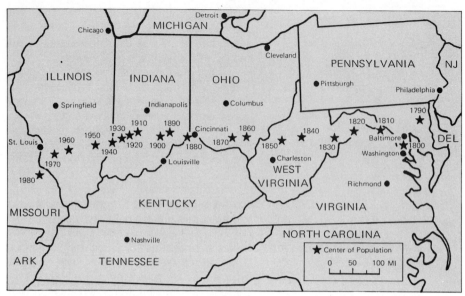

Source: U.S. Bureau of the Census

Delete this caption explaining map—not essential for grasping main points of the article

Westward Ho!

If the United States were a gigantic table, and everybody stood up right now where they lived, where would the table balance? This may seem like a question of demographic trivia, but in 1980 it will take on historical importance as the nation's center of population moves, for the first time, west of the Mississippi River.

After the first census in 1790, the center of population was just east of Baltimore. It has moved slowly westward ever since, reflecting the general migration of the population. After the 1970 census, it was just south of Mascoutah, Illinois, about 30 miles east of the Mississippi. After the 1980 head count, the center of population will move across the river and slightly to the south, reflecting the recent population shift to sunbelt states.

Journal of American Insurance (Winter 1979/80). Reprinted by permission.

After you have identified the main points, extract them from the article and, still using the language of the article, join them into a coherent working draft summary as in Figure 11.3. The necessary connective words added to the lan-

FIGURE 11.3   A working-draft summary of Figure 11.2.

Aside from the controversies about its accuracy, Americans are paying attention to the 1980 Census because there's a lot of cold, hard cash riding on the results. This massive survey will document far-reaching social changes. The twentieth census will find a majority of one- and two-person households, all the more remarkable in light of the 1790 count. The final tally will reveal important useful information available nowhere else. A housewife's decision to return to work is significant as part of a national trend, <u>and</u> even more meaningful in context. On the more pragmatic side, the census count is no longer just a means of changing boundaries <u>but</u> it also affects where $50 billion in public welfare and federal revenue-sharing will be spent. Of special interest to insurers are federal programs on vocational rehabilitation, highway safety, law enforcement assistance, and energy research. There is also much the property/casualty side of the business can gain from the census, <u>which will</u> play a major role in business—evaluating and anticipating changes. One change is that the elderly population will be increasing. This means more resources—financial and medical—in two areas where the insurance industry will play a vital role. Also, the 25 to 34 age group, which is the fastest-growing part of the population, will demand property insurance. Indeed, property/casualty insurers will glean valuable information from the questions asked on the census, more than half of all the questions are concerned with housing. <u>This</u> is an emphasis on the topic of this year's questionnaire <u>that</u> is unprecedented. How much <u>costs for houses</u> will change should be of wide interest to property insurers among others. Also of interest but of somewhat more limited use, the number and size of American houses <u>have</u> increased. Along with an increase in the number of households, <u>there is</u> a continuing decline in the average size of households. At the same time people are choosing to live with fewer other people, they are also living in larger houses. This trend has dire implications for our energy needs in the future. Fewer people in bigger living areas mean energy inefficiency. Equally ominous and of interest to automobile insurers, the 1980 census should show no let-up in America's dependence on the car as a means of transportation. Further, owning a home seems to go hand in hand with owning a car; renters are less likely to purchase a vehicle. The final report, however, may shed light on one transportation alternative. Questions on the number of trucks and vans and on whether people who use cars, trucks, or vans to go to work will ride with other people will give transportation planners as well as auto insurers some insights into the extent of car and van pooling. This information will be the first step in learning how to encourage this energy-efficient way for commuting. Insurance companies use many sources of information, yet insurers still count on the census.

guage of the original article are underscored. This working draft then has to be shortened and rewritten in your own words to produce the compact final version of your summary as in Figure 11.4. Only 152 words long, this summary is 12 percent of the length of the original article and records only major conclusions relevant to the audience for the article.

FIGURE 11.4   A final, effective summary of Figure 11.2

"Counting on the Census," Journal of American Insurance (1979/80): 13–15.

A lot of money rides on the result of the census. Information on where we live, our household size, and women in the work force affects the funding of federal programs. Because many of these programs concern public safety, health, and energy, they are of crucial importance to insurers. Census figures will also help insurers evaluate the needs of future policyholders. A larger elderly population will require more medical and financial assistance; the fast-growing adult population (ages 25–34) will need more property insurance. Since a majority of census questions deal with housing, property/casualty insurers will learn more about increasingly expensive home ownership. The census will also tell insurers that Americans will waste energy by occupying larger homes with fewer people per household. Moreover, homeowners (as opposed to renters) will buy more cars for transportation. However, information on vehicle pooling may give auto insurers encouraging news about energy conservation.

To further understand the effectiveness of the summary in Figure 11.4, review the wordy and misleading summary of the same article in Figure 11.5. The latter not only is too long but also dwells on minor details at the expense of major points. It includes unnecessary examples, statistics, and names; it even adds new information while ignoring crucial points about the function of the census to insurers. But even more serious, this summary distorts the meaning and the intention of the original article. The reader concludes that the article says the census is not very valuable for insurance agents and executives—just the opposite of the point the article makes. You can avoid such mistakes by deemphasizing minor points, by making sure that all parts of your summary agree with the original, and by not letting your own opinions cloud issues that the author of the article stresses.

FIGURE 11.5   A poor summary of Figure 11.2

Nonessential introductory material	Americans like to keep track of themselves with very advanced computers. People wonder, though, about the accuracy of the census as a counting tool since it sometimes includes information about illegal aliens. But the census, a part of America's demographic history since 1790, does serve many important functions, says Roger Herriot of the Census Bureau in Washington, D.C. The census tells us that half of all American women over the age of 16 work full-time. Also, the census establishes our congressional districts, and this is very important for our representatives, especially if they find themselves in a new district because of changes in the population. The census also helps allocate federal funds for such programs as the Cooperative Extension Service and Headstart, which are important programs to list in this summary. Furthermore, the census helps predict future insurance business, always a laudable goal. Old people and the young, too, will increase our population. But as far as property insurance is concerned, only two questions appear on this topic on the census, which is almost exclusively concerned with what home fuels, mortgages, and building materials we have. Bill Downs says the government needs this kind of information. It is no wonder since in 1976 people paid 18 percent of their income for housing and will pay 45 percent in 1980. Extravagant Americans want big houses, big cars, and will waste energy using them. Americans should use car pools. But the insurance companies, as the last crucial paragraph of the article states, will not be at too bad a disadvantage since they can rely on other sources of information than what is provided in the census.
Possible flaw in census not important to article's thesis	
Delete historical background and official's name	
Minor point in article given major attention; new information and opinion also added	
Examples not necessary; do not call attention to summary	
Omit opinion	
Ambiguous statement; misses main point that elderly population is increasing	
Distorts article, which deals with value of census for insurers	
Statistics not related to audience	
How is all this relevant to insurers?	
Distorts article, which emphasizes usefulness of census for insurers; this statement makes census sound unimportant for insurers and overemphasizes a minor point in conclusion of article	

◆ EVALUATIVE SUMMARIES

To write an evaluative summary, also called a critique, follow all the guidelines previously discussed in this chapter except one. The one major exception is that an evaluative summary includes your *opinion,* or view, of the material.

Your instructors and employers may often ask you to summarize and assess what you have read. In school you may have to write a book report or compile a critical, annotated bibliography commenting on the usefulness of the material you found in those sources. On the job your employer may ask you to condense a report and judge the merits of that report, paying special attention to whether the report's recommendations should be followed, modified, or ignored. Your company or agency may also ask you to write short evaluative summaries of job applications (see pages 154–82) or sales proposals (see pages 466–73) it has received or perhaps of conferences you might have attended.

An evaluative summary is usually short—not more than 5 to 10 percent of the length of the original. Your evaluation should blend in with your summary of the material. Rather than save all your assessments until the end of your summary, place them directly next to the summary of the points to which they apply so that your reader sees them in context. You may also want to include an especially helpful quotation from the original to emphasize the kind of recommendation you are making. In evaluating the material, include information on both the content and style of the original. Here are some questions on content and style that you should answer for readers of your evaluative summary.

Evaluating the Content

1. How carefully is the subject researched? Is the material accurate and up to date? Are important details missing? Exactly what has the author left out? Where could the reader find the missing information? If the material is inaccurate, will the whole work be affected or just a part of it?

2. Is the writer or speaker objective? Are conclusions supported by evidence? Is the writer or speaker following a particular theory, program, or school of thought? Is this fact made clear in the source? Has the author or speaker emphasized one point at the expense of others?

3. Does the work achieve the goal? Is the topic too large to be adequately discussed in a single talk, article, or book? Is the work sketchy? Are there digressions, tangents, or irrelevant materials? Do the recommendations make sense?

4. Is the material relevant to the audience for whom you are writing your evaluative summary? How would that audience use it? Is the entire work relevant or just part of it? Why? Would this work be useful for all members of your agency or only those working in certain areas? Why? What answers offered by the work would help to solve a specific problem you or others have encountered on the job?

Evaluating the Style

1. Is the material readable? Is it well written and easy to follow? Does it contain helpful headings, careful summaries, and appropriate examples?

2. What kind of vocabulary does the writer or speaker use? Are there many technical terms or jargon? Is the language precise or vague? Would your audience have to skip certain sections that are too complicated?

3. What visuals are included? Charts? Graphs? Photographs? Are they used effectively? Are there too many or too few of these visuals?

Figures 11.6, 11.7, and 11.8 contain evaluative summaries. Note how the writer's assessments are woven into the condensed version of the original. Figure 11.6 contains a student's opinions of an article summarized for a class in office management procedures. Figure 11.7 shows an evaluative summary in memo format written by an employee who has just returned from a seminar. Another kind of evaluative summary—a book review—is shown in Figure 11.8. Many journals print book reviews to inform their professional audiences about the most recent studies in their field. Reviews condense and assess books, reports, government studies, tape cassettes, films, and other materials. The short review in Figure 11.8

FIGURE 11.6   An evaluative summary of an article.

R. Alec Mackenzie and Billie Sorensen, "It's About Time . . . ," The Secretary 40 (Jan. 1980): 12-13.

According to this practical article, secretaries can find ways to decrease interruptions that rob them and their bosses of time. Instead of practicing an open-door policy, managers could save time by observing a "quiet hour" to curtail drop-in visitors and calls. Secretaries could help their bosses during this time by restricting drop-in visitors and handling minor details. Many valuable suggestions are given on how secretaries can further save their bosses' time by arranging and limiting meetings. Because secretaries' desks are located in busy areas, partitions could reduce some of their interruptions. But the authors wisely point out that managers forced to use the same arrangement lose privacy and flexibility. Partitions are unsuitable for conferences, encourage socializing, and are uneconomical. This readable and profitable article suggests techniques that will help all office personnel to save one of the manager's most valuable assets--his or her time.

FIGURE 11.7 An evaluative summary of a seminar.

SABINE COUNTY HOSPITAL
Sabine, TX 77231

TO: Marge Geberheart, R.N.   SUBJECT: Evaluation of Physical
         Director of Nurses   Assessment Seminar
FROM: Paul Danders, R.N. *P.D.*   DATE: September 14, 1990

On September 6, Doris Gandy, R.N., and Rick Vargass, R.N., both on the staff of Houston
Presbyterian Hospital, conducted a practical and worthwhile seminar on physical assessment.
The one-day seminar was divided into three units: (1) Techniques of Health Assessment, (2)
Assessment of the Heart and Lungs, and (3) Assessment of the Abdomen.

Techniques of Health Assessment

Four procedures used in physical assessment—inspection, percussion, palpation,
auscultation—were carefully defined and demonstrated. The instructors also stressed the
proper use of the stethoscope and the ways of taking a patient's medical history. We were
asked to take the medical history of the person next to us. Such return demonstration, used
throughout the seminar, meant we did not have to wait until we went back to work to
practice our skills.

Assessment of the Heart and Lungs

After we inspected the chest externally, we discussed the proper placement of hands for
percussion and palpation and the significance of various breath sounds. Using stethoscopes,
our instructors helped us identify areas of the lung. We also listened to and identified heart
sounds. The film we saw on examining the heart and lungs was ineffective since it included
too much detailed information for the seminar participants.

Assessment of the Abdomen

The instructors warned that the order of examination of the abdomen differs from that of
the chest cavity. Auscultation, not percussion, follows inspection so that bowel sounds are not
activated. The instructors then clearly identified how to detect bowel sounds, how to locate
the organs in the abdominal quadrants, and how to palpate these organs.

Recommendations

I strongly recommend a seminar like this for all nurses whose expanding role in the health
care system requires more physical assessments. Although the seminar covered a wealth of
information, the instructors admitted that they discussed only basics. In the future, however,
it would be better to offer a separate seminar on the chest cavity and another on the
abdomen instead of combining the two topics because of the amount of information involved
and the time required for demonstrations.

FIGURE 11.8   A book review.

Forty Years of Murder: An Autobiography. *By Keith Simpson. Charles Scribner's Sons, 597 Fifth Ave., New York, NY 10017. 1979. 319pp. Cloth/$12.95.*

   This is a fascinating, readable narrative of cases handled by one of the world's leading pathologists during his forty years as a medico-legal examiner for the British Home Office. In language largely devoid of technical terminology, the author presents a series of murder cases investigated throughout his career and relates how, working backward by piecing together scant bits of evidence, he reaches a logical conclusion on how a victim met a grim death and identifies the perpetrator. The clues he works with for the most part are bits of flesh, tissue, and bone; soiled or tattered pieces of clothing; or, as in one case, gallstones which were not destroyed by sulphuric acid in which the victim's body was immersed. The cases range from young women whose battered bodies were found in desolate places to a prince of Siam who was assassinated in bed. The author includes some interesting bouts in court with defense attorneys who attempted to discredit his forensic testimony and how he successfully refuted such challenges.

Reproduced from *The Police Chief* magazine, March 1980, with permission of the International Association of Chiefs of Police.

comments briefly on style, provides clarifying information, and explains how the book is developed.

Minutes

Minutes of a meeting are a special type of summary. If you are appointed secretary at an office meeting or for an organization to which you belong, you will be required to submit to members of that group an official record of the actions taken. That record, known as the minutes of a meeting, is distributed usually within twenty-four or forty-eight hours after the meeting has adjourned.

   The way in which a meeting is conducted may be governed by highly formal parliamentary procedures known as *Robert's Rules of Order.* Usually, though, business and community meetings are less formal. Still, certain matters of protocol generally are observed at meetings. For example, a chairperson usually brings a list of topics to be discussed; this list is known as the *agenda.* Participants then make *motions* (proposals) about these and other topics and then approve, modify, or vote against them. "I move that we accept the Acme Corporation's bid on the two new heating units"; "I would like to change the wording of the original motion to read 'All employees on the night shift will receive a $1.75 per hour differential.'" Each motion is then *seconded* (endorsed) by another member of the group. A motion may be *carried* (passed), defeated, withdrawn, or *tabled* (postponed).

   To be effective, minutes should be short. Obviously, you cannot repeat what everyone has said. Emphasize the decisions made or the conclusions reached. For example, do not mention any motions (or discussions of them) that have been withdrawn. Nor should you spend a great deal of time on discussions of other

FIGURE 11.9   Minutes of a meeting.

The City of Hampton

Minutes of the Hampton City Council Open Meeting
February 2, 1990

PRESENT: Thomas Baldanza, Grace Corlee (President),
         Virginia Downey, Victor Johnson, Roberta Koos,
         Kent Leviche (Secretary), Ralph Nowicki,
         Barbara Poe, Willard Ralston, Daniel Sullivan,
         Morgan Tachiashi, Ruth Vanessa, Wanda Wagner,
         and Carlos Zandrillia

ABSENT: Millard Holmes, Wendy O'Gorman

The meeting was held in Room 102 of City Hall and began
at 7:04 P.M. with Grace Corlee presiding.

OLD BUSINESS

The minutes of the previous meeting (January 5, 1990)
were approved as read. The Council returned to a
discussion of a motion tabled at the last meeting
concerning holding open meetings twice a month rather
than once a month. The motion, which was made by
Barbara Poe and seconded by Willard Ralston, was voted
on and defeated 9 to 5.

REPORTS

Two reports were given.

Victor Johnson noted that the Downtown Beautification
Committee had conferred with both the State Office of
Historical Landmarks and the U.S. Department of Housing
and Urban Development about helping Hampton (in terms
of finance and architectural planning) to restore the
Brandon Building. Johnson said he expected to hear from
both departments before next month's meeting.

---

motions. Save your readers' time by condensing, in your own words, lengthy discussions and debates (pro and con) as well as reports presented at meetings. List each motion exactly as it is worded in its *final* form and spell accurately and consistently the names of those proposing and seconding the motion. Finally, record precisely the vote for each motion (for example, "carried 11 to 2").

FIGURE 11.9   (continued)

```
Minutes                    2              February 2, 1990
```

Giving a report on the Zoning Committee, Wanda Wagner observed that fourteen requests for changes had been submitted in January. The Zoning Board has already approved ten of them, including rezoning South Evans Street from residential to medical.

NEW BUSINESS

1. The problems with the downtown parking meters were discussed. Besides the city's difficulties with maintaining them, local merchants have complained that the meters are bad for business. Roberta Koos supplied documentation that removing them would decrease city revenue and increase parking violations. But Morgan Tachiashi identified greater losses to the city from decreased business in the downtown section because of the meters. He therefore moved, and Virginia Downey seconded, that the parking meters should be removed from the downtown section of the city. The motion carried 10 to 4 by secret ballot. Grace Corlee said she would forward an official order to Police Chief Dunn for the removal of the meters effective March 15, 1990.

2. Mary Ricks, President of the Park Ridge Citizens Group, appeared before the Council requesting that automatic traffic lights be installed at the intersection of Brown and Crawford Avenues. After listening to her comments about the dangers to pupils at the Epstein School from speeding cars and the increased flow of traffic from the Granger Furniture Plant, the Council voted unanimously to install automatic signals at the intersection of Brown and Crawford Avenues. A directive was sent to J. T. Adams, Head of the Traffic Department.

Be careful not to inject your opinions into the minutes. Avoid any words that interpret (positively or negatively) rather than impartially record. "The motion was offered just in time" or "The motion was poorly stated" violate the rules of impartiality. When you cite individuals by name, do not qualify their actions, saying that "Mr. Sanders pushed the point for the third time." And resist any urge to

FIGURE 11.9 (continued)

Minutes   3   February 2, 1990

3. Congratulations were extended to Carlos Zandrillia for being honored as an Outstanding Citizen by the Hampton Chamber of Commerce.

4. A committee to study ways to increase tourism to Hampton was formed. The committee members appointed were Ruth Vanessa (Chairperson), Ralph Nowicki, and Victor Johnson. President Corlee, speaking for the Council, requested that the committee pay special attention to the use of Lake Hughes in tourism advertisements and asked for a preliminary report in two months.

5. Thomas Baldanza moved, and Virginia Downey seconded, a motion to set aside $3700.00 from the Recreation Department budget for the improvement of equipment at Alice V. Davis Park. The motion carried by a vote of 12 to 1, with 1 abstention.

There being no further business, the meeting was adjourned at 9:37. The next open meeting of the Hampton City Council was set for March 2 at 7:00 P.M. in Room 102 of City Hall.

Respectfully submitted,

Kent Leviche

Kent Leviche, Secretary

Minutes approved,

Grace Corlee

Grace Corlee, President

---

summarize the usefulness of a discussion or the meeting itself: "The proceedings cleared up a lot of doubts the subcommittee had expressed"; "The meeting was productively short and simple."

What to Include in Minutes

1. The subject and type of meeting—regular monthly meeting, special sales meeting, rules committee meeting.
2. The date, time, and place of the meeting.
3. The names of those present and those absent (if your list does not exceed twenty or twenty-five individuals).
4. The approval or amendment of the minutes of the previous meeting, or that their reading is waived by a majority of those present.
5. Any old business: further discussion and votes on motions tabled at previous meetings.
6. The new business of the meeting: motions proposed, seconded, and voted on. Indicate briefly the discussion preceding the motion and then the names of those making and seconding the motion. Indicate how the vote is taken—by secret ballot, a show of hands, by voice—and its results, including the number of *abstentions* (decisions not to vote on a motion), if any.
7. The business to be continued at the next meeting: reports to be made, motions to be voted on.
8. The time the next meeting is to be held, and where.
9. The time the meeting is officially concluded.

Figure 11.9 shows the minutes of a meeting incorporating each of these nine parts. Not every meeting, of course, will require all of them.

◆ ABSTRACTS

The Differences Between a Summary and an Abstract

The terms *summary* and *abstract* are often used interchangeably, resulting in some confusion. This problem arises because there are two distinct types of abstracts: *descriptive abstracts* and *informative abstracts*. The informative abstract is another name for a summary; the descriptive abstract is not. Why? An informative abstract (or summary) gives readers conclusions and indicates the results or causes. Look at the summary in Figure 11.4. It explains why the census is important for insurers: the census helps insurers provide better coverage to specific groups. Informative abstracts are found before long reports, such as the report on robots in industry found on page 532.

A descriptive abstract is short, usually only two or three sentences; it does not go into detail or give conclusions. Hence it is not a summary. A descriptive abstract provides table-of-contents information—what topics a work discusses, but not how or why they are discussed. Here is a descriptive abstract of the article summarized in Figure 11.4 (page 332).

The census will provide information about changes in America's housing preferences, transportation, and energy needs. This data will be valuable to insurers.

Figure 11.10 contains a group of descriptive abstracts about books of interest to professionals in public welfare. In a few words each abstract tells what kinds of information the books contain, but does not reveal the solutions, plans, views, or recommendations that the authors of these books advance.

FIGURE 11.10   Some descriptive abstracts of books.

Adult Illiteracy in the United States: A Report to the Ford Foundation
By Carman St. John Hunter and David Harman. New York: McGraw Hill, 1979. 206 pp. $10.95.
Defines the scope of illiteracy in the U.S.—a problem of major proportions that prevents many disadvantaged poor from being able to deal positively with the demands made by society—and calls for a long-range national strategy to eradicate the problem.

The Adoption of Black Children: Counteracting Institutional Discrimination
By Dawn Day. Lexington, Mass.: D.C. Heath, 1979. 156 pp. $15.95.
Looks at how the adoption system works and suggests realistic ways of raising the adoption rate of black children.

Community Mental Health in the Social Work Curriculum
By Allen Rubin. New York: Council on Social Work Education, 1979. 84 pp. $4.
Describes the place of community mental health in our nationwide service delivery system, evaluates suitability of the MSW level curriculum in the U.S., and offers examples of curriculum innovations.

Public Welfare 32 (Spring 1980): 49. Reprinted with permission of the American Public Welfare Association.

Where Abstracts Are Found

1. At the beginning of an article, report, or conference proceedings; on a separate page; or on the title page of the report
2. On the table-of-contents page of a magazine, briefly highlighting the features of the individual articles in that issue, or at the beginning of the chapter in a book or in advertisements
3. In reference works devoted exclusively to publishing collections of abstracts of recent and relevant works in a particular field (e.g., *Abstracts of Hospital Management Studies, Science Abstracts, Sociological Abstracts*). See Chapter 9 (page 268) for a discussion of the usefulness and limitations of abstracts.

◆ CONCLUSION

By following the process of writing a summary presented in this chapter you will acquire an invaluable skill. If done concisely and accurately, your summary will save readers a great deal of time and demonstrate your ability to provide the big picture. This skill will help you in preparing the types of documents stressed in subsequent chapters: questionnaire reports, proposals, and short, long, and oral reports.

◆ EXERCISES

1. Summarize a chapter of a textbook you are now using for a course in your major field. Provide an accurate bibliographic reference for this chapter (author of the textbook, title of the book, title of the chapter, place of publication, publisher's name, date of publication, and page numbers of the chapter).

2. Summarize a lecture you heard recently. Limit your summary to one page. Identify in a bibliographic citation the speaker's name, date, and place of delivery.

3. Listen to a television network evening newscast and also to a later news update on the same station. Select one major story covered on the evening news and indicate which details from it were omitted in the news update.

4. Write a summary of the research paper on stress and computer programmers (pages 305–17) or on robots in the workplace (pages 530–50).

5. Bring to class an article from the *Reader's Digest* and the original material it condensed, usually an article in a journal or magazine published six months to a year earlier. In a paragraph or two indicate what the *Digest* article omits from the original. Also point out how the condensed version is written so that the omitted material is not missed and does not interfere with the reader's understanding of the main points of the article.

6. Assume that you are applying for a job and that the personnel manager asks you to summarize your qualifications for the job in two or three paragraphs. Write those paragraphs and indicate how your background and interests are suited for the specific job. Mention the job by title at the outset of your first paragraph.

7. Write a summary of one of the following articles:
   a. "Microwaves," in Chapter 1, pages 22–23.
   b. "Intensive Care for Your Typewriter," pages 343–45.
   c. "Electronic Publishing: The Next Great Office Revolution," pages 345–48.

Intensive Care for Your Typewriter
By W. Tim Meiers

Are you guilty of carelessness with your typewriter? Carelessness can result in a typewriter that doesn't operate properly and in needless repair calls.

Although typewriters with mistake-correcting capability are becoming increasingly widespread, most secretaries must still cope with hand corrections by

W. Tim Meiers, "Intensive Care for Your Typewriter," *Today's Secretary* (Nov. 1980): 31. Reprinted with permission of Today's Secretary, Gregg Division, McGraw-Hill Book Company, copyright November 1980.

(1) erasing, (2) using strike-over correction paper, or (3) using paint-over correction fluid. Surprisingly, these methods for correcting errors can lead to service calls.

How many times, for example, have you been told to move the carriage to one side or the other when erasing and to brush the erasings away from the machine? How often do you follow that suggestion? There's actually a practical, valid reason for such advice. Erasings that fall into the segment can cause slow-striking type bars. The slow striking type bars will usually be those bars located near the center of the segment where most of the erasings will fall.

Strike-over paper also presents a similar debris problem but less can be done about it; the carriage has to be positioned wherever the strike-over is to be made. When you insert and withdraw strike-over paper, however, patience is indeed a virtue. The coating on the correction paper scrapes off on the cardholders, the type bar guide, and the ribbon vibrator. Like erasings, the scraped off coating can fall into the segment, causing slow-striking type bars.

If patience is advisable when you use correction paper, it's definitely a necessity when you use correction fluid. When mistakes on a page you are typing are "painted over" and the paper is rolled back into typing position *before* the correction fluid has dried, some of the fluid probably will come off onto the feed rolls. Over a period of time, as the feed rolls become coated with correction fluid, they become slick and paper slippage begins to occur. Such slippage is especially noticeable when you are typing near the bottom of a page because the paper is being held by only the front feed rolls.

How frequently do you wave various liquids above your typewriter? As you might guess, liquids spilled into a typewriter can result in expensive service calls. Simply put, soft drinks and sweetened coffee, when spilled, are absolute demons. They act like glue all over your typewriter. Some of the troubles that spilled liquids can cause include slow-striking bars (segment glued), sluggish keys (keyboard glued), and utter mechanical chaos (internal mechanical components glued).

You can also avoid service calls by not using your typewriter as a work bench. While seated at a typewriter, it is not unusual to clip, un-paper clip, hand staple, or unstaple stacks of papers. A common tendency is to perform these tasks near or above the typewriter. A paper clip or staple dropped into a machine can dislocate the springs, lodge under the keyboard, and bind moving parts.

When dealing with paper clips and staples, make an effort to work away from your typewriter. Certainly it takes only a second to use a paper clip or remove a staple, but equally true, it takes only a second to drop one.

Inevitably, certain office situations will require that your typewriter be unplugged and moved. It also seems inevitable that after a typewriter has been moved, it won't operate correctly. But if you are aware of a few simple trouble areas when moving a typewriter (or supervising one being moved), you can prevent more needless service calls.

Most typists know that typewriter keys cannot be depressed when the machine switch is off. This is because connected with the on-off switch of most typewriters is a device called a line lock, which "locks" the keyboard when the switch is off but "unlocks" the keyboard when the switch is on.

What frequently happens when a typewriter is unplugged and moved is that the on-off switch accidentally gets turned on. Remember that on many typewriters the keys *can* be depressed when the typewriter is turned on *even if* the machine is unplugged. The keys that get depressed when a typewriter is being moved are usually the ones near the edge of the keyboard, such as the carriage return, tabulator, shift, and space. Thus when the machine is plugged in again, it jams.

When moving a typewriter, be conscientious of the on-off switch and make certain that it stays off. When carrying a typewriter, keep your thumbs away from the keyboard.

Although this may seem ludicrous, another cause of service calls is a typewriter that is not plugged in. Believe me, it happens. It happens mostly when a typewriter has been unplugged but not moved. Custodians, construction workers, or even fellow office workers might unplug your typewriter for whatever reason and forget to plug it back in. Sure enough, it can be a perplexing situation when your typewriter won't even turn on.

A service call that necessitates merely plugging in a machine can be both embarrassing to you and expensive to a business. Depending on service contracts, a business can be billed—and probably will be billed—for such a service call. Check the plug if your typewriter won't turn on. One final hint is to try a different outlet if your typewriter is plugged in but still won't turn on. Electric outlets can go bad.

Despite all of your efforts to avoid service calls, repairs will occasionally be needed. But even then, you can help if you will learn the names of the different parts of your typewriter as explained in the owner's manual. That way you can be more specific when describing a typewriter malfunction to a repair person. You'll make this person's work easier and have your typewriter back into use sooner.

Electronic Publishing: The Next Great Office Revolution
By William M. Winsor

Desktop publishing may be the greatest productivity tool in a modern office environment since the introduction of spreadsheet software in the 1970s. Spreadsheet software was the catalyst that brought the microcomputer into the office environment because office workers embraced it with such enthusiasm.

Desktop publishing hasn't quite reached that plateau, but the writing is on the wall. The total desktop publishing market was approximately $453 million in 1986. Not bad, considering desktop publishing really didn't exist until late 1984. By 1990, the total market should reach $4.9 billion, an increase of more than 1,000 percent in just four years! Clearly, desktop publishing has a bright future for a number of reasons:

- Desktop publishing enables people and businesses to develop their own brochures, newsletters and other documents at a fraction of the cost and time expended sending the work out to a professional graphics studio.
- Desktop publishing doesn't require a great deal of artistic skill, although the ability to conceptualize is helpful.
- Desktop publishing is opening doors to people who never had the ability to produce documents before.

People who had no interest in publishing suddenly discovered they could produce documents after spending a short time learning the technology. For instance, a church secretary can develop the Sunday bulletin in an afternoon, business executives can quickly generate product documentation at the office and marketing specialists can produce a product brochure in a fraction of the time previously required.

There also has been an emergence of new customer and trade publications that use desktop publishing technology. A publisher can now put together an entire magazine at a personal computer without incurring the cost of hiring production artists or designers. All the publisher has to do is print out the pages, leave empty "knockout windows" for the printer to insert photos, and take the pages to the printer. The printer then adds the photos and prints the pages. Instant magazine!

Logical Evolution

Desktop publishing is the result of a logical evolution in publishing. It started with ancient scribes laboriously copying books by hand and evolved into the printing press revolution. Things heated up with computer-generated "cold" type which debuted in the 1950s.

With this process, type was set by computer, pasted on an art board by a layout person, photographed by a printer and transferred to a sheet on the printing press. That concept is moved forward several generations by desktop publishing.

Now an individual can assemble an entire page on a personal computer and produce a finished document. Text is first developed on a word processor and transferred to the screen, then graphics, photos and other art can either be added or developed through several graphics-generating peripherals, such as light pens.

Dot-matrix and laser printers produce a sharp document that is easily reproduced through a photocopy machine. If a large press run is needed, the print-out can be taken to a commercial printer who reproduces the document in quantity. The latter technique is also useful when photographs are used in the document.

Standards Needed

From a base of virtually zero just three years ago, nearly every major hardware and software developer is now involved with desktop publishing. As a result, the same controversy over computer industry standards that have been discussed for years, are now associated with desktop publishing.

The main alternatives are the Apple MacIntosh and MS/DOS machines, which includes IBM personal computers and a host of clones. Apple pioneered desktop publishing and currently enjoys an edge, but the corporate world is populated by MS/DOS.

Manufacturers recognize the standards issue and are making efforts to overcome compatability problems so that different machines can "talk" with one another. This is challenging, however, since most MS/DOS machines were not designed to handle the high-resolution graphics and page descriptor languages necessary to utilize desktop publishing technology.

Setting Up

No matter which system is selected, the basics are the same. Hardware requirements should include a personal computer with at least 512K of RAM (random access memory), a high resolution monitor, a "mouse," and a dot-matrix or laser printer. The printer is especially important because it determines the final product's quality.

A dot-matrix printer has a 100 dpi (dots-per-inch) resolution, which is adequate for simple projects, such as newsletters. More sophisticated projects, such as brochures, magazines and documentation require a laser printer that produces 300 dpi text, which is still less than the 1000 dpi-and-up resolution provided by professional printers.

As you would expect, there's a price for performance. Dot-matrix printers can be purchased for about $500, while laser printers go for at least four times that much. In either case, the long-term savings are significant compared with outside typesetting charges of $50 to $100 per page.

Virtually every desktop publishing system relies on a hand-held "mouse" as the principal tool for developing a layout. The mouse is a movable device which is connected to the computer by a small cable. It can be pointed in different directions to select menus and options on the computer screen and build a document.

A mouse is especially helpful when selecting "clip" art and electronically assembling a page. (The term "clip" art originates from the newspaper practice of keeping clip sheets containing drawings that were clipped with scissors and pasted on the page.) The clip art can be selected from a software program and electronically "pasted" onto a page. Because the range of clip art is somewhat limited, an optical scanner enables more complex art to be used.

An optical scanner is a necessary option if photos or other previously produced art is used in the final product. The scanner reads the image and transfers it on to the page. Many scanners are able to read various tones which provide texture to the art. Scanners don't come cheap, however, costing $3,000 to $5,000, which is still considerably less than their $30,000 price tag three years ago.

A light-emitting pen is another option that enables graphics to be hand-drawn on the screen. This art can be original and crisp and works best if the user is an accomplished graphic artist or has access to one. Drawing on a computer requires some of the same skills as drawing on paper, so artistic talent is a definite plus.

Choosing Software

As with any computer system, the software determines how desktop publishing can be used. A basic piece of desktop publishing software will enable a person to layout the text and art on the page but requires the manual reformatting of text to accommodate graphics. A second generation desktop publishing software program will automatically reformat the text to accommodate graphics.

The availability of font designs in software is another factor. Fonts are the type styles available for printing, such as Gothic, Courier, Helvetica or Old English. Each style has a certain look and it is up to the individual taste of the person designing the document to determine which font is appropriate. Obviously, the more fonts available, the more flexibility the user has.

Perhaps the most important software element is its capacity. First generation software can create documents up to 32 pages in length, while second generations handle up to 96 pages. Other features to look for in software are:

- Kerning, or the ability to automatically adjust the amount of space between letters.
- Automatic page numbering.

* Ability to change type styles within a line.
* Ability to change graphic size without distortion.

If a simple newsletter is all that will be produced, a first generation software program in the $100–$200 range will be adequate. However, if reports, documentation, and brochures will be the main focus of the system, then a sophisticated program costing $500 or more may be necessary.

Avoiding Pitfalls

Although desktop publishing opens the world of publishing to everyone, not everyone has the innate conceptual ability to use desktop publishing. A major complaint many layout specialists have is the overuse of graphics. Fortunately, most software programs come with a tips section that outlines how to develop publications. More sophisticated programs may require seminars and professional instruction. See the figure below for typical business uses of desktop publishing.

---

10 Typical Business Uses for Desktop Publishing

· Internal employee newsletter.
· External customer newsletter.
· Business forms, such as invoices, puchase orders, etc.
· Product documentation, such as owner manuals and instructions.
· Company capability brochures.
· Product sales brochures.
· Product price lists.
· Magazines.
· Meeting information packets.
· Sales kits.

William M. Winsor, "Electronic Publishing: The Next Great Office Revolution." *CPA Journal* Feb. 1988: 90–91.

---

8. Write a descriptive abstract of the article you selected in Exercise 7.

Preparing a Questionnaire and Reporting the Results

A questionnaire asks carefully selected respondents to supply answers to a list of questions. Properly designed, questionnaires can be valuable reference tools that measure the changing winds of opinion, help forecast trends, and record a wide range of statistical data. Opinion sampling can be a very elaborate operation requiring expertise in psychology, statistics, and computer science. Some questionnaires, therefore, are costly, sophisticated measuring devices prepared by firms that specialize in gathering information. Other questionnaires, including the ones described in this chapter, are shorter, less formal ones for use on the job or in school. Chapter 12 shows you how to design this type of questionnaire, distribute it, and summarize the results.

◆ THE USEFULNESS OF QUESTIONNAIRES

Questionnaires play a particularly practical role in schools, business and industry, and government. As a student, you may have completed a questionnaire recently asking you to evaluate a course or a program. You can find questionnaires on campus about extracurricular activities, the hours a pool or tennis court is open, the quality of food at a cafeteria. These questionnaires seek to measure student opinion to improve campus life—both academic and social. In addition to answering a questionnaire, you may at some point in your college career have to design one to gather information for a report or paper.

Questionnaires in business can increase a company's or agency's sales and profits by determining the consumer's needs. A customer's likes and dislikes readily translate into buying power. To determine what consumers say they want, a store can distribute a questionnaire asking for specific comments on store hours, a particular line or brand of merchandise, credit policies, effectiveness of salesclerks, services after the sale, and the like. A brief questionnaire left in hotel guest

FIGURE 12.1　A short questionnaire.

We hope that you enjoyed your stay at the Happiness Hotel. In order to make your return visit even more pleasurable, would you please take a few minutes to fill out this questionnaire? Thank you. We hope to see you again—soon.

1. How did you find out about the Happiness Hotel?
   ☐ friends　☐ travel agent　☐ magazine ads　☐ billboard　☐ telephone directory
   ☐ other (please indicate)

2. What condition was your room in when you checked in?
   ☐ spotless　☐ satisfactory　☐ unsatisfactory

3. How would you describe your maid service?
   ☐ excellent　☐ good　☐ fair　☐ poor

4. How was the food in our dining room?
   ☐ superior　☐ good　☐ satisfactory　☐ needs improvement (please specify)

5. Please rank in order of preference the recreational facilities you used at Happiness Hotel.
   ☐ pool　☐ tennis courts　☐ golf course　☐ horseback riding

Name ＿＿＿＿＿＿＿＿＿＿＿＿＿＿＿　Room number ＿＿＿＿＿＿
(optional)

rooms is found in Figure 12.1. By analyzing the answers to the short questions, the hotel will know better where to advertise, what to stress in those advertisements, and what to correct or expand in its dining room and recreational facilities.

The government is actively engaged in gathering facts and opinions from its citizens. Every ten years a long questionnaire from the Bureau of the Census asks detailed questions about occupation, income, health, language, and household size. The answers to this lengthy questionnaire help determine how many representatives are sent to Congress and how much of the tax dollar returns to the communities. At the local level, elected officials may distribute questionnaires asking whether a street should be converted into a four-lane highway, a residential area rezoned for shopping facilities, or a new water treatment plant constructed.

Mail Questionnaires Versus Personal Interview Questionnaires

There are some important practical differences between gathering information by mailing a questionnaire and by conducting an interview. Questionnaires have the following advantages over interviews.

1. A mail questionnaire can save time and money; it will reach individuals whether they live in your town or across the country. Contrast this method of collecting information with personal interviews, which require appointments, travel, and time.

2. Mail questionnaires can be completed in the privacy of the home or office by respondents who will not be embarrassed by an interviewer's eye-to-eye questions about age, income, grievances, or preferences. A questionnaire can assure respondents of anonymity and give them more time to answer. Interviews require immediate responses.

3. Properly worded, mail questionnaires can elicit honest, unthreatened responses. An interviewer, on the other hand, might unintentionally sway a respondent by gesture, tone of voice, or facial expression.

Mail questionnaires do have drawbacks. The response rate can be very low, because people may think that filling out the questionnaire is a waste of time. Even if they do fill it out, you never know when respondents plan to return the questionnaire. Generally, though, a mail questionnaire is a much more efficient method of gathering information than an interview is. You can reach more people in less time with less expense. Reserve interviews for times when you have a very small number of people to reach (not more than ten or fifteen) and when those individuals are authorities in the field rather than a cross section of a population.

Another "personal" type of interview can be conducted over the telephone. Telephone interviews are used when an individual or a company wants to sample a large segment of an audience. Polls about preferences for a candidate or a product are examples. Telephone interviews can be expensive and have drawbacks similar to face-to-face interviews. They also require the interviewer to have skills in asking questions especially suited to the ear rather than the eye.

A Questionnaire's Two Audiences

You have two primary audiences to keep in mind when you prepare a questionnaire: (1) the respondents who will fill out your questionnaire and (2) the individuals who will read your report based on responses to the questionnaire. You may later share the results (or, occasionally, even the report itself) with respondents, but they are not the primary audience for whom you write your report. The primary audience is the person or people who will read your report and make decisions based on it. Respondents usually do not make decisions on how to translate opinions into action. The questionnaire links both groups. For example, students, employees, patients, or customers complete a questionnaire to give facts, express opinions, or emphasize the need for change. Using their responses, you write a report for an employer or elected official who can decide what changes, if any, need to be made.

How carefully you poll your questionnaire audience will determine how successful you are with your report audience. You will not meet the needs of either group if your questionnaire contains gaps. Questionnaires that are vague or confusing will produce a report containing these same weaknesses. When questions are clear, concise, and relevant, respondents have a better opportunity to voice their opinions. Your report readers will not have the time or the inclination to read every questionnaire; they will depend on you to summarize the results accurately, arrange them into neat categories, and provide pertinent recommendations.

Chapter 12 emphasizes the needs of both audiences. It first discusses choosing a restricted topic, writing effective questions, and preparing a successful, attractive questionnaire. It then outlines how to select respondents, distribute the questionnaire, and tabulate the results. How to meet report readers' specific expectations constitutes the second part of the chapter and includes guidelines on how to condense information, record numbers properly, incorporate direct quotations, and make recommendations.

◆ CHOOSING A RESTRICTED TOPIC

Before constructing your questionnaire, settle on a restricted topic. The key to finding such a topic is remembering that successful questionnaires solicit answers to help solve a particular problem or initiate a specific change. Responses to precise questionnaires can help you to formulate a knowledgeable recommendation to your employer or teacher. The more precise your topic, the more accurate your recommendation will be. A school, business, or agency would soon go bankrupt if it were concerned only with the vague or the general. The topic of your questionnaire should lead to specific action.

If you decided to write a questionnaire on working conditions in your place of employment, you might have found a practical subject but not a precise one. What, specifically, are you interested in learning? You certainly could not write a report on every aspect of your working conditions. Too much is involved. You would spread yourself, your recommendations, and your respondents' answers too thin if you tried to tackle this vast subject. Using the prewriting strategies discussed in Chapter 2 (pages 27–29), you might want to begin by asking yourself what is included in the topic. What smaller, more precise topics can you find in the large issue "working conditions"? Here are some that might be found on a brainstormed list.

supervisors	eating facilities
co-workers' responsibilities	lighting
schedules	safety measures
grievance committees	temperature
union involvement	profit sharing
fringe benefits	machinery
salaries	coffee/rest breaks
parking	promotions

You would then choose a restricted topic from these subjects and build your questionnaire around it. You will more easily determine respondents' opinions when you ask them about fringe benefits or safety measures than when you ask a series of general questions. The results from your questionnaire, consequently, will be more precise, easier to organize, and more understandable and useful to readers.

Another example might be helpful. Perhaps you want to question respondents about television. That is a roomy topic, so you will have to narrow the range. For example, are you interested in the following different kinds of television stations?

> Public Broadcasting System affiliates
> stations owned by the three major networks (ABC, CBS, NBC)
> local television stations
> foreign language stations
> cable television networks

Each of these types of television stations is also a broad subject. You will have to ask yourself exactly what you want the respondents to say about one aspect of television. Again, brainstorm to narrow your focus and restrict your topic.

editorials	personalities
children's programs	news broadcasts
schedules	community service messages
advertising rates	sporting events
reception in your area	movie offerings

By developing a questionnaire on one of these much more limited subjects, you will achieve useful results.

◆ WRITING THE QUESTIONS

Relevant Questions

Once you have a topic, ask this question: "Exactly what kinds of information about this topic am I looking for?" Determine the types of information you need and then include only relevant questions. A useful technique for evaluating the relevance of a question is to make a short list of possible answers to the question. Do the answers provide useful information? If not, the question is probably irrelevant. Since many of the questionnaires you will have to write are brief (ten to twenty questions), make every question count. However interesting a side issue may be, keep it off your questionnaire. Why ask respondents to write more than is necessary? And why risk distracting them with irrelevant issues?

To illustrate the process of selecting only relevant questions, let's assume that you work for Speedee Tax Consultants and that your manager wants you to write a questionnaire to determine whether first-time customers approve of what

Speedee is doing. You are to ask them questions about your service, the time and money they invested, and their suggestions for improving your service. Anything else is unnecessary. The questions on the left side below would be relevant for your questionnaire; those on the right would not.

Relevant questions	Irrelevant questions
Did anyone help you fill out your return last year?	Were you good in high school mathematics?
Did you earn any income outside this state?	Do you consider yourself a blue- or white-collar worker?
Did you have to file a state form this year?	Do you find the state or federal form more confusing?
How did you hear about Speedee?	Have you ever been audited by the IRS?
Did you make an appointment to speak to a Speedee consultant?	Should the IRS extend the filing deadline to June 1?
Was there ample parking room?	What make of car do you drive?
How long did you have to wait if you did not have an appointment?	Did you think the Speedee office was tastefully decorated?
Was the Speedee consultant courteous?	Do you know how much training our employees receive?
Were the consultant's explanations clear or were they given in terms you did not understand?	What kind of computer did the Speedee consultant use?
On the federal return, were you told whether the short or long form was better for you?	Are there too many tax loopholes for the rich to escape paying their fair share?
Which form (long or short) did you file?	Are you currently employed?
Did the consultant show you how you could lawfully reduce the amount you owed? Increase your refund?	What will you do with your refund, if you receive one?
Were the costs for Speedee's services clearly explained?	Will you have to live on a tighter budget next year?
Did you find those costs fair?	Do you know the name of the owner of Speedee's or how many people we helped last year?
Would you come to Speedee next year?	Would you write your representative in Congress if you had to pay back more than five hundred dollars?

The relevant questions stick to the issue of most concern to the Speedee Tax Consultants—transforming first-time customers into repeat business. The irrelevant questions stray from the issues of service and costs.

Two Basic Types of Questions

In preparing a questionnaire you can write two kinds of questions: open-ended (or essay) questions and closed (or fixed alternative) questions. The following sections define each type of question, provide examples, and point out their benefits and drawbacks.

Open-Ended Questions

An open-ended question asks respondents to formulate their answers without being given certain answers to choose among, thus allowing considerable freedom of expression. Open-ended questions use verbs that elicit amplified, extensive responses: *appraise, comment on, compare, describe, discuss, estimate, evaluate, explain, judge.* Here are some sample open-ended questions.

> Describe the changes you would make in the registration process at Mesa College.
>
> Explain which part of your job is the hardest to perform and why.
>
> Discuss your reasons for attending Monmouth College.
>
> Judge the effectiveness of a family health practice in which a registered nurse screens patients and decides which ones will see a doctor.
>
> Comment on how you would correct abuses in the food stamp program in Taylorsville.

Open-ended questions are useful for a variety of purposes. They provide a practical means of soliciting information on subjects that would otherwise require options too numerous (or impossible) to list one by one. For example, the question on why students attend a particular college might bring back ten or twelve different and valid answers, some of which might never have occurred to you. Open-ended questions may also be helpful in gathering information on sensitive professional issues. Furthermore, respondents will reveal how knowledgeable they are, thus allowing you to gauge the value of their opinions.

Open-ended questions can be useful to you even before you write the final version of your questionnaire. You can send a few open-ended questions to a small sample of your respondents who, in their answers, can suggest the topics and options to include on the final questionnaire. And on the final copy of your questionnaire, the last question can be an open-ended one asking respondents to comment in detail on any topic covered in the questionnaire or on any topic you may have overlooked.

Finally, open-ended questions are valuable for lengthy studies searching for in-depth responses. If you have much time and relatively few (under fifteen or twenty) respondents, a questionnaire composed mainly of open-ended questions can be rewarding.

But open-ended questions can also pose problems for you and your respondents. This type of question requires a great deal of effort from respondents, who will have to organize, compose, and write their answers. If your question is not direct and sufficiently focused, you could easily get many irrelevant answers from respondents. Moreover, valuable answers might be mixed with these irrelevant comments. Finally, responses to open-ended questions are challenging to summarize (especially when large groups are surveyed) and these responses must be properly coded. (A later section of this chapter, pages 371–73, discusses one way to code, record, and tabulate responses.)

Closed Questions

Closed questions offer respondents a limited number of choices. Because closed questions are easier to answer, code, and tabulate, they are used more often than open-ended questions. Closed questions fall into the five categories discussed on the next pages.

1. Questions that offer only two choices. These are sometimes called *dichotomous questions* because they present the respondent with a dichotomy, a division of the subject into two mutually exclusive parts. The respondent's choice is limited to one of these two parts. Use this type of question only when the topic can be reasonably understood and explained in either/or terms.

(a) Yes/no questions

Should women be required to register for the draft?   yes _____ no _____

Is there a history of breast cancer in your family?   yes _____ no _____

Have you already taken Banking 117—Principles of Banking Operations?   yes _____ no _____

(b) True/false questions

People who smoke in public places should be fined.   true _____ false _____

Licensed Practical Nurses should, after special training, be allowed to start IV's.   true _____ false _____

Lanse Street must be changed into a one-way street.   true _____ false _____

(c) Two specific objects or types identified

Which kind of radio station do you prefer?   AM _____ FM _____

What kind of coffee do you drink most often?   regular ____ decaffeinated ____

What kind of stove does your apartment have?   gas _____ electric _____

2. Multiple-choice questions. These questions usually offer respondents three to five answers from which to choose. One of those answers can include a category marked "other," asking respondents to list "option not given," "do not know," "undecided," or "none."

What type of domesticated animal would you choose for a pet?
dog _____ cat _____ bird _____ fish _____ other (please specify) _____

Which kind of music do you like to listen to most often?
rock 'n' roll _____ country/western _____ jazz _____ classical _____ blues ____
New Age _____

Which agent called on you last month?
Ms. Kelly _____   Mr. Tumbrel _____   Ms. Baldwin _____   Mr. Lopez _____
No one called _____

How many times a day do you use the fax machine?
1 _____   2 _____   3 _____   4 _____   more than 4 (please specify) _____

3. Rating-scale questions. These questions ask readers to rate (or evaluate) an individual, program, policy, or option according to a carefully graduated scale. The respondent indicates the degree or extent of his or her opinion by marking an appropriate number on the scale. Always make sure that you specify precisely what the numbers on a scale mean. Usually this involves defining the items at either end of the scale. If the scale has an odd number of gradations, the middle position is considered a "neutral" opinion, as the following examples illustrate.

What is your overall view of Mayor Smith's administration?

Excellent   Poor
1   2   3   4   5

Central College should move from a semester to a quarter calendar.

Strongly   Strongly
agree   disagree
1   2   3   4   5

Figure 12.2 includes a questionnaire that uses rating-scale questions exclusively.

4. Ranking questions. With these questions a respondent is asked to assess the relative significance of a series of options and to assign each a value, often by labeling them 1, 2, 3, 4.

Indicate your order of preference for the kind of nursing you would like to do after graduation.
acute care _____   industrial _____   home health _____   school _____

Please rank in order of importance the following reasons for your decision to do your banking at First National.
Superteller _____   Saturday hours _____   Free checking _____   Location _____
Investment accounts _____

Rank the following types of cuisine in terms of their appeal to you.
Chinese _____   Mexican _____   Italian _____   French _____   German _____

5. Short-answer questions. These questions require respondents to fill in the blank or write a brief answer.

Give your date of birth (day, month, year): _____

How long have you lived at your current address? _____

Give the names of any community groups to which you belong: _____

What was your chief reason for accepting a job at Peterson's? _____

Which types of power tools do you use most often in your job? _____
_____

What magazine do you read most often? _____

Reliable and Valid Questions

Writing questions that work requires much thought and testing. Questions must be reliable *and* valid. A reliable question has the same meaning each time it is asked. It stands the test of time and is precisely and objectively worded so that respondents do not answer it one way on Monday and another way on Wednesday, depending on their mood. Reliable questions are not tricky or filled with loaded words; they are firm and constant. Valid questions do the job the writer intended; that is, they elicit the desired information. An invalid question contains ambiguous, vague words, thus calling into doubt any response made to it. Valid questions are ·worded so that respondents can understand exactly what the questioner wants to find out. To write reliable and valid questions, follow these suggestions.

1. Phrase your questions precisely. Specify exact quantities, times, or money. The following questions are vague.

Is there enough free swim time at the pool?   yes _____ no _____

If you were offered a good salary, would you
work inside a nuclear power plant?   yes _____ no _____

Is industry responsible for pollution?   yes _____ no _____

Words like *enough, good, industry,* and *pollution* are vague. Someone trying out for the swim team will interpret "enough" to mean far more hours than does the respondent who goes to the pool two times a week for relaxation. A "good" salary is equally imprecise. The final question does not identify the industry (plastics, textile, oil refinery, paint, rubber), the type of responsibility (through releasing waste into water, into the air, burying contaminants), and the kind of pollution (air, water, food, soil) involved. To correct vague questions, use exact words, as the following revised examples show.

How many hours of free swim time
would you use at the pool each day?   1 _____ 2 _____ 3 _____ 4 _____

Would you work inside a nuclear power
plant for a salary of $35,000 a year?   yes _____ no _____

Has All-Fix, Inc., dumped any oil in the
marsh near your home within the last
six weeks?   yes _____ no _____

2. Ask manageable questions. Broad questions, such as those below, ask respondents to write ten pages just to begin answering them. As a result, respondents will either leave them unanswered or write brief, often vague answers.

What do you think of our government?

What is your view of the economy?

What insurance does a homeowner need?

Like a vague question, a broad question offers the respondent no direction. The words *government, the economy,* and *insurance* cover a multitude of issues. Wide open, general questions like these really list the whole subject of the questionnaire rather than having each question cover one restricted part of the topic. That one large question needs to be cut into many smaller, more manageable queries. For example, by "government" does the writer mean federal, state, county, or local? And which governmental function, agency, or service (or lack of service) is involved? "The economy" also covers a lot of territory—should the respondent comment on the rate of inflation last month, current interest rates for new home loans, the percentage of unemployment in one city or in one profession, the national trade deficit, or what? When you ask about insurance for a home buyer, do you expect your respondents to discuss all kinds of insurance— life (term and whole life), medical, personal property, and even burial? A request for such an extensive amount of information in a single essay answer would overwhelm even an actuary (an expert in computing statistics on insurance risks and premiums). Replace a broad question with a more manageable one, such as the following examples show.

Do you agree or disagree with a congressional plan
to replace an income tax with a flat-rate tax?   agree _____ disagree _____

Should the United States government store nuclear
wastes in salt domes in Blanton County?   yes _____ no _____

What percentage of your monthly house payment
goes for mortgage insurance?   _____ %

3. Write questions that let respondents decide for themselves. Avoid using loaded words, such as those in the following questions.

Should we continue to waste taxpayers' money on the construction of the George Street Bridge?

Do you believe we have elected too many weirdos to City Council?

Isn't it useless to keep making agriculture majors submit daily reports?

Should the government reinstate the draft to make sure we have quality and quantity in America's armed services?

You reveal an emotional bias and thereby prejudice respondents with words like *waste, weirdos, useless,* or *quality and quantity.* The last example is particularly unfair because it suggests that those who answer "no" are against a strong America. Keep the language of your questions impartial, as in these revised examples.

Would you vote for continuing work on the George Street
Bridge?   yes _____ no _____

Do you believe your neighborhood is adequately
represented on the City Council?   yes _____ no _____

Do you want agriculture majors to submit daily reports?   yes _____ no _____

Do you believe that there should be a draft?   yes _____ no _____

A question like the following one demands a "yes" response.

Residents of Lake Mills need better sewerage facilities, don't they?

Rephrase the question to eliminate bias:

Do Lake Mills residents need more sewerage facilities?   yes _____ no _____

4. Your questions should not insult or indict the respondent. No matter how a question such as "Have you stopped picking fights with your spouse?" is answered, it accuses the respondent of the deed. The following two questions are worded improperly.

Are you still getting speeding tickets?

Have you missed many payments lately?

Do not assume that respondents have ever received speeding tickets or missed payments. Instead, ask if they ever did get a ticket or miss a payment.

Did you ever receive a ticket for
speeding?   yes _____ no _____

Have you ever missed a payment?   yes _____ no _____

If the answer is yes, you can ask the number of tickets or missed payments in a following question.

5. Do not write a question that requires the respondents to do your research. Courtesy requires that you not ask them to go to any more trouble than it takes to fill out the questionnaire. Avoid questions such as the following.

Ask your immediate superior to supply you with the number of models sold last month and please list that number.

After checking your files and last year's order book, indicate the differences between this year's engine specifications and last year's.

You are imposing on respondents when you require them to speak to other people or when you make them search their records to answer your question. Your respondents will probably end up throwing away the entire questionnaire. If you want information from a supervisor, send the supervisor a questionnaire also. Furthermore, if the information you seek is already available to you from other sources (your company's records for last month, for example), do not ask others for it.

6. Limit your questions to recent events. Do not ask respondents to search their memories to recall opinions they held years ago or to discuss details of an event they may not now clearly remember. The following questions are inappropriate.

Was your apartment building constructed with energy conservation in mind?

What was your exact gas mileage for city driving when you purchased your brand-new Cougar in 1984?

What kinds of meals did you eat on your vacation two years ago?

7. Write questions in language appropriate for your audience. A questionnaire directed to specialists may well include a few technical terms, but if respondents are not familiar with your jargon, avoid it. Patients asked about hospital service would have difficulty understanding this question.

Did you receive p.r.n. meds stat?   yes _____   no _____

Reworded as follows, the question is easier to answer.

Were you given medication when you
needed it?   yes _____   no _____

Avoid pretentious vocabulary as well.

Did the policy of merit raises exacerbate
the crew's feelings?   yes _____   no _____

Translated into understandable terms, this question reads easily.

Did the policy of merit raises anger the
crew?   yes _____   no _____

8. Each question should cover only one item. Do not confront respondents with a question that may demand an unnecessary, misleading, or contradictory choice. For example, "Do you prefer the Beatles or the Rolling Stones?" asks respondents to choose between the two. But respondents may like both groups and could not register their preference as the question is worded. Make two separate questions to be sure of obtaining a reliable response. The following question is also poor, because it assumes that respondents will automatically agree with both adjectives.

Are the new models more streamlined
and economical than last year's?   yes _____   no _____

Some may think that the new models are more streamlined but less economical than last year's, while others think just the reverse. Again, ask two separate questions, and do not use more than one adjective per question.

Overloading a question with a series of short interrogative words (*why? how? where? when? what?*) at its close should also be avoided.

Approximately how many times have you visited Baltimore in the last year? Why?
When? For how long? How did you travel?

If you need the additional information, ask a series of related questions.

9. Do not ask the same question twice. A question writer may think that there is a fine, subtle difference between two questions, but respondents may be unable to detect any difference. Check one question against another. Make sure, for example, that a question 2 does not duplicate a question 7.

(2) What is your favorite television program?
(7) Which program do you like to watch most on television?

(2) State your opinion about when placebos should be used.
(7) What are the values of placebos?

The writer of the first set of redundant questions failed to see that a favorite program means the one you like to watch. In the second pair the writer wrongly saw a difference between the use of placebos and their value. If they are prescribed for specific patients or used in different kinds of tests, these uses automatically characterize the placebo's value.

10. In multiple-choice questions supply respondents with clearly differentiated options. The following question confusingly presents overlapping choices.

What kind of car do you think gets the best mileage in the city?

(a) a compact _____
(b) a subcompact _____
(c) a foreign-made car _____
(d) an American car _____
(e) a diesel _____

These choices are not distinct. A compact or subcompact may also be either a foreign or an American car. The same is true of the diesel. Confronted with these options, respondents are asked two or three questions at the same time. Any answer they would give will be invalid and incomplete. Turn such a question into three separate questions.

(1) Do you think that a compact or a subcompact gets better mileage in the city?   compact _____   subcompact _____
(2) Name any American-made car that equals or surpasses the best import in city mileage. _____
(3) Would a diesel or a gasoline engine be more economical in city driving? diesel _____   gasoline _____

Be especially careful that questions containing an age category do not overlap as the following example does.

In which age group do you belong?

18–25 _____
25–37 _____
37–45 _____
45–59 _____
59 and over _____

Revised, the question will elicit clear and distinct responses:

In which age group do you belong?

18–25 _____
26–37 _____
38–45 _____
46–59 _____
over 59 _____

Figure 12.3 contains an effective example of nonoverlapping categories for age.

11. Include all necessary options in multiple-choice questions and those that ask respondents to rank items. Omissions are especially dangerous when respondents are forced to choose between two extremes and are not given enough options for qualified agreement or disagreement. Give respondents the option of saying that they have no opinion or that they see no change. Here are some ineffective questions because they have limited (omitted) options.

Do you favor the death
penalty?   yes _____   no _____

How do you feel about the new
uniforms we are required to
wear?   I like them _____   I do not like them _____

When is the busiest time at
your factory?   morning _____   afternoon _____

Respondents might favor the death penalty only in certain cases, they may approve of one part of a uniform code and not another, and workers may find a night shift the busiest or want to say that the workload varies from one week to another. As these questions are worded, valid responses are impossible. Make the first question, for example, valid by including differentiated options, as follows.

never _____   for murder of a police officer _____   for any murder _____
other _____   undecided _____

◆ WRITING EFFECTIVE INSTRUCTIONS

A clear and brief set of instructions should appear at the top of the first page of your questionnaire. To emphasize instructions, you might want to use boldface type or capital letters for certain points. In addition to showing respondents how to fill in their answers, instructions can summarize the topic of the questionnaire. A clear set of instructions will emphasize how easy a questionnaire is to answer and will increase your chances of respondents completing it.

Specifically, what should you tell respondents in your instructions? Indicate the kinds of questions they will be answering: multiple-choice, ranking, fill-in-the-blank, essay. Clearly specify how respondents are to indicate their choices—are they to put a check ($\sqrt{}$) or an X, circle a response, or underscore their answers? Look at the questionnaire in Figure 12.2 for an example of helpful instructions. Also, be consistent in the kinds of questions you use and the method respondents are to employ to answer them. For example, do not force respondents to jump from a group of multiple-choice questions to a set of ranking ones and then back to multiple-choice. Do not have respondents circle some answers and check others. As was noted earlier, many questionnaires composed of one type of closed question do conclude with an open-ended question. However, this shift in question type is so commonly used that it is not disturbing to respondents.

Indicate whether respondents are to sign their names or remain anonymous. If their signatures are optional, say so. Tell respondents the date by which you would like them to return the questionnaire and include a postage-paid envelope. Give your name, address, and telephone number and offer any assistance. Even though this information may duplicate what you have written in a cover letter (discussed on pages 369–70 of this chapter), give it anyway. It is safer to repeat the information than to risk having the respondent not know when and where to return the questionnaire.

FIGURE 12.2 A portion of a questionnaire with explicit instructions.

National Restaurant Association
1976 Travel Study

Name _____   Code _____

City _____

Directions: Listed below are a number of statements, some of which deal with eating out and restaurants and some of which deal with general life-style factors. For each statement listed, we would like to know whether you personally agree or disagree with the statement.

After each statement, there are five numbers from one to five. The higher the number, the more you tend to disagree with the statement. The lower the number, the more you tend to agree with the statement. The numbers 1–5 can be described as follows:

1. I strongly agree with the statement.
2. I generally agree with the statement.
3. I neither agree nor disagree.
4. I generally disagree with the statement.
5. I strongly disagree with the statement.

For each statement, please circle the number that best describes your feelings about that statement.

(After you complete the questionnaire, please place this form into the attached stamped, self-addressed envelope and mail.)

	Statement	Strongly Agree				Strongly Disagree
1	I prefer to order a la carte rather than order a dinner.	1	2	3	4	5
2	I prefer a service charge be automatically added to my bill rather than having to tip.	1	2	3	4	5
3	I like to try new and different menu items.	1	2	3	4	5
4	I prefer a self-service salad bar to being served a salad at the table.	1	2	3	4	5
5	I usually tip a fixed percentage of the bill regardless of the service I get.	1	2	3	4	5
6	Atmosphere is just as important as the quality of the food in selecting a restaurant.	1	2	3	4	5
7	I love to eat.	1	2	3	4	5
8	I usually look for the lowest possible prices when I shop.	1	2	3	4	5
9	Information I get about a product from a friend is usually better than what I get from advertising.	1	2	3	4	5
10	I have annual physical check-ups.	1	2	3	4	5
11	If a new restaurant opened in town, I would probably be among the first to try it out.	1	2	3	4	5
12	My days tend to follow a definite routine, such as eating meals at a regular time, etc.	1	2	3	4	5
13	I exercise regularly.	1	2	3	4	5
14	I enjoy most of my business trips.	1	2	3	4	5
15	Sometimes I like to do things on the "spur of the moment."	1	2	3	4	5
16	I would like to take a trip around the world.	1	2	3	4	5
17	Most people are in too much of a rush.	1	2	3	4	5
18	I like fast-food restaurants.	1	2	3	4	5
19	When I must choose between the two, I usually dress for fashion, not for comfort.	1	2	3	4	5
20	I often wish for the good old days.	1	2	3	4	5
21	I like to be considered a leader.	1	2	3	4	5
22	A party wouldn't be a party without liquor.	1	2	3	4	5
23	I would rather spend a quiet evening at home than go to a party.	1	2	3	4	5
24	I like to pay cash for everything I buy.	1	2	3	4	5
25	I love the fresh air and out-of-doors.	1	2	3	4	5
26	I follow at least one sport very closely.	1	2	3	4	5
27	I enjoy a cocktail before dinner.	1	2	3	4	5
28	I often check prices, even for small items.	1	2	3	4	5
29	I eat more than I should.	1	2	3	4	5
30	No matter how fast our income goes up, we never seem to have enough.	1	2	3	4	5
31	I often seek out the advice of my friends regarding which brands to buy.	1	2	3	4	5
32	I like to try new and different things.	1	2	3	4	5
33	I feel uneasy when things aren't neat and organized.	1	2	3	4	5
34	I just can't relax when eating out.	1	2	3	4	5
35	I prefer to use a credit card rather than cash when eating out.	1	2	3	4	5
36	Business takes me away from home more often than I'd like.	1	2	3	4	5
37	I am an impulsive individual.	1	2	3	4	5
38	I'd like to spend a year in some foreign country.	1	2	3	4	5

The Restaurant Habits of the Business Traveler, prepared by Edward J. Mayo for National Restaurant Association Consumer Attitudes Survey Series, June 1976. Reprinted with permission of the National Restaurant Association.

Make your instructions as clear as possible. Respondents will be annoyed if they are frequently interrupted by new instructions. If you use a term or concept that must be defined or explained, do it in the question itself.

Is there any encumbrance (lien, mortgage, judgment, or
easement) on your property?   yes _____ no _____

A question may require some kind of clarification for a respondent to answer it properly.

Which three-hour session is best for you to attend? (*To clarify, add:*
10:00 A.M. _____   2:00 P.M _____   8:00 P.M. _____)

◆ PRESENTING AN ATTRACTIVE QUESTIONNAIRE

The visual impression your questionnaire makes may determine whether or not respondents complete it. If your questionnaire looks sloppy and is difficult to read and follow, respondents will not bother with it. Therefore, strive to make your questionnaire neat, clear, and easy to read and answer. One of the best routes to take is to have your questionnaire done using desktop publishing software. It will look like it was typeset by a professional printer. The result may so impress your readers that it could improve your chances of having them respond. Also consider having the questionnaire copied on attractive paper. Undoubtedly, a questionnaire printed on a faded mimeo sheet or on a copying machine that leaves smudges will not invite quick replies, if any. Avoid reducing the size of your questionnaire on a copying machine in an attempt to save space; the small print will be hard to read and also intimidating. Use plenty of white space, which will be pleasing to the respondents' eyes. Proofread meticulously. Also make sure that your questionnaire contains a title, a place for the respondent's name, if desired, and instructions.

To review the material discussed so far in this chapter, examine Figure 12.3, a questionnaire distributed by Auburn University. It is a useful example of a carefully worded, clearly arranged questionnaire. Note that because travelers complete this questionnaire while resting at an Alabama hospitality center, the questionnaire does not contain instructions on where and when it should be returned.

◆ SELECTING RESPONDENTS

Once you have restricted your topic and have determined who will read the results of your questionnaire and why, you will have a better idea about the kinds of individuals you need to question. To receive useful answers, you have to exercise great care in selecting your respondents; you cannot do it haphazardly. Finding appropriate respondents for extremely technical questionnaires involves sophisticated sampling strategies far beyond the scope of this book. Texts on statistics and audience surveys will contain detailed instructions explaining the specialized methods used by pollsters like George Gallup or Lou Harris; such poll-

FIGURE 12.3   A carefully worded, clearly arranged questionnaire.

AUBURN UNIVERSITY TRAVEL SURVEY
In Cooperation With
Alabama Bureau of Publicity and Information

Dear Traveler: Thank you for traveling in Alabama. We would like to make Alabama a more enjoyable travel destination or vacation state.   Please help us by completing this form **if you have not already done so on this trip.** There is no need to sign your name.

1 Season of travel: 1 ☐ Dec.-Feb.   2 ☐ Mar-May   3 ☐ June-Aug   4 ☐ Sep.-Nov.

2 Home: City _____   State/Country _____

4 Major point *away from home* you are now traveling to/returning from:

6 City/Place _____   State _____

8 Principal mode of travel: 1 ☐ Highway   2 ☐ Air   3 ☐ Bus   4 ☐ Rail

Number and age of persons in party:

Males	Females
9 _____ Under 14	15 _____ Under 14
10 _____ 14-17	16 _____ 14-17
11 _____ 18-29	17 _____ 18-29
12 _____ 30-49	18 _____ 30-49
13 _____ 50-64	19 _____ 50-64
14 _____ 65 or over	20 _____ 65 or over

Activities engaged in while in **Alabama only**—check as many as apply:

21 ☐ Passing thru only
22 ☐ Passing thru, but engaging in the following activities checked
23 ☐ Visiting friends/relatives
24 ☐ Visiting historical sites/places
25 ☐ Beaches/swimming
26 ☐ Commercial attractions (gardens, amusement parks/centers, etc.)

27 ☐ Business
28 ☐ Golfing
29 ☐ Camping
30 ☐ Boating/fishing
31 ☐ Watching sports
32 ☐ Personal affairs
33 ☐ Attending show or event
34 ☐ Attending convention/meeting

35 _____ How many days spent in Alabama on this trip?

37 _____ How many nights spent in Alabama on this trip?

39 _____ How many days spent on entire trip?

Nights in **Alabama** were (or will be) at:
41 ☐ Home of friend or relative
42 ☐ Motel
43 ☐ Hotel
44 ☐ Rented house/apartment

45 ☐ Cabin/cottage
46 ☐ Tent
47 ☐ Recreational Vehicle
48 ☐ Travel Trailer

While in **Alabama only**, how much will your party spend on this trip for:

49 _____ Lodging

52 _____ Food and beverages

55 _____ Auto expenses (gas, oil, etc.)

58 _____ Entertainment/sightseeing

61 _____ Recreation/sports

64 _____ Other purchases

67 Annual family income (for statistical purposes only):

1 ☐ Under $5,000	4 ☐ $15,000-20,000	7 ☐ $30,000-40,000
2 ☐ $5,000-10,000	5 ☐ $20,000-25,000	8 ☐ $40,000-50,000
3 ☐ $10,000-15,000	6 ☐ $25,000-30,000	9 ☐ $50,000 or over

We welcome your comments. Please write them on the back side.

THANK YOU FOR YOUR HELP

Reprinted by permission from Dr. James W. Adams, Department of Marketing and Transportation, Auburn University.

sters can survey small sections of the population and predict outcomes with less than a 2 percent margin of error. Although not offering this kind of statistical information on sampling techniques, the following discussion does suggest guidelines you can follow when selecting respondents.

To how many people must you send a questionnaire in order to have reliable results? The answer depends on your statistics. If you are interested in finding out how technicians in a particular hospital feel about rotating shifts, then your respondents would be all the technicians in that one hospital. Similarly, if you want to determine whether your sorority chapter should have a barbeque or dance at the end of the spring term, you would question every member of your chapter. But your respondents may not always belong to such a limited and easily accessible group. Many times you will have to consider a larger audience, whose members could not all be reached and questioned individually. You might want to find out how customers at a certain store feel about a warehouse branch that would sell merchandise at a reduced rate. Certainly you could not question everyone who shops at this store. Or you might be interested in surveying how a certain profession (dairy farmers, dietitians, medical secretaries) would react to a piece of impending legislation. Being unable to question everyone in a particular profession, you would use some form of sampling.

Systematic Random Sampling

The most respected, and valid, way of finding respondents is to follow a *systematic random sampling* technique. Much marketing research is done this way. According to this technique, you choose your target audience or population (all the nurses in your hometown, all students attending your college, all holders of credit cards from a department store), and from this large target population you obtain a cross section by selecting names at random from the group. A random sampling is not like picking names out of a hat. It is far more systematic and fair. For example, from a college directory listing the names of all students enrolled at your school you can choose by random selection every tenth name or, for a smaller margin of error, every fifth name. Thus all respondents (all students listed in the school directory) have an equal chance of being selected for your sample. This equal chance is the heart of the random sampling technique. Figure 12.6 (to be discussed in detail later in this chapter) contains a report on student opinions of a campus newspaper. Because the editors of the paper could not question the entire student body, they sent a questionnaire to every sixth name in the directory and had a 66.66 percent response rate.

Citing another example, let's say that you wanted to find out the customers' preferences for shopping hours at your store. You could stand outside the store and ask everyone who happens to walk by. However, you might talk to people who are visitors to your town and who never have or never will shop at the store, or you could select residents of the town who just stopped to avoid the rain and who never have shopped at the store. To obtain a cross section of those who in fact are customers of the store, you must select as your target population those who are on record as having purchased goods from the store. Perhaps their names are on record as credit card holders. You could then go through the store's list of credit card holders and by random selection pick out names of individuals to whom you will send your questionnaire.

Another way to get a statistically valid sample is to pick names randomly out of the residential listings of your town's telephone book. This selection technique would be a good one if you wanted to find out how a relatively small town or suburb (under 30,000 people) felt about a bond proposal or welfare services.

Stratified Random Sampling

Another valid sampling technique is known as *stratified random sampling*. This approach is used when you have a number of different groups or subgroups to question; it means that you survey each group proportionately. For example, say you want to determine opinion about college facilities at a school that was formerly all female but a few years ago became coed. Now the student body is composed of 70 percent women and 30 percent men. In order to obtain a fair cross section of these two groups, you need to question each group according to the same percentage it occupies in the college population. Accordingly, if you sent questionnaires to 100 students, you would make sure that 70 questionnaires went to women and 30 to men to reflect the enrollment percentages at the college.

Quota Sampling

Still another type of sampling technique is known as *quota sampling*. Use this technique with great care. Here you choose an audience almost as one would select a quota. You might question the first twenty-five males and first twenty-five females you meet. Such a sampling might be helpful if, for example, it consisted of customers in a store who all saw a demonstration of a dishwasher, and you wanted to get their opinions of that dishwasher. The population is chosen arbitrarily and not selected as carefully as it would be with random sampling, but such a group can help answer your questions, since everyone has seen the product. The problem with quota sampling is that it can lead to a distorted sample in many circumstances. If you wanted to poll student opinion about a campus radio station and all you did was ask for the opinion of ten of your friends who you knew did not like the station, your sample would be biased. These ten friends are a homogeneous (presorted) group that may not truly represent the view of the student body. To get a valid sample, you would have to obtain a larger sample to ensure coverage of a variety of ideas and opinions.

◆ DISTRIBUTING A QUESTIONNAIRE

Before submitting your questionnaire to respondents, have someone evaluate it. Ask a student in your major, a teacher, or a co-worker to read your questionnaire and tell you whether any of your questions are vague, misleading, or irrelevant.

You should pretest your questionnaire on a small representative sample of the larger group you want to survey. Have these individuals pay particular attention to the options you list for multiple-choice questions; make sure that the options are reasonable and sufficient. Such screening may take a few days, but in the long run you will save time and energy. If you send out a questionnaire flawed by poorly worded or irrelevant questions, the answers you receive will be of dubious value. You will have to redo the questionnaire, or you may find yourself busy explaining the questions verbally to respondents who call you for help.

Once you are sure that the questionnaire is right, deliver or mail it to your respondents. Decide which approach is more feasible. Delivering the questionnaire in person may create goodwill and may increase your chances of receiving a completed questionnaire back from these individuals. However, when you think a personal visit might influence the content of a reader's response, mail your questionnaire. In any case, make sure your questionnaire reaches respondents at times convenient for them, not just for you. Do not give questionnaires to respondents when other commitments prevent their answering you. For example, students preparing for final or state board examinations will not postpone their studies to fill out your questionnaire. Some large companies close for two weeks in the summer and give all employees and supervisors a vacation. Sending a questionnaire to anyone just before or during that shutdown would be pointless. Asking for completed questionnaires around the Christmas holidays is equally ill advised. If you are aware that respondents will be on vacation, busy, or out of town on business, send your questionnaire at another time.

If you mail your questionnaire, send it by first-class mail and include a stamped, self-addressed envelope. Respondents are far more likely to answer when you make it as easy as possible for them. Make certain that the respondents' names and addresses are correct. People will not be inclined to respond if you spell their names incorrectly or if you address someone with a Mr. when that person is a Ms., or vice versa. Some given names (Pat, Leslie, Terry) apply to both men and women. If you are uncertain, omit the courtesy title and write "Dear Pat Hayes" or "Dear Terry Bronti."

When you mail the questionnaire, enclose a cover letter and follow these procedures.

1. Introduce yourself and tell why you are writing.
2. Explain why you are sending the questionnaire.
3. Emphasize how important the respondent's answers are.
4. Tell what benefits the respondent can gain by answering—the most important function of the letter.
5. Discuss the kind of questionnaire you have devised.
6. Ask that the questionnaire be returned by a specified time.
7. Perhaps promise a gift for returning the questionnaire or even send a gift along with the questionnaire. A coupon, a crisp dollar bill, even a shiny quarter can improve your rate of return.
8. Thank the respondent and promise, if practical to do so, to inform him or her of the outcome.

Depending on your topic and the questionnaire you have constructed, you may also want to assure respondents that their answers will remain confidential. Or you might want to promise them anonymity. Not being required to sign their names, respondents will not worry that anyone, including you, knows what they have answered. Figure 12.4 illustrates a sample cover letter sent with a questionnaire.

FIGURE 12.4   A cover letter sent with a questionnaire.

CASSON'S DEPARTMENT STORES
1800 South Paulina
Topeka, KS 66620

June 4, 1990

Mr. Howard Anderson
73 Crestway Park Drive
Topeka, KS 66621

Dear Mr. Anderson:

Thank you for purchasing your new Clearview television set from Casson's. Your opinions about our store and its service policies are important to us.

For this reason, I hope you will complete the enclosed questionnaire. It should not take more than ten minutes of your time, and your answers will help us provide you with even better service for your set. You will find twelve multiple-choice questions; but elaborate on any of your answers, if you wish, on the back of the questionnaire.

The questionnaire is easy to return. Just put it in the enclosed postage-paid envelope and drop it in the mail. Please return the questionnaire by June 29, if at all possible. If you have any questions, feel free to call me at 783-3423, extension 41.

Once again, thanks for shopping at Casson's. We will let you know how the results of the questionnaire will improve our service to you.

Sincerely yours,

Susan Shapiro

Susan Shapiro
Customer Services

Encl. Questionnaire

◆ TABULATING RESPONSES

A new phase of your research begins with the return of your questionnaire. You will have to count the completed questionnaires and keep a record of specific responses. Tallying is an important link between the questionnaire and the report; a mistake here can distort (or defeat) all your other efforts.

Responses to closed questions can be tallied in numerous ways. If the number of your respondents is large and your employer has a computer to tabulate the answers, consult someone in the computer department during the design stage of a questionnaire and before you start to count or categorize responses. A computer consultant can suggest different ways of coding options to your questionnaire to make sure the computer will assess them properly. Responses may be translated into numerical (or alphabetical) symbols to represent various responses.

If you are using a small number of respondents for a school or a civic project, or if you lack access to a computer, you will have to tabulate by hand. Your record keeping will be relatively easy if you follow a consistent and orderly system for listing and categorizing information. One good method is to buy a yellow, legal-size note pad and use a separate tally sheet for each question on your questionnaire. Write the question and its number at the top of the sheet; directly beneath the question, list horizontally the options (the range of choices) that the question offers. For dichotomous questions you will have two columns; for multiple-choice, as many columns as there are choices. Be sure to include the category "no response" in a separate column. If respondents give two contradictory answers to one question, indicate "no response" in your tally since you do not know which answer was intended.

The use of separate tally sheets for each question offers these advantages.

1. You are better able to tabulate, organize, and summarize responses for each question, since all answers to that question are on one sheet.
2. You can more easily check responses against individual questionnaires, since each response is coded by identification and question number.
3. You have the flexibility of comparing responses to various questions by simply pulling tally sheets for these questions and laying the sheets side by side.
4. You have a record of the number of questionnaires returned by any specific date.
5. You can conveniently keep a running tally and will not have to wait until all questionnaires are in to begin counting.

With a separate tally sheet for each question, you will be ready to tabulate responses. When a questionnaire comes in, assign it a code number. The first questionnaire to be returned could be labeled 01, the second 02, the third 03, and so forth. List the identifying numbers (and the names of respondents, if requested, after the numbers) vertically on the left-hand side of each tally sheet. Then, as you check each questionnaire in, you can record a respondent's answer to an individual question in the correct column on the appropriate tally sheet. Figure 12.5 illustrates a sample master tally sheet for the first question.

FIGURE 12.5   A tally sheet.

		YES	NO	
	Question 1: Have you ever served in the Armed Forces ?			
01	John Malone		X	
02	Bill Brownly	X		
03	Kathy Rivers	X		
04	Ruth Tapes		X	
05	Henry Stuart		X	
06	Tim Gordon	X		
07	Shirley McManus		X	
08	Debbie Buzak	X		
09	Donald Shatz		X	
10	Willa Jackson		X	
11	Bruce Page	X		
12	Mary Holka		X	
13	Frances Watts		X	
14	Richard Saperstein	X		
15	Terry Myers		X	
16	Roberta Zimmerman		X	
17	Paula Huppard		X	
18	Chris Sholds	X		
19	John Tzarki	X		
20	Billy Lamar	X		
21	Lucy Bennini		X	
22	Marge Appleby	X		
TOTALS		10	12	

Coding and tabulating open-ended questions may present problems. You will have to make option columns as you go along, but still impose some type of manageable limits on these options. When you read essay answers, use a highlighter pen to mark the exact comments that most relevantly answer the question. Those comments may be buried in useless remarks; the highlighter pen will make the most relevant remarks stand out. A different color highlighter pen can be used to identify statements you foresee quoting directly in your report, thus making them easier to find later.

◆ WRITING EFFECTIVE QUESTIONNAIRE REPORTS

After tabulating the responses, you will have to write a report on your findings. The report should accomplish three functions: (1) summarize the range of responses, (2) draw conclusions, and (3) make recommendations. The report may be brief; a one-page memo or a two-page letter will suffice. At first you may wonder if such a memo or letter is long enough, considering the time and effort you have devoted to the project. But the chief function of the report is to consolidate responses and comment on them. The report should give readers the big picture, of which individual questionnaires are only a part. Providing generalizations based on individual responses, the report does not duplicate every response you have obtained or identify every individual who made a response. If you repeated every scrap of information you obtained, it would be like giving readers the complete set of questionnaires without any necessary summary or commentary.

Writing a report means being selective. Selectivity is not a problem with responses to closed questions. Unless a respondent provides two choices for a dichotomous or multiple-choice question, you will simply tabulate his or her response with all the others you receive. Open-ended questions are more challenging to summarize. Some respondents will include more than you can use; while some of their information may be extremely interesting, it may also be irrelevant. Remember, the report is not a catchall for every comment written in response to an open-ended question. It should reflect only those answers that will help readers reach a decision. Figure 12.6 contains a sample questionnaire survey report and the questionnaire on which it is based. Study this report to see how information is selected and condensed. You might want to refer to this report throughout the following discussion.

Rules for Writing Numbers

Your report will rely heavily on numbers, especially percentages. Spell out the word *percent* in a report; do not use the symbol (%). When listing responses in terms of percentages, express the specific percentage in numbers, not words.

> Incorrect: Because of inflation, fifty-eight percent of the workers will not buy a new car this year.

> Correct: Because of inflation, 58 percent of the workers will not buy a new car this year.

FIGURE 12.6   A report and the questionnaire on which it is based.

TO: Professor Marion Andretti
           Faculty Adviser, the Campus Informer

FROM: Debrah H. Hinkel, Bob Banks, Joe Moore, Alice Wong

SUBJECT: Student Opinion of the Campus Informer

DATE: September 28, 1990

PURPOSE AND SCOPE OF THIS SURVEY

Since a number of us have recently joined the staff of the Informer, we
wanted to assess student opinion of the campus newspaper in order to guide
our future editorial decisions. To obtain a clearer sense of students'
needs, we distributed the enclosed questionnaire to a random sample of 300
of the 1,800 students at Detroit Community College (DCC) during the week of
September 4-11.

Two hundred students replied, giving us a fair cross section. Respondents
came from every major in occupational education, with a slight majority (42
percent) representing three areas—nursing, automotive mechanics, and retail
merchandising. Since many of our respondents (53 percent) have spent at
least two semesters at DCC, they are familiar with the campus.

RESULTS OF SURVEY

For the most part, these respondents are loyal readers of the Informer.
Fifty-four percent read each issue of the paper, while 31 percent noted they
look at the paper at least once a week. Only 7 percent said they rarely read
the Informer. Of most interest to our readers are articles on campus events
and sporting activities, the two areas ranked first and second by 76 percent
of the students. Sixty-nine percent of the students noted that the ads were
the third most significant reason for reading the paper. News of academic
programs and school clubs ranked fourth and fifth in student interest,
according to 71 percent of the respondents.

Most students (68 percent) think the Informer should continue to be
published twice a week, although a small percentage of these students (21
percent, or 27 students) want to see the Informer come out on Monday and
Friday rather than on Tuesday and Friday. Little support exists for a daily
paper (20 percent) and even less for a weekly or bimonthly one (12 percent).
Students may think that there is not enough news for a daily paper, and that
news would be too old if it appeared a week or two late.

FIGURE 12.6 (continued)

-2-

The Informer did not receive high marks on its appearance. Forty-six percent of the students thought the layout was only average, while 23 percent of the students believe that the size of our type is too small, that the blue color of our paper is too dark, and the placement of articles is inconsistent. Mildred Potter, a sophomore welding major, offered this representative comment: "It's hard to follow a story when it is continued on one or two other pages, because the subsequent headlines aren't always clear." A related complaint deals with our photographs. Although 27 percent of the students thought we use enough pictures, 42 percent would like to see us include more. "Stories are more enjoyable when an accompanying picture clarifies or highlights the action," stated a business student who has been at DCC for three semesters. Students were much more satisfied with the way articles are written. Seventy-two percent thought that the language was easy to understand.

Students reached a consensus about retaining our "Faculty Profile" feature. Eighty-two percent said they like to know about the faculty. As one electronics major put it: "I find it interesting to learn about a teacher's family, hobbies, and professional accomplishments."

RECOMMENDATIONS

Based upon the responses to our questionnaire, and especially to the last question on proposed major changes in the paper, we offer the following recommendations:

1. Increase the point size of type and change the color of our paper from blue to white or cream for easier reading.
2. Use more photographs, especially in covering sports events.
3. Expand our ads section and group similar types of ads--e.g., jobs, items for sale, housing, entertainment--and supply a heading for each group.
4. Run our "Faculty Profile" in each issue, rather than printing it only once or twice a month.

Thank you for considering these recommendations. We would like to have a meeting with you early next week to get your opinion about these changes. If you approve them, we can incorporate these changes in the Informer as early as next semester.

FIGURE 12.6   (continued)

-3-

QUESTIONNAIRE

Please take a few minutes to fill out the following questionnaire about the Campus Informer, our student newspaper. We on the newspaper staff are eager to know what you think about the paper so that we can make sure that it serves your needs. Please return your questionnaire to Debrah H. Hinkel, the editor, at Scott Hall 107 by Tuesday, September 18. If you have any questions, drop by by the newspaper office in Scott Hall or call 264-3450 between noon and 6:00 p.m. Your viewpoints are important to us and will count. Thanks. Please feel free to sign or not sign your name.

Name _____

1. How many semesters have you attended Detroit Community College?
   ___ 1
   ___ 2
   ___ 3
   ___ 4
   ___ more than 4

2. What is your major? _____

3. How often do you read the Informer?
   ___ twice a week, or every time it comes out
   ___ once a week
   ___ once every two weeks
   ___ I rarely look at it

4. Rank your reasons for reading the Informer (first = 1, second = 2, etc.)
   ___ find out about sports events
   ___ learn more about academic programs
   ___ look at the ads
   ___ follow campus events
   ___ learn more about campus clubs

5. How often would you like to see the Informer published?
   ___ daily
   ___ twice a week (as it is now)
   ___ once a week
   ___ once every two weeks

FIGURE 12.6   (continued)

-4-

6. How would you evaluate the <u>Informer</u>'s layout (its physical appearance)?
   ___ outstanding
   ___ very good
   ___ average
   ___ poor

7. Is the <u>Informer</u> written in clearly understood language?
   ___ yes
   ___ no

8. What do you think of the number of pictures used in the <u>Informer</u>?
   ___ not enough
   ___ just right
   ___ too many

9. Should the <u>Informer</u> continue to run its "Faculty Profile" feature?
   ___ run as is (once or twice a month)
   ___ run more often (every issue)
   ___ run less often (once every two months)
   ___ delete it

10. What one major change would you like to make in the <u>Informer</u>? Why?

Remember one exception to listing percentages as figures. If a percentage begins a sentence, write the percentage as a *word:*

Incorrect: 55 percent of the sales force thought that the new lights were easy on their eyes.

Correct: Fifty-five percent of the sales force thought that the new lights were easy on their eyes.

You can also list a percentage parenthetically.

Correct: A majority of students (75 percent) prefer the quarter to the semester system.

The word *percentage* should not be used for *percent. Percentage* is used without numbers to indicate a range or a size.

Incorrect: A large percent of the residents favored the new health care policies.

Incorrect: A thirty-five percentage of the residents favored the new health care policies.

Correct: A large percentage of the residents favored the new health care policies.

Correct: Thirty-five percent of the residents favored the new health care policies.

Explaining What the Numbers Mean

Numbers in your report will make it effective and impressive. However, beware of letting figures speak for themselves. Your report is not a statistical table. Organize and assess the numbers you include by telling readers what those numbers mean, why they are significant, and how they characterize various opinions. Numbers are most meaningful when they are placed in a context readers will understand and welcome. Avoid writing a wooden opening that provides no background information.

Poor: A fifteen-question questionnaire was distributed to forty students at Coe Community College between the dates of February 14 and February 28, 1990.

Provide a brief explanation of the reasons why you constructed and distributed the questionnaire. Supply information that will help readers connect your topic to the need you saw to question people about it. The lifeless opening just cited could be transformed for the reader's benefit into this kind of introduction.

Effective: For the last two semesters, students at Coe Community College have complained about the textbook rental service. In order to determine what types of changes students wanted, I constructed a questionnaire and sent it to forty students from seven different majors.

In discussing responses to specific questions, use numbers selectively. Prepare readers for the numbers you cite. Do not overwhelm readers with a series of unorganized and uninterpreted figures. If you simply list every response to every question, you will confuse readers. It is your job to impose some order by briefly and simply summarizing the responses.

Poor: Question 2 asked respondents: "How long have you lived in the Hillcrest subdivision?" Twenty-seven percent said they lived in Hillcrest for more than five years; 17 percent indicated they were residents there for at least three years; 34 percent said they lived in Hillcrest for more than one year; and 22 percent said they lived in Hillcrest for less than one year.

Effective: A clear majority of the respondents (78 percent) have lived in the Hillcrest subdivision for more than one year.

Here is another example in which unorganized responses are thrown at the reader.

Poor: For question 3 ("How would you evaluate the service you received after the sale?"), respondents answered as follows: 35 percent said it was all right but a little slow; 25 percent thought it was not adequate; and 40 percent said they had no complaints.

To eliminate confusion, divide the responses into two manageable groups. Readers will profit from a conclusion such as the following.

Effective: Customers were generally satisfied with the service after the sale; only 25 percent answered that it was inadequate.

The revision above shows the writer's desire to present only essential facts. For example, in reporting responses to yes/no questions, there is no need to give percentages for both the yes answers and the no answers: "75 percent liked the new office hours; 25 percent did not." When you write that 75 percent liked the new office hours, you do not have to tell the reader that 25 percent did not. Of course, if a number of respondents left the question blank, you will have to state that fact.

Using Direct Quotations

In addition to recording percentages, you may want to include a few direct quotations for emphasis. A direct quotation, if it is carefully worded, can serve three useful functions: (1) it can precisely capture the views of an entire group, (2) it might contain a colorful expression that can enliven your report, and (3) it can lend support to your recommendation, especially if it comes from a recognized authority. Because of their summary power, direct quotations will make your report more compact, relevant, and credible.

Choose direct quotations carefully and use them sparingly. Figure 12.6, for example, contains only three quotations. To avoid bias, try not to use the same person for each quotation you include; your report will appear prejudiced if you do not give equal time to both sides. If you are distributing a questionnaire on grading procedures at your college, you might ask whether students prefer one comprehensive final examination to a number of tests. By recording only the following quotation, you would present an unfair picture of students as lazy.

Students in favor of a single comprehensive final examination liked the freedom from daily preparation and weekly quizzes. As a sophomore majoring in environmental resources noted, "You're playing Russian roulette, but it's worth it for the extra time you have during the semester."

By adding the following observation, you will be giving a more balanced view.

> Those opposed to a single comprehensive examination, however, worried that they could have a bad day or not know what the instructor was looking for. A junior plant science major summarized much of this group's thinking when she wrote, "I want to have more than one chance to make a good grade."

Before using a direct quotation, always obtain permission. If given, put the exact words of the person you are quoting in double quotation marks. And, whenever possible, identify the respondent by name, status, position, or major.

Writing a Recommendation

A recommendation should show readers how to transform respondents' answers into action. You can recommend that readers perform certain actions (often by a set time), refrain from performing actions, or choose between alternatives.

Make your recommendations specific and clear-cut. Readers will not benefit from general or indecisive comments. Since profits, customer satisfaction, and improved service may depend on your recommendations, be precise. If you hedge, you betray both respondents and readers. To say that you are not sure what should be done reveals shortcomings. The following recommendations leave no doubt concerning a definite course of action.

> Based on the respondents' answers, I recommend that we do three things:
>
> ♦ expand the employee parking lot to include space for one hundred more cars by August 1, 1990.
> ♦ install a fence around the parking lot.
> ♦ station a security guard on Norris Street between shifts to direct traffic.

Keep your recommendation section short. A single concluding paragraph should be enough. You might want to list recommendations as separate items, each preceded by a raised bullet, as the example above shows, or by numbers, as in Figure 12.6. Or you may want to give your recommendations without itemizing them, as in Figure 12.7. Do not repeat unnecessary percentages and comments you have already listed in your report. Focus instead on the way readers can accomplish what respondents do or do not want. Usually your recommendation will be easy to formulate. It will entail implementing what the majority of respondents want done. Your hardest job will be finding a practical solution to the problem as the respondents define it. It would be foolish to express the opposite of what respondents want without hard facts to back up your opposition. By so doing, you invalidate your questionnaire and discredit yourself. Your recommendation should help readers who are looking for facts to support the right decision.

In some instances, however, you will find that opinions on a crucial issue are almost equally divided. With no majority opinion to guide you (and your readers), your recommendation will take on added significance. Make a recommendation, but admit that opinion is divided. Mary Snyder in Figure 12.7 endorses the city of Madison as the convention site but includes a necessary warning. There

FIGURE 12.7   A report, the questionnaire on which it is based, and a cover letter.

TO: Gerald Morgan, President, Northern Chapter WREA

FROM: Mary Snyder

SUBJECT: Report on Convention Preference Questionnaire

DATE: February 9, 1990

PURPOSE OF CONVENTION QUESTIONNAIRE

Four weeks ago, when the state office asked us to poll our chapter members about their preferences for this year's Wisconsin Real Estate Association convention, I volunteered to prepare, distribute, and summarize the results of a questionnaire. Judging from the responses to that questionnaire (a copy of which is attached), distributed over the last three weeks, next year's convention will be well attended and productive. One hundred of our 136 members returned the questionnaire: 22 secretaries/receptionists, 57 salespersons, 12 brokers, and 9 builders. Eighty-five percent of these individuals attended last year's convention in Green Bay.

RESULTS OF QUESTIONNAIRE

Opinion sharply divided between Madison (38 percent) and Milwaukee (35 percent) for the site of the convention. Respondents were more in agreement when it came to the length of the convention; 69 percent want it to last $2\frac{1}{2}$ days during the week, not the weekend. Pat Laskey, a salesperson from Door County, added later in his questionnaire that "if the convention were any shorter, we could not get our business completed; if it were any longer, we would be away from the office too long." Many members want to get back home the third day.

To get to the convention, 64 percent of our members will come by car. Actually, the total number of cars will be less, since twenty respondents expressed an interest in forming a car pool when asked for further suggestions in question 13. Sixty-one percent of our members will bring spouses with them. This preference plus the fact that some of our members will be sharing rooms may account for the large request for single rooms with two double beds (41 percent) and twin beds (33 percent).

FIGURE 12.7   (continued)

-2-

An impressive majority (88 percent) wants the annual presidential address scheduled during the banquet. This may be one of the few times our chapter members see each other at meals. Sixty-seven percent disliked the idea of having meals included in the price of the convention. A representative comment comes from Marsha Jabolowicz, a receptionist from Rhinelander, "I want to be able to go to different places suited to my schedule; I do not want to be tied to a rigid itinerary." If they miss each other at meals, members may likely see each other at night spots. Forty percent prefer going to a nightclub for convention entertainment; and 32 percent voted for dancing ("a swinging disco") to be included.

Our members will represent our chapter in force on state committees. Seventy-two percent have agreed to serve on a committee; the committee on marketing captured the attention of 59 members.

RECOMMENDATIONS

On the basis of these responses, I think we should tell the state office that our members prefer a $2\frac{1}{2}$-day convention in Madison, although Milwaukee is a strong alternate location. We will need a large block of double-occupancy rooms; and meals should not be part of the convention package, but dancing or a nightclub should. Further, our members want the presidential address delivered at the banquet.

Our members' preferences are clear in most instances. In forwarding their responses to the state office, I would recommend that we try to charter a bus for those individuals (36 percent) who did want group transportation provided.

Please let me have your comments on these recommendations by February 21 so that we can start making plans for this year's convention.

FIGURE 12.7   (continued)

-3-

A Questionnaire on
Preferences for 1990 Convention of
the Wisconsin Real Estate Association

Dear Members of the Northern Chapter of the WREA:

Please complete the following questionnaire so that our state office will be
better able to plan for this year's convention. Your comments will help make
this year's gathering even more productive than last year's.

Thank you for returning your questionnaire to me by January 31. A
stamped, addressed envelope is included for your convenience. If you have
any questions, please write or call me.

Cordially,

Mary Snyder

Mary Snyder
Mary's Realty
742 Kane Avenue
Superior, WI 54880-2607
(715) 882-5030

Name _____

Business address _____

Business telephone _____

Home address _____

Home telephone _____

FIGURE 12.7   (continued)

-4-

1. What kind of membership do you hold in the WREA?
   ___ secretary/receptionist
   ___ salesperson
   ___ broker
   ___ builder

2. Did you attend last year's WREA convention in Green Bay?
   ___ yes
   ___ no

3. Where would you like the 1990 WREA convention to be held?
   ___ Milwaukee
   ___ Madison
   ___ Eau Claire
   ___ La Crosse
   ___ other (please specify) _____

4. How long would you like the convention to last?
   ___ 1 day
   ___ 1½ days
   ___ 2 days
   ___ 2½ days
   ___ 3 days

5. When would you like the convention to be held?
   ___ during the week
   ___ on the weekend

6. How would you like to travel to the convention?
   ___ by car
   ___ by bus
   ___ fly
   ___ have group transportation provided

7. Will your spouse accompany you?
   ___ yes
   ___ no

8. What kinds of accommodations will you need?
   ___ single room (one double bed)
   ___ single room (two twin beds)
   ___ single room (two double beds)
   ___ two rooms

FIGURE 12.7   (continued)

-5-

9. When should the presidential address be given?
    ___ at a breakfast meeting
    ___ at a luncheon meeting
    ___ at a banquet
    ___ alone, at a separate meeting

10. Would you prefer to see meals included in the cost of the convention fees?
    ___ yes
    ___ no

11. What type of entertainment do you think the WREA should provide at the convention?
    ___ dancing
    ___ theater
    ___ nightclub
    ___ other (please specify) _____

12. Which state committees would you be willing to serve on?
    ___ finance
    ___ marketing
    ___ appraisal
    ___ planning
    ___ I do not wish to serve on a committee

13. Please add any further comments about any of the previous questions or any other relevant topic you think the WREA should consider.

    _____

    _____

    _____

    _____

    _____

    _____

may be times, too, when a majority opinion still calls for qualification. In recommending that a chartered bus be ordered, Ms. Snyder at once acknowledges the majority's wishes, but still allows for the most flexible interpretation of the responses. No one loses by the recommendation that she submits.

At the end of your report, tell readers exactly what you would like them to do next—approve your recommendations, meet with you (specify a date) to discuss the recommendations, and the like. See page 201 of Chapter 8 for some ways to conclude your report.

◆ CONCLUSION

Questionnaires are valuable tools that can help you in school and on the job. You need to follow a careful process to prepare an effective questionnaire and summarize the results. Most important, revise and pretest your questions to make sure they are reliable. In selecting your respondents, follow a systematic plan to sample a significant number of people who have the appropriate background to answer your questionnaire knowledgeably. After tabulating the results of the questionnaire, you are ready to write your survey report. The report should concisely summarize respondents' major opinions without burdening readers with unnecessary details. Any recommendations your report offers must be precise to help readers make the most effective use of your respondents' opinions.

◆ EXERCISES

1. Write a memo (see pages 197–201 for format and organization) to an employer—previous or current—about a specific problem that needs investigation. Indicate why a questionnaire would be the best means of gathering information and stress how the results would lead to increased sales, better service, or greater productivity. In your memo specify whom you will question, how you will get their names and addresses, and the timetable you will follow in constructing the questionnaire, distributing it, tallying the results, and writing the report.

2. Select some area of interest to a civic organization, club, fraternity or sorority, union, or church group to which you belong. In a letter to the president of this organization, explain how a questionnaire on this specific area would help the group—in membership, long-range planning, meetings, dues, etc. Volunteer to construct a questionnaire and to distribute it to members of the organization.

3. Write an appropriate closed question (dichotomous, multiple-choice, rating-scale, ranking, or fill-in-the-blank) for each one of the following topics. Where necessary, supply appropriate options.
   a. marital status
   b. general health
   c. income
   d. religion

e. credit rating
f. expectation for promotion
g. vacation preferences
h. a household product
i. college tuition
j. local liquor laws
k. medical costs

l. security on campus
m. airplanes vs. buses for travel
n. writing a résumé
o. senior citizen discounts
p. garbage pickup
q. a local television station
r. telephone service

4. The following closed questions (and some of their options) are incorrectly worded. Rewrite the questions and the options to eliminate vague terms, loaded words, jargon, overlapping responses, double adjectives, an insufficient range of responses, and the other kinds of errors discussed in this chapter.

   a. Should our city risk legalizing gambling?   yes ___   no ___

   b. Are people upset with the new leash laws?   yes ___   no ___   maybe ___

   c. I find everything I need at one store.   agree ___   disagree ___

   d. What kind of classes do you like?
   morning ___
   afternoon ___
   evening ___
   fifty-minute ___
   seventy-minute ___

   e. Do you regularly read a newspaper or current events magazine? yes ___   no ___

   f. Would you characterize yourself as being carpophagous?   yes ___   no ___

   g. Do you agree that teaching sex education in our schools has led to more teenage pregnancies and abortions and to looser morals in our already too permissive society?   agree ___   disagree ___

   h. Are you married or divorced?   yes ___   no ___

   i. What kind of beverage do you like?
   coffee ___
   tea ___
   milk ___
   soft drinks ___
   carbonated drinks ___

   j. Do you vote in all elections as a patriotic citizen?   yes ___   no ___

   k. Have you purchased any articles of clothing recently?   yes ___   no ___

   l. Into which group would you place yourself?
   full-time employee ___
   part-time employee ___
   work weekends only ___
   work nights ___

   m. Don't you think our government has spent too much money on relocating refugees?   yes ___   no ___

   n. Did you see the recession coming six years ago?   yes ___   no ___

   o. Give the name of the person who, in your opinion, cheats most on the time card:
   _____

p. How often do you ride your bicycle?
not very often ___
a few times ___
several times ___
as much as I can ___

q. Rank the following in their order of importance to you.
fringe benefits ___
health insurance policy ___
two weeks paid vacation ___
company car ___

r. Is your education meaningful to you now?   yes ___ no ___

s. Where do you live?
with my parents ___
in a trailer court ___
in a condo ___
by myself ___
in an apartment building ___
in a house ___

t. All housing loans should be guaranteed by the federal government, shouldn't they?   yes ___ no ___

u. Do you like to swim and to fish?   yes ___ no ___

v. Did the RPT come in the morning or the afternoon?   A.M. ___ P.M. ___

w. Do you understand enough mathematics to be able to complete this simple form by yourself?   yes ___ no ___

5. Rewrite the following open-ended questions to make them more precise and answerable.
a. What kinds of experiences have you had in the hospital?
b. What improvements in city services are necessary in the future?
c. Describe your philosophy of life.
d. What kinds of entertainment do you like?
e. Compare and contrast the kinds of housing opportunities in your town.
f. What appeals to you about your career?
g. Comment on any changes you have seen in the last year.
h. Describe in detail all the lectures you have attended this term.
i. What kinds of investments should a family make today?
j. Comment on the state of the environment.
k. Tell me all you know about horse husbandry.
l. What aspects of transportation in our town should be changed?
m. What kinds of regulations does the government impose on senior citizens?
n. What are some problems in higher education today?
o. What agencies are most successful today?

6. The following questionnaire contains unclear instructions, an inconsistent format, poorly worded and irrelevant questions, and inappropriate options. Rewrite the instructions and the questionnaire.

Hi, how are you today? We think that it would be a good idea for everyone to participate in a coffee fund soon. Complete the enclosed questionnaire soon and return it to me. You will have to circle some of the responses, check others, and write in still some other answers. Answer all the questions you feel confident about. If you check "I do not drink coffee" for any of the responses, use a red pencil; this will help flag your answer. If you do not check this as a response, use a blue or black pen. When you see questions asking for opinions you would rather not give, answer them anyway.

1. Do you like working here?   yes ___   it's all right ___   no ___

2. How long have you worked in this office?   0–1 month ___
   3–12 months ___   1–3 years ___   3–8 years ___   more than 8 years but less than 12 years ___   more than 12 years ___

3. What is your current salary? _____   Is it fair? _____

4. Do you have a cup of coffee before work?   yes ___
   I do not drink coffee ___   sometimes ___   no ___   it varies ___

5. When do you drink most of your coffee?   A.M. ___   P.M. ___   nights ___

6. Where do you get your coffee while at work?
   ___ I bring a thermos bottle from home.
   ___ I purchase it before coming to work.
   ___ I stop off at a restaurant and have it.
   ___ I borrow some.
   ___ I do not drink coffee.

7. How much coffee do you drink at work?
   ___ 0–2 cups a day   ___ 1–2 cups   ___ 3–5 cups   ___ more than 5 cups a day   ___ I do not drink coffee   ___ I seldom drink coffee at work

8. How do you like your coffee? Circle one of the following:
   a. black
   b. black with sugar
   c. freshly perked
   d. decaffeinated
   e. cream
   f. instant's OK
   g. milk
   h. dry roasted
   i. freeze-dried
   j. decaffeinated freeze-dried
   k. mellow roast blend

9. Would you like to have a coffee fund in our office?
   a. Yes, right now.
   b. Yes, not right now.
   If you circled (b), answer one of the following:
   ___ within the next month
   ___ within the next six months
   ___ within the next year
   c. No, but I would not oppose a coffee fund.
   d. No, I think it is a bad idea.

10. Do you think a coffee fund would be a good idea?   yes ___   no ___

11. Would a coffee fund bring people together?   yes ___   no ___   I do not know right now ___

12. Should we let people buy coffee by the single cup? If so, how much should we charge per cup?
    ___ we should charge .05¢ a cup
    ___ twenty cents a cup
    ___ thirty-five cents
    ___ whatever they want to contribute

13. Should we allow people outside our office to participate in the coffee fund?
    yes ___   no ___   on a limited basis ___   it depends ___

14. How much should we charge people outside the office for a cup of coffee?
    ___ ten cents   ___ thirty cents
    ___ fifteen cents   ___ thirty-five cents
    ___ twenty cents   ___ the same as we pay
    ___ twenty-five cents   ___ twenty to thirty cents a cup
    ___ I do not want them to buy our coffee

15. Who should prepare the coffee and collect for it?
    ___ Let's hire a caterer.
    ___ Everyone in the coffee fund should take a turn.
    ___ We should appoint two people.
    ___ We should draw lots.
    ___ Each of us should share the responsibility by drawing lots.

16. Please add any other comments. You might want to state again whether you are in favor of the fund, how much coffee you drink, and whether the office manager should provide the funds or the time to prepare the coffee.

7. Construct a questionnaire for the topic you selected in either Exercise 1 or Exercise 2 above. Distribute it, and then, after tabulating the responses, prepare a report about your findings for your employer or the president of the organization to which you belong. Also supply your employer or president with a blank copy of the questionnaire and a sample cover letter you have sent with your questionnaire.

13

Designing Visuals

Experts estimate that as much as 80 percent of our learning comes through the sense of sight. The written word, of course, forms a large part of our visual information. In conjunction with words, visual aids (hereafter shortened to "visuals") convey a giant share of the facts we receive. Visuals are especially useful on the job because they help readers to see what you are discussing. Chapter 13 surveys the kinds of visuals you will encounter most frequently and shows you how to read, construct, and use them. A discussion of visuals, however, is not confined to just this chapter. They are important in preparing successful instructions, proposals, and written and oral reports.

The kinds of visuals we will deal with can be divided into two categories—tables and figures. A table lists information in parallel columns or rows for easy comparison of data. Anything that is not a table is considered a figure, including graphs, circle charts, bar charts, pictograms, organizational charts, flow charts, maps, photographs, and drawings. Before looking at the various kinds of visuals, you may find it helpful to know more about the benefits they offer and the caution you must exercise in using them.

◆ THE USEFULNESS OF VISUALS

What can visuals do to improve your written work? Here are four reasons why you should use them. Each of the four points is graphically reinforced in Figure 13.1.

1. Visuals arouse immediate interest. Their size, shape, color, and arrangement are dramatic. They also offer readers relief from looking at sentences and paragraphs. Note how eye-catching (in both number and shape) the symbols are for the world's ten most populous countries represented in Figure 13.1. A visual captures readers' attention by setting important information apart.

2. Visuals simplify concepts. Because many readers are visually oriented, graphics unlock doors of meaning. A visual shows ideas in action when a verbal

FIGURE 13.1 A visual showing the ten most populous countries in the world.

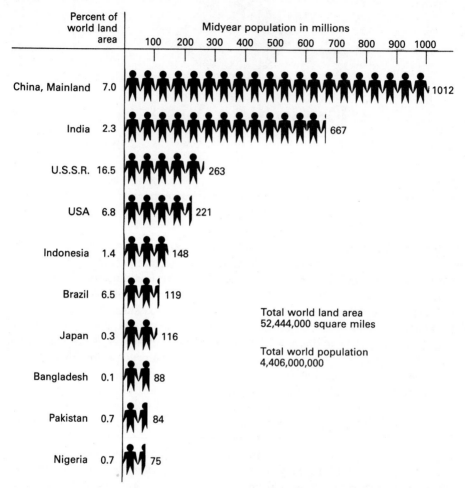

U.S. Department of Commerce. *Pocket Data Book USA 1979* (Washington, D.C.: U.S. Government Printing Office, 1979): iv.

description may be less forceful or more difficult to understand. A visual can make technical information easier to comprehend. Moreover, visuals can simplify densely packed statistical data. The vastness of a country's population and how that population compares with other nations' is much easier to grasp and to remember because of the pictogram (picture symbols) in Figure 13.1. Other kinds of visuals also make learning easier. For example, a visual could show the interior parts of a machine or enlarge one element of a piece of equipment to clarify its function or relationship to another part. Readers would therefore feel more confident about operating the machine or performing a procedure.

3. Visuals condense a large quantity of information into a relatively small space. Figure 13.1 collects twenty different pieces of information—the population and amount of land occupied by ten countries—and records the data in far less space than it would take to describe these facts in words. In a discussion of the populations of these countries, how many times would a writer have to repeat the words *population, land area, percent, more, less, greater, lower, in comparison,* or *in contrast*? And even if the writer transcribed all the facts in Figure 13.1 into words, readers would not be able to understand the percentages as easily as they can the rows of symbols.

4. Visuals emphasize relationships. Through the use of arrangement and form, visuals quickly show contrasts, similarities, growth rates, downward and upward movements, fluctuations in price and time, and the influence of one variable on another. Figure 13.1 shows not only how countries compare in population, but also how population compares with land area. India, for example, has about two and one-half times more people than the Soviet Union does, but occupies about one-eighth the space. Other kinds of visuals (pie and bar charts, discussed on pages 404–10) show the relationship of parts to the whole. And the curve of a graph can indicate the sequence of various events, such as average annual snowfall.

◆ CHOOSING EFFECTIVE VISUALS

You will have to select visuals very carefully. The following suggestions may help you to answer two important questions: (1) When should I use a visual? and (2) How many of them will I need?

1. Use visuals only when they are strictly relevant for your purpose and audience. Visuals should not be included simply as decoration for impressing readers. A short report on fire drills does not need a picture of a fire station to enhance it; a list of instructions on how to prepare a company report does not require a picture of an individual writing at a table.

2. Use visuals in conjunction with, not as a substitute for, written work. Visuals do not always take the place of words. You may need to explain information contained in a visual. A set of illustrations or a group of tables alone will not satisfy readers looking for summaries or evaluations.

3. Make sure that visuals do not interfere with your message. Too many visuals (some of them duplicating information in your text) will distract readers. If something is self-explanatory, do not include a visual. Avoid visuals that include many more details than you discuss or, worse yet, that present information that contradicts your work.

4. Consider carefully how a specific visual will help your readers. Elaborate graphs are unnecessarily complex for a community group interested only in a clear representation of the rise in food prices over a three-month period. If you have to include a detailed, complex visual to make an important point, be prepared to explain it to your readers, especially if they are not familiar with your work or the technical discipline you are writing about. Generally, the less technical your audience, the more helpful a simple visual is.

5. Never include a visual of poor quality; each should be clear and easy to read. Do not assume that readers will have magnifying glasses on their desks or that they will tolerate a messy drawing or a faded blueprint. If you photocopy a visual, make sure the copy is readable and that it does not cut off important parts of the original.

6. If you construct your own visual, do a model or sample first. It is hard to make a perfect visual on the first try.

7. Consider how your visuals will look on the page layout. Visuals should add to the overall appearance of your work, not detract from it. Observe generous margins. Don't cram visuals onto a page. If you type your paper and intend to add visuals later, make sure you leave enough room for them.

◆ THE GRAPHIC ARTIST'S DESK

When you prepare your own effective visuals, you will need the right tools. That does not mean that you must purchase elaborate equipment to produce clear and professional-looking visuals to accompany your assignments. The materials to do the job can easily be obtained at your college bookstore or your local office supply store. If you are preparing your own visuals by hand, you may want to purchase the tools and materials discussed in this section.

The basic tools of the illustrator's trade include a straightedge (or twelve-inch ruler), a plastic triangle to measure and make angles, a protractor, and a compass to make arcs. Also it is a good idea to have scissors, glue, and transparent tape.

You may also need some high-quality writing instruments. You might want to invest in an artist's pen set containing various points for lettering, sketching, and making elegant designs in a variety of colors. (If you do not anticipate using the pen set often, then buy a fine felt-tipped pen, or perhaps a few of them in different colors.) Use the artist's pens for your final copy, but for rough sketches have a supply of pencils in hard and soft leads. If you make a mistake, soft lead erases easily.

Not only must visuals be designed effectively, they should appear on suitable paper. Depending on your needs, you might want to purchase a drawing pad, some graph paper, maybe a pasteboard, and even some tracing paper.

One of the most serviceable materials you can buy for any graphic work will be templates. These are clear plastic sheets that contain a variety of cutout designs that can be traced onto a sheet of paper. Templates offer such basic shapes as circles, triangles, rectangles, trapezoids, dollar signs, and crosses. Other templates offer chemical and mathematical symbols. Depending on your technical needs and interests, you can find a template to suit any purpose. Figure 13.2 shows some sample templates.

If you are using a computer to prepare your visuals, the chances are that a particular graphics software package will make various template shapes available to you. See pages 423–27.

FIGURE 13.2   Templates for office planning, for traffic control, and for chemistry.

◆ WRITING ABOUT VISUALS

Never include a visual without mentioning it in your paper or report. Readers should be told where the visual is located and why it is there. The following guidelines on identifying, inserting, introducing, and interpreting visuals will help you use them more efficiently.

1. Identifying visuals. Each visual must have a number, title, or both, that indicate the subject and the way in which it is discussed. An unidentified visual is meaningless. Tables and figures should be numbered separately throughout the text.

> Table 1: Paul Jordan's Work Schedule, January 15–23.
> Figure 2: The Proper Way to Apply for a Small Business Loan.
> Figure 5: Income Estimation Figures for Weekdale Shopping Center.

If you use a visual that is not your own work, you must identify your source (a specific newspaper, magazine, textbook, federal agency, or individual). If your paper or report is intended for publication, you are required by law to obtain permission to reproduce copyrighted material from the copyright holder.

2. Inserting visuals in the text. Place visuals as close as possible to the discussion of them. Never introduce a visual before a discussion of it; readers will wonder why it is there. By placing an appropriate visual at the beginning of your discussion, you will help your readers understand the discussion better than if you place it near the end. Be sure to tell readers where the visual is found—

"below," "on the following page," "to the right," "at the bottom of page 3." If the visual is small enough, insert it directly in the text rather than on a separate page. If your visual occupies an entire page, place that page containing your visual immediately after the page that makes the first reference to it.

3. Introducing visuals. Refer to the visual by its number and, if necessary, mention the title as well. In introducing the visual, though, do not just insert a reference to it; relate the visual to the context of your discussion. Here are three ways of writing a lead-in sentence for visuals.

> Poor: Our store saw a dramatic rise in the shipment of electric ranges over the five-year period as opposed to the less impressive increase in washing machines. (See Figure 3.)

This sentence does not tie the visual (Figure 3) into the sentence where it belongs. The visual just trails insignificantly behind.

> Better: As Figure 3 shows, our store saw a dramatic rise in the shipment of electric ranges over the five-year period as opposed to the less impressive increase in washing machines.

Mentioning the visual in Figure 3 at the beginning is distracting. Readers will want to stop and look at the visual immediately before they know what it is or how you are using it.

> Best: Over the last five-year period, our store realized a dramatic rise in the shipment of electric ranges as opposed to the less impressive increase in the shipment of washing machines, as shown in Figure 3 below.

This sentence is the best of the three because the figure reference and the explanation are in the same sentence, but the reference is not a distraction.

4. Interpreting visuals. Sometimes the figures in a visual tell an incomplete or misleading story and you will need to interpret them in context. In a study on the benefits of vanpooling one writer supplied the following visual.

Travel Time (in minutes): Automobile versus Vanpool

Private automobile	*Vanpool*
25	32.5
30	39.0
35	45.5
40	52.0
45	58.5
50	65.0
55	71.5
60	78.0

Source: U.S. Department of Transportation, *Increased Transportation Efficiency Through Ridesharing: The Brokerage Approach* (Washington, D.C., January 1977, DOT-OS-40096): 45.

The writer then called attention to what the visual did not say.

Although it is estimated that the travel time in a vanpool may be as much as 30% longer than in a private automobile (to allow for pickups), the total trip time for the vanpool user can be about the same as with a private automobile because vanpools eliminate the need to search for parking spaces and to walk to the employment site entrance.[1]

In addition to mentioning a visual by number and title, it may also be necessary to tell readers why it is there and what specifically to look for. Of course, you should not spend time repeating information that is obvious from looking at the visual. But occasionally you will want to interpret the visual for an audience. A director of an alumni association, eager to sell alumni life insurance, used the following table and then supplied a "sales" conclusion for it.

Consider this table based upon the U.S. Department of Labor Consumer Price Index for the past ten years. The value of insurance-benefit dollars decreases right along with dollars used in everyday expenses.

Average Annual Inflation Rates

Year	Inflation rate	Relative dollar value
1976	15.8	$1.00a
1977	6.5	.94
1978	7.7	.87
1979	11.3	.78
1980	13.5	.69
1981	10.4	.63
1982	6.1	.60
1983	3.2	.58
1984	4.3	.56
1985	3.6	.54
1986	1.9	.53

If you haven't looked at your life insurance coverage recently, you may be surprised. Benefit levels thought sufficient just a few years ago may be inadequate for current and future needs. For example, a $10,000 benefit from 1976 would have to be increased to $18,868 in 1986 to provide the same level of protection.

Example used courtesy of Department of Alumni Relations, Northwestern University, Evanston, Illinois.

◆ TABLES

Tables are parallel columns or rows of information that present statistical data compiled over several weeks or months. The figures are then organized and arranged into categories to show changes in time, distance, cost, employment, or some other quantifiable variable.

But the tabular form can present more than numerical information. Lists of words can also be put into tables. Tables in textbooks summarize material for

---

[1] James A. Devine, "Vanpooling: A New Economic Tool," *AIDC Journal* 15 (Oct. 1980): 13. Reprinted by permission.

TABLE 13.1 Comparison of Forms of Business Organization

	Single proprietorship	Partnership	Corporation
Ease of organization	Easiest	Moderately difficult	Most difficult
Availability of capital	Least	Intermediate	Most (best able to raise capital)
Responsibility	Centered in one person	Spread among partners	Policy set by directors; president supervises day-to-day operation
Incentive to succeed	Centered in one person	Spread among partners	Spread among many
Flexibility	Greatest	Intermediate	Least
Ability to perform varied functions	Dependent on one individual's versatility	Dependent on capabilities of two or more	Best able to employ versatile individuals
Possibility of conflict in management	None	Most prone to conflict	Chain of command reduces internal conflict; wide ownership minimizes disagreement
Taxation	No corporate income tax	No corporate income tax	Corporate income tax
Distribution of profits or losses	All to proprietor	Distributed to partners in accordance with partnership agreement	Profits retained or distributed to stockholders as dividends; losses reduce price of stock
Liability for debts in event of failure	Unlimited	Unlimited, but spread among partners	Limited to each stockholder's investment
Length of life	Limited by one individual's life span (or until he or she goes out of business)	Limited (partnership is reorganized upon death or withdrawl of any partner)	Unlimited (with ownership of shares readily transferable)

Source: Reprinted by permission from Sanford D. Gordon and George G. Dawson, *Introductory Economics*, 6th ed. Lexington, MA: D.C. Heath, 1987: 83.

Table number   Column heading   Subcolumn heading

TABLE 13.2   Veterans Attending Lincoln-area VFW Posts[a]

| Period of service | Years attending | | | |
	1975	1980	1985	1990
World War I	59	55	22	12
World War II	1330	1309	1100	963
Korean Conflict	240	230	205	186
Vietnam[b]	423	570	598	614

Source: Lincoln VFW Association ⟵——— Origin of data
[a] Does not include Bayside, Morton, or Westover } Footnotes
[b] August 1964–May 1975

⟍— Stub

easy recall—causes of wars, symptoms of diseases, provisions of a law. Various forms of business organizations are compared in Table 13.1. Observe how the table easily summarizes much information and arranges it in quickly identifiable categories.

To prepare a table properly, you must know how to construct and label it. Refer to Table 13.2 as you read the following instructions.

Preparing a Table

First determine the size of the table. If it is small (two or three columns) and you include it within the text, center the table on the page. Leave at least one inch of white space above and below the table. If the table has a title, place it at the top (figure titles go above or below the visual), and triple space before and after the table. You might first want to determine a border and then very neatly put in the columns. Then you will have the right spaces and slots in which to insert your numbers or words. Leave adequate space between columns so that the table will not look crowded or be difficult to decipher.

If the table is large (running to five or six columns), place it on a separate sheet of paper. Again, depending on the size of the table, list the columns at the top of the page or turn the piece of paper broadside and then do the table that way. If possible, use the same margins as with the text of your paper. Make sure that the reader can easily see the numbers and letters of your table.

Labeling a Table

Provide headings for both the column and subcolumns; in Table 13.2 the column is entitled "Years attending," and the subcolumns are the years (1975, 1980, 1985, 1990) about which the table gives data. Also provide a title for the *stub,* the first vertical column on the left-hand side. The stub heading is "Period of service" in Table 13.2. The stub lists the items (the wars and conflicts in which the

Lincoln-area veterans participated) that are broken down under the subheadings. To separate the stub title and column/subcolumn headings from the body of the table, draw a rule (a line) across the table as in Table 13.2.

Label the categories appropriately and consistently. If some form of measurement is consistently involved, include the unit of measurement as part of the column heading—weight (in pounds), distance (in miles), time (per hour), quantity (per dozen). The unit of measurement should not be repeated for each entry in a column. Also, units should be consistent; do not jump from miles to meters, pounds to ounces.

Wrong:	Weight	Height
	120 lbs	165 cm
	132 lbs	5' 9"
	122 lbs	5' 7"
	58.5 kg	172 cm
Correct:	Weight (in kilograms)	Height (in centimeters)
	54.0	165
	55.2	176
	54.9	166
	58.5	172

If something in the table needs to be explained or qualified, put in a footnote (often signaled by a small raised letter: [a] or [b]) in the table where the information is to be further identified or qualified. The letter will then refer readers to an explanation directly below the table. In Table 13.2 the [a] after the title points to the qualification that three communities were not considered in the Lincoln area when data for the table were gathered. The [b] after the Vietnam entry in the stub clarifies the official dates for that conflict.

◆ FIGURES

As we pointed out at the beginning of this chapter, any visual that is not a table is classified as a figure. We will now look at nine types of useful figures, starting with graphs.

Graphs

Graphs transform numbers into pictures. They take statistical data presented in tables and put them into rising and falling lines, steep or gentle curves. Graphs vividly portray changes, fluctuations, trends, increases and decreases in profits, employment, energy, temperatures, or any other statistics that change frequently. The way the lines rise and fall in the graph depicts the kinds of changes and sometimes helps readers forecast trends. The resulting pictures are more dra-

FIGURE 13.3   A graph of the amount of snowfall in Springfield.

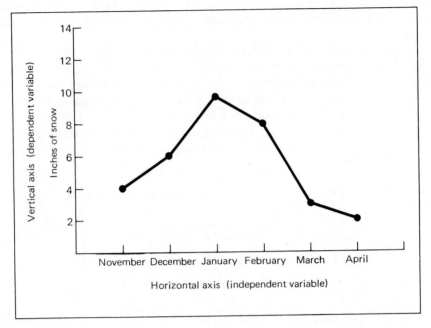

matic than tables and are easier to read and interpret. Many issues of the *Wall Street Journal,* for example, contain a graph on the first page for the benefit of busy readers who want a great deal of financial information summarized quickly.

Basically, a graph consists of two lines—a vertical axis and a horizontal axis—that intersect to form a right angle as in Figure 13.3. The space between the two lines contains the picture made by the graph (in Figure 13.3 the amount of snowfall in Springfield between November 1989 and April 1990). The vertical line represents the dependent variable; the horizontal line, the independent variable. The dependent variable is influenced most directly by the independent variable, which is almost always expressed in terms of time or distance. Hence, in Figure 13.3 the given month affects the amount of snow Springfield received. The vertical axis is read from bottom to top; the horizontal axis is read from left to right. When the dependent variable occurs at a particular time on the independent variable (horizontal line), the place where the two points intersect is marked, or plotted, on the graph. After the points are plotted, a line is drawn to connect them; the resulting curve gives a picture of which months had the greatest snow and which the least and what the overall pattern of snowfall was in Springfield.

The way in which scales are set up is crucial to the success of a graph. Many graphs may not have ranges indicated by equally spaced lines (tick marks):

But on most of the graphs you construct, use tick marks as a scale to show values, distances, or time, as in Figure 13.3. The topic will dictate the intervals to use. The time scale (independent variable) can be calculated in minutes, hours, days, or years.

A temperature-pulse-respiration graph is illustrated in Figure 13.4. The day is divided into six four-hour periods, and seven days are represented on one sheet. The temperature axis is divided into degrees (with .2° differences), and a heavy black line shows the normal line, making it easier to spot dangerous elevations. The pulse measurements are registered in two-beat differences (each dot represents two beats within the larger grouping of tens). And the respirations are also measured in twos, each dot there representing every time a patient takes two

FIGURE 13.4 A temperature-pulse-respiration graph showing the breakdown within ranges.

breaths. Note that the temperature and pulse scales have a *suppressed zero line*; they begin with 95° and thirty beats, not with zero. It would be impossible to have lower numbers for pulse and temperature and expect a patient to live. But the respiration scale begins with zero because it has a lower range (0–60). If these recordings were expressed in tabular form, they would be hard to follow because they would deprive the reader of a curve depicting much information quickly and impressively.

The graphs in Figures 13.3 and 13.4 contain only one line per category. But a graph can have multiple lines to show how a number of dependent variables (conditions, products) compare with each other. The relative productivity of corn, wheat, and soybeans in American agriculture can be seen in the graph in Figure 13.5. The graph contains a separate line for each of these three crop groups. At a glance readers can see how the three crop groups compare and also how many billions of bushels of each group were produced annually. Note how every group is clearly differentiated from the others by means of dots, dashes, or an unbroken line. Color, if available, can also help distinguish lines. Also, note how each line is clearly labeled so that the label does not cover up other lines or their points of intersection. If the lines do run close together, a *legend*, or explanatory note, underneath or above the graph identifies individual lines. Never put the legend within the graph; readers may confuse legend information with

FIGURE 13.5   A multiple-line graph showing how the production of corn, wheat, and soybeans compare.

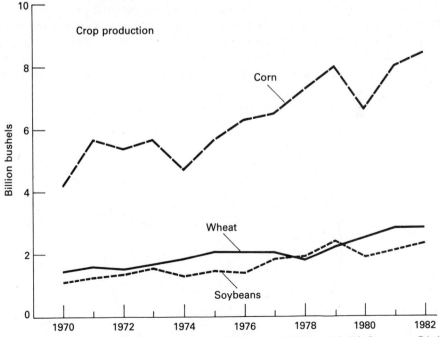

U.S. Bureau of the Census, *Statistical Abstract of the United States* (Washington, D.C.: U.S. Government Printing Office, 1984) xxviii.

the data depicted in the graph. Although some graphs may contain as many as five or six lines, it is better to limit multiple-line graphs to two or three lines (or dependent variables) so that readers can interpret the graph more easily.

Keep in mind the following guidelines when you construct a graph.

1. Inform readers what your scale is: how many dots, boxes, or spaces equal what amounts or times. If you are drawing your own graph, you may want to use graph paper that has tick marks or carefully divided lines.
2. Keep the scale consistent and realistic. If you start with hours, do not switch to days or vice versa. If you are recording annual rates or accounts, do not skip a year or two in the hope that you will save time or be more concise. Do not jump from 1979, 1980, 1981–1983, 1985, 1987, 1990. Put in all the years you are surveying.
3. For some graphs there is no need to begin with a zero, as was seen in Figure 13.4. For others, you may not have to include numbers beyond seven or eight.
4. Do not draw a line or plot a curve that goes outside the limits of the graph and extends beyond the margin of the page.

Circle Charts

Circle charts are also known as pie charts, a name that descriptively points to their construction and interpretation. Figure 13.6 shows an example of a circle chart. The full circle, or pie, represents the whole amount (100 percent) of an industry, profession, or population group. The full circle can stand for the entire budget of a company or family, or it can represent just a single dollar of that budget and show how it is broken down for various expenses. Each slice of the pie, then, stands for a part of the whole. A circle chart effectively allows readers to see

FIGURE 13.6   A circle chart showing the proposed Midtown city budget for 1991.

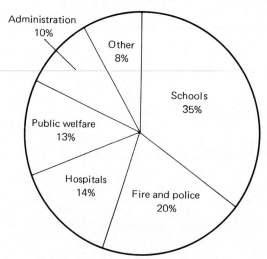

two things at once—the relationship of the parts to one another and the relationship of the parts to the whole.

The circle chart is one of the most easily understood illustrations. For that reason, it is popular in government documents (the Bureau of the Census relies heavily on it), financial reports, and advertising messages. Although many circle charts are based on tables, tables can be very complex and dry and also more detailed than circle charts. The circle gives percentage totals; the table shows how those percentage groups are broken down.

To construct a successful pie chart by hand, you will need a compass to make your circle and a protractor to measure sections of it. The mathematical principle underlying the construction of the circle chart is simple. A circle contains 360°. Translated into percentages, 100% = 360°, 10% = 36°, and 1% = 3.6°. To determine how much space you need for each of your slices, or wedges, figure out the percentage of the whole it expresses and then multiply that number by 3.6. For example, if you are constructing a circle chart to represent a family's budget, the percentage/degree breakdown might be as follows.

Housing	25%	90.0°
Food	22%	79.2°
Energy	20%	72.0°
Clothes	13%	46.8°
Health care	12%	43.2°
Miscellaneous	8%	28.8°

Don't forget that all the individual slices of the pie must total 100 percent. Now follow these four rules to construct your circle chart.

1. Do not divide a circle, or pie, into too few or too many slices. If you have only three wedges, consider using another type of visual to display them (a bar chart, for example, which will be discussed later). If you have more than seven or eight wedges, you will divide the pie too narrowly, and the overcrowding will destroy the dramatic effect of the illustration. Instead, combine several slices of small percentages (2 percent, 3 percent, 4 percent) into one slice labeled "Other," "Miscellaneous," or "Related Items."

2. Put the largest slice of the pie first, at the 12 o'clock position, and then move clockwise with proportionately smaller slices. Beginning with the biggest slice, you call attention to its importance. The one exception is that the "Other" category (see above) should be placed last, even when it is largest, as in Figure 13.6.

3. Label each slice of the pie. If the slice is large enough, write the identifying term or quantity inside, but make sure that it is horizontal and big enough to read. Do not put in a label upside down or slide it in vertically. If the individual slice of the pie is small, do not try to squeeze in a label. Connect a line to the outside of the pie nearest the slice and insert the appropriate label there, as in Figure 13.6.

4. You can shade or color alternating slices of the pie to further separate the parts. If you do, be careful not to obscure labels and percentages; also make certain that adjacent slices can be distinguished readily from each other.

Bar Charts

A bar chart shows a series of vertical or horizontal bars to indicate comparisons of statistical data. For instance, vertical bars are used to show increases in quantities (students using a library) in Figure 13.7; horizontal bars depict increases in distance (the number of feet the shotput is thrown by a women's track and field team) in Figure 13.8. Bar charts make a dramatic visual impression on the audience. They are valuable tools in sales meetings to demonstrate how well (or poorly) a product, a service, the company, or a salesperson has done. You often see bar charts at an office recording the financial goals for the United Way or other charitable drives.

Bar charts are less exact than tables, as Figures 13.7 and 13.8 show. Note that the number of students using the library or the number of feet the shotput is thrown are not expressed in precise figures, as they would be in a table, but are approximated by the length of the bar. Do not assume, however, that the bar chart is inaccurate; many bar charts are based on tables. What you lose in precision with a bar chart, you gain in visual flair. Another advantage of a bar chart is that it is easier to construct than a line graph. Finally, a bar chart is much more fluid and dynamic than a circle. The circle is static; the bar chart (like the graph) presents a moving view.

When should you use a bar chart rather than a table or graph? Your audience will help you decide. If you are asked to present statistics on costs for the com-

FIGURE 13.7 A vertical bar chart showing the number of students using the Adams Memorial Library.

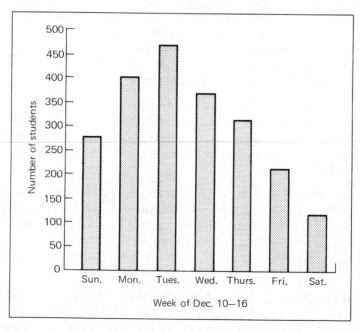

FIGURE 13.8. A horizontal bar chart showing length of shotput throws by a women's track and field team.

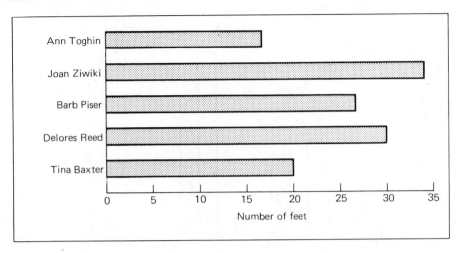

pany accountant, use a table. In that situation the reader demands a precise listing; an accountant does not judge a visual by its eye appeal. However, if you are presenting the same information to a group of stockholders or to a diverse group of employees, a bar chart may be more relevant; such readers are interested in seeing the statistics in action. They are more concerned with the effects of change than with underlying causes and precise statistical details. Since it is limited to a few columns, however, a bar chart cannot convey as much information as a table or graph.

Types of Bar Charts

One of the most common types of bar charts is the type shown in Figure 13.7. Each bar represents one day of the week, and the height of the bar corresponds to the number of students using the library on that day. To read the chart effectively, you simply note where the top of the bar is in relation to the vertical scale on the left. The chart compares one type of data (the number of students using the library) over a period of time (one week in the school year).

Another type of chart—a multiple-bar chart—is represented in Figure 13.9. Four differently shaded bars are used for each year to represent the amount of money spent on different types of advertising in America. A legend at the top of the chart explains what each bar stands for. This chart measures the amount of money spent over a period of time (fifteen years) on different media. A word of caution is in order about multiple-bar charts: never use more than four bars in a group for any one year. Otherwise, your chart will become crowded and difficult to read.

Still another kind of bar chart is the segmented, or cross-hatched (divided), bar, used to show differences within a given category for each comparison. The

FIGURE 13.9 A multiple-bar chart showing advertising expenditures by selected media: 1975 to 1990.

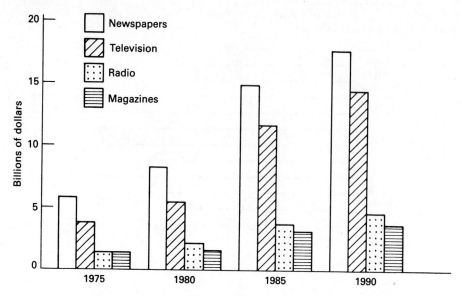

FIGURE 13.10. A segmented-bar chart showing per capita hospital care spending by funding source.

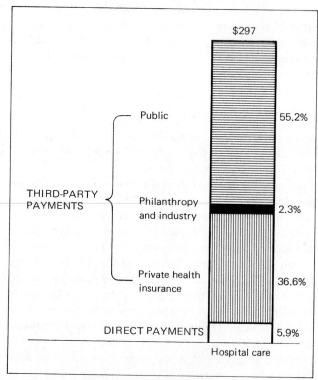

Robert M. Gibson and Charles R. Fisher, "National Health Expenditure 1977," *Social Security Bulletin* 41 (July 1978): 10.

differences are the components, percentages, or subgroups that make up the whole. A single segmented bar representing the per capita cost for hospital care is seen in Figure 13.10. The entire bar totals the payment of $297, which came from four sources (direct payments, private health insurance, philanthropy and industry, and the public). Each of these sources is represented by a different type of shading on the one column. Combined, the multiple sources account for all hospitalization payments. A group of segmented bars can be used to show multiple comparisons among many categories, as in Figure 13.11, which depicts energy consumption levels and types in five states.

Making a Bar Chart

To construct an accurate bar chart, follow these instructions.

1. Make all the bars the same width; vary only the height (or length) to show differences.

2. Select an appropriate scale and inform the readers about proportions. Be realistic. Do not construct a bar chart in which columns go off the page or are so small that readers cannot easily note differences. Look at the scale in Figure 13.7, where each division of the vertical column represents fifty students.

FIGURE 13.11 A multiple-bar, segmented-bar chart showing energy consumption by sector in five states that consumed the most energy in a given year.

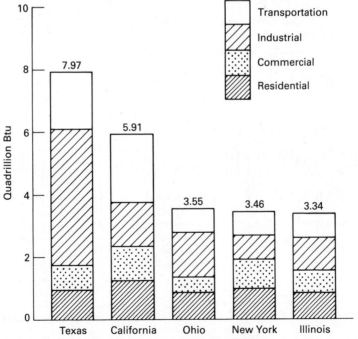

U.S. Energy Information Administration, *Monthly Energy Review,* Mar. 1984.

Keep such divisions consistent; do not make one ten students and another twenty. Also, begin with zero so that the reader can correctly chart fluctuations. Use appropriate proportions on the horizontal scale as well.

3. Identify and use distinctive markings, shadings, or colors on divided bars. Supply a clarifying legend for readers or otherwise indicate the meaning of different portions of a single cross-hatched bar, as in Figure 13.10. But do not introduce unnecessary marks or decorations.

Pictograms

Similar to a bar chart, a pictogram uses pictures instead of bars to represent differences in statistical data, as in Figure 13.1. The pictures or symbols appropriately represent the item(s) being compared. Sometimes the number of pictures indicates change, as in Figure 13.12, where the cartoon figures show Social Security recipients and workers. By increasing the size of the picture or symbol for each year, a pictogram can also show quantities, as in Figure 13.13, rather than increasing the number of symbols. However, it is usually better to increase the number of symbols rather than their size because differences in sizes are often difficult to construct accurately and hard for the reader to interpret. Whatever type of pictogram you use, though, always indicate the precise quantities involved by placing numbers after the pictures so that the reader knows exactly how much the pictures represent.

FIGURE 13.12   A pictogram indicating change in the relationship between Social Security recipients and workers.

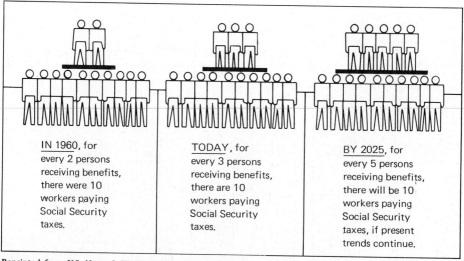

IN 1960, for every 2 persons receiving benefits, there were 10 workers paying Social Security taxes.

TODAY, for every 3 persons receiving benefits, there are 10 workers paying Social Security taxes.

BY 2025, for every 5 persons receiving benefits, there will be 10 workers paying Social Security taxes, if present trends continue.

Reprinted from *U.S. News & World Report,* 12 Jan. 1981: 65. Copyright, 1981 U.S. News & World Report, Inc. Reprinted by permission.

FIGURE 13.13   A pictogram indicating increases in U.S. peanut production.

Congressional Quarterly Weekly Report, 34 (Sept. 11, 1976): 2483. Reprinted by permission.

Organizational Charts

Unlike the charts discussed so far, the organizational chart does not contain statistical data; nor does it record movements in space or time. Rather, it pictures the chain of command in a company or agency, with the lines of authority stretching down from the chief executive, manager, or administrator to assistant manager, department heads, or supervisors to the work force of employees. The organizational chart also shows the various offices, departments, and units through which orders and information flow in the company or agency. Organizational charts help to inform employees and customers about the composition of the company and also help to coordinate employee efforts in routing information to appropriate departments.

An organizational chart shows relationship by using lines to connect rectangles or circles to each other, starting at the top with the chief executive and moving down to lower-level employees. (Sometimes the name of the individual holding the office is listed in addition to the title of the office.) Examine the organizational chart in Figure 13.14. Positions of equal authority are on parallel lines, and all jobs under the supervision of one individual are joined by bracketing lines. Individuals who serve in advisory capacities or who are directly responsible to a higher administrator are listed with broken or dotted lines, as depicted in the unit secretary positions in Figure 13.14.

When you prepare an organizational chart, first determine how much of the company or agency you want to depict. Just one branch of nursing services at a large metropolitan hospital—the division of critical care nursing—is presented in Figure 13.14. Note that the intensive and cardiac care units work two shifts a day (8 A.M. to 8 P.M.; 8 P.M. to 8 A.M.), while the cardiac rehabilitation unit works three shifts in a twenty-four-hour period.

FIGURE 13.14   An organizational chart showing critical care nursing services at Union General Hospital.

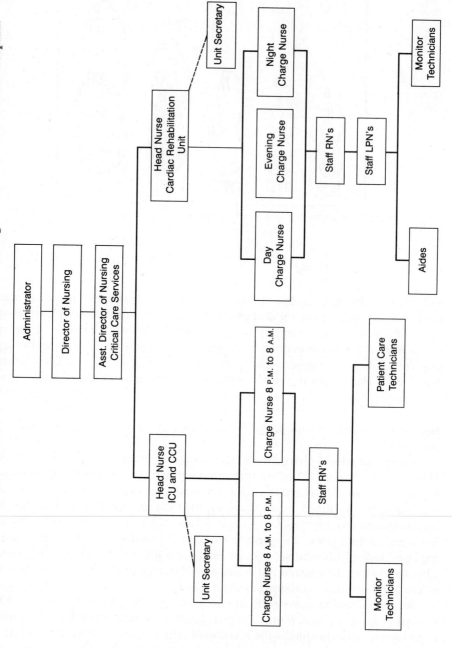

Select the extent to which you want to visualize the organization. Then select appropriate circles or boxes to represent units. The shapes should be large enough to contain the titles of the offices they represent. Make sure you label each shape; otherwise, the reader will not know which unit is being depicted. If you represent just a portion of your organization, say so in your text.

Flow Charts

Like the organizational chart, a flow chart does not present statistical information. But as its name implies, a flow chart does show movement. It displays the stages in which something is manufactured, accomplished, or produced from beginning to end. Flow charts can also be used to plan the day's or week's activities or, for accounting purposes, to show how income data go into a balance sheet.

A flow chart tells a story with arrows, boxes, and sometimes pictures. Boxes are connected by arrows to visualize the stages of a process. The presence and direction of the arrows tell the reader the order and movement of events involved in the process. Flow charts often proceed from left to right and back again, as in the flow chart below, showing the steps to be taken before graduation.

Flow charts can also be constructed to read from top to bottom. Computer programming instructions frequently are written in this way. See, for example, Figure 13.15, which uses a computer programming flow chart to show the steps a student must follow in writing a research paper. The flow chart in Figure 13.16 depicts a more complex procedure—the stages in the operation of a nuclear power plant; readers are asked to follow arrows in several directions. The jagged lines show the contents of the cooling coil and reactor. The cooling water enters from and returns to sources (a pond, a pool, the ocean) not shown at the right-hand side of the chart.

A flow chart should clarify, not complicate, a process. Do not omit any important stages, but at the same time do not introduce unnecessary or unduly detailed information. Do show at least three or four stages, however. And make sure the various stages appear in the correct sequence.

FIGURE 13.15 A computer programming flow chart showing steps in writing a research paper.

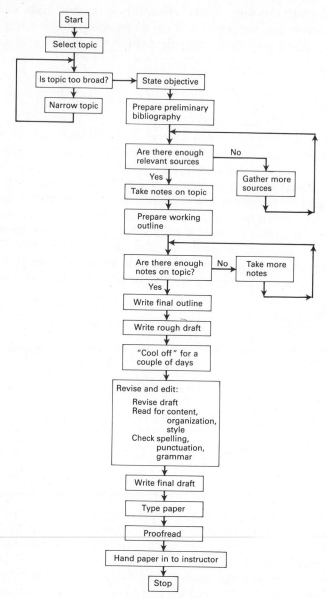

Maps

The maps you use on the job may range from highly sophisticated and detailed geographic tools to simple, hand-drawn sketches. You may use a small-scale map that shows large areas (a continent, a state, a county) in rough outline without great detail, such as the map in Figure 13.17. Or you may need a large-scale map

FIGURE 13.16 A complex flow chart showing the operation of a nuclear power plant.

Reprinted by permission of the publisher from *An Environmental Approach to Physical Science,* by Jerry D. Wilson (Lexington, Mass.: D.C. Heath, 1974): 363.

FIGURE 13.17 A small-scale map showing location of world's record water depth for petroleum exploration.

World Oil Dec. 1979: 87. Reprinted by permission.

FIGURE 13.18   A large-scale map showing location of Smithville Water Department's filter plants and pumping stations.

that displays a good deal of social, economic, or physical data (such as population density, location of retail businesses, hills, expressways, or rivers). That kind of detail is given in the map used by the Smithville Water Department in Figure 13.18. Look at the campus map included in your college catalog. How much detail does it supply and of what kind?

Your job requirements will dictate how detailed your map should be. Architects and builders need extremely detailed maps showing the location of pipes, telephone cables, and easement lines. An urban planner involved in developing a new community or an employee submitting site plans for a company's new location will use less detailed maps. For example, see Figure 16.9 on page 501. Between these two extremes, the individual working for a government agency investigating fire or flood damage to a neighborhood may require a map that indicates individual houses without presenting detailed features of those dwellings.

You may have to construct your own map or find one in a published source (a government document, an atlas, or a publication of an auto club). If you photocopy the map from your source, remember that you may not be able to reproduce colors or fine shading. When preparing a map to include in a report, follow these steps.

1. Provide a distance scale that identifies the proportion of inches to miles or inches to feet (e.g., 1″=10 miles).

2. Use dots, lines, colors, symbols (△,×, ○, □) or shading to indicate features. Markings should be clear and distinct.

3. If necessary, include a legend providing an explanation to dotted lines, colors, shadings, or symbols. Note the legend for water filter plants and pumping stations in Figure 13.18.

4. Eliminate any features (rivers, elevations, county seats) that do not directly depict the subject you are discussing. For example, a map showing the crops grown in two adjacent counties need not show all the roads and highways in those counties. A map showing the presence of strip mining needs to indicate elevation, but a map depicting population or religious affiliation need not include topographical (physical) detail. Reservoirs, lakes, and highways are essential in a map locating fire-damaged zones, details easily omitted in a map depicting strip mines.

5. Indicate direction by including an arrow and then citing the direction to which it points, for example N ↑.

Photographs

Correctly prepared, photographs are an extremely helpful addition to job-related writing. The photograph's chief virtues are realism and clarity. To a reader unfamiliar with an object or a landscape, a photograph may provide a much more convincing view than a simple drawing. Photographs of "before and after" scenes are especially effective.

The company you work for may have a photography or art department to assist you with your picture taking and preparation. A photograph can be touched up by enlarging crucial sections, deleting unnecessary parts (called *cropping*), or inserting white arrows on a black-and-white glossy to draw a reader's attention to relevant details.

If photographic cosmetics are unavailable, however, you will have to use special care when you take a picture. The most important point to remember is that what you see and what the camera records might be two different sights. Before you take a picture, decide how much foreground and background information you need. Include only the details that are *necessary and relevant* for your purpose. Inexperienced photographers need to remember the following four points.

1. Keep the camera in focus. Make sure that the lighting is proper.

2. Select the correct angle. Choose a vantage point that will enable you to record essential information as graphically as possible.

3. Give the right amount of detail. Pictures that include too much clutter compete for the reader's attention and detract from the subject. A realtor wanting to show that a house has an attractive front does not need to include sidewalks or streets. At the other extreme, do not cut out a necessary part of a landscape or object. Avoid putting people in a photograph when their presence is not required to show the relative size or operation of an object.

4. Take the picture from the right distance. The farther back you stand, the wider your angle will be, and the more the camera will capture with less detail. If you need a shot of a three-story office building, your picture may show only one or two stories if you are standing too close to the building when you photograph it. Standing too far away from an object, however, means that the photograph will reduce the object's importance and record unnecessary details.

To get a graphic sense of the effects of taking a picture the right and the wrong way, study the photographs in Figures 13.19–13.22. A clear and useful picture of a hydraulic truck (often called a "cherry picker") used to cut branches can be seen in Figure 13.19. The photographer rightly placed the truck in the foreground, but included enough background information to indicate the truck's

FIGURE 13.19 An effective photograph—truck in foreground, enough background information, and a worker to show size and function of truck.

FIGURE 13.20 A poor photograph—taken from the wrong angle so that everything merges and becomes confusing.

Photograph by David Longmire.

Photograph by David Longmire.

function. The worker in the gondola helps to show the size of the parts of the truck and also enables the reader to visualize the truck in operation.

In Figure 13.20 everything merges because the shot was taken from the wrong angle. The reader has no sense of the parts of the truck, their size, or their function. Another kind of error can be seen in Figure 13.21. Here the photographer was more interested in the person than in a piece of equipment. But looking at this picture, the reader has no idea where the worker came from or what he is doing up there. Finally, the reader looking at Figure 13.22 has a view of work going on, but no idea of the truck from which the worker is performing the job.

Drawings

A drawing serves many functions. For example, it can show where an object is located, how a tool or machine is put together, or what signals are given or steps taken in a particular situation. A drawing can explain the appearance of an object to individuals who may never have seen it. A drawing is also helpful to individuals who may have seen the object but do not have it in front of them as they read your work. By studying your drawing and following your discussion, readers will be better able to operate, adjust, repair, or order parts for equipment. As you will see, drawings are essential in giving instructions (pages 440–42).

FIGURE 13.21 A poor photograph—focus is on worker, but there is nothing else to identify person or work going on.

FIGURE 13.22 A poor photograph—focus is on work going on, but there is nothing to indicate that worker is operating from a hydraulic truck.

Photograph by David Longmire.

Photograph by David Longmire.

Generally speaking, drawings have two advantages over ordinary photographs.

1. You can include as much or as little detail as necessary in a drawing. The eye of the camera is not usually so selective; it tends to record everything in its path, including details that may be irrelevant for your purpose.
2. A drawing can show interior as well as exterior views, a feature that is particularly useful when the reader must understand what is going on under the case, housing, or hood.

A drawing can be simple, such as the one in Figure 13.23 showing readers exactly where to place smoke detectors in a house. A photograph could not give such an uncluttered picture. Stick figures may also be a useful part of a drawing, as in Figure 13.24, which shows correct landing and take-off signals for pilots.

FIGURE 13.23   A drawing showing where to place smoke detectors in a house.

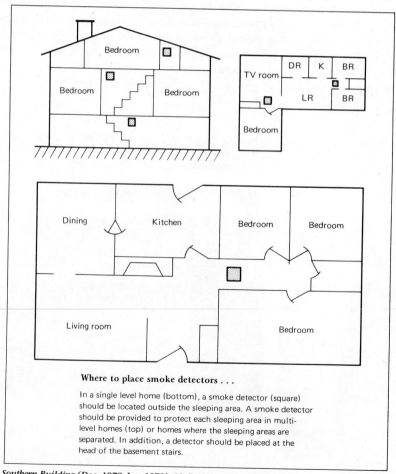

Where to place smoke detectors . . .

In a single level home (bottom), a smoke detector (square) should be located outside the sleeping area. A smoke detector should be provided to protect each sleeping area in multi-level homes (top) or homes where the sleeping areas are separated. In addition, a detector should be placed at the head of the basement stairs.

Southern Building (Dec. 1978–Jan. 1979): 10. Reprinted by permission.

FIGURE 13.24   A drawing using stick figures to show correct landing and take-off signals.

U.S. Department of Transportation, *Flight Training Handbook*, AC 61–21A: 54.

A more detailed drawing can reveal the interior of an object. Such sketches are called *cutaway drawings* because they show internal parts concealed from view. The underground pipes and service lines in a sanitary sewer are shown in Figure 13.25. The earth banking left in the foreground of the sketch shows where these pipes are buried.

Another kind of sketch is known as an *exploded drawing.* This drawing blows the entire object up and apart to show how the individual parts, each kept in order, are arranged. An exploded drawing of a chair is seen in Figure 13.26. The owner can better see how the chair is assembled and can more easily determine how to repair it. Figure 13.26 also uses *callouts,* or labels identifying the components of whatever is being depicted. These labels are often attached to the parts with arrows or lines. As the name suggests, the labels "call out" the parts so readers can identify them quickly. See Figure 14.4 on page 437 for an additional example of an exploded drawing.

FIGURE 13.25   A cutaway drawing showing construction of sanitary sewers with a steel trenching box.

August A. Guerrera, "Grounding of Electric Circuits to Water Services: One Utility's Experience." Reprinted from *Journal of the American Water Works Association* 72 (Feb. 1980): 86 by permission. Copyright 1980, the American Water Works Association.

FIGURE 13.26   An exploded drawing of a chair.

Dowel joints

Mortise and tenon joints

Mortise and tenon joint

Dowel joint

Dowel joints

Every chair has many interlocking parts and joints that must be kept tight.

From Reader's Digest *Fix-It Yourself Manual,* p. 67. Courtesy of Reader's Digest Association, Inc.

When you prepare your own drawings, follow these rules.

1. Whenever necessary, indicate which view of the object you are presenting (for example, aerial, frontal, lateral, reverse, exterior, or interior).

2. Keep the parts of the drawing proportionate unless you are purposely enlarging one section. Then provide readers with a scale.

3. Do not include any extra details. Even the addition of a line or two might distort the reader's view. Do not add decorations to make a drawing look fancy.

◆ COMPUTER GRAPHICS

For years computers have been used for a variety of data and word processing functions. Today, however, computers are also being used to produce visuals of all kinds. Numerous computer software packages offer graphic capabilities and there are also special graphics software packages. (Be cautioned, though, that some of these software packages can be quite expensive.) Moreover, advances in computer hardware technology have made creating computer graphics easy. With a *mouse* (a hand-held cursor) or a *stylus* (electronic pen) you can create all kinds of visuals. If you have a special (and expensive) attachment—a two- or six-pen plotter—your computer can produce visuals in high resolution colors. And you can even make colored transparencies that can be used with an overhead projector. Scanners, discussed below, are another piece of computer hardware used to prepare visuals. In years to come, computer assisted design (CAD) will surely replace hand-drawn visuals.

Thanks to such technology you can create sophisticated visuals that once had to be done by an artist or a printer. Sitting in front of your own personal computer (provided you have the right software and hardware) you can produce in a few minutes professional-looking graphics in a striking array of colors, shapes, sizes, and dimensions. One software manufacturer advertises that users can select more than 500 different visual configurations and that they can make numerous changes in these visuals. Figures 13.27 and 13.28 show two of the diverse types of computer visuals.

Two Ways to Produce Computer Graphics

Using appropriate software and hardware you can prepare visuals by charting them yourself or by scanning existing ones.

FIGURE 13.27   Examples of computer graphics.

Printed by permission of the Qume Corporation, a subsidiary of ITT.

FIGURE 13.28   Examples of computer graphics.

Printed by permission of VersaCAD Corporation.

Charting

When you chart you create your own visuals. The charting capabilities on a computer are almost endless. All you have to do is plug in the raw numerical data into your computer's data base and then, with a few simple keyboard commands, select the most appropriate visual shape (bar or pie chart, pictogram, graph) to display this statistical data. Following your commands, the computer will analyze and plot the data into a proportionately accurate chart or graph from the data you keyed in. The particular visual will then appear on the computer's VDT screen and with the assistance of a printer it can be produced on hard copy (paper) in black and white or in color. You do not have to be an experienced artist or mathematician to achieve high-quality results.

Scanning

If your computer is equipped with a page recognition and reproduction attachment, called a *scanner,* you can copy any type of visual (graphs, photographs, charts, pictograms, diagrams). You simply place the document/visual face up on the base of the scanner, and by touching the appropriate keys you instruct the computer to make an exact image of it and to store in your computer's memory. You can then call up this visual whenever you want and make any changes, if necessary. For example, you might want to reproduce a table exactly, then update it or delete information from it.

The Capabilities of Computer Graphics

Computers give you enormous charting, drawing, and other graphic capabilities. Using a computer you can create any of the visuals in this chapter plus numerous others. Here is a brief overview of the kinds of visuals you can produce with a computer and the types of alterations you can make in those visuals.

- You can produce black and white visuals as well as multicolored graphs, charts, drawings, etc. Some software packages even have what is called a "paintspray" feature that allows you to shade in different parts of a visual (or the entire visual) with small, densely placed black or grey dots. Such a feature helps you to distinguish one bar or bar segment from another in a bar chart.
- You can create three-dimensional drawings and designs to show different angles, shapes, and even aerial views; this visual capability clearly helps to distinguish exterior from interior views.
- You can move, delete, switch, or explode a part of a visual to make it more effective for the audience and to emphasize an idea in your text.
- You can rotate a part of a visual to see if a different point of view might be more effective.
- You can zoom in on a visual to enlarge it or scale it to make it appear smaller. With scaling you can vividly and accurately represent topographical features or even the same visual in two different scales.
- You can crop a photograph, reproduce part of it for an insert at the bottom of the visual, or even eliminate something in the middle of a photograph.
- You can join two objects from two separate visuals to show a side-by-side view which otherwise would not be possible.
- You can call up numerous geometric shapes and symbols to clarify, emphasize, or enhance a visual.
- You can display on your VDT screen both the visual (say a graph or table) and the statistical data upon which it is based in two or more "windows" (divisions or files) represented on the screen.
- You can select from among many different fonts (typeface designs) and sizes for legends, callouts, and captions.
- You can simulate what something might look like. Through computer-simulated projections you can see what a house may look like with a different shaped roof on it or how someone might look with a new hairstyle or wearing a particular piece of clothing.

Advantages of Using Computer Graphics in Your Research and Writing

Computer graphics offer more advantages than just striking visual effects. They can also significantly help you in your research and written work. In the process of preparing your work, you can experiment with a variety of visuals to see which one most accurately represents your ideas and which most convincingly displays that data for your audience. After you key in the numerical data, you can, for example, easily switch from a bar chart to a pie chart to a graph. Computer graphics increase your editing capabilities, too. You can delete irrelevant items in a visual or add features of your own. You might update a chart or graph or move information around, add new headings, etc. Also, you do not have to worry about whether you will ever find the exact visual you need or whether you will have to wait for someone to prepare it. Thanks to the computer, you will be able to design and produce the exact kinds of visuals your report calls for. Finally, using graphics software can lessen your anxiety about where and how you will place your visuals in your text. Creating your own visuals, which are stored in the computer's memory and thus ready to be used at any time, you can easily merge a visual anywhere in your document and not have to worry about whether you have left too much room or not enough.

While there is no doubt that computer graphics will help you on the job, you still need to rely on the basic information on visuals—their kinds and their usefulness—presented in this chapter. These fundamental principles will always apply, no matter how your visuals are created.

◆ GLOSSARY

By way of review, the following is a glossary of terms used in this chapter.

bar chart   a visual using vertical or horizontal bars to measure different data in space and time; bars can also be segmented to show multiple percentages within one bar. Bar charts are used to show a variety of facts for easy comparison.

callouts   labels that identify the parts of an object in a visual.

captions   titles or headings for visuals.

circle chart   a visual shaped in a circle, or pie, whose slices represent the parts of the whole. Circle charts portray budgets, expenditures, shares, and time allotments.

computer graphics   a variety of visuals generated by a computer; software (programs) and hardware (computer screens, plotters, scanners) create these visuals.

cropping   the process of eliminating unnecessary, unwanted details of a photograph by reproducing only the desired portion.

cross-hatching   the process of marking parts of a visual with parallel lines that cross each other obliquely; used to differentiate one bar or slice of a circle chart from another.

cutaway drawing   a sketch in which the exterior covering of an object has been removed to show an interior view.

dependent variable   the element (cost, employment, energy) plotted along the vertical axis of a line graph and most directly influenced by the independent variable.

exploded drawing   a sketch of an entire object that has been blown up and apart to show the relationship of parts to one another.

figures any visuals that are not tables—charts, drawings, graphs, pictograms, photographs, maps.

flow chart a sketch revealing the stages in an activity or process.

graph a picture that represents the relationship of an independent variable to one or more dependent variables; produces a line or curve to show their movement in time or space. Graphs are used to depict figures that change often—temperatures, rainfall, prices, employment, productions, and so forth.

independent variable the element, plotted along the horizontal axis of a graph, which most directly and importantly affects the dependent variable; most often, the independent variable is time or distance.

large-scale map a map that shows a great deal of detail, whether physical (elevations, rivers), economic (income levels), or social (population, religious affiliation).

legend the explanation, or key, indicating what different colors, shadings, or symbols represent in a visual.

organizational chart a visual showing the structure of an organization from the chief executive to the work force of employees. An organizational chart reveals the chain of command with areas of authority and responsibility.

pictogram a visual showing differences in statistical data by means of pictures varying in size, number, or color.

pie chart see **circle chart.**

small-scale map a map that depicts large areas without detail (a town with no streets or subdivisions represented or a state with no cities shown).

stub the first column on the left-hand side of a table; contains line captions, listing those units to be discussed in the columns.

suppressed zero a graph beginning with a larger number, when it would be impossible or impractical to start plotting at zero.

table a visual in which statistical data or verbal descriptions are arranged in rows or columns.

templates clear plastic sheets containing a variety of symbols, shapes, and designs which can be traced on paper.

tick marks equally spaced marks drawn on the vertical or horizontal scale of a graph to show units of measurement; see **cross-hatching.**

◆ EXERCISES

1. Record the highest temperature reached in your town for the next five days. Then collect data on the highest temperature reached in three of the following cities—Boston, Chicago, Dallas, Denver, Los Angeles, Miami, New Orleans, New York, Philadelphia, Phoenix, Salt Lake City, San Francisco, Seattle—over the same five days. (You can get this information from a newspaper.) Prepare a table showing the differences for the five-day period.

2. Go to a supermarket and get the prices of four different brands of the same product (hair spray, aspirin, a soft drink, a box of cereal). Put your findings in the form of a table.

3. One government agency supplied the following statistics on the world production of oranges (including tangerines) in thousands of metric tons for the following countries during the years 1985–1988: Brazil, 2,005, 2,132, 2,760, and 2,872; Israel, 909, 1,076, 1,148, 1,221; Italy, 1,669, 1,599, 1,766, 1,604; Japan, 2,424, 2,994, 2,885, 4,070; Mexico, 937, 1,405, 1,114, 1,270; Spain,

2,135, 2,005, 2,179, 2,642; and the United States, 7,658, 7,875, 7,889, 9,245. Prepare a table with this information and then write a paragraph in which you introduce the table and draw conclusions from it.

4. Keep a record for one week of the number of miles you walk, ride, or drive each day. Then prepare a line graph depicting this information.

5. Prepare a table to show the following statistical data. According to the 1980 Census, the town of Ardmore had a population of 34,567. By the 1990 Census the town had decreased its population by 4,500. In the 1980 Census the town of Morrison had a population of 23,809, but by the 1990 Census the population had increased by 3,689. The 1990 Census figure for the town of Berkesville was 25,675, which was an increase of 2,768 from the 1980 Census.

6. Prepare a line graph for the information in Exercise 5.

7. Prepare a bar graph for the information in Exercise 5.

8. Write a paragraph introducing and interpreting the table printed below.

Year	Soft drink companies	Bottling plants	Per capita consumption (gallons)
1935	750	750	10.3
1940	578	611	12.5
1945	457	466	18.6
1950	380	407	17.2
1955	231	292	15.9
1960	171	229	15.4
1965	118	197	16.0
1970	92	154	18.7
1975	54	102	21.1
1980	43	88	23.1
1985	45	82	25.3

9. Prepare a circle chart showing the breakdown of your budget for one week or one month.

10. According to a municipal study in 1990 the distribution of all companies classified in each enterprise industry in that city was as follows: minerals, 0.4%; selected services, 33.3%; retail trade, 36.7%; wholesale trade, 6.5%; manufacturing, 5.3%; and construction, 17.8%. Make a circle chart to represent this distribution.

11. Construct a segmented bar chart to represent the kinds and numbers of courses you took in a two-semester period or during your last year in high school.

12. Prepare a bar chart for the different brands of one of the products in Exercise 2. Write a paragraph introducing this illustration.

13. Find a pictogram in a math or business textbook or in a magazine (try *Newsweek* or *U.S. News & World Report*) and make a bar graph from the information contained in it. Then write a paragraph introducing the bar graph and drawing conclusions from it.

14. Make an organizational chart for a business or agency you worked for recently. Include part-time and full-time employees, but indicate employees' status with different kinds of shapes or lines. Then write a brief letter to your employer, explaining why such an organizational chart should be distributed to all employees.

15. Prepare a flow chart for one of the following activities.
    a. jumping a "dead" car battery
    b. giving an injection
    c. crocheting an afghan
    d. painting a set of louvered doors
    e. making an arrest
    f. putting out an electrical fire
    g. calling up a computer program
    h. any job you do

16. Make a map representing at least two blocks of your neighborhood. Include with appropriate symbols any stores, police or fire stations, churches, parks, or schools. Supply a legend for your readers.

17. Draw a map for a visitor who wants to know how to get from your college library to the downtown area of your city. Supply a distance scale.

18. Draw an interior view of a piece of equipment you use in your major; then identify the relevant parts using callouts.

19. Prepare a drawing of one of the following simple tools and include appropriate callouts with your visual.
    a. golf club
    b. hammer
    c. pliers
    d. stethoscope
    e. swivel chair
    f. computer terminal, keyboard, and printer
    g. ballpoint pen
    h. soldering iron
    i. table lamp
    j. pair of eyeglasses

20. Prepare appropriate visuals to illustrate the data listed below. In a paragraph immediately after the visual explain why the type of visual you selected is appropriate for the information.
    a. Life expectancy is increasing in America. This growth can be dramatically measured by comparing the number of teenagers with the number of older adults (over age 65) in America during the last few years and then by projecting these figures. In 1970 there were approximately 28 million teenagers and 20 million

older adults. By 1980 the number of teenagers climbed to 30 million and the number of older adults increased to 25 million. In 1990 there are 27 million teenagers and 31 million older adults. By the year 2000 the number of teenagers will level off to 23 million, but the number of older adults will soar to more than 36 million.

b. The percentage of women in the work force is steadily increasing. According to the U.S. Department of Labor of all women sixteen years and older 37.7 percent of them were employed in the work force in 1960. In 1965 there were 38.9 percent; by 1970 43.3 percent; by 1975 46.3 percent; by 1980 51.5 percent; and by 1985 the percentage had reached almost 55.

c. Researchers estimate that for every adult in America 3,985 cigarettes were purchased in 1970; 4,100 in 1975; 3,875 in 1980; and 3,490 in 1985.

21. Find a photograph that contains some irrelevant clutter. Write a letter to the photography department of a company for which you presumably work that wants to use the photograph. Tell the department what to delete and why.

22. Make a simple line drawing of only the relevant portions of the photograph in Exercise 21. Explain in two paragraphs why the drawing is better than the photograph.

Instructions,
Proposals, and
Reports

Chapter 14: Writing Clear Instructions
◆
Chapter 15: Proposals
◆
Chapter 16: Short Reports
◆
Chapter 17: Long Reports
◆
Chapter 18: Oral Reports

14

Writing Clear Instructions

Clear instructions are essential if work is to get done in business and industry. This chapter contains suggestions on how to prepare, organize, write, and format instructions.

◆ THE IMPORTANCE OF INSTRUCTIONS

Instructions tell, and frequently show, how to do something. They indicate how to perform a procedure (draw blood); operate a machine (run a forklift); assemble, maintain, or repair a piece of equipment (a photocopier; a carburetor); or locate an object (coils in a circuit). Readers use instructions for reasons of safety, efficiency, convenience, and economy. Product labels in a medicine chest, for example, inform users when and why to take the medications and how much to take. Owners' manuals instruct buyers on how to avoid the inconvenience of a product breakdown by keeping the product in good working order. Magazines such as *Popular Mechanics, Popular Photography,* and how-to books offer consumers money-saving instructions on topics ranging from repairing their homes to training guard dogs. You might want to read some of these how-to publications and manuals to see how they identify and meet the needs of the reader trying to perform a certain procedure.

As part of your job, you may be asked to write instructions for your co-workers as well as for the customers who use your company's services or products. Or for long, complex instructions you may be part of a team of artists, technicians, and marketing specialists. But whether the instructions are brief or lengthy, your employer stands to gain or lose much from the kinds of instructions you write. Imagine how costly it would be if employees had to stop their work each time they could not understand a set of instructions, or if they made a number of serious mistakes because of confusing directions. Clearly written instructions can save your company costly service calls. Even more important, poorly written instructions may result in injury to the person trying to follow them and thus lead to damage claims or even lawsuits.

◆ THE VARIETY OF INSTRUCTIONS: A BRIEF OVERVIEW

Instructions vary in length, complexity, and format. Some instructions are one word long: *stop, lift, rotate, print, erase.* Others are a few sentences long: "Insert blank diskette in external disk drive"; "Be sure to close after using"; "Store in an upright position." Short instructions are appropriate for the numerous, relatively nontechnical chores performed every day. For more elaborate procedures, however, detailed instructions may be as long as a page or a book. When your firm purchases a new mainframe computer or a piece of earth-moving equipment, it will receive an instruction pamphlet or book containing many steps, cautionary statements, and diagrams. Many businesses prepare their own training manuals containing instructions for 200 or 300 different procedures.

Instructions can be given in paragraphs or in lists, and you will have to determine which format is most appropriate for the kinds of instructions you write. Figures 14.1 and 14.2 show two sets of brief instructions written in paragraph for-

FIGURE 14.1   Instructions on how to prepare and administer a sitz bath.

First, adjust water temperature dial to 105–110°F. Then turn on the faucet and fill sitz tub with enough water to cover the patient's hips. Before assisting the patient into the tub, place bath towel in the bottom of the tub. Allow the patient to sit in the tub for 15–20 minutes. At the end of this time, help the patient out of the tub. Then dry the patient thoroughly.

FIGURE 14.2   Instructions on how to repair a halyard.

Easy Temporary Join for Synthetic Ropes

If you are faced with the problem of reeving a new halyard on a flagpole or mast, or through a block or pulley in an inaccessible location, the solution can be easy if both old and new lines are made of nylon or polyester (Dacron, Terylene, etc.). Simply join the ends of the old and new lines temporarily by melting end fibers together in a small flame (a little heat goes a long way). Rotate the two lines slowly as the fibers melt. Withdraw them from the flame before a ball of molten material forms, and if the stuff ignites, blow out the flame at once. Hold the joint together until it is cool and firm.

R. I. Standish, *Parks* 51 (Apr.–June 1980): 21.

mat. In Figure 14.1 hospital employees are told how to prepare and administer a sitz bath; in Figure 14.2 park rangers are given instructions on how to repair a halyard, or tackle, used to raise a flag or move a pulley.

The instructions shown in Figures 14.3 and 14.4 are printed in list form. In Figure 14.3 readers will find directions on how to change a typestyle font (all the letters and symbols of a specific size of typeface) on an IBM "Quietwriter" printer; the directions in Figure 14.4 give details on how to assemble an outdoor grill.

◆ BEFORE WRITING INSTRUCTIONS

Regardless of their format (paragraphs or lists), instructions have to be clear, complete, and easy to follow. In most instances you will not be available for readers to ask you questions when they do not understand something. Consequently, they will have to rely on your written instructions. Your goal in writing those instructions is to get readers to perform the same steps you followed and, most important, to obtain the same results you did. Writing instructions is like teaching. You have to understand the material yourself and know the best way of presenting it.

To make sure that your instructions are clear and accurate, plan them carefully. You must first completely understand the job or procedure that you are asking someone else to perform. Make sure you know the reason for doing something, the parts or tools required, the steps to be followed to get the job done, and the results of that job. If you are not completely sure about the procedure, watch an expert perform it.

Next, actually perform the procedure (assembling, repairing, maintaining, ordering, dissecting) yourself. If possible, go through a number of trial runs. Take notes as you go along and be sure to divide the procedure into simple steps for readers to follow. You should not give the reader too much to do in one step. Transform your notes into a draft(s) of the instructions you want readers to follow.

To test your rough draft, ask someone from the intended audience (consumers, technicians) who may never have performed the procedure before to follow it to complete the task. Ask this individual to identify any places in your instructions that are vague, hard to follow, inconsistent (steps bunched up or out of order), or incomplete. Then revise your draft for the final copy of the instructions that you will give to readers.

As you revise, pay special attention to the technical language and the amount of detail you include. Try to determine your reader's level of experience and education. A set of instructions accompanying a chemistry set would be much different in terminology, abbreviations, and detail from a set of instructions a professor gives a class in organic chemistry.

General Audience: Place 8 drops of vinegar in a test tube and add a piece of limestone about the size of a pea.

Specialized Audience: Place 8 gtts of $CH_3 COOH$ in a test tube and add 1 mg of CO_3.

FIGURE 14.3 **Instructions on how to replace a typestyle font on an IBM "Quietwriter" printer.**

Replacing a Typestyle Font

1. Place the font in the font holder.

2. Place your finger on top of the font.

3. Press down and toward you until the font is securely latched into the font holder. (If this is your active font, the **font** light will go off. This is also normal.)

4. Close the printer cover.

Font Holders

Reprinted by permission from *Guide to Operations for the IBM "Quietwriter" Printer* by International Business Machines Corporation.

FIGURE 14.4 **Instructions on how to assemble an outdoor grill.**

ASSEMBLY INSTRUCTIONS

The instructions shown below are for the basic grill with tubular legs. If you have a pedestal grill, or a grill with accessories, check the separate instruction sheet for details not shown here.

NOTE: Make sure you locate all the parts before discarding any of the packaging material.

TOOLS REQUIRED ... A standard straight blade screwdriver is the only tool you need to assemble your new Meco grill. If you have a pedestal grill, you will need a 7-16 wrench or a small adjustable wrench.

1. Before you start, take time to read through this manual. Inside you will find many helpful hints that will help you get the full potential of enjoyment and service from your new Meco grill.

2. Lay out all the parts.

3. Assemble roller leg (1) to bottom rear of bowl (2) with 1¼" long bolts (3) and nuts (4).

4. Assemble fixed leg (5) to bottom front of bowl (2) with 1¼" long bolts (3) and nuts (4).

5. Place fire grate—ash dump (6) in bottom of bowl (2) between adjusting levers.

6. Place cooking grid (7) on top of adjusting levers. Make sure top grid wires run from front to back of grill.

Meco Assembly Instructions and Owners Manual, Metals Engineering Corp., P.O. Box 3005, Greenville, TN 37743. Reprinted by permission.

Do not assume that your readers have done the procedure or have operated the equipment as many times as you have. (If they had, there would be no need for your instructions.) No writer of instructions ever disappointed readers by making directions too clear or too easy to follow. Use language and symbols that will be readily understood. If someone is puzzled by your directions, you defeat the reasons for writing them.

◆ SELECTING THE RIGHT WORDS

To write instructions that readers can understand and turn into effective action, follow these guidelines.

1. Use verbs in the imperative mood. Imperatives are commands that have deleted the pronoun "you." Almost all the sentences in Figures 14.1–14.4 contain imperatives: "adjust water temperature" for "you adjust water temperature"; "fill the sitz tub with enough water" for "you fill the sitz tub with enough water"; "lift the cover" for "you lift the cover." Deleting the "you" is not discourteous, as it certainly would be in a letter or a report. Instructions are best expressed as commands to show that the writer speaks with authority. Instructions say "These steps work, so do it exactly this way." Imperatives also get the reader to do something specific without hesitation. Don't water down your directions with statements such as "Please see if you can remove the outside panel"; "Try to allow the mixture to cool for five minutes"; or "If at all possible, adjust the thermostat to 78°." Wishy-washy statements may lead the reader to believe that there are some choices involved, when in fact there are none. For this reason, avoid *might, could, should:* "You might want to ignite the fire next" does not have the force of "ignite the fire next." Instead, choose action verbs (*apply, close, cut, drain, drop, insert, push, rotate, rub, shut off, turn, wipe*).

2. Write clear, short sentences. Since readability is especially important in instructions, keep sentences short and uncomplicated. Sentences under twenty words (and preferably under fifteen) are easy to read. Note that the sentences in Figures 14.1–14.4 are, for the most part, under fourteen words. Avoid the passive voice. In place of "The air blower is to be used last," write "Use the air blower last." Also avoid addressing the reader as "one" or "the user": "The user should apply the air blower last" or "One must use the air blower last" are, again, best listed as "Use the air blower last."

You can keep your sentences clear by avoiding ambiguity. Do not write a sentence that sends the reader a message opposite from what you intend. A direction such as "Before using the soldering iron on metal, clean it with Freon" may mislead the inexperienced welder to put Freon on the iron rather than on the metal that is to be cleaned. Similarly, "Perform venipuncture with the arm in a downward position" does not clearly specify whose arm is to be in that position; appropriately revised, the instruction reads "Put the patient's arm in a downward position."

3. Use precise terms for measurements, distances, and times. Indefinite, vague directions leave users wondering if they are doing the right thing. (Review pages 100–2 in Chapter 5.) The following imprecise directions are better expressed through the revisions listed in parentheses: "Turn the distributor cap a little." (How much is "a little?" "Turn the distributor cap three-quarters of an inch."); "Let the contents stand for a while." (How long? "Let the contents stand for ten minutes.") Precise timing is essential to the success of many kinds of instructions ranging from baking a cake to completing an experiment in a chemistry laboratory.

4. Use connective words as signposts to specify the exact order in which something is to be done (especially when your instructions are written in paragraphs). Words such as *first, then, before* in Figure 14.1 help readers stay on course, telling them how and why the various procedures are connected to produce the desired results.

5. Label each step with a number when you present your instructions in a list (as in Figure 14.4). You may also use bullets, as shown in the box on page 447. Plenty of white space between each step also distinctly separates steps for the reader. If circumstances permit the use of color, employ it sparingly to set off important elements of your instructions. Color is especially effective for safety notices (see page 451).

◆ USING VISUALS EFFECTIVELY

Readers welcome visuals in almost any set of instructions. Visuals are graphic and direct, showing readers precisely what they must do. A visual can simplify a process, reinforce or even save you words, and help readers get the job done faster and with more confidence. For example, the illustration in Figure 14.2 reinforces the process of joining the two parts of the halyard by fire and the sketch in Figure 14.3 labels the printer parts that the users must understand if they are to replace a typestyle font. Another frequently used visual in instructions is the exploded drawing, such as the one shown in Figure 14.4, to help consumers see how the various components of the grill fit together for easy assembly.

The number and types of visuals you include will of course depend on the procedure or equipment you are explaining. Some instructions, such as those in Figure 14.5, use a visual to illustrate each step. Others may require only one or two (such as in Figures 14.2–14.4). Gear the type of visual you include to the task you want the reader to perform and to the reader's knowledge of that task. Note in Figure 14.6 how symbols (triangle, square, circle) graphically portray the proper use of fire extinguishers.

Regardless of the number and type of visuals you include, follow these guidelines to use them effectively.

FIGURE 14.5   Instructions on inserting and removing videocassettes.

To Insert: Push the cassette through the door until the VCR mechanism pulls it into the compartment. VCR power automatically turns on and the cassette-in indicator turns on when the cassette is in place.

To Eject: Power must be on to eject the cassette. Rewind the cassette before ejecting it. Press *EJECT*.

To Remove: The cassette will come partially out of the compartment so you can pull it out. Put the cassette in its box and store it upright.

RCA/Thomson Consumer Electronics.

1. Whenever possible, place the visual next to the step the reader is to perform, not on another page or buried at the bottom of the page. To gain the most from visuals, readers must be able to see the illustrations or diagrams immediately before and after reading the directions they clarify.

2. If you are using many visuals, assign each one a number (Figure 1, Figure 2, etc.) and in your directions tell readers where those visuals can be found ("to the left of these instructions"; "see the sketch at the right").

3. Make sure that the visual looks like the object the user is trying to assemble, maintain, run, or repair.

4. Wherever necessary, label parts of the visual. The drawing in Figure 14.3 does this very carefully for readers.

5. Inform readers if a part of an object is missing or reduced in size in your visual.

6. Set each visual off with white space so it is easy to find, read, and reread.

FIGURE 14.6   Instructions on the proper use of fire extinguishers.

KIND OF FIRE

DECIDE THE CLASS OF FIRE YOU ARE FIGHTING... →

...THEN CHECK THE COLUMNS TO THE RIGHT OF THAT CLASS →

A CLASS A FIRES
USE THESE EXTINGUISHERS

ORDINARY COMBUSTIBLES
• WOOD
• PAPER
• CLOTH
ETC.

B CLASS B FIRES
USE THESE EXTINGUISHERS

FLAMMABLE LIQUIDS, GREASE
• GASOLINE
• PAINTS
• OILS, ETC.

C CLASS C FIRES
USE THESE EXTINGUISHERS

ELECTRICAL EQUIPMENT
• MOTORS
• SWITCHES
ETC.

APPROVED TYPE OF EXTINGUISHER

MATCH UP PROPER EXTINGUISHER WITH CLASS OF FIRE SHOWN AT LEFT

	FOAM Solution of Aluminum Sulphate and Bicarbonate of Soda	CARBON DIOXIDE Carbon Dioxide Gas Under Pressure	SODA ACID Bicarbonate of Soda Solution and Sulphuric Acid	PUMP TANK Plain Water	GAS CART-RIDGE Water Expelled by Carbon Dioxide Gas	MULTI-PURPOSE DRY CHEMICAL	ORDINARY DRY CHEMICAL
Class A	A B	X	A	A	A	A B C	X
Class B	A B	B C	X	X	X	A B C	B C
Class C	X	B C	X	X	X	A B C	B C

HOW TO OPERATE

FOAM: Don't Play Stream into the Burning Liquid. Allow Foam to Fall Lightly on Fire.

CARBON DIOXIDE: Direct Discharge as Close to Fire as Possible First at Edge of Flames and Gradually Forward and Upward

SODA-ACID, GAS CARTRIDGE: Direct Stream at Base of Flame

PUMP TANK: Place Foot on Footrest and Direct Stream at Base of Flames

DRY CHEMICAL: Direct at the Base of the Flames. In the Case of Class A Fires, Follow Up by Directing the Dry Chemicals at Remaining Material That is Burning

IMPORTANT! USING THE WRONG TYPE EXTINGUISHER FOR THE CLASS OF FIRE MAYBE DANGEROUS!

NATIONAL INSTITUTE FOR OCCUPATIONAL SAFETY AND HEALTH

National Institute for Occupational Safety and Health.

◆ THE FOUR PARTS OF INSTRUCTIONS

Except for very short instructions, such as those illustrated in Figures 14.1–14.4, a set of instructions generally contains four main parts: (1) an introduction, (2) a list of equipment and materials, (3) the actual steps to perform the process, and (4) a conclusion (when necessary).

The Introduction

Whether you need an introduction depends on the particular process or machine you are describing. Short instructions require no introduction or only a brief one- or two-sentence introduction, such as the one in Figure 14.4. More complex instructions require lengthier introductions. For instance, a ninety-page manual may contain a two- or three-page introduction. An introduction should be proportional to the kinds of instructions that will be given. For example, instructions on how to sand a floor will not need a one-page introduction on how friction works.

The function of an introduction is to provide readers with enough *necessary* background information to understand why and how your instructions work. An introduction must make readers feel more comfortable and better prepared. Accordingly, you can do one or all of the following in your introduction.

1. State why the instructions are useful for a specific audience. Here is an introduction from a safety procedure describing the protective lockout of equipment: "The purpose of this procedure is to provide plant electrical technicians with a uniform method of locking out machinery or equipment. This will prevent the possibility of setting moving parts in motion, energizing electrical lines, or opening valves while repair, set-up and adjustment, or cleaning work is in progress." Many instructions in training manuals contain introductions that stress the educational benefits to the user: "These instructions will serve as a valuable training tool for the beginning draftsperson, showing him or her the proper ways of preparing detailed drawings that will be useful in woodwork manufacturing today."

2. Indicate how a particular machine or procedure works. A brief discussion of the "theory of operation" will help readers understand why something works the way your instructions say it should. Such discussion sometimes describes a scientific law or principle. The introduction to instructions on how to run a machine begins by stressing the function of the machine: "These instructions will teach you how to operate an autoclave. The autoclave is used to sterilize surgical instruments through live additive-free steam." Laboratory experiments usually begin with a discussion of reasons why a particular effect will occur or how something develops under certain circumstances. For example, the following paragraph introduces an experiment on osmosis, the process by which fluids flow from one cell to another.

The distribution of water among the various fluid compartments of the body is determined in part by the solute [dissolved substance] content of these fluids. Since most solutes penetrate cell membranes relatively slowly, water, because of its abundance and permeability, plays an important role in establishing osmotic equilibrium between cells and their environment. When placed in a solution whose water concentration is different from that in its own protoplasm, a cell either gains or loses water. The process of direct migration of solvents through membranes is called osmosis. This experiment will demonstrate the movement of water across a membrane because of differences in solute concentration across the two sides.[1]

3. Establish how long it should take the user to complete all steps of the instructions. If users know how long a procedure should take, they will be better able to judge whether they are doing it correctly—if they are waiting too long or not long enough between steps or if they are going too slowly or too quickly: "It should take about three and one-half hours from the time you start laying the floor tiles until the time they dry well enough to walk on."

4. Stress any advantages or benefits the reader will gain by performing the instructions. Make the reader feel good about buying or using your product by explaining how it will make a job easier to perform, save the reader time and money, or allow the reader to accomplish a job with fewer mistakes or false starts. Note how the following introduction to a set of instructions on using an auto dial/auto answer modem encourages the reader to want to learn how to operate this computer-based telephone system.

Welcome to high-speed telecommunications and congratulations on choosing the Signalman EXPRESSi. You've made an excellent choice. The EXPRESSi is the ideal link between your computer and the ever-expanding world of information utilities, data bases, electronic mail, bulletin boards, computer time sharing, and more.

The EXPRESSi can be used in the IBM Personal Computer, PC XT, PC AT, and other PC-bus compatible computers. And because the EXPRESSi fits inside your PC, it saves valuable desk space and eliminates expensive, bulky cables.[2]

---

5. Inform the user about any special circumstances to which the instructions apply. Some instructions precede others or are used only on special occasions. Readers must be informed about those changes or emergency situations. A supervisor of a large chemical plant sent employees the memo contained in Figure 14.7 to describe operating procedures to be followed during energy shortages. Note the brief introduction emphasizing the special circumstances.

Not every introduction to a set of instructions will contain facts on all the categories of information listed above. Some instructions will require less detail. You will have to judge how much background information specific instructions call for.

---

[1] Byron A. Schottelius, John D. Thomson, and Dorothy D. Schottelius. *Physiology: Laboratory Manual,* 4th ed. St. Louis: C. V. Mosby, 1978. 11. Reprinted by permission.
[2] Courtesy of Anchor Automation, Inc., Chatsworth, CA.

FIGURE 14.7   Instructions alerting readers to special circumstances.

 HERCULES

TO: All Shift Supervisors
               All Firefighters
FROM: Robert A. Ferguson   *Robert A Ferguson*
SUBJECT: Operating Procedures During Energy Shortages
DATE: October 10, 1982

The following policy has been formulated to aid in maintaining required pressures during periods of low wood flow and severe natural gas curtailment.

All boilers are equipped with lances to burn residue or no. 6 fuel oil as auxiliary fuels. When wood is short, no. 6 oil should be burned in no. 2 and no. 3 boilers at highest possible rate consistent with smoke standards. To do this, take these steps:

1. Put no. 6 oil on no. 3 boiler lances.

2. Shut down overfire air.

3. Shut down forced draft.

4. Turn off vibrators.

5. Keep grates covered with ashes or wood until ash cover exists.

These steps will result in an output of 25,000 to 35,000 lbs./hr. steam from no. 3 boiler and will force wood on down to no. 4 boiler.

If required, the same procedure can be repeated on no. 2 boiler.

List of Equipment and Materials

Immediately after the introduction, inform readers of all equipment or materials they will need. This list should be complete and clear. Do not wait until the readers are actually performing one of the steps in the instructions to tell them that a certain type of drill or a specific kind of chemical is required. They may have to stop what they are doing to find this equipment or material; moreover, the procedure may fail or present hazards if users do not have the right equipment at the specified time.

Do not expect your readers to know exactly what size, model, or quantity you have in mind. Tell them precisely. For example, if a Phillips screwdriver is necessary to complete one step, specify this type of screwdriver under the heading *"Equipment and Materials"*; do not just list "screwdriver." Here are some additional examples of unclear references to equipment and materials, with more helpful alternatives listed in parentheses after them: solution (0.7% NaCl solution); pencils (two engineering pencils); electrodes (four short platinum wire electrodes); file (cheese-grater file); sand (10-lb. bag of sand); needle (butterfly needle); water (10 gallons untreated sea water).

If you are concerned that readers will not understand why certain equipment or materials are used, give the explanation in parentheses after the item. For example, listing alcohol and cotton as materials needed to take a blood pressure might confuse readers not familiar with the uses of these materials. A clarifying comment after the materials such as "used to clean stethoscope headphones" would help. The following example, "Instructions for Absentee Voters," contains such helpful comments.

This absentee ballot package has been sent to you at your request. It contains the following items:

1. sample paper ballot (for information only)
2. official ballot (this is a punch card)
3. punching tool
4. envelope with attached declaration
5. addressed return envelope

Voters will know that the punch card is their official ballot and that it does not look like the sample ballot because of the parenthetical information in numbers 1 and 2. The point is reinforced later in the directions by this statement.

IMPORTANT

◆ Punch only with tool provided, never with a pencil or pen.
◆ Your vote is recorded by punching this ballot card, not by marking the paper ballot.
◆ Do not return the sample paper ballot.

Read the following instructions on refinishing a piece of wood, which provide a very detailed list of materials used to clean and smooth wood surfaces.

Preparing the Surface

Before attempting to refinish a wood item, be sure the surface is smooth and free from dirt, dust, and grease.

Materials
The following materials are suitable for cleaning and smoothing wood surfaces:

Abrasives

- *Sandpaper.* Sandpaper is not made of sand as the name suggests. It is made of various kinds of abrasive material applied to paper or cloth backing and made in sheet, drum, belt, and other forms. Sandpaper comes in various grades ranging from No. 4/0 to No. 1. No. 4/0 is used when an extra fine finish is required; No. 2/0 for a fine finish; No. 1/2 for rubbing down undercoats of paint and varnish in preparation for final finish; and No. 1 to No. 3 for sanding down old coats of paint too badly chipped to repaint.
- *Sanding disks.* Sanding disks are flat, circular pieces of sandpaper of various types, sizes, and coarseness for use on a power sander. These disks can also be used either on a disk or rotary hand sander.
- *Commercial steel wool.* Steel wool is a fluffy or wool-like mass of steel turnings. It is made in grades No. 00, 0, 1, and 3, ranging from extra fine to coarse. It is a mild abrasive for rubbing down and smoothing wood and is well suited for removal of light rust from metal prior to repainting.

Cloth and Sponges

- *Jute burlap.* Jute burlap is a coarse, heavy, loose-woven material, used for all general purpose cleaning.
- *Osnaburg cotton cloth.* Osnaburg cloth is a coarse, heavy cloth used as a substitute for jute burlap and serves the same purposes.
- *Cotton wiping cloth.* This cloth is relatively free from lint. It is used as a substitute for cotton waste, especially when lint deposits are undesirable, and as a substitute for sponges when washing wood and metalwork. It can be used to apply strong soap, lye, soda ash, or other solutions, which destroy sponges quickly.
- *Cellulose sponge.* This is a synthetic material. It *cannot* be used with solutions containing soda ash, trisodium phosphate, or caustic soda (lye) because they will break down the fibers and ruin the sponge.
- *Natural sponge.* This is a natural material that has great liquid-absorption capacity. It becomes soft when wet without losing its original toughness and is used with mild cleaning solutions. Solutions of soda ash, trisodium phosphate, and caustic soda affect the natural sponge the same as the synthetic sponge.[3]

---

[3] U.S. Army Manual FM 43-4, *Repair of Wood Items.*

The Steps in Instructions

The heart of your directions will consist of clearly distinguished steps that readers must follow to achieve the desired results. To make sure that you help your readers understand your steps, observe the following rules.

1. Put the steps in their correct order. If a step is out of order or is missing, the entire set of instructions can be wrong or, worse yet, dangerous, as the cartoon in Figure 14.8 humorously illustrates. Double-check your steps before you write them down. Each step should be numbered to indicate its correct place in the sequence of events you are describing. Never put an asterisk (*) before or after a step to make the reader look somewhere else for information. If the information is important, put it in your instructions; if it is not, delete it.

FIGURE 14.8   A cartoon emphasizing the importance of putting instructions in proper order.

2. Group closely related activities into one step. Sometimes closely related actions are grouped into one step to help the reader coordinate activities
and to emphasize their being done at the same time, in the same place, or with
the same equipment. Study the following instructions listing the receptionist's duties of a ward clerk in a hospital.

1. Greet patients warmly and make them feel welcome. Never fall into the trap of
   groaning and saying "not another one." Remember the patient probably did not
   want to come to the hospital in the first place.
2. Check the identity bracelet against the summary sheet and addressograph plate. If
   the bracelet is not on the patient's wrist, place it there immediately. Set about correcting any errors you may find in any of this information at once.
3. If asked, escort the patient to his or her room. Explain the signal light, answer any
   questions, and introduce the patient and roommate, if any.
4. Notify the head nurse and/or the nurse assigned to that room of the patient's arrival.
5. Notify the admitting physician by phone of the patient's arrival and location. If the
   patient lacks admission orders, mention this to the physician's secretary at this
   time.[4]

Note how step 3 contains all the duties the ward clerk performs once patients are
taken to their rooms. It is easier to consolidate all the activities that take place in
the room—explaining the signal light, answering questions, making introductions—than to list each as a separate step. But be careful that you do not over-
work a single step. To combine steps 4 and 5 would be wrong (and impossible)
because those two distinct steps require the ward clerk to speak to someone in
person and to make a phone call. These two actions are two separate stages in a
process. On the other hand, don't divide an action into two steps if it has to be
done in one. For example, instructions showing how to light a furnace would not
list as two steps actions that must be performed simultaneously to avoid a possible explosion.

Incorrect: Step 1: Depress the lighting valve.
             Step 2: Hold a match to the pilot light.
Correct: Step 1: Depress the lighting valve while holding a match to the pilot
             light.

Similarly, do not separate two steps of a computer command that must be performed simultaneously.

Incorrect: Step 1: Press the CONTROL key.
             Step 2: Press the BREAK key.
Correct: Step 1: While holding down the CONTROL key, press the BREAK key.

**3. Give the reader hints on how best to accomplish the proce-
dure.** Obviously, you cannot do this for every step, but if there is a chance that
the reader might run into difficulties or may not anticipate a certain reaction, by
all means provide assistance. For example, telling readers that a certain aroma or

---

[4] Myra S. Willson, *A Textbook for Ward Clerks and Unit Secretaries.* St. Louis: C. V. Mosby, 1979: 70.
Reprinted by permission.

color is to be expected in an experiment will reassure them that they are on the right track. Particular techniques on how to operate or service equipment are also helpful: "If there is blood on the transducer diaphragm, dip the transducer in a blood solvent, such as hydrogen peroxide, Hemosol, etc." If readers have a choice of materials or procedures in a given step, you might want to list those that would give the best performance: "Several thin coats will give a better finish than one heavy one."

4. State whether one step directly influences (or jeopardizes) the outcome of another. Since all steps in a set of instructions are interrelated, you could not (and should not) have to tell readers how every step affects another. But stating specific relationships is particularly helpful when dangerous or highly intricate operations are involved. You will save the reader time, and you will stress the need for care. Forewarned is forearmed. Here is an example.

> Step 2:   Tighten fan belt. Failure to tighten the fan belt will cause it to loosen and come off when the lever is turned in Step 5 below.

Do not wait until Step 5 to tell readers that you hope they did a good job in tightening the fan belt. That information comes after the fact.

5. Insert warning, caution, and note statements only where absolutely necessary. A warning statement tells readers that a step, if not prepared for or performed properly, can endanger their safety.

 WARNING: UNPLUG THE MONITOR BEFORE CLEANING ANY PART WITH DAMP CLOTH.

 DO NOT APPLY PRESSURE UNTIL SAFETY VALVE IS COMPLETELY SEALED.

A caution statement tells readers to take certain precautions: wear protective clothing, check an instrument panel carefully, use special care in running a machine, measure weights or dosages exactly, save a document on a computer.

CAUTION
MAKE SURE BRAKE SHOES WON'T RUB TIRE AND THAT
SHOES MATE WELL WITH RIM WHEN BRAKES ARE APPLIED.

 BE SURE TO ENTER CORRECT CODE FOR WORD SMART. TYPING THE WRONG CODE WILL ERASE DOCUMENT.

Because of the extremely important information they impart, warning and caution statements should be graphically set apart from the rest of the instructions. There should be no chance that readers will overlook them. Put these statements in capital letters, in boldface type, in boxes, in different colors (red is especially effective). Use one or all of these devices. Distinctive symbols, such as a skull and crossbones or an exclamation point inside a triangle, often precede a warning notation. Warning and caution statements should not be used just because you want to emphasize a point. Putting too many of these statements in your instructions will decrease the dramatic impact they should have on readers. Use them sparingly—only when absolutely necessary—so readers will not be tempted to bypass them.

A note statement simply adds a clarifying comment.

> *Note:* All models in 3500 series have a hex nut in the upper right, not left, corner.

 Drive B disk indicator will glow and the drive will make a few clicking sounds as the disk is formatted.

The instructions in Figure 14.9 on how to paint a garage floor contain steps that offer hints on how best to do the job, comment on how one step affects another, and issue warning, caution, and note statements. Not every instruction requires this amount of detail. Use such comments and signals only when the procedure you are describing calls for them and when they will help your readers.

The Conclusion

Not every set of instructions requires a conclusion. For short instructions containing a few simple steps, such as those in Figures 14.1–14.4, no conclusion is necessary. These instructions usefully end with the last step the reader must perform. For longer, more involved jobs, a conclusion can help readers finish the job with confidence and accuracy. For example, a short conclusion like the following might help users who have just followed the step-by-step instructions on painting a garage floor given in Figure 14.9.

> With proper care this procedure should have to be repeated only once every three years. To keep the floor in top shape, sweep it at least twice a month to prevent gritty materials such as sand from scaling the painted surface. If possible, wipe up grease and oil immediately to prevent them from soaking into the paint. Make sure you dispose of rags properly to avoid chance of fire.

When they are necessary, conclusions can help the reader in a variety of ways. They might either provide a succinct wrap-up of what the reader has done or end with a single sentence of congratulation. A conclusion might tell readers what to expect once a job is finished, describing the results of a test, or explaining how a piece of equipment is supposed to operate. Conclusions can also give readers practical advice on how to maintain a piece of equipment, as the conclusion above does, or how to follow a certain procedure.

FIGURE 14.9   Instructions on how to paint a garage floor.

Cleaning the Floor

(1) Remove all objects from the floor.
(2) Scrape areas where there is old chipped paint with a metal scraper. For hard-to-reach places such as corners or underneath pipes, use a 3-inch wire brush. New paint will not stick to the floor if old paint is not first removed.
(3) Sweep the floor first with a broom; then to make sure that all particles of dust and dirt are removed, use a vacuum sweeper.
(4) Open all windows for proper ventilation. Fumes from cleaning solution used in Step 5 should not be inhaled.

CAUTION: USE PROTECTIVE EYEWEAR AND RUBBER GLOVES FOR NEXT STEP.

 WARNING: DO NOT USE DETERGENTS CONTAINING AMMONIA. AMMONIA ADDED TO THESE INGREDIENTS WILL CAUSE AN EXPLOSION.

(5) Mop the entire floor with a solution composed of the following ingredients:
$\frac{1}{3}$ box of Floorex
1 quart of bleach
10 quarts of water
1 cup powdered detergent
Note: Do not worry if the mixture does not appear soapy; it does not need suds to work.
(6) For any grease spots that remain, sprinkle enough dry Floorex powder to cover them entirely. Scrub these spots with a 5-inch wire brush.
(7) Rinse the entire floor thoroughly with water to remove cleanser. Allow floor to dry (30 min.) before painting.

Painting the Floor

(8) Mix the paint with a stirrer ten or fifteen times until the color is even.
Note: If the paint has not already been shaken by machine before being opened, shake the can for about three minutes, open, and stir the contents for about five to ten minutes or until the paint is mixed.
(9) Pour the paint into the paint tray.
(10) With the 3-inch paint brush, paint the floor around the baseboard. Come out at least two to three inches so that roller used in the next step will not touch the baseboard.
(11) Paint the rest of the floor with a roller attached to an extension handle. A roller handles much more easily than a brush and distributes the paint more smoothly. Move the roller in the same direction each time. Overlap each row painted by one-half inch to avoid spaces between rows of paint.

(12) Allow two hours to dry. The floor will be ready to walk on.

> **CAUTION:** DO NOT DRIVE VEHICLES ONTO FLOOR FOR 24 HOURS. TIRES WILL PICK UP NEW PAINT.

◆ INSTRUCTIONS: SOME FINAL ADVICE

Perhaps the most important piece of advice to leave you with is this: Do not take *anything* for granted when you have to write a set of instructions. It is wrong and on occasion dangerous to assume that your readers have performed the procedure before, that they will automatically supply missing or "obvious" information, or that they will easily anticipate your next step. No one ever complained that a set of instructions was too clear or too easy to follow.

To make sure that your instructions are clear and complete, draft, revise, edit, proofread, and test them with your reader in mind. Give the reader all the appropriate information needed for the task—and in the right order. Make sure your instructions have all the parts the reader must have to do the job safely and accurately: introduction, list of materials, the steps, and conclusion. Use visuals to clarify a tricky step or to simplify a procedure, and always insert warning, caution, or note statements where needed.

◆ EXERCISES

1. Bring to class two examples of short directions that require no introduction, list of materials and equipment, or conclusion. Look for these two examples on labels, carton panels, or backs of envelopes. Evaluate the effectiveness of these instructions by commenting on how precise, direct, and useful they are.

2. Find at least one example of long instructions containing an introduction, list of materials and equipment, statements of warning, caution, or note, and a conclusion. Bring this example to class and be prepared to show how the various steps in this set of instructions follow the principles outlined on pages 448–51 in this chapter. You can find a set of full instructions in many technical manuals and in some manuals to help consumers assemble or maintain large or complex home appliances.

3. Find a set of instructions that does not contain any visuals, but which you think should have some graphic materials to make it clearer. Design those visuals yourself and indicate where they should appear in the instructions.

4. From a technical manual in your field or from an owner's manual, locate a set of instructions that you think are poorly written and illustrated. In a memo to

your instructor, explain why those instructions are unclear, confusing, or badly formatted. Then revise the instructions to make them easier for the reader to carry out. Submit the poor instructions with your revision.

5. Write a set of instructions in numbered steps (or in paragraph format) on one of the following relatively simple activities.
   a. tying a shoe
   b. brushing your teeth
   c. unlocking a door with a key
   d. making a long distance collect telephone call
   e. planting a tree or shrub
   f. logging on to a computer
   g. removing a stain from clothing
   h. pumping gas into a car
   i. building a campfire
   j. checking a book out of the library
   k. parallel parking a car

6. Write a set of full instructions on one of the following more complex topics. Identify your audience. Include an appropriate introduction, a list of equipment and materials, numbered steps with necessary warning, caution, and note statements, and an effective conclusion. Also include whatever visuals you think will help your readers.
   a. outfitting a kayak for a sea expedition
   b. changing a flat tire
   c. designing a computer program
   d. developing black-and-white film
   e. shaving a patient for surgery
   f. changing the oil and oil filter in a car
   g. making a blueprint
   h. installing a wind turbine on a roof
   i. filling out an income tax return
   j. surveying a parcel of land
   k. pruning hedges
   l. jumping a dead car battery
   m. using the Heimlich maneuver to help a choking individual
   n. filleting a fish
   o. arranging a footlocker for inspection
   p. taking someone's blood pressure
   q. changing a cash register tape
   r. finding and plugging a leak in a tire
   s. taking reservations at a hotel/motel
   t. painting a car
   u. cooking a roast
   v. flossing a patient's teeth after cleaning
   w. sewing on a button

7. The following set of instructions is confusing, vague, and out of order. Rewrite these instructions to make them clear, easy to follow, and correct. Make sure that each step follows the guidelines outlined in this chapter.

Reupholstering a Piece of Furniture

(1) Although it might be difficult to match the worn material with the new material, you might as well try.

(2) If you cannot, remove the old material.

(3) Take out the padding.

(4) Take out all of the tacks before removing the old covering. You might want to save the old covering.

(5) Measure the new material with the old, if you are able to.

(6) Check the frame, springs, webbing, and padding.

(7) Put the new material over the old.

(8) Check to see if it matches.

(9) You must have the same size as before.

(10) Look at the padding inside. If it is lumpy, smooth it out.

(11) You will need to tack all the sides down. Space your tacks a good distance apart.

(12) When you spot wrinkles, remove the tacks.

(13) Caution: in Step 11 directly above, do not drive your tacks all the way through. Leave some room.

(14) Work from the center to the edge in Step 11 above.

(15) Put the new material over the old furniture.

P.S. Use strong cords whenever there are tacks. Put the cords under the nails so that they hold.

Proposals

A proposal is a detailed plan of action that a writer submits to a reader or group of readers for approval. These readers are usually in a position of authority—supervisors, managers, department heads, company buyers, elected officials, civic leaders—to endorse or reject the writer's plan. Proposals are among the most important types of job-related writing. Their acceptance can lead to improved working conditions, a more efficient and economical business, additional jobs and business for a company, or a safer and more attractive environment.

◆ WRITING SUCCESSFUL PROPOSALS

Proposals are written for many purposes. You might write a proposal to your boss seeking authorization to purchase a new piece of equipment for the office; for example, a copier with a reduction mode to handle the special printing needs you see on the job. William Tisch's memo in Figure 2.5 (page 34) is a proposal persuading his boss to purchase a fax machine. Proposals also routinely go to potential customers offering a product or a service. For instance, you might write a proposal to a manager of a high school cafeteria to convince her to stock your company's brand of potato chips or to a fire chief offering to supply special firefighting gear. Government agencies (e.g., Department of Interior, Health and Human Services) regularly request and receive proposals from individuals hoping to gain funding for research projects that might study the mating habits of a particular animal species or determine the mercury levels at a certain lake.

Depending on the job, proposals can vary greatly in size and in scope. A proposal to your employer could easily be conveyed in a memo of a page or two. A proposal to do a research project for a class assignment can also be successfully completed in a brief memo. To propose doing a small job for a prospective client—redecorating a waiting room in an accountant's office—a letter with information on costs, materials, and a timetable might suffice. But for an extremely large and costly job—constructing a ten-story office building, for example—the

456

customer would require a long, detailed report with appendixes containing sections on engineering specifications, detailed budgets, and even résumés of all key personnel working on the project.

Long, complex proposals and reports might be written by a team of individuals instead of by one writer. Collaborative (or team) writing on long projects is frequent in the business world. But for collaborative writing to be effective, every member of the team must:

- understand and share the same goals and priorities.
- clearly identify the main audience and its needs.
- perform the specific duties assigned to him or her, whether it is gathering data, drafting and editing the document, preparing visuals, or coordinating the efforts of several members of the team.
- adhere faithfully to an agreed upon timetable.

A discussion of long, elaborate proposals is beyond the scope of this chapter. But the principles and techniques of audience analysis, organization, and drafting that this chapter does cover apply equally well to any longer project you may be called upon to prepare individually or as part of a team.

◆ PROPOSALS ARE PERSUASIVE PLANS

Proposals, whether large or small, have one thing in common. They must be highly persuasive to succeed. Without your audience's approval, your plan will never go into effect, however accurate and important you think it is. Through the details of your proposal you must convince readers that your plan will help them either improve their businesses or generally make their jobs easier. The tone of your proposal should be "Here is what I can do for you." Stress the precise benefits your plan has for the reader. Show readers how approving your plan will save them time and money or will improve their employees' morale or their customer relations.

Competition is fierce in the world of work, and a persuasive proposal frequently determines which company receives a contract. Demonstrate to your reader why your plan is better—more efficient, practical, economical—than a competitor's. In a sense, a proposal combines the persuasiveness of a sales letter (see Chapter 8), the documentation of a report (see Chapters 16 and 17), and the binding power of a contract, for if the reader accepts your proposal, he or she will expect you to live up to its terms.

◆ TYPES OF PROPOSALS

Proposals are classified according to how they originate and where they are sent after they are written. Distinctions are made between *solicited* and *unsolicited* proposals based on how they originate and between *internal* and *external* proposals based on where they are sent. Depending on your audience and your purpose, you may write an internal solicited or unsolicited proposal; or you may write an external solicited or unsolicited proposal.

Solicited and Unsolicited Proposals

When a company has a particular problem to be solved or a job to be done, it will solicit, or invite, proposals. The company will notify you and other competitors by preparing a Request for Proposals (an RFP), which is a set of instructions that specify the exact type of work to be done along with guidelines on how and when the company wants the work completed. Figure 15.1 contains a sample RFP. RFPs are mailed to firms with track records in the area the company wants the work done. RFPs are also printed in trade publications to attract the highest number of qualified bidders for the job.

An RFP helps you to know what the customer wants. It is often extremely detailed and even tells you how the company wants the proposal prepared; for example, what information is to be included, where it needs to appear, and even how many copies of the proposal you have to submit. Your own proposal will be judged according to how well you fulfill the terms of the RFP. For that reason, follow the directions in the RFP exactly. (Note how the solicited proposal in Figure 15.3 directly refers to the terms of the RFP.)

With an unsolicited proposal, you—not the reader—make the first move. You identify a problem for readers and prepare a proposal to solve it. Doing that is not as difficult as it sounds. See how the writers of the unsolicited proposals in Figures 15.2 and 15.4 identify a problem for their readers.

FIGURE 15.1   A sample RFP.

REQUEST FOR PROPOSALS

Mesa Community College solicits proposals to construct and to install fifty individual study carrels in its Holmes Memorial Library. These carrels must be highly serviceable and conform to all specification standards of the ALA. Proposals should include the precise measurements of the carrels to be installed, the specific acoustical and lighting benefits, and the types and amount of storage space offered. Work on constructing and installing the carrels must be completed no later than the start of the fall semester, August 27, 1990. Proposals should include a schedule of when different phases of work will be completed and an itemized budget for labor, materials, equipment, and necessary tests to ensure high quality acoustical performance. Contractors should state their qualifications, including a description of similar recent work and a list of references. Proposals should be submitted in triplicate no later than May 15, 1990 to:

Mrs. Barbara Feldstein-Archer
Director of the Library
Mesa Community College
Mesa, NV 89203-0996

Before you write an unsolicited proposal, though, you may want to speak with an appropriate manager at the company or write an inquiry letter to that individual to determine if he or she would be interested in receiving your proposal. Many times companies are eager to learn about a problem and how the writer proposes to solve it for the company. Sometimes the company will even help by giving you information through an interview or a tour. If so, acknowledge that assistance in your proposal.

Unlike a solicited proposal in which the company knows about the problem, an unsolicited proposal has to convince readers in the first place that there is a problem and in the second place that you and your firm are the ones to solve it. Accordingly, your unsolicited proposal has to document the existence of the problem and demonstrate how solving it is in the best interest of the readers. If they accept your identification of the problem, you have greatly increased your chances of their accepting your plan to solve it. On the other hand, if you do not convince readers that a problem exists, your solution, and hence your proposal, will be rejected or ignored.

Internal and External Proposals

An internal proposal is written to a decision maker within your own organization. As you will see on pages 460–65, this type of proposal can deal with a variety of topics, including changing a policy or procedure or requesting additional personnel or equipment.

An external proposal, on the other hand, is sent to a decision maker outside of your company. It might go to a potential client you have never worked for or to a previous or current client. An external proposal can also be sent to a government funding agency such as the Department of Agriculture. External proposals tend to be more formal than internal ones.

◆ GUIDELINES FOR WRITING A SUCCESSFUL PROPOSAL

Regardless of the type of proposal you are called on to write, the following guidelines will help you to persuade your audience to approve your plan. Refer to these guidelines both before and while you formulate your plan.

1. Approach writing a proposal as a problem-solving activity. Your goal is to solve a problem that affects the reader. Do not lose sight of the problem as you plan and write your proposal. Everything in your proposal should relate to the problem, and the organization of your proposal should reflect your ability as a problem-solver. Psychologically, make the reader feel confident that you can solve the problem.

2. Regard your audience as skeptical readers. Even though you offer a plan that you think will benefit readers, do not be overconfident that they will automatically accept it as the best and only way to proceed. To determine the feasibility of your plan, readers will question everything you say. They will withhold their approval if your proposal contains errors, omissions, or inconsistencies. Consequently, try to examine your proposal from the reader's point of view.

3. Research your proposal carefully. A winning proposal is not based only on a few well-meaning, general suggestions. All your good intentions and enthusiasm will not substitute for the hard facts readers will demand. Concrete examples persuade readers; unsupported generalizations do not. To make your proposal complete and accurate, you will have to do a lot of homework, for example, reading previous correspondence or research about the problem, doing comparative shopping for the best prices, verifying schedules and timetables, interviewing customers and/or employees, making site visits.

4. Prove that your proposal is workable. Your proposal should be well thought out. It should contain no statements saying "let's see what happens if we do X or Y." By analyzing and, when possible, by testing each part of your proposal in advance, you can eliminate any quirks and revise the proposal appropriately before readers evaluate it. What you propose should be consistent with the organization and capabilities of the company. It would be foolish to recommend, for example, that a small company (fifty employees) triple its work force to accomplish your plan.

5. Be sure that your proposal is financially realistic. This point is closely associated to and follows from guideline 4. Do not submit a proposal that would require an unnecessarily large amount of money to implement. For example, it would be unrealistic to recommend that your company spend $20,000 to solve a $2,000 problem that might not ever recur. Most short proposals, the type you will most likely be writing, offer plans that can be put into effect for under $10,000 or $15,000.

6. Package your proposal attractively. Make sure your proposal is letter-perfect, inviting, and easy to read (for example, use plenty of headings and other visual devices discussed on pages 16–17). The appearance as well as the content of your proposal can determine whether it is accepted or rejected. Remember that readers, especially those unfamiliar with your work, will evaluate your proposal as evidence of the type of work you want to do for them. Take advantage of any software programs dealing with desktop publishing (see pages 345–48) that may be available to you.

◆ INTERNAL PROPOSALS

The primary purpose of an internal proposal, such as the one included in Figure 15.2, is to offer a realistic and constructive plan to help your company run its business more efficiently and economically. On your job you may discover a better way of doing something or a more efficient way to correct a problem. You believe that your proposed change will save your employer time, money, or further trouble. (Angie Quinn in Figure 15.2 has discovered a more efficient way to get mail delivered in her company.) You decide to notify your department head,

FIGURE 15.2   An internal unsolicited proposal.

MIDWEST PETROCHEMICAL CORPORATION
Des Moines, IA 50351-0100

TO: O. L. Higgins, Office Manager
FROM: Angie Quinn, Accounting Department   A.Q.
DATE: June 15, 1988
SUBJECT: A Proposal to Change Mail Delivery by Using a Golf Cart

PURPOSE

I am writing to propose a cost-effective solution to what I believe is a growing problem at Midwest: the inefficiency of our current mail distribution system. I recommend the purchase of a motor-driven golf cart and the partial reassignment of a mail-room clerk for twice-daily delivery and pickup of mail and packages to each of the fifteen buildings within our operation.

THE COSTLY PROBLEM WITH CURRENT MAIL SERVICE

Currently, each office dispatches an employee to the mail room in the Administration Building to send and pick up mail. Considering the seven-acre size of our operation, the employees traveling the greatest distance to the mail room spend at least 50 minutes a day in this activity. I estimate that for all 42 offices, an average of 20 minutes per office a day is spent in mail delivery and pickup.

20 minutes/day × 42 offices = 840 minutes/day, or 14 hours/day

Fourteen employee-hours per day is a costly investment of time to spend for mail service. This activity translates into 70 hours per week just for mail service. At an average rate of employees' pay ($5.50) per hour, this task costs the company $385 (70 hours × $5.50) a week. The amount of money and time per year is even more staggering—$385 × 52 weeks = $20,020. A more cost-effective and efficient method of mail delivery needs to be found.

A SOLUTION TO THE MAIL PROBLEM

By using a golf cart to deliver mail and small packages to each of our fifteen buildings twice each day, the company can realize significant savings. Mr. A. J. Pandolf of Smith's Hobby Port informed me that a cart can be delivered within five days of ordering it.

No special training or license is necessary to operate a golf cart. A mail-room clerk earning entry-level wages ($4.50 per hour) could easily make the deliveries. Each delivery would require no more than 75 minutes per trip, or a total of $2\frac{1}{2}$ hours a day.

FIGURE 15.2   (continued)

We will need to construct a mail drop in front of each of the fifteen buildings. Janis Leeds, of our Buildings and Grounds Department, assures me that these mail drops are large enough for our purposes, are relatively inexpensive, and can be purchased and installed within two weeks.

The reduction in walk-in traffic resulting from this new delivery system will decrease the work load in our mail-room, thus allowing a clerk to be reassigned easily to this delivery work with very little loss of efficiency to the mail-room. Moreover, the efficient use of one clerk for mail-drop service can significantly reduce the amount of frustration employees have experienced in waiting for mail.

COSTS

The costs of implementing my proposal are as follows:

1 Golf Pro golf cart, model 750, with gasoline engine and canvas canopy (from Smith's Hobby Port)	$2,900.00
Purchase and installation of mail drops in each building ($250.00 × 15 buildings)	3,750.00
Salary for mail clerk/driver ($4.50/hr × 12$\frac{1}{2}$ hrs/wk × 52)	2,925.00
Maintenance (Plant Motor Pool estimate for 1 year)	100.00
Gasoline/oil	75.00
Total	$9,750.00

Compared with the $20,020 the company now spends in employees' time to receive and deliver mail, this cost reduces by more than half the amount of money the company will have to spend on mail service.

The company will have a futher financial benefit. Because employees will spend less time away from each office picking up and sending the mail and small packages, they can devote more time to their office duties and thereby increase the productivity of each office.

CONCLUSION

Using a golf cart for our mail service is both feasible and cost-effective. Adoption of this proposal will save our company more than $10,000 in wasted time. I will be happy to discuss this proposal with you at any time at your convenience.

manager, or supervisor, or your employer may ask you for specific suggestions to solve a problem he or she has already identified. Trudy Snowden's memo in Figure 8.3 (page 200) responds to such a request from her employer.

Generally speaking, your proposal will be an informal, in-house message, so a brief (usually one- or two-page) memo should be appropriate.

An internal proposal can be written about a variety of topics such as:

♦ purchasing new or more advanced equipment: word processors, transducers, automobiles
♦ hiring new employees or training current ones to handle a new technique or process
♦ eliminating a dangerous condition or reducing an environmental risk to prevent accidents—for employees, customers, or the community at large
♦ revising a policy to improve customer relations (eliminating an inconvenience, speeding up a delivery) or employees' morale (offering vanpooling; adding more options for a schedule)

As this list shows, internal proposals cover almost every activity or policy that affects the day-to-day operation of a company or agency.

Your Audience and Office Politics

Writing an internal proposal requires you to be aware of and sensitive to office politics. To be successful, your internal proposal should be written with the needs and likes of your audience in mind. Remember that your boss will expect you to be very convincing about both the problem you say exists and the solution you propose to correct it. You cannot assume that your reader will automatically agree with you that there is a problem or that your plan is the only way to solve it.

Your reader in fact may feel threatened by your plan. After all, you are advocating a change. Some managers regard such changes as a challenge to their administration of an office or department. Or your reader may be indifferent, not even wanting to give your work serious consideration. Or your manager-reader may have certain "pet" projects or ways of doing things that you must take into account. To surmount these and other obstacles, show that the change you propose is in everyone's best interest. Do not overlook the possibility that your boss may have to take your proposal up the organizational ladder for commentary and, eventually, approval.

Before you write an internal proposal, consider the implications of your plan for your boss and for other offices or sections in your company. A change you propose for your department or office (transfers; new budgets or schedules) may have sweeping and potentially disruptive implications for another office or division within your company. It is wise to discuss your plan with your boss before you put it in writing.

Never submit an internal proposal that offers an idea you think will work but relies on someone else to supply the specific details on *how* it will work. For example, do not write an internal proposal that says payroll, community relations, maintenance, or advertising departments can give the reader the details and costs he or she needs about your proposal. That pushes the responsibility onto some-one else, and your proposal could be rejected for lack of concrete evidence.

The Organization of an Internal Proposal

A short, internal proposal follows a relatively straightforward plan of organization, from identifying the problem to solving it. Internal proposals usually contain four parts, as shown in Figure 15.2. Refer to this proposal as you read the following discussion.

The Introduction

Begin your proposal with a brief statement of why you are writing to your boss: "I propose that . . ." State why you think a specific change is necessary now. Then succinctly define the problem and emphasize that your plan, if approved by the reader, will solve that problem. Where necessary, stress the urgency to act—within the next week? month?

Background of the Problem

In this section prove that a problem does exist by documenting its importance for your boss and your company. As a matter of fact, the more you show how the problem affects the boss's work (and area of supervision), the more likely you are to persuade him or her to act. And the more concrete evidence you cite, the eas-ier it will be to convince the reader that the problem is significant and that action needs to be taken now.

Avoid vague (and unsupported) generalizations such as "we're losing money each day with this procedure (or piece of equipment)"; "costs continue to esca-late"; "the trouble occurs frequently in a number of places"; "numerous com-plaints have come in"; "if something isn't done soon, more difficulty will result."

Instead, provide readers with quantifiable details about the number of dollars a company is actually losing per day, week, or month. Emphasize the financial trouble so that you can show how your plan (described in the next section) of-fers an efficient and workable solution. Indicate how many employees (or work-hours) are involved or how many customers are inconvenienced or endangered by a procedure or condition. Verify how widespread a problem is or how fre-quently it occurs by citing specific occasions. Rather than just saying that a new word processor would save the company "a lot of money," document how many work-hours are lost using other equipment for the routine jobs your company now has employees perform.

The Solution or Plan

In this section describe the change you want approved. Tie your solution (the change) directly to the problem you have just documented. Each part of your plan should help eliminate the problem or should help increase the productivity or efficiency you think is possible.

Your reader will again expect to find factual evidence. Do not give merely the outline of a plan or say that details can be worked out later. Supply details that answer the following questions: (1) Is the plan workable—can it be accomplished here in our office or plant? and (2) Is it cost effective—will it really save us money in the long run or will it lead to even greater expenses?

To get the boss to say yes to both questions, supply the facts that you have gathered as a result of your research. For example, if you propose that your firm buy a new piece of equipment, do the necessary homework to locate the most efficient and cost-effective model available, as Angie Quinn does in Figure 15.2. Supply the dealer's name, the costs, major conditions of service and training contracts, and warranties. Describe how your firm could use this equipment to obtain better results in the future. Cite specific tasks the new equipment can perform more efficiently at less cost than the equipment now in use.

If you are proposing that your company hire or reassign employees, indicate where these employees will come from, when they will start, what they will be paid, what skills they must have, where they will work and for how long. If you propose to assign current employees to a job, keep in mind that their salary will still have to be paid by your company. Just because they are coworkers does not mean they will work for nothing. Note in Figure 15.2 how Angie Quinn handles the reassignment of one of the employees in the mailroom.

A proposal to change a procedure must include the following details:

1. how the new (or revised) procedure will work
2. how many employees or customers will be affected by it
3. when it will go into operation
4. how much it will cost the employer to change procedures
5. what delays or losses in business might be expected while the company switches from one procedure to another
6. what employees, equipment, or locations are available to accomplish this change

As these questions indicate, your boss will be concerned about schedules, working conditions, employees, methods, locations, equipment, and the costs involved in your plan for change. The costs, in fact, will be of utmost importance. Make sure that you supply a careful and accurate budget so that your reader will know what the change is going to cost. Moreover, make those costs attractive by emphasizing how inexpensive they are as compared to the cost of not making the change, as Quinn does in her section labeled "Costs."

The Conclusion

The conclusion to your internal proposal should be short—a paragraph or two at the most. Your intention is to remind the reader that the problem is serious, that the reason for change is justified, and that you think the reader needs to take action. Select the most important benefit and emphasize it again. In Figure 15.2, Angie Quinn again emphasizes the savings that the company will see by following her plan. Also be willing to discuss your plan with the reader.

◆ SALES PROPOSALS

A sales proposal is the most common type of external proposal. Its purpose is to sell your company's products or services for a set fee. Whether short or long, a sales proposal is a marketing tool that includes a sales pitch as well as a detailed description of the work you propose to do. Figures 15.3 and 15.4 contain sample sales proposals.

The Audience and Its Needs

Your audience will usually be one or more business executives who have the power to approve or reject a proposal. Unlike readers of an internal proposal, your audience for a sales proposal may be even more skeptical since they may not know you or your work. Your proposal may also be evaluated by experts in other fields employed by your prospective customer. Readers of a sales proposal will evaluate your work according to (1) how well it meets their needs and (2) how well it compares with the proposals submitted by your competitors. Your proposal must convince readers that you can provide the most appropriate work or service and that your company is more reliable and efficient than any other firm.

The key to success is incorporating the "you attitude" (see pages 132–37) throughout your proposal. Relate your product, service, or personnel to the buyer's exact needs as stated in the RFP for a solicited proposal or through your own investigations for an unsolicited proposal. You cannot submit the same proposal for every job you want to win and expect to be awarded a contract. Different firms have different needs. The most important question the reader will raise, therefore, about your work is, "How does this proposal meet our company's special requirements?" Some other fairly common questions readers will have as they evaluate your work include the following.

- Does the writer's firm understand our problem?
- Can the writer's firm deliver what it promises?
- Can the job be completed on time?
- What assurances does the writer offer that the job will be done exactly as proposed?

Answer each of these questions by demonstrating how your product or service is tailored to the customer's needs.

Organizing a Sales Proposal

A sales proposal can have the following parts: introduction, description of the proposed product or service, timetable, costs, qualifications of your company, and conclusion.

FIGURE 15.3   An external solicited proposal.

REYNOLDS INTERIORS
250 Commerce Avenue, S.W.
Portland, OR 97204-2129
763-2000

January 14, 1989

Mr. Floyd Tompkins, Manager
General Purpose Appliances
Highway 41 South
Portland, OR 97222

Dear Mr. Tompkins:

In response to your Request 7521 for bids for an appropriate floor covering at your new showroom, Reynolds Interiors is pleased to submit the following proposal. After carefully reviewing your specifications for a floor covering and inspecting your new facility, we believe that the Armstrong Classic Corlon 900 is the most suitable choice. I am enclosing a sample of the Corlon 900 so that you can see how it looks.

CORLON'S ADVANTAGES

Guaranteed against defects for a full three years, Corlon is one of the finest and most durable floor coverings manufactured by Armstrong. It is a heavy-duty commercial floor 0.085 inch thick for protection. Twenty-five percent of each tile consists of interface backing; the other 75 percent is an inlaid wear layer that offers exceptionally high resistance to everyday traffic. Traffic tests conducted by the Independent Floor Covering Institute repeatedly proved the superiority of Corlon's construction and resistance.

Another important feature of Corlon is the size of its rolls. Unlike other leading brands of similar commercial flooring—Remington or Treadmaster—Corlon comes in 12-foot-wide rather than 6-foot-wide rolls. This extra width will significantly reduce the number of seams in your floor, thus increasing its attractiveness and reducing the danger of tile split.

INSTALLATION PROCEDURES

The Classic Corlon requires that we use the inlaid seaming process, a technical procedure requiring the services of a trained floor mechanic. Herman Goshen, our floor mechanic, has over fifteen years of experience working with the inlaid seam process. His professional work has been consistently praised by our customers.

INSTALLATION SCHEDULE

We can install the Classic Corlon on your showroom floor during the first week of March, which fits the timetable specified in your request. The tile will take three and

FIGURE 15.3   (continued)

one-half days to install and will be ready to walk on immediately. We recommend, though, that you not move equipment onto the floor for twenty-four hours after installation.

COSTS

The following costs include the Classic Corlon tile, labor, equipment, and tax:

750 sq. yards of Classic Corlon at $12.50 /yard	$ 9,375.00
Labor (28 hr. @ $15.00/hr.)	420.00
Sealing fluid (10 gal. @ $10.00/gal.)	100.00
Total	9,895.00
Tax (5 percent)	494.75
Grand total	$10,389.75

Our costs are $250.00 under those you specified in your request.

REYNOLDS'S QUALIFICATIONS

Reynolds Interiors has been in business for more than twenty-five years. In that time, we have installed many commercial floors in Portland and its suburbs. In the last year, we have served more than sixty customers, including the new multi-purpose Radon plant in Portland.

CONCLUSION

Thank you for the opportunity to submit this proposal. We believe you will have a great deal of success with an Armstrong floor. If we can provide you with any further information, please call me.

Sincerely yours,

M.T. Chin

M. T. Chin
Sales Manager

FIGURE 15.4   An external unsolicited proposal.

National Business Equipment   **N B E**
470 Rodgers Rd. ■ Camden, NJ 08104-0826 ■ (201) 568-1100

September 20, 1988

Mr. Daniel Taylor
Business Manager
Madison Tool and Die Company
3400 Veterans Boulevard
Camden, NJ 08104

Dear Mr. Taylor:

While we were servicing your Piko 2500 copier last week, it occurred to me
that you might be interested in purchasing a newer model that will give you
state-of-the-art features to make your copying work more efficient and
reliable. In the past three years since you purchased your 2500, copier
technology has advanced tremendously, giving users many benefits at
surprisingly low cost.

Knowing that you want the most reliable office equipment available, I am
submitting for your consideration this proposal to supply Madison Tool and
Die with our latest copier, the Piko 4000.

ADVANTAGES OF THE PIKO 4000

With the Piko 4000, your cost per single copy will be reduced to only $1\frac{1}{2}$
cents, compared with approximately 5 cents per copy with your present
machine. The following description of the main features of the Piko 4000 will
show you its other advantages over your current copier.

Printing Technology

The Piko 4000's dry toner capability and double-sided copying option will
save you time and money. Your copies will never again be smudged because

FIGURE 15.4 (continued)

of liquid toner problems. In addition to the standard paper sizes—$8\frac{1}{2} \times 11$, $8\frac{1}{2} \times 14$, and 11×17—the 4000 functions effectively with other paper sizes and shapes, including heavyweight sheet stock suitable for specifications and drawings.

Feeding/Sorting Capacity

The 4000 includes as standard equipment both an automatic feeder and an automatic sorter. These features can reduce the time spent on large copying jobs by as much as 50 percent.

Printing Quality

The new Piko 4000 offers top-quality, high-resolution reproduction. Since seeing is believing, I am enclosing a copy of this proposal made on the 4000 as well as copy of a blueprint to show you how both copied documents look.

Size

The Piko 4000 measures $4' \times 3' \times 4'$, occupying one-quarter less space than your present copier. Once the machine is installed, you will find this extra space useful for your storage needs.

INSTALLATION, TRAINING, AND SERVICE

We will deliver and install your new Piko 4000 within one week of receiving your purchase order. The installation requires approximately forty-five minutes.

Our local sales representative, Darlene Simpson, is available to instruct your employees in the operation and routine maintenance of the 4000. A phone call will set up a mutually convenient date. If a problem occurs, we offer customers our "hot-line" service on business days from 8:00 a.m. to 5:00 p.m. We guarantee that a service representative will arrive at your office within three business hours from the time of your request.

FIGURE 15.4   (continued)

COSTS

Below is the price of the Piko 4000 and appropriate initial supplies:

Piko 4000	$7295.00
Toner (tube)	18.00
Paper (500-sheet box of regular $8\frac{1}{2} \times 11$)	2.70
Service contract—optional	
($780 per year, parts and labor included)	780.00
Total	$8095.70

The installation of your new Piko 4000 is free.

NATIONAL'S REPUTATION

Over the past twenty-two years, National has supplied copiers to more than ninety companies in the greater Camden area, including Biscayne Industries, Northeast Manufacturing, and Aronson Accounting, Inc. In addition to providing quality products, we are dedicated to giving our customers fast and efficient service long after a sale.

We appreciate your using National Business Equipment for your repair needs and hope that you will decide to purchase the new Piko 4000. Please call me if you have any questions about the Piko 4000 or National.

If this proposal is acceptable, please sign and return a copy of this letter.

Sincerely yours,

Marion Copely

Marion Copely

I accept this proposal made by National Business Equipment.

_____

for Madison Tool and Die Company

Introduction

The introduction to your sales proposal can be a single paragraph in a short sales proposal or several pages in a more complex one. Basically, the introduction should prepare readers for everything that follows in your proposal. The introduction itself may contain the following sections, which sometimes may be combined.

1. Statement of purpose and subject of proposal. Tell readers why you are writing and identify the specific subject of your work. If you are responding to an RFP, use specific code numbers or cite application dates, as the proposal in Figure 15.3 does. If your proposal is unsolicited, indicate how you learned of the problem as Figure 15.4 does. Briefly define the solution you propose.

2. Background of the problem you propose to solve. Show readers that you are familiar with their problem and that you have a firm grasp of the importance and implications of the problem. In a solicited proposal, such as the one shown in Figure 15.3, a section outlining the problem is usually unnecessary, because the potential client has already identified the problem and just wants to know how you would handle it. In that case, just point out how your company would solve the problem, mentioning your superiority over your competitors if possible (see the third paragraph of Figure 15.3). In an unsolicited proposal, on the other hand, you need to describe the problem in convincing detail, identifying the specific trouble areas. However, if it is an external proposal to a current customer, such as the one in Figure 15.4, it would be unwise to point out explicitly past problems your client may have had with your company's service or products. In Figure 15.4, note how the problems of the Piko 2500 model are described mainly as a way to sell the advantages of the Piko 4000.

Description of the Proposed Product or Service

This section is the heart of your proposal. Before spending their money, customers will demand hard, factual evidence of what you claim can and should be done. Here are some points that you should cover.

1. Carefully show your potential customers that your product or service is right for them. Stress specific benefits of your product or service most relevant to your reader. Blend sales talk with descriptions of hardware.

2. Describe your work in suitable detail—what it looks like, what it does, and how consistently and well it will perform in the readers' office, plant, hospital, or agency. You might include a brochure, picture, or, as the writer of the proposal in Figure 15.3 does, a sample of your product for customers to study. Convince readers that your product is the most up-to-date and efficient one they could select. Note how the proposals in Figures 15.3 and 15.4 accomplish this.

3. Stress any special features, maintenance advantages, warranties, or service benefits. Highlight features that show the quality, consistency, or security of your work. For a service, emphasize the procedures you use, the terms of that service, and even the kinds of tools you use, especially any "state-of-the-art" equipment. Be sure to provide a step-by-step outline of what will happen and why each step is beneficial for readers.

Timetable

A carefully planned timetable shows readers that you know your job and that you can accomplish it in the right amount of time. Your dates should match any listed in an RFP. Provide specific dates when the work will begin, how long it will continue, and when you will be finished installing equipment, testing equipment, or training employees to use equipment. For proposals offering a service, specify how many times—by the hour, week, month—customers can expect to receive your help; for example, spraying three times a month for an exterminating service or making deliveries by 10:00 A.M. for a trucking company. Indicate whether follow-up visits or service calls will be provided.

Costs

Make your budget accurate, complete, and convincing. Don't underestimate costs in the hope that that a low bid will win you the job. You may get the job but lose money doing it, for the customer will rightfully hold you to your unrealistic figures. On the other hand, don't inflate prices; competitors will beat you in the bidding.

Give customers more than the bottom-line cost. Show exactly what readers are getting for their money so they can determine if everything they need is included. Itemize costs for specific services, equipment, labor (by the hour or by the job), transportation, travel, training you propose to supply. If something is not included or is considered optional, say so—additional hours of training, replacement of parts, and the like. If you anticipate a price increase, let the customer know how long current prices will stay in effect. That information may spur them to act favorably now.

Qualifications of Your Company

Emphasize your company's accomplishments and expertise in using relevant services and equipment. You might list previous work you have done that is identical or similar to the type of work you are proposing to do for the customer. You may even want to mention the names of a few local firms for whom you have worked that would be pleased to recommend you.

Conclusion

This is the "call to action" section of your proposal. As with the conclusion in an internal proposal, encourage your reader to approve your plan. Stress the major benefits your plan has for the customer. Notice how the last paragraphs of Figures 15.3 and 15.4 do this effectively. Offer to answer any questions the reader may have. Some proposals end by asking the reader to sign and return a copy of the proposal thus indicating their acceptance of it, as the proposal in Figure 15.4 does.

◆ PROPOSALS FOR RESEARCH PAPERS AND REPORTS

You may have to write a proposal like the one in Figure 15.5 when your instructor asks you to submit a report or research paper, a topic for an independent study, or some other type of major term project.

Writing for Your Teacher

The principles guiding internal and sales proposals also apply to research proposals. As with internal and sales proposals, you will be writing to convince your reader—the teacher—to approve a major piece of work. But otherwise the goals of your teacher/reader will be considerably different from those of other proposal readers. A teacher will read your proposal to help you write the best possible paper or report. In examining your proposal, the teacher will want to make sure of four things:

1. that you have chosen a significant topic
2. that you have a sufficiently restricted topic
3. that you will investigate important sources of information about that topic
4. that you can accomplish your work in the specified time

Your proposal gives your teacher an opportunity to spot omissions or inconsistencies and to provide helpful suggestions.

In order to prepare an effective proposal for a research project you must do some preliminary research. You cannot pick any topic that comes to mind, or guess about procedures, sources, or conclusions. As other proposal readers do, your teacher will want convincing and specific evidence for your choice of topic and your approach to it. Be prepared to cite key facts to show that you are familiar with the topic and that you can handle it successfully.

Organization of a Proposal for a Research Paper

Your proposal for a school research project can be a memo divided into five sections, as illustrated in Figure 15.5: introduction (or purpose), scope of the problem or topic to be investigated, methods or procedures, timetable, and request for approval. However, be ready to reverse or expand these sections if your teacher wants you to follow a different organizational plan.

FIGURE 15.5   A proposal for a research paper.

TO: Professor Barbara Felton-Parks
           Business Management 200

FROM: James Salinas

DATE: February 5, 1988

SUBJECT: Proposal for a report on the advantages and
           disadvantages of electronic mall

Purpose

For my term project, I propose to research and write a report
on the advantages and disadvantages for an office in switching
to an electronic mail system.

Electronic mail is being used increasingly by many private
companies and government agencies. It has been estimated that
more than five million workers today use electronic mail
through the services of such vendors as Western Union
(EasyLink) or Tymshare (OnTyme). David Basten, Executive Vice
President of Wordplex Corporation, has enthusiastically
predicted that electronic mail "may end up running second only
to the word processor when it comes to leading business
applications" (The Office [Feb. 1986]: 56).

Although electronic mail has brought many companies closer to
the paperless office of the future, it also poses some major
problems. The United States Postal Service discontinued its
express E-COM service, as did Federal Express its ZapMail. An
understanding of the benefits as well as the drawbacks of
electronic mail is important for any office manager thinking of
converting to it. My paper will serve as a background report
for an office manager considering electronic mail.

Problems to Be Investigated

At this stage of my research, I think my report needs to answer
the following questions:
(1) How does electronic mail work as compared to conventional
    methods?
(2) What kinds of special applications does it offer users in
    preparing and sending routine messages (invoices, monthly
    sales reports) or special ones?

FIGURE 15.5   (continued)

2

(3) Will electronic mail provide the same level of security
    and confidentiality as conventional mail?
(4) Do the costs of switching to electronic mail--keyboarding
    problems, terminals, modems, hookups--offset the costs of
    conventional preparation, forwarding, and storing of mail?

I propose, therefore, to divide the body of my paper according
to the four key issues of operation, application, security,
and costs.

Methods of Research

I will rely heavily on literature dealing with electronic
mail. Judging from the number of entries on this topic in the
Business Periodicals Index from 1982 to early 1988, the
subject is popular and significant. For these years, I located
more than 140 entries. Of course, not all of them focus on
comparisons and contrasts with conventional mail systems. From
a preliminary check of some articles available in our library,
I think the following may be most useful to me:

Barks, J. V. "Can You Count on Electronic Mail?" Distribution
      83 (Mar. 1984): 72, 78-79.

"Bidirectional Electronic Mail System Helps Account for Firm's
      Increased Productivity." Communication News 21 (Feb.
      1984): 54.

Canning, B. "Electronic Mail Systems Can Develop Costly
      Problems." Office Administration Automation 44 (Apr.
      1983): 98-99.

Foley, M. J. "Hardware Vendors Adapt to Changing E-Mail
      Market." Electronic Business 1 May 1987: 40, 42.

Kay, Susan S. "Electronic Mail Growth Rests on Its
      Acceptance." The Office 97 (Aug. 1982): 48, 52, 60.

Kelly, R. L. "Electronic Mail: Will It Work on Your System?"
      The Office 99 (Apr. 1984): 42, 47.

"Limitations of Electronic Mail." Training and Development
      Journal 39 (June 1985): 10.

FIGURE 15.5   (continued)

3

McQuillan, J. M. "The Market for Electronic Mail: Turbulence and Change." The Office 99 (Jan. 1984): 104.

Panko, R. R. "Electronic Mail: The Alternatives." Office Administration Automation 45 (June 1984): 37—40.

Stevenson, Patricia. Telecommunications: An Introduction. Pittsburgh: Data Processing Press, 1987.

Walker, Philip M. "Electronic Mail Offers Growing Range of Uses." The Office 106 (Jan. 1988): 120.

"Why ZapMail Finally Got Zapped." Business Week 13 Oct. 1986: 48—49.

I intend to interview two office managers in Springfield whose companies switched to electronic mail in the last year. My choices right now are Alice Phillips at Dodge & Spenser Hydraulic Systems and Keith Wellbridge at General Dynamics. But because of their possible schedule conflicts, I may have to interview two other individuals.

Timetable

I hope to complete my library research by April 2 and my interviews by April 8. Then I will spend the following two weeks working on a rough draft, which I will submit by April 19, the date you specified. After receiving your comments on my rough draft, I will work on the final copy of my paper and turn it in by May 12, the last day of class. I will submit two progress reports--one when I finish my research and another when I decide on the final organization of my paper.

Request for Approval

I ask that you approve my topic and approach to it. I would appreciate any suggestions on how you think I might best proceed.

The Introduction

Keep your introduction short—a paragraph, maybe two, pinpointing the subject and purpose of your work.

> I propose to do research on and write a report about the "hot knife" laser used in treating port wine stain and other birthmarks.

> I intend to investigate the relationship that exists in today's office between office design and the employee's need for "psychological space."

Then briefly indicate why the topic or the problem you propose to study is significant. In other words, be prepared to explain why you have chosen that topic and why research on it is relevant or worthwhile for a specific audience or course objective. Note how James Salinas in Figure 15.5 states how and why his paper will be useful to an office manager.

Supply your teacher/reader with a few background details about your topic; for example, the importance of using a laser as opposed to conventional ways of treating birthmarks or why psychological space plays a crucial role in employee productivity and morale. Prove that you have thought carefully about a suitable topic.

The Scope of the Problem or Topic to Be Investigated

The second section, which might be entitled "Problems to Be Investigated" or "Areas to Be Studied," shows how you propose to break the topic into meaningful units. Tell your reader what specific issues, points, or areas you hope to investigate. Doing this, you show how you will limit your topic to establish an appropriate scope for your work.

Some instructors ask students to formulate a list of questions their research paper or report intends to answer. The topics included in these questions, or a list of areas or problems to be covered, might later become major sections of your paper. Make sure that the issues or questions do not overlap and that each relates directly to and supports your restricted topic. Note how the student in Figure 15.5 hopes to divide his study of electronic mail into four distinct and useful areas.

Methods or Procedures

In the third section of your proposal inform your teacher how you expect to find the answers to the questions you raised in the previous section, or how you intend to locate information about your list of subtopics. It's not enough to write, "I will gather appropriate information and analyze it." Specify what data you hope to include, where they are located, and how you intend to retrieve them. Most students gather data from literature published about their topics. (In fact, many research papers are based exclusively on library work.) This literature can include books, encyclopedias or other reference materials, articles in professional publications, newspapers, bulletins, manuals, or audiovisual materials. Inform your teacher what indexes, abstracts, or even computer searches you intend to use (review pages 257–66) as part of your literature search. To document your preliminary library work, provide your instructor with a list of a few appropriate titles on your topic following the style of documentation used for a Works Cited page (discussed on pages 292–98).

In addition to library materials, you might collect information from experiments you will perform in a laboratory or from a field test, interviews with experts, replies to letters of inquiry, questionnaires, or a combination of any of these sources.

Timetable

Your proposal should indicate when and in what order you expect to complete the different phases of your project. Your teacher needs this information to keep track of your progress and to make sure that you will turn in an assignment on time. Specify tentative dates for completing your research, rough draft(s), and final copy.

Some instructors also ask students to turn in progress reports at regular intervals. If you are asked to do this, indicate when those progress reports will be submitted, as James Salinas did in Figure 15.5.

Request for Approval

End your proposal with a request for approval of your topic. You might also indicate that you would appreciate any suggestions from your teacher on how you might restrict, research, organize, or write about your topic.

◆ PREPARING PROPOSALS: A FINAL REMINDER

This chapter has given you some basic information and specific strategies for writing proposals. Keep in mind that a proposal presents a plan to a decision maker for his or her approval. To win that approval, your proposal must be *realistic, carefully researched,* and *highly persuasive.* These essential characteristics apply to internal proposals in memo format written to your employer, more formal sales proposals sent to a potential customer, and research proposals submitted to your instructor.

◆ EXERCISES

1. In two or three paragraphs identify and document a problem (in services, safety, communication, traffic, scheduling) you see in your office or plant or at your school. Make sure that you give readers—a school official (chairper-

son; dean) or employer (section or department head; manager)—specific evidence that a problem does exist and that it needs to be corrected.

2. Write a short internal proposal, modeled after Figure 15.2, based upon the problem you identified in Exercise 1.

3. Write a short internal proposal, similar to Angie Quinn's in Figure 15.2, recommending for a company or a college a specific change in procedure, equipment, training, safety, personnel, or policy. Make sure that you provide an appropriate audience (a college administrator or department manager or section chief) with specific evidence about the existence of the problem and your solution of it. Here are some possible topics:

* providing more and safer parking
* extending the bookstore or company credit union hours
* purchasing new office or laboratory equipment
* hiring more faculty, student workers, or office help
* reorganizing or redesigning the school yearbook or company annual report or sales catalog
* changing the decor in a student or company lounge
* expanding the number of weekend or night classes in your major
* adding more offerings to a school or company cafeteria menu
* altering the programming on a campus radio station
* improving access for handicapped students or employees
* decreasing waiting time at school registration or in a computer lab

4. Rewrite the following vague and unconvincing internal proposal to make it more effective. Supply any details you think necessary.

```
TO:  Holly Gordon        SUBJECT:  Changes at Acme Corp.

FROM: K. T. Smith        DATE:  April 10, 1990

For some time now I have noticed a problem with the way the
office handles information. Things are often out of place and
sometimes hard to find. I know that it took me more than 15
minutes one day to find an important report for Mr. Swanson.
Others in the office too have been complaining about this prob-
lem. I propose that we do something about the way information is
conveyed in our department.

Having the right kind of equipment would save us hours and money.
I suggest that we call a few of the office equipment supply
offices for their opinion about the kinds of changes we need to
make.

We should also call one of the new assistant managers in the
engineering department to find out how that office is run. I have
been there a number of times and things seem to be going very
```

smoothly. Clearly they do not have the organizational problems
we do.

Along with these investigations, I suggest that we have someone from accounting give us an estimate about how much we could
afford to spend this year.

As for costs, though, I don't think the investment would be bad
and the company would be getting a lot for its money, more than
they are now with our outmoded communication system in this
office.

Please let me know what you think of my idea. I think it is worth
pursuing.

5. Write an unsolicited sales proposal, similar to the one in Figure 15.4, on one
   of the following services or products you intend to sell, or on a topic your
   instructor approves.

   - providing exterminating service to a store or restaurant
   - supplying a hospital with rental televisions for patient rooms
   - doing typing or word processing for students
   - offering temporary office help or nursing care
   - providing landscaping and lawn care work
   - testing for noise, air, or water pollution in your community or neighbor-
     hood
   - furnishing transportation for students, employees, or members of a commu-
     nity group
   - providing consulting service to save a company money
   - designing business forms for a local bank or hospital
   - digging a septic well for a small apartment complex
   - supplying insurance coverage to a small (five to ten employees) firm
   - cleaning the parking lot and outside walkways at a shopping center
   - selling a piece of equipment to a business
   - making a work area safer
   - offering a training program for employees
   - increasing donations to a community or charitable fund

6. Write a solicited proposal for one of the topics listed in Exercise 5 or on a
   topic that your instructor approves. You might want to review Figure 15.3.

7. Write an appropriate proposal—internal or solicited or unsolicited sales—
   based upon the information contained in one of the following articles. Assume that you or your prospective customer's company or community faces
   a problem similar to one discussed in one of these articles. Use as much of
   the information in these articles as you need and add any details of your own
   that you think are necessary.

Turning Schoolgrounds Green

"If our conservation district doesn't take the initiative to show our children and school leaders how to stop erosion on their playgrounds, then who will?" said Bobby Joe Ganey, Chair of the Lasalle Soil and Water Conservation District in Lasalle Parish, Louisiana.

Ganey, along with other conservation district board members, was tired of seeing bare, eroded soil outside classroom doors so the district board initiated a project to put cover on the schoolgrounds.

The district board members talked with school principals in the parish about erosion problems on their school campuses. The district board determined that six school campuses were suffering from a lack of vegetative cover, and erosion was keeping their playgrounds bare. Board members asked the Soil Conservation Service to prepare a plan for the schools.

"School grounds get a lot of foot traffic from the students, so it was necessary for us to establish a species of grass that could withstand this problem," Ganey said.

The Lasalle Soil and Water Conservation District supplied the funds to buy bermuda grass seed and fertilizer.

"It was our intention from the beginning to have the students take an active part in establishing vegetative cover on the playgrounds," said Ganey. "In this way not only could they see the value of erosion control at their school but they also could learn how erosion is bad for the community and for their futures."

The district board and Soil Conservation Service introduced the students to erosion problems through a slide show. More than 650 students from the six elementary schools participated in the erosion control work on their campuses. They helped till, seed, and fertilize the eroding areas.

To be sure that the newly established grass would be properly maintained, the plan included cutting height and fertilizer requirements.

Soil and Water Conservation News (Oct. 1984): 9.

Self-illuminating Exit Signs

The Marine Corps Development and Education Center (MCDEC), Quantico, Virginia, submitted a project recently, to replace incandescent illumination exit signs with self-illuminating exit signs for a cost of $97,238. The first-year savings were anticipated to be about $37,171 with an anticipated payback time of 2.6 years—an excellent prospect. The contractor bid much lower, however, and the actual payback will be about 1.5 years.

What are the benefits of these self-illuminating exit signs? The primary benefit is that virtually all operation and maintenance expense is eliminated for the life of the device, normally from 10 to 12 years. Power failures or other disturbances will not cause them to go out.

In new construction, expensive electrical circuits can be totally eliminated. In retrofits, the release of a dedicated circuit for other use may be of considerable benefit. Initial total cost of installing circuits and conventional devices approximately equals the cost of the self-illuminating signs. Installation labor and expense for the self-illuminating signs is about that of hanging a picture.

The amount of electricity saved varies and depends on whether your existing fixtures are fluorescent (13 to 26 watts) or incandescent (50 to 100 watts). Multiply the number of fixtures × wattage/fixture × hours operated/day × days/year = KWH/year savings. For example assume:

$$400 \text{ incandescent fixtures}$$
$$0.08 \text{ \$/KWH } 0.05 \text{ KW/fixture}$$
$$24 \text{ hours/day } 365 \text{ day/year operation}$$
$$400 \times 0.1 \times 365 = 350400 \text{ KWH/year}$$
$$350400 \times 0.08 = \$28,032/\text{year for electricity}$$

Now add in savings achieved from:

- reducing labor to change bulbs
- avoiding bulb material, stocking, and storage costs
- avoiding transportation costs involved in bulb changes
- reusing existing bulbs

The above savings can be significant. For the MCDEC Quantico project, estimates of bulb change interval and savings were 700 hours (29 days) and $13,512/year when all factors were considered.

The cost of a self-illuminating sign depends on whether one or two faces are illuminated primarily and varies between different suppliers. Single-face prices will likely be $100 to $150 while double-face prices may be $250 to $330. The contractor at Quantico found better prices than these ranges indicate. The labor cost should be about $10 per sign.

If you can use an exit-sign system with high dependability, no maintenance, and zero operations cost in your retrofit on new construction projects, try a self-illuminating exit-sign system in your economic analysis today. "Isolite" signs, by Safety Light Corp., are listed as FSC (Fire Safety Code) Group 99, Part IV, Section A, Class 9905, signs and are available through GSA contract. Contact Gerald Harnett, Safety Light Corp., P.O. Box 266, Greenbelt, MD 20070 for more information.

Lt. James F. McCollum, CEG, USN. "Self-illuminating Exit Signs Equal High Payback." *Navy Civil Engineer* (Summer 1983): 30–31.

8. Write a suitable research proposal upon which the research paper on "Stress and the Computer Programmer" (pages 305–17) could have been based.

9. Write a research proposal to your instructor seeking approval for a major term project. Do the necessary preliminary research to show that you have selected a suitable topic, that you have narrowed it, and that you have identified the sources of information you have to consult. Identify at least six or seven relevant articles and one or two books on your topic.

Short Reports

This chapter will show you how to write short reports, also called informal, semi-formal, or semi-technical reports. The skills necessary for writing these reports are among the most important ones you can develop because you will be expected to prepare short reports very often on your job. In Chapter 17 you will learn how to write a long report.

◆ WHY SHORT REPORTS ARE IMPORTANT

Business and industry cannot function without short written reports. A report may be defined as an organized presentation of relevant data on any topic—money, travel, time, personnel, equipment, management—that a company or agency must keep track of in its day-to-day operations. Reports tell whether schedules are being met, costs contained, sales projections met, clients and patients efficiently served. Reports also are likely to be required if unexpected problems occur.

You may write an occasional report in response to a specific question, or you may be required to write a daily or weekly report on routine activities about which your readers expect detailed information. Many organizations—businesses, clinics, mass transportation systems, schools—must submit regularly scheduled reports in order to maintain their accreditation or funding by state or federal agencies.

◆ TYPES OF SHORT REPORTS

To give you a sense of some of the topics that you may be required to write about, here is a list of various types of short reports that are found in business and industry.

appraisal report	medicine/treatment error report
audit report	operations report
construction report	periodic report
design report	production report
evaluation report	progress report
experiment report	recommendations report
incident report	research report
investigative report	sales report
laboratory report	status report
library report	test report
manager's report	trip report

Discussing each of these reports is too large a task for one chapter. Instead, Chapter 16 will concentrate on six of the most common types of reports you are likely to encounter in your professional work:

1. periodic reports
2. sales reports
3. progress reports
4. trip reports
5. test reports
6. incident reports

The first five reports can be called *routine reports* because they give information about planned, ongoing, or recurring events. *Incident reports,* on the other hand, describe events that writers did not anticipate—accidents, breakdowns, environmental mishaps, delivery delays, or work stoppages. All six, however, may be termed "short" reports. They deal with current happenings rather than with long-range forecasts. Short reports focus on the "trees," not the "forest."

◆ HOW TO WRITE SHORT REPORTS

The most important point to keep in mind is that reports are written for readers who need information so that they can get a job accomplished. Never think of the reports you write as a series of short notes jotted down for *your* own convenience. And also do not believe that because they are short that you can dash these reports off quickly. An effective short report needs the same careful planning that goes into other types of on-the-job writing. Prepare a brief outline or a preliminary draft first to make sure you get all your ideas down and in the most useful order for your audience. Then do some rewriting and revising to make sure your report is clear and concise.

Under each of the following categories you will find specific guidelines applicable to writing *any* short report you encounter. More specific information pertinent to particular types of reports is given within a discussion of those reports later in this chapter.

1. Audience. Short reports are written to co-workers, employers, and customers. The needs of each audience will vary. Consider how much your audience knows about your project and its reason for reading your report *before* writing it. While it is likely that co-workers in your department will be familiar with your project, readers in another department or section of your company may not be. Even employers, who will constitute the largest group of readers for your short reports, may not always know about the details of your work. These managers will use your reports to help them make decisions. Always give readers the details most relevant for their job. In a report for a business manager about equipment failure, your reader will be less concerned with the technical details about what went wrong than with the costs of parts replacement or the amount of lost work time.

2. Length. Short reports are *brief*—one paragraph to two or three pages. They get right to the point and do not waste a busy reader's time. Some test reports ask for nothing but numbers; for example, the glucose level on a blood test. A progress report, however, calls for written evaluations.

3. Format. Since so many short reports are done within a company, the memo is the most frequently used format. Review pertinent sections of Chapter 8 dealing with memos (pages 197–201). When you are writing to individuals outside your business, you will generally use a letter format. Prepared forms can also be used (or may be required) for reports. Regardless of format—letter or memo—be sure that you use headings to help readers follow your work and also help you classify information into easily understood and labeled categories. Most of the examples in this chapter employ headings to highlight and preview information for readers.

4. Content. The emphasis is on the objective reporting of the facts: costs, eyewitness accounts, observations, statistics, test measurements. Impressions, unsupported personal opinion, and guesswork are outlawed. Readers want a straightforward account of current events. Past activities may sometimes be mentioned, but only to clarify the present and to help readers follow current details. Always give dates and specify the exact period the report covers and indicate A.M. or P.M. Just listing "Thursday" is often not enough. Give the date. To record time in compact and specific terms, employers may use a twenty-four-hour clock: 1:00 A.M. is 0100 hours; 1:00 P.M. is 1300 hours. An event occurring on February 19, 1990, at 2:30 P.M. is written 90/2/19/1430—year, month, day, time (hours/minutes). Give precise locations as well. "Highway 30" is not as helpful as "Highway 30, three miles southeast of the Morton exit." Call a machine by its precise technical name. Never use "thing," "gizmo," or "contraption" to refer to parts or tools. Keep any appropriate manuals or other reference materials handy to check on technical names, serial numbers, or codes. Refer to individuals by their proper names, not nicknames (Buddy, Red, Sis).

5. Organization. Organization means order. Effective organization of a short report means that you include the right amount of information in the most appropriate places for your audience. The organization of a short report will not be as elaborate as that for a long report. Many times a simple chronological or sequential organization will be acceptable for your readers' needs. Or you may follow one of the patterns of organization discussed in Chapter 3, pages 61–66.

Here is a fairly standard outline to follow when you are not required to submit a specially prepared form.

Purpose. Always begin with a statement of purpose. Tell readers why you are writing to them and alert them to what you will discuss. When you establish the scope (or limits) of your report, you help readers zero in on the specific times, places, procedures, or problems you will discuss. You may also need to provide necessary background information (for example, a summary of an earlier report or occurrence) to assist readers.

Findings. The data that you collected goes under the section on findings. Data includes the facts you have gathered about prices, personnel, equipment, events, locations, incidents, or experiments. Gather this data from your research, personal observations, interviews, or conversations with clients, co-workers, or employers. Many times you will find it convenient and helpful to readers to list your data in an appropriate visual, especially a table. See how visuals are used in the reports contained in Figures 16.3, 16.9, and 16.12. Some short reports even attach a computer printout with statistical data, as in Figure 16.2.

Conclusion. The conclusion can be a brief summary of what has happened or a review of what actions were taken. In a conclusion you might also explain the outcome or results of a test, a visit, or a program. The conclusion tells readers what your data means.

Recommendations. A recommendation tells readers what specific actions need to be taken: when, where, what, why, and how. Recommendations must be based upon the data you have collected and the conclusions you reached. The placement of recommendations in a short report can vary. Some employers prefer to see recommendations at the beginning of a report, others want them listed last. Some short reports (for example, those included in Figures 16.1, 16.2, 16.5, 16.8) do not require a recommendation. Be sure to find out if your reader will expect you to make one.

◆ PERIODIC REPORTS

Periodic reports, as their name signifies, provide readers with information at regularly scheduled intervals—daily, weekly, semimonthly (twice a month), monthly, quarterly. They help a company or agency keep track of the quantity and quality of the services it provides and the amount and types of work done by employees. Information in periodic reports helps managers make schedules, order materials, assign personnel, budget funds, and, generally speaking, determine agency or corporate needs.

You may already be familiar with some kinds of periodic reports. For example, if you have ever punched a timecard and turned it in at the end of the week, or if you have ever taken inventory in a stockroom, you have prepared a periodic report.

Periodic reports are used for numerous jobs. Delivery services require drivers to keep a daily record documenting the number of packages delivered, the time, and the location. A log, another kind of periodic report, is shown in Figure 16.1. At the end of a tour of duty, for example, law enforcement officers submit a daily activity log showing hours worked and actions taken. Often information from these daily logs is stored in a computer to allow for easy retrieval. Employees at television and radio stations may have to keep weekly reports of calls received by the station to aid management in determining the types of programming to offer.

Periodic reports follow no single format. Employers often supply routine forms on which to list information. These forms, such as the one illustrated in Figure 16.1, are relatively easy to complete. They ask for numbers, dates, codes, and expenses; occasionally a few clarifying or descriptive comments have to be added. Clearly distinguished categories on routine forms help to organize information for readers.

Other kinds of periodic reports may require more writing. You may be responsible for compiling a report based on individual periodic reports. Figure 16.2, a report submitted to a police captain, summarizes, organizes, and interprets the data collected over a three-month period from individual activity logs similar to the one in Figure 16.1. Such a report answers the reader's questions about the frequency and types of crimes committed and the work of the police force in the community. Because of this report, Captain Alice Martin will be better able to plan future protection for the community and to recommend changes in police services.

◆ SALES REPORTS

Sales reports provide businesses with a necessary record of accounts, purchases, and profits over a specified period of time. Sales reports might be considered a special type of periodic report, but because of their importance in the world of business they deserve a separate category here. They are important at various levels of business. Retail stores require a daily sales report in which purchases, coded by clerks on the cash register tapes, are arranged into major categories. Salespersons often submit weekly reports on the types and costs of products sold in a given district. Branch managers write monthly reports based on the figures given to them by their sales force. Higher up the business ladder, the president of a company sends stockholders an annual report assessing the financial health of the business. A report sent to someone at the same level of management as the writer (branch manager to branch manager) is known as a *lateral report.* A report sent to a higher executive level than the level of the writer (branch manager to vice president of marketing) is known as a *vertical report.*

Sales reports help businesses assess past performance and plan for the future. In doing this they fulfill two functions: financial and managerial. As a financial

FIGURE 16.1 A log, a type of periodic report.

DENVER POLICE DEPARTMENT

DAILY ACTIVITY LOG

Page ____ of ____ pages

Name					Ser. No.	Name			Ser. No.

Date	Mo.	Day	Yr.	Unit No.		Unit No.	Class 1 Actions	No.	Min.	ON DUTY TIME Assgnd. & O'time:		Sgt. Approved:	Ser. No.
Detail				Mileage Off		Mileage Off	Class 2 Actions			Total Time Used: All Action Classes		Clerk Recapped:	Ser. No.
From: To				Mileage On		Mileage On	Class 3 Actions			Patrol Time		Captain Approved:	Ser. No.
Dist. & Precinct	/			Total		Total	Total Class Actions						

Act. Cl.	Call Code	Time Out	Time In	Time Used	LOCATION, KIND OF ACTION AND DISPOSITION: Names, License, Citation No., etc.	
						CLASS 1 Felony Arr.
						CLASS 1 Misc. Arrests
						CLASS 2 Felony Arrests
						CLASS 2 Misc. Arrests
						CLASS 2 DUI Arrests
						CLASS 2 Open Door
						Recovered Units
						Contact Cards
						Offense Reports
						Other Reports
						Moving Violations
						Parking Violations
						Warning Violations
						Accident Violations
						Accident Reports

UNIT INSPECTION RECORD

Date	Unit No.	Car No.	Speedometer Reading	DAMAGE Old New	Officer	Ser. No.	Officer	Ser. No.	Supervisor

COMMENTS OR DEFECTS:

Right Side Left Side Front Rear

FIGURE 16.2 A quarterly periodic report.

GREENFIELD POLICE DEPARTMENT
"To Serve and To Protect"
Greenfield, TX 77003

TO: Captain Alice Martin

FROM: Sergeant Daniel Huxley *DH*

SUBJECT: Crime rate for the first quarter of 1990

DATE: April 12, 1990

From January 1 to March 31, 1,276 crimes were committed in Greenfield, representing a 25 percent increase over the 1,021 crimes recorded during the previous quarter.

The following report, based on the enclosed computer printout, discusses the specific types of crimes, organized into three categories: felonies, traffic, and misdemeanors.

<u>FELONIES</u>

The greatest increase in crime was in robberies, 20 percent higher than last quarter's figure (126 robberies). Downtown merchants reported 75 burglaries totaling more than $650,000. The biggest theft occurred on January 21 at Weisenfarth's Jewelers when three armed robbers stole more than $50,000 in merchandise. (These suspects were apprehended three days later.) Home burglaries accounted for 43 crimes, though the thefts were not confined to any one residential area. We also had 39 car thefts reported and investigated.

The number of homicides decreased from last quarter. During the first quarter, we had 8 homicides as opposed to 9 last quarter. Charges for battery, however, increased to 82--15 more than we had last quarter. There were 5 charges for arson, 11 for carrying a concealed weapon, and 37 for possession of a controlled substance. The number of rapes for this quarter was 8, fewer than last quarter (9). Three of those rapes happened within one week (February 3-8) and have been attributed to the same suspect, now in custody.

---

record, sales reports list costs per unit, discounts or special reductions, and subtotals and totals. Like an accountant's ledger or spreadsheet, sales reports show gains and losses. They may also provide statistics for comparing two quarters' sales. The method or origin of a sale, if significant, can also be recorded. In selling books, for example, a publisher keeps a careful record of where sales originate—direct orders for single copies from readers, adoptions for classroom use,

FIGURE 16.2   (continued)

Captain Martin
April 12, 1990
Page 2

TRAFFIC

     Traffic violations for this period were lower than last quarter's
figures. The 319 citations for moving violations for the first quarter
represent a 5 percent decrease over last quarter's 335 violations. Most were
issued for speeding (158) or for failing to observe signals (98). Officers
issued 45 citations to motorists for DUI. These citations point to an
impressive decrease over the 78 issued last quarter. The new state penalty
of withholding for six months the driver's license of anyone convicted of
driving while under the influence appears to be an effective deterrent.

MISDEMEANORS

The largest number of arrests in this category were for disturbing the
peace--53. Compared to last quarter, this is an increase of 10 percent.
There were 48 charges for vagrancy and public drunkenness, a decrease from
the 59 charges brought last quarter. We issued 32 citations for violation of
leash laws, which represents a sizable increase over last quarter's 21
citations. Fifty citations were issued for violations of city codes and
ordinances; 37 of those 50 citations were issued for dumping trash at the
Mason Reservoir.

Encl. computer printout

---

purchases at bookstores, or orders from wholesale distributors handling the book.
     Sales reports are also a managerial tool, since they help businesses make both
short- and long-range plans. By indicating the number of sales, the report alerts
buyers and managers about which items or services to increase, modify, or discontinue. The sales report illustrated in Figure 16.3 guides the restaurant owners
in menu planning. Knowing which popular dishes to highlight and which unpopu-

FIGURE 16.3   A sales report in tabular form.

The Palace
Dayton, OH 43210

TO: Gina Smeltzer   DATE: June 27, 1990
          Frank Drew, Owners

FROM: Sam Jelinek _SJ_   SUBJECT: Analysis of entrée
          Manager   sales, June 10–24

As we agreed at our monthly meeting on June 4, here is my analysis of entrée sales for two weeks to assist us in our menu planning. Below is a record of entrée sales for the weeks of June 10–17 and June 18–24 that I have compiled into a table for easier and more valid comparisons.

	Portion Size	June 10–17		June 18–24		2 weeks combined	
		Amount	Ratio	Amount	Ratio	Amount	Ratio
Strip Steak	12 oz.	168	12%	198	11%	366	11%
Veal à la Viennoise	8 oz.	112	8	182	10	294	9
Shrimp Newburg	8 oz.	154	11	217	12	371	12
Brook Trout	12 oz.	56	4	70	4	126	4
Prime Rib	10 oz.	343	25	413	23	756	24
Lobster Tails	2–4 oz.	147	10	161	9	308	10
Delmonico Steak	10 oz.	182	13	252	14	434	13
Beef Stroganoff	8 oz.	238	17	307	17	545	17
		1,400	100%	1,800	100%	3,200	100%

Recommendations

Based on the figures in the table above, I recommend that we do the following:

1. order at least one hundred more pounds of prime rib each two-week period to be eligible for further quantity discounts from the Northern Meat Company
2. delete the brook trout entrée because of low acceptance
3. introduce a new beef or pork entrée to take the place of the brook trout item; I would suggest stuffed pork chops.

Please give me your reactions within the next week. It shouldn't take more than two weeks to implement these changes.

Table from *The Financial Ingredient in Foodservice Management*. Lexington, MA: D. C. Heath, 1976. Reprinted with permission from The National Institute for the Foodservice Industry.

FIGURE 16.4   A narrative sales report.

CCCCCCCO   HAMILTON COIN SHOP
Erie, PA 17321-3636

TO: Harry T. Udall   DATE: September 7, 1990
       Owner

FROM: Jessica Alonzo *JA*   SUBJECT: Favorable August sales
       Manager

Our sales were brisk during August. Sales of mint sets and proof sets totaled
$1,634. The sale of individual coins came to $2,340. Commemorative coin sales
were $521. These sales total $4,495.

The most impressive sales came from our offer to sell pennies by the pound. We
placed ads in the Erie Times-News and in Coin World Today. Our ads over WTOR AM
may also have helped sales. Although it is hard to determine what portion of our
walk-in business came from the radio announcements, possibly it was as much as a
third. The total sales for the pennies by the pound were $5,930.

Sales for the month of August come to $10,425. Detailed breakdowns of these
figures will appear in the September 30 quarterly report.

---

lar ones to delete, the owners can increase profits. Note how the recommendations follow from the figures Sam Jelinek gives to Gina Smeltzer and Frank Drew, the owners of the Palace Restaurant.

To write a sales report, keep a careful record of order forms, invoices, and production figures. Sales information might be arranged in list form, as in Figure 16.3, or in narrative form, as in Figure 16.4. If you use the narrative format, make sure you do not overload your readers with numbers. Underlining key numbers will emphasize them for a reader, as Jessica Alonzo does in Figure 16.4.

◆ PROGRESS REPORTS

A progress report informs readers about the status of an ongoing project. It lets them know how much and what type of work has been completed by a particular date and how close the entire job is to being completed. A progress report emphasizes whether you are keeping on schedule, staying within a budget, using the proper equipment, making the right assignments, and completing the job efficiently and correctly. Almost any kind of ongoing work can be described in a progress report—research for a paper, construction of an apartment complex, preparation of a fall catalog, documentation of a patient's rehabilitation.

A progress report is intended for people who are generally not working alongside you, but who need a record of your activities in order to coordinate them with other individuals' efforts and to learn about problems or changes in plans. For example, since local management or supervisors at the home office cannot be in the field or branch office or at the construction site, they will rely on a progress report for much of their information. Customers, too, will expect a report on how carefully their money is being spent.

The length of the report will depend on the complexity of the project. A short memo about organizing a time management workshop, such as that in Figure 16.5, might be all that is necessary. A report to a teacher about the progress a student is making on a research paper could easily be handled in a one-page memo, such as James Salinas's report in Figure 16.6 for his paper proposed on pages 475–77. Similarly, Dale Brandt's assessment of the progress his firm is making in renovating Dr. Burke's office is given in a two-page letter in Figure 16.7.

Progress reports should contain information on (1) the work you have done, (2) the work you currently are doing, and (3) the work you will do.

They can be written daily, weekly, monthly, quarterly, or annually. Your specific job and your employer's needs will dictate how often you have to keep others informed of your progress. Nurses have to write progress notes for each eight- or twelve-hour shift; management trainees may have to submit a weekly report of their accomplishments. A single progress report is sufficient for Philip Javon's purpose in Figure 16.5. On the other hand, James Salinas has been asked

FIGURE 16.5   A one-time progress report.

| **R** | **REPUBLIC INDUSTRIES** | P.O. Box 5073
Trenton, NJ 08542-5073 |

TO: Kathy Sands   DATE: September 12, 1990

FROM: Philip Javon *P.J.*   SUBJECT: Preparations for the
                                                  Time Management
                                                  Workshop

As you requested last week, I called the managers of all departments on Thursday (September 6) to alert them to the time management workshop we will offer on October 2–3. I also sent follow-up notices to the managers today.

I have reserved the cafeteria annex for both October 2 and 3 and ordered all the supplies we will need. The management kit will have the company brochures on organization policies, the time sheets used in the plant, the report forms we used last March, notepads, and ballpoint pens. I have also arranged with Ms. Suarez in the audiovisual department to set up the projector on the morning of October 2. By tomorrow I hope to complete a list of all those who will participate in the workshop.

Plans are going according to schedule.

FIGURE 16.6 A progress report from a student to a teacher.

TO: Professor Barbara Felton-Parks

FROM: James Salinas

DATE: April 10, 1990

SUBJECT: First Progress Report on Research Paper

This is the first of two progress reports that you asked me to
submit about my research paper on the advantages and disadvantages
of electronic mail.

From March 8 until April 6, I gathered information from library
materials and from an interview. Of the twelve references listed on
my proposal, I found only nine. Stevenson's <u>Telecommunications: An
Introduction</u>, the articles by Barks ("Can You Count on Electronic
Mail?") and Foley ("Hardware Vendors Adapt to Changing E-Mail
Market"), and "Bidirectional Electronic Mail . . ." (<u>Communication
News</u>) are not in our library. I have ordered them through
interlibrary loan.

On February 23, I had an extended interview ($1\frac{1}{2}$ hours) with Mr.
Keith Wellbridge of General Dynamics, who gave me some brochures as
well as a copy of a report on electronic mail he wrote for General
Dynamics--materials I hope to use in my paper.

Because of a long business trip to Denver, Ms. Alice Phillips of
Dodge & Spenser could not meet with me. At her suggestion, I am
trying to schedule an interview with Ms. Gloria Miller, the office
manager at Mid-Atlantic Power Company. Her firm has recently
switched to electronic mail.

Even if Ms. Miller cannot meet with me, I believe that Mr.
Wellbridge gave me enough information about a business manager's
view of electronic mail systems. However, not having the Stevenson
book and the articles cited above may slow my work a little.

Starting tomorrow, I will begin organizing my paper. I will be able
to submit a rough draft by April 27. You will receive my second
progress report on the organization of my paper by April 20.

FIGURE 16.7 The second of three progress reports from a contractor to a customer.

BRANDT CONSTRUCTION COMPANY
Halsted at Roosevelt
Chicago, Illinois 60608-0999
312-572-3700

April 28, 1988

Dr. Pamela Burke
1439 Grand Avenue
Mount Prospect, IL 60045-1003

Dear Dr. Burke:

Here is my second progress report about the renovation work at your new
clinic at Hacienda and Donohue. Work proceeded satisfactorily in April
according to the plans you had approved in March.

REVIEW OF WORK COMPLETED IN MARCH

As I informed you in my first progress report on March 31, we had torn down
the walls, pulled the old wiring, and removed existing plumbing work. All
the gutting work was finished in March.

WORK COMPLETED DURING APRIL

By April 8, we had laid the new pipes and connected them to the main sewer
line. We had also installed the two commodes, the four standard sinks, and
the utility basin. The heating and air-conditioning ducts were installed by
April 13. From April 18 to 23, we erected soundproof walls in the four
examination rooms, the reception area, your office, and the laboratory. We
had no problems reducing the size of the reception area by five feet to make
the first examination room larger, as you had requested.

PROBLEMS WITH ELECTRICAL SYSTEM

We had difficulty with the electrical work, however. The number of outlets
and the generator for the laboratory equipment required extra-duty power
lines that had to be approved by both Con Edison and county inspectors. The
approval slowed us down three days. Also, the wholesaler, Midtown Electric,
failed to deliver the recessed lighting fixtures by April 25 as promised.

FIGURE 16.7   (continued)

2

These fixtures and the generator are now being installed. Moreover, the cost of these fixtures will increase the material budget by $425. The cost for labor is as we had projected--$69,450.

WORK REMAINING

The finishing work is scheduled for May. By May 9, the floors in the examination rooms, laboratory, washrooms, and hallways should be tiled and the reception area and your office carpeted. By May 13, the reception area and your office should be paneled and the rest of the walls painted. If everything stays on schedule, touch-up work is scheduled for May 16–20. You should be able to move into your new clinic by May 23.

You will receive a third and final progress report by May 13.

Sincerely yours,

Dale Brandt

Dale Brandt

to submit two progress reports, the first of which is in Figure 16.6. Contractor Brandt in Figure 16.7 has found that three separate reports, spaced four to six weeks apart, are needed to keep Dr. Burke posted.

How to Begin a Progress Report

In a brief introduction indicate why you are writing the report. Provide any necessary project titles or codes and specify dates. Help readers recall the job you are doing for them. If you are writing an initial progress report, supply background information. Philip Javon's first two sentences in Figure 16.5 quickly establish his purpose by reminding Kathy Sands of their discussion last week. Similarly, James Salinas in Figure 16.6 reminds his teacher of the purpose and scope of his work in the first paragraph. If you are submitting a subsequent progress report, show where the previous report left off and where the current one begins. Make sure that the period covered by each report is clearly specified. Notice how Dale Brandt's first paragraph in Figure 16.7 calls attention to the continuity of his work.

How to Continue a Progress Report

The body of the report should provide significant details about costs, materials, personnel, and times for the major stages of the project. Emphasize completed tasks, not false starts. If you report that the carpentry work or painting is finished, readers do not need an explanation of paint viscosity or geometrical patterns. Omit routine or well-known details ("I had to use the library when I wanted to read the back issues of *Safety News*") in your progress report. Describe in the body of the discussion, too, any snags you encountered. See Dale Brandt's section on electrical problems in Figure 16.7. It is better for the reader to know about trouble early in the project, so that appropriate changes or corrections can be made.

How to End a Progress Report

The conclusion should give a timetable for the completion of duties or when the next progress report can be expected. Give the date by which work will be completed; be realistic. Do not promise to have a job done in less time than you know it will take. Readers will not expect miracles, only informed estimates. Any conclusion must be tentative. Note that the good news Dale Brandt gives Dr. Burke about moving into her new clinic is qualified by the words "if everything stays on schedule." A recommendation may also find a place in the conclusion. Such a recommendation might advise readers, for example, of a less costly, equally durable siding than the one originally planned, suggest that a joint meeting of two committees would expedite production of a college yearbook, or show that hiring an additional part-time salesclerk would help ease the busy workload over the holi-day sales period.

◆ TRIP REPORTS

Reporting on the trips you take is an important professional responsibility. Trips can range from a brief afternoon car ride across town to a one-month long jour-ney across the country. These reports inform readers about your activities out-side the office, plant, clinic, or agency. In documenting what you did and saw, these trip reports help your readers to better understand what has happened and even give them information they can use for later reports. Specifically, a trip re-port should answer the following questions for your readers.

1. Where did you go?
2. When did you go there?
3. Why did you go there?
4. Whom did you see?
5. What did they tell you?

For a business trip you are likely to have to inform readers how much the trip cost and to supply them with receipts for all your expenses.

Common Types of Trip Reports

Trip reports can cover a wide range of activities and are called by different names to characterize those activities. Undoubtedly, you will encounter the following three types of trip reports.

1. Field trip reports. These reports, often assigned in a course, are written after a visit to a local plant, military installation, garage, hospital, forest, detention center, or other facility. Their purpose is to show what you have learned about the operation of these places. You will be expected to describe how an institu-tion is organized, the equipment or procedures it uses, the ecological conditions present, or the ratio of one group to another. The emphasis is on the educational values of the trip, as Mark Tourneur's report in Figure 16.8 demonstrates.

2. Site inspection reports. These trip reports are written to inform man-agers, department heads, or section chiefs about conditions at a branch office or plant, a customer's business, or at an area directly under an employer's jurisdic-tion. Site inspection reports tell how machinery or production procedures are working or provide information about the physical plant, environment (air, soil, water), and computer or financial operations. A site inspection report will be written for an employer or a customer who wants to relocate or build new facili-ties (a record shop, a halfway house, a branch office) to assess the suitability of a particular location. After visiting the site, you will determine whether it meets your employer's (or customer's) needs. Figure 16.9, which shows a report writ-ten to a manager interested in acquiring a new site for a fast-food restaurant, be-gins with a recommendation.

FIGURE 16.8   A student's field trip report.

TO: Katherine Holmes, RN, MSN   DATE: November 12, 1990
      Director, RN Program
FROM: Mark Tourneur   SUBJECT: Field Trip to
      RN Student   *M.T.*   Water Valley
                                                  Convalescent Center

On Tuesday, November 6, I visited the Water Valley Convalescent Center,
1400 Medford Boulevard, in preparation for my internship in a nursing
home next semester.

Before my tour started, the Director, Sue LaFrance, explained the
holistic philosophy of health care at Water Valley and emphasized the
diverse kinds of nursing practiced there. She stressed that the agency
is not restricted to geriatric patients but admits anyone requiring
long-term care. She pointed out that Water Valley is a medium-sized
facility (150 beds) and contains three wings: (1) the Infirmary, (2)
the General Nursing Unit, and (3) the Ambulatory Unit.

My tour began with the Infirmary, staffed by one RN and two LPN's,
where I observed a number of life-support systems in operation--IV's,
oxygen setups, feeding tubes, and cardiac monitors. Then I was shown
the General Nursing Unit, a forty-bed unit that is staffed by three
LPN's and four aides. Patients can have private or semiprivate rooms;
bathrooms have wide doors and lowered sinks for patients using
wheelchairs or walkers. The ambulatory section cares for ninety
patients who can provide their own daily care.

Before lunch in the main dining room, I was introduced to Doris Betz,
the dietitian, who explained the different menus she coordinates. The
most common are low-sodium and restricted-calorie. Staff members eat
with the patients, reinforcing the holistic concern of the agency.

After lunch, Jack Tishner, the pharmacist, discussed the agency's
procedures for ordering and delivering medications. He also explained
the kinds of patient teaching he does and the in-service workshops he
conducts. I then observed patients in both recreational and physical
therapy. Water Valley's full-time physical therapist, Tracy Cook, works
with stroke and arthritic patients and helps those with broken bones
regain the use of their limbs. In addition to a weight room, Water
Valley has a small sauna that most of the patients use at least twice a
week. The patients' spiritual needs are not neglected, either. A small
chapel is located just off the Ambulatory Unit.

From my visit to Water Valley, I learned a great deal about the health
care delivery system at a nursing home. I was especially pleased to
have been given so much information on emergency procedures, medication
orders, and physical therapy programs. My forthcoming internship will
be much more useful, since I have firsthand knowledge about these
available services.

FIGURE 16.9   A site inspection report using a map.

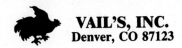

VAIL'S, INC.
Denver, CO 87123

TO: Dale Gandy   DATE: July 2, 1990
        District Manager

FROM: Delores Marshack *DM*   SUBJECT: New site for Vail's #8
        Development Department

RECOMMENDATION:

The best location for the new Vail's Chicken House is the vacant Dairy World
shop at the northeast corner of Smith and Fairfax Avenues--1701 South
Fairfax. I inspected this property on June 21 and 22 and also talked with
Marge Bloom, the broker at Crescent Realty representing the Dairy World
Company.

THE LOCATION:

Please refer to the map below. Located at the intersection of the two
busiest streets on the southeast side, the property allows us to take
advantage of the traffic flow to attract customers. Being only one block
west of the Cloverleaf Mall should also help business. Customers have easy
access to our location.

FIGURE 16.9   (continued)

Dale Gandy
July 2, 1990
Page 2

They can enter or exit the Dairy World from either Smith or Fairfax, but
left turns on Smith are prohibited from 7 A.M. to 9 A.M. However, since most
of our business is done after 11 A.M., the restriction poses few problems.
Only two other fast-food establishments are in a one-mile vicinity.
McGonagles, 1534 South Kildare, specializes in hamburgers; Noah's, 703
Zanwood, serves primarily fish entrées. Their offerings will not directly
compete with ours. The closest fast-food restaurant serving chicken is
Johnson's, 1.8 miles away.

PARKING FACILITIES:

The parking lot has space for 45 cars. The area at the south end of the
property (38 feet x 37 feet) can accommodate another 11 to 15 cars. The
driveways and parking lot were paved with asphalt last March and appear to
be in excellent condition. We will be able to make use of the drive-up
window on the north side of the building.

THE BUILDING:

The building has 3,993 square feet of heated and cooled space. The
air-conditioning and heating units were installed within the last fifteen
months and seem to be in good working order; nine more months of
transferable warranty remain on these units. The only major changes we would
have to make are in the kitchen. To prepare items on the Vail's menu, we
would have to add three more exhaust fans (there is only one now) and expand
the grill and cooking areas. The kitchen also has three relatively new sinks
and ample storage space in the fourteen cabinets. The restaurant has a
seating capacity of up to 54 persons; ten booths are covered with red vinyl
and are comfortably padded. A color-coordinated serving counter could seat 8
to 10 patrons. The floor does not need to be retiled, but the walls must be
painted to match Vail's color decor.

3. Home health or social work visits. Nurses, social workers, and probation officers report daily on their visits to patients and clients. Their reports describe clients' lifestyles, assess needs, and make recommendations. A report from
a social worker to a county family services agency can be seen in Figure 16.10.
The report begins with the information Jeff Bowman acquired from his visit with

FIGURE 16.10   A social worker's visit report.

Green County
Family Services _____ Randall, VA 21032

TO: Margaret S. Walker, Director
           Green County Family Services

FROM: Jeff Bowman, Social Worker *JB*

SUBJECT: Visit to Mr. Lee Scanlon

DATE: October 12, 1989

PURPOSE OF VISIT

    At the request of the Green County Home Health Office, I visited Mr. Lee Scanlon at his home at 113 West Diversy Drive on Tuesday, October 10. Mr. Scanlon and his three children (ages six, eight, and eleven) live in a two-bedroom apartment above a garage. Last week, Mr. Scanlon was discharged from Methodist General Hospital after leg surgery and has asked for financial assistance.

DESCRIPTION OF VISIT

    Mr. Scanlon is a widower with no means of support except a monthly Social Security check of $405 and unemployment compensation totaling $130 a month. He lost his job at Baymont Manufacturing when the company went out of business four weeks ago and wants to go back to work, but Dr. Canning-Smith advised against it for six to seven weeks. His oldest child is diabetic, and the six-year-old daughter must have a tonsillectomy. Mr. Scanlon also told me the problems he was having with his refrigerator; it "was off more than it was on," he said.

    Mrs. Alice Gordon, the owner of the garage, informed me that Mr. Scanlon had paid last month's rent but not this month's. She also stressed how much the Scanlons need a new refrigerator and that she had often let them use part of hers to store their food.

    Mr. Scanlon's monthly bills and income are as follows:

Expenses	Income
$270 rent	$405 Social Security
65 utilities	130 unemployment
350 food	$535
60 drugs	
80 transportation	
$825	

FIGURE 16.10   (continued)

Margaret S. Walker
October 12, 1989
Page 2

ACTION TAKEN

To assist Mr. Scanlon, I have done the following:

1. Set up an appointment (10/20/89) for him to apply for food stamps.
2. Talked with Blanche Derringo regarding Medicaid assistance.
3. Asked the State Employment Commission to aid him in finding a job as soon as he is well enough to work.
4. Visited Robert Adkins at the office of the Council of Churches to obtain food and money for utilities until federal aid is available; he also will try to find the Scanlons another refrigerator.
5. Telephoned Sharon Muñez at the Green County Health Department to have Mr. Scanlon's diabetic daughter receive insulin and syringes gratis.

the Scanlons and concludes, not with a recommendation, but rather with a list of the actions this social worker has taken.

How to Gather Information for a Trip Report

Regardless of the kind of trip report you have to write, your assignment will be easier and your report better organized if you follow these suggestions.

Before You Leave for the Site

1. Obtain all necessary names, addresses, and telephone numbers.
2. Check the files for previous correspondence, case studies, terms of contracts or agreements.
3. Locate a map of the area or a blueprint of the building.
4. Look for brochures, work orders, instructions, or other documents pertinent to your visit.
5. Make sure you have a notebook and a pen with you. Depending on your job, you may also need to bring a tape recorder, camera, or calculator. Use these instruments to record important data.

When You Return

1. Write your report promptly. If you put it off, you may forget important items.
2. When a trip takes you to two or more widely separated places, note in your report when you arrived at each place and how long you stayed.
3. Do not include in your report everything you saw or did on the trip. Exclude irrelevant details, such as whether the trip was enjoyable, where you stayed overnight, what you ate, or how delighted you were to meet people.

◆ TEST REPORTS

Much physical research (the discovery of facts) is communicated through reports. These reports have various names. Depending on your profession's terminology, they may be called experiment, investigation, laboratory, operations, or research reports. They all record the results of tests, whether the tests were conducted in a forest, computer center, laboratory, parking lot, shopping center, or soybean field.

No doubt you have already written a test report (or laboratory report) after performing an experiment in a science class. Writing an effective test report involves specific training in a scientific or technological field.

Objectivity and accuracy are essential ingredients in a test report. Readers want to know about your empirical research (the facts), not about your feelings (the "I"). Record your observations without bias or guesswork in a laboratory journal or log book and always include precise measurements. When you draft

FIGURE 16.11   A laboratory (or test) report with recommendations.

CHARLESTON CENTRAL HOSPITAL
CHARLESTON, WV 25324-0114

TO: James Dill, Supervisor   DATE: December 4, 1990
     Housekeeping

FROM: Janeen Cufaude   *JC*   SUBJECT: Routine sanitation
       Infection Control Officer   inspection

As part of the monthly check of the psychiatric unit (11A), the following areas
were swabbed and tested for bacterial growth. The results of the lab tests of
these samples are as follows:

AREA   FINDINGS

1. cabinet in patients' kitchen   1. positive for 2 colonies of strep germs

2. rug in eating area   2. positive for food particles and yeasts
                                         and molds

3. baseboard in dayroom   3. positive for particles of dust and fungi

4. medicine counter in nurses'   4. negative for bacteria--no growth after
   station   48 hrs.

5. corridor by south elevator   5. positive for 4 colonies of staph germs

ACTIONS TO BE TAKEN AT ONCE

1. Clean the kitchen cabinet with K-504 liquid daily, 3:1 dilution.

2. Shampoo rug areas bimonthly with heavy-duty shampoo and clean visibly soiled
   areas with Guard-Pruf as often as needed.

3. Wipe all baseboards weekly with K-12 spray cleanser.

4. Mop heavily traveled corridors and access areas with K-504 cleanser daily, 1:1
   dilution.

your report, tell readers why the test was made, under what circumstances (or controls) it was made, and what the outcome was. When you sign the final copy of your test report, you are certifying that things happened exactly when, how, and why you say they did.

Figure 16.11 contains a relatively simple and short test report in memo format regarding sanitary conditions at a hospital psychiatric unit. This report follows a direct and useful pattern of organization:

- statement of purpose
- findings
- recommendations

Submitted by an infection control officer, the report does not provide elaborate details about the particular laboratory procedures used to determine if bacteria were present; nor does it describe the pathogenic (disease-causing) properties of the bacteria. Such descriptions are unnecessary for the audience (the housekeeping department) to do its job.

A more complex example of a short test report is found in Figure 16.12; it studies the effects of four light periods on the growth of paulownia (a flowering tree cultivated in China) seedlings. This report, published in a scientific journal, is addressed to specialists in forestry. To meet the needs of this expert audience, the writers had to include much more detailed information than Janeen Cufaude did about the way the test was conducted and about the types of data the audience would need to confirm and use the scientific data from the author's tests. Such a test report follows a different pattern of organization than the one in Figure 16.11 and includes the following parts:

- an informative abstract (see pages 404–5)
- an introduction to provide background information about the importance of the test and perhaps to review previous research on the topic
- a materials and methods section to describe the exact scientific procedures and equipment the author(s) used to conduct the test
- a results and discussion section (sometimes separated into two sections) to record the data obtained from the test and to explain the significance of the data. Many times a test report will conclude by confirming previous studies, emphasizing the need for further tests, or offering researchers new interpretation of the evidence
- a list of references cited in the study

Notice how the needs of two different audiences as well as the authors' purpose control the way each report is organized and how much and what type of information is included. Janeen Cufaude's reader is a nonspecialist, less interested in scientific theory than in the practical application of that theory; Immel, Tackett, and Carpenter's readers are experts demanding scientific documentation and commentary. As these two reports show, you should always determine how much technical knowledge an audience has about your field and how they will use your report to accomplish *their* specific job.

FIGURE 16.12   A short test report published in a scientific journal.

Paulownia Seedlings Respond to Increased Daylength
M. J. Immel, E. M. Tackett, and S. B. Carpenter

Abstract
Paulownia seedlings grown under four photoperiods were evaluated after a growing period of 97 days. Height growth and total dry weight production were both significantly increased in the 16- and 24-hour photoperiods.

Introduction
Paulownia (*Paulownia tomentosa* [Thunb.] Steud.), a native of China is a little-known species in the United States. Recently, however, there has been increased interest in this species for surface mine reclamation *(1)*.* Paulownia seems to be especially well adapted to harsh micro-climates of surface mines; it grows very rapidly and appears to be drought-resistant. In Kentucky and surrounding states, paulownia wood is actively sought by Japanese buyers and has brought prices comparable to black walnut *(2)*.

This increased interest in paulownia has resulted in several attempts to direct seed it on surface mines, but little success has been achieved. The high light requirements and the extremely small size of paulownia seed (approximately 6,000 per gram) may be the limiting factors. Planting paulownia seedlings is preferred; but, because of their succulent nature, seedlings are usually produced and outplanted as container stock rather than bareroot seedlings. Daylength is an important factor in the production of vigorous container plants *(5)*. Our study compares the effects that four photoperiods—8, 12, 16, and 24 hours—had on the early growth of container-grown paulownia seedlings over a period of 97 days.

Materials and Methods
Seeds used in this study were stratified in a 1:1 mixture of peat moss and sand at 4°C for 2 years. Following cold storage, seeds were placed on a 1:1 potting soil-sand mix and mulched with cheesecloth. They were then placed under continuous light until germination occurred. Germination percentages were high, indicating paulownia seeds can survive long periods of storage with little loss of viability *(3)*. Thirty days after germination, 3- to 4-centimeter seedlings were transplanted into 8-quart plastic pots filled with an equal mixture of potting soil, sand, and peat moss. Seventy-five seedlings were randomly assigned to each of the four treatments. Treatments were for 4 photoperiods—8, 12, 16, and 24 hours—and were replicated three times in 12 light chambers. Each chamber was 1.2- by 1.2-meters with an artificial light source 71 centimeters above the chamber floor.

The light source consisted of eight fluorescent lights: four 40-watt plant growth lamps alternated with four 40-watt cool white lamps. Light intensity averaged 550 foot-candles (1340μ einsteins/m^2/sec) at the top of each pot and the temperature averaged 23°C ($\pm$ 2°C).

Tree Planters' Notes 31 (Winter 1980): 3–5.
* All actual references have been omitted to save space.

TABLE 1. Height, diameter, root length, total dry weight, and R/S ratio for paulownia seedlings grown under four photoperiods after 97 days.

Photo-period (hrs.)	Height (cm)	Diameter (cm)	Root length (cm)	Total dry weight (gm)	R/S ratio
8	13.1b	0.48	16.0	1.65c	0.18
12	17.8b	0.67	34.7	7.27b	0.32
16	27.3a	0.93	31.1	15.92a	0.39
24	29.2a	0.90	43.9	18.56a	0.33

Seedlings were kept watered and were fertilized after transplanting with a 6-gram 14–4–6 agriform container tablet. Beginning 1 month after transplanting, two seedlings were randomly selected and harvested from each chamber for a total of 24 trees. Height, root collar diameter, length of longest root, and oven-dry weight (at 65°C) were determined for each seedling. Harvests continued every week for 5 additional weeks.

Results and Discussion

Results indicate that early growth of paulownia is influenced by photoperiod, as shown in Table 1. Expanding the photoperiod from 8 to either 16 or 24 hours increased height growth by 100 percent. Height growth in the 12-hour treatment also increased, but did not differ significantly from the 8-hour treatment. Heights under photoperiods of 8, 12, 16, and 24 hours were 13.1, 17.8, 27.3, and 29.2 centimeters, respectively.

Previous studies have also shown that photoperiod affects the growth of paulownia seedlings (4, 6). Sanderson (6), for example, found that paulownia seedlings grown under continuous light averaged 27.2 centimeters in height after 101 days compared with 29.2 centimeters for our 24-hour seedlings. Other corresponding photoperiods were equally comparable. Downs and Borthwick (4) also concluded that height growth of paulownia was affected by extending the photoperiod.

The greatest treatment differences were shown in total dry weight production. Refer again to Table 1. The mean weight of 1.65 grams for seedlings in the 8-hour treatment was significantly less than that of any of the other photoperiods. The 16- and 24-hour treatments did not differ significantly. In fact, they more than doubled the average weight for seedlings in the 12-hour treatment.

Root-to-shoot ratio (R/S) indicates the relative proportion of growth allocated to roots versus shoots for the seedlings in each photoperiod. In this study, shoots were developing at nearly three times the rate of the roots for seedlings in the 12-, 16-, and 24-hour photoperiods. The 0.18 R/S ratio for seedlings in the 8-hour treatment was much lower, indicating that relative growth of the shoot is approximately five times that of the root. The shorter photoperiod therefore decreased root development relative to shoot development as well as significantly reduced total dry weight production.

Although root collar diameter and root length did not significantly differ under the different photoperiods after 97 days, there was a trend for greater diameter and root growth with longer photoperiods.

Conclusions
Results indicate that the growth of paulownia seedlings is affected by changes in the photoperiod. Increasing the photoperiod significantly increased height growth and total dry matter production. The distribution of dry matter (R/S ratio) was altered by increasing the photoperiod; the ratio was larger in the longer photoperiods. In contrast to earlier studies (4), we found paulownia seedlings subjected to extended photoperiods were still growing after 97 days.

◆ INCIDENT REPORTS

The reports discussed thus far in this chapter have dealt with routine work. They have described events that were anticipated or supervised. But every business or agency runs into unexpected trouble that delays routine work. Employers, and on some occasions government inspectors, insurance agents, and attorneys, must be informed about those events that interfere with or threaten normal, safe operations. A special type of report known as an *incident report* is submitted when there is an accident, law enforcement offense, environmental danger, machine breakdown, delivery delay, cost overrun, or production slowdown.

Protecting Yourself Legally

The incident report can be used as legal evidence. It frequently concerns the two topics over which powerful legal battles are waged—health and property. The report can sway the outcome of insurance claims, civil suits, or criminal cases. To ensure that what you write is legally proper, follow these three guidelines.

1. Be accurate, objective, and complete. Never omit or distort facts; the information may surface later, and you could be guilty of a cover-up. Do not just write "I do not know" for an answer. If you are not sure, state why. Also be careful that there are no discrepancies in your report.

2. Give facts, not opinions. Provide a factual account of what actually happened, not a biased interpretation of events. Indirect words, such as "I guess," "I wonder," "apparently," "perhaps," or "possibly," weaken your objectivity. Stick to details you witnessed or that were seen by eyewitnesses. Indicate who saw what. Keep in mind that stating what someone else saw will be regarded as hearsay, and therefore not be admissible in a court of law. State only what *you* saw or heard. When you describe what happened, avoid drawing uncalled-for conclusions.

Wrong The patient seemed confused and caught himself in his IV tubing.
 Right The patient caught himself in his IV tubing.
Wrong The equipment was defective.
 Right The bolt was loose.

Be careful, too, about blaming someone. Saying that "Baxter was incompetent" or that the "company knew of the problem but did nothing about it" are libelous remarks.

3. Do not exceed your professional responsibilities. Answer only those questions you are qualified to answer. Do not presume to speak as a detective, inspector, physician, or supervisor. Do not represent yourself as an attorney or claims adjuster in writing the report.

Parts of an Incident Report

You will use either a memo or a specially prepared form with spaces for detailed comments. Figure 16.13 contains an incident report written in memo format; Figure 16.14 shows a typical incident report form used to report an accident. Regardless of the format, all incident reports will ask for the following information.

1. Personal details. Record titles, department, and employment identification numbers. Indicate if you or your fellow employees were working alone. For customers and victims, record home addresses, phone numbers, and places of employment. Insurance companies will also require policy numbers. Note that the first four questions in Figure 16.14 request this kind of information.

2. Type of incident. Briefly identify the incident—personal injury, fire, burglary, delivery delay, equipment failure. In the case of injury identify the part(s) of the body precisely. "Eye injury" is not enough; "injury to the right eye, causing bleeding" is better. "Dislocated shoulder," "punctured left forearm," and "twisted left ankle" are descriptive and exact phrases. A report on damaged equipment should list model numbers. Note how Ned Roane's report (Figure 16.13) specifies the grain car numbers. For thefts, supply colors, brand names, quantities, and serial numbers. "A stolen watch" will not help detectives locate the right object; "a seven-jewel lady's Benrus" will.

3. Time and location of the incident. Follow the advice given at the beginning of this chapter, page 486.

4. Description of what happened. This section is the longest part of the report. Some forms ask you to write on the back, to attach another sheet, or to add a photograph or diagram. Put yourself in the reader's position. If you were not present or did not speak directly to witnesses, would you know by reading the report what happened exactly and why, how it occurred, who and what were involved, and what led up to the incident?

The two most common errors writers make are that they do not give (1) enough information or (2) the right kinds of information. Recount what happened in the order in which it took place. What you (or eyewitnesses) saw, heard, felt, and smelled are the essentials of your description. Describe what happened before the incident, if that is relevant—for example, environmental or weather conditions for storm damage or an automobile accident, or warning signals for a malfunctioning machine. If you are depending on an eyewitness ac-

FIGURE 16.13   An incident report.

THE GREAT HARVESTER RAILROAD
P.O. Box 4005
Des Moines, IA 50306-4005

TO: Angela O'Brien   DATE: March 2, 1990
        District Manager
        James Day
        Safety Inspector
FROM: Ned Roane *NR*   SUBJECT: Derailment of Train 28 on
        Engineer   March 1, 1990

DESCRIPTION OF INCIDENT

At 7:20 A.M. on March 1, 1990, I was driving Engine 457 traveling north at a speed of fifty-two miles an hour on the single main-line track four miles east of Ridgeville, Illinois. Weather conditions and visibility were excellent. Suddenly the last two grain cars, 3022 and 3053, jumped the track. The train automatically went into emergency braking and stopped immediately. There were no injuries to the crew. But the train did not stop before both grain cars turned at a 45° angle. After checking the cars, I found that half the contents of their load had spilled. The train was not carrying any hazardous chemical shipments.

I notified Supervisor Bill Purvis by AMAX telephone at 7:40 A.M., and within forty-five minutes he and a section crew arrived at the scene with rerailing equipment--a bulldozer and a derrick. The section crew removed the two grain cars from the track, put in new ties, and made the main-line track passable by 9:25. At 9:45 a vacuum car arrived with Engine 372 from Hazlehurst, Illinois, and its crew proceeded with the cleanup operation. By 10:25 A.M. all the spilled grain was loaded onto the cars brought by the Hazlehurst train. Bill Purvis called Barnwell Granary and notified them that their shipment would be at least three hours late.

CAUSES OF INCIDENT

Supervisor Purvis and I checked the stretch of train track where the cars derailed and found it to be heavily worn. We believe that a defective fisher joint slipped when the grain cars hit it, and the track broke.

RECOMMENDATIONS

We made the following recommendations to the switch yard in Hazlehurst to be carried out immediately:

1. Check the section of track for ten miles on either side of Ridgeville for defective fisher joints.

2. Repair all such defective joints at once.

3. Instruct all engineers to slow down to five to ten mph over this section of the road until the rail check is completed.

FIGURE 16.14   An accident report form.

DIVERSIFIED INDUSTRIES, INC.
Baltimore, Maryland

ACCIDENT REPORT

1. Name of the employee (last, first, middle) _____

2. Employee identification number _____

3. Social Security number _____

4. Home address and telephone number _____

5. Time of injury _____ A.M. P.M. Location _____

6. Type of injury (specify exact body part[s]) _____

7. What kind of treatment did injured party receive? Where was treatment given?

8. Describe what happened (give a narrative of events before, during, and after; describe materials or tools involved in accident):

9. Provide names and addresses of eyewitnesses:

10. What caused the accident?

11. What action should be taken to prevent similar accidents from occurring in the future?

12. Which company employees (e.g., supervisor, union representative) were notified?

Signature of person filling out form _____

Date form is filled out _____

Send one copy to Home Office; one copy to Safety Department; and one to Personnel Department.

count, use quotation marks to set off statements by the witness. But delete any emotional reactions of eyewitnesses—how much an object meant or how surprised they were to see something happen. Filter out other irrelevant details. If you are reporting a work stoppage, it is unnecessary to indicate what the employees did while waiting for machinery to be repaired. Do not duplicate information found elsewhere in the report—license numbers, times, employee identification numbers. Finally, if necessary, give information about expenses.

5. What was done after the incident. After describing the incident, be concerned with the action you took to correct conditions, to get things back to normal. Readers will want to know what was done to treat the injured, to make the environment safer, to speed delivery of goods, to repair damaged equipment, or to satisfy a customer's demands.

6. What caused the incident. Make sure that your explanation is consistent with your description in number 4. Pinpoint the trouble. In Figure 16.13, for example, the defective fisher joint is discussed under the heading "Causes of Incident." In the following example, the two causes cited in a report of an accident involving a pipe falling from a crane are exact and helpful.

1. The crane's safety latch had been broken off and was never replaced.
2. A tag line was not used to guide the pipe onto the truckbed.

7. Recommendations. Readers will be looking for specific suggestions to prevent the incident from happening again. Recommendations may involve discussing the problem at a safety meeting, asking for further training from a manufacturer, adapting existing equipment to meet customers' needs, doing some emergency planning for the next storm damage, modifying schedules, or cutting back on expenses. In the example of the falling pipe in number 6, the writer of an incident report listed the following two appropriate recommendations.

1. Order safety latches to replace the broken latch and have additional spare latches on hand.
2. Have a pipeshop supervisor conduct a safety meeting for employees and use a representative drawing of the incident as an aid.

◆ MAIN POINTS TO REMEMBER ABOUT SHORT REPORTS

Before considering long reports, the subject of the next chapter, let's review the main points about short reports.

1. They are a few pages at most and get to the point quickly and concisely.
2. They can be prepared in a variety of formats—memo, letter, or special form.
3. Their content will vary with the type of report—periodic, sales, progress, trip, test, or incident. In all types of short reports, however, the emphasis is on facts and objectivity.
4. They are generally organized to include information on purpose, data, conclusions, and recommendations.

◆ EXERCISES

1. Bring to class an example of a periodic report from your previous or present job or from any community, religious, or social organization to which you belong. In an accompanying memo to your instructor, indicate who the audience is and why such a report is necessary, stressing how it is submitted and organized and what kinds of factual data it contains.

2. Assume that you are a manager of a large apartment complex (200 units). Write a periodic report based on the following information—There are 26 units vacant, 38 ready to become vacant, and 27 soon to be leased (by June 1). Also add a section of recommendations to your boss (the head of the real estate management company for which you work) on how vacant apartments might be leased quickly.

3. Assume you work for a household appliance store. Prepare a second-quarter sales report based upon information contained in the following table.

	Numbers Sold	
Product	1st Quarter	2nd Quarter
Kitchen appliances		
Refrigerators	72	103
Dishwashers	27	14
Freezers	10	36
Electric Ranges	26	26
Gas Ranges	10	3
Microwave Ovens	31	46
Laundry appliances		
Washers	50	75
Dryers	24	36
Air treatment		
Room air-conditioners	41	69
Dehumidifiers	7	2

4. Write a progress report on the wins, losses, and ties of your favorite sports team for last season. Address the report to the Director of Publicity for the team and stress how the director might use these facts for future publicity.

5. Submit a progress report to your writing teacher on what you have learned in his or her course so far this term, which writing skills you want to develop in greater detail, and how you propose doing so. Mention specific memos, letters, instructions, reports, or proposals you have written or will soon write.

6. Compose a site inspection report on any part of the college campus or plant, office, or store in which you work that might need remodeling, expansion, or new or additional air-conditioning or heating work.

7. You have been asked to write a short preliminary inspection report on the condition of a historic building for your state historical society. Inspecting the building, the home of a famous late nineteenth-century governor, you discover the following problems. Include all these details in your report.

   - Eight front columns are all in need of repair; two of them in fact may have to be replaced.
   - The area below the bottom window casements needs to be excavated for waterproofing.
   - The slate tile on the roof has deteriorated and needs immediate replacement.
   - The front stairs show signs of mortar leaching requiring attention at once.
   - Sections of gutter on the northwest and northeast sides of the house need changing; other gutters are in fair shape.
   - Wood louvers need to be repainted; four of the twelve may even need to be replaced.
   - All trees around the house need pruning; an old elm in the backyard shows signs of decay.
   - The siding is in desperate need of preparation and painting.
   - The brick near the front entrance is dirty and moss covered.

8. Assume that you are a social worker, law enforcement officer, or youth counselor. Write an appropriate trip report based on the following information. Make sure to include your reasons for the visit, a description of the visit, and some appropriate recommendations based on the visit.

   George Morrow, age 15, was put on probation last August for stealing. He has missed a number of school days this term. The principal at his high school said he also got into some trouble about library books—defacing them or not returning them. George's parents were recently divorced, and he lives with his mother. His mother has requested some help and wants to know what kinds of programs are available. George is very eager to go to technical school and become an electrician. He feels as though his misdeeds will hurt him. George has to report to the court at least once a month for the next year.

9. Write a report to an instructor in your major about a field trip you have taken recently. Indicate why you took the trip, name the individuals you met on the trip, and stress what you learned and how that information will help you in course work or on your job.

10. Submit a test report on the purpose, procedures, results, and recommendations of an experiment you conducted on one of the following subjects:

a. soil	h. computers
b. machinery	i. forests
c. water	j. food
d. automobiles	k. money
e. textiles/clothing	l. transportation
f. animals	m. blood
g. recreational facilities	n. noise levels

11. Write an incident report about a problem you encountered in your work in the last year. Use the memo format or use the form reprinted in Figure 16.14.

12. Write an incident report about one of the following problems. Assume that it has happened to you. Supply relevant details in your report. Identify the audience for whom you are writing and the agency you are representing or trying to reach.

   a. After hydroplaning, your company car hits a tree and has a damaged front fender.

   b. You have been the victim of an electrical shock because an electrical tool was not grounded.

   c. You twist your back lifting a bulky package in the office or plant.

   d. Your boat capsizes while you are patrolling the lake.

   e. The crane you are operating breaks down and you lose a half day's work.

   f. The supplier shipped the wrong replacement part, and you cannot complete a job without renting an expensive tool.

13. Choose one of the following descriptions of an incident and write a report based on it. The descriptions contain unnecessary details, vague words, insufficient information, an unclear cause-and-effect relationship, or all of these errors. In writing your report, correct the errors by adding or deleting whatever information you believe is necessary. You may also want to rearrange the order in which information is listed. Use the form in Figure 16.14 or a memo format to write the report.

   a. After sliding across the slippery road late at night, my car ran into another vehicle, one of those fancy imported cars. The driver of that car must have been asleep at the wheel. The paint and glass chips were all over. I was driving back from our regional meeting and wanted to report to the home office the next day. The accident will slow me down.

   b. Whoever packed the glass mugs did not know what he or she was doing. The string was not the right type; nor was it tied correctly. The carton was too flimsy as well. It could have been better packed to hold all those mugs. Moreover, since the bus had to travel across some pretty rough country, the package would have broken anyhow. The best way to ship these kinds of goods is in specially marked and packed boxes. The value of the box was listed at $350.

Long Reports

This chapter will introduce you to long reports—how they differ from short reports, how they are written, and how they are organized. It is appropriate to discuss long reports in one of the last chapters of *Successful Writing at Work.* The long report is often assigned last in class because writing one gives you an opportunity to use and combine many of the writing skills and strategies you have already learned. In business, a long report is the culmination of many weeks or months of hard work on an important company project.

The following skills and strategies will be most helpful to you as you prepare to study long reports; appropriate page numbers appear below where these topics have already been discussed.

- gathering and summarizing information, especially from reference works (pages 250–85; 323–33)
- organizing, drafting, and revising your ideas (pages 26–35)
- reporting the results of your research accurately and concisely (pages 373–86; 485–87)
- writing a variety of paragraph patterns and sentence types (pages 61–66; 72–87)
- creating and introducing visuals (pages 391–427)
- using an appropriate method of documentation (pages 289–304)
- preparing an informative abstract (pages 341–42)

Having improved these skills, you should be ready to write a successful long report.

◆ HOW A LONG REPORT DIFFERS FROM A SHORT REPORT

Both long and short reports are invaluable tools in the world of work. They provide essential information to help a company or agency function. Both should be written in formal, standard English and have an objective, professional tone.

Basic differences exist, though, between these two types of reports. A short report is not a watered-down version of a long report; nor is a long report simply an expanded version of a short one. These reports differ in purpose, scope, format, and, many times, audience. The following section explains some of the key differences between these two reports. By understanding these differences, you will be better able to follow the rest of Chapter 17 as it covers the process of writing a long report and the organization and parts of such a report. A model long report is included in Figure 17.3.

1. Scope. A long report is a major study that provides an intensive and in-depth view of the problem or idea. For example, a long report written for a course assignment may be eight to twenty pages long; a report for a business or industry may be that long or much longer, depending on the scope of the subject. The implications of a long report are wide-ranging for a business or industry—relocating a plant, adding a new line of equipment, changing an accounting system. While the long report examines a problem or idea in detail, the short report covers just one part of the problem. Unlike a short report, a long report may discuss not just one or two current events, but rather a continuing history of a problem or idea (and the background information necessary to understand it in perspective). For example, the short test report on paulownia in Figure 16.12 (pages 508–10) would be used with many other test reports for a long report for a group of industrialists on the value of planting trees to prevent soil erosion at mine sites.

The following titles of some typical long reports further suggest their extensive (and in some cases exhaustive) coverage: "A Master Plan for the Recreation Needs of Syracuse, New York," "The Transportation Problems in Kingsford, Oregon, and the Use of Monorails," "The Revolutionary Advances in the Manufacture and Use of the Compact Disc Player."

2. Research. A long, comprehensive report requires much more extensive research than a short report does. The research provides writers with the detailed documentation readers of a long report expect and need. Such research can be gathered over time from questionnaires, laboratory experiments, library research, on-site visits, interviews, and the writer's own observations. For a course report, you will have to do a great deal of library research and possibly interviewing to identify a major problem or topic, to track down the relevant background information, and to discover what experts have said about the subject and what they propose should be done.

Information gathered over many short reports can also be used to help prepare a long report. In fact, as the example of paulownia shows, a long report can use the experimental data included in a short report to arrive at a conclusion. Also for a long report writers often supply one or more progress reports (one type of short report—review pages 493–99).

3. Format. Another significant difference between a long and short report is in format. Because a long report contains extensive documentation, it is too detailed and complex to be adequately organized in a memo or letter format. The product of thorough research and analysis, the long report gives readers detailed discussions of large quantities of data. To present this information in a logical and orderly fashion, the long report contains more parts, sections, headings, subheadings, and supplements (appendixes) than would ever be included in a short report. The long report often includes many graphs, charts, and tables to provide readers with extensive background information and documentation. The long report also incorporates many summaries of data at the beginning, at the end, and at key points in between for the reader's convenience.

4. Timetable. The two types of reports also differ in the time it takes to prepare them and in the way in which they are written. Writers of the two types of reports are working under different expectations from their readers and under different kinds of deadlines. A long report is generally commissioned by a company or agency to explore in detail some subject involving personnel, locations, costs, safety, or equipment. Many times a long report is required by law; for example, investigating the feasibility of a new missile system or a change in the ecosystem. The long report is so important that it becomes a record a company will keep on file for executives and employees to consult. A short report is often written as a matter of routine duty where the writer is given little or no advance notice. The long report may take weeks or even months to write. Over this period the researchers have to gather the extensive documentation readers will expect. When you prepare a long report for a class project, make sure that you select a topic that really interests you, for you will spend a good portion of the term working on it.

5. Audience. The audience for a long report is generally broader—and goes higher in an organization's hierarchy—than that for a short report. Your short report may be read by your co-workers or a first-level supervisor, but a long report may be read by people in the top levels of management—presidents, vice-presidents, superintendents, directors—who make long-range financial and organizational decisions. In addition, copies of long reports may be sent to appropriate department heads for their information and commentary. A long report written about a campus issue or problem may at first be read by your teacher and then sent to an appropriate decision-maker, such as a dean of students, a business manager, a director of athletics.

6. Collaborative Effort. Unlike many short reports, the long report in the business world and industry is not always the work of one employee. Rather, it may be a collaborative effort, the product of a committee or group whose work is reviewed by one main editor to make sure that the final draft is consistently and accurately written. (As we saw, proposals also may be written by a group of writers—see page 457.) Individuals in many departments within a company—art, computer programming, engineering, public relations, industrial safety—may cooperate in planning and producing a long report, which may reflect their various skills: graphics production, statistical analysis, interviewing. Your instructor may ask you to work in a group (or alone) in preparing your long report.

◆ THE PROCESS OF WRITING A LONG REPORT

As we just saw, writing a long report requires a lot of time and effort. Your work will be spread over many weeks, and you need to see your report not as a series of static or isolated tasks but as an evolving and accomplishable project. Before you embark on that project, review the information on the writing process found in Chapter 2. You may also want to study the flow chart found on page 414, illustrating the different stages in writing a research paper.

The first steps involve choosing a broad subject area to explore. You can do this by doing some preliminary research—general reading, consulting relevant indexes, talking to experts about the subject. From this preliminary research you are better able to arrive at a restricted topic, the second major step in the process. After that, you need to assemble information (the documentation) on that topic and read and think about it carefully. From this information and your analysis of it you can prepare one or more outlines. Then you may want to start drafting, though you may return to outlining later on. Through revisions, your drafting will ultimately lead to the final copy of your report. (Some writers find it helpful to outline and draft at the same time, moving back and forth between drafting and outlining.)

In the process of writing the long report, expect to revise your work often— and sometimes extensively. You will have to reexamine and rethink your ideas. While you do this, your organization and analysis may change. You may have to consult new sources and arrive at a *new interpretation* of those sources. Not everything you need will be available to you right away. You may have to order materials from a company or through interlibrary loan, or you may have to reschedule an interview. Also, as you narrow your purpose and scope, you may find yourself deleting information. You may even substitute a better source for a weaker one. At the earlier stages of outlining and preparing rough drafts, you may move material around a great deal to avoid unnecessary duplications and to ensure adequate coverage. At the later stages, you will be revising sentences and paragraphs to make them read more smoothly and logically. At this stage you should also pay increasing attention to the transitions between and among sentences and paragraphs.

Keep in mind, even as you work on your rough drafts, that a long report is not written in the order in which the parts will finally be assembled. You cannot write in "final" order—abstract to appendix. Instead you will write in "loose" order to reflect the order in which you gathered information and assembled it for the final copy of the report. Accordingly, the body section is usually written first, for authors must obtain material included here in order to construct the rest of the report. However, you may want to sketch in parts of your introduction first. The abstract, which appears very early in the report, is always written last, after all the facts have been recorded and the recommendations made or the conclusions drawn. Introductions are usually written later as well, since authors can then make sure that they have not left anything out.

To keep track of your work, prepare both a work calendar and a checklist. Keep both posted where you do your work—above your desk, typewriter, or word processor. The calendar should mark the dates by which each stage of your work must be completed. Match the dates on your calendar with the dates your instructor or employer may have given you for a copy of the outline, for progress reports, for the final copy. Your checklist should contain the major parts of your report. As you complete each section, check it off. Before assembling the final copy of your report for readers, use the checklist to make sure that you do not accidentally omit something.

◆ PARTS OF A LONG REPORT

A long report may include some or all of the following twelve parts, which form three categories: *front matter,* the *text of the report,* and *back matter.* The entire report may be placed in a clear plastic folder or other suitable cover.

Front Matter

As the name implies, the front matter of a long report consists of everything that precedes the actual text of the report. Such elements introduce, explain, and summarize to help the reader locate various parts of the report.

1. Letter of transmittal. This three- or four-paragraph letter states the purpose, scope, and major recommendation of the report. If written to a teacher, the letter should additionally note that the report was done as a course assignment. Sometimes the letter of transmittal is bound with the report as part of it; most often it comes before the report, serving as a kind of cover letter. Figure 17.1 is a sample letter of transmittal for a business report; Figure 17.3 contains a letter of transmittal for a student's long report.

2. Title page. The title, which should be listed in all capital letters, indicates a specific subject and how or why you studied it. This page also gives the name of the company or agency preparing the report, the name(s) of the report writer(s), the date, any agency or order numbers, and the name of the firm for which the report was prepared. Figure 17.3 shows a typical title page for a long report.

3. Table of contents. The major sections of the report are listed on the contents page. By looking at the table of contents in Figure 17.2, for example, the reader sees at a glance how the report, "A Study to Determine New Directions in Women's Athletics at Coastal College," is organized and can find the location of the various sections of that report. When preparing a table of contents, use lower-case roman numerals for front matter elements as in Figures 17.2 and 17.3. Never list the contents page itself, the letter of transmittal, or the title page in your table of contents, and never have just one subheading under a heading. You cannot divide a single topic by one.

FIGURE 17.1   A letter of transmittal for a long report.

α

ALPHA CONSULTANTS
1400 Ridge
Evanston, California 97213-1005

August 1, 1990

Dr. K. G. Lawry, President
Coastal College
San Diego, California 93219-2619

Dear Dr. Lawry:

We are happy to send you the enclosed report, "A Study to
Determine New Directions in Women's Athletics at Coastal
College," that you asked us to prepare. The report contains
our recommendations about strengthening existing sports
programs and creating new ones at Coastal College.

After studying Coastal's sports facilities and the college's
plans for expansion, we interviewed the coaching staff and
many of the women athletes. We also polled the coaching staffs
and 100 women athletes at three local colleges—Baystown
Community College, California State University of Arts and
Sciences, and Central Community College.

Our recommendation is that Coastal should engage in more
active recruitment to establish a competitive women's baseball
team, start to offer athletic activities in women's track and
field by August 1991, and create a new interdisciplinary
program between the Athletic Department and the Women's
Studies Program.

We hope that you find our report useful in meeting students'
needs at Coastal College. If you have any questions or if you
would like to discuss any of our recommendations, please
call us.

Sincerely yours,

Barbara Gilchrist
Barbara Gilcrest

Lee T. Sidell
Lee T. Sidell

Encl. Report

FIGURE 17.2   A table of contents for a long report.

CONTENTS

LIST OF ILLUSTRATIONS iii

ABSTRACT iv

INTRODUCTION 1
  Background 1
  Problem 1
  Purpose of Report 4
  Scope of Report 5

DISCUSSION 6
  Women's Athletics at Area Colleges 7
    Baystown Community College 7
    California State University of Arts and Sciences 9
    Central Community College 10
  Coastal's Sports Facilities 12
    North Campus 12
    South Campus 14
  Coastal's Coaching Staff 16
    Freshmen Teams 16
    Varsity Teams 18
  Performance of Coastal's Women Athletes 19
  Coastal's Recruitment Strategies 20
  Women's Athletics and the Curriculum 22
    Interdisciplinary Women's Studies Program 23
    Physical Education Program 25

CONCLUSION 28
  Views of the Students 29
  Views of the Coaches 31

RECOMMENDATIONS 32

REFERENCES CITED 34

APPENDIXES 37
  A. Sample Questionnaire for Coaches 38
  B. Sample Questionnaire for Athletes 39
  C. Profile of Women Athletes' Achievements 40
  D. Cost Estimates for Physical Plant Additions 41

Incorrect	EXPANDING THE SPORTS PROGRAM
	Basketball
	BUILDING A NEW ARENA
	The West Side Location
Correct	EXPANDING THE SPORTS PROGRAM
	Basketball
	Track and Field
	BUILDING A NEW ARENA
	The West Side Location
	Costs

4. List of illustrations. This list of all the figures and tables indicates where in the report they are found. Figure 17.3 shows a list of illustrations.

5. Abstract. As discussed in Chapter 11 (pages 341–42), an abstract presents a brief overview of the problem and conclusions; it summarizes the report. An informative abstract is far more helpful to readers of a report than is a descriptive one, which gives no conclusions or results.

Not every member of your audience will read your entire report. But almost everyone will read the abstract of your long report. For example, the president of the corporation or the director of an agency may use the abstract as the basis for approving the report and passing it on for distribution. Thus the abstract may be the most important part of the report.

Abstracts may be placed at various points in long reports. They may be placed on the title page, on a separate page, or on the first page of the report text.

Text of the Report

6. Introduction. The introduction may constitute as much as 10 or 15 percent of your report but should not be any longer. If it were, the introduction would be disproportionate to the rest of your work, especially the body section. The introduction is essential because it tells readers why your report was written and thus helps them to understand and interpret everything that follows. Do not regard the introduction as one undivided block of information. It includes the following related parts, which should be labeled separately in the introduction with subheadings. Keep in mind, though, that your instructor or employer may ask you to list these parts in a different order.

(a) Background. To understand why your topic is significant and hence worthy of study, readers need to know about its history. This history may include information on such topics as who was originally involved, when, and where, how someone was affected by the issue, what opinions have been expressed on the issue, what the implications of your study are. See how the report on robots (page 532) provides useful background information.

(b) The problem. Identify the problem or issue that led you to write the report. Since the problem or topic you investigated will determine everything you write about in the report, your statement of it must be clear and precise. That statement may be restricted to a sentence or two.

(c) Purpose statement. The purpose statement, crucial to the success of the report, tells readers why you wrote the report and what you hope to accomplish or prove. In explaining why you gathered information about a particular problem or topic, indicate how such information might be useful to a specific audience, company, or group. Like the problem statement, the purpose statement does not have to be long or complex. A sentence or two will suffice. You might begin simply by saying, "The purpose of this report is . . . ."

(d) Scope. This section informs readers about the specific limits—number and type of topics, times, money, locations, personnel, and so forth—you have placed on your investigation. For example, a report on waste disposal might include a scope statement such as, "This report examines the recent techniques involved in the disposal of liquid and solid wastes; gaseous wastes are not discussed in this report." In your report, you may not have studied individuals in an adjacent town or counties because of time or may not have reviewed certain types of electronic equipment because of their costs or availability. If so, indicate this in your scope section. A careful statement of the scope should tie in with the purpose of your report.

7. The body. Also called the discussion, this section is the longest part, possibly making up as much as 70 percent of your report. The body of your report should supply readers with statistical information, details about the environment, physical descriptions, as well as the various interpretations and comments of the authorities whose work you consulted as part of your library research. (Follow the method of documentation discussed on pages 298–302.)

The body of your report should be carefully organized to reveal a coherent and well-defined plan. Your goal is to impose a rational order on your material to help readers understand it easily and accurately. To do that, you have to separate the material in the body of your report into meaningful parts. Make sure that you identify the major topics as well as subtopics in your report. These topics and subtopics must be clearly related to each other. Headings help your reader identify major topics more quickly.

Your organization should be carefully reflected in the different headings (and maybe even subheadings) included in your report. Use them throughout your report to make it easy to follow. These organizational headings will also enable someone skimming the report to find specific information quickly. These headings, of course, will be included in the table of contents page.

The order in which you present these topics is equally important for your readers. Divide your information based upon the categories into which it logically falls. For example, in tracing an idea or a program through various stages, you might follow a straight chronological order. If you were writing a feasibility report, one in which you study and weigh conflicting options (locations, equipment, programs) for readers, you would devote a section of the body to each one of the options being studied. If you were investigating the usefulness of a piece of equipment, you might divide your discussion according to the value of each major part of that equipment. An investigation of the public transportation of a community might be divided into the modes of transportation you have investigated: "Rail," "Buses," "Cabs," "Van- and Carpooling," and "Private Automobiles." Study the way in which the body of the model report included in Figure 17.3 is organized.

In addition to headings, use transitions to reveal the organization of the body of your report. At the beginning of each major section of the body tell readers what they will find in that section and why. Summary sentences at the end of a section will tell readers where they have been and prepare them for any subsequent discussions. The report in Figure 17.3 does an effective job of providing these internal summaries.

8. Conclusion. The conclusion should tie everything together for readers by presenting the findings of your report. These findings will explain to readers what the data you have gathered mean. Findings, of course, will vary depending on the type of research you engage in. For a library research report, the conclusion should summarize the main viewpoints of the authorities whose works you have cited. For a marketing report done for a business or industry, you must spell out the implications for your readers in terms of costs, personnel, products, location, and so forth. Regardless of the type of research you do, your conclusions should be based on the information and documentation you presented in the body of the report. To write an effective conclusion, you will have to summarize carefully a great deal of information.

9. Recommendations. A research report for a course may not require a recommendation section. But for a business or scientific report, the most important part of the report, after the abstract, is the recommendation(s) section, which tells readers what should be done about the findings recorded in the conclusion. Review the principles of writing effective recommendations in Chapter 12 (pages 380–86).

Back Matter

Included in this section of the report are all the supporting data which, if included in the text of the report, would bog the reader down in details and cloud the main points the report makes.

10. Glossary. An alphabetical list of the specialized vocabulary with its definitions appears in the glossary (see pages 427–28). A glossary might be unnecessary if your report does not use highly technical vocabulary or if all members of your audience are familiar with the specialized terms you do use.

11. References cited. Any sources cited in your report—books, articles, television programs, audiovisual materials, interviews, and reviews—must be listed in this section (see Chapter 10, pages 292–98, on preparing a Works Cited page).

12. Appendix. The appendix contains all the supporting materials for the report—tables and charts too long to include in the discussion, sample questionnaires, budgets and cost estimates, correspondence about the preparation of the report, case histories, transcripts of telephone conversations. Group like items together in the appendix, as the examples under "Appendixes" in Figure 17.2 show.

◆ THE MODEL LONG REPORT IN THIS CHAPTER

The long report in Figure 17.3 is a research report written by a student for a communications class. It deals with robots in American industry, a popular topic about which the student gathered relevant data primarily through library work. It contains all the parts of a long report discussed on pages 522–27 except a recommendation, glossary, and appendix. Intended for a general audience unfamiliar with robot technology, the report consequently avoids the technical terms and descriptions for which a glossary might be necessary. Because the student is surveying authorities' opinions, he does not supply a recommendation section of his own.

The student's main task is to investigate what has been said about robots in American industry and to report the results of his research in a logically organized discussion. Notice how the body section of his report is divided into four closely related areas—employment, safety in the workplace, benefits to employers, and future advances from robot technology. A number of these areas are further subdivided, as you will see from the table of contents and the subheadings in the report.

This report shows how one writer researched, organized, and discussed a major problem (or topic) suitable for a long report.

FIGURE 17.3   A long report.

345 Spruce Lane
Apt. 34-C
Gunderson, NE 68345

May 17, 1988

Professor Dorothy Ridgely
Communications Department
Fairmont Central College
Fairmont, NE 68339-6717

Dear Professor Ridgely:

With this letter I am enclosing my research report on the
robotics topic you approved six weeks ago. My report discusses
the various contributions robots can make to American
industry, both for workers and for employers.

Robotization offers significant and widespread technological
benefits. Contrary to some views, robots will not take jobs
away from American workers but instead will increase
employment opportunities. Robots will also make the work
environment safer and offer employers many financial benefits.
Finally, robots of the future will radically improve American
industry and the life-style of workers.

I hope that you will find this report interesting and
carefully researched. If you should need to discuss it with
me, I can be reached at 678-3400 during the day and at
456-8294 after 6:00 P.M.

Sincerely yours,

John Mark Russell

John Mark Russell

Enclosure

FIGURE 17.3   (continued)

THE POSITIVE EFFECTS OF ROBOTS IN AMERICAN INDUSTRY

John Mark Russell

Communications 102

Professor Dorothy Ridgely

May 17, 1988

FIGURE 17.3   (continued)

Table of Contents

LIST OF ILLUSTRATIONS iii

ABSTRACT iv

INTRODUCTION 1

  Background 1

  Problem 2

  Purpose of Report 2

  Scope 3

DISCUSSION 3

  Robots Will Encourage, Not Threaten, Employment 3

    Unjustified Fears About Unemployment 3

    Fewer Robots Mean Fewer Jobs 5

    Increased Employment Because of Robots 6

  Robots Provide Efficiency and Safety in the Workplace 7

    Robots Can Improve Workers' Efficiency 8

    Robots Will Make the Workplace Safer 8

  Robots Offer Employers Benefits 9

    Robots Can Increase Output and Quality 10

    Robots Can Decrease Manufacturing Costs 11

  What Robots Will Do in the Future 13

CONCLUSION 16

WORKS CITED 17

ii

FIGURE 17.3   (continued)

LIST OF ILLUSTRATIONS

Table 1: Estimated Number of New Robot-related Jobs,
1985–1995 7

Figure 1: Costs for Robot and Human Workers as of 1988 12

ABSTRACT

After twenty-five years of rather slow growth, the robot
worker in American industry is finally becoming an
indispensable part of our technology. This robot revolution
has created fears that many human workers will lose their
jobs. Most industry experts agree, however, that only a small
displacement of human workers will occur and that most of
these workers will be transferred to related or upgraded jobs.
Through their greater productivity, robots are expected to
create more jobs than they eliminate. They will also make the
workplace safer for human employees and improve their
effectiveness. Robots will reward employers by giving them
improved efficiency and productivity at lower costs. Moreover,
robots will bring even greater benefits to workers through
better jobs and a higher standard of living.

FIGURE 17.3   (continued)

INTRODUCTION

Background

    For centuries people have been fascinated by amazing stories of machines that could be programmed through remote control to do superhuman feats. However, we have seen less enthusiasm about robots in such places as an assembly line or a chemical plant. The name robot itself (from the Czech word meaning "compulsory labor, drudgery") symbolizes the reaction many people have to mechanical devices that perform human jobs in the workplace.

    The first industrial robot was used in 1959, and shortly thereafter, in 1962, General Motors installed its first Unimation robot (Ayres and Miller 4). But the growth of robots in American industry was slow. By 1970 only a few hundred robots were in use in American plants. It was not until the 1980s that industry readily accepted them (Teresko 35). The successful introduction of robots by several major companies, especially Detroit automakers, encouraged other industries to make the same investment (Aronson 22–23). In the early 1980s, more than 5,000 robots were found

FIGURE 17.3   (continued)

2

in the United States, with a growth rate projected by
the firm of Bache Investments to be 35 percent annually
(Ayres and Miller 5). More recently, TechTran
Consultants have predicted that by 1995 there may well
be over 550,000 robots at work in America (Koelsch 49).
In fact, Robert Lund, senior research associate at the
MIT Center for Policy Alternatives, stresses that the
new robotics technology is the only salvation for
American industry if it is to match and surpass the
production levels of other countries in the world market
(Dodd 691).

Problem

    Robotics technology is not universally understood
or accepted. Although this new technology will certainly
shape American industry in the future, many workers and
some managers fear it and do not understand its
benefits.

Purpose of Report

    The purpose of this report is to discuss the
benefits robots offer American industrial workers and
their employers.

FIGURE 17.3   (continued)

3

Scope

This report includes information on how robots can establish new jobs, make the workplace safer for employees, improve production for employers, and create a better future for American workers through advanced technology.

DISCUSSION

Robots Will Encourage, Not Threaten, Employment

Unjustified Fears About Unemployment

A recurrent fear about the widespread use of robots is that they may put American workers out of a job. Some industrialists have predicted that by the year 2000 robots will replace 16 to 18 percent of all manufacturing workers, resulting in millions of lost jobs (Cromie 16). According to Toepperwein et al., each robot installed in the early 1980s displaced about two workers a day, but as robot capabilities increase, they may displace more than three workers a day (312).

FIGURE 17.3 (continued)

4

These statistics are misleading, however. Most industry experts, including officials of the United Auto Workers, consider these projections to be excessively high (Jones 23). These and other experts "predict that robots will never displace more than 5 percent of the work force" (Aronson 26). And some experts believe that by 1995 less than one percent of the American work force may be laid off because of robots (Koelsch 49—50; Jones 22). To date, robots have displaced only about 15,000 workers in America, most of whom were shifted into related or more technologically advanced positions.

Fortunately, nearly all of these workers should be "retrained for new jobs within their companies" ("Robots to Create. . ." 15). This occupational relocation, together with a declining birthrate over the next few decades, should remove any fears of widespread unemployment caused by robots (Aronson 26—27; Rice interview). Ironically enough, it is the outmoded robots that most likely will be laid off as sophisticated, newer models take their places (Williams 23).

FIGURE 17.3   (continued)

5

Fewer Robots Mean Fewer Jobs

When American companies do not use robots, they
jeopardize the jobs of American workers. James Albus, an
expert in industrial systems and robotics, has precisely
identified the cause-and-effect relationship between
advanced technology, such as robotics, and employment:

> It is in the industries that fall behind in
> productivity that job layoffs are prevalent.
> Inefficient industries lose market-share to
> competitors, shrink, and eventually die. Thus,
> the biggest threat to jobs is not in
> industries that adopt the fastest robot
> technology but in those that do not (27).

To illustrate this principle on an international
scale, consider that "Britain's sagging economy employs
fewer than 200 robots; Japan's booming economy employs
nearly 8000 robots" (Cromie 16). Applying this principle
closer to home, R. Weisel of Prab Robots proposed that
United States automakers will lose 400,000 jobs to
foreign competitors by trailing them in the use of
robots (Teresko 39). American workers are unemployed
because of the robots in Japan, not the robots in
Detroit (Albus 27). More than one expert has predicted

FIGURE 17.3   (continued)

6

that by failing to use robots, certain industries will

become "obsolete" (Coates and Coates 32) and that

workers in these industries will suffer.

Increased Employment Because of Robots

Not only will the robot boom help to prevent

unemployment but it may, in all likelihood, increase

employment. Thomas Weekly of the United Auto Workers sees

"new types of jobs created" because of robots (qtd. in

Cromie 15). Robotics should, like earlier automation in

industry, create more jobs than it eliminates through

increased production (Aronson 26). Greater industrial

productivity means more human involvement in the decision-

making, manufacturing, and marketing processes. Moreover,

robot technology will create new opportunities for workers

in maintaining and repairing these machines (Cromie 13;

Toepperwein et al. 308) as well as in constructing them.

Additional human supervisors will be needed if problems on

the assembly or transportation line result (Teresko 36).

As Table 1 on the following page indicates, the Robotics

Delphi Report estimates that more than 45,000 new jobs

will be available by 1995 because of robots. Thus, it

seems safe to conclude that robots "will complement, not

compete with, humans" (Albus 27).

FIGURE 17.3   (continued)

7

Table 1 Estimated Number of New Robot-related Jobs			
	1985	1990	1995
ROBOT INDUSTRY	1300	2300	3050
SUPPLIER INDUSTRIES	1000	2200	4500

USERS—
  MAINTENANCE
  PROGRAMMING
	
	5500
	3700
		
		18,000
		6000
			
			25,300
			12,650

TOTAL EMPLOYMENT
  ASSOCIATED
  WITH USE OF ROBOTS
	
	11,500
		
		28,500
			
			45,500

From Robotics Delphi Report: 1985			

Source: Nagler 59.

Robots Provide Efficiency and Safety in the Workplace

   Some authorities believe that the robot revolution
will, in the long run, provide vast improvements and
benefits for Americans in their workplaces. Not only
will new and better jobs result because of robots but
they will enhance many existing jobs. Vary T. Coates,
an expert on technology assessment, speculates that
companies will purchase robots to help especially in
those environments that "may be inefficient, unsafe,
and inhospitable for human workers" (qtd. in Coates and
Coates 32).

FIGURE 17.3 (continued)

8

Robots Can Improve Workers' Efficiency

Coates's first area of concern--inefficiency--is
one in which robots on the job site can be of great
help. A robot can assist a human worker to accomplish
specific duties much more carefully and precisely. For
example, robots can be designed to reach into very small
or awkward places that would be impossible or
extraordinarily difficult for human workers. A robot can
also precisely measure the insides of a pipeline (Coates
and Coates 31) or test the interior components of a
machine without disassembling the machine. Robots are
also used to sample products (such as Coca-Cola) for
uniformity, thus "eliminating the monotony experienced
by technicians performing [such] routine analyses"
("Robot and Weighing System. . ." 115).

Robots Will Make the Workplace Safer

Perhaps the ultimate contribution of robots will be
in making the workplace safer for human beings. Thanks
to robots, human beings may not have to be exposed to
occupational environments that threaten their health.
Robots do not have lungs, skin, ears, or eyes to

FIGURE 17.3   (continued)

9

protect. Nor do they have to worry about noise levels, dust or asbestos particles, or eyestrain and headaches from uninterrupted work. Robots on hazardous work sites will therefore help to decrease employment-related injuries and illnesses (Coates and Coates 31).

Robots can be invaluable in providing safety nets in potentially dangerous industries such as nuclear power plants. Countless human lives could be spared because of robots. For example, if there were a leak of lethal radioactive material, robots rather than human beings would be exposed at the power plant. Likewise, robots would reduce hazards to human workers at factories that produce toxic chemicals or explosives. Robots can also safely load and transport toxic materials (Coates and Coates 31–32; Toepperwein et al. 207). In addition, "Robots can be important in assisting individuals who work in mines, one of the most dangerous occupational sites in America" (Rice interview).

Robots Offer Employers Benefits

Robots also offer employers numerous benefits. They improve the quality and output of the employer's plant, and they reduce the cost of materials.

FIGURE 17.3   (continued)

10

Robots Can Increase Output and Quality

An important benefit of robotization is the increased output and amazingly high quality that a robot can provide. While human welders can keep their torches on the job only 30 percent of the time, robot workers can keep going 90 percent of the time. Robots used for welding also have the capability of correcting errors during a job, saving time and increasing production. When General Dynamics started using a robot in 1978 to prepare and install sheet-metal parts for the F-16 fighter jet, the production of the jet quadrupled (Sugarman 54). By 1987 robots at the Garrett Turbine Engine Company in Phoenix could measure noise levels at eighty locations in a power turbine unit in fourteen minutes, a job that takes nine hours for human workers (Tolman 6).

Robots on the job also improve the quality of work done for an employer. T. E. Baker of General Electric convincingly describes one of the robot's chief virtues:

> The robot is a maddeningly demanding and consistent machine. . . . If materials fed to it are not completed, uniform, and reasonably flawless, it will either correct the problem

FIGURE 17.3   (continued)

11

        itself, summon its human supervisor with a

        bell or whistle, or just quit. (qtd. in

        Teresko 39)

A robot can deliver high quality by also being extremely

accurate. It is capable of drilling sets of holes within

.005 inch of error and can machine 250 different parts.

A human worker on the job produces 6 parts per shift

with 10 percent rejections, while a robot in the same

job makes 24 to 30 parts with zero rejections (Dodd

691). Used in the electronics industry, robots can

insert microchips without "deviating so much as a

millimeter's space" (Jones 27).

    Every aspect of our economy benefits from the

increased production and improved quality of American-

made products. Certainly two of the most welcome

advantages will be more orders for American goods and

increased employment for American workers.

      Robots Can Decrease Manufacturing Costs

    As the initial price of purchasing a robot falls

with improved technology, lower labor cost becomes a

principal argument for the robotization of American

factories. Joseph Engleberger, president of the largest

FIGURE 17.3   (continued)

12

U.S. robot manufacturer, estimates that the cost per
hour of a medium-priced hypothetical robot is $6.00.
This figure represents only a 50 percent increase since
1967, while hourly rates for human laborers have
increased by 180 percent over the same period (Ayres and
Miller 72). The graph in Figure 1 (from Jones) records
the differences in labor costs between human and robot
workers up to 1988. Moreover, as the production of

Figure 1. Costs for robot and human workers as of 1988.
Source: Jones 32.

FIGURE 17.3 (continued)

13

robots increases, the cost per unit will surely decrease

(Sugarman 53). And businesses can also expect to pay

less for their robots thanks to a number of recent tax

incentives and low-interest government loans (Farnum 56;

Nagler 60).

Significant savings can also result from a robot's

efficient use of materials. At one General Electric

factory, a robot used for painting saved $19,000 worth

of paint in one year while improving coverage and finish

(Ayres and Miller 77). Because of their mechanical

capabilities, robots waste fewer parts and less

materials (die, plastic for moulding, bolts) and energy

in any manufacturing process (Toepperwein et al.

307–308). This increased cost efficiency may be the

chief method of protecting American industry from

foreign competitors.

What Robots Will Do in The Future

So far this report has emphasized the current

advantages robots offer industrial workers and

employers. Compared to what robots will do for us in the

future, these benefits are relatively small. David

Nitzan, the program manager at the robotics research and

FIGURE 17.3 (continued)

14

development firm of SRI International, claims that
despite their amazing current feats, robots are in their
"infantile" stage of development (qtd. in Dodd 689). In
the 1970s and early 1980s, robots had limited
capabilities and applications. For the most part they
were restricted to performing pick-and-place operations
(Aronson 26). But new markets are opening up in the late
1980s and early 1990s for robots outside of auto
assembly lines and manufacturing.

Although experts say that we are many years from
seeing highly skilled robots (Albus 22—23), experimental
laboratories are already using robots that have
extraordinary vision and tactile sensory systems (Jones
24—25). The next generation of robots will have sensory
capabilities unmatched by their human counterparts. Like
the Bionic Woman, the Six Million Dollar Man, and
Superman, they will be able to see, touch, smell, and
hear perfectly and do so under extremely dangerous
conditions. Within the next decade some robots will be
equipped for voice recognition. Robots will be used
extensively in space exploration, crime-detection work,
medicine, and all types of engineering.

This growth in capabilities will be matched by the
increase in the number of robots in industry. Robots

FIGURE 17.3 (continued)

15

will be found in almost every manufacturing process in the 1990s. As we saw, TechTran Consultants are projecting implementation of 550,000 robots in the United States by 1995. With such large corporations as General Electric, General Motors, IBM, and Texas Instruments entering the robotics field, these estimates may not be unreasonable (Ayres and Miller 8).

All of these technological advances will translate into a better life for workers. According to Thomas Weekly, robots will soon give workers "shorter hours, longer vacations, and higher wages" (qtd. in Cromie 16). Looking further into the future, James Albus predicts that "If all humans could own the equivalent of one or two robots, they would be financially independent, regardless of whether they were employed or not" (27). Robots may not make everyone rich, but one thing is certain: "Combined with other emerging technologies, robotics can contribute to a transformation of society-- both in the United States and throughout the world-- that is as encompassing a change as the Industrial Revolution" (Coates and Coates 32). As Jones points out, robots will join the computer as "the two most essential tools of the late 21st century" (32).

FIGURE 17.3 (continued)

16

CONCLUSION

The steadily increasing use of robots in American industry will benefit workers and employers. Although some individuals have worried about potential jobs being lost to robots, many industrialists and union leaders maintain that robots will create more jobs than they eliminate. Previous successes with automation confirm this assessment. Despite a temporary displacement of a small percentage of the work force, industrial robots can improve overall working conditions for employees. Robots help human workers to perform more efficiently and to escape hazardous jobs and work sites. Employers find robots desirable because they will make it possible to cut costs, to reduce errors, and to improve quality and output. As robot technology improves, it will offer numerous future benefits, including a higher standard of living for the American industrial worker.

FIGURE 17.3   **(continued)**

17

Works Cited

Albus, James. "Robots in the Workplace." The Futurist
    17 (1983): 22—27.

Aronson, Robert. "The Robot Boom Is On." Machine Design
    52 (1980): 22—24, 26—28.

Ayres, Robert, and Steven Miller. Robotics Applications
    and Social Implications. Cambridge, MA: Ballinger,
    1983.

Coates, Vary, and J. F. Coates. "The Potential Impacts
    of Robotics." The Futurist 17 (1983): 28—32.

Cromie, William. "Robots: A Growing, Maturing
    Population." SciQuest 54 (1981): 12—16.

Dodd, John. "Robots: The New Steel-Collar Worker."
    Personnel Journal 60 (Sept. 1981): 688—695.

Farnum, Gregory T. "Industrial Robots--The Next Ten
    Years." Manufacturing Engineering 95 (Dec. 1985):
    55—56.

Jones, Sue-Ellen. "The Social and Economic Impact of
    Robots in the American Workplace." Journal of
    Business and Engineering Technology 9 (1988): 22—37.

Koelsch, James R. "The Steel-Collar Worker: Friend or
    Foe?" Product Engineering 33 (1986): 48—50.

FIGURE 17.3   (continued)

18

Nagler, Ben. "Career Paths in Robotics." Manufacturing
   Engineering 95 (Dec. 1985): 59–60.

Rice, Barbara. Industrial Technology Professor,
   Fairmont Central College. Personal interview, 30
   Mar. 1988.

"Robot and Weighing System Reduce Sample Testing Cost
   50% at Coca-Cola." Chilton's Food Engineering 57
   (Dec. 1985): 115.

"Robots to Create 44,500 Jobs by 1995." Modern
   Materials Handling 40 (1985): 15, 17.

Sugarman, Robert. "The Blue-Collar Robot." IEEE
   Spectrum 17 (1980): 53–57.

Teresko, John. "Robots Come of Age." Industry Week 25
   Jan. 1982: 35–36, 38–39, 42.

Toepperwein, L. L., et al. Robotics Applications for
   Industry: A Practical Guide. Park Ridge, IL: Noyes
   Data Co., 1983.

Tolman, Alan G. "Sound Intensity Measurements in
   Hazardous Areas." Sound and Vibration 21 (1987): 6.

Williams, David. "Steel Collar Layoffs as Robots
   Decline." Automotive Industries 166 (Oct. 1986): 23.

◆ EXERCISES

1. Write a memo to your instructor on how one of the short reports in Chapter 16 could be useful to someone who has to write a long report.

2. Using the information contained in Figures 17.1 and 17.2, write an introduction for the report "A Study to Determine New Directions in Women's Athletics at Coastal College." Add any details you think will be relevant.

3. What kinds of research did the student do to write the long report in Figure 17.3? As part of your answer, include the titles of any specific reference works you think the writer may have consulted. You may want to review Chapter 9.

4. Study Figure 17.3 and answer the following questions.
   a. Why can the abstract be termed informative rather than descriptive?
   b. How has the writer successfully limited the scope of the report?
   c. Where does the writer use internal summaries especially well? (See page 527 for a discussion of the values of such summaries.)
   d. What visual devices does the writer employ to separate parts of the report and divisions within each part?
   e. How does the writer introduce, summarize, and draw conclusions from the expert opinions he cites in order to substantiate the main points?
   f. What are the ways in which the writer documents information he has gathered?
   g. What functions does the conclusion serve for readers? Cite specific examples from the report.

5. Come to class prepared to discuss at least two major problems that would be suitable topics for a long report. Consider an important community problem—traffic, crime rate, air and water pollution—or a problem at your college. Then write a letter to a consulting firm or other appropriate agency or business, requesting a study of the problem and a report.

6. Write an outline of the report appropriate for one of the problems listed in Exercise 5. Use major headings and include the kinds of information listed on page 526.

7. Have your instructor look at and approve the outline you prepared for Exercise 6. Then write a long report based on the outline.

Oral Reports

Every job requires employees to have carefully developed speaking skills. In fact, in order to get hired, you have to be a persuasive speaker at your job interview. On the job you will have oral communication responsibilities that will vary in the amount of preparation you have to do for them, the time they last, and the audience and occasion for which they are intended. This chapter offers practical advice on how to become a better, more assured communicator in informal briefings and formal speeches.

◆ INFORMAL BRIEFINGS

If you have ever given a book report or explained laboratory results in front of a class, you have given an informal briefing. Such semiformal reports are a routine part of many jobs. Nurses and law enforcement officers, for example, give their colleagues or supervisors end-of-shift reports, summarizing major activities for the previous eight or twelve hours.

Another kind of briefing involves explaining a new procedure or policy to other departments. As a personnel officer, you may have to inform plant employees of extended coverage on an insurance policy. If your company has just purchased a new piece of equipment, you may have to demonstrate it. Or you may introduce a speaker, a visitor to your agency, or a new employee or report on a convention you attended. Finally, you may give a brief report at a public hearing—before a school board, group of county supervisors, or government agency.

These informal reports are usually short (one to seven minutes, perhaps), and you always will be given advance notice. Make your comments brief and to the point. When the boss tells you to "say a few words about the new Minivac (or the new parking policy)," you are not expected to give a lengthy formal speech. For example, the personnel officer informing employees about extended insurance coverage should not read the fine print in the policy, but rather cover its key points, saving detailed questions for a private conference.

Rather than writing down all your comments in full sentences, make a few rough notes and jot them down on a three-by-five note card you can easily hold in the palm of your hand. Your notes should consist of only the major points you want to mention, preferably in chronological order or from cause to effect (see pages 62; 65). A note card with key facts used by an employee who is introducing Ms. Rizzo, a visiting speaker, to a monthly meeting of safety directors might include the following items.

- Diana J. Rizzo, Chief Engineer of the Rhode Island State Highway Department for twelve years.
- Experience as both a civil engineer and safety expert.
- Consultant to Secretary Taft, Department of Transportation
- Member of the National Safety Council and author of "Field Test Procedures in Highway Safety Construction."
- Designed specially constructed aluminum posts used on Rhode Island highway system.

Similarly, a note card used by a personnel officer to inform employees about new insurance coverage might list the following major points.

- American Democratic Insurance has changed some of the coverage on employees' policies.
- If you are hospitalized, American Democratic will pay up to $221.75 per day on your room. This is an increase of $38.35 per day from the old policy.
- Outpatient lab benefits are also increased. American Democratic will now pay $500 a year rather than the $375 under the old policy.
- Premiums will also increase by about $3.40 a week, but Iramco, the employer, will pay $1.40 of that increase, meaning employees will have $2.00 more deducted from weekly checks.
- Currently we are exploring a dental rider on the American Democratic policy.
- If any questions, call me or Mr. Blackwell at extension 3452 or drop by the Personnel Office in the Administration Building.

◆ FORMAL SPEECHES

Whereas an informal briefing is likely to be short, generally conversational, and intended for limited numbers of people, a formal speech is likely to be longer, less conversational, and intended for a wider audience. Therefore, it involves more preparation and less interaction between speaker and audience; it is, in other words, more "formal."

Most of us are uncomfortable in front of an audience because we feel frightened or embarrassed. Much of this anxiety can be eased, though, if you know what to expect. The two areas you should investigate thoroughly before you begin to prepare your speech are (1) who will be in the audience and (2) why they are there.

Analyzing Your Audience

The more you learn about your audience, the better equipped you will be to give them what they need. First, determine what unites them as a group. For example, are they all members of one profession (computer programming or mechanical engineering) or do they have similar professional interests (court reporters, paralegals, and legal secretaries)? Or your audience may be linked by place of employment; for instance, all the employees—mechanics, bookkeepers, salespeople—in a car dealership. Other bonds, too, may unite an audience—ethnic background, hobbies, membership in clubs, age, sex, or religion.

Once you have defined your audience, assess how much they will know about your topic. Everything depends on what your audience will understand and need—the terms you use, how many details you have to give, the number of explanations and definitions you supply, and the amount of background information required. Terms taken for granted in one group must be explained or never used with another group.

Speaking for the Occasion

Understanding why your audience is there will help you deliver a successful speech. An audience may be present for a variety of reasons—for a social gathering, a business meeting, or an educational forum. Shape your remarks to fit the occasion.

Consider also how much time is allotted for your speech and whether you are the only speaker scheduled. It makes a big difference in your preparation if you are the first speaker at an 8:00 A.M. breakfast meeting or the last of four speakers at an evening meeting.

The number of people in your audience is also significant. A formal presentation to a small group—five or six supervisors or buyers—seated around a conference table can nonetheless be made more intimate; you can walk around or stop your talk a few times to ask if there are any questions. You will obviously have much less flexibility when addressing a large group—seventy or eighty people—in an auditorium.

Ways of Presenting a Speech

Your effectiveness depends directly on the extent of your preparation. Of the four approaches below, the extemporaneous is best suited to most individuals and occasions. But first we will examine three other possibilities and their advantages and disadvantages.

1. Speaking off the cuff. The professional speechmaker may be comfortable with an off-the-cuff approach, but for most of us, the worst way to deliver a speech is to speak without any preparation whatsoever. You may know a subject very well and think that your experience qualifies you for an on-the-spot performance. But you will only be fooling yourself if you think you have all the details and explanations in the back of your head. It is equally dangerous to believe that once you start talking, everything will fall into place smoothly. The "everything works out for the best" philosophy, unaided by a lot of hard work, does not operate in public speaking. Without preparation, you are likely to forget or to confuse important points entirely. Mark Twain's advice is apt here: "It takes three weeks to prepare a good impromptu speech."

2. Memorizing a speech. The exact opposite of the off-the-cuff approach, a memorized speech does have some advantages for certain individuals—tour bus drivers, guides, or salespeople—who must deliver the same speech many times over. But for the individual who has to deliver an original speech just once, a memorized speech contains pitfalls. First, the hours spent memorizing exact words and sentences would be better devoted to organizing your speech or gathering information for it. Second, if you forget a single word or sentence, you may lose the rest of the speech. Third, a memorized delivery can make you appear mechanical. Rather than adjusting to an audience's reactions, you will be obligated to speak the exact words you wrote before you saw your audience.

3. Reading a speech. Reading a speech may be appropriate if you are presenting information on company policy or legal issues on which there can be no deviation from the printed word. Most speeches, however, will not require this rigid adherence to a text. Your speeches will be more acceptable, socially and professionally, when you interact with the audience. In reading, you set up a barrier between yourself and the audience. You will not establish eye contact with your audience for fear of losing your place.

4. Delivering a speech extemporaneously. An extemporaneous delivery is best for the widest variety of occasions. Unlike a speaker using a memorized or written speech, you do not come before your audience with the entire speech in hand. *By no means, though, is an extemporaneous delivery an off-the-cuff performance.* It requires a great deal of preparation. But what you prepare is an outline of the major points of your speech, as discussed later in this chapter. You will rehearse using that outline, but the actual words you use in your speech will not necessarily be those you have rehearsed. Stand confidently in front of the audience with your outline reminding you of major points but not the precise language to express them. In this way you can establish contact with the audience.

The rest of this chapter will discuss various effective ways of preparing and delivering an extemporaneous speech.

Preparing the Parts of a Speech

The Introduction

The most important part of a speech, your introduction should capture the audience's attention by answering these questions: (1) Who are you? (2) What are your qualifications? (3) What topic are you speaking about, and how is that topic restricted? and (4) How is that topic relevant to the audience? An effective introduction is proportional to the length of your speech. A ten-minute speech requires no more than a sixty-second introduction; a twenty-minute speech needs no more than a two-minute introduction.

You will probably begin by introducing yourself, emphasizing your professional qualifications. (This self-introduction may be unnecessary if someone else introduces you or if everyone in the room knows you.) Never apologize for taking up your audience's time or for your limitations as a professional speaker.

Thank the audience for the opportunity of addressing them and indicate at once what your topic is and how it is divided. The most interesting speeches are the easiest to follow. Restrict your topic to ensure that it will be organized carefully. Focus on one major (and restricted) idea; e.g., a tasty diet under 1200 calories a day or a course in canoeing.

Give listeners a "road map" at the beginning of your talk so that they will know where you are, when you are there, and what they have to look forward to or to recall: "Tonight I will discuss the three problems a foodstore manager faces when deciding to stock inventory: (1) the difficulty in predicting needs, (2) the inability of the production department to record current levels of stock accurately, and (3) the uncertainty of marketplace conditions."

Moving from your announcement of the topic to your presentation of it requires skill at inducing an audience to listen. Use a variety of tactics to get the audience to "bite" on the "hook." The simplest is to ask a question: "Do you know how much actual meat there is in a hot dog?" "How many of you have taken Graphics 201?"

Another often used technique is to cite some interesting statistics. Listeners' curiosity should be so piqued that they will stay tuned in for an explanation or description: "In 1990 two million heart attack victims in America lived to tell about it." "By 1992, more than half of America's population will be over thirty-five."

You might also begin with an anecdote, or brief story, that illustrates the main points of your speech. Sometimes effective speakers start with something humorous. But be careful about using jokes to get the audience in a good mood. Some may not find your joke amusing, in good taste, or relevant.

The Body of the Speech

The body is the longest part of your speech just as it is in a long report. It supplies the substance of your speech by (1) explaining a process, (2) describing a condition, (3) telling a story, (4) arguing a case, or (5) doing all of the above.

To get the right perspective, recall your own experiences as a member of an audience. How often did you feel bored or angry because a speaker tried to overload you with details? The Peanuts cartoon in Figure 18.1 points out the consequences of boring an audience.

When you prepare the body of your speech, consider your audience as a group of listeners, *not* readers. Readers have more time to digest the ideas in your work. They can read as slowly or as quickly as they want, reread and double-check details, or skim wherever they want. Listeners, however, cannot absorb as much as readers can. The speaker's audience has a shorter attention span. You cannot include every fact you gathered in preparing the speech. Select only details that are relevant to your audience and purpose.

Here are a few helpful ways you can present and organize information in the body of your speech. In writing a report, you assist readers by supplying head-

FIGURE 18.1   How to find out if you are a boring person.

© 1980 United Features Syndicate, Inc.

ings, underscorings, and bullets. In a speech, switch from purely visual devices to aural ones, as in the following.

1. Give signals (directions) to show where you are going or where you have been. These signals will convince an audience that your speech does not ramble. Enumerate your points: "first," "second," "third." When you tell a story, follow a chronological sequence and fill your speech with signposts: *before, following, next, then.*

2. Comment on your own material. Tell the audience if some point is especially significant, memorable, or relevant. "This next fact is the most important one in my speech." "The best determiner of pressure is the amount of liquid present in the chamber."

3. Repeat key ideas. You can repeat a sentence or a word for emphasis and to help the audience remember it. But do this sparingly; repeating the same point over and over again bores an audience.

4. Provide internal summaries. Spending a few seconds to recap what you have already covered will reassure your audience and you as well. For example, "We have already discussed the difficulties in establishing a menu repertory, or the list of items that the food-service manager wants to appear on the menu. Now we will turn to ways of determining which items should appear on a menu and why."

The Conclusion

Plan your conclusion as carefully as your introduction. Stopping with a screeching halt is as bad as trailing off in a fading monotone. An effective conclusion leaves the audience feeling that you have come full circle and accomplished what you promised. Conclusions, even for long speeches (twenty minutes), should never run more than sixty to ninety seconds. Moreover, you should clearly inform your audience when you are approaching the end of your speech: "finally," "in conclusion," "to wrap up."

A conclusion should contain something lively and memorable. Do not introduce a new subject or simply repeat your introduction. A conclusion contains a restatement and reemphasis of your most important points (or the conclusions you reached about them). For example, "The installation of the stainless steel heating tanks has, as we have seen, saved our firm 32 percent in utility costs, since we do not now have to run the heating system all day." If you are delivering a persuasive speech, issue a call for action, just as in a sales letter (see Chapter 8). Stress what you want your listeners to do and why it is beneficial for them to do it or harmful (or less desirable) if they do not follow your advice.

The Speech Outline

Construct a speech outline to represent the introduction, the body, and the conclusion. As we saw, in an extemporaneous speech you do not write out the entire speech you are going to deliver. Instead you will have a speech outline to guide you. The speech outline has great psychological value in that it gives you enough facts to handle your speaking engagement confidently, yet it is not so detailed that it places you in a straitjacket.

The speech outline illustrated in Figure 18.2 contains the appropriate amount of detail to represent the introduction, body, and conclusion of a speech given by Tim Phalen, an assistant cashier at a savings and loan. A roman numeral designates each major point; capital letters indicate appropriate supporting facts. Be careful about crowding too much into a speech outline. You do not need an outline as highly structured as the following.

Not every point will require four or five capital letters. But each point, whether indicated by a roman numeral or a capital letter, should be written as a complete sentence. Since your outline must be easy to read and follow, leave wide margins and double space between your points. Mark, perhaps with a red pen or capital letters, where visuals appear in your speech. That way, you won't forget them.

Using Visuals

You may use a variety of visuals during your talk: photographs, maps, chalkboards, models, pasteboards (large, two-by-three-foot, stiff pieces of white cardboard), diagrams, or slides. Visuals are used in a speech for the same reasons as in a report: to explain quickly, condense information, and add interest and variety. But visuals in an oral presentation must be constructed even more carefully than for a written report. Unlike a reading audience, a listening audience cannot refer to a visual again and may not have time to study the visual in detail.

The size and shape of your visuals are important. If they cannot be seen clearly from a distance and understood at once, they are not very useful. If possible, before using any visual, mount it in the front of the room and sit in the last row of chairs in the room in which you will speak to see if your audience will be able to decipher it. You might decide to increase the size of your visual (enlarge a photograph, for example), hold it up higher, or show it to different sections of your audience by walking from one side of the room to another.

Determining How Many Visuals to Use

Use visuals sparingly. A brief speech may not require any visuals and even a very long speech may need only two or three visuals. Their purpose is to clarify (or supplement), not to compete with what you say. (Note Tim Phalen's limited use of visuals in Figure 18.2.) Too many visuals will distract your audience.

FIGURE 18.2   A speech outline.

AUDIENCE: Madisonville Optimist Club

PURPOSE: To encourage members of the Optimist Club to do business
           with Madisonville Savings and Loan

INTRODUCTION

  I. Is there a secret to financial success?

     A. Authors of books on "how to make a million dollars" say
        that readers will profit from their advice.

     B. Fashion designers claim that the way we dress determines
        our success.

     C. Psychologists maintain that the key to success rests with
        how well we manipulate people.

     D. Real success is knowing how to turn your dreams into
        reality.

     E. Madisonville Savings and Loan can show you how to make your
        dreams of financial success come true. SHOW POSTER WITH
        WORDS "MADISONVILLE SAVINGS AND LOAN," "DREAMS," AND
        "REALITY" TO EMPHASIZE RELATIONSHIP FOR AUDIENCE.

BODY OF THE SPEECH

 II. Madisonville Savings and Loan will help you find the best way
     to save.

     A. We pay the highest interest rates allowed by law.

     B. Our staff of financial counselors will assist you in
        selecting the right savings account.

     C. Madisonville Savings and Loan currently offers customers
        five types of savings accounts.

        1. The Basic, or Standard, Account is the most flexible; it
           pays interest daily from the day of deposit and requires
           no minimum balance.

FIGURE 18.2   (continued)

    2. A Payroll Savings Account automatically deposits money into your account.

    3. An Ambassador Account allows you to get money away from home when you need it.

    4. A Certificate Account pays more interest than the Basic Account but requires a $500 minimum.

    5. A Money Market Account, requiring a $10,000 balance, pays the highest interest rate.

  D. Our Retirement Plan assures you of trouble-free years to travel; you will have a steady income when you need it.

  E. All savings accounts and retirement plans are insured by the Federal Savings and Loan Insurance Corporation.

  F. With any account you select, you will receive a quarterly statement showing the interest earned and, where appropriate, maturity dates.

III. Madisonville Savings and Loan will help you to borrow as well as to save money.

  A. Savings and loans have been in the lending business for 100 years.

  B. Madisonville Savings and Loan is a leader among local financial institutions in giving home owners and businesses long-term loans. STOP. SHOW GRAPH.

  C. Most of our savings are invested in mortages.

  D. In fact, 45 percent of all houses in Madisonville in the last fifty years were built or bought with mortgage money obtained from Madisonville Savings and Loan.

  E. Madisonville Savings and Loan offers customers four types of mortgages.

FIGURE 18.2   (continued)

3

   1. VA loans give veterans interest rates fixed by the U.S.
      government, no closing costs, and no down payments.

   2. FHA loans, another federally assisted program, also
      offer fixed interest rates below the conventional
      market, but buyers must purchase insurance to protect an
      FHA loan.

   3. Conventional mortgages allow buyers to obtain their
      money in Madisonville; on a month-to-month basis they
      are cheaper than FHA loans.

   4. Adjustable Rate Mortgages (ARMs) offer home owners
      flexible rates, which help to lower monthly payments.

IV. Our new Fast Account gives you checking benefits you have not
    had before.

   A. You can write checks and earn interest on the same account.

   B. You can pay your bills by telephone--no postage to worry
      about.

   C. You receive a monthly statement of all transactions,
      including the interest your money has earned.

   D. If your checking account has ever been overdrawn, you will
      like the automatic line of credit a Fast Account gives you.

CONCLUSION

   V. Let Madisonville Savings and Loan help you to find your most
      successful financial opportunities.

   A. The three services we offer--savings, loans, and checking--
      are interrelated. SHOW TRIANGLE DEPICTING RELATIONSHIP.

   B. Come to Madisonville Savings and Loan and allow us to show
      you how to take advantage of all our services.

Thank you for the opportunity to be with you today. I will be happy
to answer any questions you may have.

Getting the Most from Your Visuals

The following practical suggestions will help you get the most from your visuals.

1. Do not set up your visuals before you begin speaking. The audience will try to determine how you are going to use them and so will not give you full attention.

2. Firmly anchor any maps or illustrations. Having a map roll up or a picture fall off a stand during your presentation is embarrassing.

3. Never obstruct the audience's view by standing in front of the visuals you are explaining. Also, when you finish with a visual, do not leave it standing to block the audience's view of you or of other visuals for the rest of your talk.

4. Avoid crowding three or four visuals onto one pasteboard to save space or time. Use different pasteboards instead.

5. Do not put a lot of writing on a visual. Elaborate labels or descriptions defeat your reason for using the visual. Your audience will spend more time trying to decipher the writing than attempting to understand the visual itself.

6. Be extra cautious with a slide projector. Check beforehand to make sure that all your slides are in the order in which you are going to discuss them and that they are right side up.

Rehearsing a Speech

An efficient writer never submits a rough draft of a paper or report as final copy to an employer. Rather, the draft is revised, edited, and carefully checked before it is typed to produce the final copy. Similarly, a careful speaker does not write a speech and march off to deliver it. Between the time you write a speech and deliver it, rehearse it several times. Going over your ideas aloud may help you to spot poor organization and to correct insufficient or inaccurate content.

Rehearsing will also help you to acquire more natural speech rhythms, pitch, pauses, and pacing. Try speaking in front of a full-length mirror for at least one of your rehearsals to see how an audience might view you. At another time, speak into a tape recorder to determine if you sound friendly or frantic, poised or pressured. You can also catch and correct yourself from going too quickly or too slowly. Time yourself so that you will have a fairly accurate idea if your talk falls within the time allotted you. Practice with the visuals or equipment you intend to use in your speech for valuable "hands-on" experience.

Delivering a Speech

A poor delivery can ruin a good talk. When you speak before an audience, you will be evaluated on the image you project by how you look, talk, and move (your body language). Do you mumble into your notes, never looking at the audience? Do you clutch the lectern as if to keep it in place? Do you shift nervously from one foot to another? All these actions betray your nervousness and detract from your presentation.

The following suggestions on how to present a speech will help you to be a well-prepared speaker.

Before You Speak

Your name is called, and within a minute or two you will have to begin addressing the audience. You will be nervous. Accept the fact and even allow a few seconds for a "panic time." But then put the nervous energy to work for you. Chances are, your audience will have no idea how fearful you are; they cannot see the butterflies in your stomach. If you have to go to a lectern, walk slowly so you do not trip.

Once you are before the lectern, remove any pitchers or glasses of water if you are worried about spilling them. Always have a wristwatch with you. Before speaking, lay it on the desk or lectern so that you can occasionally glance down to see how much time you have left. This unobtrusive act is far preferable to reminding the audience that you are running out of time by noticeably raising your arm to look at your watch.

Giving Your Talk

Begin your speech slowly. Give listeners a chance to sit back in their chairs and establish a mental connection with your topic. Rushing into your speech may be startling, causing you to lose the audience from the start. To speak effectively, pay attention to the following four points.

1. Establish eye contact with your listeners to form a special relationship with them. Burying your head in notes signals your lack of interest in the audience or your fear. Some timid speakers think that if they look only at some fixed place or object in the back of the room, the audience will still regard this as eye contact. But this kind of cover-up does not work. Another tactic poor (or frightened) speakers use is to look at only one member of the audience or to focus, with frequent sidewise glances, on the individual next to them on the stage, perhaps the person who has introduced the speakers.

Establish a pattern of gazing at your notes and then looking up at various individuals in the audience. If the group you are addressing is small (five to ten people), look at each person in the course of your talk. When you speak to a large audience (fifty or more individuals), visually divide this group into four or five sections, and look at each section a number of times as you speak.

2. Make the volume, tone, and rate of your delivery a favorable part of your image. Speak in a natural, conversational voice, but avoid such "verbal tics" as "you know" or "I mean" repeated several times each minute. Such nervous habits will make your audience nervous too and make your speech less effective. Talk slowly enough for your audience to understand you, yet quickly enough so that you don't sound as if you are emphasizing each word.

Talk loudly enough for everyone to hear, but be careful if you are using a microphone. Your voice will be amplified, so if you are already speaking loudly, you will boom rather than send messages pleasantly to your audience. Watch out for the other extreme—speaking so softly that only the first two rows can hear you.

3. Watch your posture. If you stand motionless, looking as if rigor mortis has set in, your speech will be judged as cold and lifeless, no matter how lively your words are. Be natural; move, and let your body react to what you are saying. Smile, nod your head, move your arms, point your fingers at an object, stand back a little from the lectern. This is not to say that you should be a moving target. Never sit on a desk or lean on a lectern in front of your audience. Listeners will be waiting to see if you fall off your newly discovered perch.

4. Let your gestures be a help, not a hindrance. Be natural and consistent. Do not startle an audience by suddenly pounding on the lectern for emphasis. Any quick, unexpected movement detracts from what you are saying. Let your material suggest appropriate movements. If you are itemizing four or five points, hold up the appropriate number of fingers to indicate which point you are discussing. Using your hands and arms to indicate direction, size, or relationships is also a way to use body language to comment on your material.

Avoid any gesture that will distract your audience; do not provide your own sideshow. The following nervous habits, engaged in frequently during a speech, can divert the audience's attention: scratching your head, rubbing your nose, twirling your hair, pushing up your glasses, fumbling with your notes, or tapping your foot.

When You Have Finished Your Speech

Don't just smugly sit down, walk back to your place on the dais or in the audience, or, worse yet, march out of the room. Thank your listeners for their attention, and stay at the lectern for them to applaud, ask questions, or perhaps give the person who introduced you a chance to thank you while you are still in front of the group. If a question-and-answer session is to follow your speech, give your audience a time limit for questions. For example, you might say, "I'll be happy to answer any questions you may have now before we break for lunch in ten minutes," or "I have set aside the next ten minutes for questions." By setting limits, you reduce the chances of engaging in a lengthy debate with members of the audience, and you also can politely leave after your time elapses.

◆ SPEECH EVALUATION FORM

A large portion of Chapter 18 has given you information on how to construct and deliver a formal speech. As a way of reviewing that advice, study Figure 18.3, an evaluation form similar to those used by instructors in speech classes. Note that the form gives equal emphasis to the speaker's performance and to the organization and content of the speech.

FIGURE 18.3   A speech evaluation form.

Name of speaker _____   Date of speech _____

Title of speech _____   Length of speech _____

PART I: THE SPEAKER (circle the appropriate number)

1. Appearance: 1   2   3   4   5
                   sloppy   well groomed

2. Eye contact: 1   2   3   4   5
                    poor   effective

3. Voice: 1   2   3   4   5
                  monotonous   varied

4. Posture: 1   2   3   4   5
                    poor   natural

5. Gestures: 1   2   3   4   5
                  disturbing   appropriate

6. Self-confidence: 1   2   3   4   5
                   nervous   poised

PART II: THE SPEECH (circle the appropriate number: 1 = poor; 5 = superior)

A. Overall performance

   1. Speaker's knowledge of the subject—carefully researched; factual errors; missing details:

           1   2   3   4   5

   2. Relevance of the topic for audience—suitable for this group:

           1   2   3   4   5

   3. The speaker's language—too technical; filled with cliches or slang expressions; or crisp and descriptive:

           1   2   3   4   5

   4. Use of visuals—too many or too few; well placed; appropriate size; handled with care; interfered with speech:

           1   2   3   4   5

FIGURE 18.3   (continued)

B. Parts of the speech

  1. The introduction—brief and attention getting; informative about division and presentation of topic:

      1   2   3   4   5

  2. The body—carefully organized and easy to follow; appropriate amount of information; message developed and conveyed clearly:

      1   2   3   4   5

  3. The conclusion—brief, effective summary of the main points:

      1   2   3   4   5

PART III: YOUR FINAL REACTIONS (briefly complete the following)

1. Of all the speakers on the platform today, this speaker should be ranked:

    _____

2. The speaker's main strengths were: _____

    _____

    _____

    _____

3. The speaker needs to improve on: _____

    _____

    _____

    _____

◆ **EXERCISES**

1. Prepare a three- to five-minute talk explaining how a piece of equipment that you use on your job works. If the equipment is small enough, bring it with you to class. If it is too large, prepare an appropriate visual that you can use in your talk.

2. You have just been asked to talk about the students at your school. Narrow this topic and submit a speech outline to your instructor, showing how you have limited the topic and supplied appropriate evidence. Use two or three

appropriate visuals (tables, photographs, etc.). Follow the format of the outline in Figure 18.2.

3. Prepare a ten-minute talk on a controversial topic that you would present before some civic group—a local PTA, local chapter of an organization, a post of the Veterans of Foreign Wars, a synagogue or church club. Submit a speech outline similar to that in Figure 18.2 to your instructor, together with a one-page statement of your specific call to action and its relevance for your audience.

4. Using the information contained in the research paper in Chapter 10 (pages 305–17) or the long report in Chapter 17 (pages 530–50), prepare a short speech (five to seven minutes) for your class.

5. Using the evaluation form contained in Figure 18.3, evaluate a speaker; this person can be someone in a speech class, a local politician, or perhaps someone delivering a report at work. Specify the time, place, and occasion of the speech.

Index

Abbreviations, 107–8
  for states, 125–26
  when not to use, 107–8
Abstracts
  descriptive, 341
  informative, 320–32, 341
  for long reports, 521, 525
  of specific reference works, 268,
    284–85
  for test reports, 507
Acceptance letters, for a job, 187–88
Accident report, 485, 510–14
Active voice, 76–77
Adjustment letters
  saying "no," 232–35
  saying "yes," 229–32
Administrative Management Society
    (AMS) letter format, 119, 122–23,
    203, 204
Advertisements, for jobs, 153–54
Alphabetizing, 250–51
  references in Works Cited list, 297–98
American Heart Association, 5–7
Apostrophes, use of, 95
Appendix, for long reports, 527–28
Application forms, for jobs, 179–80
Application letters, 174–79
Applied Science & Technology Index,
    260, 261
Artist's tools, for visuals, 394–95
Asterisks, 17, 448
Attention line, on envelopes, 131
Audience analysis, 4–10, 83–87, 155,
    171, 173, 196, 197, 214–15, 334,
    554
  for formal speeches, 554–58
  for instructions, 435, 439–42
  for letters, 117, 131–37, 206–10,
    210–14
  for long reports, 520
  for memos, 197

for proposals
  internal, 460, 463–64
  sales, 466
  research, 474
for questionnaires, 351–52, 361
questions to ask about, 6–8
for short reports, 486, 493–94
Audiovisual materials, 273–75
Author card, 251–52
Author-date method of documentation,
    303

Back matter, in long report, 527–28
Bibliographic Retrieval Service (BRS),
    265
Bibliography cards, 275–76
Blind ads, for jobs, 153
Body
  of business letters, 127
  of formal speeches, 557–58
  of long reports, 526–27
Body language, 563–64
Book reviews, 335, 337
Brainstorming, 29, 51, 155, 165, 353,
    414, 521
Bullets, use of, 17, 380, 440
Business Periodicals Index, 260, 262–63

Call numbers, for books, 255, 256
Capitalization, of proper nouns, 125, 156
Card catalog, 250–55
Career objective statement, 158, 160–62
Caution statement, 450–51
Charting, 425
Charts, 404–10, 411–15
Clauses, 72–75
  definition of, 72
  dependent and independent, 72–73
  relative, 81
  subordinate, 74, 81
Clustering, 27–28, 155, 165

Code words, on note cards, 277
Collaborative writing, 457
Collection letters, 235–40
Comma splice, 74–76
    four ways to correct, 75–76
    how *not* to correct, 76
Complaint letters, 224–28
Complimentary close, 128
Computer graphics, 423–27
Computer hardware, 36
Computer programming flow chart, 414
Computer software, 36, 37, 424
Computers
    to check spelling, 93
    in formatting résumés, 156, 168
    in letter writing, 119
    in library searches, 250, 263–66
    in preparing visuals, 394, 423–27
    in writing process, 35–40
Computerized bibliographic searches,
        263–66
Computerized library catalog, 250
Conciseness, 102–5
    of reports, 486
Conclusions
    in adjustment letters saying "no," 235
    in adjustment letters saying "yes," 232
    in formal speeches, 558
    in long reports, 527
    in progress reports, 498–99
    in sales letters, 214
    after speeches, 565
Congratulation letters, 221–22
Conjunctions, 72–75
    coordinating, 75
    subordinate, 72
Contemporary language, in letters, 139–41
"Copyrights Approved for Colorization,"
        321
Correspondence. *See* Letters
"Counting on the Census," 325–30
Cover letters, 369–70
Customer relation letters, 214–40
    direct approach, 217–18
    indirect approach, 217–18

Dangling modifiers, 81
Data sheet. *See* Résumé
Date line, 123–24, 199
Delivery of speeches, 563–65
Dependent clause, 72–73
Descriptive phrases, in incident reports,
        511
Dewey decimal system, 255, 256
DIALOG, 265

Dictionaries
    English language, 267
    specialized, 283–84
Direct quotations, 290
    on note cards, 278–80
    in questionnaire reports, 379–80
Documentation, 289–304
    author-date method, 303
    importance of, 289–90
    material to document, 290
    MLA guidelines for, 291–302
    ordered references method, 303–4
    parenthetical vs. footnoting, 291–93
    preparing Works Cited page, 292–98
    within the text, 298–302
Dossier, 149–53
Double consonants, 93–94
Dow Jones News/Retrieval, 265
Drafting
    in documenting sources, 290
    in instructions, 438
    in letters of application, 174–79
    in paragraphing, 44–45
    in proposals, 457
    of sentences, 138
    in short reports, 485
    in summaries, 324, 331
    in long reports, 521
    in the overall writing process, 29–33,
        314
Drawings, 419–23
    in instructions, 440–42
Dummy subject, 84

"Electronic Publishing: The Next Great
        Office Revolution," 345–48
Ellipsis, 278–79
"Emergency Preparedness via Cable TV,"
        69–70
Employment agencies, 154
Employment evaluations, 187–90
Enclosure line, in letters, 129
Encyclopedias, 267, 281–83
Envelope format, 129–31
Evaluation
    of formal speeches, 565–67
    of résumés, 172
Exploded drawings
    in instructions, 440
    as visuals, 422
Extemporaneous speeches, 555–56
Eye contact, 555, 564

Facts on File, 321
False plurals, 94–95

"Fatal assumptions," of job seekers, 148–49
Fax machines, 30–32
Figures, 400–23
    part of long report, 520
    usefulness in occupational writing, 15–16
Findings in short reports, 487
Flex time, 28, 64
Flow charts, 413–14
Follow-up letters, 186–87, 222–23, 224, 225
Footnotes, 291–92
Formal speeches, 554–67
    delivery of, 563–65
    evaluation of, 565–67
    extemporaneous, 555–56
    forms of presentation, 555–56
        memorized, 555
        off-the-cuff, 555
        read, 555
    outlining, 558–59, 560–62
    preparation of
        body, 557–58
        conclusion, 558
        introduction, 556–57
    rehearsal of, 563
    visuals in, 559, 563
Forward instructions, on envelopes, 131
Fragments, of sentences, 73–74
Front matter, in long report, 522–25
Full block format, for letters, 119–20, 122

Gallup, George, 365–67
Gestures. See Body language
Glossary
    for long reports, 527
    of terms to describe visuals, 427–28
Goodwill, importance in business correspondence, 118, 131–33, 206, 220, 229
Government documents, 268–71
Graphs, 400–4

Handbooks, manuals, almanacs, 268
Harris, Lou, 365–67
Headings
    for figures and tables, 399–400
    importance of
        in long reports, 526
        in memos, 201
        in proposals, 460
    in short reports, 486
    in writing, 16
Heparin, descriptions of, 12–13
Horizontal axis, of a graph, 401

Illustrations list, for long report, 525, 532
Imperatives, in instructions, 439
Incident reports, 510–14
Independent clause, 72–73
Indexes, references works, 257–66, 280–81
Informal briefings, 552–53
Initials, 125, 128, 199
Inside address, 125
Instructions
    guidelines for writing, 439–42
    importance of, 435
    parts of
        actual steps, 447–51
        conclusion, 451
        introduction, 442–44
        list of equipment and materials, 444, 446–47
    for questionnaires, 363–64, 365
    variety of, 436–38
    before writing, 438–39
"Intensive Care for Your Typewriter," 343–44
Interviews, for jobs, 183–87
Introductions
    to formal speeches, 556–57
    to instructions, 442–44
    to long reports, 525–26
    to progress reports, 498
    to proposals, 464, 472, 478
    to a test report, 507
    of visuals, 396
Italics, use of, 16

Jargon, 106–8, 323
Job hunting
    application forms, 179–82
    dossier, 149–53
        letters of recommendation in, 149–52
        where stored, 149, 151–52
    identifying qualifications for, 148–49
    interviews, 183–87
    letters of application, 171–79
    placement offices, 149–51, 153
    restricting job search, 148–49
    résumés, 154–72
    sources for jobs, 153–54

Journal of Employment Counseling,
171, 172
Journals, as opposed to magazines, 257

Landers, Ann, 108
Legal notification for collection letters, 238
Legal significance of long report, 520
Legally proper writing, 435, 510–11
Legibility, 179, 275
Letterhead, 119–20
Letters
  of acceptance and refusal, 187, 188, 189
  adjustment, 229–35
  of application, 171–79
  of assessment, 190
  collection, 235–40
  complaint, 224–28
  of congratulation, 221–22
  cover letter for questionnaires, 369–70
  customer relations, 214–40
  definition of, 117
  effective language in, 137–41
  follow-up, 186–87, 222–23, 224, 225
  formats, 119–23, 124, 142
  functions of, 117–18
  general content, 131–37, 142
  of inquiry, 204–5
  order, 201, 202–4
    external, 203, 204
    internal, requisition, 204
  parts of
    body, 127
    complimentary close, 128
    copy distributed notation, 129
    date line, 123–24
    enclosure line, 129
    inside address, 125
    reference initials, 128
    salutation, 125, 126–27
    signature, 128
    subject line, 127
  of recommendation, 149–51
  request for letter of recommendation, 150–51
  sales, 206, 208–14
    comparison with speeches, 557
    the "four A's," 210–14
  special request, 206, 207
  thank-you, 218–20
  thank-you, after job interview, 186–87
  of transmittal, 522, 523, 529
Libraries
  card catalog, 250–55

author card, 251–52
subject card, 253–55
title card, 252–53
circulation desk, 250
the stacks
  call numbers, 255, 256
  shelves, 255, 257
Library of Congress classification system, 255, 256
Library research, 257–85
  note taking, 275–80
  quoting and paraphrasing, 278–80
  reference works, 257–75, 280–85
Long reports
  back matter
    appendix, 527–28
    glossary, 527
    works cited, 527
  difference from short reports, 518–20
  documentation in, 519
  format for, 519–20
  front matter
    abstract, 525
    letter of transmittal, 522, 523
    list of illustrations, 525
    table of contents, 522–25
    title page, 522
  model of, 529–48
  purpose of, 518
  text of
    body, 526–27
    conclusion, 527
    introduction, 525–26
    recommendations, 527

Magazines, *See* Reference works: periodicals; popular press
Mail questionnaires, 350–51
Maps, 414–17
Margins, 118, 168, 366, 399, 404, 559
Measurements, significance of, 17, 439–40, 486, 505
Melville, Herman, 107
Memorized speeches, 555
Memos, 197–201, 202
  definition of, 197
  formats for, 197–99
  function of, 197
  strategies for organization, 199–201
  suggestions on writing, 199, 201
  used for proposals, 463, 474
  used for short reports, 486
  versus letters, 198–99
Message, 10–12, 117–18, 127, 174–75, 352–53
Microfiche, 274–75

Microfilm, 273–74
"Microwaves," 22–23
Military time, 486
Minutes of meetings, 337–40
Misplaced modifiers, 81–82
MLA Handbook, 291
Modifiers, 81–82, 86
  dangling, 81
  misplaced, 81–82
Multiple-bar charts, 407, 408, 409
Musty expressions, 139

NewsBank, 272–73
Newspapers. *See* Reference works: popular press
Note cards, 276–78
  for formal speeches, 553
Numbers
  percents, 373, 378
  in questionnaire reports, 378–79
  rules for writing out, 373, 378
  significance in reports, 488–91
  in table of contents, 522

Objectivity, importance of, 14–15, 358, 366–68, 486, 505, 510–11
Omissions, in incident report, 510
Oral reports, 552–67
Order letters, 201, 202–4
Ordered references method of documentation, 303–4
Organization
  of headings, in long reports, 526–27
  of memos, 199–201, 202
  of steps, in instructions, 447–51
  of *Successful Writing at Work,* 20
  of summaries, 323–25
Organizational charts, 411–13
Outlines
  for business correspondence, 215
  for formal speeches, 558–59, 560–62
  for long reports, 521
  importance in the writing process, 29, 31, 414, 521

Pagination
  second or subsequent pages, 123
  table of contents, 522, 524
  title page, 522
Paragraphs, 43–70
  appearance of, 59–61
  coherence in, 54–57
  definition of, 43
  importance of, 43–44
  length of, 59–61
    job acceptance letter, 187

  in application letters, 175
  in business letters, 127
  in letters of congratulations, 221
  in proposals, 465, 472, 478
  in questionnaire reports, 380
  in sales letters, 210
  in short reports, 486
  order in letters of application, 175–79
  patterns of organization
    cause-to-effect, 65
    classification, 64–65
    comparison/contrast, 63–64
    definition, 64
    description, 62
    effect-to-cause, 66
    examples, 61
    space, 63
    time, 62
  topic sentences
    finding one, 51
    importance of, 51
    placement in paragraph, 51–52
    restricting one, 52–53
  transitional devices in
    parallelism, 57
    repetition of key ideas, 56
    transitional words, 54–56
    use of pronouns, 56–57
  T-shaped, 48–49
  types of
    concluding, 50
    introductory, 49
    supporting, 47–49
    transitional, 49–50
  unity in, 53–54
Parallelism
  to achieve coherence in paragraphs, 57
  in sentences, 78–80
Paraphrases, 278–80
Passive voice, 76–78
Periodic reports, 487–88
Periodical holdings and indexes, 257–63
Personal interview questionnaire, 350–51
Persuasion
  in proposals, 457, 466, 472–73
  in sales letters, 210, 213, 214
  use of in occupational writing, 18–19
Photographs, 417–19
Phrases, 72–73
  definition of, 72
  prepositional, 74, 81, 104
Pie charts. *See* Visuals
Placement office, for job information, 149–51, 153

Plagiarism, 289–90
Plurals, 94–95
"Positive Effects of Robots in American
    Industry," 530–48
Precise words, 100–2
Preliminary screening, for questionnaire,
    368–69
Prepositional phrases, 74, 81, 104
Prewriting strategies, 27–29, 36, 155,
    165, 352
Process of writing. *See also* Writing pro-
    cess
  general guidelines, 25–35
  for letters of application, 174–79
  for long reports, 414, 521–22
  for progress reports, 498–99
  restricting a topic, 352–53
  for summaries, 323–32
  for topic sentences, 51
Progress reports, 493–99
Pronunciation, in a speech, 563–65
Proofreading
  importance of, 118
  letters, 118–19, 174
  questionnaires, 365
  résumés, 172
  ways to do it effectively, 119
Pronouns, misplaced or faulty, 82–83
Proposals, 456–83
  appearance, 460
  audiences for
    internal proposals, 32, 460, 463–64
    research papers, 474
    sales proposals, 466
  cost sections in, 465, 473
  definition of, 456
  formats of, 463, 474
  guidelines for writing, 459–60
  as persuasive plans, 457, 466
  purposes of, 456–57
  qualifications of writer/company, 473
  request for proposals (RFP), 458, 466
  statement/solution of problem,
    464–65, 472, 478
  timetables in, 473, 479
  types
    external, 459
    internal, 459, 460–65
    for research papers, 474–79
    sales, 466–74
    solicited, 458
    unsolicited, 458–59
Punctuation, 72–76, 125, 128–30
  apostrophe, 95
  colon, 125
  comma, 74–76, 125, 128

  period, 74–76
  semicolon, 74–76
Purpose
  of instructions, 435
  of proposals, 456–57
  of résumés, 154
  of sales letters, 206, 209–10
  of short reports, 484, 487
  in summaries, 322
  in writing on the job, 8, 10, 13–19
  in writing questionnaires, 349–50

Questionnaires, 349–86
  cover letter for, 369–70
  definition of, 325
  distribution of, 368–70
  restricting topics for, 352–53
  selecting respondents for, 366–68
  tabulating responses from, 371–73
  usefulness of, 349–50
  writing instructions for respondents,
    363–64, 365
  writing questions for, 353–63
  writing reports based on, 373–86
Questions
  about audiences, 4, 5–8
  closed, 356–58
  open-ended, 355–56
  in sales letters, 211
Quota sampling, 368

Reader's Digest, 320–21
Readers' Guide to Periodical Literature,
    257–58, 259, 260
Reading a speech, 555
Recommendations
  in incident reports, 514
  in long reports, 527
  in questionnaire reports, 380, 386
  in short reports, 487, 507
  in summaries, 322
  in trip reports, 499
Recommendations, securing for a job,
    149–51
Redundancy, 103–5
Reference, pronoun, 82–83
Reference works
  abstracts, 268, 284–85
  audiovisual materials, 273–75
  dictionaries, 267, 283–84
  encyclopedias, 267, 281–83
  government documents, 268–71
  handbooks, manuals, almanacs, 268

periodicals and indexes, 257–66
for popular press, 271–73
Refusal letter, for a job offer, 187, 189
Rehearsing a speech, 561
Reliability, of questions, 358
Reports, 373–86, 484–514, 518–48,
   552–67
  accident (*see* Incident reports)
  field trip, 499, 500
  incident, 485, 510–14
  lateral, 488
  periodic, 487–88
  progress, 493–99
  questionnaire, 373–86
  routine, 485
  sales, 488–93
  site inspection, 499, 501, 502
  social work or health visits, 501,
    503–5
  test, 505–10
  trip, 499–505
  unusual occurrence (*see* Incident re-
    ports)
  vertical, 488
Request for proposals (RFP), 458
Research
  importance in writing process, 26–27
  library, 249–85
  for long reports, 519, 521
  for proposals, 460, 478–79
  for short reports, 487
  for test reports, 505, 507
Responsibility
  of readers, 17–18
  of writers, 17–18
Résumé
  audience for, 154–55
  by chronology, 157–61, 165
  color of, 172
  difference from letters of application,
    172–73
  by function or skill areas, 165–68
  organization of, 165–168
  parts of
    career objective, statement of, 158,
      160–62
    education, 162–63
    experience, 163–64
    heading, 156–57
    hobbies and interests, 164
    personal data, 164
    references, 165
    skill areas, 165
  typing of, 168–69, 172
  what to exclude, 156
  what to include, 156

Revising
  for clarity, 137
  importance of, 35
  in the overall writing process, 35
  for sentences, 79, 83
  steps in developing paragraphs, 44–46
  for words, 103
Robert's Rules of Order, 337

Sales reports, 488–93
Salutation, 125, 126–27
  avoiding sexist use of, 106
Sampling
  quota, 368
  stratified random, 368
  systematic random, 367–68
Scanning, 425–26
"See also" card, 254
Semiblock format, for letters, 119, 121
Sentences, 71–87
  active verbs in, 86
  appropriate context for, 81
  avoiding *that/which* clauses, 86–87
  in business letters, 127
  definition of, 72
  in descriptive abstracts, 341
  fragments, 73–74
  graceful and positive, in letters,
    136–37
  guidelines for writing, 83–87
  imperative, 439
  in instructions, 419
  lead-in, for visuals, 396
  length of, 83, 85–86
  logic within, 84–85
  in sales letters, 210
  subject-verb-object pattern, 83
  for summary in long report, 527
Sexist language
  ways to eliminate, 105–6
Short reports
  definition of, 484–85
  how to write, 485–87
Signature, 128
"Size Standards for Domestic Mail," 11,
  129
Slang, 108–9
Slide projectors, use of, 563
Speaking off-the-cuff, 555
Special mailing instructions, 131
Speech outline, 558–59, 560–62
Spell-checking programs, 93
Spelling correctly, rules for, 92–95
*Standard and Poor's Corporation
    Record,* 173, 174

Stratified random sampling, 368
"Stress and the Computer Programmer,"
    305–17
Stub, part of a table, 399–400
Style
    easy to read, 83–87
    nontechnical, 13
    technical, 12–13
Stylus, 424
Subject card, 253–55
Subject line, 127, 199
Summaries. *See also* Abstracts
    contents of, 322–23
    definition of, 320–21
    evaluative, 334–37
    internal, in formal speech, 558
    length of, 320
    preparation of, 323–33
    of questionnaire reports, 373
    usefulness of, 320–21
Suppressed zero, 402, 403
Systematic random sampling, 367–68

Table of contents page, 522, 524–25,
    531
Tables, 397–400
Taking notes, 276–77
Talks. *See* Oral reports
Tape recorder
    in rehearsing a speech, 563
    for trip reports, 505
Technical audience, 6–7, 12–13, 507
Technical language, 6–7, 12–13, 361,
    437, 507, 527
Telephone interviews, 351
Templates, 394–95
Test reports, 505–10
Thank-you letters, 186–87, 218–20
Tick marks, 401–2
Title card, 252–53
Title page, for long reports, 522
Titles, underscoring, 175
Tone
    in adjustment letters, 229, 232
    in complaint letters, 225–26
    definition, 12
    in test reports, 505
Tools, artist's, 394–95
Transmittal letter, for long reports, 522,
    523, 529
Trip reports, 499–505
Typewriter maintenance, 343–44
Typing
    of business letters, 118–23
    of envelopes, 130
    of résumés, 156, 168–69, 172

Underscoring, 16, 175, 201
Use of computer in library research,
    263–64

Vague pronoun reference, 82–83
Vague words, 100–2
Validity
    of questionnaires, 380
    of questions, 334
Verbs, selecting graphic, 101–2
Vertical axis, of graph, 401
Vertical files in library, 271
Visuals, 391–428
    charts, 404–14, 415
        bar, 406–10
        circle, 404–5
        flow, 413–14
        organizational, 411, 413
    computer graphics, 423–27
    criteria for using, 393–94
    definition of, 391
    drawings, 419–23
    for formal speeches, 559, 563
    glossary for, 427–28
    graphs, 400–4
    in instructions, 440–42
    maps, 414, 415–17
    photographs, 417–19
    pictograms, 392, 410–11
    tables, 397–400
    use in long reports, 520, 525
    usefulness of, 15–17, 391–93
    writing about, 395–97
Vita. *See* Résumé
Voice
    active, 76–78
    passive, 76–78

Warning statement, 450
WILSONLINE, 265
Word processors, 36–37, 93, 119, 156
Wordiness, 102–5
Words
    contextually appropriate, 81
    general, 101
    homonyms, 96–100
    precise, 100–2
    selection for instructions, 439–40
    sexist, 105–6
    specific, 101–2
    spelling of, 92–95
    unnecessary, 102–5
Working bibliography, 275, 276
Writing, job related
    characteristics of, 13–19
    importance of, 3

measurements in, 17
responsibilities for, 17–18
Writing process, 25–35, 44–47, 51, 83,
    92, 155, 175, 215, 241, 290,
    323–25, 352, 414, 437, 485,
    498–99, 521–22

Writing process and the computer,
    35–40

"You attitude," 132–37, 174, 199, 210,
    226, 241, 466